THE INSIDER'S GUIDE TO

INDIA

THE INSIDER'S GUIDES

AUSTRALIA • BALI • CALIFORNIA • CHINA • EASTERN CANADA • FLORIDA • HAWAII •
HONG KONG • INDIA • INDONESIA • JAPAN • KENYA • KOREA • NEPAL • NEW ENGLAND • NEW
ZEALAND • MALAYSIA AND SINGAPORE • MEDITERRANEAN FRANCE • MEXICO • PORTUGAL •
RUSSIA • SPAIN • THAILAND • TURKEY • VIETNAM, LAOS AND CAMBODIA • WESTERN CANADA

The Insider's Guide to India
First Published 1990
Second Edition 1995
© 1995 Kümmerly + Frey AG

ISBN: 0-86190-563-6

Moorland Publishing Co Ltd
Moor Farm Road, Airfield Estate, Ashbourne, DE61HD, England
published by arrangement with Kümmerly + Frey AG

Created, edited and produced by Allan Amsel Publishing
53 rue Beaudouin, 27700 Les Andelys, France
Telefax: (33) 32 54 54 50
Editor in Chief: Allan Amsel
Original design concept: Hon Bing-wah/Kinggraphic
Picture editor and designer: Michelle Chan
Text and artwork composed and information updated
using Ventura Publisher software

Printed by Samhwa Printing Co Ltd, Seoul, Korea

THE INSIDER'S GUIDE TO
INDIA

by Kirsten Ellis
Photographed by Robert Holmes

MPC

Contents

MAPS
India	10—11
Delhi	68
Agra and India's Heartland	103
Varanasi (Benares)	114
Jaipur	121
Rajasthan	132
The Mountain Trail	158
Bombay	186
The West	200
Calcutta	226
The Eastern Trail	242
Orissa	252
Bhubaneswar	253
Hyderabad	271
Bangalore	277
Mysore	282
Madras	294
The Deep South	324

WELCOME TO INDIA   13

THE HISTORICAL LEGACY   19
Ecology is History   21
Ancient India   22
The Arrival of the Aryans   23
The Western Challenge   23
The Growth of Religion   24
The Mauryan Age and Ashoka   26
    The Birth of Bureaucracy • The
    Enlightened Emperor
Post-Empire Opportunism   28
The Classical Age   29
The Legacy of the South   30
The Impact of Islam   31
    The First Muslim Invasions
Mughal Power and Decadence   32
    Decline and Transition
The Arrival of the Europeans   35
    A Profitable Trade
The Birth of the Raj   36
The Sepoy Revolt   37
The Seeds of Rebellion   37
Gandhi and Independence   38
An Indian Dynasty   39
India Today   41

INDIA AND HER CULTURE   43
The Artistic Legacy   45
The Sacred Flame   46
    The Religions of India • Hinduism •
    Jainism • Buddhism • Islam •
    Sikhism • Zoroastrianism •
    Christians and Jews
Indian Pleasures   54
    Festivals and Fairs • Festival Footnote
Dance And Music   60
Elephants and Man-Eaters   61
    Wildlife Directory
Spicy Pleasures   62
    Indian Food and Drink

DELHI AND THE NORTH   67
The Capital: A Tale of Two Cities   69
The Northwest Citadel   70
Visiting Delhi   72
Getting Around   74
Hotels   75
Restaurants   76
Nightlife   78
Sightseeing   78
    Old Delhi: Mosques and Moneylenders •
    Civil Lines: The Cusp of Old and New •
    New Delhi: Imperial Inheritance • The
    Historic Trail • Museum Round-Up
Shopping   88
General Information   89
Corbett National Park   89
Punjab   89

AGRA AND INDIA'S HEARTLAND **91**
Agra and the Taj Mahal 93
  Access • Hotels • Restaurants •
  Sightseeing • Shopping •
  Excursions
Fatehpur Sikri 100
Keoladeo National Park, Bharatpur 102
Khajuraho 103
  Access • Hotels • Restaurants •
  Sightseeing
Gwalior 108
  Datia and Orchha
Varanasi (Benares) 110
  City of Light • When to Go • How
  to Get There • Where to Stay •
  Where to Eat • The Ghats • The
  City • Sarnath • Shopping and
  Crafts • General Information

JAIPUR AND RAJASTHAN **119**
Jaipur 121
  Access • Hotels • Restaurants •
  Sightseeing • Shopping • General
  Information
Samode 128
Ranthambhore National Park 128
Alwar and Sariska Wildlife Reserve 128
The Fresco Trail 129
Ajmer and Pushkar 130
Jodhpur 130
  Access • Hotels • Restaurants •
  Sightseeing • Village Safaris
Khimsar, Osian, and Nagaur 137

Jaisalmer: Fortress of Gold 137
  Access • When to Go • Hotels •
  Restaurants • Sightseeing
Bikaner 144
  Access • Hotels • Sightseeing
Udaipur 147
  Access • Hotels • Restaurants •
  Sightseeing • General Information
Chittaurgarh 150
Mount Abu 152
  Access • Hotels • Sightseeing

THE MOUNTAIN TRAIL **155**
Shimla 157
  Access • Where to Stay • Out and
  About • General Information
The Kulu Valley and Manali 159
Kashmir 161
Srinagar 162
  Access • When to Go • Houseboats •
  Where Else to Stay • Getting Around •
  Srinagar a la Carte • Sightseeing •
  Shopping • Srinagar After Dark •
  General Information
Mountain Retreats 173
  Gulmarg • Pahalgam
Jammu 175
  Hotels • Restaurants • Sightseeing •
  General Information
Ladakh 176
  Access • General Tips • When to
  Go • Where to Stay and Eat •
  Leh Town • Going to the *Gompas*

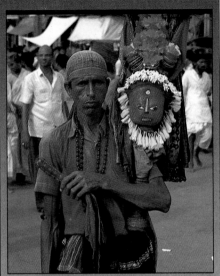

BOMBAY AND THE WEST   **185**
Bombay   187
  A Port City's Past • Early Settlers •
  The City • Climate • Touring
  Bombay • Hotels • Restaurants •
  Nightlife • Sightseeing • Out of
  Bombay • General Information
The Western Trail   200
Goa   201
  Balmy Days and Portuguese Relics •
  When to Go • How to Get There •
  Getting Around • Sightseeing •
  Where to Stay • Goa a la Carte •
  General Information • How to Get
  There • Museums and Art Galleries
Maharashtra   208
  Legacy of Stone
Aurangabad   208
  Getting There • Hotels • Eating Out •
  Getting Around • Sightseeing •
  General Information
Gujarat   215
  Woven Colors and Creeds • when to
  Go
Ahmedabad: Gateway to Gujarat   217
  How to Get There • Where to Stay •
  Eating Out • Sightseeing • Out of
  Ahmedabad: Lothal • General
  Information
Jain Footsteps   221
  Palitana

Junagadh   221
  General Information
Somnath   222
Sasan-Gir   222
  General Information
Vadodara (Baroda)   223
  Sightseeing

CALCUTTA AND THE EAST   **225**
Calcutta   227
  When to Go • A Bird's Eye View •
  Transport • Access • Hotels •
  Restaurants • Sightseeing • City
  Tour • A Patchwork of Legacies •
  Culture and Crafts Round-Up •
  Shopping
Around Calcutta   240
  The Banyan Boulevard • The Belur
  Math • Mangroves and Tigers
The Eastern Trail   242
Bihar: The Buddhist Trail   242
Darjeeling   242
  Permits • How to Get There • Room
  With a View • Orientation • High
  on the Himalayas • Flora and Fauna •
  Tea Plantations • Recreation
Sikkim   248
The North-East   250
  Assam • Wildlife Parks • Meghalaya •
  Manipur • Entry Formalities

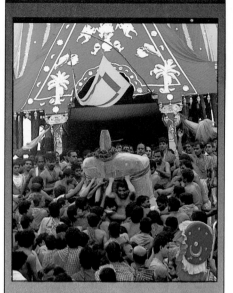

Orissa 252
  Getting There
Bhubaneswar 253
  Getting Around • Where to Stay •
  Eating Out • The Temple Trail • Out
  of Town • Shopping for Crafts
Puri 257
  On the Beach • Where to Stay •
  The Main Drag
Up the Coast 261
Konarak 261
Andaman and Nicobar Islands 262
  Entry Formalities • Access • When to
  Go • Hotels • Sightseeing • Harbor
  Cruises • Beach Paradise and Coral
  Reefs

ACROSS THE DECCAN **267**
Hyderabad 269
  Access • Hotels • Restaurants •
  Sightseeing • General Information
The Deccan Trail to Bangalore 274
Bangalore 276
  Access • Hotels • Bars and
  Restaurants • Sightseeing •
  General Information
Mysore 280
  Access • Hotels • Restaurants •
  Sightseeing

The Hoysala Temples 284
  Hassan • Belur • Halebid •
  Somnathpur
Karnataka's Wildlife Sanctuaries 285
Ootacamund (Ooty) 285
  Access • Hotels • Restaurants •
  Sightseeing • Ooty Excursions •
  General Information

MADRAS AND THE TEMPLE TOWNS 291
Tamil Nadu 293
Temple Architecture of the South 293
South Indian Cuisine 293
Madras: The Southern Gateway 295
  Access • The City • Getting Around •
  Hotels • Restaurants • Sightseeing •
  Entertainment • Shopping • General
  Information
The Temple Towns 305
  Kanchipuram • Tirukkalikundram •
  Mahabalipuram (Mammallapuram) •
  Madurai

THE DEEP SOUTH TRAIL	**315**
Kerala: Coconuts and Cathedrals	317
Trivandrum	317
Access • Hotels • Restaurants • Sightseeing • Excursions from Trivandrum • General Information	
Kovalam	320
Access • Hotels • Restaurants • Beaches	
The Backwaters	322
Quilon • Alleppey • Kottayam • Periyar (Thekkady) • Access • Hotels • Sightseeing	
Cochin	326
Access • Where to Stay • Restaurants • Sightseeing • Kathakali • General Information • Out of Cochin: Trichur	
TRAVELERS' TIPS	**331**
Getting There	332
Air India • From Europe • From Australasia • From the United States	
Visas	332
Customs	333
Currency	333
When to Go	333
What to Take	334
Health	334
Immunizations	

On the Road	335
Accommodation	336
Tourist Information	336
Getting Around	337
Domestic Airlines • Riding the Rails • Buses • Urban Transport	
Communications	339
Time • Postal Services • Telephones • Telex, Telegrams, and Facsimile • Media	
India's Nightlife	340
Beneath the Whirling Fan	340
Baksheesh, Begging and Bargaining	341
Travelers' Hindi	342
Glossary of Common Foods, Cuisines and Dishes	343
QUICK REFERENCE A–Z GUIDE	**345**
To Places and Topics of Interest with Listed Accommodation, Restaurants and Useful Telephone Numbers	

JAMMU AND KASHMIR
Indus
agar
Leh
Pahalgam
Batote
Jammu Tawi
Kuku
HIMACHAL
PRADESH
Shimla
Chandigarh
ritsar
AB
Bhatinda
Hardwar
Corbett
National Park
HARYANA
Rohtak
DELHI
Rewari
Ganga
Fategarh
Alwar
Agra
UTTAR
Lucknow
Ayodhya
Fatehpur
Sikri
Gwalior
Kanpur
PRADESH
Mau
kar
Jaipur
Datia
Etawah
Oral
Sarnath
Ajmer
Ranthambhore
National Park
Orchha
Yamuna
Varanasi
ttaurgarh
Khajuraho
MADHYA PRADESH
pur 2
Bodhgaya
Bhopal
Bandavgarh
Indore
Jabalpur
Natarhat
Melghat
Bilaspur
Ellora
Raipur
Saputara
Ajanta
Wardha
Aurangabad
MAHARASHTRA
Shirdi
Nanded
rla Caves
Madhya
Warangal
Bhadrachalam
Hyderabad
Bijapur
Srisailam
Rajahmundry
Vijayawada
nhata
Aihole
Pattadkal
Hampi
ANDHRA
PRADESH
KARNATAKA
OR
Jog Falls
Chitradurga
Tirupathi
Halebid
Bangalore
Belur
Hassan
Kanchipuram
Mangalore
Srirangapatna
Sravanabelagola
Mamallapuram
Mysore
Somnathpur
Chenglpattu
Cannanore
Udagamandalam
Pondicherry
Ootacamund
(Ooty)
Chidambaram
KERALA
Trichur
Tiruchchirappalli
TAMIL NADU
Cochin
Kottayam
Madurai
Alleppey
Periyar
Quilon
Courtallam
Rameswaram
Trivandrum
Kovalam Beach
Kanya Kumari

Indus
Ranthambore
INDIAN OCEAN

CHINA
NEPAL
SIKKIM
Gangtok
BHUTAN
ARUNACHAL
PRADESH
Lumbini
Darjeeling
Manas
Itanagar
Brahmaputra
Kariranga
NAGALAND
Patna
Dispur
ASSAM
Kohima
Rajgir
Bharatpur
Shillong
MEGHALAYA
Imphal
BIHAR
BANGLADESH
MANIPUR
Chittaranjan
Aizawl
Ranchi
WEST
TRIPURA
MIZORAM
BENGAL
BURMA
Calcutta
Simlipal
National Park
Digha
Bhubaneswar
Konark
ORISSA
Puri
BAY OF BENGAL
Simhachalam
Visakhapatnam

Andaman and
Nicobar Islands

SRI LANKA

N

250 km
158 miles

✈ Airport
〰 River
National Highway
Railway
International Boundary
State Boundary

Welcome
to India

A PERSON who tells you they found what they expected in India is probably not telling the truth. No traveler is ever fully prepared for the first experience of India, nor leaves feeling untouched. Many approach their arrival with excited anticipation — for here, they have been told, exists all that is most extraordinary and shocking, most marvelous and bizarre.

The first glimpse of the vast subcontinent is very often misleading. This is the India revealed in the bright fluorescence of its international airports, where jet-lagged newcomers usually land during the early hours of the morning — the arrival time of most international flights. As the doors of the air-conditioned airport close behind them, they feel enveloped by waves of sticky heat and pungent, unfamiliar scents from the darkness — and unsteadily step into what seems a flickering Hades of shouting Indians, bundle-like pavement sleepers, car horns bleeping in unison and urgent scrums of taxi touts pulling at your shirt sleeves. Most travelers feel being instantly caught off guard, catapulted into confrontation with a strange alien land.

Yet India has many guises. India offers its visitors majestic temples and tombs, erotic sculptures, forlorn royal palaces, fabled mountains and great natural beauty.

A tour through this ancient, vast and crowded land is always an authentic adventure — sometimes daunting, often moving, but always stimulating and memorable. This colossal pendant-shaped continent is a place where breathtaking extremes are accepted almost as commonplace, and where the traveler learns to expect the unexpected.

India covers a land mass roughly the size of Europe and is home to one fifth of humanity — more than 800 million people — who form a diverse multitude of cultures, languages, religions and dress. Its domain extends 3,300 km (2,000 miles) from the northern snow-capped peaks of the Himalayas to the steamy palm-dotted plains of the southern tip of Kanniyakumari, and sprawls for 2,700 km (1,700 miles) between the mountainous frontiers of China and Burma to the arid desert wasteland at the borders of western Rajasthan. Its people speak a total of 1,652 dialects, of which only 15 are officially recognized. It has a present-day society with a paradoxical inner core: while it prides itself as the world's largest democracy and a leader of the Third World, it remains overwhelmingly a peasant nation rooted in often brutal traditions that have barely changed for centuries. It is the cradle of one of the greatest ancient civilizations — and during its heyday, one of the

wealthiest — with a history that spans more than 4,000 years and that today offers its visitors a glimpse of an infinitely diverse, rich cultural heritage.

Above all, India is a flesh and blood encounter with the Indian people — for no country can ever be judged by its spectacle alone, nor can a traveler be insulated from its ocean of faces. It is they who will reveal India to you in all its baffling, rich, and often exasperating complexity. There will be moments on your travels when you will feel intoxicated by the diversity and splendor that India has to offer, and others when you just want to fly home as quickly as possible. India demands much patience and tolerance from its visitors. It can seem just too big and overwhelming to understand.

In a headlong rush to get visas and immunization jabs, many tourists overlook two very essential items of luggage for travel in India: an open mind and a well-developed sense of humor. If you manage to keep these intact throughout your stay, you will have mastered the knack of appreciating India.

While you'll probably never see the entire country, or ever completely understand it, you'll come away with an enduring fascination, exerting a pull that may bring you time and time again. Memories of India's pageant-like street-life, teeming with endlessly moving crowds and infused with dust-laden light, vivid flashes of color and spicy scents, and its landscape layered with majestic relics of lost empires, leave an indelible impression, touching a human hunger for all that is most exotic, bizarre and elusive.

The purpose of this guide is to present the most worthwhile and accessible Indian destinations, and help plan your itinerary within a broad framework of travel options. Whether you are backpacking, traveling in luxury, or taking a mid-way compromise between the two, this guide contains up-to-date information on hotels, restaurants and transport to help you fully appreciate each place.

Unless you plan to stay for several months — and there are plenty of enthusiastic travelers who end up staying in India for years — you'll need to be very selective in your choice. It is usually best to focus on one or two main regions, rather than attempting a crammed all-encompassing tour of India, a nation best appreciated on a loose schedule. An itinerary that looks good on paper may not account for

OPPOSITE: India's trains. TOP, at a remote hamlet in Rajasthan and BOTTOM, the *Dehradun* refuels while villagers scavenge for unburnt coal.

ever-lurking complications of traveling in India, such as an odd "off-key" day due to about of the notorious "Delhi-belly", or missing a crucial connection due to an unforeseen act of God.

To do justice to the country, an Indian expedition should be at least three weeks long. Most people take at least three or four days to acclimatize after arrival, not just from the usual jet-lag, but to the overwhelming "strangeness" of India's climate, pace and culture. Many who undertake a flying visit have a frantic encounter with a country that yields richer and more varied experiences the longer one stays, when a certain buoyant adventurousness takes root. Conversely, few newcomers to the subcontinent tend to stay longer than six weeks. Most people find it both exhilarating and exhausting, a place that rivets the senses and triggers such a complex array of reactions to its varied sights that one can feel rather mentally pommeled. Experiences are foisted upon travelers as it is not a place where one can just drift through passively, expecting things to function as elsewhere. Responding to India's idiosyncrasies — as baffling or downright frustrating these may seem at the time — is what makes the country such a special destination. If you maintain a fairly relaxed attitude, plenty of fresh enthusiasm and enough sang-froid to put it all down to experience, than you will most certainly love India, and have some of the most fantastic and unforgettable experiences of your life.

Hardy but fun-loving Rajasthani nomads of the arid Thar desert, swaddled against the sands in colorful camel-hair rugs.

The Historical Legacy

TO VISIT INDIA is to be given a tantalizing glimpse of one of the world's most ancient and complex cultures. The 4,000 to 5,000 years of India's recorded past have seen its soil annexed countless times by history's shifting fortunes. Dynasty has usurped dynasty, empire has followed empire, and the lives of ordinary people have been plunged into suffering and turmoil from one century to the next. India's civilization has been of crucial importance to world history and culture, particularly within the context of central and south-east Asia. Westerners may find it hard to believe, but India's creative and intellectual tradition has produced more major works than the entire European tradition — even more impressive considering its extraordinarily destructive tropical climate which has devoured vast quantities of sculpture, painting and manuscripts.

A holidaying traveler, whose interest in India's history is often sparked by a desire to learn more about the people he has begun to encounter, or about the awe-inspiring relics of fallen empires that stand before him, may find that trying to understand India can be a maddeningly elusive occupation. Even if you travel from the proverbial "Kashmir to Kanniyakumari"; pride yourself on taking the rugged trail through the "real" India of mud-hut villages and earthy peasants, or arrive well-primed by novels and history books, you'll probably find India still skittishly defies comfortable definition. Perhaps in the end, only a lifelong scholar of things Indian could come to grips with the question: What makes India, India? The best that can be done in a book such as this is to give India's past a comprehensible perspective. The history as recounted here deals not just with India's present boundaries with Pakistan and Bangladesh, but with the entire subcontinent.

ECOLOGY IS HISTORY

Just as some people hold that biology is destiny for individual human beings, so too it may be said that ecology has determined the history of India. The story begins with the Indus river, the very lifeblood of prehistoric India, from which the country's name is derived. Along its lushly forested banks, the early Indus Valley civilization flourished more than four thousand years ago. The early settlers — and many future conquerors — were lured by the region's fertile soil: the legacy of the physical forces that shaped the surfaces and the climate of the subcontinent long before man existed. Nature bequeathed India with the mighty 2,692-km (1,600-mile) -long chain of the Himalayas, the "resting place of the snows", without which

the land would be little more than a desert. The Indus and northern India's other two great river systems, the Ganga–Yamuna and the Brahmaputra, all fed by Himalayan glaciers, still continue to sweep vast quantities of sedimentary topsoil downstream to form rich alluvial valleys and plains right across the northern plains. Worshipped as goddesses by Hindus, these formidable rivers gave rise to India's greatest ancient cities. Their inhabitants were able to tap the river waters to irrigate a crop-growing hinterland and also to set off on them to distant destinations for trade. It was in the most bountiful region, watered by five

upper tributaries of the Indus, and hence called "land of five rivers" (Panch-ap, or Punjab) that the immigrant Aryans composed India's first ancient literary work, the *Rig Veda,* some 3,000 years ago.

India's destiny was shaped by the idiosyncrasies of its geographical isolation. It was cut off from its Asian neighbors by the sea around its coasts, by the protective natural barriers imposed by the Himalayas in its northern frontier with Tibet and China, and by the vast stretches of virtually impenetrable jungle-clad hills blocking contact with Burma. In the south, the spine-like wall of the Vindhya and Satpura mountain ranges presented another barrier to easy communication between north and south India, encouraging the development of almost completely independent cultures and empires. Even today, few people in the Tamil-speaking south can speak Hindi, the national language, for example. But most significantly, India's earliest migrants and invading armies swept in from its most accessible corner — and its historical Achilles' heel — the northwest frontier. They came along a series of well-known passes — the

ABOVE: Sunset over Dal Lake in Srinagar, Kashmir.
OPPOSITE: Shy village belle stands in the courtyard of a temple in Khajuraho, Madhya Pradesh.

Khyber, the Bolan and the Khurram — now shared by Afghanistan and Pakistan. For this reason, India's northwestern corner has always been the most turbulent historical battleground, with each invasion sowing fresh seeds into India's ethnic patchwork — whether zealously spurred on by visions of conquered wealth and glory — or more recently, by the zeal of Islam or Christianity, or by profits of commercial enterprise and power.

ANCIENT INDIA

Evidence suggests that pro-human life existed in India during the Paleolithic Age when nomadic tribes of primitive men first began drifting across the subcontinent, leaving stone implements and crude hand axes as the only clue to their existence. A sketchy evolutionary trail, fueled by finds in the Sind province of Pakistan of terra-cotta pots, mother goddess figurines, phallic symbols, fragments of bronze as well as copper, suggests that some sort of village culture might have developed as long ago as 4000 BC. Exactly how long it took for India's early villagers to make the extraordinary leap to urban settlement is not known.

Although a lot of India's early history lies in legend, it's not disputed that its earliest major civilization was established in fertile, forested pockets beside the Indus River, and that it thrived for at least a thousand years from around 2500 BC. Its people were thought to be Dravidians, whose descendants still inhabit the far south of India today. The ruins of its major cities — located at Harappa (Hara is one of Shiva's names) and Mohenjo-daro ("Mound of the Dead"), now in present-day Pakistan, and to a lesser extent at Lothal and Kalibangan in Gujarat, Ropar in Punjab — all indicate highly rigorous town planning. As many as 70 unearthed sites have also been found right across the northwestern region of Punjab and Sind. Informed speculation has it that some buried cities still await discovery beneath Indian soil.

Archaeologists compare the systematically laid-out sites to what has been unearthed at Pompeii. Excavations reveal that large-scale commercial operations flourished in these ancient cities. Their citizens, who enjoyed a hitherto unknown high standard of living, subscribed to religious beliefs and had some knowledge of script. Kiln-baked bricks, as opposed to simple mud bricks, were the standard building material. (In contemporary Mesopotamia in Egypt, kiln-baked bricks would have been regarded with fascinated awe). Mining and working of several metals such as bronze, copper, lead and tin were undertaken. Some cities, like

Mohenjo-daro must have existed for centuries, as nine layers of construction were unearthed. Streets and lanes were laid out according to an axis grid running from north to south; houses were spacious units based around a central courtyard that ensured privacy; a bathroom and kitchen were de rigueur; evidence of stairs suggests double stories. Well-covered sewage drains existed, both inside private homes and on the streets, as did hot and cold public baths, deep wells, public buildings, trading posts and harbor ports. Indeed, Lothal, now in southwest Gujarat, was once a port, whose inhabitants bartered with their northern neighbors at Harappa and Mohenjo-daro, as well as the Persian Gulf and Sumeria (Iran), in the Indian currency of the day — ornamental conch shells, bone inlay goods, cotton, pearls, and possibly even in peacock feathers and apes.

Discovery of these ancient ruins came relatively late in the mid-nineteenth century — when India's history was commonly believed to have begun only from the time of Alexander the Great's invasion in the fourth century BC. British engineers laying a railway between the Punjab and Karachi observed that local laborers seemed to have an unlimited supply of bricks with which to build the track's foundations. The time-worn bricks remained an enigma until the 1920's when archaeologists explored the region and changed history books with uncovering of Mohenjo-daro along the Indus and Harappa on the Ravi.

Surviving artifacts offer intriguing glimpses into the art and culture of the Indus people. Perhaps one of the most famous finds is that of a bronze naked dancing girl striking a provocative pose. Large numbers of excavated female figurines with their overemphasized hips, protruberant breasts and pudenda seem to indicate fertility worship. Among the discoveries are hundreds of small, ornately inscribed steatite seals with pictographic portraits of Brahmanic bulls, "unicorns" tigers and other animals, and also pictographic signs, thought to have been used by merchants to brand their wares, as an early form of trademark. Despite extensive ongoing research, comparatively little is known about the Indus Valley civilization's development and eventual decline, nor has their script ever been able to be deciphered. The current theory has it that sometime after 1750 BC, the efficient, wealthy settlements at Harappa and Mohenjo-daro suffered a series of earthquakes and floods, spelling complete disaster. Evidence at Mohenjo-daro suggests that, as with Pompeii, homes were hastily abandoned, cooking pots scattered across kitchen floors, and crushed skeletons of people attempting to flee have been found caught in the debris of walls and ceilings.

THE ARRIVAL OF THE ARYANS

Sometime after 2000 BC, semi-barbaric tribes of fair-skinned Aryans swept into India, probably from northeastern Iran and the region around the Caspian Sea. By 1500 BC they had snatched control from the Harappans, whose developed way of life had all but collapsed, and had become well ensconced in the Punjab. The Aryans were a pastoral race, who had stormed the fortified cities of the Indus wielding bronze axes and riding in horse-drawn chariots. Unlike the Harappans, they lived in tribal villages with their migrant herds, and these dwellings, made from bamboo or light wood, have not survived the ravages of time. The Aryans became known as Hindus, from the word "Indus" and they worshipped a pantheon of gods, most of them nature's elements, such as the sun, wind, water and fire. These gods did not replace the mystical fertility or earth gods of the Dravidians — both found room within the same evolving religious faith that eventually became Hinduism.

It's thought that Aryans were the original architects of the caste system, invented to ensure that their racial distinctiveness was kept "pure". Early Aryan society was broadly divided into four hereditary social strata, called *varna* or "colors". The priestly Brahmans, were the aristocrats of the social pyramid. Next came the Kshatriyas, the warriors, whose duties involved warfare and government, and the Vaishya, who tended to be farmers, merchants or skilled artisans. At the bottom were the Sudras, the menial laborers. Beneath them were the indigenous dark-skinned slaves, scoffed at by the sharp-featured, fair Aryans as the "noseless ones". Each *varna* was associated with a distinguishing color: white for Brahmans, red for Kshatriyas, brown for Vaishya and black for Sudras.

Along with their Caucasian genes, the Aryans brought with them a new, rich and precise language: Sanskrit. This was a branch of the Indo–European family of languages and it was later perfected to express in literary form the hymns and epics of the Vedas, the Upanishads and the Bhagavad Gita. These huge compilations of myth and folklore were the seminal religious texts of virtually the whole of Indian thought to follow. Even the unorthodox religions, Buddhism and Jainism, were influenced by the Vedas to some extent. Before Sanskrit was written, however, the Aryans had to rely for a long time entirely on rote learning of hymns and rituals by the priestly caste, the Brahmans. From the epics written by these Vedic Aryans, it seems they were an earthy bunch, who adored gambling, music and large quantities of *soma*, an alcoholic drink heavily laced with hashish, as

well as war and chariot racing. The Mahabharata, whose epic core is thought to reflect Indian life at about the time of 1000 BC, starts with King Santanu's obsessive love for the beautiful goddess Ganga, whom he "marries", symbolizing the Aryan advance east across the Ganges river.

At about this time too, the Aryans had mastered the art of smelting iron ore for tools and weapons and had ventured further inland — perhaps lured there by rumor of large iron ore deposits — to Uttar Pradesh, Bihar and Orissa. New cities rose to prominence: Indraprasatha, (site of present-day Delhi), Kashi (Varanasi) and Pataliputra, (Patna in Bihar). All this eastward colonizing meant that they failed to maintain their crucial hold on the north-west frontier. Inevitably this led to invasion and yet further cross fertilization of cultural influences.

THE WESTERN CHALLENGE

The first invaders were Persians under Cyrus, followed by Darius (521–485 BC) who occupied the Indus Valley region of Punjab and Sind. They later recruited Punjabi soldiers who fought with Darius' son Xerxes in the Persian invasion of Greece (479 BC). Fantastic tales of India had been circulating ever since the return of their first official envoy, Scylax, a decade previously. Darius the Great, Emperor of Persia had deposited him near the head-waters of the Indus and instructed him to sail down the river to its mouth and make his way home by the Red Sea. In so doing, Scylax was to follow the same route as the Phoenicians of the Levant who traded with Western India as early as 975 BC and went on forays for ivory, apes and peacocks. Scylax's account of his adventures were taken up by Heredotus who had a great deal to tell about India at the time: for instance, that there were two races, the dark aboriginals and the fair Aryans, "white like the Egyptians". He told of "gold-digging ants who labored in gold-strewn plains"; of the crocodiles of the Indus, the extremes of temperature in the Punjab, and the novel cotton clothes of the Indians. He also described a religious sect which ate nothing which had life and lived on grain — a reference perhaps to the Jains. Scribes also described the existence of marriage markets, where impoverished parents sold their daughters, and the practice of immolation of widows on the funeral pyres of their dead husband — the economically motivated tradition known as *suttee*.

No wonder the world's greatest young general, Alexander the Great of Macedon was spurred to lead his armies, estimated at some

25,000 to 30,000 men, on his epic march from Greece to this exotic, distant land across the Indus in the spring of 326 BC. Alexander first occupied Taxila, now in Pakistan, then usurped the Persians and proceeded further inland, defeating the Aryan King Porus and his vast army of elephants. Following this crushing defeat, no Indian ruler seriously contested Alexander's advance, but the further inland he moved, the more mutinous his travel-weary army became. Drunk on conquest, Alexander was anxious to venture on to the "Eastern Sea", which may have been the Ganges river, but was forced to accept the will of his men. Leaving behind a few officers as petty princes in the Upper Indus Valley, the Greek army turned homeland back to the homeland that Alexander himself never lived to see again. He died in 323 BC at the age of 36 in Babylon. Despite the sowing of seeds into India's gene pool by his soldiers (still said to be the cause of blond hair and blue eyes among children in the upper Himalayas), Alexander's most lasting legacy to India was the development of Gandharian art, a mixture of Roman–Hellenic artistic ideals — including the draped toga-like garments and the bare torso — and Buddhism, the emerging "radical" religion of the time.

THE GROWTH OF RELIGION

The Aryan epoch marked the emergence of Hinduism, the subcontinent's greatest religion, and the two born in revolt against it: Buddhism and Jainism. Few religions in the world can claim such an ancient tradition as Hinduism. Its essential beliefs can be traced to the Indus Valley civilization, when it is thought that Shiva was revered by lingams, or phallic stones, excavated at Indus sites. It was left to the nature worshipping, priest-dominated Aryan society to lay the framework for the development of Hinduism. They wrote their sacred religious text, the Vedas, written around 1500 to 1200 BC, which is thought to refer to actual historical events. This epic tells of the victory of Brahma over Indra, the god of thunder and warfare — a fable that is thought to refer to the revival of Brahmanism (the Indus Valley's embryonic form of Hinduism) in the wake of the Aryan invasions.

The majority of Indians today still believe in the idea the Aryan priests formulated of karma, meaning "one's deeds", with its notion of cause and effect in the reincarnation of the soul — what is done in one life has direct repercussions

OPPOSITE: Procession of high-ranking Hindu priests during the Kumbh Mela, India's holiest and most spectacular religious gathering, which is held every four years.

for the next, for better or for worse. This posed a Catch 22 situation to society's underdogs, since any protest about oppression or injustice in one's present life could be easily attributed to bad behavior in one's past life, for which punishment was required to earn a better life in the next.

In the sixth century BC two contemporary figures emerged — first Mahavira, then Buddha — both challenging orthodox Vedic solutions to the question: Why is there so much suffering in life? Buddha, like Mahavira, was born into the Kshatrias, the warrior class, which permitted religious learning, but precluded priesthood. Both these two great religious reformers rejected Hinduism's central ethos and its rigid caste system, but from this point their paths diverged: Mahavira's led to Jainism, a relatively hermetic faith; while Buddhism emerged as a formidable religious force, supplanting Hinduism as the official religion under Emperor Ashoka, and gradually adopted throughout Asia. At this time Hinayana, or "lesser vehicle" Buddhism was in vogue, in which the image of Buddha himself was never revealed, in case it inspired physical desire, thus causing attachment to life on earth and distracting from the striving towards nirvana (release from the cycle of birth and rebirth). Instead, Buddha was alluded to through such symbols as stupas, footprints, trees or animals. The more populist, less monkish schism, Mahayana, or "greater vehicle" form of Buddhism, (which exists more or less in its original form among Buddhists today), emerged several centuries later, with its more tactile images of Buddha's various incarnations, from animal to human, as well as to Bodhisatta, the potential Buddha.

THE MAURYAN AGE AND ASHOKA

The departure of Alexander the Great left a power vacuum that was rapidly filled by India's first imperial family, a mighty Aryan clan who used the peacock as their totem. These were the Mauryas, (326–184 BC) who rose to prominence under the leadership of Chandragupta, perhaps inspired by Alexander's catalytic invasion of the Indus. From their capital at Magadha, built on the site of ancient Pataliputra and present-day Patna in Bihar, they were to unify the warring kingdoms and tribes along the Ganges under a single imperial umbrella for 140 years.

A fascinating insight into the contemporary Mauryan society and India's earliest foreign policy ploys was given by the contemporary

OPPOSITE: Honey-colored gateway within the medieval fortress of Jaisalmer in Rajasthan.

Greek ambassador, Megathenes at the court of Chandragupta's son, Bindusara. He cites a rather amusing correspondence between Bindusara and the Greek ruler Antiochus I: the former had apparently requested Antiochus not only to send him samples of Greek wine and raisins, but also philosophers to teach him the art of arguing. Antiochus replied dryly that the wine and raisins had been dispatched, but that the Greeks drew the line at trading in philosophers.

THE BIRTH OF BUREAUCRACY

It's thought that the genius behind the Mauryan throne was Chandragupta's chief minister Kautilya Chanakaya, who wrote the *Arthashastra,* or *"Science of Material Gain,"* a treatise on the art of government and taxation written around 250 BC. He was diabolical and shrewd enough to have given even Machiavelli a few pointers. Kautilya realized that the path to a powerful empire lay in a strong civil administration and punishment of those who trespassed its laws — he also introduced a state tax on everything from land and harvested crops to gambling and prostitution.

Mauryan society marked a unique transition from a rural monarchy to a strictly enforced civil administration — an indication that bureaucracy took indigenous root in India then and not after the arrival of the British, as it is commonly argued. Megathenes noted seven "classes" within Mauryan society, the highest class being royal councilors, whom he ranked above the priests or Brahmans. The others were agriculturists, soldiers, artisans, police (including spies) and last but not least, the bureaucrats. At the peak of $Ihistory;MauryasMauryan power it is thought that more than a million men acted as imperial administrators, soldiers and spies. The Mauryan state controlled all the major industries — everything from wine-making to road-building — with strict pay-scales and taxes imposed on artisans and professionals alike. The great Magadhan capital was administered by the traditional *panchayat* (five member) council of elders, a structure that was repeated throughout the Mauryan empire to govern India's villages, guilds and castes as well as towns and cities. Even today it remains a strong force in modern Indian villages.

THE ENLIGHTENED EMPEROR

The Mauryan empire reached its zenith under Chandragupta's grandson, the legendary Ashoka, "Sorrowless One". During his reign from 269 to 232 BC, Ashoka emerged as India's most powerful and possibly, most enlightened emperor. In its heyday, Ashoka's empire ruled over

more of India than any other invader until the British some 2,000 years later, claiming revenue from Kashmir to Mysore and Bangladesh to Afghanistan. Only three Dravidian kingdoms — Kerala, Chola and Pandya — remained independent in the far south.

Following the advice of the *Arthashastra*, which instructed that "any power superior in might should launch into war", Ashoka invaded the frontier tribal kingdom of Kalinga to the south, in modern Orissa, subduing it after the bloodiest war of his era. The sight of the battlefield's terrible carnage was to haunt him for the rest of his life, causing him to renounce violence as an instrument of policy. He became a Buddhist, and spread his faith by inscribing some 5,000 words of moral advice across 30 pillars (of which only 10 survive) and 18 rock faces across his enormous domain, notably in Orissa, Gujarat, Delhi, Sarnath and Sanchi. The most famous of his pillars, adorned with lions, has now been adopted as the symbol of modern India.

Ashoka's reign is best distinguished by his paternalistic toleration to his subjects of every faith and tongue. He abandoned the traditional annual royal hunt in favor of a *dharma yatra* or "pilgrimage of religious laws", which involved long journeys throughout his realm. An off-shoot of this was that India gained an early network of tree-lined highways, leading from the capital. Ashoka is said to have informed his subordinates that wherever he was, whether eating or in his harem, he was always "on duty" to carry out the business of the state. His Mauryan capital Pataliputra became Asia's foremost center of art and culture, while Mauryan administrators were posted to every far-flung region of the empire, rotated regularly to avoid corruption — a system with many similarities to the way British "collectors" later operated.

Under Ashoka, Buddhism spread throughout the society — his own son Mahendra became a monk and took the gospel of Buddha to Ceylon, now Sri Lanka. Another by-product of Ashoka's conversion to *ahimsa* or non-violence, was that vegetarianism was adopted by the masses.

POST-EMPIRE OPPORTUNISM

Fifty years or so after the death of Ashoka in 232 BC, the Mauryan empire had collapsed. Some historians would have it that his pro-Buddhist stance led to insidious resistance from power hungry Brahman priests, while others believe that his pacifist ways allowed the military strength of the empire to wane leaving it highly vulnerable to fortune hunters from central Asia. Possibly it might just have been that Ashoka's successors were weak and ineffectual, lacking what it takes to hold a vast empire together.

Whatever the reason, the Mauryan empire had collapsed by 184 BC. Confusion and warfare reigned as various triumphant central Asian and Persian tribes warred to take advantage of the political void. For more than five centuries, from 232 BC to AD 320, power shifted from one dynasty to another, ushering in half a millennium of unsettled, often barbaric rule which largely undermined the great civilization and unity of the Ashokan era.

First had come Alexander the Great's successors, the Bactrian Greeks. They captured Peshawar in 190 BC, and a decade later, with the collapse of Mauryan rule, established control throughout the Punjab. Many of these Greeks accepted Indian religions, the most famous conversion being that of their powerful king, Menander (circa 150 BC) who embraced Buddhism. The most enduring legacy of this Bactrian bridge between east and west can be seen in their distinctive classical Buddhist art, known as the Gandhara school, examples of which can be seen in many of India's national museums. Then, around 50 BC, the Greek Bactrians fought in vain against a double-pronged attack by two foreign nomadic tribes: the Scythians, or *Sakas* over the Kabul Valley in the north, and the Parthians, or *Pahlavas* over the Bolan Pass further south, who both managed to win solid power bases in the Indus Valley in the following century. Neither proved a match for the next spate of invasions by the more powerful central Asian Kushan warriors. The Parthians fell in battle, while the Scythians simply melted away inland, adopting Kshatriyan names and becoming Indianized.

The Kushans (circa AD 50–240) sent their armies along the Ganges as far as Benares, now Varanasi. Their most famous king, Kanishka had a utopian fantasy that his dynasty would rule forever. He gave India a new calendar, intended as a historical *tabula rasa* that began with the year he commenced his reign in AD 78. Like Ashoka and Menander, Kanishka converted to Buddhism, and he hosted the Fourth Great Buddhist Council in Kashmir, which gave rise to the radical new schism of Mahayana Buddhism. During Kanishka's reign, the very first carved images of Buddha began to appear.

Meanwhile, against this backdrop in the north, Brahman rulers had established themselves further south-east in the Indo-Gangetic plains; the former Mauryan domain in Bihar had been directly inherited by the Sungas

(184–70 BC), while the central Deccan was ruled for four and a half centuries after 230 BC by the Telugu-speaking Andhras.

Although for some five centuries, post-Mauryan era India was thrown into political fragmentation, many impressive artistic and scientific contributions emerged at this time. Foreign influence — in the form of the Bactrian Greeks — allowed Hellenistic ideas to percolate into Indian thinking, and vice versa. In particular, medicine and astrology flourished. In medicine, India was already rather advanced, being based on the ancient Hindu science of ayurvedic medicine, with its many herbal medication and "magic" potions, was widely accepted in India. Interesting enough, during Ashoka's reign, yoga gained imperial patronage — an indication perhaps of how seriously longevity was taken in those days. In astronomy, the solar calendar, with its seven day week and the hour, seem to have been Hellenistic imports, along with the zodiac, which the Indian adopted zealously.

This was also an era of greatly expanded trade via the sea and the fabled Silk Road, the long and often perilous overland trading route traipsed by merchants, camels, oxen and donkeys that crisscrossed the subcontinent. It began near what is now the port of Tyre in Lebanon and crisscrossed through what is now northern Iran, Afghanistan, Soviet Central Asia, and China, making India the economic center of Sino-Roman trade. Increased trade and wealth inspired Indian thought and art in various ways. Indian merchants, who set aside some of their fortunes as donations to religious orders, usually Buddhist, in the belief that such piety would be well rewarded in the next life, or preferably by attaining blissful "ultimate release" or nirvana from life's cycle of re-births. Consequently virtually all the great artistic and architectural remains from this period are Buddhist. The Buddha image, which first emerged under Kanishka under the new Mahayana sect, sparked an artistic religious fervor to represent the Enlightened One in all his many guises and symbolic poses with varying hand gestures (*mudras*) to depict his various messages, including his most famous gesture of reassurance, the "forget fear" gesture, which Gandhi later adopted as one of his favorite symbols. This prompted Buddhist monks to raise monasteries, temples and beautifully decorative stupas, of which the most famous can be seen at Sanchi with its gateway of voluptuous *yakshi* (mother-goddess figures), dancing elephants and other carved figures intended to depict stories of the Buddha's previous incarnations.

Perhaps the most extraordinary Buddhist legacy can be seen in a series of great monolithic rock-hewn temples throughout the Deccan, the most magnificent of which are hewn from crescent-shaped ridges at Ellora and Ajanta, near Aurangabad in Maharashtra state, where the earliest temple caves date back to 200 BC. The tradition of creating these fabulous cave grottoes was to continue over the centuries until the thirteenth century. Yet it was during the imperial reign of the Guptas that artisans working here executed the most ambitiously monumental temples together with the most exquisite relief sculptures and large-scale fresco paintings, all constructed for the greater glory of Buddha.

THE CLASSICAL AGE

India's greatest Hindu dynasty, the Guptas (320–700) is noted for its grand cultural contribution to Indian history. Under its auspices, the arts blossomed as never before, while Sanskrit poetry and literature reached celebrated heights of sophistication. The Guptas, like the Mauryas, established their base of imperial power in Magadha, in present-day Bihar, where they controlled rich sources of iron ore. The dynasty was founded by Chandragupta I, and although their empire never matched that of the Mauryan's, these powerful rulers lost no time in usurping pettier princelings and could soon claim a territorial triangle extending from Punjab to the north, Bengal to the north-east and the southern Deccan plateau, with imperial cities rising throughout the domain, most importantly at Ayodhya. Soon, Kashmir too was claimed — a rare and highly coveted jewel in the Gupta crown.

With the Guptas on the throne, India entered its so-called "classical age", a golden

Dravidian women walk bare-footed through the ancient temples of the Five Rathas in Mahabilpuram, Tamil Nadu.

epoch of peace, prosperity and stability. This era produced India's "Shakespeare", the brilliant court poet-playwright, Kalidasa, whose seven major Sanskrit classics marked the flowering of purely secular literature. Many new theories in algebraic mathematics and astronomy also surfaced. Ironically, the Guptan astronomer Aryabhatta I, who calculated that earth moved around the sun and not the other way around, as was commonly believed at the time, was completely ignored. Royal patronage was tolerant, extending to Hindu, Buddhist and Jain faiths, as can be seen in the cave art and sculpture perfected at Ajanta. However, the Guptas artistic effort

reached in culmination in the classical architecture of the Hindu temple.

Importantly, the Guptas brought about a wholesale revival of Hinduism. Its popularity had sagged in the post-Mauryan era, when Buddhism predominated amid a bevy of other fashionable "alternative" sects, ranging from fatalistic determinism to ritualized human sacrifice — with everything else in between. The rise of Hinduism automatically reconditioned the caste system, tightening up the social hierarchy and regulating its conduct. Untouchables and slaves became little more than two-legged chattels. They were confined to the outskirts of towns and villages, and designated the "unclean" menial jobs of scavenging, cleaning, tending the dead and making leather goods. Even accidental contact with an untouchable by a high-caste person was a contamination and required ritual cleansing. The visiting Chinese Buddhist pilgrim Fa-hsien, who traveled though India for six years at the beginning of the fifth century was rather taken aback to find that untouchables carried gongs to warn passing upper castes to stand clear in order to avoid being "polluted" by their presence. Another important social change under the Guptas concerned the status of women. The Guptas were the first to legalize the practice of arranged marriages, and

codified a system which had existed for centuries, making women legal wards under the power of fathers, husbands, sons and brothers.

Perhaps one of the most fascinating windows on the world of the equivalent of the upper castes during this time is the *Kama Sutra* by Vatsyayana, referred to by the Guptas as a classic textbook on the art — and gymnastics — of love. It also describes the highly hedonistic lifestyle a wealthy young man of the time might well pursue for the benefit of his education. According to the *Kama Sutra,* days should also be spent appreciating poetry, music, sculpture and painting and delectable food, all in a haze of delicate perfume, fresh flowers and elegantly coiffeured young women. However, it's important to stress that the *Kama Sutra* dealt with only one aspect of a courtier's life — the period of being a "good householder" — sandwiched in between "celibate studenthood" and "sagacious old age!"

Ultimately, the Gupta empire was weakened by invading barbaric White Huns. By the sixth century they had gained control of Punjab and Kashmir and splintered the former Gupta stronghold across north India into a number of separate Hindu kingdoms which would not be united again until the coming of the Muslims.

THE LEGACY OF THE SOUTH

Few of the political intrigues occurring in north India had much, if any, bearing on the contemporary political climate of the south. At this time the south was divided into three major ancient Tamil "kingdoms," the Cholas on the east coast at Tanjore near present-day Madras, the Cheras, or Kerala, in the west, and the Pandyas in the center, based at Madurai with a domain reaching down to Kanya Kumari in Tamil Nadu. Madurai, still one of south India's greatest temple cities, was the center of Tamil literary culture with its prestigious *sangams* or academies where some 500 poets are reputed to have congregated, also attracting philosophers and artists.

In the face of attacks from the north, these three Tamil kingdoms formed political alliances, but during rare moments of peace they schemed and plotted against one another. Early in the fourth century, another Tamil dynasty appeared on the scene, the Pallavas ("robbers") who managed to oust the Chola monarch from Kanchipuram, and set about leaving an incredible architectural legacy, as the vast *goporams* or gateways so distinctive of the south testify.

Unlike the Aryan caste system, the Tamils had their own pyramidal social structure, divided into "castes" that were really a kind of geographical identity, for instance, hills people, plains people, and forest, coastal and desert dwellers. Within each of these five groups were divisions relating to employment, including pearl divers, fishermen, boat-makers and boatmen. At society's apex sat the supreme ruler, the monarch who was considered part-deity. These Tamil Dravidians also had a tradition of matrilineal succession — which survived right up until the nineteenth century. They also had the custom of cross-cousin marriage — and were repelled by the northern practice of arranged marriage to "strangers."

This was a prosperous and cosmopolitan region, with well established seaborne trading links with other civilizations, notably the Romans and the Egyptians, and later Bali, Sumatra and Java. Spices, teak, ivory, exotic birds, onyx, precious gems, cotton goods, silks, and even Ayurvedic medicine were bartered for gold coins, while India's art, philosophies and religions were inadvertently exported into the bargain.

A new and important foreign influence in the south was Christianity, brought by St Thomas the Apostle when he arrived in Kerala in AD 52. He was said to have been martyred at Mylapore, a suburb of Madras in AD 68, and ever since, Christianity has retained a foothold in India's deep south. The tiny Jewish community of Cochin is also thought to have been founded in the first century.

THE IMPACT OF ISLAM

The Muslim conquest of India had the most profound impact on the political, social and culture life of the country. Islam spread like wild fire, and India was never the same again. With Hinduism and Islam being as incompatible as fire and water, the blend of religions was far from amicable. To somewhat puritanical Muslim eyes, the whole Hindu way of thinking was suspect. Hindus were seen as caricatures: caste-bound cow-worshippers, with a slavish devotion to thousands of different gods who they worshipped in the form of idols — anathema to followers of the monotheistic Islam. Hindus, on the other hand, saw Muslims as gross over-simplifiers, with a doggedly single-minded perception of a complex elemental cosmos. They saw no need to recruit fresh converts, since anyone not born a Hindu was automatically excluded from the faith. Conversely, Muslims were great proselytizers. Proselytizing was not always peaceful, as Muslims not only brandished the Koran but battle swords as well. Islam did not acknowledge that

any person was better than another by reason of race, skin color or social class, although women did not enjoy the same status as men. Evidence given by a woman, for example, was (and still is today in Islamic countries), only half as credible as that given by a man.

THE FIRST MUSLIM INVASIONS

The first Muslims to arrive were peaceable Arab traders who landed on the west coast from what is now Saudi Arabia as early as the seventh century, not long after the death of the Prophet Muhammed, the founder of Islam, in

632. Although Muslim merchants returned home laden with exotic imports and tales of India's wealth — creating the impression that the country was ripe for plundering — more than two centuries passed before Islamic armies launched a full-scale invasion. This was left to Mahmud of Ghazni, "the Sword of Islam," who mounted 17 separate attacks between 1000 and 1027, leaving a bloody trail as he and his Turkic hordes zealously smashed countless Hindu temples to dust and descending upon India's cities in a frenzy of murder and rapine. His most successful campaign netted him so much booty from the holy Shiva temple at Somnath, on the Arabian sea in Gujarat, that not even a giant caravan of elephants, camels and mules was able to carry it all away. Mahmud's court chronicler may have exaggerated, but he recorded that more than 50,000 Hindus were slaughtered that day. Certainly his credo was convert or die, for in his opinion, Islam tolerated no rivals. Vanquished Hindu chieftains were lucky if Mahmud spared them their lives — and even if he did, he was known

OPPOSITE: Lonely, boulder-strewn moonscape surrounding the Thikse monastery in Ladakh.
ABOVE: Detail of the Taj Mahal, considered the most sublime architectural achievement of the Mughal Emperors.

to severe their fingers as trophies for his ever-growing collection. As much as he enjoyed these periodic sprees of acquisitive mayhem, Mahmud was a bandit at heart, and had no great political designs on India.

It was not until 1192 that Muslim power took firm root in India, this time with another fierce Turko-Afghan Muslim warlord at the helm, Muhammed Ghauri. Within a decade, his armies had forced the Hindu kingdoms of the Gangetic valley to collapse, one by one, like dominoes. Only the valiant Rajputs never completely surrendered, although they suffered horrific losses. During this expansion, Buddhists were especially vilified, with monasteries destroyed and thousands monks sent fleeing to Nepal and Tibet. Exiled from the land of its birth, Buddhism was not to be restored in any significant way in India until the twentieth century. Subjugated Indians were treated as second-class citizens, and were forced to pay their new rulers hefty tax. The Muslim title, *zaminder* or landlord dates from this period of feudal rule.

After Ghauri's death in 1206, his slave lieutenant, Qutb-ud-din-Aibak, declared himself the Sultan of Delhi, commemorating the event with a towering victory tower, the Qutb Minar, and what is supposed was India' first mosque — symbolically constructed from the remnants of 27 Hindu temples. His Sultanate is also known as the "Slave Dynasty" referred to martial slavery, which allowed ambitious low-born young men an opportunity to rise above their status. During the 320 years of its existence the throne of the Delhi Sultanate changed hands among six successive Turko-Afghan dynasties. Next came the Khilji monarchs, notably Ala-ud-din-Khilji, (1296–1316), whose reign spanned 20 years, and together with his general, Malik Kafur, not only conquered the Deccan, but also the kingdoms of south India — although these did not stay subjugated long. Despite their iconoclastic and almost wholesale destruction of Hindu architecture, these Muslim sultans imported the imposing building styles of Central Asia, introducing two features without which Islamic architecture would later be unrecognizable: the minaret and the dome.

The Delhi Sultanate was beginning to weaken by the fourteenth century, during the reign of the next Turkic dynasty, the Tughlaqs, who ruled 1320–97. The first of Tughlaq rulers was Muhammed bin Tughlaq, who was notorious for his insane zealousness, a sort of Indian "Grand old Duke of York" who first marched his subjects to his new capital in the Deccan, then marched them all back again. Discontent and rebellion pock-marked the 26 years of his reign, and two southern regions of his Sultanate broke away and formed independent kingdoms

in the north of present-day Karanataka, one Hindu, one Muslim. The Hindu Vijayanagar kings built a magnificent capital at Hampi, forming a united Hindu front against the flood-tide of Islam in the north. Meanwhile the Bahmani Muslim empire emerged, later splitting into the warring provincial kingdoms at Berar, Ahmednagar, Bijapur, Golconda and Ahmedabad, all leaving behind impressive medieval fortresses.

The waning Delhi Sultanate proved an irresistible lure to one of the most dreaded names roaming the wilderness beyond the north-west frontiers, the ruthless warlord Tamerlane or "Timur the Lame." His devastating raid across the Punjab to Delhi in 1399, left "towers built high" of severed heads and mutilated bodies, and Delhi itself laid waste with famine and pestilence. His invasion resulted in a catalytic shift of power — severing India once more into two parts. The north reverted to the Turkic Afghan princes, while the south one more regained its independent status as a conglomerate of Hindu kingdoms. Slightly more than a century later, Timur's great grandson, Babur, an Uzbek prince, would return to found his Mughal dynasty on the same site.

MUGHAL POWER AND DECADENCE

No other age in India's history has ever been as dazzling, as affluent or ultimately as decadent as that of the Mughals, a two-century-long era of six major emperors that reached its zenith while Elizabeth I ruled in England. The period saw a remarkable blend of Indian, Persian and Central Asian influences, manifested in an impressive legacy of magnificent palaces, forts, tombs and landscaped gardens, including India's most famous building, the Taj Mahal.

Mughal is a corruption of *Mughul*, the Persian word for Mongol, since the Mughal rulers were partly descended from the great medieval Mongol leaders, Genghis Khan and Timur. But the Mughals were more Persianized Turks than Mongols, and they spoke a language among themselves known as Turkic.

The Mughal chieftain Babur in 1526 swept down on the Hindu plains from current-day Afghanistan and at the Battle of Panipat his army killed Ibrahim Lodi and 20,000 soldiers, laying open the road to Delhi where the young warlord proclaimed himself emperor.

"Do not hurt or harm the flocks or herds of these people, not even their cotton ends or broken needles", Babur was recorded as telling his soldiers. "Beware not to bring ruin on its people by giving way to fear or anxiety. Our eye is on this land and on this people. Raid and rapine shall not be."

Babur dispatched his son, Humayan, to capture Agra, where the conquerors acquired the fabulous Koh-i-noor diamond from the disintegrated armies of the Lodi dynasty. Babur's legacy in Agra is the Ram Bagh garden, where the emperor liked to compose poems. Despite his success, Babur disliked India and the Indians, writing in his diary: "Three things oppressed us in India, heat, violent winds and dust." All he found to praise was India's countryside, its monsoon and its gold. He died, homesick for the cool fragrant air of Kabul, where his body was later taken for burial.

Humayan succeeded Babur at the age of 23 but was a natural recluse who lacked his father's military skills and acumen required to hold together the new empire. He preferred to study languages, mathematics, philosophy and astronomy, and was also fond of illuminated manuscripts and opium. Humayan was ousted in 1540 by a brilliant Afghan commoner, Sher Shah Suri, who captured Delhi and slaughtered 8,000 Mughal soldiers. While Humayan skulked in exile in Persia, Sher Shah earned popularity during his five-year reign for impressive civil policies; the construction of Delhi's sixth city, Shergarh, numerous state highways, and for active promotion of Hindu employees and Rajput soldiery.

Humayan recovered sufficient experience in statesmanship during his 15-year exile, and in 1556 he again brought Delhi and Agra back under Mughal rule. His taste of victory was to be brief. Just a few weeks after reinstating himself in Delhi, he died from a fall down some stairs, aptly enough in his library. Humayan's contribution to Mughal architecture is his impressive name-sake tomb in suburban Delhi that strongly resembles the Taj Mahal.

Akbar, destined to be mightiest emperor, was only 13 when he succeeded his father in 1556, although he took six years to shake off power-hungry guardians. Born of exiled parents, Akbar's unsettled childhood denied any chance of a formal education and he remained illiterate throughout his life, yet he was soon able to memorize vast tracts of Persian and Arabic poetry, displaying the brilliant intellect that later earned him the sobriquet "Akbar the Great". Historian Philip Mason wrote that Akbar "tried to give India the unity she had nearly attained under Ashoka, and once again under the Gupta dynasty; his was the third attempt and the fourth was to the British."

Akbar, through a series of military campaigns, pushed the borders of the Mughal empire three-quarters of the way across the subcontinent, always creating an efficient bureaucracy

in conquered areas. He encouraged harmony between Hindus and Muslims, setting an example by marrying a Rajput princess from Jaipur and appointing her Hindu kinsmen to powerful positions. He patronized the arts on a grand scale and had such a fascination for other religions that his courtiers privately expressed doubts that he was a Muslim at all. He devised his own faith, the Din-i-Allahi, a mélange of Islam and Hinduism and other dogmas with himself as the supreme god-head. This enlightened experiment proved short-lived, but its memory is preserved in Akbar's greatest architectural achievement, his beautiful city of **Fatepur Sikri,** abandoned just 14 years after it was built 37 km (23 miles) from Agra.

When Akbar died in 1605, his powerful empire passed to his son, the despotic and frequently drunk Jehangir, who expanded his domain with calculated brutality. He once coolly calculated that his hunting exploits had killed a total of some 17,000 animals and 14,000 birds. Yet at the same time, he was an aesthete whose patronage of painters produced gauche miniatures illustrating court life, love life and natural history of unsurpassed delicacy. He also built exquisite marble tombs, mosques and Mughal gardens, but did not share his father's vision for a united, secular India.

The fifth Mughal, Shah Jehan executed all possible rivals as soon as he sat on the throne in 1627, and further unraveled Akbar's achievements by destroying sacred Hindu temples and waging brutal wars against the Hindu Rajputs and the Deccan Muslims. Yet now he is remembered for the elegant beauty of his architectural masterpieces; the infamous Taj Mahal, the Pearl Mosque in Agra Fort and the Jama Masjid and Red Fort in Old Delhi. His colossal expenditure on grandiose architecture became so profligate that his son Aurangzeb finally locked him up to save the dynasty from financial ruin. Shah Jehan spent his last years imprisoned in Agra Fort, where from his quarters he could gaze across the Yamuna River to the Taj Mahal.

Aurangzeb took the throne in 1658 and his 51-year-long reign is remembered for fanatical imposition of Islamic orthodoxy. He aroused the hatred of his Hindu subjects by making them second-class citizens, building mosques with the rubble of their holy temples. Although he extended the Mughal empire's boundaries to their furthermost, he also paved the way for its eventual collapse by alienating the rulers from the ruled. Aurangzeb lived frugally, never touching opium or visiting his harem, and banning dancing girls and musicians from his court. His paranoia about losing power led him to systematically exile, imprison, and in some

The lakeside Shiv Niwas Palace and City Palace complex in Udaipur. Of all the ruling Rajput clans, only the Udaipur Mewars managed to remain virtually independent of the Mughal yoke.

cases execute his male relatives. He even imprisoned his favorite wife and daughter and had them deliberately insulted by eunuchs. Aurangzeb died in 1707 and his grave is a spartan affair covered only with earth and open to the sky at Khuldabad, near Aurangabad.

DECLINE AND TRANSITION

After Aurangzeb, the Mughal dynasty fell into slow decay. Eleven successive kings ruled over its dwindling fortunes, each as ineffectual and profligate as the last. Fresh contenders for power sensed that the Mughals were on their last legs, and the first serious body blow came in 1739 when the Persian king Nadir Shah stormed Delhi. He slaughtered more than 30,000 people and returned home with 1,000 elephants, 7,000 horses and 10,000 camels laden with booty, including the symbol of Mughal power, the fabulous Peacock Throne.

The seams of the Mughal empire were splitting, and by the middle of the eighteenth century, India had seen numerous shifts in power and influence, with many regions falling to strong Hindu rulers. Some subject Indians revolted, such as the Sikhs and the Jats, but the most formidable were the west-Indian Marathas, the militant anti-Muslim group that rose to prominence under the low-caste warrior Shivaji. Villagers in present-day Maharashtra state still relate anecdotes of Shivaji's daring military exploits. The Marathas gradually controlled succeeding in his dream to rediscover the fabled Indies related by Marco Polo 200 years previously. His men set about zealously converting Indians to Christianity and sending home ship-loads of exotic spices, which reaped colossal profits in European markets. The Portuguese enjoyed a century-long monopoly on this lucrative trade before other European powers followed suit and began to sail East. Pepper became known as "black gold" and spices in Europe were highly valued as preservatives and flavoring. The Portuguese established bases at Damen and Diu in Gujarat, and made their headquarters at Goa, an enclave captured in 1510 and kept under Lisbon's rule until 1961.

The Dutch inadvertently brought about the British Raj, as Elizabethan Englishmen grew envious of their coastal neighbor's success in the Indonesian spice trade and resolved to compete for the booming markets in the East Indies. A series of bruising battles forced them to retreat to India, where they were enticed by tales of the decadent Mughals' treasures. Stories percolated back to England of kings who weighed themselves in gold, of stores of silver, silks and jewels in ornate palaces filled with dancing girls, eunuchs and exotic animals such as peacocks and elephants.

Queen Elizabeth I in 1600 granted the British East India Company a trade charter, and eight years later the corporation of wealthy English merchants landed a vessel at Surat in Gujarat during the reign of Emperor Jehangir. The Portuguese, Dutch, French and Danes were all active in the East during this period but it was the English who were fated to found an Indian empire. By the end of the seventeenth century, the Company's various settlements were dominated by three Presidencies: Madras, founded in 1640, Bombay in 1668, and Calcutta in 1690.

The British East India Company expanded during the next 250 years, exporting cotton, cloths, silks, saltpeter and indigo, and opium from poppies, which was sent to China in exchange for that other valuable commodity, tea. From the outset the Company had a structured hierarchy upon which the Indian Civil Service was gradually superimposed. At the bottom were the "writers", or clerks whose starting salaries were 10 a year, the minimum age a young man could come out from England being 16. At the top were governors, who ruled like mini-emperors from palatial mansions. In order to bolster official salaries, private enterprise flourished and created the breed of social-climbing Company-men known as "nabobs" who accumulated vast fortunes and returned to England to build themselves country estates, hobnob with aristocrats and often, to enter Parliament.

most of north India except Punjab. They were soon to face a challenge by new and unexpected rivals from across the seas, and one that would eventually prove more formidable than the declining Mughals — the British East India Company.

THE ARRIVAL OF THE EUROPEANS

A PROFITABLE TRADE

The European vanguard arrived even before the Mughals, when adventurous Portuguese explorers made forays into India in the late fifteenth century. Six years after Christopher Colombus discovered America, Lisbon's own Vasco da Gama landed at modern day Kerala in 1498,

By mid-eighteenth century, tensions between England and France were simmering in Europe when the War of Austrian Succession began, followed by the Seven Years War. Hostilities broke out on Indian soil in 1746 when a French army based at the trading post of Pondicherry captured British Madras, only to lose it back to the East India Company three years later. Tension between French and British posts remained long after peace returned in Europe, and both sides frequently provided local Indian rulers with arms, supplies and expertise in attempts to hasten each other's end.

The Company's first full-scale military intervention in Indian politics was both accidental and decisive. Bengal was one of the several independent kingdoms that arose as the Mughal empire disintegrated, and in 1756, its nabob, Suraj-ud-daula, captured the British garrison at Calcutta and the infamous Black Hole incident took place (see CALCUTTA, page 225). One year later, Robert Clive's forces easily defeated the nabob and his French supporters on the field of Plassey, and finding himself in control of Bengal, Clive put his own candidate, Mir Jafar on the throne. In the south, the so-called "Tiger of Mysore", Tipu Sultan and his father Hyder Ali inflicted a series of defeats on the British, but were overcome in 1799, opening up the region for British exploitation. In the west, British forces defeated the Marathas in 1803, and after two Sikh Wars left Punjab in British hands in 1849, the Company had become the effective sovereign of most of India. English armies also defeated Nepalese troops and annexed Burma.

THE BIRTH OF THE RAJ

British domination of the subcontinent by the late eighteenth century stemmed both from timely opportunism as the Mughal empire collapsed and their pragmatic policy of toleration towards the conquered, indirectly employing the same rules Akbar had employed so successfully. The British initially made no attempt to interfere with Indian religions, customs and culture, and made it clear that their interest in India was making fortunes, not conversions.

With British muskets at their throats, so to speak, local rulers saw no choice but to accept British suzerainty. For the next 50 years, the British focused their attention on gaining complete political control. In 1803 the blind Moghul emperor Shah Alam was formally taken under British protection. Deference continued to be paid to him as the Great Mughal and it was officially he who ruled an empire but in reality

he was a puppet of the British Resident in Delhi. Disgust with the Mughals was no secret among the British. Lord Thomas Macaulay derided Aurangzeb's heirs as "a succession of nominal sovereigns, sunk in indolence and debauchery, sauntering away life in secluded palaces chewing bang, fondling concubines and listening to buffoons."

The British froze the borders of numerous Indian kingdoms, ranging from the largest and grandest, like Hyderabad and Kashmir, bigger in area than many European nations, to smallest and most insignificant enclaves. On the up side of the coin, rulers of these so-called princely or native states enjoyed a security of tenure that their predecessors had never enjoyed. The aristocratic Rajput maharajas, the Muslim nizams and nabobs, and the few remaining Maratha generals were obliged to swell British coffers with generous annual revenues and acknowledge British paramountcy, but were otherwise autonomous in the administration of their territories.

Company agents were amassing enormously inflated personal fortunes, often by highly unscrupulous tactics. Tales of greedy excess filtered back to London, resulting in the India Act in 1784, which established the British government's control over the Company, although the Company was retained as a full partner in trade. London appointed a Board of Control to supervise all civil, military and revenue matters, and the body was presided over by the Company's Governer-general, the first being Warren Hastings who ruled from 1774 to 1785.

The British poured their mercantilist energies into large-scale iron and coal mining, developing tea, coffee and cotton production, and creating a vast network of railways, highways, postal and telegraph services, irrigation and agricultural programs. English was the official language of the civil service and education, and still remains the lingua franca among India's administrative classes. By the mid-nineteenth century, some 1,000 Englishmen governed the affairs of some 221 million people. The British never allowed Indians into the upper government echelons, but they established numerous schools and universities that led to the birth of an educated Indian elite.

Governor-general William Bentinck, influenced by philosophies of humanitarian liberalism fashionable in London in the 1830s, for the first time introduced laws against certain Indian cultural practices. He outlawed human sacrifice; the practice of suttee, or the ritual suicide of widows upon the death of husbands; and took actions against the Thugs, a secret society estimated to have strangled some 30,000 travelers a year in obeisance to the Hindu goddess of destruction, Kali. Not all British reforms were destined for success, and their tactics of delegating responsibility had dubious success in many rural areas. They bestowed administrative powers on zamindars, local landowners who generally abused their authority and forced many peasants into bonded labor in order to pay exorbitant taxes. The short-sighted policy gave birth to a class of impoverished landless peasantry, whose plight of living in near-slavery is still rife across India.

THE SEPOY REVOLT

British missionary zeal in reforming India led to considerable Hindu and Muslim antipathy, which in 1857 and 1858 took the conquerors completely by surprise. The revolt of the sepoys, British-employed foot-soldiers, is called the "Indian Mutiny" in the West, but titled the "War of Independence" in modern Indian school primers. Either way, both sides spilled much blood. The rebellion's unlikely symbolic figurehead was the last Mughal emperor, Bahudur Shah II, whose talents were more suited to perfecting poetry than revolutions.

The rebellion began in Meerut, near Delhi, where sepoys were incited by a rumor that new bullets being issued were greased with animal fat from pigs, which are deemed unclean to Muslims, and cows, which are sacred to Hindus. In the space of an afternoon, 47 battalions mutinied and began a spontaneous bloody trail of destruction across the north, killing every feringhi, or foreigner, they could find. A cheering mob proclaimed Bahudur Shah II the Emperor of Hindustan, and reinstated the octogenarian Mughal in Delhi's Red Fort.

The British contained the rebellion to the northern plains by disarming sepoys based in other areas, and recruiting Sikhs and tribal irregulars to assist them in reasserting control. The campaign was marked by extreme brutality on both sides, and it took the expeditionary force six months to reach numerous besieged garrisons and eventually recapture Delhi in January 1858. Bahudur Shah was banished to Burma, signaling the final defeat of the Mughal Empire.

THE SEEDS OF REBELLION

The traumatic experience of the mutiny made London reassess its position in India. The Company was abolished in 1858 and its authority replaced by the British Crown. Queen Victoria was proclaimed Sovereign Empress of India, where a Viceroy would be her representative and chief executive. The industrial revolution was in full swing in England, and India — the "jewel in the crown" — became a key source of raw materials for the "workshop of the world".

From 1858 until 1900 was the full-blown era of the Raj, Hindi for "rule". Ironically, British-founded educational institutions created an Indian intelligentsia, who justifiably became incensed that principles of democracy fastidiously upheld in the United Kingdom were not applicable to Indian subjects.

National pride was also fueled by a growing awe for India following numerous revelations on its grandeur and complexity as the site of ancient civilizations. Archaeologists unearthed cities twice as old as Rome and discovered that Buddha was an Indian. Scholars deciphered ancient Sanskrit texts that revealed several millennia of formerly unknown kings and emperors. They pieced together the significance of coins, paintings and sculptures, and uncovered long-lost philosophical, artistic and literary achievements.

The Hindu renaissance and will for social reform was spearheaded by a handful of modern-thinkers: Ram Mohan Roy, Ramakrishna, Swami Vivekananda, Dayanada and even the English Annie Beasant, president of the Theosophical Society and founder of the Central Hindu University, which later became Benares Hindu University. They preached a common philosophical ground between modern Hinduism and Western thought, and called for the religion to break away from its domination by high-caste Brahmans.

ABOVE: Shah Jehan's Red Fort in Delhi, which saw the dethronement of the final Mughal emperor, Bahudur Shah in the aftermath of the 1857 Mutiny.

The movement found its voice in the Indian National Congress, started in 1885 from the efforts of another reformist Englishman, Allan Hume. The Congress gradually came to articulate Indian desires for self-rule, and its creation led to the 1906 birth of the All-India Muslim League, whose founders derided plans of an India dominated by Hindu "Brahmans, money-lenders and shopkeepers", and called for separate political representation.

Violence flared between the two communities and intensified under Lord Curzon's ill-conceived plan to divide Bengal into eastern and western administrative zones respectively

dominated by Moslems and Hindus. The British also passed, in 1909, the Morley–Minto reforms, which called for separate electorates for Hindus and Moslems. Clashes between Moslem separatists and mostly Hindu unionists prompted Curzon in 1911 to reverse his Bengal partition plan, but the two British schemes, intended to placate the demands of the two communities, had instead exacerbated the rift.

GANDHI AND INDEPENDENCE

Self-rule demands widespread at the turn of the century, were temporarily abandoned during World War I. Thousands of Indians served the British with honor and wanted their loyalty to be recognized by an act of imperial generosity granting similar terms to India as Australia and Canada, which enjoyed considerable self-rule as dominions within the empire. When London offered nothing in 1918, disillusionment among educated Indians turned to anger.

ABOVE: Two icons of twentieth century Indian history: A fast-weakened Mahatma Gandhi with Nehru's daughter Indira, who later succeeded her father as prime minister of India.

Congress began to expand its appeal, largely due to the inspiration of Mohandas Karamchand Gandhi, a young lawyer who returned to India in 1915 fresh from campaigning for human rights in South Africa. Gandhi called for the Congress to broaden its attitudes and membership, and include the rural classes and the illiterate poor. He realized the near-impossibility of ousting the British through armed might, and instead insisted that all agitation by based on *ahimsa* or non-violence, and *satyagraha*, or passive resistance. Gandhi's inspired views earned him the title of Mahatma, or "Great Soul", and he undertook a series of famous fasts to urge Hindus and Muslims to lay aside their differences and create a national unity that would cut across caste, community and religious barriers. He insisted on the dissolution of untouchability, and called upon Brahmans to remove their sacred threads that symbolized their place in the elite caste.

Gandhi dreamed that India would once more be Rama Raj, a mythical golden age under the benign Hindu god, Rama, when food was abundant and all people lived in peace and equality. He wanted the Indian flag to bear the spinning wheel, the symbol of his philosophy, and hoped that once the British left, India's economic future would be assured through small-scale cottage industries in which the rural masses could happily produce handicrafts, enjoying the utility derived from their labor.

With Gandhi's prompting, Indian women first began to involve themselves in politics and social movements. One of the most effective tactical weapons he used against the British was the ancient Hindu custom of *hartal*, or boycott, in which the daily functioning of the government ground to a halt due to nationwide strikes affecting all sectors of the economy.

A horrifying event in 1919 proved catalytic to the independence movement. General Reginald Dyer ordered his Gurkha troops to open fire on a peaceful but illegal protest meeting in Amritsar, killing 379 people and wounding 1,200 others in the sealed courtyard of Jallianwala Bagh. Sikhs, whose loyalty to the British had remained steadfast even throughout the Indian Mutiny, largely changed their alliance to Congress. Gandhi shrewdly began campaigning against products and practices that made the British presence in India profitable. He agitated against taxes on Indian-produced salt and urged boycotts against British manufactured textiles, symbolizing his protest by learning to spin cotton thread and by wearing only handwoven cloth, or *khadi*.

Although Gandhi spent several years in jail for his efforts, the British gradually accepted they must relinquish India, but plans for their departure were complicated by their official control being over about three-quarters of the subcontinent. Roughly one fifth of the population lived in some 600 princely states, whose rulers mostly did not relish the thought of sacrificing their typically lavish lifestyles.

Confrontations escalated between the Congress Party led by Jawaharlal Nehru and the Muslim League's leader, the sharp-witted Muhammed Ali Jinnah, who rallied the large Muslim minority behind his call for independent Islamic homeland.

Viceroy Lord Wavell further infuriated Indians by announcing without consultation that they would fight for the empire in World War II, but many rallied to the cause and fought in Africa, Europe and Asia against the Axis. The war stymied the independence movement, but peace was marked a new wave of Congress civil disobedience marked by mass arrests, riots and bloodshed.

All parties now conceded that independence was inevitable, but Gandhi's call for the British to "Quit India" was now matched by Jinnah's slogan "Divide and Quit". The results of central and provincial elections in India — as well as intensifying bloody clashes between Hindus and Muslims — made it clear that India's future lay either with partition or a possible civil war.

A new British Viceroy, Lord Louis Mountbatten, was charged with the responsibility of handing over full control of India and the date was set for midnight, 14th August 1947. Both Nehru and Jinnah preferred partition to the alternative of a loose federation which had been proposed by the British as early as 1945. Jinnah in particular refused to budge, proclaiming, "I will have India divided or India destroyed." Only Gandhi remained unmoved by the mood of jubilation, believing that India should be fully united.

Princely states were released from British sovereignty and obliged to decide which nation to join. The evacuation of some 200,000 British Sahibs and Memsahibs in India was surprisingly smooth, almost anti-climactic as India exploded with celebrations to mark its newborn freedom. However, the euphoria was soon overshadowed by the holocaust of partition.

The subcontinent was sliced into two new nations, its geographical boundaries imposed by religion. Pakistan was comprised of two completely separate regions; West Pakistan, which included half of the fertile, affluent Punjab, Sind province and several mountainous tribal states; and more than a thousand miles away, East Pakistan, made up of the eastern half of Bengal, which has became Bangladesh. At the time of partition, India was home to 35 million Muslims, while the newly-created Pakistan housed millions of Hindus In the months-long upheavals triggered by partition, more than ten million people migrated in each direction across the divided Punjab — the largest human exodus in history. The price of the operation was to be paid in frenzied communal bloodshed and suffering. Estimates of how many people, mostly villagers, died in the terrible slaughter range between 200,000 and one million. Communal violence between Hindus, Sikhs and Muslims spread so fast and so far that the Indian Army without the aid of British troops was quite unable to contain it. Trains were found in the middle of nowhere, their carriages spilling with mutilated corpses. Convoys of trucks were ambushed, and entire villages wiped out to last man, woman and child.

So extreme was the murderous madness that Jawaharlal Nehru, India's first prime minister, saw no option but to hand back responsibility to Mountbatten, who had by then become the first Governor-General of the independent nation. Gandhi came to Delhi and went on a prolonged hunger strike for reconciliation and an end to communal violence. His assassination by a Hindu fanatic, on January 30, 1948, so shamed the nation that the blood-letting ceased. "The light has gone out of our lives", Nehru announced in a voice choked with grief. The impact of Gandhi's assassination was national psychological shock, sapping the will for communal violence and allowing Nehru time to turn his attention to the task of building a new India. One of his most pressing concerns was resolving the status of the 362 major princely states. Kashmir, the last state to join India, had at its helm a vacillating Hindu maharaja governing a predominantly Muslim population, who refused to make his mind about which side he wanted to go. His decision was made for him when the strategic state was invaded by Pakistan-backed tribals in October 1948, and he was forced to seek help from the Indian Army. New Delhi's forces halted the invaders, but lost about one third of Kashmir, which is now divided by a U.N.-mediated frontier.

AN INDIAN DYNASTY

The 1950s were the golden years of Indian independence, during which Prime Minister Jawaharlal Nehru formed what he hoped would be the guiding principles of his modern nation — secularism, democracy, social justice and political non-alignment. His great personal charm and integrity, his intellectual stature and his westernized sophistication singled him out as the leading international spokesman for newly-independent Third World nations. A Socialist, but not a Marxist, Nehru's goal was to create a modernized, self-sufficient India that would never again be beholden to another power. Nehru's socialist stance softened somewhat after consultations with the industrialists and Congress-backers, J.R. Tata and G.D. Birla, the Indian equivalents of Ford and Rockerfeller. He established a protected and centralized economy through a series of Five Year Plans aimed at encouraging massive industrialization and agricultural reforms.

Despite Nehru's policy of non-alignment, India increasingly found itself linked to the Soviet Union — partly in response to its month-long rout by China in 1962, and America's increasing support for its arch foe, Pakistan. Gandhi's belief in peaceful neutrality was laid to rest when Beijing's forces poured across their mutual Himalayan frontier, and relations between the world's two most populous nations remain bedeviled by disputes over two border areas.

Nehru died in 1964, and one year later his successor, Lal Bahudur Shastri, successfully repulsed Pakistan's twin attack on India — in the Rann of Kutch and in Kashmir. In January 1966, Shastri died, and Indira Gandhi, Nehru's daughter and no relation to the Mahatma, won a landslide victory at the polls to replace him. Skeptics darkly predicted that Indira would share the fate as India's only other woman ruler, the thirteenth century Muslim Slave Queen, Razia, whose three and a half year-long reign ended with a palace coup and her murder at the hands of her armed protectors.

With her election slogan "India is Indira and Indira is India", she was to prove them all wrong. During her 15 years in power she was both revered and severely criticized. Writer Salman Rushdie observed, "Her use of the cult of the mother — of Hindu mother-goddess symbols and allusions.... was calculated and shrewd." Mrs. Gandhi's most trying problem was sectarianism, in the form of Congress Party splits or conflicts with neighboring powers. Agitation in East Pakistan against subjugation of the Bengali population by Islamabad erupted in 1971 into a civil war, that culminated in Indian involvement. New Delhi's troops fought Islamabad's forces in both Kashmir and East Pakistan, from where nine million refugees flooded into India. After 12 days of fighting, Islamabad yielded its shaky hold over its eastern section and sued for peace, resulting in the creation of the independent nation of Bangladesh.

Mrs Gandhi's travails were by no means over. National debt, caused by the war and the refugee crisis, mounting inflation and unemployment caused popular opposition to her rule. Sensing that the tide was turning against her and prompted by a low-level indictment that she had used government money for electioneering, the prime minister imposed an 18-month-long state-of-emergency involving suspension of civil liberties and imprisonment of thousands of her political opponents. India ceased to be a democracy during this period. Indira's zealous son, Sanjay, who she was grooming as her successor, incensed the populace with radical programs of forced sterilization of more than 11 million villagers and clearing slums with bulldozers.

Mrs Gandhi called an election in 1977 under the misguided belief that she remained popular, and was ousted in a wave of support for the newly-formed Janata Party, largely comprised of disgruntled, Congressmen. Its elderly, pedantic leader, Moraji Desai, is remembered largely for his idiosyncratic habits of drinking urine, protecting cows and banning alcohol and Coca-Cola, than solving India's pressing economic problems. After their brief honeymoon, the Janata Party crumbled into squabbling factions, and a 1980 election placed "Mrs G" back on her pedestal in the nation's hearts and on its ruling seat.

Mrs Gandhi valiantly tried but failed to conquer escalating economic and social ills, as well as bitter inter-communal unrest. Extremist Sikhs began agitating for the creation in northern Punjab of a theocratic nation named "Khalistan", or "Land of the Pure". The radicals began stockpiling arms in Amritsar's Golden Temple, Sikhdom's holiest shrine. Mrs Gandhi retaliated in June 1984 with "Operation Bluestar", a massive week-long army assault on the shrine that left some 600 people dead, mostly Sikhs.

The carnage and desecration of the shrine enraged Sikhs and led to the Oct. 31, 1984 retaliatory assassination of Mrs Gandhi by two of her Sikh security guards. Communal violence raged across northern India, where an estimated 3,000 Sikhs died at the hands of Hindu mobs. The mantle of the Nehru dynasty was passed onto Mrs Gandhi's oldest son Rajiv, a former Indian Airlines pilot inducted into politics since the death of Sanjay in a 1980 plane accident.

Rajiv Gandhi was swept to power in 1984 on an unprecedented wave of popularity. Dubbed "Mr. Clean," he began with radical plans to liberalise the Indian economy, but soon ran into opposition. He was accused of accepting kickbacks in an arms contract — an investigation that is still being debated in the Swiss courts — and he unceremoniously lost his mandate in 1989. Two years later, Rajiv Gandhi himself was assassinated, this time in a suicid-bomb attack allegedly mastermined by the Tamil Tigers, his death adding even greater dimensions to the Greek tragedy style saga of the Gandhi family.

India's current helsman — Narasimha Rao — presides over an increasingly fragmented Congress party; and meanwhile the Hindu nationalist parties, the Bharatiya Janata Party and the Shiv Sena are becoming more militant. Mr. Rao's economic policies have been acclaimed by foreign bankers and businessmen; with widespread liberalisations and lifting of controls, India is currently experiencing an industrial boom.

INDIA TODAY

Take a glance at the front page of any Indian newspaper for stories of mayhem and excess matched by few other nations. Political unrest could come from any region — perhaps from Sikh separatists in the Punjab, from the remote northeast, where there are several tribal insurgencies, from near-feudal Bihar, where peasant militia clash with private armies funded by land-owning families, or anywhere where the centuries-old enmity between Hindus and Moslems may flare.

In the capital, headlines may cry of corruption in high places, prompting opposition members to walk out of Parliament, "amid uproarious scenes". Farmers, lawyers or students may have called for hunger-strikes, processions or sit-ins that have brought the nation's businesses grinding to a halt. There may be another of God's terrible acts — drought or floods, ferries over-turning or buses plunging off ravines. There may be bizarre stories of a child being revered as a God, a movie star turning to politics, a widow throwing herself on her husband's funeral pyre, girls cutting off their tongues to honor Lord Shiva, or an elephant stampede destroying a remote village.

However startling to a Western eye, none of these yarns mean India is falling apart. The nation still lives in the shadow of the utopian dreams of Gandhi and Nehru, whose legacy lives in the yet unshaken ideals of unity, secularism and social justice, maintained imperfectly perhaps, but nonetheless cherished as necessities. Beyond the story of sectarian violence is the telling fact that Hindus, Sikhs, Muslims, Buddhists, Parsis, Jains and many other groups have lived together in India's nearly 600,000 villages for many centuries. Hinduism, the nation's most pervasive religion with some 600 million adherents, exerts a strong binding moral and spiritual force. Its central world-view is of flexibility and absorption.

India can point to impressive economic modernizations, but it can not shake the growing burdens of the rural poor or its untrained and unemployable people flooding the cities. In a nation of 800 million people there are only 24 million wage-paying jobs. Seventy per cent of Indians live in the villages, yet their water supply is barely adequate, and they have no electricity, nor can many of them read or write. One statistic simply speaks for itself: one in every ten people who walk on this earth is an illiterate Indian.

But the single-most problem facing the nation today is its ever-growing population. India's population is estimated to be about 800,000 million, and with one baby born every two seconds, it adds an Australia to its ranks each year. Demographers say the next generation has already been born, and nothing can halt the population reaching 1 billion by the year 2000. But they warn that steps must now be taken to stop an extra 200 million people being born by the year 2000.

India is very proud of its scientific community, the world's fourth largest, be it locally-made space rockets, battleships, atomic power stations or computer software.

And they are sure that India, with its massive population and resources, is well on its way to being a leading power on the world stage comparable to China. At the same time India's burgeoning middle class — an estimated 80 million people — is regarded as one of the world's last great consumer markets.

ABOVE: Dapper regiments at the annual Republic Day in New Delhi when India proudly shows off its latest military hardware and martial might.

India
and her
Culture

THE ARTISTIC LEGACY

India's spectacular artistic heritage began 6,000 years ago when ancient tribesmen began fashioning buxom mother goddesses from clay: the earliest surviving artifacts to have been dug up at the Indus Valley sites in present-day Pakistan. It was not until the Mauryan age in the third century BC that India experienced a burst of artistic brilliance, notably in Buddhist art during the reign of Ashoka. The remarkable stone-carving of this period can be seen at its most impressive at Sarnath and Sanchi, in Madhya Pradesh. Succeeding dynasties — the Sungas and Satavahanas — adapted Mauryan motifs and techniques and were very keen on using symbols to indicate Buddha's all-seeing eye, such as a footprint, the sacred wheel and the stupa.

The next artistic wave was Alexander the Great's legacy from his subcontinental foray near present-day Peshawar: Gandharan art was classic East meets West, a mixture of Greco-Roman know-how and Buddhist inspiration. Gandharan art is recognizable by its classical Grecian-style torsos, draped toga-like folds that are thought to be the inspiration behind saris and dhotis, and its "avant-garde" depiction of Buddha in human form. At the same time, a major school developed in Mathura, mid-way between Delhi and Agra, that reflected the revival of Hinduism and also featured busty Iyakshinis, or nymphs who were the dumpy forerunners to the sophisticated ladies of Khajuraho.

During the "golden age" of the Guptas (AD 320–600), an artistic renaissance created the so-called classical style of Indian art. The paintings and sculpture of this time have a fluid and sensuous look, with a consummate fascination for detail yet contriving an effect of utter simplicity. During this period, images of Buddha's stylized attitudes, clothing and hand positions evolved to perfection, and are today mimicked by modern mass-produced images in Buddhist countries. Just as the Guptas were taking Buddhist art to its zenith, Dravidian craftsmen in the south were developing a strongly Hindu tradition with new sculptural forms crafted in stone and bronze.

The next millennium saw a steady evolution from stylized, rather static Buddhist art towards almost decadent freneticism as the medieval Hindu revival entered full swing, perhaps best illustrated at the rock-cut caves of Ajanta and Ellora in modern Maharashtra. By then, sculpture had become an inseparable part of architecture, with every surface dripping with carved activity — as seen at the Hoysala temples at Karanataka, the Sun Temple at Konarak, and the celestially carnal temples at Khajuharo.

The arrival of the temple-bulldozing Muslims undoubtedly wiped out great chunks of the Hindu artistic tradition. In their zeal to build empires these early invaders had little time for art, and only under the Mughal Emperor Akbar did a truly creative style of art emerge. This was miniature painting, concocted from a blend of Islamic and Persian styles, and primarily depicting portraits, courtly life, battles and under Jehangir, exquisite wildlife and nature studies were produced. An artist's palette included malachite, lapis lazuli, gold, silver and an ingenious substance called peori, a yellow dye extracted from the urine of cows fed on mango leaves.

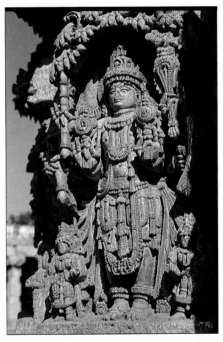

Throughout the Hindu states of north India, artists were quick to take their cue from the Mughals, combining their own religious and artistic traditions with those established by the Mughal school. Provincial styles differ greatly and are divided into different schools, notably Rajastani or Mewar, Jammu or Pahari, Basolhi and Kangra, all former hill states of the Punjab.

Although best remembered for their remarkable architecture, the Mughals represent the last great period of exclusively Indian artistic

ABOVE: Stylized stone carving dating from the Hoysala dynasty (1006–1310) who marked a peak in Dravidian temple architecture that can be seen at Somnathpur, Belur and Halebid. OPPOSITE: A towering *goporum*, or gateway, typically adorns the giant temple complexes of South India.

activity. During the British Raj, the British East India Company commissioned Indian artists to paint picturesque landscapes in oils and water-colors, and this became known as the Company school. Modern Indian painting gained impetus in the 30's with the so-called Bengali school, a distinct style of painting developed by a group of artists who took inspiration from traditional water-color techniques and folk art motifs. India's most famous twentieth century artists include Amrita Shergill, M.F. Husain and Krishen Khanna, whose work is rooted in the Indian tradition, yet reflect western influences.

THE SACRED FLAME

THE RELIGIONS OF INDIA

The nation's founding Prime Minister, Jawaharlal Nehru once described India as "a mad-house of religions". He was only half in jest. Religion is the heart-beat of the nation, and its influence, symbolism and superstition pervade every facet of life.

Four of the world's most influential religions — Hinduism, Buddhism, Islam and Christianity — have flourished on Indian soil, the first two born in India. In addition, India also saw the rise of Jainism, Sikhism and countless minor sects and tribal cults, as well as playing host to Judaism and Zoroastrianism.

India has long been perceived as a land of mystic wisdom and spirituality, standing

The spectrum of faith in India is as infinitely varied, startling and mysterious as the country itself. ABOVE: Totemic image of Kali, the fearful Hindu goddess of destruction. OPPOSITE TOP: Sikh clerics within the exquisitely ornate sacred citadel of the Golden Temple at Amritsar. OPPOSITE BOTTOM: Unorthodox Hindu temple with Belgian chandeliers and slumbering devotees in Goa.

in contrast to Western society with its emphasis on material gain. Yet outsiders often find it near bewildering to grasp how important religion is to the average Indian — as sustaining and inseparable to their existence as air, water and food. As casual spectators to this fairground of faiths, tourists will catch glimpses of its influences almost every day they spend in India. Glittering ornate temples are found even in the most remote villages, some ancient and exquisite, others modern and gaudy, but always atmospheric — busy with devotees making puja offerings to brightly painted deities, chiming temple bells, and filling the nostrils with wafts of incense and marigold blossoms. In the courtyard, sacred poems are read, hymns are chanted, dances are performed. Just as noticeably, on Fridays, the Muslim Sabbath, the nation's mosques throng with white-capped Muslims who chant verses from the Koran, bow and cup their hands to Allah. Drivers adorn their dashboards with incense sticks, flowers and the images of their faith — Sikhs enshrining the image of Guru Nanak, their religion's founding father; Hindus painting swastikas, the ancient Aryan symbol around gaudy pictures of favorite gods or goddesses. Many homes have shrines, or even a room, set aside for worship. The Indian calendar is peppered with religious festivals, some of them drawing pilgrims by the million. The Hindu religion has the most — 360 with an average of a festival a day. Just as important are the innumerable commonplace rites and observances performed almost unconsciously each day — a Hindu's pre-dawn *puja*, a Muslim's Mecca-facing five prayers, a Sikh piling up his hair and re-winding his turban.

Indian society is dominated by Hindus, who make some 83 percent of the population; Muslims comprise some 10 percent; Sikhs and Christians combined make up a further five percent, while a handful of other minorities, namely Jains, Parsis and Buddhists, make up the remainder.

HINDUISM

The world's most ancient living faith, Hinduism is not so much a religion as a system of philosophy. It has more adherents than any other religion in Asia: more than 500 million Indians are Hindus.

Although its origins can be traced back to the fertility cult of the Indus Valley civilization, Hinduism formally emerged as a distinct religious tradition with the Sanskrit-speaking Aryan invaders some 3,500 years ago. It is rare among major religions since it neither claims a specific founder nor can point to a single "holy book" as its ultimate spiritual reference. Instead it has many — the earliest being the four sacred Vedas,

India and her Culture.

notably the Rig Veda, composed between 1600 and 1000 BC, formally marking the birth of Hindu mythology. Other scriptures include the Upanishads, the Bhagavad Gita (described by Mahatma Gandhi as his "spiritual dictionary"), the Puranas, and two remarkable epic poems, the Mahabharata and the Ramayana — written in a tradition that would later be echoed in Homer's Iliad and Odyssey.

Hinduism has survived numerous periods of both prosperity and decline, demonstrating a resilient capacity to absorb and assimilate opposing faiths, rather than forcefully seeking converts. Its central view of religious tolerance was encapsu-

lated in the Upanishads, (800–400 BC) which states: "The Great God is One, and the learned call him by different names." Far from diluting itself out of existence, Hinduism seemed to gain strength from its flexibility and religious synthesis. It allows an astonishing freedom of worship. Under its umbrella can be found monotheists, polytheists, pantheists, totemists, animists, agnostics and even the odd atheist!

Despite its inherent pluralism, Hinduism has several essential beliefs that tie the various creeds together. The ultimate objective of life is essentially life's renunciation of life by achieving *moksha*, or perfection, thus breaking the soul's cycle of birth and re-birth. The passage leading to this desirable state is determined by an individual's karma, which roughly translates as "actions", but meaning a law of cause and effect whereby a person's deeds in this and previous lives tally up to influence their status in the next life; and dharma, an individual's moral duties to perform in life. Both are inextricably bound up with the concept of reincarnation, which offers both solace and hope in the belief that present troubles are the wages of a former life's sins and that pious and unselfish actions hold the key to a better life in the future.

The rules for reincarnation can be extraordinarily complex. Some 2,000 years ago, the great legal scholar Manu wrote learned treatises codifying ancient precepts of law and sacred duty — then punctuated them with digressions on what kind of rebirth is punishment for which sin. For example, if a man steals silk he becomes a partridge; if he steals cotton cloth he becomes a crane; if linen, a frog, and so on.

Although the larger esoteric concept of attaining an unblemished soul is important, Hinduism has its feet firmly on the ground, and encourages its adherents in kama, or earthly pleasures, including sex, and *artha*, or prosperity and material wealth. According to Hindu beliefs, life passes through four stages — the stage of the learner, demanding self-control and abstinence; the stage of the householder, when *kama* and *artha* are healthy pursuits; the stage of detachment or gradual turning away from worldly things; and the stage of ascetic renunciation, when a person becomes devoted only to spiritual meditation and yoga, preparing for *moksha*.

An interesting feature of Hinduism is its cult of its peripatetic sadhus or holy men, who are rarely seen outside their mountain retreats where they endure great hardships to show renunciation of the material world, occasionally congregating at large religious festivals. Foreign visitors to India have for centuries been mystified by sadhus' bizarre acts, such as lying on beds of nails and being buried for weeks on end. Many deliberately cultivate their bedraggled appearance by smearing their half-naked bodies with ash and growing their hair and beard in matted dreadlocks. Many brandish tridents in obeisance to Lord Shiva to whom they ritually smoke hashish.

A Pantheon of Gods

Hinduism recognizes an ultimate omnipotent force, known as the Supreme Universal Soul, or Parabrahma, who has three physical manifestations — Brahma, the Creator, Vishnu, the Preserver and Shiva the Destroyer. All three are represented with four arms, while Brahma also has four heads to depict his all-seeing wisdom and he is said to have delivered the four sacred Vedas from each of his mouths.

Orthodox Hinduism is divided into two main sects: Shaiviam, comprised of those who worship Shiva, and Vaishnaiviam, comprised of those who worship Vishnu. Unlike these two, the other member of holy trinity, Brahma has almost no temples, save for a unique shrine at Pushkar, where you can see his "stead" or so-called vehicle, the sea turtle. This trinity symbolizes the main basic stages of life — birth, life and death — and presides over a vast pantheon of some 330 million Hindu gods. Despite such a profuse array of gods, most people concentrate their devotional energies on just a select few.

Vishnu, the most revered of the gods, possesses cosmic powers more formidable than Einstein's Theory of Relativity: when Vishnu sleeps, the universe goes into spasms of agitated flux that only normalize when he wakes up again. Vishnu is usually depicted sitting on his vehicle, a human-faced eagle called a *"garuda"*. Vishnu has already visited earth in nine incarnations (*avatars*); as a fish, a tortoise, a boar, a half-man, a beggar-dwarf and as the axe-wielding Parasurama, and is scheduled to return once more as the horse-headed Kalki. On his seventh call, he came as Rama, with his Herculean mission to destroy the demon king

nation was Buddha himself, apparently the result of an inventive ploy to lure break-away Buddhists back to the Hindu fold.

Shiva's main symbol is the cobra, the deadly snake of death and destruction, and he usually rides around on the bull Nandi. He is worshipped as the Lingam, the phallic symbol of creativity and fertility. Shiva's formidable temper resulted in the odd appearance of his elephant-headed son Ganesh. When Shiva returned from many years absence, he hoped to surprise his beloved wife Parvati in her bedroom. Instead he discovered her talking to a young man — imagining himself cuckolded and not recogniz-

of Ravanna of Lanka (Sri Lanka). The remarkable story of his success, aided by the faithful monkey-god Hanuman became one of India's greatest epics, the Ramayana. Vishnu made his eighth visit as Krishna, the handsome blue-skinned cow-herder god, who like Christ is said to have lived on earth in human form. Unlike Christ however, Krishna was something of a Casanova, who decked himself out in yellow silk, peacock feathers and jasmine-bud garlands. He was the heart-flutter of all the Mathura *gopis* (milk-maids), whom he married en masse after delivering them from the clutches of the demon king Naraka. Krishna is said to have had some 16,000 girlfriends, but Radha was his favorite and their romantic love was woven into Hindu myth to symbolize the relationship between the human soul with the Divine Spirit. Vishnu's ninth and most daring incar-

ing his own son, he furiously swiped off Ganesh's head with a sword. Mortified to discover that he had decapitated his own child, Shiva replaced the severed head with that of the first creature he could find — an elephant. Thus "lucky" Ganesh re-emerged as one of the most popular of all deities, affectionately known as the "Divine Remover of Obstacles", whose animal vehicle is the bandicoot or rat.

Each of the Hindu trinity has a consort, representing the feminine side of their powers. Brahma is married to his own daughter, Saraswati, Goddess of Knowledge, who travels about

ABOVE: This pilgrim takes elaborate measures to preserve her precious cargo of water from the Ganges River in Varanasi, which Hindus believe has the power to cleanse the soul. OPPOSITE: Restoring the frescoes of a Rajput temple requires both skill and a certain religious fervor.

on a swan. Vishnu's consort is the gorgeous Lakshmi, the Lotus Goddess of wealth and prosperity, Shiva's first wife was Sati, but after her tragic demise as India's first suttee victim, he married the beautiful Parvati, Goddess of Cosmic Energy, whose soul splintered into innumerable incarnations — Kali, the terrifying Goddess of Destruction, capable of inflicting disease and misery, but also to heal and bless, depicted with a necklace of writhing snakes and skulls; Durga, the Slayer of the Buffalo Demon, a female warrior usually depicted riding around on a tiger and waving weapons from each of her ten hands; and Shakti, the

Goddess of Creative Energy. As well as Ganesh, Parvati had another son by Shiva, the six-headed god of war, Kartikeya.

Modern-day Hinduism is steeped in elaborate legends about the courageous exploits and playful idiosyncrasies of these flamboyant, larger-than-life gods and goddesses, as well as heroes and demons. Mythology is inseparable to all Indian art — sculpture, paintings, classical music and dance — and the tradition continues to be kept alive today through fairs, festivals and folk songs.

Caste
One of the most pervasive aspects of Hinduism is caste, the schematized division of society into four castes or *varnas*, or "colors": Brahmans, (priests and teachers), Kshatriyas (leaders and warriors), Vaishyas (merchants) and Sudras (farmers, craftsmen and laborers). Caste was invented as a form of social apartheid by the fair-skinned Aryans, (see THE ARRIVAL OF THE ARYANS, page 23). A more romantic explanation for the system is that the four castes sprang from the mouth (Brahmans), arms (Kshatriyas), thighs (Vaishyas) and feet (Sudras) of the creator, Brahma. Over the centuries, these four categories of caste splintered into thousands of sub-castes or *jatis*, so that

their original job-definitions have lost their meaning. Only the Brahmans, by virtue of their high-caste status, have preserved their exclusivity, and regardless of their profession, they tend to occupy privileged positions within society.

Inextricably bound to the notion of caste are the concepts of purity and pollution. Higher castes, especially Brahmans, have their lives regulated by a bewilderingly complex laundry list of prohibitions. Cardinal "don't do's" include the eating of beef and any contact with lower-castes or items of food, water or objects touched by them. High-born castes often refuse to perform tasks that is deemed polluting. This is why many Indian households employ a bevy of servants — a Brahmia cook, a Sudra sweeper, and sub-Sudra toilet cleaner and so on. To transgress these rules requires rigorous ritual, such as bathing in holy waters, and extra time spent at the temple. However the most infamous aspect of the caste system lies outside its boundaries — untouchability. Traditionally, untouchables have always been considered social pariahs, and designated tasks considered lowly and contaminating to all other castes, such as sweeping houses and streets, cleaning sewers and removing corpses. Since independence, the new constitution abolished untouchability, renaming members of the out-caste, harijans or "children of god" and giving them full democratic and human rights.

However breaking customs that have existed for thousands of years is difficult. Caste still determines the kind of work a man accepts, the woman he will marry, the people he will and won't mix with and the type of religious observances he will perform.

Religion in Revolt
From Hinduism emerged two different breakaway ideologies — one propounded by Gautama Buddha and the other by Vardhamana Mahavira, each opposed to extravagance, hierarchical rule and violence. Both philosophers were Kshatriyas, who stood against the complications and in-built prejudices of caste and advocated a return to a simpler, more direct lifestyle, and boundless compassion for all beings — an ascetic approach focused on the belief in the "One Soul", namely the belief that everything that exists within the material world lives on an equal plateau.

JAINISM
Jainism was the first major sect to rise in rebellion from Hinduism and was founded around 500 BC by Vardhamana Mahavira, an older contemporary of Buddha and the last of the 24th Jain saints or *tirthankaras*. He rejected

the Hindu gospel that a Supreme Creator had engineered the universe, believing instead that it was infinite and eternal. Mahavira preached the complete renunciation of desire and the material world as the most direct path to spiritual salvation, encouraging his adherents to follow the path of asceticism, austerity and non-violence. Jain monks became noted for their extreme asceticism, many of them adopting the habits of the Hindu sadhus or holy men, taking to the road dressed in just a loin-cloth with just a begging bowl and a stave as possessions. The Jain's cardinal doctrine of *ahimsa*, non-injury to any living creature stems from their belief that all matter is eternal and that every object has a soul, even pebbles or a grain of sand. Plants and trees have at least two souls, while animals are thought to have three. This leads some of them to wear thin muslin masks over their mouths to prevent them from breathing in small insects. These devotees do not eat after dark in case insects should accidentally fall into their food and die. Many sweep the ground before them as they advance to avoid treading on small creatures.

The Jains are just as preoccupied as Hindus with the theory of rebirth, and becoming a monk is thought to provide a fast track to release. Lay Jains traveling the slower route, try to refrain from telling lies, being devious and from indulging in sensual pleasures.

In the first century AD the Jains split into two sects: the white-clad Shevetambaras and the misogynist, sky-clad Digambaras. The latter were literally "sky-clad", so zealously disdainful of possessions that they refused to don clothes at all, and also regarded women the scourge of humanity, whose charms were evil temptation to those trying to tread the path of straight and narrow. Jain temples are frequently exquisite, with ornately carved marble pillars and sculptures. The most impressive of these can be seen in Rajasthan (Mount Abu), Gujarat (Palitana and Junagadh) and Bombay, the three main Jain centers. The Jains have more than three million adherents in India today. Despite their ascetic beliefs, the Jain community has a strong presence in the business world as traders, bankers and philanthropists, and run rest houses for pilgrims, homes for widows and orphans and even hospitals for sick birds.

BUDDHISM

The Buddhist religion was the second religious schism to emerge from Hinduism, and proved far more influential. The Lord Buddha was born Siddhartha Gautama, the son of a local prince, between 563 and 556 BC in what is now Nepal. Living at first in luxury, he had married

and fathered a son before, at the age of 29, he left the palace to embark on a long quest for truth, human mortality and suffering. After several years of rigorous asceticism, he sat down under a bodhi tree at Uruvela, near Gaya in Bihar state, and achieved "enlightenment" or nirvana. He spent the next 45 years of his life preaching his new philosophy. His message was that everyone, not just priests or ascetics, was capable of aspiring to enlightenment in their own lifetime, without having to passively await a better incarnation in the next life.

Gautama's answer to the problem of suffering was contained in his "Four Noble Truths".

In this doctrine, he offered the diagnosis that human suffering is rooted in terminal dissatisfaction and insatiable desire, and the solution, that in order to remove suffering you must escape desire, and that the way to escape desire is to follow the Eight-fold Path. This path details the ways to become disentangled from all desire for worldly gratification.

At Sarnath's Deer Park near Benares (Varanasi) Gautama met five Brahmans who became his disciples. Called the "Buddha" or the Enlightened One, Gautama reputedly died at the age of eighty, having eaten poisoned food.

ABOVE: An infamous Indian "sacred" cow, elaborately clad for the harvest festival of Pongol in South India. OPPOSITE: An elephant fresco in Shekhavati district, Rajasthan.

Buddhism was clearly a radical departure from Hinduism or Jainism, which held that rebirth, rewards and deliverance came after death. Instead Buddhism renounced the need for extreme asceticism, and instead emphasized living in the present.

Buddhism at first flourished in India, adopted by the great Emperor Asokha (231–198 BC). It was carried to every part of his extensive empire, and spread in time to Burma, Thailand, Sri Lanka, Korea, China, Vietnam, Nepal, Tibet, Central Asia and notably in present-day Japan.

Buddhism was soon divided by a schism, leading to two main schools of Buddhist thought. The Hinayana or "lesser vehicle" held that enlightenment was an individual pursuit and referred to Buddha in external symbols (the lotus for his birth, the bodhi tree for his enlightenment, the wheel of law for his first sermon, and the stupa for his enshrinenment). The Mahayana or "greater vehicle" held that it was a collective one, with the ultimate aim of bringing humanity to salvation, who took Buddha's last words as gospel, "Be a lamp unto yourselves, be a refuge unto yourselves, seek no refuge outside of yourselves".

Buddhism later waned in popularity in India, the land of its birth, largely because of the challenges it faced from Hinduism and Islam. Although Hinduism and Buddhism were almost diametrically opposed theories, these religions and Jainism still co-existed relatively peacefully for many centuries until the advent of Islam.

ISLAM

Muslims are the largest religious minority group in India, with more than 95 million adherents, almost the same as that of Pakistan. They are mainly scattered throughout northern India. Only in Kashmir are they a regional majority. The Muslims first came to India as powerful, iconoclastic conquerors, making the bulk of their converts from low-caste Hindus. Today the most visible legacies of Islam can be seen in the nation's Mughal forts, mosques and domes, and in the Mughali cuisine and art.

Arab traders sowed the first seeds of Islam in India when they beached their sailing vessels along the southern coast during the seventh century AD — bringing news of the recently-founded faith of the Prophet Muhammed. They also brought the Muslim canon, the Koran, a collection of messages from Allah (God) spoken to Muhammed. The overwhelming feature of Islam was its forceful zeal to spread the word — by the sword if required. Beginning in Arabia, Islam spread east over the centuries and eventually took firm root in three continents. Unlike the Hindu religion, which requires its adherents

to be born Hindus, conversion to Islam is easy — to become a Muslim merely requires saying the words "There is no god but Allah and Muhammed is his prophet."

Early in its history, Islam experienced a schism that remains to this day. The majority of Muslims are Sunnites, whose allegiance is to the descendants of Muhammed's direct successor, the Caliph — while other Muslims are Shias or Shi'ites who follow the descendants of the prophet's son-in-law, Ali. Both aspire to make a pilgrimage to Mecca — the prophet Muhammed's birthplace in AD 570 — and become a haji.

SIKHISM

The Sikh religion is fairly new, having broken away from Hinduism in the sixteenth century. Sikhs became increasingly martial towards the end of the seventh century due to Muslim persecution. The Mughal Emperor Aurangzeb so detested the Sikhs that he offered a reward of gold coins for any citizen who brought him a severed head of a Sikh. Provoked by this, the sixth Guru of the line, Guru Gobind Singh (1675–1708) turned the Sikh religion into a military brotherhood, whose members all took the surname Singh or "Lion". He enjoined male Sikhs to observe and wear "the five K's" or *Kakkari* (symbols): *kesh*, uncut hair (normally wrapped in a turban) and beard; *kara*, a steel bangle; *kachh,* short boxer shorts; *kangha*, a wooden or ivory comb and a *kirpan*, a dagger.

Although Sikhs make up only two percent of the population, with some 14 million adherents, they are a very proud and visible community in India. Sikhism grew in response to frictions between Hindus and Muslims in the Punjab, and was founded by Guru Nanak (1444–1538). Sikhism originated as a bhakti or pacifist caste-rejecting movement, seeking to fuse the best from both Hinduism and Islam. It is based on the teachings of ten gurus and contains its essential message in the Sikh Bible, the Granth Sahib. The Sikhs have one god, have temples known as *gurdwaras*, and have had a total of 10 gurus whose collected writings, as well as various Hindu and Muslim scripts form the Granth Sahib. The holiest Sikh shrine is the Golden Temple in Amritsar, in northern Punjab state.

Sikhs are notable for their pragmatism, their earthy good humor, capacity for hard work and skill in mechanical matters.

ZOROASTRIANISM

The tiny community of Zoroastrians, more popularly known as Parsis, are mostly concentrated in Bombay, and are thought to number around 10,000. Their religion is one of the world's oldest, founded by the prophet Zoroaster in modern-day Iran around 800 BC. After the Islamic conquest of Iran many intrepid Zoroastrians left their homes and sought refuge in India. The first group is said to have reached Diu, in Gujarat around AD 766. There was no tension or religious conflict probably because they made no attempts to convert. They were considered desirably fair-skinned and they were astute — as they are still considered to be — in business and intellectual matters.

Their scripture is the Zend-Avesta, which describes the on-going battle between good and evil, and their god is Ahura Mazda, who is symbolized

century of Christ's own lifetime. St Thomas, one of the Disciples, arrived in Kerala in AD 54, and spread the Syrian Christian faith, so that Christianity was by no means unknown when Catholic and Protestant missionaries made converts from various Portuguese, Dutch and English settlements during the sixteenth century, mainly amongst low-caste Hindus. Today India has some 18 million Christians, many of them living in the ex-Portuguese enclave of Goa, as well as a quarter of the population of Kerala. Two small northeastern states — Mizoram and Nagaland — were also sufficiently impressed by intrepid Christian missionaries to convert in large numbers.

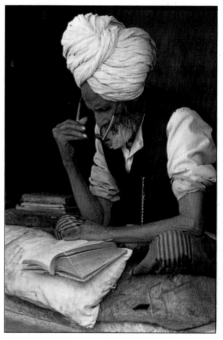

by fire. Parsis worship nature's elements and are fire-worshippers, keeping the symbol of their belief burning in their temples. They are probably best known for their rather macabre habit of leaving their dead in "Towers of Silence" to be devoured by vultures, thus avoiding polluting the sacred purity of the elements — fire, earth, water or air —by burying or cremation.

The numbers of Parsis are on the wane today due to intermarriage becoming more common. Indira Gandhi was married to a Parsi but her son Rajiv could not be a Parsi even if he wanted to — it takes two to tango and two Parsi parents to make a Parsi child.

CHRISTIANS AND JEWS

Many people are surprised to learn that Christianity first took root in India within half a

In Kerala again, the Jews of Cochin should get a special mention — their ancestry dates back to 973 BC when King Solomon's merchant fleet began trading for spices and other fabled treasures. Scholars say that the Jews first settled in Craganore, along Kerala's Malabar Coast, soon after the Babylonian conquest of Judea in 586 BC. The immigrants were well received and the Dravidian king of Cochin granted a title and small principality to one Joseph Rabban, a Jewish leader. Although only a handful of so-called White Jews remain in Cochin, it's possible to see their synagogue, which is the oldest in the Commonwealth.

ABOVE: A diptych of elderly bibliophiles.
LEFT: A monocled Sikh huddled over the holy Granth Sahib. RIGHT: A Rajput gent lost between the pages of his yellowing book.

INDIAN PLEASURES

FESTIVALS AND FAIRS

The Indian calendar brims with thousands of festivals and many fairs all year round. For its most special days, India explodes with dazzling color, religious pageantry, trumpets, fireworks, tinsel, feasting, glorious costumes, brocade-showered idols, and magic outdoor processions of caparisoned elephants. There are festivals to celebrate everything under the sun, from the

latest military hardware to the arrival of the monsoons, even festivals to honor sacred cows and cobras. There are Muslim, Sikh, Buddhist, Jain, Parsi and Christian festivals. But the infinite pantheon of Hindu gods generate the most. Every temple has its own special festival, often occasions when its deities take a bath, require a ritual anointment, or are re-united with a spouse.

In a nutshell, Indian festivals are an excellent excuse for most Indians to put their work aside, forget their hardships, dress up and have fun. The major arts festivals attract the country's best performers of classical and folk dance, music and theater. Many attract thousands of pilgrims, strolling players, and the merely curious, from all over India. The party spirit extends to all aspects of Indian life — from cities to villages, from the annual Republic Day parade to individual wedding celebrations.

The dates of most festivals are calculated according to the Indian lunar calendar, and can be determined only by around October the previous year. At this time your nearest Government of India tourist office should have the full list of upcoming festival dates.

The most interesting and worthwhile festivals and fairs, together with their approximate dates and the best place to see them are listed below. You'll find more details in the relevant section covering the destination.

JANUARY

Pongol, or **Sankranti,** is south India's most exuberant harvest festival. It lasts three days and is best seen in Tamil Nadu and Karnataka. Villagers decorate cattle with fragrant blossoms, ghee, and mango leaves, feeding them *pongol,* or sweet rice, and parade them in lively processions with drums and music. Its highlight is a sort of Dravidian rodeo, when local lads try to wrest bundles of currency from the horns of ferocious bulls.

Republic Day, on January 26, is an important national festival celebrated all over India, but the most spectacular is in New Delhi: a magnificent military parade with regiments in full dress, bands, richly caparisoned camels and elephants, floats and colorful folk dancers rolling along Rajpath. It is followed by a two-day festival of music and dance, and culminates with the famous dusk "Beating the Retreat" held on January 29 at Raj Bhawan.

JANUARY/FEBRUARY

Vasant Panchami honors Saraswati, the Hindu goddess of knowledge, and is celebrated with colorful processions and kite-flying, best seen in West Bengal. Paint-brushes, ball-point pens and musical instruments are reverently placed at Saraswati's shrine, as if to encourage continued creativity.

Float Festival is held in the famous temple town of Madurai in south India, marking the birth anniversary of Tirumali Nayak, the city's seventeenth-century ruler.

Desert Festival, Jaisalmer's popular three-day festival coincides with the full moon and brims with a carnival Rajput atmosphere. Highlights include camel polo, camel races, turban-tying competitions, desert music and dance (See page 138).

Nagaur Livestock Fair, located half a day's drive from Jodhpur, rewards adventurous travelers with four days of camel races, livestock competitions and colorful Rajasthani dancing and singing. Old India hands rate it just as highly as its better-known cousin, the Pushkar Fair.

Goa's Carnival (see page 201) is no longer as exuberantly spectacular as in former days, but still attracts devotees for its free-flowing feni and party atmosphere.

FEBRUARY/MARCH
Shivrati marks the day when Hindus across India pay their respects to Shiva, the religion's father figure. The most colorful pageantry occurs at the largest Shiva temples at Khajuraho,

may not enjoy the experience of being sloshed with buckets of paint from rooftop pranksters. Go prepared like everyone else by purchasing plenty of powder, paint and water-pistols, and wear clothes that can be thrown away the next day. Don't despair — you may resemble a walking artist's palette for days, or even weeks later — but the color will eventually come out!

Khajuraho Dance Festival is held early March in the famous temple, with a week-long program of evening performances by the country's best artists to a backdrop of flood-lit temples and glittering stars.

Varanasi, Mandi, Chidambaram and Kashmir. Devotees fast for a day, then fall upon dates, fruits, nuts, sweet potatoes and rice — Shiva's favorite snack.

Holi is India's color-doused version of April Fools day. Spring is celebrated with explosive Bacchanalian, paint-squirting revelry that breaks down all traditional barriers of caste and religion in an atmosphere of playful flirtation. Picasso never visited India, but he was so impressed by the idea of Holi that he once staged it at his Spanish villa. It's best to soak up the carnival atmosphere of a "real" rural Holi in one of the smaller Rajasthan towns, where you'll be drawn into exuberant folk dance, music and gentle pelting with clouds of saffron, emerald, turquoise, pink and red powder. Large cities are often not so much fun — and unwary foreigners

MARCH/APRIL
Gangaur is best seen in Rajasthan, especially Jaipur and Udaipur, West Bengal and Orissa. It pays tribute to Shiva's wife Parvati, in her incarnation of Gangaur, goddess of marital happiness, abundance and fertility. *Gauri* means yellow, the color of ripened wheat. In Jaipur, idols of Shiva and Gangaur are paraded on floats pulled by caparisoned horses and elephants, amid trumpeting and singing. Everywhere else, marriage parties add to the atmosphere.

Festival fun. ABOVE: Sikhs LEFT don traditional attire to celebrate the birthday of Guru Gobind Singh. RIGHT: At Pushkar Camel Fair. OPPOSITE: A smiling paint-splattered youth after a busy morning of Holi festivities. OVERLEAF: Dazzlingly colorful elephant parade in Jaipur.

Mahavir Jayanti is a Jain festival dedicated to Mahavira, the 24th Jain Thirthankara or saint, best seen at Jain shrines at Jain centers in Gujarat or at Mount Abu in Rajasthan.

APRIL/MAY

Urs Festival, Ajmer. Held for six days in April to May, the Urs Festival is a dramatic annual display of *quwwali* singing, exuberant fairs and feasts (see page 130).

Baisakhi celebrates the beginning of the Hindu solar New Year. Hindus throng to the sacred Ganges River to bathe and worship, since the

goddess Meenakshi and Shiva with ten days of non-stop revelry in the courtyards of the famous Meenakshi Temple. Artists dance, priests chant, children dress as gods, and musicians play enchanting devotional music.

MAY-JUNE

Buddha Purnima celebrates Buddha birth, death and enlightenment, and is best at the famous Buddhist centers of Sarnath and Bodhgaya.

Hemis Festival is held at the largest monastery in Ladakh, and celebrates the birth anniversary

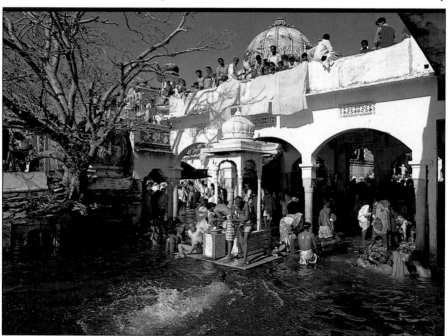

goddess Ganga is thought to have descended to earth on this day many millennia ago. Festive processions are best seen in the holy cities along the Ganges river in north India, as well as in Srinagar's Mughal Gardens and in Tamil Nadu. Sikhs also celebrate it to commemorate the day in 1689 that Guru Gobind Singh founded the Khalsa or militant brotherhood of the Sikhs. In Punjab farmers start harvesting and perform the *bhangra* dance, as wild and vigorous as that of the cossacks.

Pooram in Trichur, Kerala, is one of India's temple festival highlights with its 30 decorated elephants, dhoti-clad priests, trumpets and fireworks (see page 329).

Meenakshi Kalaynam in Madurai, celebrates the annual mock-marriage of the "fish-eyed"

of the Guru Padmasambhava. Masked dances, fairs and the ornately-dressed Ladakhis are the highlights (see page 181).

JUNE/JULY

Id-ul-Fitr, also known as Ramazan-Id, is a major Muslim celebration which marks the end of Ramazan, the Islamic month of fasting. Thousands of devout Muslims stream into the major mosques to pray, then rejoice and feast. It's best seen in Delhi, Lucknow, Hyderabad and Calcutta.

Rath Yatra, held in Puri, Orissa, is the most spectacular of all temple festivals, with a cast of devout thousands, like an Indian version of a Cecil de Mille epic. Held in honor of Lord Jagannath, three enormous temple chariots carrying the idols of Jagannath and his siblings,

Balabhadra and Subhadra, are dragged by sweating devotees (see page 252).

JULY/AUGUST

Naag Panchami is held in honor of Naga, the great thousand-headed serpent on which Vishnu reclined in contemplation. It's most dramatic in Jodhpur, where giant colorful effigies of Naga are erected, and women worship visiting snake charmers for fertility. Throughout India, cobras are fed with milk and sweets.

Teej celebrates both the onset of the monsoon

Dussehra is a 10-day festival celebrated with performances across India, but the most colorful pageantry takes place in Kulu, Mysore, and West Bengal. In Delhi and Varanasi it is known as **Ram Lila.**

Diwali, or the "festival of lights" traditionally takes place on the full moon night after Dussehra. It's the gayest and most riotous of all Indian festivals, with a night-long display of fireworks, illuminations and general pageantry. Throughout India, houses are cleaned and re-painted to honor Lakshmi, the goddess of wealth and the home, then bedecked with hundreds of oil-

and the reunion of Shiva and his wife Parvati, (Gangaur). Nubile girls dress up in tinsel-fringed saris, jewelry and bright green veils, playfully push each other on garland-bedecked swings, and pray for a faithful loving husband. It's best seen at Jaipur, where gaily, vividly dressed villagers swarm to see the pageantry as caparisoned elephants, dancers and musicians escort the Parvati idol from her parent's home into Shiva's waiting arms.

Independence Day on August 15, is celebrated all over India, notably in New Delhi.

SEPTEMBER/OCTOBER

Ganapati (Ganesh Chaturthi) honors the elephant-headed god of good luck and inspires grand processions everywhere, but especially in Bombay (see page 196).

lamps. It's best seen in north India and at Mysore in the south.

NOVEMBER/DECEMBER

Pushkar's Cattle Fair. A definite "must-see" tourist highlight (see page 130).

Christmas Day, December 25. Exotic piety is most spectacular in Goa, where glorious sixteenth-century cathedrals stage candle-lit mass, hymns and pompous religious celebrations.

Madras Dance and Arts Festivals last from mid December to early January and offer a potpourri

OPPOSITE: Villagers undergo a ritual bath in the holy lake at Pushkar. ABOVE: Naked Naga sadhus, clad only in marigold garlands and Rastafarian dreadlocks converge at Hardwar for the Kumbh Mela.

of excellent performances by the nation's best artists.

FESTIVAL FOOTNOTE

India's **Kumbh Mela** is the most ancient and spectacular religious carnival on the planet, revealing to astonished Western eyes all that is most mysterious, bizarre and awesome about Hinduism, a faith that was born some 3,000 years ago. It is held every three years consecutively in one of the four places: Allahabad (Uttar Pradesh), Nasik (Maharashtra), Ujian (Madhya Pradesh) and Hardwar (Uttar

Pradesh). Ancient legend relates that demons once stole sacred nectar of immortality from the gods in a kumbh, or vessel, and during the ensuing battle between the gods and the thieves, the nectar spilled at 12 spots in the universe — eight in the heavens and four on earth — forming the four most sacred Indian cities. The Kumbh Mela begins when the astrological positions of the sun and moon are most auspicious, and millions of pilgrims and thousands of holy men (sadhus) of every order descend in order to bathe in holy rivers, believing the holy rivers suddenly run with life-preserving nectar. Ash-smeared, leopard skin-clad "gurus" preside over captive audiences; "god" children bestow regal blessings; naked ascetics perform miraculous feats of endurance amid a temporary city erected from tents on huge sand belts near the river. The holiest of all the Kumbh Melas occurs every 12 years at Allahabad, the confluence of the Ganges, Yamuna and the mythical Saraswati rivers.

ABOVE: A master musician instructs his pupils in a Madras school. OPPOSITE: A lone tiger in Rajasthan's Ranthambhore National Park.

DANCE AND MUSIC

India has extraordinarily rich traditions of both classical and folk dance and music, woven inextricably together. It also offers a wealth of gifted artists, and performance festivals, sometimes against the original backdrops of ancient temples. In the large cities, five-star hotels often lay on performances in their restaurants as an extra draw for tourists, but more authentic happenings can be found by scanning details of events in the English-language newspapers.

There are several well-defined classical dance forms, each having evolved from a particular part of the country. All are rooted in the ancient religious tradition of dance as a form of worship, and their themes tend to concentrate on Hindu myths and the legendary exploits of the gods. In fact dance is said to have originated with Lord Shiva, who in the form of Nataraja, the Lord of the Dance, performed the energetic *tandava* or cosmic dance.

The most ancient classical form is BHARAT NATYAM, performed for centuries by *devadasis*, girls who were dedicated to Dravidian temples in Tamil Nadu. It is performed solo by a woman, who begins with *alarippu*, a dance symbolizing that she is offering her body for the pleasure of the gods. The fluid, sensuous style combines *nritta*, or "pure dance" with expressive facial and hand movements, as well as jingling ankle bells, to depict maidenly love, accompanied by musicians.

KATHAKALI, literally "dance-drama" comes from neighboring Kerala, is derived from a form of strenuous yoga. It is easily the most spectacular of all India's dances, always performed by males in outrageously burlesque Mikado-like costumes that require hours of preparation.

ODISSI, from the eastern state of Orissa, is the most lyrical, erotic of all devotional temple dances.

KUCHIPUDI, from southern Andhra Pradesh is a form of decorative dance dramas.

KATHAK, from northern India is a fast-paced Muslim-influenced north Indian dance with complicated footwork, whirling pirouettes and rhythmic sensuality — performed by *nautch* or dancing courtesans in the Mughal court.

Apart from these main styles are many regional folk dances, tribal martial art and drama traditions, such as Manipur's graceful Manipuri style, Bengal and Orissa's tradition of *Chahau* masked dance. There are many others — ritualist dances to welcome the birth of a child, or chase away demons — and some involving balancing tricks with jugs of water or juggling knives.

Dance in India is unthinkable without music and song. According to legend, *nada* (sound)

was the cosmic boom that accompanied earth's creation, while musical, rhythmical chanting of holy scriptures is as old as India's earliest civilization. Classical Indian music and its accompanying singing has a timeless, spiritual quality that must be experienced to be understood. Broadly speaking, it can be divided into two distinct styles; northern Hindustani and southern Carnatic, the former being more earthy and improvisational, steeped in Muslim and Persian influences, while the latter is more melodic and devotional. The music has two basic elements, the *tala* and the *raga*. *Tala* is the rhythm and is characterized by the number of beats, while the *raga* provides the melody. Best known of the Indian instruments are the sitar and the tabla. The sitar is the large stringed instrument popularized by Ravi Shankar, while the tabla, a twin drum, is rather like the western bongo. Other less known instruments include the stringed *sarod* and *sarangi*, the latter played with a bow, and the reed trumpet-like *shehnai* and *tampura.*

ELEPHANTS AND MAN-EATERS

India offers the chance to walk on the wild side, to see and photograph some of the world's most majestic creatures — tigers, lions, elephants, rhinos, leopards and wild bears — getting as close as you dare to be in their natural habitats. India has a rich variety of wildlife — over 350 species of mammals, 900 species of reptiles, 2,000 species of birds and over 30,000 varieties of insects and butterflies, to be exact — enough to fascinate serious naturalists and casual tourists alike.

Although aristocratic maharajas and topeed British colonialists adored *shikar*, the sport of tiger shooting and netting countless mounds of dead animals and birds, conservation of wildlife actually has a very long history in India. It began over 2,000 years ago when Emperor Ashoka forbade his subjects to destroy forests or slaughter wildlife. He called forests "abhayaranya", meaning places "free from fear" — an ethic that anticipated the wildlife sanctuaries of the modern era. Ancient Aryan nature worship wove animals into Hindu myth, legend and religious belief. Animals were the sacred steads of the Hindu gods, on which they could roam the universe. Lord Shiva, god of creation, rode about on a Nandi or bull; Saraswati, goddess of knowledge on a swan; Vishnu, god of preservation, on a garuda, a sun bird with golden wings. Others were part-gods themselves, like the elephant-headed Ganesh, god of wisdom, or the monkey god Hanuman. Today, something of this ancient harmony between man and nature endures with the Bishnois

community in west Rajasthan, who have a remarkable rapport with the black buck antelope, believing the animals are their reincarnated ancestors.

Presently, India has 20 major wildlife sanctuaries, 121 national parks and nine bird reserves, scattered from Ladakh in the Himalayan mountains to the southern tip of Tamil Nadu, and covering a combined total of 90,000 sq km (35,000 sq miles), some three percent of India's total land. They are vital to the conservation of endangered species, such as the Bengal Tiger, the Asiatic Elephant and Lion, the Snow Leopard and the Siberian Crane. India's most successful conservation

effort is Project Tiger, launched in 1973 by the government and the World Wildlife Fund to create strongholds for the tiger, the very symbol of India, when the beast was on the edge of extinction. There are now 15 of these throughout the country, and some 4,000 tigers. The most famous (and accessible) of all Project Tiger reserves is Corbett National Park, a six hour drive from Delhi on the edge of the Himalayas.

Sanctuaries offer rewards of great natural beauty as well as magnificent wildlife. They all seem to have good lodges — particularly located within former princely hunting reserves — facilities, adequate restaurants and almost always offer excellent tours for visitors, often with the option of hiring jeeps, tame elephants or in some cases, boats for exploring. Each sanctuary usually has a Forest Department with a raft of local guides and trackers. If arranged in advance, it's possible to stay in the Department's rest-houses and hideaways, usually tucked within dense forest — marvelous for safe, comfortable "spying" at very close quarters. You will almost never be allowed to meander off into the jungle without an experienced guide.

Go well-prepared with binoculars, a good camera (preferably with a wide-angle and zoom lens), rolls of camera film, plenty of mosquito repellent and/or a mosquito net for slumbering comfort in jungle lodges. Camouflage clothes — olive green, khaki, and dull brown colors — are in; lurid Hawaiian shirts, transistor radios, strong after-shave and loud conversations are definitely out — they'll send most wildlife running for cover.

WILDLIFE DIRECTORY

Delhi and the North

UTTAR PRADESH   Corbett National Park (see page 89), Dudhwa National Park.

MADHYA PRADESH   Shivpuri Wildlife Sanctuary, Bandhavgagh National Park, Kanha National Park, Panna Wildlife Sanctuary.

Rajasthan

Keoladeo National Park, Bharatpur (see page 102), Ranthambhore National Park (see page 128), Sariska Tiger Reserve (see page 122).

The Mountain Trail

KASHMIR   Dachigam National Park (see page 172).

Bombay and the West

GUJARAT   Sasan-Gir (see page 201).

Calcutta and the East

ASSAM   Kaziranga Wildlife Sanctuary (see page 251), Manas Wildlife Sanctuary (see page 251).

WEST BENGAL   Sunderbans Tiger Reserve, (see page 240), Jaldapara Wildlife Sanctuary, Sajnakhali Bird Sanctuary (see page 242).

BIHAR   Hazaribagh and Palamau Sanctuaries.

ORISSA   Simliphal Reserve.

Across the Deccan

KARNATAKA   Bandipur and Nagarhole Wildlife Sanctuaries (see page 285), Ranganathittu Water Bird Sanctuary.

TAMIL NADU   Mudumalai Wildlife Sanctuary (see page 288).

The Deep South Trail

TAMIL NADU   Vedanthangal Water Bird Sanctuary, Point Calimere Bird Sanctuary.

KERALA   Periyar, Thekkady Wildlife Sanctuary (see page 318), Mundanthurai Tiger Sanctuary, Anamalai Tiger Sanctuary.

SPICY PLEASURES

INDIAN FOOD AND DRINK

Visitors soon awaken to the fact that Indian food is infinitely more than merely curry. The word is an English mispronunciation of *kari* or spice sauce. In fact curry is only one of many techniques used in India's countless kitchens. Housewives from Kashmir and Kanya Kumari are further apart cuisine-wise than those from Scandinavia and Spain. Even curry itself is more than its seems. The Indian cook uses an enormous armory of more than 30 freshly ground spices like an artist's palette to make endlessly inventive combinations of masala sauces, which like each basic ingredient, varies from region to region.

The fabled furnace-like heat of Indian food, particularly in the South — causing the unwary eater to turn bright red and blink back tears — can be an occupational hazard of experimentation, better soothed by *raita* (yogurt side-dish) or coconut milk than water. How Indian stomachs cope with this every day is a mystery.

India's great religions — Hinduism, Buddhism and Jainism — have long advocated vegetarianism, and this has led to the development of what is surely the world's most delicious vegetarian cuisine. In Gujarat, the Jains refuse to eat meat (even insects) and even shun the color of blood. Although not all Hindus are vegetarian, you will probably end up eating more vegetable dishes during your stay, particularly in south India. Table manners in India dictate that if you adopt the local custom of eating with your fingers, you do so only with your right hand, the other being considered "unclean" and used for something completely different altogether. There is always somewhere to wash, and many restaurants bring finger-bowls to the table.

Broadly speaking, the cuisine of India divides the nation.

Northerners, whose paunches tend to be more developed, adore their traditional rich Mughali cuisine, redolent of yogurt, fried onions, saffron and nuts — brought by the Mughals from Persia in the sixteenth century. *Rogon josh,* (curried lamb), *gushtaba* (spicy meat pounded to paté-consistency, formed into balls and simmered in spiced yogurt) and *biryani* (chicken or lamb in orange-flavored rice, sprinkled with rose water, almonds and dried fruits) are well known. The world-renowned clay oven-baked tandoori cooking (chicken, meat or fish marinated in herbs and baked in a clay oven) and charcoal-grilled kebabs also hail from north India. *Naans, paratha,* stuffed *kulcha,* and hankerchief-thin *romali roti* breads are served alongside.

Longevity-conscious southerners, who are almost exclusively vegetarian, traditionally serve an array of light, but fiercely hot curries with steaming rice, chutneys, pickles and *puris* — either on a well-washed banana leaf or on a *thali*, a large round metal tray filled with little bowls that are constantly refilled. Other specialities include the breakfast staples — the popular *dosa*, a form of crepe made from lightly fermented rice flour and stuffed with spiced potato, and steamed rice-cake *idlis*, both eaten with fresh coconut chutney and *sambhar*, a chilli-laced lentil soup.

There are several staples without which no meal on the sub-continent would be complete. A day without bread for most Indians would be unthinkable — like a Frenchman without his baguette. Certain unleavened breads such as the common *chapati, roti* and millet *paratha*, originated 4,000 years ago and these slapped to the side of a tandoor oven or fried over charcoal braziers, still dominate most meals. Dairy products are liberally used in both the North and South — so that it is not difficult to understand why the Indians regard the cow as sacred.

Desserts are mainly very sweet milk/curd-based puddings and confections like mouth-watering *kulfi* ice-cream, flavored with cardamom, pistachio nuts and saffron, *rasgullas* (cream cheese balls in rose syrup), and *burfi* halva sweets, covered in wafer-thin silver paper. *Gulab jamun* (spongy ground almond balls), and *jalebi* (cartwheel-shaped sweets), both come dripping with honeyed syrup.

There is a spectacular variety of fresh fruit — mangoes, pomegranates, melons, pineapples, fig-like pitchouts, bananas, coconuts, Kashmiri apples and tangerines — found right across India, most of it extremely cheap. Always buy complete fruits and peel them yourself. If grapes and tomatoes look appetizing, wash them in sterilized water first.

It's common to end your meal by chewing palate-cleansing handfuls of *sof*, or aniseed. The mildly addictive *paan* is also served — a mixture of betel nut and spices wrapped in a betel leaf — and the cause of all those red-stained lips and teeth.

India's national drink is *chai*, the army-style brew made from boiled up tea, buffalo milk and spoonfuls of sugar, served at every railway station and *dhaba* or roadside café, usually in red clay cups which are supposed to be shattered afterwards. If you ask for "tray tea", it is served the conventional way. If you don't like sugar, ask for "*ek chai neh chini*" (one tea, no sugar). Local south Indian coffee is excellent, and is available

from the extensive network of Indian Coffee Houses in most cities and towns.

For thirst-quenchers, *nimbu* or lime soda, served sweet, salt or plain, or freshly squeezed juices are the most refreshing "safe" beverages. Yogurt-based *lassis* and milk straight from the king coconut are also very cooling and cleansing. Fizzy bottled soft drinks — with improbable names such as Limca, Thrills, Campa Cola and Thumbs Up — can be bought virtually anywhere and consumed with relative safety, but are very sickly. A bag of oranges are probably a healthier, more satisfying alternative. Bottled mineral water is widely available,

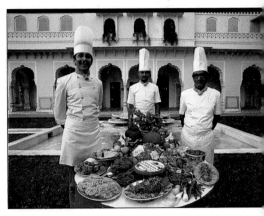

but check first that its seal has not been tampered with.

Imported wine and spirits is available in top hotels, but is very expensive, which is why bottles of Scotch are so gratefully received as presents in India. Indian alcohol is cheaper, craftily confusing matters by its name: Indian Made Foreign Liquor or Foreign Liquor for short. Indian-made beer, wines and whiskey are not terribly memorable (except the morning after) and are served in most hotels except in "dry" Gujarat and Tamil Nadu states, where liquor permits must be collected from the nearest tourist office. Popular brands of beer, good for drinking along with spicy curries, include Golden Eagle, Punjab, Kingfisher, Rosy Pelican and London Pilsner. Bangalore has excellent draught beer served on tap in many English-style pubs. In the ex-Portuguese enclave of Goa, coconut and palm-leaf *toddy*, and cashew-nut *feni* make a piquant, interesting variation — and goes down very well with fresh grilled seafood on a tropical star-filled night.

ABOVE: Chefs display tantalizing Mughali fare at the famous Rambagh Hotel in Jaipur. OVERLEAF: Communal bread-baking at a Sikh festival in the Punjab.

Delhi
and
the North

THE CAPITAL: A TALE OF TWO CITIES

New Delhi, India's capital and its third largest city, plays host to the nation's political elite, influential tycoons, *dhoti*-clad bureaucrats and Mercedes-driven diplomats. It is the political and administrative powerhouse of the world's largest democracy, grafted on an ancient relic-dotted hinterland that once formed the seat of the mighty Mughal empire. Its origins are thought to extend as far back as 1200 BC, and since then, no less than seven cities have risen and fallen, phoenix-like from the abandoned ruins of the last. Across Delhi's skyline, centuries-old monuments, lapis-domed mosques, and magnificent forts are surrounded by elegant Raj-era architecture, modern government blocks, embassies and stark concrete tenements.

Visitors to Delhi are immediately struck by the immense contrast between its ancient and modern character, for it is really two distinct cities merged into one. The more historic, medieval Old Delhi was built by the Mughal Emperor Shah Jehan, drawing tourists to its imposing seventeenth century Red Fort, the Jama Masjid mosque and network of tangled bazaars. It is an oriental hubbub laced with dust and sneeze-inducing spices, teeming with both human and animal life. Here pavement ear-cleaners ply their trade; squads of *burqa*-clad women move like shiny black shadows into narrow secret lanes; strings of sure-footed coolies strain under giant sacks; and indolent merchants sell everything from brass utensils to wedding turbans.

To the south of the old city lies New Delhi, which was laid out during the early twentieth century by the British as an imperial capital from which to direct affairs on the subcontinent. This spacious eighth Delhi was designed by British architects Sir Edwin Lutyens and Sir Herbert Baker, and is dominated by a vast sandstone presidential palace, larger than Versailles, which is linked to the Arc de Triomphe-like India Gate by a sweeping ceremonial avenue, called Rajpath, or King's Way. From these pompously grand architectural icons radiate concentric rings of wide, well-paved tree-lined boulevards, flanked by handsome white bungalows and landscaped gardens. Completed at the tail-end of the British Raj in 1931, New Delhi was a ready-made capital inherited by India's new leaders 16 years later. It still manifests a perceptible hangover from the Raj-era, not only in much of its old-world architecture, but in the British systems of parliament, law and bureaucracy which survive more or less intact, albeit idiosyncratically. An early illustration of this, just after India became independent

in 1947, was when many of the original 6,000 servants who kept the Viceroy's Palace pristine during the Raj, and lived behind the palace in a township of their own, were first dismissed in a show of egalitarianism, but soon asked to resume their old jobs in the newly-named Rashtrapati Bhawan. These days New Delhi's colonial architecture has a seedy, decaying air, seen everywhere but most noticeable in the central spoke-like Connaught Place where the once-grand colonnaded arcades have become dirty, peeling pissoirs, covered with crow-infested *tatties* or giant rattan curtains to shield shops from sun and rain. Fast-food parlors and handicraft

emporiums ensure a steady flow of tourists who learn to negotiate pavements covered with blood-like betel stains spat from pedestrians, child beggars and prowling touts hawking extraordinary junk.

The social life of Delhi's rich and powerful is played out against a backdrop of genteel clubs, five-star hotels and Raj-era bungalows, where gossip is spiced with the latest wafts of scandal and sycophancy. On the flip-side, Delhi also houses thousands of homeless on its streets, many of them Rajasthani villagers fleeing the ravages of drought to find work as laborers on the city's numerous construction sites. After a day or so

ABOVE: Lutyen's India Gate remains the emblem of British-built New Delhi. Beyond stands the empty Rajput-style *chhatris* where a statue of King George V used to stand before it was removed after Independence.

in Delhi, you'll see these hordes of gaunt workers, who look like sun-blackened skeletons draped in bright rags, who balance impossible loads on their heads on sites resembling biblical epics. At night, you'll see their makeshift cardboard hovels go up on pavements and traffic islands next to slumbering cows, barely a stone's throw from the capital's luxury hotels and embassy colonies.

Delhi can be a rather deceptive introduction to India — with its built-up urban sprawl, large influx of foreign tourists and sten-gun toting security patrols — but its historic sights merit a stay of at least four or five days. Of all the large

Indian cities, it offers the most gentle transition to life on the subcontinent with some of the country's best hotels and restaurants. It's also the most efficient center from which to make bookings and gather information, and a convenient base for exploring northern India, with easy access by air and train to the ever-popular "Golden Triangle" route of Agra and Jaipur; to the rest of Rajasthan; to Varanasi and Khajuraho, and to Kashmir and Ladakh.

THE NORTHWEST CITADEL

Historically, Delhi represented a crucial foothold on the subcontinent that none of India's prospective invaders could afford to ignore. It commanded the strategic north-eastern routes from Central Asia and the high valleys from Afghanistan, where Delhi's early conquerors came from — many of them in the footsteps of Alexander the Great — and provided a bastion for plundering the rich lowlands of the Ganges delta.

Competition for the mastery of Delhi began in the eleventh century, much of it marked by gruesome Oriental despotism and valiant victories — the city was raised, fought over, destroyed, deserted and re-built no less than seven times, although archaeologists argue that

as many as eight other cities existed, and also put forward the hypothesis that idol-smashing Muslims may have wiped out remnants of ancient Hindu settlements.

The antiquity of Delhi may be traced to the legendary city of Indrapratha, the capital of the Pandavas, the mythical heroes of the Mahabharata epic. Legend has it that their city was founded on the banks of the river Yamuna over 3,000 years ago, although archaeologists trace the earliest settlements in Delhi to 1200 BC. Indrapratha was said to be located where the sixteenth century Purana Qila now stands — where shards of fine grey earthenware have been found that seem to give substance to this myth.

Invading Rajput dynasties were responsible for the first "Dillis", whose decaying ruins can be seen 10 km (about six miles) south of Connaught Place near the Qutb Minar. Of these, the first was Lal Kot, built by the Tomar Rajputs in AD 1060, who brought with them the mysterious Iron Pillar with its fourth or fifth century Sanskrit script, said to be more than 2,000 years old and made of such pure iron that it has never rusted. Even more enigmatic than the origin of the Iron Pillar, is the only great ancient Hindu shrine left intact in Delhi's environs, 17 km (10.5 miles) south of Delhi, known as Suraj Khund. Thought to have been constructed by the Tomar Rajputs, it is a pool surrounded by wide amphitheater-like steps, with the remains of a large temple nearby dedicated to the sun-god, Surya.

Feudal battles ensured that Lal Kot soon fell to another Hindu Rajput clan, the Chauhans, in the twelfth century. They considerably expanded this original domain, re-naming it Quila Rai Pithora.

Then in 1206, Delhi trembled to the rumblings of India's "Spartacus", the former Turkic slave, Qutb-ud-din-Aibak who became Delhi's first Muslim Sultan. He pounded his predecessor's cities to rubble before laying the base for Delhi's second city with his two significant edifices: — the Quwwat-ul-Islam, one of India's first mosques, built from the remains of 27 Hindu temples with the looted Iron Pillar given pride of place in its courtyard — and his famous tower of victory, the Qutb Minar, situated south of New Delhi and celebrating the Muslim defeat of a Hindu king.

The line of the so-called Slave Kings ended with assassination in 1296, when Sultan Ala-ud-din of the Afghan Khiljis stormed through India, capturing the Rajput fortress of Chittaugarh and founding Siri, Delhi's second city, leaving a magnificent sprawling fort that visitors will find surrounded by encroaching modern tenements in the present-day Hauz Khas suburb.

By 1321, the Afghans, were ousted by the Muslim Tughlaqs, a formidable Islamic warrior dynasty, who constructed no fewer then three cities here during the fourteenth century, The first, Tughlaqabad, built by Ghiyas-ud-Din, is now a ruined ghost fort city, dotted with tombs and fortified by massive sloping walls, 10 km (about six miles) southeast of the Qutb Minar. Whether or not the city is haunted — as the story goes — by the ghost of a vengeful saint, is a matter for speculation, but it was abandoned only five years after its construction due to a shortage of water. Today it is inhabited only by the Gujars, a gypsy tribe. The second city, Jehanapanah, was also rapidly deserted. Its founder was the mad quixotic Sultan Muhammed Shah, an Indian "Nero", renowned for fiendish ways — among his many exploits, the most vicious was crushing his elderly father to death beneath a specially-constructed "ceremonial welcome" archway. Acting on imperial whim he decided to quit his father's domain, and force-marched his subjects 1,100 km (563 miles) all the way to his new capital at Daulatabad, near present-day Aurangbad. According to an eye-witness account, two subjects attempted to evade the Sultan's Long March, and suffered the ruler's wrath. The first, a cripple, was butchered, and the other, who was blind, was prodded all the way to Daulatabad by soldier's lances. It was later observed that only the poor man's severed leg, a macabre trophy, eventually arrived. Seventeen years later, the Sultan grew tired of debauched amusements at his Deccan fortress, and marched his subjects all the way home to Delhi again.

Delhi's fifth city, was the final and most impressive achievement of the Tughlaq rulers, founded in 1351, by the Sultan Muhammed's considerably more tolerant cousin, Feroz Shah. His 37 year-long reign was relatively peaceful, and he was able to indulge his hobby for building, and repairing the existing buildings of the Qutb complex. Today visitors explore the crumbling ruins of his historic capital's core in the site known as Feroz Shah Kotla, just to the south of the Red Fort, where you can see one of two ancient third century pillars which bears the edicts of the Emperor Ashoka in the Brahmanic script deciphered by James Prinsep in 1837.

After Feroz's death, confusion about the succession of the Tughlaq line weakened the kingdom, and when in 1398 Timur the Lane, the dreaded Tamerlane, the emir of Samarkand and conqueror of Persia, Afghanistan and Mesopotamia, invaded India, he met with only slight resistance. But after two weeks sacking the city, Timur led his armies back to Samarkand, taking 120 elephants as useful booty, but not bothering to set himself on Delhi's throne. The last of the Tughlaqs died in 1414, and power passed to the Sayyids, descendants of the Prophet, who

barely made a dent in Delhi's history, and to three generations of Pathan Lodhi kings, who built a necropolis of tombs and mosques but little else, and moved to Sikander, just outside Agra in 1504.

The first of the Great Mughals to arrive in Delhi was Babur, a feudal overlord from Samarkand who claimed the blood of both Genghis Khan and Timur ran in his veins. He swept through Delhi briefly before marching his armies onto Agra, where he acquired the Koh-i-noor diamond and founded the Mughal dynasty before dying in 1530. His son Humayan moved north to Delhi, building a fort-capital,

known as Purana Qila on the banks of the Yamuna river, where his magnificent tomb stands today. Humayan called his capital Din-Panah or Asylum of the Faith, but had to flee to Persia (using the Koh-i-noor to bribe his way out in safety) when an Afghan adventurer, Sher Shah Suri arrived on the scene in 1540. The usurper was able to add several impressive monuments to what became Delhi's sixth city, Shergarh, before Humayan reclaimed his throne with a vengeance in 1555.

From then on, into the seventh century, Delhi and Agra became twin jewels in the Mughal crown, and not until 1638 did Humayan's

ABOVE: Mahatma Gandhi depicts the "Father of the Nation" in a characteristically stalwart pose.
OPPOSITE: Decaying colonial colonnades in Connaught Place.

great-grandson, Shah Jehan transfer the seat of his empire to Delhi. Completed over a decade, the seventh Delhi, Shahjahanabad, became India's regal center. It was dominated by a magnificent euchre sandstone walled fortress, now called the Red Fort, the giant Jama Masjid mosque and the broad processional avenue, Chandni Chowk, or "moonlight bazaar", named for a wide canal which once ran down its center. Chandni Chowk was described by the contemporary American traveler Robert Minturn as the "gayest scene in India" filled with "scarlet ladies" and gloriously-clad "natives" gadding about on howdahed elephants and Arab steads. With this in mind, it's easy to picture the pride of Mughal Delhi's architect Shah Jehan, who inscribed his famous claim: "If there is paradise on the face of this earth, it is here, Oh! It is here!" in gold above his marble audience hall in the Red Fort.

However, the Mughal empire was fated to fall into decay, and a century later in 1739, Delhi's prized gem-studded Red Fort fell to the plundering Nadir Shah, the emperor of Persia.

By this time the weakened Mughals were no match for the British, who had long ago established footholds in Madras and Bengal. By 1803, the British placed under their yoke the last Mughal, the blind old poet, Bahudur Shah, who was in reality only a puppet king. All that remained to him was his title, palace and a pension bestowed by the new rulers. But the British suffered a severe setback with the year-long Indian Mutiny in 1857 — sparked in Meerut by protesting sepoys, or native soldiers, whose principal objection seems relatively straightforward in retrospect — pig and cow fat to grease Muslim and Hindu cartridges. The British reaction was one of classic hubris, and the enraged sepoys went on a murderous spree, arriving in Delhi after a day's gallop to bayonet every European in sight. The sepoys secured the reluctant support of their symbolic emperor, Bahudur Shah in their bid to oust the feringhi or foreigners. The insurgents were later strung up by avenging British troops, so incensed at the sight of their mutilated womenfolk and children that they not only blew up mutineers by placing them over the mouths of their cannons, but seriously debated blowing up the Jama Masjid too, with the notion of raising a Christian cathedral in its place. At Kashmir Gate, slightly north of the Red Fort, you can still see the pock-marks of shot and shell, where the dwindling number of British were forced to retreat to defend themselves. Bahudur Shah was packed off in disgraced exile to Rangoon, but a vigilante British officer "bagged" the last Mughal's sons for

the greater glory of Empire during a spate of cross-firing at Humayan's Tomb. Delhi remained a provincial town set amid hyena-infested wilds and magnificent relics, until 1911, when for the first and only time, a ruling English monarch came to India to be crowned Emperor in Delhi at the Coronation Durbar. This was where the new King George V broke the news of the shift of India's imperial capital from Calcutta to "this beautiful and historic city". His words so traumatized the British in Calcutta that they omitted to print the numbing news in the next day's newspapers, fearing perhaps that their new Emperor was suffering from a bad bout of sun-stroke.

VISITING DELHI

New Delhi's grid-like boulevards are relatively easy to find your way around — roads are well signed and all the street names uniformly belong to the post-Independence era — but the city is very spread out, leaving many travelers with the impression that they've spent much of their time in Delhi just getting from one place to another. To a large extent, whether you stay in Old Delhi or New Delhi has a significant effect on which aspect of the city you end up experiencing.

Travelers tend to concentrate their sightseeing efforts in three major areas: in and around the central hub of **Connaught Place** and **Janpath** where you'll find all the banks, shops, emporiums, tourist and airline offices, and many tourist-orientated restaurants and budget hostels — near the **Red Fort** for exploring the old walled city's bazaars and sights, which is located close to Old Delhi Railway Station, and a little further north, the Interstate Bus Terminal near Kashmiri Gate — and around the **Paharganj** area, situated two kilometers (a mile and a quarter) north of Connaught Place next to New Delhi Railway Station with a reputation as a back-packer's haunt for its cheap accommodation and cafés. Unless you are staying at one of the five-star hotels within Lutyens' residential New Delhi to the south of the city, it's often easy to neglect this exceptionally pleasant area, but it's well worth making time to explore the tranquil **Lodhi Gardens**, the tombs of **Safdarjang** and **Humayan**, and the imperial **Rashtrapati Bhawan complex**.

The best time to visit Delhi is between mid-September and March, when the days are crisp, fine and sunny and the evenings cool. Winters can be surprisingly chilly — so if you plan to arrive between December and January, you'll need woolens, socks and sweaters. Winter is also India's marriage season — a good time for seeing spontaneous processions of brocade-clad turbaned grooms resplendent on white horses and their glittering brides with an entourage of

---

OPPOSITE: Humayan's Tomb, the majestic prototype of the Taj Mahal, is one of Delhi's best preserved monuments.

drunken guests, lamp-wallahs and trumpet-tooting bandsmen in old epauletted uniforms. Delhi has a fleeting but beautiful blossoming splendor during the spring months of February and March.

One of Delhi's most spectacular annual festivals is Republic Day, held on January 26th, when India displays its martial might along the Rajpath with parades of dapper regiments (including the famous Camel Corps), brass bands, folk dancers and India's latest military hardware. Don't take along anything valuable, as all baggage has to be left with security. At dusk, crowds watch silently as camel-mounted soldiers perform their ritual for Beating the Retreat. Delhi is also particularly lively during the 10-day Ram Lila (Dussehra) festival in October. Continuous plays, marathon readings, music and dance are performed by weird and wonderfully dressed actors on chariots in Old Delhi, recounting episodes from India's epic poem, the Ramayana, which tells the story of the god Rama's victory over the Lankan demon king Ravana and the rescue of Rama's abducted wife Sita. The festival culminates in a procession of immense, firework-padded, brightly painted effigies of the evil ten-headed Ravana and his henchmen to the Ram Lila fairground (located where Old Delhi ends and New Delhi begins), where they are set ablaze to the roar of thousands of onlookers. The Muslim festival Bakr Id in April is also very dramatic, with hundreds of thousands of devotees kneeling in prayer outside the Jama Masjid. The only festival you might want to avoid in Delhi is Holi in March — which is possibly India's most delightful festival in small villages or amongst friends — but can turn nasty in big, impersonal cities, when gangs of young men use it as an excuse to pelt unwitting passer's by, particularly young women and tourists, with paint, colored water, stones or even kerosene and battery acid.

GETTING AROUND

Of all the Indian cities, Delhi's varied and spread-out attractions require you to be selective and organized about sightseeing. It helps to have a good city map so that you have at least some idea where your driver is supposed to be taking you, otherwise you may find yourself being taken for a ride! You can begin on a city-wise note as soon as you arrive in Delhi's airport terminal by heading for the "Pre-Paid Taxi" booth, and utilizing the no-hassle system on paying your fare in advance, with the rate calculated against your desired destination. The fare from the airport to Connaught Place is around US$7.

It might take a while to adjust to the anarchic haphazardness on the capital's roads, where a combination of relatively well-paved roads and erratic horn-bleeping driving often proves fatal. According to statistics, Delhi's roads are the second most dangerous in the world after Nairobi, and there seems every indication that they will stay that way. You'll need to adopt a little Hindu fatalism to stay cool, but you'll soon get used to seeing lurching over-crammed sardine-can buses or snail's-pace motor-scooters atop which an entire family have arranged themselves. After a few days of observation on Delhi's roads, you'll come away with some new discoveries about the Average Indian vs. the Law of Physics and some new ideas about different ways of utilizing vehicles. You should have learnt how to detect subtle suicidal urges in potential auto-rickshaw or taxi-drivers. For instance, glazed blood-shot eyes are tell-tale signs that they have recently been sipping *bhang*, which is a marijuana-based concoction, to which many drivers are addicted. It's also worth noting that it's not always wise to follow up your driver's invitation to change money on the black market, as a good number of them are paid as police informers. Just put it all down as good character assessment practice for being out in the "field"!

You may wish to ride a Delhi bus just for the experience. But they are very crammed and often downright unpleasant, particularly for women. It's far more fun to watch the macho sport that young Indian men seem to regard as a sort of rite of passage — they'll go to astonishing lengths to self-consciously loiter until the bus has begun to accelerate, then sprint after it for a highly competitive (highly amusing) last-ditch effort to hurl themselves aboard, often left desperately half-dangling to the cheers of watching onlookers!

Auto-rickshaws provide the cheapest, most convenient way of negotiating short distances in Delhi. They tend to be slow and kidney-rattling, and so are obviously less practical for longer distances, like going out to the airport or to the Qutb Minar.

With any motorized transport, always agree on the price first (this deflects the driver's inclination to waste his petrol on driving you around in circles) or make sure that the meter is being used. Drivers will wait quite happily if you want to retain them, while you hive off for an hour of so of sightseeing or shopping — but you must agree on the waiting charge — usually about Rs 20 an hour for taxis. Taxi-drivers are legally entitled to charge you 25 percent "night charge" after 11 pm, but their "ten percent extra charge" story is bosh at all other times. You're free to tip drivers liberally if they have been particularly helpful. In Old Delhi, you can get about the bazaars by cycle-rickshaw or horse-drawn tonga — both are good for laid-back, open-air sightseeing.

HOTELS

Delhi is one of India's busiest entry points for foreign visitors, expatriates and business people. It has a fleet of fine international-standard five-star luxury hotels, most of them hastily built to house athletes and politicians for the Asian Games in 1982 and the Non-aligned Movement conference a year later. Even so, few travelers stay longer than a few days in Delhi before heading off for their chosen destinations. One reason for this is that, by Indian standards, hotel rates are expensive — beginning at around US$150 a night in most of the top tourist and business class establishments. Facilities in the five-star hotels are top-notch, with a range of excellent restaurants, 24-hour coffee shops, recreational facilities and swimming pools (a definite plus during summer), business desks, travel agents, shopping arcades, bakeries, bars, astrologers and discotheques.

Most of the luxury hotels are miles away from the center of town (close to the city's Fort Knox grid of diplomatic embassies at Chanakyapuri), which makes sightseeing much less spontaneous in sprawling Delhi. It's always essential to advance-book five-star accommodation, especially so during the peak season months between October and March. In the range of US$160 and up you can take your pick of the following luxury hotels:

Maurya Sheraton (Welcomgroup), ((011) 301-0101, fax (011) 301-0908, Diplomatic Enclave.
Taj Mahal Hotel, ((011) 301-6162, fax (011) 301-7299, 1 Mansingh Road.
The Taj Palace Hotel, ((011) 301-0404, fax (011) 301-1252, 2 Sardar Patel Marg.
The Oberoi, ((011) 436-3030, fax (011) 436-0484, Dr Zakir Hussain Marg.
Hyatt Regency Delhi, ((011) 688-1234, fax (011) 688-6833, Bhikaji Cama Place.
The Holiday Inn Crowne Plaza, ((011) 332-0101, fax (011) 3325335, Connaught Plaza.
Le Meridien Hotel, ((011) 371-0101, fax (011) 371-4545, Windsor Place, Janpath.
Ashok Hotel, ((011) 600412, fax (011) 687-3216, Chanyakapuri.
Centaur Hotel, ((011) 545-2223, fax (011) 545-2256, Delhi Airport.

Several impeccably-kept colonial hotels offer less expensive elegance with plenty of period flair as well as efficiency for those arriving in Delhi to embark on their Indian adventure: The fairly central **Claridges,** ((011) 301-0211, fax (011) 301-0625, 12 Aurangzeb Road, price: moderate; the delightful, pukka Georgian-style **Oberoi**

Maidens, ((011) 252-5464, fax (011) 252-5420, 7 Sham Nath Marg, built in 1900 just north of Old Delhi in the former Raj-cantonment of Civil Lines, and where Lutyens stayed as he planned his new city with spacious comfortable rooms. price: moderate; and the **Hotel Imperial,** ((011) 332-5332, fax (011) 332-4542, a peaceful garden retreat right on central Janpath, with quirky, recently refurbished 1930's decor, a good shopping arcade, swimming pool, period bar and pretty terrace and lawn for al fresco meals and afternoon teas, prices: moderate to expensive. The Imperial Hotel, like the Ashok, Claridges, Maurya and the Kanishka hotels, allow non-guests to use their pool for a small fee.

Comfortable inexpensive priced hotels that are relatively convenient to the city include the **Hotel Ambassador,** ((011) 463-2600 fax (011) 463-2252, Sujan Singh Park, with air-conditioned rooms and the advantage of having New Delhi's best South Indian restaurant downstairs; **Lodhi Hotel,** ((011) 436-2422, also in south Delhi on Lala Rajput Rai Marg has comfortable rooms and an excellent restaurant; **Nirula's,** ((011) 332-2419, L Block, Connaught Place is as central as it is possible to be, located right next to one of New Delhi's most popular restaurant complexes. Continuing anti-clockwise is the **Hotel Marina,** ((011) 332-4658, fax (011) 332-3138, G 59 Block, with quiet, clean rooms. A cheaper central option is the ITDC-run **Ashok Yatri Niwas,** ((011) 332-4511, 19 Ashok Road, a giant 556-roomed complex with basic but adequate rooms and a good South Indian restaurant.

The most popular of Delhi's four "Y's" is the **YMCA Tourist Hostel,** ((011) 311915, fax (011) 374-6032, near the Regal Cinema on Jai Singh Road, which offers excellent value comfortable single rooms with hot and cold water in the cheap to very cheap range, a good restaurant, gardens, and room rates include breakfast. If this is full, try the similarly priced **YWCA International Guest House,** ((011) 311561, in Parliament Street (also known as **Sansad Marg**), where you'll be given basic clean rooms, or the lesser-known **Blue Triangle Family Hostel,** (310133, on Ashoka Road just off Parliament Street, where rooms with attached bath and including breakfast are fall within the cheap range. All the "Ys" will accept a temporary membership fee and they take both sexes.

There are plenty of budget (cheap to very cheap) lodges scattered around Janpath, but few are reliably clean, friendly or reasonable — in fact, most are downright grim, and over the decades have fueled thousands of travelers' tales about disastrous encounters with the sub-continent. However, there is one worthwhile lodge to try in Janpath, **Roshan Villa**

Guest House, ℂ (011) 331-1770, at 7 Babar Lane, which offers basic, well-kept rooms, plus US$2 for an attached bath, and there's also a dormitory. Otherwise take yourself down to the Paharganj area near New Delhi Railway Station, which is a rabbit warren of very cheap (and often nasty) lodges in and around the Main Bazaar Road. If you have a definite aversion to creepy-crawlies this may not be the place for you, but if there's any reasonable accommodation under US$7 to be had in Delhi this is where you'll find it. It's really a matter of combing through several such places yourself since one man's squalor can be another's mansion. But one seems to get consistent praise from back-packing tourists: **Vivek Hotel,** ℂ (011) 523015, at 1541-50 Main Bazaar, where rooms have an attached "bath" (euphemism for "tap" and "hole!") where the natives are friendly and helpful!

RESTAURANTS

As the nation's cosmopolitan capital, Delhi offers some great eating experiences. You can either dine at its luxury hotels which employ top chefs and usually have a varied range of Indian, Western and Chinese restaurants and coffee shops, or there's a wide choice of well-established eating houses scattered across town.

Delhi is probably the best place in the world to sample delicious, authentic north-Indian Mughali food. This strongly meat-based cuisine is very rich, redolent of thick yoghurt, onions and exotic spices which the Mughals brought with them when they quit Persia in the sixteenth century. It's served with a variety of breads to mop up its sauces, most popularly the delicious fluffy, yoghurt-leavened naan which is baked clinging to the side of a tandoor clay oven; whole wheat rotis; roomali (handkerchief) rotis or parathas, layered and stuffed with minced meat or paneer cheese, and really a meal in themselves. Tandoori mutton, poultry and fish are a famous Mughal speciality, and these dishes attain their distinctive succulence from being marinated in a mixture of yogurt, crushed garlic, tumeric, sometimes papaya pulp and salt, and then skewered over the tandoor's glowing coals. Don't be alarmed by the fiery red of your tandoori chicken — the color comes from the marinade, not from being smothered with chilies! Then there's the classic biryani of basmati rice and spiced meat cooked with saffron to sticky, fragrant perfection in a sealed pot, or popular chicken Mughali which has a thick creamy sauce with onions, cashews and raisins. Mughali vegetable dishes tend to be equally sumptuous. Try *dal makhni*, rich spiced lentils with coriander, *shahi paneer*, cheese in cream and tomatoes, *khatte alloo*, spiced potato, or *baingan mumtaz*, stuffed eggplant. Desserts are generally prepared from milk or Indian cottage cheese flavored with cardamom or saffron. *Firni* is the most popular, a kind of exotic rice pudding served in earthenware bowl. There's also *kheer*, a rich thickened milk with raisins and nuts, and a summer favorite is *khulfi*, Indian ice-cream accompanied by transparent sweet vermicelli called *falooda*.

Foreigners and diplomats who live and work in Delhi swear that the major hotels offer the best cuisine — and they rate the Maurya Sheraton and the Oberoi Intercontinental as two of the very best. Arguably, these two hotels offer the most memorable Mughali cuisine in town: the Maurya Sheraton's very elegant **Dum Pukht** for aristocratic sixteenth century Lucknowian specialities cooked by India's most famous chef, Muhammed Imtiaz. Also at the Sheraton is the popular **Bukhara** — renowned for its delicious north-west frontier dishes, notably its succulent *raan* or roasted spiced lamb, chicken *tikka* and charcoal-grilled kebabs, all served in mock-rustic surroundings where guests are invited to slip on aprons, eat with their fingers like baronial Mughals, sip frothy Indian beer from pewter goblets, and watch chefs deftly gouging rows of skewers behind huge glass windows. This place is so popular, they don't take bookings after 8:30 pm.

The Oberoi's **Kandahar** has similar excellent fare served in classic European surroundings where the tone is set by bow-tied waiters, subdued lighting and elegant silver platters, although true to Mughal form, you'll find no knives or forks on the table. Although these restaurants are fairly expensive by Delhi standards, at around US$15 per head (including liberal quantities of beer), it's absurdly good value if you consider what a comparable meal would cost at home. It's only when you start ordering imported wines or spirits at hotels that you'll really start paying through the nose. Delhi, like the rest of India, only sells foreign liquor in hotels, priced up to four times more than their original value. Another pointer — it's also advisable to advance-book at any of the main hotels, as all the popular restaurants are lionized by socializing Delhites.

You'll also find classic, hearty Mughali fare at the Taj Mansingh's **Haveli**, where classical dancers and musicians perform while you eat; at Claridges' **Dhaba** which has a real-life truck incorporated into its decor; and the Hotel Ashok's **Frontier** which has strumming minstrels who doggedly serenade your table (something you either adore or suffer). More authentic restaurants outside the hotels tend to have unpretentious surroundings, but can be surprisingly good.

Try especially the **Khyber**, ℂ (011) 252-0867, 1514 Kashmiri Gate, for good, reasonably priced Afghani dishes, and ring in advance to order their excellent raan, and both branches of **Karims**, the more classy air-conditioned one at Nizamuddin West, ℂ 698300, or the other located on the south side of Jama Masjid along Motia Mahal, which is more popular with locals. (As with any eating house in Old Delhi, if you're there later than 9 pm, you'll observe rows of urchins patiently congregating outside — after the last diner has left, they'll be given the night's scraps!)

For exceptional south Indian food, (which tends to be much lighter on the palate if you're

If you're in Connaught Place on the prowl for a solid meal, try one of Delhi's oldest, most eccentric haunts, **Gaylord**, 16 Regal Building, Connaught Place, (it began in the early 1950's, and still retains the original waiting staff, damask tablecloths and chandeliers), or **Kwality**, just around the corner on Parliament Street — both are air-conditioned havens where you can feast on good Indian food for about US$8 for two. Or go to the **Imperial Hotel** where you can sit under umbrellas on the lawn for a lunch of chicken *tikka*, *naan* and sip *nimbu* soda. Unlike most other Indian cities, Delhi also has a rash of pseudo-American fast-food parlors, complete

still adjusting to the Indian diet), head for **Dasaprakash**, located in a cavernous, lamp-lit dome in the lobby of the Ambassador Hotel, and always crammed with avidly eating locals. Trt their three-course *thali* meal; waiters are always hovering to refill your platter with varieties of *subze*, or spiced vegetable dishes and puffed *puri* bread — as much as you can put away. Fresh grape juice, *lassis* and creamy mango milk shakes are the house specialities. Other good places include Delhi's branch of the famous **Woodlands** chain of restaurants at the Lodhi Hotel; the **Coconut Grove** for delicious non-vegetarian South Indian and Bengali dishes at the Ashok Yatri Niwas Hotel; at **Sona Rupa**, 46 Janpath, good for sampling a typical Madras-style breakfast of steamed *idlies* (rice cakes) in spicy *sambar* gravy, and at the very cheap, prompt South Indian Boarding House, opposite Shankar Market.

with french fries, "buffalo" burgers, thick-shakes and ersatz pizzas — great if you need a complete change from Indian food. They're also the "in" place with gum-chewing, jean-clad Indian yuppies, and the place to meet other hungry tourists. Best of all is **Nirula's**, located in L Block, Connaught Place, where there's also a popular vegetarian lunch buffet. The complex also includes Delhi's oldest Chinese restaurant, a cake and pastry shop, an ice-cream parlor and two popular stand-up fast-food annexes, selling everything from *dal* and *chapatis* to pizzas and India's very own **Campa-Cola** and **Thumbs Up**. Another novelty is the **Wimpy Bar** in Connaught Place, just along from the

ABOVE: Tea House of the August Moon at the Taj Palace is typical of elaborate restaurants in Delhi's five-star hotels.

Tourist Office at 5 Janpath, which serves burgers made from almost everything except beef, but still taste okay. Numerous snack bars in the city serve local favorites: *khulcha bhatura*, a soft doughy bread eaten with spicy chick-peas; the South Indian *dosa*, a crisp rice pancake often with a mashed potato filling served with *sambhar*; *pakoras* or fruit *chaat*, prepared by roadside vendors and made up of potato, papaya, apple and tomato chunks, tossed with piquant chutney, lemon juice and salt.

It's possible to dine well on Chinese food in Delhi — virtually all the main hotels employ Chinese chefs, who usually hail from Calcutta where most of India's Chinese community live, and the best restaurants will send to Hong Kong for essential ingredients. For stylish and fairly authentic fare, try the **Tea House of the August Moon** at the Taj Palace, which has eye-catching décor mocked up like a pagoda garden, good *dim sum* and a variety of regional dishes; the Oberoi's **Taipan**, the Hyatt's **Pearls**, and the Taj Mansingh's **House of Ming**. For something a little different, you might try classic French cuisine at the Oberoi's pricey **La Rochelle**, where you can dine on quails, oysters and steaks and imported wines, or to the Maurya's **Bali Hi** for good Polynesian, and South East Asian dishes, stunning rooftop views and live band. The ultra-smart **Valentino's** at the Hyatt has an Italian chef behind its excellent pasta creations and *zabaglione* and there's Mediterranean food at the Ashok Hotel's **Taverna Cyprus**. If you yearn for seafood in land-locked Delhi, **Fisherman's Wharf**, ((011) 698123, at A-1 Moolchand Shopping Complex, Defense Colony, is one of Delhi's few exceptional independent eateries, and probably the best place to satisfy cravings for fresh fish, king prawns, mussels and lobster. Standards of hygiene (you can never be too fussy about seafood!) and preparation are high — and their tandoori pomfret, sold at seasonal cost price, is a real winner.

The truly adventurous will enjoy a visit to the **paratha-wallah gully** or "the alley of bread sellers", which is wedged in Chandni Chowk's lanes. Originally established in 1875, this row of historic "cafés" is run by high-caste Brahmans, employing Fagan-like urchins as adept street "chefs", and over the decades has catered to everyone from colonial British administrators to jailed opposition party leaders. Its fame rests on its fresh unleavened *paratha*, sprinkled with cumin, sesame, caraway, or stuffed with peas, onions or potato. While the restaurants barely conform to Western standards of cleanliness, you'll dine extremely well here on insatiable amounts of sizzling, fragrant *parathas*, all served with rounds of delicious, freshly cooked *subze* (spiced vegetable) banana chutney and curd. It's

Chandni Chowk's most popular lunch-time spot, and has an enthusiastic clientele of travelers disillusioned with the expensive, less authentic fare of New Delhi's five-star hotels. No one I know has ever got "Delhi-belly" here! Here's how to find it: start with the Red Fort behind you, walk a hundred yards or so up Chandni Chowk's boulevard until you see a large State Bank of India building on the other side of the road. This is your cue to turn left into a lane directly opposite and this should lead you directly to the spice-smelling cul-de-sac of your search. Don't worry if you seem to be getting impossibly lost — everyone in Chandni Chowk knows "paratha wallah gully" and should be able to point you in the right direction.

NIGHTLIFE

While Delhi is not as lively as cosmopolitan Bombay, top classical dancers and musicians perform here far more regularly. If you're determined to experience at least something of India's dazzling cultural heritage — be it dance, drama or music — scan the morning's *Times of India* or *Indian Express* for their daily listing of what's on, the *Delhi Diary* sold at most newsstands, or consult the tourist office's fortnightly *Program of Events*. Performances tend to start around 6:30 pm and there's a central ticket office at Cottage Industries Emporium, Janpath. One regular event to catch is the Dances of India program at the **Parsi Anjuman Hall**, ((011) 331-8615, Bahudur Shah Zafar Marg, Delhi Gate, a popular showcase of *bhavai*, *kathak* and *bharat natyam* styles, and starts at 7 pm every night, at US$2.50 a ticket. If you want to experience the technicolor thrills, wet saris and outrageous fortunes of Hindi movies, join the scrums of flared-trousered youths at the **Regel Cinema** complex in Connaught Place or the modern **Sheila** opposite New Delhi Railway Station.

At night, you can always try the city's discotheques — dark, flashing pits full of be-bopping turbaned Sikhs, African students, and other night lizards dancing to the latest pop music. The best is the **Ghungroo** at the Maurya, but the Taj Mansingh's **Number One** has a regular following amongst Delhi's mon-eyed young. The Hyatt Regency has a flashy basement disco, but is open only to members or guests.

SIGHTSEEING

Most travelers are still working off jet-lag when they arrive in Delhi, and need time to ease into ambitious sightseeing. Besides, it's often interesting enough just getting acquainted with the Indian sights, sounds and smells of your immediate neighborhood. If you feel you're not quite in a mood to go charging off into the Old City, or scrambling over ramparts out at Tughlaqabad, then you might like to try the tourist office's four-hour morning conducted tour, which whisks you about to many of Delhi's far-flung places of interest, so that you get to see a good deal of the city and many of its most famous sights without much effort or expenditure on your part. (See GENERAL INFORMATION page 89, on where to book conducted tours). If you want to tackle Delhi's sights at your own pace, then the suggested routes below should serve as a useful framework, best spread over three or four days.

OLD DELHI: MOSQUES AND MONEYLENDERS

Make **Shah Jehan's Medieval Walled City** your first sightseeing stop in Delhi for a taste the "real" India — a total contrast to Lutyen's spacious green city — of vibrant color, tangled alleys, pungent scents and frenetic crowds. Here you can linger in Chandni Chowk's bazaars, visit Jama Masjid and old Delhi's majestic centerpiece, the Red Fort — and this one combined destination will probably fill an entire day.

Old Delhi is dominated by the gigantic rust-colored **Red Fort**, or Lal Qila, which looms 18.5 m (60 ft) at its highest watchtowers, and is enclosed by nearly two and a half kilometers (one and a half miles) of snaking battlements. The fortress-palace became the courtly hub of the Mughal empire when Shah Jehan decided to shift the seat of power from Agra to Delhi, sparking a construction boom between 1638–48 to create his new capital — Shahjahanabad. The emperor-architect prided himself on the unequaled grandeur of the Red Fort — no small thing for the man who designed the Taj Mahal — and tantalizing reports of his precious gem-studded palace, pietra dura inlay, marbled fountains, ceremonial pomp, and above all, his solid gold jewel-encrusted Peacock Throne, spread the Red Fort's fame. Shah Jehan was soon deposed by his fanatical son, Aurangzeb who was the last of the Great Mughals to rule from Delhi. Shah Jehan's palace, once considered a symbol of monumental wealth, now has a desolate, plundered look — all its precious gems, gilt and silver were plucked bare in the aftermath of the 1857 mutiny.

Entry is through the massive **Lahore Gate**, so-named because it faces Lahore in what is now Pakistan, which leads you into the vaulted shopping arcade known as **Chhatta Chowk**, formerly where royal memsahibs would inspect the latest creations of court goldsmiths, jewel-

ers and weavers, but today full of "antiques" (usually "aged" by pros down in the old city) tourist junk and frantically gesticulating touts. At the end of this is the two-storied **Naubat Khana**, where court musicians used to serenade passing nobles on their way across the garden to the colonnaded **Diwan-i-Am**, or public audience hall. This was a sort of impromptu law court where any commoner had the right to plea their case before the emperor, who gazed down from an ornate palanquined platform. Beyond lies a large formal garden and six palace *mahals*, through which ran the network of lotus-shaped marble fountains Shah

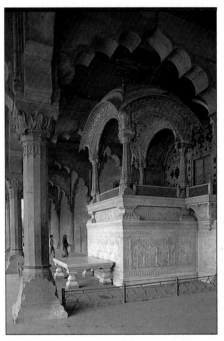

Jehan named Naher-i-Bahisht or "Stream of Paradise", which has sadly been allowed to fall into disrepair. To the far right is **Mumtaz Mahal**, now a museum open from 9 am to 5 pm, and close to it is Rang Mahal, once an elaborate painted boudoir. As you move left, you'll pass through the emperor's former trio of apartments known collectively as the Khas Mahal. The palace's citadel was the adjoining **Diwan-i-Khas**, the majestic private audience hall, where the emperor received his most important visitors seated on his priceless Peacock Throne. This was given its name from two peacock forms outlined in jewels forming the main part of the

ABOVE: The emperor's marble canopied throne in the Red Fort's Diwan-i-Am. OVERLEAF: Impregnable and forbidding, the Lahore Gate looms at the entrance to the Red Fort, flanked by crenelated battlements.

design. After the plundering Nadir Shah took it back with him to Persia, it was broken up and so no longer survives. Shah Jehan's famous inscription can still be seen above the entrance to the hall. Close by are the *hamams*, or baths, where royal parties took hot saunas and perfumed baths and could cool off by parading down the fort wall, which overlooks the Yamuna River. Aurangzeb's Moti Masjid, or Pearl Mosque was built in 1622 for his own private worship. It's worth returning for the excellent sound and light show dramatizing the Red Fort's history held at 8:30 to 9:30 pm within the central courtyard.

Directly opposite the Red Fort sprawls **Chandni Chowk**'s arterial row of bustling bazaars. It was laid out in 1648 by Shah Jehan's daughter Jehanara Begum with a central canal flanked by merchants and nobles' mansions. If you took away the multitude of jangling cycle-rickshaws and humpbacked Ambassador cars, you'd swear that little had altered its inexorably oriental character for centuries. Residents know its web of narrow alleys like an intimate secret — but newcomers often get lost quite happily for hours, fascinated by its explosive street life, wafting smells and bizarre sights, every second humming with activity in every direction. Scrawny coolies weave in and out like human oxen here, pavement barbers lather and snip there. Street photographers huddle in Victorian cameras to immortalize clients against surrealistic landscapes, while matrons scrutinize silver jewelry for timid brides. Wobbling rickshaws pull wooden cages of giggling kohl-eyed schoolchildren, while ash-smeared ascetics trudge through with tridents and begging bowls. Almost everything can be found here, but the historic lanes are most fun to browse — **Pul-ki-Mandi** for flowers, **Dariba Kalan** for moneylenders, weight-priced gold and silver, **Kinari Galli** for wedding garb, tinsel and turbans, and Nai Srak for perfume. Don't forget **paratha-wallah-gully** (see RESTAURANTS, page 78) if all this walking has given you an appetite. The moment you start to feel slightly fractious having to side-step speeding rickshaws, clumsy cows and bubbling vats of ghee, climb aboard a cycle-rickshaw — it's exactly the right pace, and it enables you to see far more without constantly glancing behind or beneath you.

At the top of the Chowk is the seventeenth century **Digambar Jain Mandir**, better known by tourists for the **Bird Hospital** within its grounds, where hundreds of sick birds are administered splints and medicine and even given ceremonial cremations on the banks of the Yamuna if they die. Non-vegetarian birds, like vultures, are considered spiritually unclean, and are only allowed in as "out-patients!" Visitors

are welcome and donations help keep the birds in grain. From here, just let your feet wander — but landmarks include the seventeenth century **Sikh Gurudwara Sisgani**, dedicated to Tegh Bahudur, a Sikh guru beheaded by Aurangzeb and the *kotawali* (police station) where mutineers were hung by the British after the 1857 Mutiny. Make sure you pay a visit to the lively **Spice Market** at the end of the Chowk near Fatepuri Masjid.

It's impossible to miss the tapering minarets and onion domes of the **Jama Masjid**, India's largest mosque opposite the Red Fort. Built predominantly from red sandstone and white marble, and adorned with exquisite Mughal inlay, it was commissioned by Shah Jehan in 1644 and completed by Aurangzeb 14 years later. There are three main gateways, each approached by steep flights of stairs — the magnificent eastern gate reserved for the Emperor riding in magnificent procession to attend Friday prayers. It's the epicenter of India's Muslim community — you'll notice black flags which mourn the death of Muslims in communal violence — and on Fridays and Islamic festivals thousands of white-capped devotees prostrate themselves in its central courtyard — which accommodates up to 20,000. A small booth at the entrance sells tickets to the 46-m (150-ft) -high **South Minaret**, where a 122-step climb earns you one of the best views across the old city. Women must be accompanied by "responsible family members" — a rule imposed after several incidents of molestation up in the tower. Within the courtyard is a small marble crypt containing various treasures — an alleged whisker from the Prophet's beard, the imprint of his foot at Mecca, and ancient Urdu parchments.

CIVIL LINES: THE CUSP OF OLD AND NEW

Civil Lines was the British cantonment in Delhi before New Delhi was dreamt up. North of the old city near Kashmiri Gate, the area is dotted with crumbling historic homes — the scene of brutal murders of Europeans during the 1857 Mutiny — worth a stroll if you are especially fascinated by the Raj era in India. Places of interest include the Greco-colonial **St James Church** (consecrated in 1836), built by the larger than life Sir James Skinner, the son of a Scotsman and his Rajput mistress, who founded the Indian Army's yellow-clad Skinner's Horse Cavalry Regiment. Inside are beautiful stained-glass windows, oak pews and fascinating plaques to a deceased "Who's Who" of nineteenth century Anglo-Indian families, swarms of whom perished at the sepoy's hands. Skinner's own tomb is by the altar — and his many family members were buried outside — when he died 64 men contested his estate claiming they were his sons. Sunday services are held in English, but at all other times, between 8 am and 5 pm, a church attendant should be on call to let you in with a key. Nearby also see the nineteenth century **Lothian Road** and **Nicholson Cemeteries** and the once select, now seedy **Raj-era Mall** near Kashmiri Gate.

On Rani Jhansi Marg which winds uphill onto North Ridge, you'll see the **Mutiny Memorial,** known as "Jeetgarh," or victory fort which looks like a lopped-off Gothic cathedral spire. It marks the spot where the party of cholera-stricken, beleaguered British, Gurkha and Sikh soldiers camped out for several weeks before mounting their assault and commemorates those who died in the attempt. Further up the road on your right is a motley-looking **Ashokan Pillar,** (273-236 BC) patched up after being broken in many pieces, with most of its Brahma script worn away. It was brought to Delhi by Feroz Shah Tughlaq, a Sultan of the fourteenth century. **Flagstaff Tower** stands on the crest, slightly off the road, with a gate entrance. Terrified British memsahibs and children fled here on May 11th 1857, as sepoys began rampaging in Civil Lines. The nearby **Oberoi Maidens Hotel** is a good place for a tea break.

Several other Raj-era treasures lurk nearby, difficult to hunt down unless you are especially zealous. Closest are the **Old Secretariat,** just north of here, and the once-magnificent **Metcalfe House** located not far from Delhi University at the northern end of Mahatma Gandhi Marg. Built in 1835, it was the museum-piece home of Sir Thomas Metcalfe, British Resident of the Mughal Court, who transferred all his family art treasures from England to India. Metcalfe died in this house in 1853, which was later occupied by his nephew, Sir Theophilus, Joint Magistrate and a key figure in rousing Delhi's Europeans to arms against the mutineers.

NEW DELHI: IMPERIAL INHERITANCE

Start with **Connaught Place,** built to commemorate the Duke of Connaught's visit in 1920. This paint-splintered ring of ever-widening colonial arcades is lined with dusty-shop fronts, airline offices, restaurants and squatting merchants selling everything from piles of books to (inexplicably) whips and knuckle-dusters. Other eccentric Raj-era oddities can still be fossicked out, like solar topees, military attire and old regimental silver — or you can pick through Janpath's overflowing Tibetan market — and there's plenty to occupy an entire morning.

Leaving Connaught Place, turn down Parliament Street to arrive at the **Jantar Mantar,** the astronomical observatory of Maharaja Jai Singh I of Jaipur. Built of sandstone and marble in 1724, this was the experimental prototype of five similar structures scattered across India, the most famous of which can be seen in Jaipur. It comprises four "instruments", including the huge "Prince of Dials" sun-dial, each designed to exactly measure the position of sun, planets and stars, as well as to predict eclipses. Set in pretty gardens, it's open from sunrise to 10pm daily.

Hail a rickshaw to visit the garish elaborate **Laxmi Narayan Temple,** on Mandir Marg, west of Connaught Place, built by the industrialist Birla family in 1938, and usually referred to as the **Birla Temple.** A "modern" Hindu, Birla wanted his temple to symbolize unity of faith, so he broke all the traditional rules and caste barriers and came up with something completely different. Constructed from a medley of different stones instead of the usual sandstone or marble, it is a mixture of many different types of Hindu architecture, but more radically, it's open to all Hindus, including harijans, or untouchables, and instead of being dedicated to just one god, it not only worships a whole gamut, but incorporates icons of other religions too — Buddhist and Sikh wall frescoes and a giant Chinese Buddhist bronze bell. The main attraction is Krishna's mirrored shrine, designed to reflect the deity's face from which ever way you look at it.

It's a short rickshaw hop to **Sansad Bhawan,** the circular colonnaded house of parliament designed by Lutyen's colleague, Sir Herbert Baker. Originally created for the Chamber of Princes, the Council of State and the Legislative Assembly, it now houses the Rajya Sahba (Upper House) and Lok Sahba (House of the People). It's quite easy to arrange a visit to watch India's political turbines churning — sessions are often, in *Times of India* parlance, "uproarious", and when tempers run high, certain members of parliament have been known to hurl their shoes in rage. Contact your embassy or the tourist office for details on acquiring a pass for front row seats.

Beyond is Lutyen's magisterial Indo-Baroque **Rashtrapati Bhawan,** the former Viceroy's Palace now used as the official residence of India's president and flanked by imposing secretariat blocks, both inaugurated in 1931. As pompous and awe-inspiring as this sprawling apparatus of empire was, the British proved only temporary tenants and its keys were handed to India's politicians only 16 years after its inauguration. Somewhere beneath the palace lies a foundation stone originally laid by King George and Queen Mary at a site at some distance north which was later deemed impractically far away from the old city, so, to save face, the stones were secretly exhumed at night and carted off to the new site. Lutyens never really forgave his collaborator, Sir Herbert Baker, for miscalculating the steep gradient of the slope upon which this complex stands — the result of which obscured the view from India Gate up to Lutyen's Rashtrapati Bhavan. You can wander through the main entrances of Baker's secretariat buildings, now North and South blocks, where crucial executive decisions are made in an ambience rendered eccentric by nesting pigeons, aged shuffling tea "boys" and huge stacks of yellowing files. Curious tourists aren't allowed inside Rashtrapati Bhavan (where servants still use bicycles to get from one wing to another) but you can visit the adjacent four-hectare (10-acre) **Mughal Gardens** between February and March when they are gloriously in bloom.

At the end of stately Rajpath is **India Gate**, the 42-m (138-ft) -high memorial arch with its "eternal flame" built by the British in memory of the 90,000 Indian soldiers killed during the First World War and in the ill-fated 1919 Afghan expedition. After the 1971 war with Pakistan, Indira Gandhi added a smaller arch for more war dead. Enveloping it is the **Maidan**, the imperial village green, mowed by oxen and a magnet on hot summer nights for ice-cream wallahs, lolling families and courting couples.

THE HISTORIC TRAIL

Delhi's most famous landmark, the **Qutb Minar**, is best visited in the sunlit peace of early morning (avoiding scrums of tourists and irritating "hullooing" touts). Located about nine and a half kilometers (four miles) south of New Delhi, this "tower of victory" was the Empire State Building of ancient India — and at 72.5 m (239 ft) high it's still the country's tallest man-made tower. It was built by the Turkic "Slave king" Qutb-ud-din-Aibak in 1199 to celebrate his victory over Delhi's last Hindu ruler. Modeled on the tower at Ghazni, and adorned with Islamic arches, motifs and bold script, the red sandstone and marble five-storied structure has survived lightning and earthquakes (which destroyed the topmost cupola in 1803, at that time enjoyed by Europeans as a surreptitious picnic spot). After a gruesome accident with many killed in 1981, visitors are not allowed up its tower stairway for spectacular views. Within the Qutb complex lies Delhi's first mosque, the Quwwat-ul-Islam or the Might of Islam. Begun in 1193, it was modeled on the

Prophet's house in Medina and built with many decorative remnants from 27 demolished Hindu temples — figures of gods and goddesses which the Muslims found offensive were defaced and turned inward. Within the mosque's courtyard is the Iron Pillar, erected here in the fifth century. According to lore, if you can stand back against the pillar and clasp your hands, your wish will be granted. See also the richly carved tomb of Aibak's son-in-law, Iltutish, built in 1235, and the structures erected by the Khilji ruler Alu-ud-Din, the architect of Delhi's second city at Siri: the Alai-Darwaza (south gateway) the vast base and unfinished 27-m (88-ft) -high Alai Minar tower — intended as a sequel to the Qutb Minar, and his own tomb amid the rubble of his college for Islamic studies.

From here you can either drive eastwards to the rampart ruins of **Tughlaqabad**, (from which the huge amphitheater at Suraj Kund is a convenient detour south), or head back into residential New Delhi to browse through a cluster of forlornly beautiful monuments and tombs, built at different stages of the city's history, There's no need to tackle them all at once — in fact it's best to leave these until you feel in the mood for a quiet garden stroll away from the hectic bedlam of Delhi proper. Like all Delhi's historic places, they are open from sunrise to sunset. Perhaps start with **Safdarjang Tomb** at the end of Lodhi Road, built in 1753 to 1754 for the second Nabob of Oudh, Safdar Jang, its wistful charms enchained as the last of the great garden tombs constructed by the waning Mughals. Just south is Safdarjang Airport where Indira Gandhi's son and Rajiv's brother, Sanjay, crashed his plane in 1980.

It's barely two minutes stroll to the **Lodhi Gardens**, a picturesque necropolis of over 50 large octagonal-shaped, blue-domed tombs of the Sayyid and Lodhi dynasties (1451–1526) set amid a leafy park. School-boys play cricket on the green, retired civil servants read Hindu epics to rapt cross-legged illiterates, *ayahs* wander about with toddlers in tow, and MPs and diplomats jog breathlessly here. Tombs are everywhere, often sadly debauched with graffiti and sure signs of inhabitance, but look especially for the Bara Gumbad with its large dome, the Sheesh Gumbad which still has much of its blue-tiled roof intact and exterior inlay floral designs, and Muhammad Shah's tomb erected in 1450, one of the earliest prototypes of Mughal design.

A far more sophisticated version of this basic design can be seen at **Humayan's Tomb**, located at the very end on Lodhi Road (half-an-hour's stroll) at the crossroads with Mathura Road. Flanked by four impressive archways and four garden squares, this black and white marble and

OPPOSITE: The twelfth century Qutb Minar, with its intricately fretted and embellished tower, seen through the archways of India's oldest mosque, the Quwwat-ul-Islam.

red sandstone tomb is considered the architectural precursor to the Taj Mahal — with its octagonal base plan, grand arches, lofty double dome and fountains in a central canal. It was built in 1555–69 by Humayan's senior widow, known as Haji Begum, nine years after the emperor's death. Her tomb lies here, along with those of other Mughal royals, including that of Dara Sikoh, Shah Jehan's favorite son. It was at Humayan's Tomb that the last of the Mughals, Bahudur Shah Zafar, hid then gave himself up to the British — his two sons were killed here by a trigger-happy officer. The Lodi-style tomb outside belongs to the nobleman Isa Khan, built in

take the narrow path near the police station on Mathura Road. Along with Ajmer in Rajasthan, Nizamuddin attracts flocks of pilgrims for the Urs festival (dates vary from year to year) with poetry readings, fairs and performances of Khusrau's *qawwalis* or mystical verses.

From here, it's a 10-minute rickshaw ride north along Mathura Road to **Purana Qila**, which is said to straddle the legendary city of Indraprasatha. The walled fort's original structure was initiated by Humayan, but the Afghan Sher Shah expanded it during 1538–45 in the interim decade before the ousted emperor returned from exile to wrest Delhi back. Two main

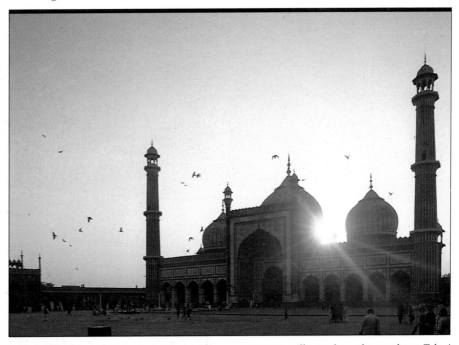

1547, and the Mughal-style one to Khan-i-Khanan, a military general under Akbar, built in 1627. Across the road, explore the fourteenth century Sufi village of **Nizamuddin** which is still an exclusively Muslim precinct which grew up around the *darger* (shrine) of the Sufi saint Sheikh Nizamuddin Christi. He died in 1325, aged 92 and his tomb is the most famous of several in the Muslim cemetery here, including those of renowned Urdu poets, Amir Khusrau and Mirza Ghalib, and Shah Jehan's daughter, Jehanara, who loyally stayed with her father when he was imprisoned in Agra by Aurangzeb. Here life follows a medieval pattern, shimmering with heat, dust and flies; women live in strict purdah, goats are tethered in mud-bricked courtyards, stalls are a jumble of perfumed rose water, embroidered caps, freshly slaughtered buffalo and hookah pipes. To reach the shrine,

gateways still stand — the northern Talaqi Darwaza or "Forbidden Gate" and the southern and Lal Darwaza which overlooks Delhi's Zoo. Inside, look for the Sher Mandal, a two-storied octagonal tower which Humayan converted into his library. A year later he stumbled on the stairs in his haste to attend the muezzin's call to prayer, dying from his injuries three days later. Just beyond is Sher Shah's **Qila-i-Kuhran** mosque (1541), and an interesting museum housing the site's archaeological finds which date back to 1000 BC.

Purana Qila is flanked on the right by the **Zoo**, India's largest and notable for its rare white tigers of Rewa and open plan (water canals instead of cages) and open daily except Fridays from 9 am to 5 pm; and on the left by the **Pragati Maiden** exhibition grounds built for the Asian Games in 1982, which is worth visiting for its excellent **Crafts Museum**. This displays traditional icons, rare religious wooden figurines, tribal *bhutas* (folk deities) of Karnataka, terracotta figures from Tamil Nadu, textiles, brass crafts and utensils. Outside is a "village" collection of rustic huts peculiar to each Indian state, and a courtyard where village artisans are invited to demonstrate how traditional Indian crafts are made. You can buy Rajasthani fabrics, terra-cotta pottery, bronze miniatures, Hyderabadi *bidri* ware and many other crafts very reasonably. It's open 9:30 am to 6 pm, and the crafts demonstration program lasts from October 1st to June 30th.

Slightly north-east of this area on Mathura Road is Delhi's fifth city, **Feroz Shah Kotla**, built during the fourteenth century by Emperor Ferozshah Tughlaq. Much of it was wrecked to build Shahjahanabad, but its ruins are still impressive and contain one of Ashoka's inscribed pillars which dates back to the third century BC. (See THE NORTHWEST CITADEL, page 70). From here it's a 10 minute walk north-east down Mahatma Gandhi Road to **Raj Ghat** on the banks of the Yamnua River. A simple black marble slab marks the place where Mahatma Gandhi was cremated following his assassination on Friday, 31 January 1948. Members of India's ruling Nehru dynasty have had their funeral pyres here: Jawaharlal Nehru, India's first prime minister in 1964, then his grandson, the heir-apparent, Sanjay Gandhi in 1980, Indira Gandhi in 1984, and Rajiv Gandhi in 1991. Various dignitaries have planted trees including Mikhail Gorbachev, Queen Elizabeth II, Gough Whitlam, Dwight Eisenhower and Ho Chi Minh. Opposite Raj Ghat is the **Gandhi Museum**, open 9:30 am to 5:30pm except Mondays.

MUSEUM ROUND-UP

If you have time, Delhi's lesser-visited sights are very worthwhile. The **National Museum**, on Janpath, just below the Rajpath intersection, contains one of the largest and most precious collections of Indian art and artifacts. It houses many key finds from the Prehistoric and Indus Valley civilizations, terra-cotta figures dating to the seventh and eighth centuries, miniature paintings, and sculpture from the Maurya, Gandhara and Gupta periods. Central Asian antiquities are well represented, (with some Tibetan objects secretly smuggled out of Lhasa during the Younghusband mission in 1904) and there's a new wing devoted to folk, classical and tribal music instruments. The museum shop offers cheap replicas of famous sculptures, and shows good films at 2:30 pm onSaturdays and Wednesdays, and is

open daily except Mondays from 10 am to 5 pm.

The **Indira Gandhi Memorial** at Number One, Safdarjang Road, the residence of India's former prime minister is preserved as a museum with many of her personal effects and a photographic display, after she was assassinated in December 1984 while strolling through her garden by two of her own bodyguards, both Sikhs. Her recorded voice follows visitors through the garden, and the site where she fell is covered by glass, her bloodstains preserved. For another chapter in India's modern history, go to the **Nehru Museum** on Teen Murti Road, near

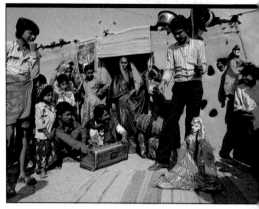

Chanakyapuri, where the residence of India's first prime minister has been converted into a fascinating repository of documents and photographs about his life. There's a sound and light show every night about Nehru and the independence movement. To see where Mahatma Gandhi was killed, visit the **Gandhi Smriti Museum** in Tees January Marg. All are open from 10 am to 5 pm and closed Mondays.

Rail-buffs won't need encouragement to visit Delhi's interesting **Rail Museum** in Chanakyapuri, (behind the Bhutanese Embassy) where highlights include an 1855 steam engine, a 1908 Viceregal dining coach and a museum stuffed with fascinating rail-lore, with its most eccentric exhibit the fractured skull of a wild elephant which charged a Calcutta-bound rail train in 1894. Original sepia plates of trains are also on sale for around US$25 to US$50, and the museum is open from 8:30 am to 11:30 pm and 4 to 7:30 pm (April to June) and 10:30 am to 5 pm (July to March).

Other notable museums are the **Doll's Museum** with over 6,000 dolls from 85 different

OPPOSITE: Dawn breaks over the medieval Jama Masjid, casting its distinctive silhouette across old Delhi's skyline. ABOVE: Itinerant street performers entertain in one of Delhi's shantytowns.

countries on Bahudur Shah Zafar Marg, the **National Museum of Modern Art** on Dr Zakir Hussain Marg, and **Tibet House**, 1 Institutional Area, Lodhi Road, which displays ceremonial items brought out of Tibet when the Dalai Lama fled the Chinese invasion. Tibetan handicrafts are sold, and there are often lecture and discussion sessions that visitors are welcome to join.

SHOPPING

If you plan to return home laden with exotic purchases, then Delhi is the best place for seri-

ous shopping. As India's competitive marketplace, its shops are overflowing with goods from all over the country. Hard bargaining pays off in Delhi, where prices are often hugely inflated for the tourist market — but often dropped just as quickly for the citywise. The biggest center is **Connaught Place**, and the best place to start browsing are at the fixed price **Government Emporiums**. Even if you don't buy anything here, you'll gain an insight into the range, quality and price of goods to expect in bazaars and shops elsewhere. The two-storied, merchandise-crammed **Central Cottage Industries Emporium** on Janpath has a fine range of fabrics, crafts, furniture, pottery, carpets, dhurrie rugs and jewelry. On the other side of Connaught Place on Baba Kharak Singh Marg you'll find the long row of government state emporiums, each specializing in the crafts

of a single state — they make a fascinating morning's excursion. Especially good are **Tamil Nadu** for colorful applique lantern and umbrellas, giant terra-cotta animals, bronzes and papier mâché masks, **Bihar** for fine raw silk, **Nagaland** for tribal woven rugs and bamboo baskets, **Orissa** for unusual *ikat* fabrics and toys and **Gujarat** for fine weaves, embroidered fabrics and lacquered furniture. The only drawback with the state emporiums (open 10 am to 6 pm) is its archaic system of sale (bills in triplicate done at one counter, collection at another). Just opposite is the **Regal Building Complex**, where it's worth visiting the **Khadi Gramodyog Bhawan**, which specializes in *khadi*, the coarse fabric that is spun, dyed, woven and printed by hand as opposed to handloom fabrics which are mill-spun, then hand-woven. Prices are government subsidized to promote cottage industry, and the whole place is festooned with pictures of Mahatma Gandhi, who as part of his Quit India campaign urged all Indians to burn British clothes and adopt khadi as a symbol of independent India. In the same block, is **The Shop** on Parliament Street for high quality leather goods, stylish linen, hand-printed fabric and pottery. Also in Connaught Place, comb through the underground **Palika Bazaar**, a warren of 300 stalls, and the **Tibetan Market** along Janpath, good for cheap clothes, ethnic jewelry, bronze, carvings and bric-à-brac.

Aside from Chandni Chowk's curio shops, (clustered around the Jama Masjid), it's fun to witness the lively Sunday market along Mahatma Gandhi Road, known as **Chow Bazaar**. Originally started during the Mughal period, this Indian version of London's Portabello Road has an extraordinary assortment of old and new, and also crowds to see itinerant circus performers doing death-defying stunts. For essential oils, rose water, henna and ornate sandstone-carved bottles — all perfect for gifts — visit the unique **Chhabra Perfumery** at R-Expo, 1115 Main Bazaar, Paharganj.

For antiques and curios, you need go no further than **Sunder Nagar Market**, located near mid-way between the Oberoi Hotel and Purana Qila on Dr Zakir Hussain Road, with some 40 antique and art shops. If you're unsure about the authenticity of an antique or item of jewelry, you and the shop-owner can always pay a visit to the National Museum or to the Government Gem Laboratory in Barakhamba Road. For the best books, head for **Khan Market** (near Lodhi Gardens) Delhi's "prestige" market, which has **The Bookshop** for up-to-date book releases, or **Oxford Book and Stationary Company**, Scindia House, in Connaught Place. All the main hotels have shopping arcades, but the best are found at the Taj Group's **Khazana** shops, at the Maurya and the Imperial. For the finest Indian tea, also prettily gift-wrapped, go to the **Tea Room Aap Ki Pasand**, Netaji Subhash Marg, opposite Golcha Cinema, Old Delhi. Stop here after exploring the old city and for delicious iced lemon tea. Shops, in general, are open from 10 am to 6 pm daily except Sundays.

GENERAL INFORMATION

Consult the monthly Delhi Diary for its extremely useful directory that covers all the information centers, travel reservation offices, restaurants, theatres, embassies, hospitals etc that you could possibly need. Delhi is the place to stock up on information for your next destinations, as well as doing as much advance-planning and booking as possible to save hassle later. The main **Government of India Tourist Office**, ((011) 332-0005 and 333-0008, at 88 Janpath is open from 9 am to 6 pm daily except Sundays offers answers to queries about all Indian destinations, and usually stocks a good map of Delhi. This is where you book conducted tours for New Delhi (morning) and Old Delhi (afternoon), run by both ITDC and DTDC. See also TRAVELERS' TIPS for addresses of appropriate Government and State tourist offices.

CORBETT NATIONAL PARK

India's most famous, gloriously scenic and well-organized tiger sanctuary is 267 km (140 miles) north-east of Delhi, in Uttar Pradesh is easily reached in six hours by car, or by rail to Ramnagar, the nearest station, 50 km away. It's named after Jim Corbett who spent a lifetime hunting down man-eaters and leopards in these parts from 1907 to 1939, and whose ripping yarns and instinctive understanding of these mesmerising beasts spawned a series of books, notably *The Man-Eaters of Kumaon*. Corbett Park has crocodiles, elephants, leopards, Himalayan black beer, hog deer, chital and spectacular birdlife (585 species). But it is the lure of seeing a tiger that draws visitors here. Stay at one of the many forest lodges, all comfortable and inexpensive with modest menus, but with confusingly identical names. In **Dhikala**, the main entrance to the park, there's a choice between the "luxury" New Forest Rest House and Annexe, New Forest Rest House, Old Forest Rest House and individual cabins. To add spice to tiger-watching, there are numerous lodges in the park, notably the Khinanauli Forest Rest House. For information and bookings contact the Reservations Director, Project Tiger (UP), PO Ramnagar, Distict

Nanital or the UP Tourist Office, ((011) 322251, Chandralok Building, 36 Janpath, New Delhi. You can explore by elephant and jeep, or hide out in machans (watch-towers). The park's Ramganga river brims with trout and mahseer, and you're free to go fishing as long as you have a permit from the Dhikala Game Warden. Best season to visit is between November and May, with the park most beautiful between January and March.

PUNJAB

Tourists are now free to travel through Punjab

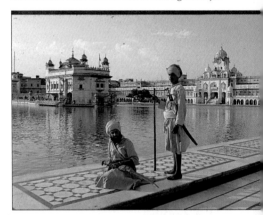

state, as the Indian government lifted its ban on foreign visitors citing a decrease in terrorist violence. In **Amritsar,** see the famous sixteenth century Golden Temple, the holiest of holy Sikh shrines. It was consecrated by the fifth Sikh Guru, Arjun, but the Sikh ruler, Maharajah Ranjit Singh created its grandiose marble structure and smothered its domes with 400 kg of gold. The city is named after its sacred pool — *amrit* (nectar) *sar* (pool). Make sure your head is covered and your feet bare, try not to swallow too much of dubious sweet prasad which temple attendants will encourage you to eat as a sign of good-will, and join the throng of pilgrims within the temple complex and see especially the **Akal Takht** or "Throne of the Timeless God" facing the Golden Temple. Also seek out **Jallianwala Bagh,** 100 yards away from the temple complex's main entrance, where on 13th April 1919, General Dyer ordered his Gurkha troops to fire on peaceful protestors. Over 300 people died and the massacre ignited anti-British hatred in the struggle for independence.

OPPOSITE LEFT: A *paan*-wallah awaits customers in Chandni Chowk. ABOVE: Sikhs in ceremonial costume guard the sacred pool lake precincts of the Golden Temple complex at Amritsar, the holiest of all Sikh shrines.

Agra
and India's
Heartland

AGRA AND THE TAJ MAHAL

Agra is the medieval Mughal city of the famous Taj Mahal, the creation of a dynasty that dedicated its spoils to building architectural masterpieces. Its origins are recounted in the epic Mahabharata — as "Agrabana" or "Paradise", it was a strategic Aryan stronghold some 3,000 years ago. Agra first rose to prominence as the capital of Sikandar Lodi during the early sixteenth century, soon usurped by the Mughals, and both Babur and Humayan made some early efforts to establish it as their power-base. In 1566, the 24 year-old Akbar ordered the construction of his red sandstone fort beside the Yamuna river, and the city of Agra grew up around its lofty crenellated battlements, massive watch-towers and giant gateways. It was the dynasty's first major architectural venture, and it remained the center of imperial activity during the early years of Mughal rule. At its peak, tales of Agra's splendor and the lavish patronage of its powerful rulers lured emissaries, traders, missionaries, musicians, scholars, artists, physician, philosophers and craftsmen from practically every civilization, ushering in a period of creativity comparable to the Italian Renaissance. The mightiest of the Mughals, Akbar not only established control across almost three-quarters of the sub-continent, but also created an efficient bureaucracy and fostered the arts on a grand scale. His rule was marked by religious tolerance towards the people he had subjugated, and he set an example by taking a Hindu wife, Jodhai Bai from Amber, and raising her Rajput kinsmen to positions of eminence. His vision of creating a secular state prompted him to devise an eclectic faith, the Din-i-allahi, or "Ultimate Religion of God", combining what he considered the best elements of Islam, Zoroastrianism, Hinduism, Jainism and Christianity into a single, unifying religion, with himself as the divine god-head.

Akbar's legacy also included the nearby city of Fatehpur Sikri, described by author Geoffrey Moorehouse as "the most enduring, elegant ghost town that man ever abandoned" from which he ruled between 1570 and 1585, before quitting, apparently due to poor water supply.

It is Akbar's grandson, Shah Jehan, (ruled 1627–58) whose name is most romantically linked to Agra. He was a compulsive builder, addicted to monumental architecture inlaid with jewels and semiprecious stones (and to his harem as well, apparently, whose population numbered some 5,000). He created the Jami Masjid and an array of lavish marble palaces, pavilion gardens and an exquisite mosque within Agra Fort—all executed with such finesse it was said of the Mughals that they "designed like giants and finished like jewelers". By far his greatest contribution however, was the Taj Mahal, the elaborate mausoleum for his beloved Empress Mumtaz Mahal, whom he called "The Light of the Palace" who died at 39 after delivering him his 14th child — only half of whom survived to adulthood. "Empire has no sweetness, life itself has no relish left for me now", Shah Jehan was said to have mourned when he heard the news. Although he was to outlive his wife by 35 years, Shah Jehan became progressively reclusive and devoted himself to what, apart from Mumtaz, had always been his passion — architecture.

As the "seventh wonder of the world", and perhaps its most enduring symbol of human love, the Taj Mahal is still India's most popular tourist attraction. For many it is one of the main reasons for visiting India, usually inspiring even the most seasoned traveler. Yet Shah Jehan grew restless at Agra, and by 1648 he had prepared his magnificent new capital of Shahjahanabad, now Old Delhi, as the new seat of Mughal power. However, Shah Jehan was fated never to reign from his imposing Red Fort in Delhi — within a decade he was deposed by his own son, the fanatical Aurangzeb, and spent the rest of his days confined to royal quarters in Agra Fort, from which the imprisoned monarch could gaze across the river to his finest creation, the Taj Mahal. Under Aurangzeb, the Mughal empire fell into slow decline, suffering random sieges by local Marathas and Jat forces, who wrecked havoc, even pillaging the Taj Mahal. By 1803, the British had marched their troops in, establishing their capital of the North-Western Province (now Uttar Pradesh). Their stately cantonment town, to the south of Agra fort, now known as **Sardar Bazaar**, is an oasis of peaceful bungalows and gardens, but was the scene of violent battles during the Mutiny in 1857.

Few visitors seem inclined to linger long in Agra, which despite its historic Mughal monuments, is also regarded as a tourist trap, swamped with assertive touts, beggars and tourist shops. It's worst at the Taj Mahal, where droves of prospecting con artists swarm up waving soiled testimonials, a bundle of smudged postcards or a mangled limb or two, and turn sightseeing into a mixture of the sublime and the ridiculous. Just when you're lost in the Taj's milky, mirage-like beauty, some smirking commission agent may sidle up, offering you anything from a cheap and nasty

---

OPPOSITE: Glowing like an opalescent pearl, the marble surface of the Taj Mahal with its floral inlaid motifs and stylized calligraphy is a masterpiece of exquisite ornamentation.

"light-up" Taj Mahal socket plug or an invitation to buy yourself a wife. Studious refusal to stop and converse, and sharp "no thank-you's" are the only tactics to ensure relative peace at the Taj Mahal. Rising at dawn helps too, and it's worth allowing time to view the Taj's chameleon-like guises in different light. You'll enjoy Agra's sights much more if you spend two or three days, rather than day-tripping from Delhi and also to cover surrounding sights such as Sikandra, Fatehpur Sikri and Bharatpur bird sanctuary. Other easily accessible destinations from Agra include Jaipur in Rajasthan and Gwailior, Datia and Orchha in Madhya Pradesh.

Like Delhi and most of central India, Agra is at its optimum best during October to March, when days are warm, nights just cool enough for a sweater, and the landscape filled with exuberant bursts of bright bougainvillea and mustard flowers. Attempting sightseeing during high summer entails distinct discomfort — temperatures can soar as high as 50°C (122°F) and choking dust storms, or *simoons*, sweep across the plains.

The Taj Mahal, the most enduring symbol of India, seen from the monsoon-swelled Yamuna River.

ACCESS

Located 204 km (126 miles) southeast of Delhi, Agra is conveniently reached by direct daily flights from Delhi, Khajuraho, Varanasi, Jaipur and Bombay. Few travelers take the half-an-hour flight from Delhi, preferring to take the Taj Express, which departs daily from New Delhi station at 7 am and returns from Agra at 7 pm, with a travel time of up to three hours each way — a convenient day trip if time is short. The Shatabdi Express also goes directly from Delhi to Agra, ending in Gwalior. It leaves New Delhi station at 6:30 am, arriving in Agra at 8:30 am, and returns the same night from Agra at 8:10 pm, arriving at New Delhi station at 10:15 pm. Its air-conditioned first-class cabins are usually luxurious, with free packed snacks and coffee. It certainly works out cheaper, and often faster than traveling by air, since flights are often delayed. A word of warning however — be wary of extra-chatty young men and pick-pockets — touts and thieves manage to make canvassing this popular tourist route worth their while, and many have quite ingenious ploys all figured out. It's a five-hour journey by bus, with hourly departures from the main Delhi inter-state bus stand, and deluxe buses leaving daily at 7 am, from the ITDC Transport Counter, L-Block Connaught Place. At Agra railway station, day-trippers may want to join the excellent daily government-run tour of Agra's key sights, including Fatehpur Sikri, Agra Fort and the Taj Mahal in air-conditioned comfort with an articulate guide, with timings linked to train arrivals and departures. Tickets can either be purchased on the Taj Express or from

near the Platform 1 inquiry window. The state tourism bus leaves the railway station at 10:30 am for Fatehpur Sikri, returning at 6:30 pm.

HOTELS

Agra's constant floods of tourists ensure that hotel rates remain India's highest. Rooms with a vista across the Taj (for moonlight gazing) are highly coveted, yet ironically, most of the luxury hotels who boast the superiority of their "Taj Views" are several miles away — you'll often find the best balcony seats in the "front-row", the less-than-basic budget hotels clustered around the back of the Taj's South Gate.

Agra's top hotel is the five-star **Mughal Sheraton**, ((0562) 361701, fax (0562) 361730, Fatehbad Road, a design award-winning marble edifice with cascading fountains, terrace swimming pool and landscaped gardens. As far as the locals are concerned, this is Agra's real "Taj Mahal", a mecca of chic restaurants and tourist-crammed "atmosphere", and, for Agra socialites where they like to see and be seen. It certainly offers some of the city's best Mughali food, accompanied by Indian musicians, as well several as good restaurants and may be the only hotel in India with a resident elephant, camel and mongoose. Rooms are in the expensive range.

The **Taj-View Hotel**, ((0562) 361171-8, fax (0562) 361179, is moderately priced, located just down the road. There's a good restaurant, swimming pool, travel desk and shopping arcade, and rooms cost from US$110 to US$150. Other "luxury" hotels are the **Clarks Shiraz**, ((0562) 361421, fax (0562) 361428, 54 Taj Road, situated within the leafy cantonment area, just next to the Indian Airlines office. It has a popular rooftop restaurant, swimming pool and comfortable "Taj-View"; also the **Agra Ashok**, ((0562) 361223, fax 361620, The Mall, both moderately priced.

In the cheap range, try either the three-star **Hotel Mumtaz**, ((0562) 361771 or the slightly cheaper **Hotel Amar**, ((0562) 360696, both on Fatehbad Road with comfortable air-conditioned rooms, and less expensive "fan-cooled" singles. Two Raj-era options in this price range have more faded charm: the **Grand Hotel**, ((0562) 364014, 137 Station Road in the Agra Cantonment area with air-conditioned rooms, and the **Hotel Lauries**, ((0562) 364536, MG Road whose eccentric High-Raj atmosphere was profiled by one of its room guests, J.G. Farrell, author of *The Siege of Krishnapur*, as "a little island of English peace" with enormously high ceilings, non-flushing toilets, lizards, and "a dining room with a horde of waiters dressed in elaborate cummerbunds and turbans serving Queen's pudding, creamed rice and jam and egg-white…".

Back-packers tend to zero in on the main cluster of budget lodges around the back of the South Gate, just outside the precincts of the Taj Mahal. The area is riddled with prowling touts, tourist shops and cheap cafés — all of whom deluge you with offers of cheap accommodation. Check out the current travelers' favorite, **Shanti Lodge**, which offers Taj "special single cheapies", and clean doubles with roof-top views. Nearby, other good very cheap lodges that get consistent praise from tourists, are the Agra Lodge, the **Shah Jehan Hotel** and the **New India Hotel**.

RESTAURANTS

As well as its legacy of Mughal architecture, Agra also offers a chance to sample fine Mughali cuisine, refined by court chefs to tantalize the taste-buds of emperors. For stylish authentic fare, try the Mughal Sheraton's **Nauratna** restaurant, excellent for succulent spiced tandoori *burra* kebabs, *rogan josh* (curried lamb), mutton *biryani*, (mutton in saffron flavored rice), and rich *rasgulla*, (cream cheese balls soaked in sugared rose water). Or opt for a *thali* platter, either for lunch or dinner, which has a delicious selection of meat and vegetable dishes. Musicians and *ghazal* singers entertain while you eat. Also within the hotel complex, you'll find Agra's best Chinese Szechuan restaurant, and an outdoor garden café for barbecue dishes. The Clarks Shiraz has good-value Rs 65 dinner buffets at its **Rooftop Restaurant**, with a choice of Indian, Chinese and Continental dishes.

Outside the hotels, try **Kwality Restaurant** at 2 Taj Road, near the tourist office, for reasonably priced, promptly served Indian food. Nearby, for excellent cheap South Indian vegetarian food, try **Lakshmi Vilas** in Sadar Bazaar, popular with locals for breakfasts of fluffy *idlis*, *vadas* and banana *lassis*, but open all day, and Agra's local cheap Chinese restaurant, the **Chungwah**. Near the main entrance to the Taj Mahal, the ITDC-run **Taj Restaurant** is good for lunch or afternoon teas after sightseeing, with a pleasant outdoor annex. Otherwise you'll find plenty of cheap cafés catering to Western tastes jumbled around the tourist lodges near the back of the Taj Mahal's South Gate.

At night, the hotel-lined Fatehbad Road transforms into a long strip of alfresco food *dhabas* or sidewalk stalls, all lit by hissing gas lamps and doing a roaring trade in meat and vegetable curries, griddle-hot chapatis, and stewed, sugary *chai*. It's very basic — with knee-high tables, rickety stools and tarpaulins overhead — but always full of appreciative locals and street-wise tourists. The best to try is the **Amar Dhawa**, near the Raj Hotel.

SIGHTSEEING

Taj Mahal

Described by Rudyard Kipling as "the embodiment of all things pure, all things holy and all things unhappy", the Taj Mahal is India's ultimate symbol. The so-called "Crown of Palaces" has been eulogized by poets and artists countless times, so much in fact that when Mark Twain visited in 1897, he felt himself "drunk on someone else's cork", but like him, most visitors still feel that the vision of its fabled splendor is more than ample compensation for traveling around the globe.

The Taj was Shah Jehan's greatest architectural project, completed in 1659 after 22 years of construction with some 20,000 artisans on the site — including many from Iran, France, Italy and Turkey. Beneath its tons of seamless white marble lies plain red sandstone, wrought to jewel-like brilliance by exquisite pietra dura inlay of precious stones and Urdu verses from the Koran, fretted marble kiosks, and bulbous domes. The marble came from Makrana in Rajasthan, and over a thousand elephants were required to transport it and work construction pulleys. Its cost in those days was well over five million rupees, and it is priceless by today's standards. Pollution smudges have done little to diminish the majesty of the building, perhaps the most photographed in the world. The Taj is ever elusive, its Makrana marble taking on different hues with changing light, emanating a ghostly phosphorescent glow in moonlight, an oleander-pink glow at dawn and dusk, and a blindingly white glare in the heat of the day.

Like lifting the veil from a beautiful woman, it was designed to tantalize the viewer with a series of coquettish glimpses as you pass through the courtyard leading to the huge red sandstone entrance gate, when all its splendor is revealed. Raised on a central marble plinth, flanked at each corner by minarets and silhouetted against the sky, the huge domed mausoleum gives the illusion of "hovering" above its reflected image in the central watercourse. Classical Mughal symmetry is achieved by precisely laid-out formal gardens and water pavilions, and by balancing the great tomb with two subsidiary buildings; one a mosque, the other an assembly hall. As remote as it might seem today, during the early years of the Agra cantonment, the early British once held moonlit balls here — although after the Mutiny in 1857 this was deemed a tad too inflammatory for local sensibilities!

As with any temple or mosque, you're required to take off your shoes before entering the cenotaph chamber — or opt to rent a pair of peculiar regulation canvas "slippers" to fit over your shoes — while they're guaranteed to make you feel like a shuffling yeti, they're a practical concession to the multitude of tourists who are sometimes (quite naturally) wary of entrusting their footwear to the official "shoe minding" service. The entrance level contains false tombs of Mumtaz and Shah Jehan, who actually were laid to rest in precise duplicates in a lower-burial vault, surrounded by a superbly fretworked marble screen decorated with thousands of inlaid semiprecious stones. Once there was a golden screen around them, but in the eighteenth

century this was looted by the Jats of Bharatpur, who also took away original silver entrance doors. The tombs are engraved with floral patterns of jaspers, emeralds, sapphires and other precious stones. But Mumtaz's sarcophagus is more elaborate, in line with an order from Shah Jehan, who wanted his wife's grave continually covered in flowers. The screen and the dangling Cairine lamp was donated by former British Viceroy, Lord Curzon in 1909. If you listen to the Indian guides, they'll tell you the story that Shah Jehan planned to build an identical tomb in black marble on the other side of the Yamuna, joining the two with a bridge. As fanciful as it sounds, this seems to be more legend than fact. It is true that on the other side of the river from the Taj, large quantities of old brickwork have been unearthed, which gave substance to the story — but they were later identified as the remains of walls and pavilions in one of Babur's gardens. Another lesser-known rumor concerns the late Shah of Iran's tour of India during the '70's, and whether or not Indira Gandhi granted his private request to be able to spend a night in the Taj Mahal with his wife, in the hope that she might conceive a heir.

Purists say the Taj Mahal is best seen in the moonlight, but after random incidents of vandalism, it's now open to the public only from dawn to dusk. The only way to see the Taj at night is to book a hotel room with a view directly overlooking it.

The Fort

Built by Akbar between 1566 and 1573, **Agra Fort** was created as his much-needed military stronghold from which to govern the burgeoning Mughal empire. Determined at any cost to have an impregnable citadel, Akbar ordered it encircled by nearly two and a half kilometers (one and a half miles) of monumental 15-m (50-ft) -high turreted walls and wide moats, constructed from sandstone slabs so skillfully joined that Akbar's court historian wrote that even "a hair could not fit between them". Aside from Akbar's sturdy earth-bound battlements, few of his original buildings remain, for his son Jehangir and grandson Shah Jehan replaced them with their more opulent structures. Most of the fort's interior belongs to Shah Jehan's reign, whose residential jewel-encrusted palaces are linked by pavilions and terraces from which to gaze across at the Taj Mahal and the plains beyond.

Entrance is through the main southern Amar Singh Gate, named for the Maharaja of Jodhpur who was killed near the gate after coming to blows with Shah Jehan's soldiers in the Diwan-i-Am in 1644. It's emblazoned with the words Allah-o-Akbar, the Islamic call to prayer, which means "God is Great". Within, the first buildings visitors see were built by Akbar; the **Akbari Mahal**, Akbar's former quarters, and his son's Jehangiri Mahal, unusual for its Hindu decorative motifs. Look for the stone pool nearby in which Jehangir's wife Nur Jehan ("Light of the World") used for her rose water baths. Within the center of the fort is Shah Jehan's **Diwan-i-Am**, the hall of public audience, a pavilion supported by 40 carved pillars where the emperor once sat in state, consulting with officials and receiving petitioners. No ordinary citizen was permitted to venture further. Beyond lies the **Moti Masjid**, the pearl mosque, where the emperor, his family and attendants

naded terraces set amid a formal garden. An adjacent sunken courtyard once served as a pool stocked with exotic species of fish, for the emperor was fond of angling. Look especially for the **Sheesh Mahal**, the royal bathing quarters, where the light of a single lamp is reflected in thousands of tiny mirrors embedded in the walls and ceiling. Water cascaded down marble chutes into vast intricately-carved Turkish-style tubs. Within the courtyard stairs lead up to the octagonal **Mussamamman Burj**, or **Jasmine Tower**, named for its adornment of mosaics, flower-wreathed columns and beautiful marble filigree screens. It was here that Shah Jehan

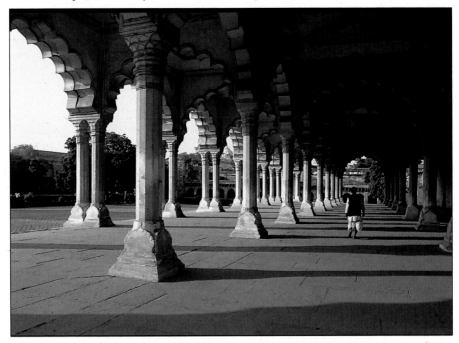

gathered for private prayer. From its domed ceiling once hung a huge priceless pearl. Near the mosque are a group of arcaded sandstone structures, the site of the annual New Year Meena Bazaar when the aristocratic ladies took on the role of flirtatious purveyors, selling exotic wares to the princes, nobles and even the emperor himself. As a local guide pamphlet rather graphically puts it, "Emperor Akbar used to attend in feminine disguise so that he could mix up with the female sex!" It was here that Shah Jehan, then a prince, met and fell in love with Mumtaz Mahal. The fort's true citadel of power was Shah Jehan's **Diwan-i-Khas**, or private audience hall, which glittered with solid gold, silver and precious stones. Here the emperor would receive important dignitaries or foreign ambassadors. Close by are the **Khas Mahal**, Shah Jehan's private pavilions, linked by colon-

spent the last eight years of his life as a prisoner, dying in 1666. Like most of Agra's monuments, the fort is open from sunrise to sunset.

Mughal Tombs

Agra Fort's **Delhi Gate** directly faces the squat domed Jami Masjid, built by Shah Jehan in 1648 and dedicated to his daughter Jehanara Begum, who loyally stayed with her father during his imprisonment.

From here, hire a taxi or auto-rickshaw for the 15 minute ride across to the opposite bank of the Yamuna River, about a kilometer (two-thirds of a mile) north-east of Agra Fort, to the **Itmad-ud-Daulah**, known as the **"Baby Taj"** — less frequented, smaller and yet somehow more delicately beautiful than its grander famous cousin. Completed in 1628, it is the resting place of Nur Jehan's father Mirza Ghiyas

Beg (alias Itmad-ud-Daulah, the "Pillar of the State").

The story attached to Ghiyas Beg is fascinating, for his family became intimately entwined with the fortunes of the Mughals. The Persian noble fell out with the Safavid king Abbas of Persia, and fled to India with his wife and small daughter, but the journey was so difficult, and money and morale so low, that they decided to abandon the little girl to speed the journey. Allah intervened, or so it seemed, when a caravan traveling behind the penniless couple, found the child and returned her to her parents. Ghiyas Beg soon rose to prominence in the Mughal court, and his rescued daughter, Mehrunissa, became the beautiful young wife of a Persian general. On her husband's sudden death in 1607, the 30 year-old, Mehrunissa returned to Agra and became a lady-in-waiting to one of Akbar's widows. Here she was spied by the young Emperor Jehangir, who made her his Empress Nur Jehan in 1611. Despite being in purdah, Nur Jehan wielded formidable power and as her frequently drunken husband became increasingly ruled by his three main passions — art, hunting and his harem — she proved herself an exceptional administrator. Many of her family members rose in the Mughal ranks, including her niece, Mumtaz, the woman who inspired the Taj Mahal.

Itmad-ud-Daulah was the first Mughal tomb to incorporate the Persian technique of *pietra dura*, the inlay of semiprecious stones in marble that was later popularized by Shah Jehan in the Taj. A feminine touch prevails in its intricate geometric and floral mosaics and lace-like pierced screens, similar in style to the tomb Nur Jehan built for Jehangir, near Lahore in Pakistan.

Further north, you'll see the **China-ka-Rauza**, the "China Tomb" notable for its giant enameled dome, constructed for posterity by Afzal Khan, a noble in Shah Jehan's court. Continuing two kilometers (one and a quarter miles) north along the riverside lies **Emperor Babur's Ram Bagh Garden**, laid out in 1528 and presently being restored to its former glory. It's said that Babur was temporarily buried here before being permanently interred at Kabul in Afghanistan as was his wish.

Finally, visit **Sikandra**, 10 km (six miles) north of Agra, to see Akbar's vast beautifully carved, but ravaged red-ocher sandstone tomb set in a lush garden and completed by his son, Jehangir in 1613. Guarded by four monumental gateways, its architecture blends Muslim, Hindu, Sikh and Christian designs, reflecting Akbar's secular faith, with the lavish, more typically Mughal *pietra dura* inlay work added out of filial duty by Jehangir.

SHOPPING

Agra brims with handicraft shops and emporiums, and is famous for its *pietra dura* marble inlay work, embroidery, carpets, and jewelry. It's also notoriously touristy, with plenty of shabbily-produced goods pumped out for impulse-buyers. Every taxi or auto-rickshaw driver will spin a story about their "brother's" shop, but if you take up their offer of visiting a certain shop, they're liable to rake up as much as 40 percent profit on anything you buy, meaning the overall price is inflated. As with most large Indian cities, make

the government emporiums your first stop, so that you'll be able to compare quality and prices when picking through curio shops later. Good shopping areas include **Sardar Market**, near the Mall, and further up Balu Ganj, where hundreds of "factories" churn out marble inlay goods, painstakingly fitting in mosaic patterns in a process little changed since the days when the Taj Mahal was built. The easiest way to tell bone-fide marble from inferior soapstone or alabaster is to scratch it surreptitiously: alabaster marks, marble remains clear.

EXCURSIONS

For an adventurous, unforgettable day, combine Agra's two most compelling surrounding sights — **Fatehpur Sikri** and **Bharatpur Bird Sanctuary** for a single day's excursion. By far the most pleasant way to do this is to hire a taxi the day before, agreeing on the rate for a round-trip beforehand — usually in the range of US$25. If so, arrange to leave about 4:30 am (you'll soon nod off in the taxi!), and arrive at Bharatpur by sunrise to see all its exotic birdlife swoop and

OPPOSITE: Mughal columns within the Diwan-i-Am at the Red Fort. ABOVE: Detail of surface exterior at Itmad-ud-Daulah's tomb.

Agra and India's Heartland

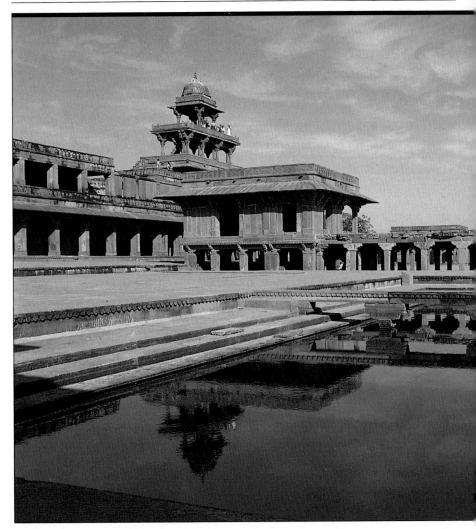

dive, fluttering brilliant plumage against the soft dawn sky. The return journey is then broken with an afternoon ramble through Fatehpur Sikri, and you'll arrive back in Agra around 5 pm in time to catch on-going connecting flights or trains. If you've more time to spare, it's much cheaper to make the hour-long bus trip to Fatehpur Sikri from Agra's Idgah bus station, and continue onto Bharatpur that afternoon for an overnight stay. From Bharatpur, which is located in Rajasthan's south-eastern corner, direct twice daily trains run to Agra, Jaipur and Delhi.

ABOVE: The magnificent citadel of Fatehpur Sikri with its stately arrangement of palaces, pavilions, gardens, shrines and administrative buildings, all in cinnabar-red sandstone. The world may not contain a larger, more beautiful and more perfectly preserved ghost city than this.

FATEHPUR SIKRI

This gigantic, forsaken sixteenth century city looms high above the dusty tableland 37 km (23 miles) southwest of Agra. It was the Mughal empire's most fleeting capital, and perhaps its most magnificent, still almost perfectly preserved. Emperor Akbar conceived it as a "modern" utopian city — a meeting place of enlightened scholars, philosophers and statesmen — and its distinctive architecture reveals far more of this ruler's brilliant and enigmatic personality than his enormous palace complex at Agra Fort.

For all his pragmatic hardheadedness, Akbar was inspired to build Fatehpur Sikri in a fit of romantic superstition. As the story goes, the emperor was is his late twenties, possessing as

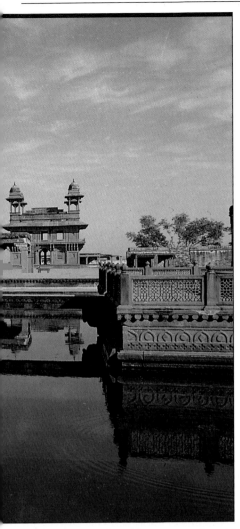

the site teemed with the empire's best architects, masons, stone-cutters and sculptors, as well as some ten thousand coolies to help build what came to be known as Fatehpur or "City of Victory", named for Akbar's victory over Gujarat in 1573. Even by the heroic and decadent standards of the Mughals, Akbar's magnificent sandstone metropolis must have seemed a sumptuous court, filled with palaces, pleasure domes, mosques, gardens, courtyards, bathhouses and stables, enclosed within a circumference of some 14 km (nine miles). A contemporary English traveler, Ralph Finch, wrote: "The king hath in Agra and Fatehpur Sikri 100 elephants, 30,000 horses, 1,400 tame deer, 800 concubines and such other store of leopard, buffaloes, cocks and hawks that it is very strange to see. Agra and Fatehpur Sikri are very great cities, either of them much greater than London". Yet by 1586, Akbar was forced to abandon Fatehpur Sikri, apparently when the water supply dried up, prompting a mass migration back to Agra.

Akbar's elegant inner citadel remains strongly evocative of his cultured Mughal court. His graceful buildings seem barely touched by the ravages of time, although only ruins remain of the original town on the periphery. There are two entrances to the city — the official one through the **Shahi Darwaza**, where licensed guides can be hired for several hours' strolling, the other up majestic steps to the monumental 54-m (177-ft) -high **Buland Darwaza**, or "Gate of Victory", visible for miles, and bearing a Koranic inscription that was to prove strangely prescient for Akbar's city: "The world is a bridge: pass over it but build no house upon it. He who hopes for an hour, hopes for Eternity, for the world is but an hour." It leads into an enormous congregation courtyard, containing the **Friday Mosque**, or **Jami Masjid**, said to be a copy of the main mosque at Mecca, and the tiny white marble jewel-like tomb of Sheikh Salim Chisthi, ornamented with latticed screens and serpentine brackets. The holy man died in 1571, but the tomb was completed some ten years later on the orders of Akbar, and given much of its exquisite pietra dura work later by Shah Jehan as an act of piety. It was built on the site of the Sheikh's favorite meditation place. Childless women of all religions come to pray at the Sheikh's tomb for his blessings. The mosque and shrine are cloistered outside the city's main secular enclosure and must be visited separately.

To the left of the Buland Darwaza is a very deep well filled with murky water into which local lads dare to dive if you give them a few rupees. From here it's a five minute stroll to the Shahi Darwaza. Within this royal citadel past the royal stables, stretch seemingly endless

much territory and wealth as a monarch could ever hope for, yet despite his many wives (and his extensive 800-strong harem) he lacked a legitimate male heir. Apparently the problem lay not in his fertility, but in the fact that his male children failed to survive. Akbar sought the advice of a Sufi Muslim saint, Sheikh Salim Chisthi, who successfully prophesied that the emperor's wives would soon produce three healthy male children. Sure enough the next year Jodhai Bai, one of Akbar's Rajput wives and the daughter of the Maharaja of Amber, gave birth to a son. He was named Salim in honor of the holy man, and became the future emperor, Jehangir. (The other two sons followed soon after.) Overjoyed that his line was secure, Akbar announced his intention to move his royal capital from Agra to a brand new city built at Sikri, the home of the holy man. Work began in 1565, and for a decade palaces, each more majestic than the last. First looms the casket-like palace that belonged to Raja Birbal, Akbar's brilliant Brahman prime minister, one of the "Nine Jewels of Akbar's Court".

To your right lies the principal harem wing for the Hindu wives, over which Akbar's Wife No.1, the Rajput princess Jodhai Bai presided imperiously from her spacious purdah-screened salon. Within the zenana (harem) were spacious gardens, fountains and a mosque, and privacy was ensured by solid gates guarded by eunuchs. Two favorite wives had separate abodes: Akbar's Christian wife from Goa, Maryam, lived in the so-called Golden Palace, named for its gilded interiors; and his Turkish wife, Sultana Begum, (who was, it is said, his favorite, despite her inability to provide him with a son) was the envy of all the harem for her elegant marble pavilion, once studded with precious jewels.

Look especially for the **Panch Mahal**, a five-storied architectural marvel and Akbar's personal citadel of pleasure, where he would wile away his evenings in the company of his harem. Close by, you'll see two of Akbar's quasi-bureaucratic chambers, the **Astrologer's Seat**, an ornamented pavilion where the resident astrologer played an important role in day-to-day court life, and the **Treasury**, or the **Ankh Michauli** (Hide and Seek) building, nicknamed for Akbar's favorite game in the harem, but functioning as the imperial repository of gold and silver.

This section leads onto the **Pachesi Court-yard** where Akbar and his courtiers used slave girls attired in brilliant dresses of different colors as pieces to play *pachesi* (a game similar to ludo), moving when ordered on a giant marble board, a notion that inspired India's famed film-maker Satyajit Ray to create his classic *The Chess Players*.

Akbar's private quarters flanked those of the Zenana, screened away from the courtyard, and his richly embellished "House of Dreams" or bedchamber is on the first floor.

Across the royal courtyard is Fatehpur Sikri's architectural gem, the **Diwan-i-Khas, (Hall of Private Audience)**. This single vaulted chamber is dominated by its massive central Lotus Throne Pillar, which supported Akbar's throne and is linked to the upper-level gallery by four suspended gangways. The central pillar is tiered with eclectic carved motifs of a pot-pourri of religions, reflecting the universal outlook of Akbar's faith. It is simultaneously the Hindu tree of life (of which the *bodhi* tree of the Buddhists is a version), the lotus flower stretching to the heavens, and the royal umbrella that protects the king and his subjects. Akbar's throne itself was designed to represent the nail of the river-god Indra, in an unmistakable allusion to the Hindu concept of the cosmos: the emperor in the middle and the universe

radiating around him. Within this resplendent honey-comb chamber, Akbar would conduct philosophical debates with adherents of diverse faiths, some Hindu, some Muslim, others mystics of no particular persuasion, and even missionaries from the Portuguese trading posts on the south-western coast of India.

Climbing to the roof of Diwan-i-Khas, you'll get a good view of the octagonal Elephant Tower to the north. Spiked with masonry "tusks", this tower is the tomb of Akbar's favorite elephant, Hiran "The Golden One". Even in Akbar's relatively tolerant court, Hiran was often called upon to perform one of the more gruesome punishments meted out by the Mughals. Convicted criminals sentenced to be "Crushed by Elephant" were placed strategically beneath his feet, whereupon he was usually ruthless. If the elephant seemed indifferent, and refused to squash the victim three times in a row, this was considered divine intervention and the happy criminal would be set scot-free. Further north, lie the remains of the caravansary, where visiting traders would stay; the Elephant Gate, (one of nine gates that dot the massive city walls), as well as the imperial workshops and market.

Coming out of the south door of the Diwan-i-Khas, you'll follow Akbar's route along a raised pavilion to the colonnaded **Diwan-i-Am**, designed for large public gatherings. Akbar sat at the center (flanked by unseen wives behind a carved *jami* screen), dispensing justice and hearing litigation. According to his biographer Abul Fazl, Akbar was "without harshness or ill-will", but if you examine the center of the lawn, you'll see the sickle-shaped stone where Hiran the elephant trampled convicted criminals to death.

You'll need a map, and may wish to hire a licensed guide — both available at the Shahi Darwaza entrance. If you're keen to stay overnight in Fatehpur, try the **Archaeological Survey Rest House**, where basic rooms are bookable through the Survey's main (informative) office at 22, The Mall, Agra.

KEOLADEO NATIONAL PARK, BHARATPUR

Located in Rajasthan's eastern corner, 17 km (10.5 miles) from Fatehpur Sikri, Bharatpur is an ornithologist's paradise: one of the world's finest bird sanctuaries with over 29 sq km (11 sq miles) of fresh water marshland, originally developed by the Maharaja of Bharatpur for his legendary duck shoots. The sanctuary was established in 1956, when it had been a royal hunting domain for more than 200 years. During British colonial times, English aristocrats and their supporting casts of young subalterns never refused an invitation to a shooting spree. Sepia photographs in the old hunting lodge, now a tourist guest house, record arch-imperialists, Lords Kitchener and Curzon at shoots in 1902, but it was Lord Linlithgow, a former viceroy, whose Bharatpur record remains unbroken and caused the demise of 4,273 birds on November 12, 1938.

Thankfully, today the park's 370 species of birds live in lushly beautiful, protected peace. The sanctuary is open from September to February, but best visited from November to January, when about 150 different types of migratory birds wing in for a temperate winter, usually from China, the Arctic Circle, Afghanistan and Siberia. Bharatpur's most famous residents are rare Siberian cranes, often as many as 40 out of some 2,000 believed to exist in the world. They take just under a week to reach India from Siberia. You'll see the Indian sarus, dazzling white egrets, hunch-back herons, water-dancing Chinese coots, gliding eagles, extravagantly-colored storks poised on treetops, lapis-blue kingfishers, and many others, dipping, diving and spiraling.

Arriving at dawn, (armed with binoculars, camera, a jersey and mosquito repellent) is an absolute must, when the mists rise and the sanctuary's feathered occupants stir into life with the first sun's rays, sending stereophonic bird-song echoing across the water. At the Forest Office at the main entrance, where tickets must be purchased, you can arrange bicycle (best for covering plenty of ground) and rowboat hire (for punting across the marshes), as well as hire one of their excellent guides, who are usually trainee ornithologists with a genuine enthusiasm for their subject. It's enticing to meander off the well-designated roads and marshland embankments — for there are plenty of established forest tracks, where you may encounter Indian antelopes and the odd wild boar, who tend to sprint away from human foot-falls. Cobras inhabit a small breeding patch within the park, and their mid-morning wriggle in the sun has become a small tourist attraction in itself — but it's wise to let your guide approach first! If you want to bone up on birdlife, take along Salim Ali's *Book of Indian Birds*. Jeeps and taxis can pick up passengers at a halt zone about eight kilometers (five miles) into the sanctuary.

After a morning's scout, you can proceed for a hot brunch at the **Forest Lodge**, the Maharaja's former hunting lodge and the sanctuary's nicest accommodation option, in the cheap range. Air-conditioning is available but usually not required in winter. To book, call ((05644) 22722, fax (05644) 22864, or contact the Forest Office. Another in-park option is the quaint **Shanti Kutir Forest Rest House,** the former maharaja's old hunting lodge, perfect for secluded bird-watch-

ing. It's best to book in writing. In Bharatpur town, opt for newly refurbished old-world palatial charm at the **Golbagh Palace Hotel** ((05644) 3783, Agra Road. This former palace guest house brims with trophies, collector's item photographs and faded frescoes. Meals are excellent, with vegetables picked straight from the garden. Rates are inexpensive. Other good options can be found in Bharatpur town, otherwise try the RTDC-run **Saras Tourist Bungalow,** ((05644) 3700, on Agra Road, with practical, clean rooms, hot showers and a basic menu, (very cheap). Aside from the sanctuary, there's plenty to see in Bharatpur, a former British cantonment town.

Its most impressive sight is the eighteenth century Lohagarh (Iron) Fort, built by the Jat ruler, Maharaja Suraj Mal, the founder of Bharatpur, and named for withstanding numerous attacks by the British. There's an interesting museum displaying artifacts from the region, open from 10 am to 5 pm, closed on Fridays. It's also worth cycling to see the Jat dynasty's imposing palace and museum, where family heirlooms are displayed. Locals describe with relish how the present Maharaja's grandfather was renowned for his eccentric manner, and how he used to don his flying goggles and take off in his World War I biplane, laughing maniacally as he strafed "moving objects" in the fields below!

KHAJURAHO

The famous erotic sculptures of Khajuraho display the most sensuous and vivacious motifs of all Indian temple architecture, ranking close to the "Golden Triangle" of Delhi, Agra and Jaipur as a major tourist destination. Built between AD 950 and 1050 by the rich and powerful Rajput Chandella rulers, these temple sculptures with their countless scenes in praise of earthly passion are the very antithesis of India's modern, more censorious sexual mores. Situated in the middle of Madhya Pradesh's dry rural plains, Khajuraho was once a magnificent temple city, clustered with some 85 spire-peaked temples, of which today only 22 remain, seeming all the more extraordinary in their desolation.

A thousand years ago, Khajuraho was encircled by a fortress-like wall with eight gates, each flanked by two gilt date palms — inspiring the Chandella's to call their capital "Khajurvahika" or "city of the golden dates". The surviving temples are remarkably intact, revealing this ancient civilization's zeal for life it all its forms: spiritually, sexuality, music, hunting, and martial

conquest. They probably owe their continued existence to their remote location, therefore escaping the destructive fury of icon-smashing Muslim armies as they swept across northern India during the eleventh century.

Why the Chandella kings — who claimed descent from the moon god, Chandra and worshipped Lord Vishnu, God of Preservation — decided to build their capital in such a remote barren spot remains a mystery. The pure technological feat of constructing these architectural marvels is impressive. The sandstone was dug from the Ken River 20 km (12 miles) away, and chiseled to crisp perfection by a laborious method involving cutting and carving every stone individually, then assembling it like a giant three-dimensional sandstone jigsaw. Believing that temple-building ensured a place in heaven, this dynasty erected the bulk of their temples in an intense burst of creative energy between the tenth and eleventh centuries. Five hundred years later, the Rajput Chandella empire was on the wane, and their fabulous capital became obscured by undergrowth, and the region notorious for its ruthless *thugs* or Kali-Worshiping bandits. The temples were recorded with dispassionate, if somewhat dismissive accuracy as "ruins" by a British military official surveying the region in 1819, leaving the discov-

ery of Khajuraho's wonders to the more adventurous Captain T.S. Burt in 1838. However his excitement at uncovering such ancient masterpieces was tempered with the realization that "the sculptor had at times allowed his subjects to grow a little warmer... than there was any absolute necessity for doing so", perhaps the most classic understatement of the Victorian era.

Today visitors are awed by the sheer intricacy, workmanship and optimism of the temple carvings. From a distance they resemble a kind of tiered, variegated beehive, but at close range, they depict a universal hierarchy seething with mythological gods and goddesses, warriors, seductive celestial nymphs or *apsaras*, animals and changelings. Certainly you will find countless loving couples locked in sexual union, *mithuna*, fondling each other, engaged in oral sex, (and even indulging in the odd bout of bestiality), yet this is presented as a natural and integral part of human nature. Above all they celebrate man's union with the divine and the pleasures of the material world.

During the British Raj, unwitting young memsahibs reportedly fainted away when faced with the more lurid of Khajuraho's couplings. Just after India's independence, when politicians were doing much soul-searching about their national heritage, they actually contemplated screening off "offensive" portions of Khajuraho's temples from public view, and classifying their famous ancient treatise on the art of sex, the Kama Sutra, as obscene literature — taking a stance towards there earthy ancestors that astonish any Western reared on notions of the "Wisdom of the East". For India is the heir to a religious tradition that took unashamed delight in sexuality, even adopting the phallic lingam and the female genital-shaped yoni as its most widespread symbols of worship.

Various theories have been put forward about the purpose of the sculptures. One story has it that the copulating couples were a test of the monk's celibacy, another that the figures were a graphic reminder to the worshipers to leave all earthly thoughts behind before entering the temple's hallowed inner sanctum. The most outlandish explanation was that the temples were built for purposes of sex education when the population was in serious decline!

Avoid Khajuraho's blistering summer, and arrive between November and February for cool comfort.

Khajuraho's highlight is its annual week-long Dance Festival, held during early March, when India's top classical dancers and musicians perform every evening against the flood-lit backdrop of ancient temples, rekindling the traditional practice of the *devadasis* (girls dedicated to Indian temples), and an unforgettable experience for performers and audience alike. Tickets range from about US$1 to US$5 per "seat", (a cushion space), and this is the time you'll need to advance book hotels and flights. While Khajuraho is small enough to see within an afternoon, it's best to plan to spend at least two days to appreciate its temple architecture by leisurely bicycling, returning for the charmed light of dawn and dusk.

ACCESS

Khajuraho is small enough to cover in a day and many visitors fly in on the shuttle flight from

The **Jass Oberoi**, ((076861) 2085, fax (076861) 2088, offers comparable accommodation, and also has a good swimming pool and shopping arcade. The best cheap range option with air-conditioned rooms is the **Khajuraho Ashok**, ((076861) 2024, slightly north of town. Of the array of budget (very cheap) lodges clustered around the town center try the **Rahil Hotel** ((076861) 2062, which has clean rooms, as well as dormitory beds and communal showers, or the **Tourist Bungalow**, ((076861) 2064, with rooms in the very cheap to cheap range for air-conditioned doubles. Otherwise try Hotel **Sunset View, New Bharat Lodge** or **Jain Lodge** (very cheap), all popular with

Delhi in the morning, and return the same evening. Daily flights also link Khajuraho with Agra and Varanasi. Arriving overland can be problematic — the most convenient railhead is Jhansi, 175 km (108 miles) away, for trains to and from Delhi, Bombay and Madras, while Satna is 120 km (74 miles), the nearest railhead for trains from Calcutta and Varanasi. Regular bus services link Khajuraho with Agra, Jhansi and Satna.

HOTELS

There are two excellent top-class luxury hotels, set in large gardens and convenient to the airport, located four kilometers (two and a half miles) away from the temples. The Taj-run **Chandella**, ((076861) 2054, has moderately priced rooms, an idyllic swimming pool, health club and serves an array of Indian, Chinese and continental food.

back-packers, clean and within a minute's walk from the Western group of temples.

RESTAURANTS

The two leading hotels offer a range of excellent Indian restaurants with Western-style coffee shops. Beyond that, locals have cottoned on to foreign tastes and set up a row of open-air cafés near the entrance to the Western Temples, prettily lit up at night with fairy lamps. The best of these is the Swiss-run Raja's Café, good for full breakfasts of eggs, toast and coffee, and popular for its cheap, delicious Indian meals as well as its apple pancakes and banana fritters. Other

OPPOSITE: An amorous couple entwined in one of Khajuraho's less explicit, perfectly chiseled embraces. ABOVE: The beehive-shaped temples of Khajuraho teem with countless *mithunas* or love-making scenes.

highly patronized spots include the Safari Restaurant with good-value *mewari thalis*, the **Madras Coffee House** and the all-vegetarian **Gupta Restaurant**.

SIGHTSEEING

The Temple Tour

For easy reference, Khajuraho's medieval temples are divided into three main areas, the most famous of which are the Western group, located at the center of town and fringed by tourist cafés, lodges and shops. The Eastern group lies one and a half kilometers (just under a mile) away

getting a copy of Krishna Devi's informative pamphlet sold at the museum.

As a general introduction, the temples follow a distinct pattern, externally resembling a sort of giant textured beehive, tiered with twisting spires or *shikaras*. Each is a compact mass of five parts, with an *ardhamanadapa* or entrance porch leading onto a pillared *mandapa* hall, then a *antarala* or vestibule, and finally an enclosed corridor, or *pradakshina* revolving around a central inner sanctum, or *garbhagriha*. The temples can be divided into two groups — those dedicated to Vishnu, Lord of preservation; and those dedicated to Shiva, Lord of destruction. Traces are

near the old village, while the Southern Temples is located some four kilometers away. The temples are open from sunrise to sunset, and it's possible to explore them in about five to six hours, best on a cycle hired from town; by autorickshaw, or a taxi for longer excursions. Enjoyment of the temples is definitely enhanced by the service of well-informed guides — you can always return to appreciate them alone. Bear in mind that the Archaeological Survey conducts free lecture tours of the Western group twice daily except on Fridays and holidays, leaving the main entrance at 9:30 am and 2:30 pm. Otherwise make your way across the road to Raja's Café, where talented graduate guides rent themselves out for about US$2 for half a day, or US$4 for a full day, as well as lunch allowance and "language allowance" if you happen to be French, German or Japanese. It's well worth

also found of Buddhism, Jainism, sun-worship, animism and various other cults that indicate the eclectic tastes of their architects. They also stand on high platforms, some two and a half meters (eight feet) above the ground, causing speculation that the Chandellas may have flooded these enclosures to create the illusion of a lake of floating temples.

Start with the famous Western group, first visiting its fascinating **Archaeological Museum**, located just outside the enclosure. It contains a rich collection of relics found within this area, and is open from 9 am to 5 pm daily except Friday. Remember to keep your ticket (with its strategic rip!) which also allows you to enter the Western group of temples. Just next door you'll see a shrine dedicated to the region's former ruling Maharaja Sri Pratap Singh Dev, touchingly laid out to recreate his personal bedroom, complete with a blown-up photograph of the deceased ruler and many personal effects.

Set within beautifully maintained gardens, the Western group represent the zenith of Chandella art. Just to the left, stands a quartet of early temples, all dedicated to Lord Vishnu. The **Lakshmana** (circa AD 930–50) is covered in rampaging sculpture, eulogizing the marital might of the Chandellas, and also notable for fine figures of *apsaras* with numerous erotic scenes on a frieze running around the temple base. Two small temples stand nearby, **Lakshmi** and **Varah**, the latter bearing a huge statue of Vishnu in his incarnation as a boar. Slightly south of the enclosure is the Matangeswara Temple, the fourth of the group, with its giant lingam. This is Khajuraho's most popular "living" temple, and on festival days comes alive with clanging bells and vividly dressed villagers laying flowers and sweetmeats around its central shrine.

Walking westwards, you'll find the **Kandariya Mahadev** (circa 1025–50) the most artistically magnificent of all Khajuraho's temples, teeming with over 900 sculptured figures, its spectacular main spire soaring to a height of 31 m (108 ft). Friezes depict deities on their cosmic plateau, observing the activities of mere mortals beneath, swarming into epic battles with phalanxes of elephants and dragons (the symbol adopted by the Chandellas), or reclining with curvaceous young women on their return home. Every detail of contemporary life is captured here, portrayed with exuberant realism and humor. Above all they celebrate the idealized woman, with her hour-glass waist and high provocative breasts, smoldering with saucy sensuality in countless poses and moods. As if caught unseen, these seductive creatures go about their toilette, combing their hair, applying eye-shadow, preening in the mirror or perhaps joyfully entwine with their lovers. Here are found Khajuraho's most energetic and explicit *mithunas* (lovemaking scenes), graphic illustrations of the Kama Sutra. Just north is the small **Dev Jagdamba** temple, thought to have been dedicated to Goddess Parvati and on close inspection, filled with formidably athletic orgiastic sequences.

In the northeastern corner is the **Chitragupta Temple**, dedicated to Surya, the sun god, portrayed driving his chariot drawn by seven horses. There are interesting exterior reliefs of hunting scenes, dancing nymphs, rural processions, and fights between incensed elephants. Inside look for the 11-headed Vishnu in the central niche, each head representing his various incarnations. Completing the temple circuit is the **Parvati Temple**, notable for its inner frieze of the Goddess Ganga using a crocodile as a carpet, and the **Vishvanath Temple**, dedicated to Shiva, and flanked by a large Nandi bull.

It takes about 15 minutes to cycle to the Eastern group of temples, following the dirt road to Khajuraho's medieval village. This walled enclosure is more evocative of the sedate influence of Jainism, lacking the frenetic erotic fervor of the Western group. The largest and finest of these Jain temples is the central **Parsavanath Temple**, with its elegantly chiseled *apsaras* engaged in prosaic day-to-day activities: fondling a child, writing a letter, applying make-up, removing a thorn from feet. Within the inner shrine stands an ornamental throne and ornate carved bull, the emblem of the first Jain Tirthankara, the saint Adinath. Just outside is a

circular museum which houses a fine collection of relics, columns and broken-off friezes from the site. The Eastern group's Hindu temples are actually scattered in the surrounding fields nearby: the **Javeri**, dedicated to Vishnu, located near the village, the **Vamana**, 200 m (217 yds) north dedicated to Vishnu's incarnation as a dwarf and notable for its bands of dazzling maidens in a variety of come-hither poses, and the **Brahma Temple**, one of the oldest at Khajuraho. Nearby, you can't miss giant luridly orange statue of Hanuman, the monkey god, guarding a modern temple on the road out to the Jain enclosure. For more, temple addicts can venture out to the

Despite its popularity with tourists, Khajuraho remains very rustic and unspoilt, with an unhurried pace of life. ABOVE: An old man soaks up the morning sun. OPPOSITE: Bullocks being used to draw water in Khajuraho village.

Southern group, four kilometers (two and a half miles) away to admire the two interesting temples, the **Duladeo** and the **Chaturbhuj**.

A highly rewarding day excursion is out to the fantasy tree-house built by Khajuraho's lovable eccentric, Gilles Bohnenblust, a Swiss who considers India his adopted home, and runs the Raja Café with his English wife Betty. His designer tree-abode has to be seen to be believed, perched high above the gushing torrents of the Ken River in Panna District, 23 km (14 miles) away. Among those eager to stay and experience life among the leaves have been actresses Julie Christie and Vivien Leigh. It's certainly a pleasant place to linger — they have possibly the world's most unique bar — and Gilles and Betty may offer guests the opportunity to experience luxurious tree life. If you're curious to see and possibly stay, contact the staff at the Raja Café.

GWALIOR

Located only 118 km (73 miles) from Agra (with regular trains and buses plying to and fro), and connected by daily flights from Delhi, Gwalior attracts few tourists, yet it offers one of India's most spectacular Rajput forts and is a good base for exploring two fabulous, deserted medieval cities nearby — **Datia** and **Orchha**.

Gwalior Fort, a colossal honey-colored sandstone citadel set some 91 m (300 ft) along a crest-like rock face, is the city's principal lure. Akbar was said to have been influenced by it when building his own Fatehpur Sikri. According to legend, the fort's history began in the fourth century AD when a sun-worshipping, but leprous Rajput chieftain named Suraj Sen encountered a faith-healing ascetic called Gwalipa on the fort's site — and after experiencing a miracle cure built the first fortress in gratitude. The ascetic also prophesied that if Suraj Sen took the name "Pal", his line would reign successfully in Gwalior. Suhan Pal and 83 of his successors did indeed rule after him, until Tej Karan failed to comply with the hermit's prerequisite for power. The Tomar king, Man Singh (1486–1516) built the six-towered Man Singh Palace, considered to be the finest example of Hindu architecture extant in India. Fresh usurpers have ensured many bloody battles for its possession, first Sikandar Lodi, then Moghul Emperor Babur, then the Marathas, whose descendants are now Gwalior's ex-First Family. Their ancestors battled with the British twice, and were twice returned to the throne. During the 1857 Mutiny, the ruling Maratha king at Gwalior was loyal to the British — but his 18,000-strong army was not. They went to war independently with the British under India's

Joan of Arc, the legendary Rani of Jhansi. She was slain alongside her troops in 1858, and the British moved into the fort, finally returning it to the Scindias in 1885.

You'll need at least a full morning or afternoon to do justice to this magnificent Boy's Own fortress, whose rambling battlements wind a five-kilometer (three-mile) -long circle. Approach it by the south-west Hindola Gate, passing the giant Jain statues carved from the rock faces (whose faces were defaced by Babur in a fit of pique). Inside is Man Singh's palace, a quintessential Oriental "wonder", with its six onion-dome cupolas, and myriad rooms adorned with dazzling lapis lazuli tiles, encrusted with broken jasper and emerald mosaics, a menagerie of carved gargoyles and peacocks, and even a natural air-conditioning system. The subterranean quarters beneath were used by the Mughals as dungeons, notable as the place where Aurangzeb hanged his brother, a possible successor to his throne. Also see the cluster of marble palaces built by the Mughals; the two eleventh century **Sasbahu Temples**, literally "mother-in-law" and "sister-in-law" temples along the eastern wall; the ninth century **Teli-ki-Mandir**, a curious temple built for newly-weds, with erotic sculptures which instruct young brides in the art of pleasing their husbands. There's an excellent museum housed in the fifteenth century **Gujari Palace**, just inside the Hindola Gate, with a fascinating collection of inscriptions, carvings, Gupta sculptures and miniature paintings. As at **Amber** (near Jaipur), caparisoned elephants carry passengers up to the fort's gate. The entire complex is open daily except Mondays, from 8 to 11 am and 2 to 5 pm. From April 1 to September 30, the schedule is 7 to 10 am, 3 to 6 pm.

Other sights in Gwalior include the ornate Italianate **Jai Vilas Palace**, built in 1872 to 1874 by the madly decadent Maharaja Jayaji, whose tastes ran to "see-through" glass furniture, gilt brocade, kitchy amusing erotica (see Leda in a loving embrace with a swan) and tiger-head trophies. Built during 1872 to 1874 while the British still occupied Gwalior Fort, it was designed by one Lieutenant Colonel Sir Michael Filose of the Indian Army as a princely showpiece for the Prince of Wales to sojourn in during his tour of India. Its gem-like **Durbar Hall** contains two immense chandeliers, reputed to be the largest in the world. Each is nearly 13 m (42 ft) high, carries 248 candles apiece, and weighs three tons. Before they could be hung, three elephants were hoisted to the roof to make sure that it was going to stand the strain. Not to be out-done, the next successor, Madhav Rao Scindia, built a silver train set that chugged its way around the dining table delivering mutton vindaloo, port and cigars. This gleeful Maharaja charmed the pants off the

British — as legendary for his school-boy pranks and unerringly accurate water pistol attacks as for enthusiastically modernizing his state. He also staged perhaps the most elaborate tiger shoots in India for the benefit of the British aristocracy. One observer estimated that if all the Maharaja's combined kills were laid out, they would stretch for more than two and a half miles — in the days when tiger slaughter was all the rage. Even more eccentrically, he managed to be the only Indian to fight with the British expeditionary force against the Chinese in Peking at the time of the Boxer uprising.

Also in town, you'll find the tomb of Tansen, the brilliant bard whom Akbar made Master of Music at his court in 1562, and according to local lore, chewing the leaves of the tamarind tree nearby gives you a mellifluous singing voice.

Stay overnight in Gwalior at the Welcomgroup's **Usha Kiran Palace**, ℂ (0751) 323213 fax (0751) 321103, Jayendragunj, a stylish palace guest house crammed with 1930's furniture, set within well-maintained grounds. Air-conditioned singles are moderately priced, with slightly cheaper fan-cooled rooms. Otherwise try the government-run **Tansen Hotel**, ℂ (0751) 340371, at 6 Gandhi Road, which has very cheap, comfortable rooms with hot water, or cheap rooms with air-conditioning.

DATIA AND ORCHHA

It's worth visiting Gwalior just to make the memorable day-trip to the hauntingly forlorn palace-cities of **Datia** (69 km or 43 miles) and **Orchha** (129 km or 80 miles) — almost completely untouched by visitors. Regular buses ply from Gwalior to the city of Jhansi, 11 km (nearly seven miles) from Orchha, but hiring a taxi makes for speedier, more relaxed sightseeing. It's nicest to leave at dawn, driving past tiny hamlets and fields of swaying wheat, arriving at Datia in the morning cool. At Datia, the seven-story hill-top **Gobinda Palace** (1614) awed even Lutyens (who failed to be moved by many Indian buildings), who went as far as calling it "one of the most interesting buildings architecturally in the whole of India". The palace is a fabulous maze of latticed corridors, verandahs, pillared cupolas and fresco-covered rooms, once studded with semiprecious gems. It's to the west of the surrounding town, encircled by a seventeenth century stone wall.

Both the Datia and the Orchha palace-complexes were financed by Raja Bir Singh Deo, a Bundela Rajput ruler based in Jhansi during the seventeenth century. This rather Machiavellian character won sway and great wealth in Jehangir's court, rewarded for his services to the emperor when he was still Prince Salim and plot-ting to depose his father, Akbar. As one of Jehangir's side-kicks, the Raja was entrusted with the task of murdering one of the heir apparent's key rivals — Akbar's personal friend and chief advisor, the influential Abul Fazal, who was also an outstanding writer whose voluminous works provide an intimate account of India under the Mughals.

Up until the 1930's Datia was a standard spectacle included in viceregal itineraries — hosting the British Governor-General Lord Hastings in 1818 and the Viceroy Lord Curzon in 1902. Today it is a forgotten masterpiece, and gypsies camp in its decaying ruins with herds of goats. Continuing onto Orchha, the most magnificent and least spoilt of the two fort cities, with its palaces and temples rising from overgrown foliage, inhabited by deer and nesting birds. It's perfect for a quiet picnic and undisturbed exploring. Tucked away at Orchha's fringes is a tiny village with small shops and tea-stalls — connected to the medieval palace by an impressive stone seventeenth century bridge. Orchha's monuments are a rich amalgam of different architectural styles, incorporating Mughal, Jain, Persian and even European features. Its most impressive structure is the perfectly symmetrical **Jehangir Mahal**, combining lofty walls with the fragile delicacy of numerous *jali* screens and ornate carvings. Close by is **Raj Mahal**, the royal chambers connected by a maze of colonnaded corridors lined with silver doors and exquisite wall paintings, even along the curving ceilings. Other palaces are linked by crossing Mughal style gardens with pavilions and fountains serviced by underground pipes. Orchha also has some beautiful and unusual temples. The **Laxmi Narain Temple**, dedicated to the goddess of wealth, Lakshmi, is covered in paintings depicting the pomp of Orchha court life, sadly defaced by graffiti, and the large **Chatturbhuj** temple dedicated to the four-armed Vishnu, with a layout that visually reproduces each of his four limbs. Along the Bewa River are rows of domed cenotaphs housing the ashes of Orchha's former rulers. The booklet *A Study of Orchha*, should be available from the Archaeological Survey Office or from the Madhya Pradesh tourist office in Jhansi. You can actually stay within the palace quarters, partly converted into the delightful **Hotel Sheesh Mahal** by Madhya Pradesh tourism authorities. Its most beautiful deluxe suite has its own sun-filled courtyard and large marble bathroom with a wall-size mirror. Suites and double rooms are in the cheap range, all with running hot and cold water and attached bathrooms — food is extra and perfectly adequate for a day or so. Book through the Madhya Pradesh Tourist Office, 19 Ashok Road, New Delhi ℂ (011) 351187.

VARANASI (BENARES)

CITY OF LIGHT

Varanasi, as Mark Twain put it in 1896, is "older than history, older than tradition, older even than legend, and looks twice as old as all of them put together." The spiritual heart of Uttar Pradesh state, it is one of the world's oldest continuously inhabited cities, and was a bustling metropolis when its main counterparts were the ancient centers of Thebes, Ninevah and Babylon.

Hindus flock to Varanasi for purification and death, to bask in the *Kasha,* or divine light that they believe emanates from the ancient holy city's thousand or more temples clustered along the Ganges river. Washing in the sacred waterway is said to cleanse away all sin. To die next to the river and have one's ashes scattered into the water is the goal of every devout Hindu, who hold that this guarantees release from the eternal cycle of birth and rebirth.

Every dawn in Varanasi involves spiritual devotion on an epic scale. As temple bells peal across the city, thousands of pilgrims throng the ghats, or stone waterside steps, leading down to the khaki-colored sacred waterway. Bearing ritual brass vessels, marigold garlands and earthen oil lamps, they immerse themselves in the Ganges and reverently cup water to their lips as the sun rises. In soft, almost evangelical light, Varanasi's teeming river-front canyon of spire-topped temples, decaying eighteenth century palaces and ashrams, presents a haunting, unforgettable sight. Behind the ghats lies a medieval maze of tangled alleys crammed with glittering bazaars, ascetic priests, dusky-skinned urchins, tumeric-smeared fakirs with rope-like hair, white-clad widows, chanting mendicants and plump painted cows.

Hinduism's umbilical attachment to the Ganges river is thought to have begun with the Aryans, who understood that the waterway saved much of north India from being a barren desert. The 2,525-km (1,565-mile) -long river begins as a spring at Gangotri in the Himalayas and snakes through the northern plains into a mammoth delta of fertility before flowing into the Bay of Bengal. With its current it carries the hopes, the prayers and, in death, the ashes of millions of Indians. Other holy towns in Uttar Pradesh also line its banks: Allahabad, Rishikesh and Hardwar. Although Ganges

water is sacred and countless people drink it, the river is severely polluted by millions of liters of raw sewage and industrial waste pumped into it each day. The problem is compounded by the Hindu practice of forbidding cremation of children, holy men and disease victims, who comprise the estimated 60,000 corpses annually thrown straight into the Ganges.

Archaeologists believe the city's mythological name, Kashi, probably derived from its earliest inhabitants, the aboriginal Kashia tribe, who settled by the river some 3,000 years ago and eked out a living by bartering woven matting made from local grass and known as *kushasans.* The mats are still made and used as umbrellas to shield meditating holy men from the often fierce sun.

The Hindu Aryans occupied the site around 800 to 900 BC, and the city soon became a magnet for philosophers, poets, mathematicians and pilgrims. Buddhism began at nearby Sarnath, where Prince Siddartha preached his first sermon in the sixth century BC after he found enlightenment by sitting under a tree.

Varanasi emerged as a prestigious and wealthy metropolis of gilded temples and shrines dedicated to the city's special deity, Lord Shiva. Local rulers constantly contested the right to claim its considerable revenue, and plundering northern invaders periodically laid siege. Varanasi's attraction had lain in more than mere intellectual or religious curiosity: its rich silks, brocades, cotton textiles and woolen cloth were coveted from China to Rome. Muslims frequently held the city to ransom from the eleventh century onwards, but the most ruthless destroyer of Hindu temples was the Mughal Emperor Aurangzeb, who converted into a mosque the Lord Vishwanath Temple, said to be the original home of Lord Shiva, god of creation and destruction. Hindu Rajas came to power in 1738, giving Varanasi a spell of local rule until it was ceded to the British in 1775.

Benares was the British corruption of a Mughal version of the old Hindu name. The ancient Hindu name Varanasi — a compound of the nearby Varuna and Asi rivers — was restored after independence.

The city has long been renowned as a center of creativity and culture, and is still the best place to hear the graceful *thrumri* and *dadra* melodies of Indian classical music. Spectacular enactments of Hindu epics have been performed since the seventeenth century, and the Benares Hindu University founded in 1916 by the nationalist Madan Mohan Malviya is now India's premier school for Sanskrit and Hindu studies. Internationally renowned musician Ravi Shankar hails from Varanasi, as do many of the country's most talented sitar and tabla

---

OPPOSITE: Pilgrims throng Varanasi's ghats or steps to bathe and pray beside the Ganges River, which devout Hindus believe has the power of cleansing away cumulative sins.

players. Tucked away in the city's medieval old center are thousands of families, many of them Muslims, engaged in making Varanasi's famous silks and brocade fabrics, intricately carved wooden toys and carpets.

WHEN TO GO

Every day in Varanasi is dedicated to one of the gods in the Hindu pantheon, and pilgrims ensure that the city is lively all year around. But the weather is best between October and March as the monsoon swells the Ganges between mid-June and September. Varanasi stages during

September to October India's most flamboyant festival, the Ram Lila or Dussehra, a 10-day extravaganza of pageants, dance and music performances. Music festivals are the best showcase for Varanasi's extraordinary talents, the best being held at the Sankat Mochan Temple in early April when top musicians perform for four to six nights as a tribute to the Monkey-God Hanuman. Others to watch out for include the Lalit Sangit Parishad in December; the Rimpa in January and the Dhrupad Mela in late February. Admission is free, but bring a blanket to wrap yourself in as evening concerts often end at dawn.

HOW TO GET THERE

Indian Airlines connects Varanasi with flights from Delhi, Bombay, Agra, Khajuraho, Hyderabad, Calcutta, Lucknow, Allahabad and Patna,

and there are also connections to Kathmandu. Vayudoot flies from Delhi and Agra. A regular bus links the airport to the city, and the 22-km (13.6-mile) -long route costs about US$7 in a taxi.

Northern and North-Eastern railways link Varanasi to major cities, and overnight sleepers from Calcutta (12 hours) and New Delhi (17 hours) are the most comfortable rail option.

WHERE TO STAY

Varanasi's few luxury hotels are frequently over-booked, so try to reserve well in advance. Top of the range is the **Hotel Taj Ganges**, ($ (0542) 42480, fax (0542) 322067, rates: moderate). Opt for a high-storey room with a view across the leafy garden, swimming pool and the adjacent Nadesar Palace of the former Maharaja, where the Queen and Prince Phillip stayed in 1955. Facilities include several excellent restaurants, a shopping arcade and travel desk. Two less expensive but comfortable options are the **Varanasi Ashok**, ($ (0542) 46020, and the **Clarks Varanasi**, ($ (0542) 46771. All these hotels are centrally located in the Raj-era Mall area and also will allow non-guests to swim in their pool for a nominal fee.

Hotel de Paris, ($ (0542) 46601; rates: inexpensive) is opposite, located halfway between the old St Mary's Church and the Tourist Office. A former guest house of the Maharaja of Benares, it has eccentric, natty charm, with a huge garden filled with hammocks and deck chairs, and a dining room crammed with sepia photographs and deer heads. Another good economy option is the popular **India Hotel**, ($ (0542) 45127, 59 Patel Nagar).

Budget travelers will find affordable space and peace at the **Tourist Dak Bungalow**, ($ (0542) 43413, rates: cheap). It's rooms are set in pretty gardens, but the food is dreadful. Back-packers tend to stay in the rock-bottom priced lodges clustered at the heart of the atmospheric old city. The **Trasmati Lodge** and the **Yogi Lodge** both have very cheap, crash-pad style accommodation right opposite the Golden Temple. You'll awake just before dawn to the sound of temple gongs, and the scent of incense and *parathas*.

WHERE TO EAT

Clarks Varanasi probably has the best restaurant, and it is pleasant to have pre-dinner cocktails in the garden before tasting their superb Mughali, Lucknowi or Chinese food that costs around US$5 per head. Lunchtime poolside barbecues are also popular. The **Taj Ganges** offers similar fare, as well as garden buffet dinners.

Locals swear by the generous portions and reasonable prices of the less glamorous

Diamond Hotel at Belapur, especially good for splurging on rich Mughali cuisine, fluffy *naans* and *kulfi* ice-cream. For light, nourishing south Indian food, seek out the **Kerala Café**, also at Belapur, open all day and excellent for lightly spiced *dosas,* lunch-time *thalis* and aromatic Mysore coffee. Other popular eateries can be found in the central Lohurabir area, including the **Tulasi Restaurant** for simple Indian cuisine. Nearby, **Kwality** has an extensive menu of Mughali, Chinese and Continental food.

Varanasi is famous for its sumptuous sweetmeats — *rasgulla, chum-chum* (oval-shaped, sprinkled with desiccated coconut and stuffed

view of the magical light filtering across one of the most spectacular scenes of devotional pageantry on earth. Rise at 4 am — you can always have a siesta — and take a cycle-rickshaw to the central **Dasaswanadh Ghat**, where you'll find plenty of boatmen willing to ferry you around at reasonable rates. A good introductory hour-long tour is to go upriver to **Asi Ghat,** and then return and proceed downstream to **Panchganga Ghat.**

You will see the faithful throng the water's edge, perform Hindu rites and energetically lather themselves with suds from head to toe. Young men strut about and limber up with

with *malai* cream), *kheer-mohan, pista burfi,* and others — best sampled from stalls in **Thatheri Bazaar** in the Chowk area. Residents often start their day with *thundai,* an aromatic concoction of milk, saffron, almonds, black pepper and ground-up marijuana or bhang. Many people are addicted to the brew, and also consume bhang in their *paan* mixtures.

THE GHATS

The city's life revolves around its seven-kilometer (4.3-mile) -long sweep of about 100 bathing ghats which skirt the west bank of the Ganges. Most were built in the eighteenth century, along with palaces and temples constructed by Hindu maharajas of Varanasi, Jaipur, Udaipur, Gwalior and Mysore. No visitor should miss taking a boat ride along the ghats at dawn for a grandstand

exercises before making dare-devil dives from temple spires. Women surreptitiously bathe in their saris. Brahman priests hold court on plinths beneath palm umbrellas and give sermons about the Hindu epics. Pavement barbers shave heads of their penitent customers, dhobi-wallahs process mountains of soapy cloth and half-naked yogis sit frozen in contorted positions. Wrestling is a favorite pastime, and crowds cheer as they watch combatants tussle in a special pit in contests to clamber up a *malkham,* or smooth wooden pole.

Most travelers return from Varanasi with graphic tales of the city's death industry. Your boatman will no doubt take particular pleasure

ABOVE: Early morning activity on the ghats.
OPPOSITE: Passengers ferried across the Ganges River silhouetted by sunset.

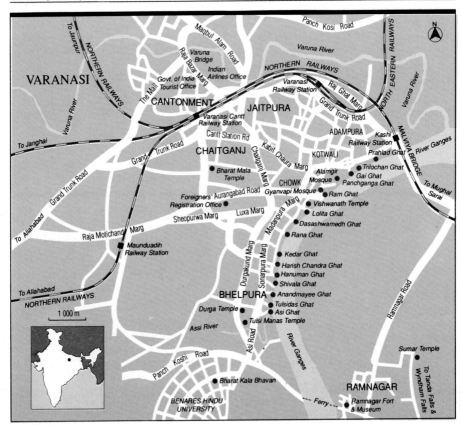

in pointing out "Ganga people," the whitened rubbery corpses which float downstream accompanied by marigolds and plastic bags. Locals shrug these sights off with Asiatic calm and humor, regarding them as all part of the flotsam and jetsam of Varanasi's great spiritual recycling of life and death. Some startled tourists may be instantly converted to vegetarianism. However, most find that fascination wins over squeamishness.

The busiest cremation or "burning" ghats are Manikarnika and Harishchandra. Corpses are wrapped in white muslin cloth and covered with orange marigold flowers, before being borne on bamboo stretchers to the pyres on the water's edge, traditionally set ablaze by the deceased's eldest son. Varanasi's caste of undertakers are the untouchable "doams," recognizable by their shaved heads and loin cloths. The Doam Raja is their hereditary leader who is held in great awe since his blessing is said to ensure a superior reincarnation. He surveys his domain from a house above Manikarnika Ghat that is decorated with two life-size plaster tigers symbolizing death's imminence.

The doams dispatch the dead with alacrity, building pyres, sloshing wood with inflamma-

ble cooking oil, and enthusiastically swinging ceremonial staffs to burst open flaming skulls and ensure the soul escapes from the body. At Manikarnika Ghat, wealthy families vie to have their relatives cremated on the Chandrapaduka slab that is believed to be marked with the footprints of the god Vishnu. Grief is rarely evident as Hindus believe that once the soul is released, the body is just a discarded shell. But do not try and photograph the proceedings, as this greatly offends the participants and has caused numerous brawls between mourners and unwitting tourists, sometimes resulting in cameras being hurled into the Ganges.

During your boat trip, make sure you see the five most sacred ghats, the Asi, Dasaswamedh, Manikarnika, Panchganga and Raj. Pilgrims who bathe in each one consecutively believe their prayers will be fulfilled.

The furthermost upstream is **Asi Ghat**, which marks the confluence of the Ganges and the Asi rivers. Next is **Tulsi Ghat** which honors the poet Gosain Tulsi Das who translated the Ramayana and died here in 1623. The city's sewage pumps out under **Janki Ghat**, and nearby is the government's first electric crematorium, an experiment which pits faith against modernization, since it de-glamorizes an event most Hindus consider sacred. **Bachra Ghat** is used by Jains, and has three Jain temples. Beside it is the ornate **Shivala,** or **Kali Ghat,** the most impressive royal ghat still used daily by the former Maharaja of Benares and distinguishable by its huge Shiva lingam. **Hanuman Ghat** attracts hordes of devotees paying their respects to the monkey-god. Nearby, the **Dandi Ghat** is used by ascetics, fakirs and yogis. Past Harishchandra's smoking pyres is **Kedar Ghat** with its fine temples. **Mansarowar Ghat** is named after a Tibetan lake at the foot of Mount Kailash, Shiva's Himalayan home. **Someswar,** or **"Lord of the Moon" Ghat,** is said to have magical healing powers and attracts droves of hopeful lepers, cronies and terminally ill. Next is the ghat of **Ahalya Bai,** an eighteenth century queen of Indore.

Dasaswamedh Ghat is Varanasi's liveliest bathing place, named to honor the site where Brahma sacrificed (*medh*) ten (*das*) horses (*aswa*). One of its many temples is dedicated to Sitala, the goddess of smallpox. Nearby is the grand **Man Mandir Ghat** and an observatory built by Jai Singh in 1710. Mir Ghat leads to a Nepalese temple which is decorated with erotic paintings, and further inland is the **Golden Temple** (see below), Varanasi's most sacred shrine. Nearby are the two holiest burning ghats, the **Manikarnika** and the **Jasain,** a favorite cremation spot for India's elite.

At the northern is **Dattatreya Ghat,** named after a Brahman saint, Panchganga Ghat, where India's five holy rivers are said to merge, **Trilochan Ghat,** marked by its two turrets, and **Raj Ghat,** the final goal of pilgrims.

THE CITY

Back on land, it's most fun to comb the city's atmospheric medieval gullies, or lanes, seeking out bazaars and temples, peering into decaying palaces and emerging at the river-front. No accurate map exists of this remarkable web of stone-paved corridors, barely more than an arm's span wide, often dark and slippery, both enchanting and claustrophobic at the same time. Getting lost is all part of the fun. If all fails, locals claim that following a sacred cow will lead you to the river.

Start from the old city's main forum, the Dasaswamedh Ghat/Chowk area, and take a stroll down Vishwanath gully which leads to the famous **Golden Temple**. Hindus believe Shiva lives here, so it's far too holy for non-Hindus to view, although tourists can peer inside from the old house next door. The original temple built in 1600 was destroyed by the Mughal Emperor Aurangzeb, who, in a display of dominance over his Hindu subjects, built his Gyanvapi

Mosque on top of the site. A Maratha queen, Ahilya Bai, in 1776 reconstructed next door the present shrine dedicated to the god held by Hindus as the lord of the universe. The solid gold plating on the towers were given by the Maharaja Ranjit Singh of Lahore in 1835. Stalls along the lane sell flowers by the kilo, horse-hair flywhisks, religious paraphernalia, ornate toys, glass bangles and filigreed jewelry.

To the south is the red-ochre **Durga Temple,** built in the north Indian Nagara style by an eighteenth century Bengali Maharani. It is dedicated to Durga, a fearsome incarnation of Shiva's wife, Parvati. She is placated by periodic

goat sacrifices, and the temple is renowned for its resident tribe of stroppy monkeys that often whisk away visitor's glasses and handbags.

Nearby is the modern shikara-style Tulsi **Manas Temple,** engraved with verses and scenes from the Rama Charit Manas, the Hindi version of the Ramayana written by the medieval poet Tulsi Das.

Further south is the **Benares Hindu University,** situated 11 km (6.8 miles) from the city center. It is open daily except Sundays from 11 am to 4 pm, and has an excellent miniature painting and sculpture collection inside its Bharat Kala Bhawan.

From here, you can either take a ferry or taxi to reach the eighteenth century **Ramnagar Fort** across the river, 16 km (10 miles) from the city center. The ex-Maharaja still lives here in a splendid suite overlooking the Ganges, although part of his ancestral home is now a well-organized museum with liveried guards and eccentric treasures giving a whiff of former glories: gem-encrusted weapons, moth-balled howdahs, palanquins, astrological clocks, decadent Kashmir vestments, ostrich eggs and vintage cars. It is open from 10 am to noon and 1 to 5 pm.

ABOVE: Faded clothes being hung out to dry at the Washing Ghat, Varanasi.

SARNATH

Sarnath is a serene Buddhist pilgrimage center about 10 km (six miles) from Varanasi that was the deer park where Buddha preached his first sermon around 528 BC to his five close disciples after receiving enlightenment at Bodhgaya in Bihar. His speech titled "Setting in Motion the Wheel of Righteousness" laid down the Buddhist doctrine of the "Middle Way," which pledged the path of righteous moderation in order to attain spiritual salvation, or nirvana.

Sarnath probably derived its name from one of Buddha's titles, Saranganath, Lord of the Deer. It became a monastic center, gaining official patronage as the capital of the Buddhist religion under Emperor Ashoka (circa 269–232 BC), the warlord turned pacifist who erected several

memorial towers or stupas and one of his famous pillars here. The Chinese Buddhist pilgrims, Fa Hsien and Hsuan Tsiang, who respectively visited in the fifth and seventh centuries, both recorded impressions of their stay. The latter wrote of Sarnath's vast monastery with 1,500 monks, the Ashokan pillar, lakes, gardens and magnificent giant stupas. Over the centuries Buddhism lost its initial momentum, and successive Muslim invasions in the twelfth and seventeenth centuries destroyed much of Sarnath's fabled grandeur, although the sprawling remains of this religious capital are still impressive. The huge swastika-covered **Dhamekh Stupa** dates from around AD 500, and is thought to mark the place where Buddha gave his sermon.

The excellent **Archaeological Museum** is open 10 am to 5 pm, except Friday. Its prize exhibit is the four-faced lion capital which decorative tapestries threaded with pure gold and silver and patterned with delicate motifs. Saris, stoles and cloth woven by craftsmen can cost up to US$1,200 a piece, but there are plenty of perfectly exquisite, much cheaper ones. For browsing or buying, you can view the finest selections at **Brij Raman Das** and **Ushnak Malmulchan** in the central Chowk area. The **Silk Corner** next to the Indian Airlines office in the Mall has a large range of reasonably priced good quality silks sold by the meter, as well as silk boxer shorts, cushion covers and ties.

The bazaars offer a plethora of goods, and it is easy to compare prices and bargain. The main **Chowk** and **Godowlia** areas are good for silks, brocade, perfume, paan and carved walking sticks; **Vishwanath Gully** for painted toys and images of gods and goddesses; **Thatheri Bazaar** for ornamental brass work and lacquered glass bangles; **Satti Bazaar** for saris.

Varanasi is also the best place in the world for sitar shopping. Serious students are welcomed by the senior sitar-maker, **Radhey Shyam Sharma,** who is a disciple of Ravi Shankar and has a workshop at 52/34E Luxmi Kund behind the New Imperial Hotel. A fine quality instrument costs around US$70 to US$200. Cheaper varieties priced around US$20 to US$50 can be found in **Nichi Bagh** off Chowk.

GENERAL INFORMATION

There are two main tourist offices: the Government of India Tourist Office, ((0542) 43189, 43744, at 15B, The Mall, Cantonment; and the Uttar Pradesh State Tourist Office, ((0542) 43486, Parade Kothi, opposite the railway station. Both are very ready with advice on city sights, shopping, music, dance and festivals, and are able to provide knowledgeable guides. At either you can buy US$1 tickets for daily morning and afternoon conducted tours — the Dawn river trip, temples, Benares University (5:30 am to noon), or Ramnagar Fort and Sarnath (2:30 to 6:30 pm).

The Indian Airlines Office, ((0542) 44537, 43116, in Mint House, Cantonment, runs a bus shuttle to the airport, but the service can be erratic if you are in a hurry. The *Northern India Patrika* newspaper has good entertainment sections. The best local guide books are *Glimpses of Varanasi* by K. Jaycees, or *Benares* by S.N. Mishra. *Benares: City of Light* by Diana Eck (Princeton University Press) has detailed information on each ghat and temple in particular, as well as Hinduism in general.

originally crowned the Ashoka pillar and is now the official symbol of modern India. It is a treasure-house of sculptures from the major periods of artistic activity at Sarnath — Mauryan, Kushan and Gupta — as well as later Hindu images from the ninth to twelfth centuries.

Sarnath's annual fete is Buddha Purnima, which commemorates Buddha's birth with a colorful fair and procession of his relics held on the full moon of May.

SHOPPING AND CRAFTS

Varanasi's famous silk and brocade fabrics are used by leading American and European designers, and have always been valued by wealthy Indians as wedding attire, to be passed down as heirlooms. Quality hand-woven silk brocades are called *kinkhab,* and are highly

Varanasi's riverside ghats stretch along the river's edge for nearly seven kilometers like a medieval canyon of plaster-peeling residences, eighteenth century palaces and ornate temples.

Jaipur
and
Rajasthan

VIBRANTLY exotic and colorful, Rajasthan — the "land of the rajas" — is in many ways India's ultimate destination. It is both a barren and an inhospitable land, laid bare to a blazing sun and shifting desert sands, and a fantastic time-worn realm of medieval fortresses. Yet everywhere throbs with a rich diversity of life and color. Rajputs are proud, handsome people. Lithe and graceful, clad in vibrantly colored cloth and glints of silver, they seem to the visitor's eye almost absurdly picturesque. In Rajasthan, one barely feels in the twentieth century at all.

JAIPUR

Known as the "Pink City", Jaipur is the bustling capital of Rajasthan. Nestled amid the rough-hewn Aravalli Hills, Jaipur was founded in 1727 by the brilliant astronomer-king Jai Singh II to replace his ancestral hill fortress of Amber, 11 km (seven miles) away. By the time Jai Singh II came to power at the age of 13, his family had earned the dubious distinction of being the first Rajput power to win sway with the Mughals by marrying one of their princesses to Emperor Akbar. Jai Singh proved a formidable statesman, and the Mughal alliance brought peace and privilege to his domain.

A man of his times, Jai Singh was an enthusiastic student of contemporary sciences. He laid out Jaipur on a grid system consisting of seven rectangular blocks of buildings fronted by seven magnificent gates, and precisely criss-crossed by broad 33.8-m (111-ft) -wide arterial avenues intersecting at the city's core — the City Palace — in keeping with the principles of the ancient Hindu architectural treatise, the *Shilpa Shastra*. In the new city, traders and artisans under court patronage were given their own lanes, a tradition that persists today. Until town planners went on a demolition binge after Independence, the city's encircling walls were completely intact — sadly, only portions now remain.

But the city retains a fairytale exuberance with its courtly palaces, colorful bazaars, and nearby fort. Its streets are spice-scented bedlams massed with bobbing turbans, cocooned women in tinsel-fringed scarlet clutching kohl-eyed babies, gamboling monkeys, camel-drawn carts, and jingling cycle-rickshaws. It's still the "highly ornamented curiosity... all in the soft, rich tint of strawberry ice-cream" described by Mark Twain when he visited the city in 1897.

Actually, Jaipur's overall "pinkness" was then only a recent phenomenon, dating from 1876 when the city was painted up for the visit of the Prince of Wales, later King Edward VII. Today, every shop-owner within the historic

"Pink City Boundary" is required by law to maintain his shop's faade.

As the final destination in the tourist's popular "Golden Triangle" of Delhi-Agra-Jaipur, the city is well endowed with hotels, restaurants, and shops — but also, unfortunately, with pushy touts and con-artists. Watch out for over-pricing and over-booking. Jaipur — indeed, all of Rajasthan — is best visited during October to February, when the days are sunny and crisp and the evenings cool. Jaipur celebrates all the major festivals, but it's especially worth visiting during *Diwali* in November, and the elephant processions and exuberant color-throwing may-

hem during March and April, when both *Holi* and the Rajasthani *Gangaur* festivals take place. Also during March, polo fever hits Jaipur, with tournaments of elephant, horse, camel, and even bicycle polo being staged.

ACCESS

Indian Airlines operates two flights daily from Delhi to Jaipur, which is also linked by direct flights to Jodhpur, Udaipur, Ahmedabad, Bombay, and Aurangabad. Vayudoot offers an alternative flight from Delhi to Jaipur en route to Jodhpur, Jaisalmer, and Bikaner. From Delhi, the *Pink City Express* departs daily at 6 am, reaching Jaipur, via Alwar, at 11 am, and returns to Delhi at 5 pm, arriving at 10:20 pm. Another late-evening train leaves Delhi and arrives in Jaipur around dawn. You'll avoid last-minute confusion if you remember that all Jaipur-bound

OPPOSITE: A crow's eye view of Jaipur, with vistas across to the surrounding Aravelli Hills.

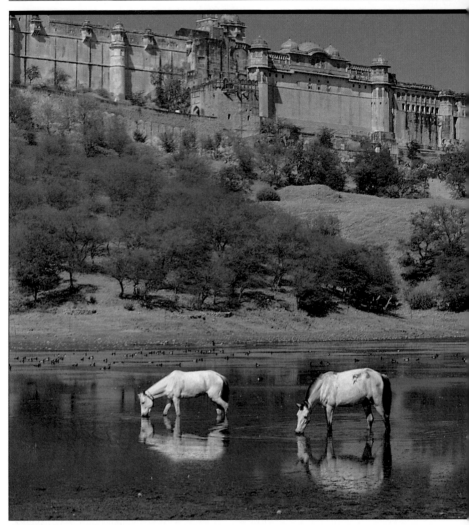

ABOVE: Horses graze in the lake beneath the majestic Amber Palace, the former capital of the royal Jaipurs.

trains leave from the Old Delhi railway station. From Agra, both the *Superfast Express* and the *Hawa Mahal Express* depart from Agra Fort Station for Jaipur each day, via Bharatpur, making daily return circuits. From Delhi and Agra, there are regular departures of both luxury air-conditioned and express buses from the main interstate bus stations.

Jaipur is a perfect staging post for exploring the rest of Rajasthan by train or bus, and has direct rail links to Alwar (for visiting Sariska Tiger Reserve), Sawai Madhophur (for visiting Ranthambhore National Park), Ajmer (for Pushkar), Jodhpur, Udaipur, Abu Road, and Ahmedabad, and Bikaner (via a stop at Sikar to link up with the Fresco Trail).

HOTELS

Jaipur offers a broad range of hotels, ranging from pure princely splendor to budget-priced hostels. Top of the market are three royal palaces — all run by the Taj Group. The most magnificent is the five-star **Rambagh Palace**, ((0141) 381919 fax (0141) 381098, Bhawani Singh Road, the late-nineteenth-century former official palace of the polo-playing maharaja Man Singh II — the world's only private residence with its own polo ground. Set amid manicured gardens, this marble palace offers royal suites with period furniture, four-poster beds, and art deco marble bathrooms. The Polo Bar — judged one of the world's most famous watering holes — and cane chair-strewn veranda are Jaipur's most relaxing oases at sunset. Facilities include an excellent maharaja. All three can be booked through any Taj Group Hotel or Utell worldwide. The **Mansingh Hotel**, ((0141) 378771 fax (0141) 377582, on Sansar Chandra Road, lacks character but has modern amenities and is reliably efficient and centrally located. efficient and centrally located.

Jaipur has a number of quaint mansions belonging to ex-nobles which have been converted into guesthouses, all set amid peaceful gardens. The most charming of these is **Narain Niwas**, ((0141) 563448, Kanota Bagh, Narain Niwas Road, built in 1881. Its decadent suites are a repository of faded finery — four-poster beds, Afghan carpets, old lithographs, and flayed tiger skins — and prices are moderate. There are two little garden cottages, and simpler comfortable rooms for US$15. Breakfast on the terrace, with preening peacocks strutting past, is as relaxed and pleasant as Jaipur ever gets. All are well-priced and well-located, with friendly, if erratic service. Meals are prepared only to order. Also highly recommended are **Samode Haveli,** Gangapole (((0141) 540370 fax (0141) 42407), located north of the old Pink City walls, beautifully maintained and furnished with a large peaceful garden; **Haveli Hotel,** Statue Circle, ((0141) 75024, a 1940's style *haveli*, or mansion, with period furnishings, spacious lawns and swimming pool. **Bissau Palace**, ((0141) 74191, Chandpole Bazaar, a charming and peaceful refuge in the heart of the old city. Guests can browse through a beautifully kept library, peer at heirlooms, cool off in a backyard pool, and sip tea on the veranda. Excellent Western breakfasts are served. Single rooms to well-furnished suites are within the inexpensive range, all with air-conditioning. Right next door is **Khetri House**, ((0141) 69183, a 1930's-style bungalow with pleasant and cheap rooms. Other cheap mansion options are **Achrol Lodge**, ((0141) 72254, Jacob Road, in quiet Civil Lines, with spacious, quirkily old-fashioned rooms overlooking the lawns; and **Khasa Khoti**, ((0141) 375151, Mirza Ismail Road (known as M.I. Marg), which has comfortable rooms and a tourist office on the premises. Other hotels include the RTDC-run **Gangaur Tourist Bungalow**, ((0141) 371641, on Mirza Ismail Road and **Teej Tourist Bungalow**, ((0141) 374373, Collectorate Road, Bani Park, neither exceptional but clean and well-priced.

health club with squash courts, a beauty salon, an excellent shopping arcade, a delightful 1930's pavilion-enclosed marble-lined swimming pool, and a jacuzzi. Modern rooms have standard five-star décor and are in the expensive range, but suites offer the proverbial lap of luxury for upwards of US$250.

Smaller, more secluded, almost as delightful and significantly cheaper (in the moderate range), are two other palatial royal mansions: the **Jai Mahal Palace**, ((0141) 371616 fax (0141) 365237, in Jacob Road, Civil Lines, and the more period-flavor **Raj Mahal Hotel**, ((0141) 381757 fax (0141) 381887, set in rambling gardens off Sardar Patel Road, a former British Residency later taken up by Jaipur's First Couple after they left the Rambagh. Prince Philip came here in 1965 and was introduced to the joys of *Holi* when he was showered with colored water by Jaipur's

RESTAURANTS

Of the four leading hotels, the Rambagh Palace offers the most spectacular candlelit dining experience at its huge Italian marble-lined **Savaran Mahal**, which has rococo cherubs and pudgy maidens daubed on the ceiling. Regally attired waiters serve excellent Mughali dishes — although it's possible to pitch for less exotic

Chinese and Western dishes — and there's an evening accompaniment of musicians and folk ballads. Dinner for two costs about US$20. The Mansingh's rooftop **Shiver** attracts scores of Jaipur businessmen for its super lunches, and has good views and evening music.

Of the dozens of restaurants clustered along Jaipur's main M.I. Marg, the best are **Niros**, **Chanakya** (for vegetarian Rajasthani dishes), and **Kwality**, all reasonably priced with prompt service. For Sino-Indian fare — "masala-style", no chopsticks — try the **Golden Dragon**, just off M.I. Marg. One place where you can be assured of good food, fast service, and a friendly atmosphere without overstretching your budget is the **LMB Hotel** in the old city near Johari Bazaar. It is always packed with discerning backpackers for its delicious vegetarian dishes, *kachori*, savoury puffs served with hot chutney, and milk-based desserts of *rasmalai* and *halwa*. To round off a splash-out meal, Jaipur's best ice-cream counter is just outside.

SIGHTSEEING

Jaipur's sights are concentrated within the old city in and around the City Palace complex. You can spend the best part of a day seeing them at your own pace, enjoying the colorful bazaars and street life in between. When this gets tiring, climb aboard a cycle-rickshaw and be whisked down Jaipur's wide boulevards — the best way to get around and still feel part of the color, scent, and activity all around you. Watch out for glint-eyed auto-rickshaw and taxi-wallahs, particularly those who besiege befuddled tourists emerging from the railway station. They have a pathological dislike of using their meters, so always agree on the fare in advance.

Jaipur has plenty of bike-rental places, including a rank outside the rail station. Enthusiasts rave about winding up the steep Aravalli ridge on the Jaipur–Delhi Road to Amber, 11 km (seven miles) away, stopping halfway to admire the eighteenth-century **Jal Mahal**, or "Water Palace", originally used by the maharajas as a summer residence.

You'll need at least two full days to see most of Jaipur's richly diverse sights and to poke through its bazaars for shopping bargains. The RTDC morning conducted tour is a good time-saver, with comfortable buses and English-speaking guides. The full-day tours can be exhausting, and the independently inclined may strain at the leash in a chronic case of too much, too quickly. Tours leave from the RTDC Tourist Office, ((0141) 69714, Gangaur Tourist Bungalow.

The Old Royal City

Start just outside the City Palace complex, with Jaipur's famous **Hawa Mahal**, or "Palace of the

Winds". Named for the cool westerly winds which blow through it, this five-tiered pink faade is ornamented with delicate overhanging balconies and gilded arches, yet this unique structure is only one room deep. It was built in 1799, so that veiled royal women could peer down through its 593 stone screens unseen by the world. You can climb to the top for a purdah-view of Jaipur, between the hours of 10 am and 4:30 pm daily. There is also a good "Jaipur Past and Present" display. On the pavement outside, Jaipur's famous "psychic parrot" will tell your fortune for Rs 10.

Behind the Hawa Mahal, a large square filled

with *chai* stalls and fluttering pigeons leads to the oleander-pink **City Palace**, the symbolic heart of the capital. It is still used as a royal residence and as a backdrop for special state festivals. Jai Singh's eighteenth-century palace is an enchanted miniature metropolis in itself, occupying one-seventh of the entire old city area. The complex — with its confection-like pink façades edged with delicate lacy white borders, arched pavilions, and marble courtyards — has been described by architecture buffs as India's "most daring and successful synthesis of Mughal and Rajput styles". The palace courtyards are full of indolent, picturesquely dressed guards with flowing red turbans, many of them old retainers of the former maharaja.

Just within the entrance courtyard of the City Palace stands the dazzling white **Mubarak Mahal**, or "Palace of Welcome". Built in 1900, it was used first as a guesthouse, then as the Royal Secretariat; now it houses part of the City Palace museum, displaying a fine collection of antique textiles and royal costumes. Among the extensive displays of Rajput weaponry are such curiosities as gold daggers with crystal handles, guns tailored for a camel-back rider, and gruesome instruments designed to spring open in the unfortunate victim's abdomen. To your right is the ornate **Singh Pol**, or Lion Gate, with its guardian marble elephants, which leads into a magnificent courtyard flanked by tiered buildings of oleander stucco, and a marble **Diwan-i-Khas**, or "Private Audience Hall", at the center.

rare Sanskrit and Quranic manuscripts. Royal palanquins, gilt-studded ivory howdahs, and one of India's largest chandeliers complete the collection. The City Palace is open daily from 9:30 am to 4:45 pm, except on public holidays and festivals.

Directly opposite the City Palace is Jai Singh's fascinating astronomical observatory, the **Jantar Mantar** (see also page 83). Jai Singh's obsession for astronomy inspired him to pore over ancient texts, to ponder the calculations of Euclid and Ptolemy, and to pick holes in contemporary European theories of astronomy. He was the first Indian astronomer to emphasize scien-

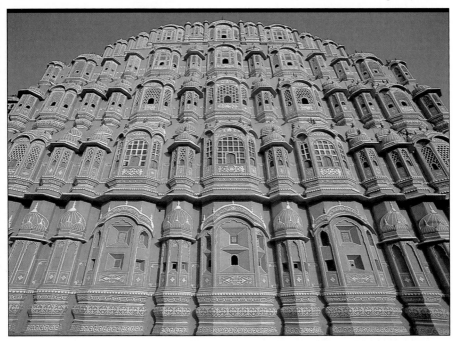

The two silver urns here, said to be the world's largest, were made to store six months' supply of Ganga water for a Jaipur maharaja who attended King Edward VII's coronation in London.

On your left, a gateway leads to the "Peacock Courtyard"; its four gateways are studded with glass mosaics and polished brass, each depicting one of the four seasons. Nearby is the seven-tiered **Chandra Mahal**, or "Moon Palace", the maharaja's personal abode. Its mirror-decorated topmost chamber affords fine views across the Jai Niwas Gardens, the eighteenth-century Sri Gobind Dev Temple, and the towering Clock Tower. Back in the main courtyard, the facing gateway leads to the **Sawai Man Singh II Museum**. On display here are some magnificent medieval carpets, most of them from Afghanistan and Pakistan, and some of the collection of Jaipur and Mughal school miniatures and

tific observation rather than theory, and he went on to revise the Indian lunar calendar and astrological tables. The observatory is open from 9 am to 5 pm daily.

One final place to visit in town is the grand nineteenth-century Indo-Saracenic-style **Central Museum (Albert Hall)**, south of the walled city in the sprawling Rang Niwas Gardens, which also contains a small zoo. This vast eccentric collection includes a fascinating display of Rajasthan's tribal groups, lore, costumes, and arts. Among its more bizarre exhibits are 100

ABOVE: The five-story pyramidal Hawa Mahal, (Palace of the Winds) in Jaipur is a classic example of traditional Rajput architecture with its *chhatris* domes, curved arches and latticed windows giving the effect of architectural embroidery in cinnabar and white. OPPOSITE: Detail of a typically ornate façade in the so-called "Pink City" of Jai Singh's time.

wax models of gruesomely contorted G-string-clad yogic sadhus or holy men, an Egyptian mummy, many bald stuffed birds, snakes rotting in bottles, hundreds of Austrian rock samples, some very decrepit stuffed crocodiles, and one inexplicable display: an ancient fish dangling in a case, with a tag marked "Fish" tied around its belly — definitely worth a giggle or two!

Amber

Few visitors fail to be moved by the dramatic Rajput grandeur of Amber, the hilltop fortress-palace 11 km (seven miles) north of Jaipur. Surrounded by fortified battlements, it straddles two sepia-hued tundra ranges in the Aravalli Hills overlooking Maota Lake. Higher still, the summit is crowned by a craggy fortress bastion, and the surrounding hills are latticed by sprawling crenellated walls. This was the citadel of the powerful Rajput Kachchwaha kings, whose illustrious descendant, Jai Singh II, founded Jaipur. Although they had ruled the region since the eleventh century, Amber palace was not built until the late sixteenth century, by which time the Kachchwahas had risen to power and wealth. You can either walk up the steep cobbled ramparts to the fort-palace complex or take the popular (but overpriced) ride on a caparisoned body-painted elephant. Passing through the main entrance gate, you'll step into a small courtyard containing the marble-pillared **Kali Temple** which has solid silver doors.

The multi-pillared **Diwan-i-Am** (Public Meeting Hall) nearby leads to Jai Singh's magnificent ceremonial **Ganesh Pol,** or "Elephant Gate" — an ornamental masterpiece of intricate inlaid mirror mosaic, fresco, and scalloped stucco-work. It leads into a charming garden courtyard flanked by royal apartments, many with elaborate frescoes, stained-glass windows, mosaics, plaster reliefs, and mirror-studded alcoves. The main attractions are the fountain-cooled **Sukh Niwas,** or "Hall of Pleasure", the glittering **Sheesh Mahal,** or "Mirror Palace", and the **Jai Mandir,** Jai Singh's royal abode, with glass and precious stones studded into a shining surface of powdered marble, egg-shells, and crushed pearls. Behind the garden court lies the elaborately latticed zenana, where each of Jai Singh's wives had a separate suite.

Amber is best visited in the crisp cool of early morning, allowing plenty of time to wander through the labyrinthine passages leading to the servants' quarters, watchtowers, and dungeons. Bring bottled water and a packed lunch and do what few tourists do — clamber up the steep, boulder-strewn slopes to the fortress ramparts, where you'll find an interesting museum, cool drinks, and sublime views in all directions.

Amber's fort-palace is open from 9 am to 4:30 pm daily.

On the way back to town you can stop at **Gaitor,** the cremation grounds of the Kachchwaha clan, to see the white marble *chhatris* or cenotaphs of Jaipur's rulers. Jai Singh II's is the most magnificent, supported by marble pillars and covered in ornamental friezes. Follow the steep road up the ridge to **Nahargarh** (Tiger) **Fort,** at the top, built by Jai Singh II in 1734 to defend his new city. Alternatively, it's a one and a half kilometer (just under a mile) climb up a paved pathway northwest of the City Palace. Either way, it's Jaipur's loveliest sunset spot.

SHOPPING

Jaipur has the most colorful variety of things to buy in all of India, ranging from enameled blue pottery, exquisite gem-studded, enameled jewelry, and traditional block-printed fabrics to brightly patterned dhurrie rugs. It is tempting to forsake Jaipur's other attractions and spend hours poking about in the spice-scented lanes, drinking sickly-sweet tea and chatting with artisans working at traditional crafts. The bazaars are concentrated to the south of the old city, while many of the modern shops and all the state emporiums are on M.I. Marg and Agra Road.

You can find the most famous of Jaipur's wares — polished gems, semi-precious stones, and exquisite enameled jewelry — in wide-open **Johari Bazaar,** near the Hawa Mahal, and in an opposite lane called **Gopalji Ka Rasta. Bapu Bazaar** and **Nehru Bazaar** are the places to find traditional tie-and-dye *bhandhani*-work and hand-printed textiles, as well as embroidered camel-skin *mojadis,* or slippers, and local

ABOVE: Outmoded underwear fashions in a Jaipur shop. OPPOSITE: Chulgiri Temple TOP and Ranaji Ki Nasia BOTTOM, in Jaipur.

perfumes. Along **Tripolia Bazaar**'s long arterial boulevard are endless rows of brassware, terracotta pots, and the famous Jaipur "blue" pottery, and **Chaura Rasta** is crammed with costume jewelry and bangles.

For quality gems and jewelry, there are two particularly good shops to visit — bearing in mind that bazaar jewelry is not always "pukka": **Gem Palace** and the **Jewels Emporium**, both on M.I. Marg. **Anokhi**, on Tilak Marg, opposite the Udyog Bhawan, is easily India's best shop for a large range of traditional hand-block printed cottons and stylish European-style dresses (it has a cult following with Delhi's diplomatic wives). There's another outlet in the Rambagh Palace Hotel, and opposite Delhi's Ashoka Hotel. To see craftsmen making block-printed fabrics, marbled paper, and Jaipur blue pottery, make an excursion out to the charming village of **Sanganer**, 16 km (10 miles) south. The village is also noteworthy for its palace ruins, imposing antique *toranas*, or gateways, and several ornate Jain temples.

GENERAL INFORMATION

Of the six Rajasthan Tourist Offices around town the one at the Railway Station, ((0141) 69714, is particularly useful and offers good local information, maps, guide services, and reasonably priced car rental for out-of-town excursions.

SAMODE

If you can spare a night away from Jaipur, make a detour 42 km (26 miles) north to Samode, where there is an enchanting eighteenth-century palace built by Jai Singh II's finance minister, and now run by his descendants as a hotel. Surrounded by barren scrubland and crowned by the battlements of an old fort up on the ridge, it has exquisite jewel-box interiors, fine murals, gilded and painted surfaces, and *meenakari*, or inlay of mirrors and stones, as fine as that of the Sheesh Mahal at Amber. It's splendidly romantic, with a grand central courtyard, carved old furniture, faded courtly photographs, old retainers, and posing peacocks. Evenings are spent in the fine Durbar Hall, being served Rajasthani cuisine and entertained by musicians. The rooms are furnished simply and well. The bathroom shutters open to reveal spectacular views. Prices are in the cheap range.

At Jaipur's railway station tourist office you can hire a RTDC car to take you there. Local buses ply there from outside the RTDC Teej Bungalow, with a change at Chomu village. It's conveniently en route to Shekhavati. Book by writing, Hotel Samode Palace ((34), Samode 303806, District Jaipur, or contact Samode Haveli, ((0141) 42407, Ganga Pole, Jaipur.

RANTHAMBHORE NATIONAL PARK

Set between the Aravalli and Vindhya hills, Ranthambhore's 411 sq km (156 sq miles) of dry deciduous forest is tiger territory, full of picturesque pavilions and ruined temples with a thousand year-old fort silhouetted against the hilltop skyline. Since the eighteenth century, the area served as a hunting ground for the Maharajahs of Jaipur, who built a series of artificial lakes as vital watering holes for wildlife. The Project Tiger park also has leopards, hyenas, jungle cats, sloth bears, sambhar, chital, nilgai and chinkara. Marsh crocodiles and monitor lizards can be seen slumbering on lakebanks, and the park attracts many migrant water birds.

Ranthambhore lies 162 km (100 miles) from Jaipur, and can be easily reached by car or train. The nearest station, Sawai Madhopur, is only 13 km (eight miles) away from the park entrance. From Delhi, Ranthambhore is directly accessible on the Delhi-Bombay line. Stay at the ex-royal **Maharaja Lodge** or the RTDC-run **Castle Jhoomer Baori Forest Lodge,** (620, both in Sawai Madophur or stay in the park at Jogi Mahal. Bookings can be made through Jaipur's RTDC offices, or the Field Director at Ranthambhore. Best season to visit is from November to May.

ALWAR AND SARISKA WILDLIFE RESERVE

A train halt lying 143 km (90 miles) northwest of Jaipur and halfway from Delhi, Alwar has a gruesome martial past, yet today is a languid town dotted with palaces and lakes, dominated by a 300-m (1,000-ft) -high battle-scarred hilltop fortress hewn from the jagged Aravalli Hills. It was founded as an independent princely state late in Rajasthan's history in 1776, but quickly made up for lost time with constant bouts of brutal warfare with Delhi's Mughals. Following an alliance with the British, Alwar's rulers concentrated their efforts on building pleasure palaces and staging extravagant tiger shoots.

Alwar makes a picturesque staging post for a visit to **Sariska Tiger Reserve**, 34 km (21 miles) away, staying overnight at either the **Sariska Palace,** (22 (Sariska), one of the largest hunting lodges in India, or the RTDC-run **Lake Palace,** (3764, which overlooks the beautiful Siliserh

Lake and wooded hills. There's plenty to see in town, starting with the opulent 105-room **Vinay Vilas Palace**, built in 1925. In its prime, its stables accommodated 3,000 thoroughbred horses and a herd of royal elephants. To the right of the palace is the magnificent two-story gilt carriage designed to straddle the backs of four elephants and carry 50 people off on a tiger shoot. Among the highlights in its fascinating museum are a cup carved out of a single emerald, enemy-scuttling weaponry, and a rich display of eighteenth- and nineteenth-century Mughal and Rajput paintings. It's open from 10 am to 5 pm, closed on Fridays and public holidays. Clamber up to the fort for an eagle's view of the **Pujan Vihar** garden and summer house, the royal *chhatris*, temples, and pavilions near the tanks.

A former royal hunting ground, the **Sariska Tiger Reserve** spans 800 sq km (300 sq miles) and is one of India's most beautiful tiger sanctuaries. You'll get as close as you would ever want to get to tigers by driving in jeeps or hiding in little *machan*-huts above the reserve's well-patronized waterholes (especially at dusk), and see plenty of leopards, sloth bear, hyenas, nilgai (blue bull), chinkara, four-horned antelope, and various birds. Stay at the **Tiger Den Tourist Bungalow**, (42, with rooms in the inexpensive range, and a good restaurant. The season is from February to June.

THE FRESCO TRAIL

In Rajasthan's northwest corner, the dust-drenched, fresco-filled region of Shekhavati lies within easy reach by road or train of Jaipur, Bikaner, and Delhi. From the fifteenth century, when Rao Sheka defied the rulers of Amber, the area remained a semi-independent collection of *thikanas*, or fiefdoms. But it is the more recent painted walls in Shekhavati that draw visitors to this exotic backwater. It was once the heartland of the wealthy Marwari merchants, from near Jodhpur, who created townships clustered with ornate walled *havelis*, or mansions, which look rather like tiny medieval fortresses but are covered in elaborate life-sized paintings. Most of the frescoes date back to the mid-eighteenth century, worked in a technique similar to that developed during Renaissance Italy of working rapidly on wet plaster — a method that has kept many of them very well preserved. The earliest frescoes are loving depictions of popular gods, martial lore, and elephants — but the later works feature such startlingly quirky subjects as a mourning Queen Victoria, the visit of King George V and Queen Mary to India, podgy pinstriped Indians waving farewell

from a train, and even the Wright brothers in their odd-looking airplane.

You'll find the largest concentration of these beguiling creations within the districts of Jhunjhunu and Sikar at three major fresco centers: **Mandawa**, **Dundlod**, and **Nawalgarh**, each within an afternoon's driving and inspection distance of moderately priced and charming palace-hotels. Of the three, try **Castle Mandawa**, (24, Located 168km (100 miles) from Jaipur, 35 km (22 miles) from Sikar. Built in 1775, it is the most special — particularly when its courtyard throbs with unbelievable pageantry during the festivals of *Holi*, *Gangaur*, and *Teej*.

From the moustached Rajput guards at the entrance to the brilliant peacocks fluttering across the rooftops, it offers a splendid base from which to explore the surrounding villages. At the end of the day, return for a hot shower, a good meal, and a delightful room with original furnishings, either in the castle or in the converted stables. The same family run a Desert Camp, perfect for large groups with its deluxe Rajput huts (with attached modern bathrooms!) and village atmosphere, located just two kilometers (a mile or so) from Castle Mandawa. Both can be booked through: Old Mandawa, Sansar Chandra Road, Jaipur 302001, ((0141) 75358. The other excellent accommodation options are **Castle Dundlod**, ((0141) 61611, located 150 km (94 miles) from Jaipur, 25 km (15 miles) from Jhunjhunu, 14 km (9 miles) from Mukundagh. Built in 1756. Can be booked through Dundlod House, Hawa Sarak, Civil Lines, Jaipur, ((0141) 66276, and **Roop Niwal Haveli**, ((0141) 75358, located 28 km (17 miles) from Sikar. The best way of exploring these fresco towns is by jeep or car. If you arrive at either Sikar or Fatepur by train, there are plenty of drivers willing to bargain on rates for driving you around.

ABOVE: Close-up of a fresco painting in Shekhavati district.

You can get there by taking the Shekhavati Express, which runs between Delhi and Jaipur daily and stops at Jhunjhunu, Mukundagh and Sikar, or opt for the erratic bus services linking Shekhavati's towns with Sikar and Jaipur.

AJMER AND PUSHKAR

Located within central Rajasthan, 130 km (80 miles) west of Jaipur and 198 km (123 miles) east of Jodhpur, the walled lakeside city of **Ajmer** is a curious Muslim toehold in a region dominated by Rajput Hindus — for it is India's

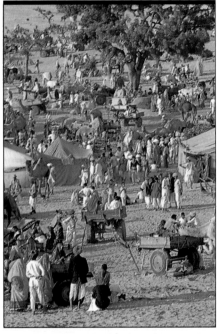

most famous Muslim pilgrimage center, with its shrine of the Sufi saint Khwaja Muinudin Chisthi (1142–1256), a direct descendant of the Muhammed's son-in-law, Ali. Its early history was scarred with bloody rampaging assaults by the Mahmud of Ghazni in 1024 and Muhammed Ghori in 1193, but it later became an important religious and strategic oasis town for the Mughal emperors. It was annexed by Akbar in 1556, who built a fort-palace which has now been turned into a museum. After 1818, it was ruled by the British, who founded the Mayo College, the first-ever Indian public school for young princes.

Rajput villagers ABOVE gather for the annual Pushkar Cattle Fair. OPPOSITE TOP: Children dressed in Rajput finery for the Pushkar fair. OPPOSITE BOTTOM: Beasts of burden and labor, camels are prized for their endurance in the harsh, sun-baked tracts of the Rajasthan desert.

The city is strewn with historic Islamic architecture, most notably the **Adai-din-ka-Jhonpra,** the remarkable mosque built by Muhammed Ghori's armies in just two days on the ruins caused by an orgy of destruction that razed an ancient Sanskrit college and 30 Hindu temples; and the **Dargah**, a grand shrine built by Humayan, containing the relics of the Sufi saint. The Dargah is the scene of Ajmer's spectacular annual festival of *Urs*, commemorating the saint's death. Held for six days in April or May, the festival draws thousands of pilgrims. Curious tourists go to witness the dramatic spectacle of continuous *quwwali* singing, exuberant fairs, and feasts cooked in iron tureens so vast that people dance in them. You can stay overnight at the RTDC **Hotel Khadim,** ((0145) 2490, moderate, or head northwest to the tiny temple-dotted township of **Pushkar,** 11 km (seven miles) away across the Nag Pahar, or Snake Mountain. Hindus believe Pushkar's beautiful lake to be sacred, second only to the Ganges River in purifying those who immerse themselves in it. According to legend, the lake was formed when Lord Brahma dropped a lotus flower while searching for a suitable place to do his yagna, or sacrifice. Pushkar also boasts the only Brahma temple in India.

But for most visitors, Pushkar means only one thing — the exuberantly colorful 10-day **Camel and Cattle Fair** staged in November, when this tiny oasis town is suddenly crammed with up to 200,000 Rajput traders and 50,000 cattle for an endless round of livestock-dealing, camel racing, fairs selling silver jewelry, embroidered shoes, camel-skin items, and woolen rugs, folk-dancing, music, and itinerant entertainers. You'll never have seen anything like it — the horizon massed with splay-legged camels and blazing with the most riotous bursts of color imaginable. It is a pageant of Rajput women in their swinging, multi-colored *ghagharas* skirts, tie-dyed blouses embellished with silver tinsel, and bedecked with silver jewelry, and turbaned men. Pushkar's modest accommodation facilities are swamped, and the RTDC sets up an amazingly civilized tented village for tourists, with a choice of double tents with shower and lavatory or communal tents, with food included in the tent price. At other times, stay at the Maharaja of Jaipur's former palace, the chaotically RTDC-run **Hotel Sarovar,** ((0145) 2040. Ask for the good air-cooled rooms.

JODHPUR

Lying on the edge of the Thar Desert and dominated by its medieval fortress citadel, this flat, sandy, leisurely paced city was the former

capital of the arid, drought-prone principality of Marwar, or "Land of Death".

The city was founded in 1459 by Rao Jodha — attracted by the natural defenses provided by its massive 125-m (400-ft) -high steep scarp — although his clannish Rathore Rajput forefathers had ruled the surrounding terrain since the twelfth century. Jodhpur's rulers rapidly amassed vast wealth as a trading post on the main camel caravan routes, and its merchant class — known as the Marwaris — are still renowned in India for their mercenary prowess. Jodhpur's main attraction is its extraordinary fifteenth-century fort, encircled along with its old city by a snaking 10-km (six-mile) -long stone wall punctuated by eight monumental gates. This fortress proved invulnerable even to the Mughals, who finally compromised by signing treaties with Jodhpur's rulers, exchanging wealth for military assistance to win Gujarat for the Mughal empire. The patronage of the Mughals reached its height in the mid-sixteenth century, when Jodhpur's Rao Udai Singh married his sister to Emperor Akbar and his daughter to the emperor's son, Jehangir. Akbar may

have secretly regretted the alliance — his Rajput wife, Jodhai Bai, managed to increase considerably the powers of the Jodhpurs, but more importantly for Akbar she made him give up "beef, garlic, onions and the wearing of a beard", according to a court chronicle.

Mughal patronage turned sour when Jodhpur's Jaswant Singh backed the losing side in a Mughal dynastic tryst for power between the waning Shah Jehan and his formidable son, Aurangzeb. One of the first commands given by the new emperor Aurangzeb was for the murder of Jaswant Singh's posthumously born boy heir to the Jodhpur throne, who was then conveniently at the royal court in Delhi. The attempt failed (the boy was hidden in a basket of sweetmeats and whisked away to safety), but Aurangzeb wreaked his revenge in 1678 by sacking Jodhpur and plundering the prosperous towns of Marwar. Ajit Singh, the boy-prince, recaptured his kingdom after an interval of 30 years, becoming in the process one of Jodhpur's greatest heroes.

Jodhpur was then thrown into a century of dynastic disarray and bloody battles with neighboring states; by the end of the eighteenth century, it was seized first by the Marathas and then by the British. During the early twentieth century, Jodhpur was ruled by the quixotic and powerful Maharaja Umaid Singh, who left the remarkable Umaid Bhawan Palace, one of the world's largest private residences, as his legacy. The palace was built to keep 3,000 of his starving population employed following a devastating famine in 1923. It was completed in 1945, just before the maharaja had to cede his princely state to a new independent India.

Jodhpur remains curiously unappreciated by many travelers, who glimpse it only in passing, usually en route either to Jaisalmer, further west, or Udaipur in the south. But old-India hands rate its charms highly, for as well as its wealth of historic attractions and colorful bazaars, Jodhpur is a place where you can stray off the beaten track for a glimpse of village India.

ACCESS

Some 336 km (208 miles) from Jaipur, Jodhpur has direct flights to and from Delhi, Jaipur, and Udaipur. Unless you're on a fly-by-night tour, Rajasthan is perfect for train trips, with the overnight sleepers providing just the right degree of novelty without being unduly tedious. Good "overnighters" ply to Jodhpur from Delhi and to the main Rajasthan centers of Jaipur, Jaisalmer, Udaipur, Abu Road, and Bikaner, as well as to Ahmedabad.

HOTELS

The magnificent oleander-colored sandstone **Umaid Bhawan Palace**, ((0291) 33316, fax (0291) 35373, residence of the former maharaja, is now India's most extraordinary luxury hotel, superbly maintained and run by Welcomgroup. Irrepressibly romantic, swathed in marble, gilt, and rich brocades, this vast 347-roomed palace is eccentric opulence on a grand scale. Massive crested brass doors usher visitors into an art deco lobby leading to spectacular soaring double-domed inner courtyards, the first with stuffed leopards poised on its sweeping twin marble staircases, the second with European gilt furniture and tiered spiraling stairwells leading up to a whispering gallery. Directly below is the basement swimming pool, and from the central courtyard branch trophy-crammed billiard rooms and libraries. It's all so grand, formal, and vast that guests feel dwarfed and almost chastened. Equally, once settled into their spacious suites and after a few moonlit courtyard barbecues, many guests simply never want to leave. Much of the palace is given over to the hotel, while the up-permost wings are inhabited by Jodhpur's former royal family. The main reception halls hold the palace museum, with its rare antique clock and watch collection, Rajput Mughal miniatures, armor, *objets d'art*, and ambitious painted murals (open 9 am to 5 pm).

Each room is different, but all are spacious and decorated with original period furnishings. The suites are positively splendid — with up to six rooms apiece and balconies overlooking the peacock-inhabited garden pavilions — and are comparatively reasonably priced. There's even a novelty suite created to resemble the interior of a ship, but by far the grandest are the two Regal Suites, formerly occupied by the maharaja and his maharanee, with mammoth beds, interior fountains, chandeliers, and glorious art deco marble bathrooms.

Evenings are best spent on the moonlit terrace, where turbaned musicians play every evening against a magical backdrop of pavilioned gardens and the illuminated fort. The excellent five-star facilities include squash, tennis, and badminton courts, with croquet and golf on request.

Ajit Bhawan, ((0291) 20409, fax (0291) 23006, near Circuit House, is Umaid Bhawan's closest rival. Built for Umaid Singh's younger brother, this bougainvillaea-covered ancestral mansion has been transformed into a charming hotel brimming with family heirlooms, Raj-era bric-brac, hunting trophies, and a friendly atmosphere. It is run with great aplomb in the guesthouse tradition by a raconteurish descendant of Ajit, Maharaj Swaroop Singh — the uncle of Jodhpur's present maharaja — who cuts a dashing figure in riding breeches, cravat, and turban. There's a choice of 25 air-cooled double rooms within the mansion, or any one of the stylish cottages scattered around the pretty gardens, each designed like a traditional village hut but with very pukka tiled bathrooms. Room prices are inexpensive. Additional quirky glamor is provided by Ajit Bhawan's staff, all startlingly authentic in their Rajput costumes. Excellent breakfasts and home-cooked dinners are served in the garden or the courtyard. Golf, squash, camel rides, and excellent village tours (see page 135) can be arranged. The maharaja is definitely the man to talk to about acquiring a pair of Jodhpur's classic jodhpurs.

Another mid-range accommodation option is the **Hotel Kalrni Bhawan**, ((0291) 30157, Defence Lab Road. This modern hotel with good amenities offers inexpensive, comfortable rooms, with a pretty breakfast courtyard. Budget travelers can take their pick of a handful of cheap, reliable lodges. The RTDC-run **Ghoomar Tourist Bungalow**, ((0291) 44010, on High Court Road near the Ajit Bhawan Gardens, is a popular travelers' halt. It also houses the Tourist Office, the Indian Airlines desk, ((0291) 28600 or 20909, and a cafeteria. Rooms are shabbily worn, but clean, and quite acceptable for a night or so and there are very public-looking dorm beds at next to nothing. Otherwise try the more central **Adarsh Niwas Hotel**, ((0291) 26936, just near the rail station which has clean rooms and a popular courtyard cafeteria.

RESTAURANTS

Try to dine at least once at both Umaid Bhawan Palace and Ajit Bhawan, for each offers a

unique style, spectacular settings, and good food. Highlights at **Umaid Bhawan** include the excellent blow-out buffet lunches in the grand Marwal Hall, with its dangling chandeliers, polished mirrors, and stuffed tigers, and afternoon teas on the terrace. **Ajit Bhawan** is perfect for sampling authentic West Rajasthani dishes in a prettily illuminated garden or courtyard — or, during Jodhpur's bitterly cold winter nights, around a blazing fire. In town are two popular eating houses: the vegetarian **Pankaj** at Jalori Gate, and the **Kalinga** restaurant near the rail station, which is good for reasonably priced Mughali dishes and as a place to linger before catching an overnight train. Don't miss out on the famous Jodhpur treat, Makhania *lassi*, a divine concoction made from whipped-up cow's milk, butterballs, and cardamom — one taste and you're hooked. It's served cheap

all over town, usually in suspiciously grimy glasses, with a lump of ice added for good measure. The **Sri Mishra Lal Hotel** at the main Sardar bazaar gateway serves the nicest and most hygienic of the genre, and are perhaps telling the truth when they claim to sell 1,000 glasses a day. Another decadent Jodhpuri dessert is *mawaki-kachori*, a baklava-like pastry stuffed with caramelized nuts and coconut, served smothered in syrup.

SIGHTSEEING

A novel, but slow, way to get around is by nag-drawn tonga or the ubiquitous cycle-rickshaw. But take a taxi or motorized rickshaw up the winding road to Jodhpur's main attraction, the magnificent **Mehrangarh Fort**, five kilometers (three miles) from the town center.

From Jai Pol (Victory) Gate, continue the steep climb on foot past cannon-scarred battlements and the souvenir shops with busking musicians. Commissioned by Rao Jodha in 1459, this fortress eyrie is a masterpiece of medieval defense. It is said that after it was completed, its unsuspecting architect was ordered buried alive so that he could not reveal its secrets.

Another grisly relic of the feudal past is in the forlorn plaster row of delicate sati palm prints beside Lohapol (Iron) Gate, marking the spot of self-immolation by women whose husbands died in battle. Sati was idealized as an act of romance, sacrifice, and devotion, so that a king's prestige was quite literally measured by the number of women who elected to throw themselves on his funeral pyre. Of all Jodhpur's rulers, Ajit Singh was to claim the greatest "honor" by having his six queens and 58 concubines share his fate of flames in 1731.

Rudyard Kipling was suitably impressed by the fortress-palace, describing it as a creation of "angels, fairies and giants", though this seems too saccharine a description of the full-blooded, larger-than-life Rajputs. The complex is beautifully maintained as a museum, and houses 18 different sections, each full of carefully displayed antiquities. Open 9 am to 5 pm daily, the entrance fee includes the very useful services of a very knowledgeable English-speaking guide. Elderly royal retainers usher visitors through cordoned passages with a proprietorial air. Within lies a maze of interlocking palace interiors, inner marble courtyards, audience halls, exquisite latticed zenana chambers, and the *pièce de résistance* — the royal boudoir, an Arabian Nights fantasy of exotic paneling, dangling colored balls, mirrored and mosaic walls with swings for romping with his favorite concubines, and an enormous bed upon which generations of Jodhpur's maharajas indulged their peccadilloes. Another highlight is the eighteenth-century Dancing Hall, the ceiling of which is plastered with 80 kg (176 lb) of pure gold.

The museum rooms house a richly diverse collection of weaponry, including the swords of Akbar and Timur, gem-encrusted gilt elephant howdahs, royal cradles, rare miniatures, and many traditional Rajasthani musical instruments, many of which have now disappeared from common use. But pride of place is taken by a huge portable tent-palace, used by Emperor Shah Jehan on his tours.

Beyond the palace lie the fort's craggy ramparts, strewn with antique cannons. The view from the edge is unforgettable, like being atop Mount Olympus and spying on the activities of the world below. From the city rises the hum of massed humanity, with stray shouts, dog's barks, and snatches of song lifted suddenly with almost unnatural clarity.

As you drive down the fort road, you'll see the dazzling white marble **Jaswant Thada**, the cenotaph to Maharaja Jaswant Singh built in 1899. He was the first of the Rathore rulers not to have his cenotaph erected at Mandore, the historic capital. It's worth finding the *chowkidar* to let you inside to see the portraits of all the Rathore rulers.

In town, wander through Jodhpur's colorful marketplace which spans out around the **Clock Tower** square until late in the evening. It's too narrow for cars, but big enough for swarms of jingling bicycles, cows, carts, and camels. This is the fabled Old Market, now known as **Sardar Bazaar**. In the general market, cows doze lethargically under giant tarpaulins, dhoti-clad merchants sprawl like odalisques amid pyramids of millet, women squat like monkeys discarding wheat from chaff, and swarms of flies and giggling children simply cannot be shaken free. Depending on which direction you take, you'll be plunged into anything from a locksmith's cul-de-sac to one stacked with oozing raw jaggery, silverware, sweetmeats, flower garlands, or medical textbooks. Good finds in Jodhpur include wooden puppets, painted horses, ivorywork, tie-dyed *bandhana* fabric, and embroidered slippers.

Tranquil strolls can be enjoyed in the leafy, well-kept **Umaid Public Gardens and Zoo**, full of bougainvillaea, mango, and rose bushes. To the northwest of the gardens is the **Government Museum**, a taxidermist's nightmare with its balding, silverfish-infested stuffed menagerie, reminiscent of the famous Monty Python "dead parrot" skit. Other exhibits include antique Indian sculpture, scrolls, royal treatises, and a decorated Durbar Hall. It's open from 10 am to 4 pm daily except Fridays.

It's worth reserving a morning or afternoon to see **Mandore**, the ancient capital of the Rathore Marwars, eight kilometers (five miles) north of town. It's a picturesque necropolis set in a lush, leafy garden, strewn with the *chhatris* of the Jodhpur rulers. The maharanees' *chhatris* are more desolately elegant, standing amid boulders along the hilltop ridge and reached by a steep winding path to the right of the garden.

Make sure you see the eighteenth-century Hall of Heroes, a gallery of 16 life-sized gods, goddesses, and Rajput warriors carved from a single rock.

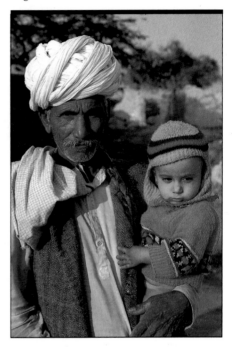

VILLAGE SAFARIS

Between tours of princely palaces and marble mausoleums, many visitors to India lament that they missed a glimpse of the real India — the rural villages where people still live by their ancient customs. Maharaja Singh of Ajit Bhawan offers a unique one-day safari aboard a 1942 U.S. Army jeep through the villages in the near-desert terrain surrounding Jodhpur. His fascinating firsthand insights into Rajasthani rural life won glowing praise from

ABOVE: A Rajput patriarch and his grandson. OPPOSITE: The circular dome within the monumental Umaid Bhawan Hotel, originally an Anglophile maharaja's fantasy palace built entirely of red sandstone in the 1920s.

Geoffrey Moorehouse, author of *India Britannica* and *Calcutta*.

"Everything in towns is evil", explains Singh. "It is on the farms, the uncorrupted areas away from electricity and telephones that the real beauties of life can be found."

The vestige of his previous role still exists, for at each stop the villagers offer an enthusiastic greeting, and still turn to him for guidance, to mediate disputes, and even to conduct wedding ceremonies. The maharaja and his small group of visitors are met by a beaming white-haired patriarch dressed in white, and clusters of curious, brightly clad tribeswomen laden with

are shown how villagers make dhurrie rugs in dug-out huts, and are encouraged to try their hand at making pots, grinding grain, and firing slingshots. The tour costs US$15 per person and is an unforgettable experience.

The Umaid Bhawan Palace can also arrange trips to these surrounding villages by putting you in touch with the energetic young men of a local Rathore noble family. Although their tours lack the vigorous personality of Maharaja Singh, they are cheaper and the pageantry of village life remains as fascinating. They are most worthwhile if combined with a night or two at the delightful sixteenth-century **Rohet Castle**,

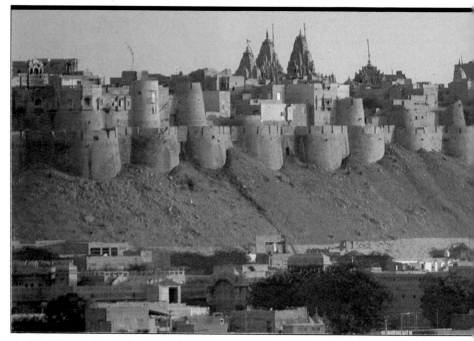

chunky silver jewelry and ivory bracelets up the length of their arms. Visitors are asked to take off their shoes before walking across the surprisingly pleasantly textured "protective" ring of mixed dried cow dung and urine around the hut — an ancient practice to ward off snakes and harness the "generative energy" of the cow, a sacred creature to the Hindus. Over spicy ginger tea — and sometimes a draught of *afion* opium, taken infused in water from the cupped hand of the host — Singh holds court on subjects as varied as the plight of the Untouchables, the desert's deepwater wells, the significance of turban colors, and local courtship rituals. Visitors

42 km (26 miles) from Jodhpur, a mini-fortress stronghold of the region's ruling Rathore clan overlooking an oasis lake. Here you'll be well looked after by the present *thakur* (ruler), Siddarth Singh, and his charming family, fed mouthwatering Rajput cuisine, and if you are part of a small group, you'll be given a truly memorable welcome, ending with an uproarious dance on the lawns with infectiously gleeful Rajput villagers. Rooms look out on to the garden and are inexpensive. Or you can opt to spend a comfortable night on the roof under a brilliant canopy of stars. For bookings, contact Rohet Castle, P.O. Rohet, District Pali (306421, Rajasthan, or Rohet House, ((0291) 21161, P.W.D. Road, Jodhpur.

If you're getting about Rajasthan by hired car, Castle Rohet can be a good place to break the trip to see **Ranakpur**'s wondrous fifteenth-

---

ABOVE: The magically medieval fortress city of Jaisalmer sits on a rocky promontory on the edge of the Thar Desert, with its amber turrets turning golden in the dusk light.

century Jain temples, 116 km (72 miles) away. Intricately sculpted from rose marble, these 29 halls form India's most complex and extensive group of Jain temples, covering over 3,600 sq m (40,000 sq ft) and containing 1,444 ornate pillars, each unique and covered with carvings. From Ranakpur, Udaipur is only 60 km (37 miles) away.

KHIMSAR, OSIAN, AND NAGAUR

On the desert route between Jodhpur and Bikaner, 240 km (150 miles) away, are three sightseeing "musts". The journey is best made

in a hired jeep, though local buses can be taken. Some 100 km (62 miles) north of Jodhpur, nestled near the (real) sand dunes of the Thar Desert, lies the fifteenth-century oasis stronghold of **Khimsar**. Its moated, fortified **Royal Castle**, (℡ 28 via Nagaur exchange) is a delightful hotel — a mix of medieval architecture and 1920's decor, taken over by the Welcomgroup and run by its ancestral owner and Rajasthan M.P., Onkar Singh, and his family. The rooms are pleasant, with very modern amenities. Evening barbecues and delicious authentic Rajput dishes are served in the ramparts of the old fort. The surrounding plains and sandy dunes are filled with romping nilgai, chinkara, desert fox, and the Great Indian Bustard, with partridges and imperial sand grouse often ending up as Royal Castle fare. For bookings, write to Onkar Singh, Royal Castle, P.O. Khimsar, District

Nagaur, or contact the Umaid Bhawan Hotel in Jodhpur.

It's 65 km (40 miles) to the ancient town of **Osian**, worth seeing for its cluster of 16 ornate Hindu and Jain temples dating from the eighth to the eleventh century. Also see **Nagaur**, 110 km (68 miles) from Bikaner, a medieval town with a very fine partridge-infested, twelfth-century Mughal fort. It's perfect for picnics and for clambering through. The zenana quarters have frescoes painted with crushed emeralds, pearls, and egg yolk; there are also mossed-over swimming pools and a mosque built by Akbar. So few visitors ever explore this remarkable fort that the guard beams with joy when they do appear, proudly producing a musty Visitors' Book for them to sign. On the full-moon cusp of January and February, Nagaur attracts thousands of Rajput villagers for its camel fair — bigger and less of a tourist trap than Pushkar — with camel races, folk dancing, strolling players, and mongoose fights.

JAISALMER: FORTRESS OF GOLD

Nothing quite prepares the traveler for the first breathtaking glimpse of **Jaisalmer**, the remote fortress city on the edge of Rajasthan's Thar Desert. (*"Thar"* means "abode of death".)

It's customary to make the journey by train, Jaisalmer's main link to the outside world. As the trip unfolds, vegetation and life are replaced by the hot and barren desert wasteland. Suddenly the walled city appears, seeming to hover above the tundra and shale. The twice-daily *Jaisalmer Express* is ingeniously timed to arrive at dawn or dusk, an hour of unsettling beauty in the desert light.

Jaisalmer, which lies 287 km (178 miles) from Jodhpur at the edge of India's western border with Pakistan, is the most magically medieval of Rajasthan's desert cities, and certainly the most extraordinary, since all the buildings — from the humblest shop to the palace and temples — are carved from a burnished golden-yellow sandstone. Even today, houses are built in the medieval manner to merge in with the old.

The Bhatti Rajput chieftain Rawal Jaisal deserted his former capital of Lodurva, 17 km (10.5 miles) away to found Jaisalmer in 1156, attracted by the site's large oasis and the natural defense provided by Trikuta (three-peak) hill. It was also a tryst with destiny — for centuries ago, Lord Krishna was said to have predicted that a distant descendant of his Lunar clan would one day rule from here. Jaisalmer's ruling family, who claimed both Lord Krishna and the moon as ancestors, kept only silver furniture in their palace quarters, believing that the moon-like color would give them talismanic strength.

Protected against the shifting sands and feudal marauders by a steep, double-tiered ring of giant stone ramparts, Jaisalmer became a prosperous, coveted stronghold on the great Spice Route from Persia and Afghanistan. It became a city of caravanserais, large buildings surrounding a central courtyard in which the merchants took shelter.

The early Muslim king of Delhi, Ala-ud-din Khilji, laid seige to the city at the end of the thirteenth century when one of his particularly well-laden caravans was pillaged by the Jaisalmer ruler. The siege lasted eight years, and in a bizarre twist of fate, the young Jaisalmer prince, Rattan Singh, befriended the enemy general, Nawab Mahboob Khan. The two were inseparable companions, and would meet to play chess until the war-horn sounded them into battle. Finally, in 1295, the Rajput clan knew that defeat was imminent. While Rattan Singh's sons were secretly delivered into the safe care of the Nawab, Jaisalmer's entire community of women and children committed *johar*, or mass suicide, as their menfolk, clad in ceremonial saffron and delirious with opium, fought to the last.

The warlike Bhattis were soon back in their citadel, waging vendettas against neighboring tribes and spinning webs of intrigue and treachery. Jaisalmer entered a more peaceful era as part of the Mughal empire in the late seventeenth century, prospering as a trading post for silks, spices, indigo, and opium. Hindu and Jain merchants, bankers, and artisans settled here, and built magnificent *havelis* mansions with elaborate honeycomb-like balconies.

Jaisalmer's fortunes dwindled with the opening of the Bombay port in the eighteenth century, but it suffered an even worse crisis in the aftermath of Partition in 1947, when the time-honored trade routes to Pakistan were suddenly deemed illegal. Only when it became an important military base during the 1965 and 1971 Indo-Pakistan wars did Jaisalmer emerge from its almost medieval seclusion to be connected by road and rail to the rest of Rajasthan.

Today, Jaisalmer's main sources of revenue are tourists who, since its "discovery" in the early seventies, go on camel safaris and buy the beautifully-woven local embroidery; the military, who linger in the bazaar smoking cheroots during periods of leave from border patrol duty; and a burgeoning illicit trade of black market goods, smuggled by camel drivers across the dunes separating India and Pakistan.

ACCESS

Indian Airlines flies to Jodhpur, the nearest airport, 287 km (178 miles) away. There is also a small light aircraft service three times a week to Jaisalmer run by Vayudoot Airlines, which can link with Jaipur, Jodhpur, and Bikaner.

There are twice-daily trains from Jodhpur; the overnight sleeper (departs 10:15 pm, arrives 6:30 am) is the most popular, and comfortable, option. Take plenty of water, oranges, and an engrossing book for the arduous 10-hour day journey, which passes through flat and monotonous desert, with gnarled fist-shaped trees, nomadic camels, and graceful lines of *paniharis*, women water-carriers. Hard-seat second-class carriages are the most entertaining, as they fill up suddenly at desert halts with spectacularly attired Rajput villagers who seem preserved from another age: tall, sinewy men jaunty in scarlet onion-dome turbans, glinting earrings, and ingeniously tied white *dhotis*; and women covered in silver jewelry and *chaori*, bracelets of ivory or bone which are worn from the shoulder to the wrist as a symbol of marriage.

Jaisalmer has become an extremely popular destination, and competition for the coveted overnight sleepers can be fierce, so it's essential to reserve tickets as soon as you reach Jodhpur.

It's possible to steam across the sands in full-blown sumptuous style — for a suitably sumptuous price. The Maharaja of Jodhpur's two white carriages, emblazoned with his coat of arms, are available for hire; one contains seven ornate coupés with baths and dining quarters for 14 people at a cost of US$3000; the other is smaller, although no less modest, and fits six people at US$540. Prices include two nights (there and back to Jodhpur), cooks, butlers, escorts from the Umaid Bhawan palace, and all meals in Jaisalmer.

Jaisalmer is connected by bus to Jodhpur, a 10-hour trip, and Bikaner, 280 km (174 miles), about 8 ½ hours. These are not exactly pleasure rides; train travel is vastly preferable.

WHEN TO GO

Ideally, visit Jaisalmer from November to February when the days are warm, the skies clear, and the nights cold enough for a driftwood fire and a warm sleeping bag. Avoid the summer months, when the temperature shoots up as high as 53°C (127°F) and the raging *simoon* (dust-storm) turns Jaisalmer into a virtual ghost-town. Jaisalmer is most popular during its annual three-day **Desert Festival**, which coincides with the full moon in February and March. It's a lively jamboree of camel polo, acrobatics and races, sword-swallowers, traditional Rajput *ghazals* (songs) and dance performances, turban-tying, and "Best Dressed Rajput" contests. Villagers from all around throng to Jaisalmer's bazaar to sell silver jewelry and hand-woven wares. Prices for necessities such as mineral water, toilet paper, and beer suddenly soar, and accommodation and train seats are hard to come by. Many hotels solve the problem by erecting impromptu canopied rooms on their roofs, and a "tourist village" of basic tents and bathroom facilities is set up on the plateau beneath the fort in a style similar to that at Pushkar's Camel Fair.

Jaisalmer is still one of the best places to witness the spectacle of **Holi** (February/March), a day of mock color battles and giggling powder-besplattered chaos. On this day, villagers cram into Mandir Palace, where they playfully pelt the ex-maharaja's family, and the courtyard fills with the sound of the reedy pipe *sheenai*, folk songs, and the clapping rhythm of swirling Rajput dances. All the important Rajasthan festivals — Dussehra, Diwali, and Gangaur — are celebrated here in the traditional exuberant way.

HOTELS

Hotel Narayan Niwas, ((02992) 2408, is Jaisalmer's most stylish hotel. A converted caravanserai with 24 rooms, the hotel is quaintly romantic, but simple, with a deep open hall where the camels used to sleep but where guests can now recline on striped cushions and listen to the traditional Rajasthani musicians in canopied culs-de-sac each evening. There's an attached restaurant with a good evening buffet, and highly exotic performances by dancers, sword-throwers, and musicians. Rooms are well-furnished, air-conditioned and moderately priced, and during the Desert Festival, colorful canopied tents, complete with beds, fresh linen, and toilets, are available.

Outside the town walls, the **Jawahar Niwas**, the ex-maharaja's former guesthouse, is now a hotel of faded charm. It has a pleasant veranda and a large billiard room. Rates: inexpensive.

Jaisal Castle, ((02992) 2362, an old 11-room courtyard house tucked into the fort's topmost ramparts, has less panache but is inexpensively priced. You'll find it—after asking for directions many times — by weaving up a sloping bottleneck of cobbled alleys. The views at sunset compensate only somewhat for the abysmal service and food — tea is served in chipped, stained cups, and the promised fresh sheets, soap, and towels never seem to materialize.

Close by is the **Sri Palace Hotel**, for highly authentic atmosphere in an old merchant's *haveli*. Its cramped but quaintly furnished rooms are very cheap.

The **Hotel Neeraj**, ((02992) 2442, set slightly outside the city walls, is the best cheapie option and far preferable to the poorly run RTDC **Moomal Tourist Bungalow**, ((02992) 2392,

which is at an inconvenient distance (two kilometers, or just over a mile) from town, and has a choice of rooms ranging from air-conditioned "deluxe" doubles to basic singles and a dormitory for budget travelers. Jaisalmer's Tourist Office is located here, but it is not terribly helpful. You'll find more enthusiastic English-speaking guides, who claim to be part of the town's "Guide Association", at the entrance gate to the fort; they will show you every place of historical interest for about US$2 a day.

Jaisalmer has become a rabbit warren of small family-run lodges that offer very cheap accommodation (including rooftop mattresses), basic local fare, and all the local information you

Jaisalmer's maze of sheltered lanes are surprisingly cool, lined with merchants *havelis* with façades of honey-colored sandstone carved to weblike delicacy.

need, as well as reserving train tickets and organizing camel treks, all with smiling desert hospitality. By far the most popular is **Fort View Hotel, ℭ** (02992) 2214, which has spartan doubles (no bathroom), a clambering waiter who serves guests their meals on the rooftop, and an endearing manager whose "no-frills" camel safaris are extremely popular. Other backpackers' havens within the fort town and worth investigating are the **Swastika Guest House**, opposite the State Bank of India, doubles with bath, the **Sunil Bhatia Rest House**, the **Hotel Pleasure**, and the **New Tourist Hotel**, all with very basic rooms and rock-bottom prices.

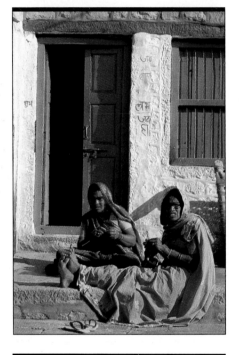

RESTAURANTS

Stick to Jaisalmer's traditional desert fare, with its simple round of spiced vegetables, robust millet *rotis*, and curd. **Hotel Narayan Niwas** has an excellent evening buffet with local specialties such as nut-textured *kar-san-gria*, made from dehydrated desert shrub beans, and *bajra ka sohita*, an unusual combination of ground millet and spiced mutton. Local sweets include *halwa*, made of lentils, and *ghewar*, a sugar-coated ball with a rich milky filling.

Clustered quite close together, Jaisalmer's other reliably good restaurants are **Kalpana's**, **8th of July Restaurant**, and **Gaylord Restaurant**, which all serve good Indian, Chinese, and Continental food. Otherwise you can take your pick of the dozens of small family-run budget eating places which have mushroomed around the market square. Some are very unhygienic-looking, but are usually safe for simple vegetarian dishes and spicy-sweet *chai*.

SIGHTSEEING

Fort and City Tour

A good walking tour begins at the fortress gate, from where a steep slope branches into a tangled maze of roughly cobbled, dim, and winding passageways. Here the bustle of life seems centuries old. Camels are herded into the shade of overhanging balconies while their owners crouch nearby over a pot of syrupy tea; goods ranging from ornate curled slippers to cartloads of fresh figs are hawked on the cobbles; and villagers, dressed in vivid Rajput costume, haggle over spice trays.

Amidst this mêlée, walking is really the only practical means of getting around, although Jaisalmer is so small and contained it can be enjoyed at a leisurely pace in a morning.

It's a 10-minute walk to the **Gadisar Tank**, the large natural oasis just below the city walls to the southwest. The lake that led Jaisal to found his city is full only in the monsoon months, but there are many temples and shrines around it to explore. The beautiful carved archway leading to the tank is supposed to have been built by Telia, a well-known *nautch* courtesan, for her Bhatti prince lover. She slyly added a Krishna temple so that the monarch's disapproving royal matrons, who refused to use the gate, could not pull it down. For glorious early morning views of the turreted fort, clamber up on to the temple roofs.

A short distance north is the **Fort** by the Gadisar Gate. This majestic sandstone fortress buttressed by 99 cone-shaped bastions is perched high on Trikuta, or "three-peak" hill. It is the second-oldest fort in Rajasthan, after Chittaugarh, and its cannonball-scarred battlements remain mute witness to several bloody conquests over the centuries, most notably by the Tughlaqs and the Mughals.

Just inside the thick gateway of the fort is the ornate seven-story city palace, which rises up from the traditional "blind" zenana ground floor to a riot of carved porticoes; and the four other *mahals* (palaces) which housed the royal queens and concubines. After a short stroll up the steep cobbled path, you'll enter a spacious square, dominated by a magnificent marble throne, the **Diwan-I-Am**, where the maharaja used to preside over public meetings, entertain visiting royalty, and celebrate weddings. It was also within this courtyard that *johar* took place.

Just beyond, past a low arched gateway, are the **Jain Temples**, an elegant group of seven interconnecting temples built by wealthy Marwari traders between the twelfth and fifteenth centuries and dedicated to the Jain saints Sambhavanathi and Rikhabdevji. Each temple is a marvel of elaborate design and intricate carvings; exteriors festooned with mythological deities and coy, curvaceous *apsaras* (celestial nymphs); and incense-laden chambers lined with rows of meditating white marble *tirthankaras*, or Jain saints, whose eyes flicker eerily with precious gems — all 6,666 pairs of them. Look especially for the priceless emerald icon of the Jain deity in the temple devoted to Mahavira.

Within the temple complex is an ancient library, the **Gyan Bhandir**, with a rare collection of manuscripts, miniature paintings, and books. The temples are only open in the morning from 9 am to noon, and only between 10 and 11 am on Sundays.

Follow the path left of the temples and you'll come to the nearby **Dop Khana**, or "place of the cannon", which offers the best views across the maze-like walled city to the desert plains below. It's an enchanting place to return to at dusk, when you see what looks like a row of bobbing glow-worms in the darkness of the surrounding desert — the lantern trail of long chains of nomads astride their camels, arriving laden with goods for Jaisalmer's markets.

Havelis and Palaces

Descendants of the wealthy traders still live in some of these beautiful *havelis*, some of which are centuries old. Jaisalmer is full of these magical eighteenth- and nineteenth-century mansions, their surfaces covered with intricate filigree carvings skillfully created by Muslim *silavats* (stone-carvers) for Hindu traders. The sandstone surface of the buildings crumbles slightly to the touch, creating an odd sensation of having breathed, for a moment, the dust of Jaisalmer's vanished opulence, the scent of silks, rich brocades, and thick incense.

Start your *haveli* tour with the **Salim Singh Haveli**, which is slightly north of the central market. Salim Singh was a despotic prime minister in the late seventeenth century who built himself this Arabian Nights-style *haveli*, with its impressive peacock-motif arched roof and unique sky-blue cupolas, to outshine the mansions of other nobles. Renowned for his cruelty, he once had 3,000 people from a nearby village massacred in order to win sway with the ruling maharaja. According to local lore, he tried to build his *haveli* as high as the monarch's palace, and even planned to build a connecting bridge to the royal chambers, but Rajput courtiers persuaded the king to destroy this skyscraping

rival, and its upper stories were blown to bits. Although its faade is stunning, the interior has been left ransacked and spartan.

Close by is the vast late-nineteenth-century **Mandir Palace**, built outside the city walls by the Maharawal Salivahan of Jaisalmer in the belief that a curse on the old city palace was killing off his family members in droves. It's unlike any other building in Jaisalmer — an Indo-Saracenic extravaganza, with fluted pillars, domed turrets, tiered filigree-work faades, and interiors of silver furniture.

In a cul-de-sac just north of the palace is the most spectacular of all Jaisalmer's beautiful

havelis, the **Patwon-ki-Haveli**, the collective name for five houses built between 1800 and 1860 by the wealthy Patwa brothers (who dabbled in opium dealing and gold smuggling, as well as trading precious gems). Two of the houses are museum showcases (open daily 10:30 am to 5 pm), one is rented by a shopkeeper who seems quite happy to show people through, and the remaining two are private residences. And do not miss **Nathamal-ki-Haveli** nearby, a late-nineteenth-century prime minister's house, with a marvelous fretted frontispiece flanked by sandstone elephants. You can ask to see the first floor, with its intricate painted walls and murals.

Spice, Slippers, and Silver

One of the most enjoyable things to do in Jaisalmer is to wander the alleys seeking out the bazaars, where fossicking can uncover some wonderful treasures, often more unusual and of better quality than those geared for the mass market in Jaipur.

In tiny niche-like shops tucked up crooked stairwells, or in *haveli* basements, you'll find

OPPOSITE: Women knitting in the afternoon sun within Jaisalmer's walled town. ABOVE: Balconies of delicate lattice patterns jut out from Jaisalmer's *haveli* walls, under eaves that provide protection from the savage sun.

Camel Safaris

Not least of Jaisalmer's attractions is the romantic lure of the camel safari. This has to be one of India's unforgettable, once-in-a-lifetime adventures: a camel trek across the desolate wastes of the Thar, the monotony broken by sudden magnificent glimpses of an age-old desert culture — encounters with nomadic tribes dressed like theatrical troubadours, ancient palace ruins etched against an azure sky; and swift packs of chinkara antelope racing across the horizon.

colorfully embroidered and mirror-inlaid cloths, decorative banners, and blankets. Jaisalmer is an excellent place to buy woolen dhurrie rugs, which are produced locally in many traditional designs and sizes. To get an idea of the selection, quality, and price, it's worth first taking a look at **Marudhar Handicrafts** in Patwon Haveli and **Kamal Handicrafts Emporium**, just near the Jain temples in the fort.

Along **Manik Chowk**, the main market square at the entrance to the fort, dozens of small stalls provide the perfect props for a swashbuckling Rajput-style desert adventure: brightly embroidered, curving camel-skin *mojadis*, or slippers; camel saddles and whips, 14-m (45-ft) - long turbans, and huge gathered *ghagras*, or skirts (taking up to 7 m, or 7.5 yds of cloth). Small items like embroidered camel-leather belts and bags make wonderful gifts, but if you're looking for exotic trophies to take home from Rajasthan, this is the place to browse for unusual antique silk, heavy silver Rajput jewelry, and the unique wall-hangings patched together painstakingly by village women with fragments of embroidery.

Whether you make it an afternoon's camel jaunt or a full-fledged three-week "Lawrence of Arabia" epic journey is up to you. For most people, a single night spent by a thorn-tree fire under a dazzling umbrella of stars, with a glorious desert sunrise, and two days of a camel's odd, lolloping gait, with earthy meals of *dahl*, millet *chapatis*, and *aloo choli* (spicy vegetables), is usually long enough to absorb the spirit of desert travel.

Virtually all Jaisalmer's hotels and guesthouses can arrange camel and jeep safaris for the most popular two-day trail which does a circuit of local places of interest. For practical advice on camel travel, pay a visit to the affable Mr Vyas of the Fort View Hotel, Jaisalmer's walking encyclopedia on the subject, and take a look at his book of tourists' comments. His well-organized tours include interesting sights, mattresses, food, potable water, and the lively company of rakishly turbaned camel drivers who sit behind you, gather firewood, prepare all

---

Few sights are as arresting in Rajasthan as the spectacle of its vivid and picturesquely dressed inhabitants. Four faces of Rajasthan: ABOVE: A young musician and a Rajput beauty, her arms covered in ivory bracelets, signifying her married status. OPPOSITE: A nomadic camel driver and a gypsy tribeswoman.

the meals, and croon desert ballads — all for the modest fee.

The Hotel Narayan Niwas offers a deluxe version more suited to those seeking the comforts of the Raj. The party consists of camels (one each, plus one for luggage), a cook, bedding, World War II-style tents, hampers packed to one's predilections, filtered water tanks, onions to keep the snakes away, nightwatchmen, and wireless contact with the police. You can even request folk dancers to entertain the party in the evenings around the campfire. Prices are considerably higher.

Essentials for a camel safari include a pair of sunglasses (for the intense desert glare), an individual water bottle, sunburn lotion, chapstick, mosquito-repellent, a bag of oranges (great thirst-quenchers), all-encompassing light cotton garments, strong comfortable shoes, protective headwear, and Lomotil tablets for emergency cases of diarrhea. A good book and a torch

to read it with, and plenty of camera film complete the ideal list.

If you're planning a long camel safari of around two weeks, it's only really practical between November and January when the desert is at its coolest and most enjoyable, but Jaisalmer's camel safari season runs from October to March.

Short two- or three-day tours from Jaisalmer usually visit a handful of several ancient monuments in the desert. A short distance north is

Bada Bagh (Big Garden), the cremation ground of Jaisalmer's rulers, dating back to the twelfth century. Here stand tiered canopied rows of marble *chattris*, or memorial cenotaphs, each carved with bas-reliefs. It's the perfect spot to take sunset photographs of Jaisalmer, blazing saffron-pink against the horizon. **Lodurva**, 16 km (10 miles) northwest, is the archaic eighth-century Rajput capital, with fine ruins and an ornate Jain temple complex. One traveler reported stepping into this temple without taking his shoes off, and being astonished to hear a voice exclaim in plummy Oxford vowels: "I say, old chap — you simply musn't wear shoes here, you know!" The owner of this astonishing voice turned out to be a scantily-clad, tumeric-smeared fakir squatting in a darkened niche! Other stops on the trail include **Amar Sagar**, six kilometers (3.7 miles) northwest, where a beautiful Jain temple stands near a dried-up oasis, and **Mool Sagar**, nine kilometers (5.6 miles) directly west of Jaisalmer, a garden and large tank. In between you'll pass many small villages of beehive-shaped mud and cow-dung huts and grinning desert dwellers who find the sight of sunburned foreigners atop cantering camels as funny as a Marx Brothers comedy.

Longer treks include the **Sam** sand dunes, 40 km (25 miles) away — where you'll see the true Sahara-like desert landscape of Rajasthan — and the exotic fortress city of Bikaner, 280 km (174 miles) away, which takes about 11 days.

Another popular excursion from Jaisalmer is **Khuri**, 40 km (25 miles) southwest of Jaisalmer and very close to the Pakistan border. Like the Sam, its chief attraction is its "real" desert landscape of smooth tidal waves of golden sand, which seems much more authentic desert than the empty scrubland surrounding Jaisalmer.

If you want to see the *real* Rajasthan, where people still live by their ancient customs, visit Khuri. The charming Rajput Sodha family — the rulers of this region for over 400 years until Independence in 1947 — run excellent camel safaris between October and March and also accommodate tourists in small, spotless mud

guest huts in the village for about US$3 a day, which includes three delicious traditional meals of homemade cheese, a wide range of breads, vegetarian dishes, and non-stop cups of sweet cardamom tea. The Sodhas are dignified, warm-hearted hosts, and the two sons, Bhagwan and Tane Singh Sodha, make articulate, humorous escorts whether on a camel safari or a tour of the village.

To get to Khuri, either hire a jeep or take the early morning bus from Jaisalmer. Bhagwan Singh is always there to meet visitors when the bus arrives.

BIKANER

Situated in the northern Thar desert, Bikaner is an ochre-colored sandstone fortress city surrounded by high medieval ramparts. It is famous for its distinctive Rajput architecture, martial camels, and exotic inhabitants. It was founded in 1488 by Rao Bikaji and his band of 300 loyal followers. Lying at the crossroads of the great medieval caravan routes, this prosperous stronghold became renowned for its military strength in withstanding a centuries-long vendetta — and many spectacular battles — with the ruling Jodhpur clan.

Like many Rajputs, the Bikaners adored indolent pleasures — and court archives note their excessive consumption of opium and the aphrodisiac *asha*, a potent brew of powdered gold, silver, ground pearls, and goat brains. During the nineteenth century, Bikaner began to curry favor with the British, donating 200 camels to the Afghan Campaign in 1842, and offering shelter to many European refugees during the Great Mutiny of 1857.

Present-day Bikaner owes many of its finest buildings to one remarkable man, the late Maharaja Ganga Singh (1880–1943), who single-handedly transformed his backward feudal domain into Rajasthan's chief granary by building the Ganga Canal to transform the surrounding desert into green fields, and by constructing a railway. This flamboyant monarch founded India's most prestigious military unit, the Camel Corps, and staged spectacular annual shoots for imperial sand grouse, complete with fleets of Rolls Royces and vast banquets. The Prince of Wales attended the shoot held in 1905. Ganga Singh's fantasy nineteenth-century Lallgarh Palace, built in rose sandstone, is now a luxury hotel and looms on the edge of the desert like a vast mirage from *Brideshead Revisited*.

ACCESS

Vayudoot operates regular flights to and from Bikaner, via Jaipur from Delhi, landing at a small airstrip 13 km (eight miles) out of town. Bikaner is also conveniently reached by twice-daily express trains — preferably by sleepers on the overnighters — which take between eight and 12 hours from Jodhpur (240 km, or 150 miles), 10 to 11 hours from Jaipur (354 km, or 220 miles), and 12 hours from Delhi (510 km, or 317 miles), arriving at Bikaner's station just as the dawn sky turns rosy. "Express" bus trips from these main cities, as well as to Jaisalmer (320 km, or 205 miles), take a little longer — mainly due to long halts at shanty tea stalls while the driver has a rollicking time with his mates — and are rather more grueling. Luxury air-conditioned coaches offer more comfort, but run only from Delhi and Jaipur.

HOTELS

Bikaner's grandest hotel is the **Lallgarh Palace**, ((0151) 61963, run by members of Bikaner's former royal family. Much of it remains uninhabited, as if magically deserted. Peacocks and squirrels make themselves at home in the echoing, marble-balustraded courtyards; the state rooms are swathed in dustcloths; and in the corridors are mounted trophies and exquisite *jali*-screened alcoves. The hotel rooms are delightful; straight out of the 1930's, they have canopied twin beds, gloomy drapes, and mahogany furniture. Rates: inexpensive. Guests are informed that the staff are at their service should they wish to go clay-pigeon shooting or play croquet! There is also a golf course, squash courts, and bougainvillaea-dotted gardens. The hotel's **Palace Museum** is brimming with royal memorabilia, including many stuffed trophies, *objets d'art*, various military outfits worn by the portly maharaja, and a massive carpet woven by Bikaner's prisoners. There is a particularly fine photographic gallery for a fascinating close-up inspection of virtually all of India's

chutney. They also serve early-morning "Brake Fast" and "Plane Tost"! For those with a sweet-tooth, Bikaner's famous *ghaver*, caramelized fudge, and the town's distinctive combination of hot milk, curd, and sugar, frothed up by sidewalk vendors with theatrical sloshes into brass beakers, can quickly become addictive.

SIGHTSEEING

As with most of Rajasthan's smaller centers, transport around town is mainly by foot or pony-drawn *tongas*, although a few unmetered

princes, stiff-collared viceroys, and their formidable vicerines. The museum is open daily except Wednesdays, from 9 am to 6 pm. The management can arrange for you to stay at **Gajner Palace, ℂ** (0151) 3239, 32 km (20 miles) away, an elegant royal hunting lodge set on the lake of a wildlife sanctuary full of gazelles, wild boar, black buck, sambhar, and imperial sand grouse.

For cheaper accommodation, avoid the cluster of squalid lodges near the railway station; head instead for the state-run **Dhola Maru Tourist Bungalow, ℂ** (0151) 5002, which also houses the friendly and informative Tourist Office.

Amber Restaurant, on Station Road, is recommended for delicious, cheap vegetarian *thalis*, creamy *lassis*, and curd. Try their unusual "Amber Special Dosa", stuffed with cashew nuts and fruit and served with fresh coconut

auto-rickshaws and taxis operate from the railway station. The city is dominated by its imposing medieval **Junagarh Fort**, built entirely with red-ochre sandstone and marble between 1588 and 1593 by Raja Raj Singh, one of Akbar's generals. Successive rulers enlarged and embellished the fort over the next 400 years. With its massive battlements and moat, it is one of the few forts in India never to have been conquered, although it was often attacked. Beyond the main **Suraj Pol**, or "Sun Gate", you can see the silver-fringed sati handmarks left by queens and concubines over the centuries. Inside is a magnificent Mughal Durbar Hall and a maze of no less than 37 ornate palaces, with marble pillared halls, delicately painted

ABOVE: Dawn silhouette of *chhatris* spires, Bikaner.
OPPOSITE: Pastel-hued walls in a quiet alley, Bikaner.

chambers, mirror-encrusted ceilings, and ivory and wood carvings.

The most sumptuous of all these palaces are the **Chandra Mahal**, or "Moon Palace", a jewel-box of delicate paintings, mirrors, and carved marble panels, and the **Phool Mahal**, or "Flower Palace", filtered with stained glass and studded with mirror mosaics. Other notable places to see within the fort include the Karan Mahal, Rang Mahal, Bijai Mahal, and the Anup Mahal palaces, the latter opposite the Har Mandir temple where royal marriages, births, and the annual Gangaur festival are still celebrated. The fort museum brims with fascinating heirlooms, including rare manuscripts, jeweled weaponry, gold howdahs, hookahs, and a number of oddities including two decaying World War biplanes purchased by the patriotic Ganga Singh. The fort is open daily, except Fridays, from 10 am to 4:30 pm, and also houses the Tourist Office.

Bikaner's old walled city has an equally medieval flavor. It is fun to spend an afternoon combing the filthy, chaotic bazaars clustered around **Kote Gate**, full of turbaned desert nomads, colorfully clad women, and pigeon-hole stalls hawking everything from antique doors and cauliflowers to lacquer-work, camel-skin lampshades, and ivory bangles. The **Ganga Singh Golden Jubilee Museum**, in Gandhi Park near the Tourist Bungalow, is well worth visiting for its rich collection of pre-Aryan archaeological finds, antique Indian sculpture, and fine Bikaner school miniatures. It's open from 10 am to 5 pm, and closed on Fridays and public holidays.

If **Bikaner Jail**'s Superintendent J.K. Sharma is in an affable mood, he will allow you to tour through this massive nineteenth-century stone prison, where some 400 inmates — a mixture of petty thieves and *dacoitish*-looking murderers — create US$3000 worth of carpets annually in a system first begun by Maharaja Ganga Singh during the 1920's. The prison yard presents an unforgettable Kafkaesque spectacle: hundreds of surly calico-clad men sit in dug-out troughs amid a 40-m (130-ft) -long mesh of foot-pedalled pulley contraptions and water wheels which process raw wool into clean threads for the weaving looms — all beneath the burning sun under the watchful eye of a pockmarked Tamburlaine-like jailor. Hand-knotted carpets can be purchased from the prison storeroom.

Out of town, don't miss a visit to the state-run **Camel Breeding Farm**, 10 km (six miles) west of Bikaner, home to about 300 gambolling baby camels and their parents. India's regimental Camel Corps plucks the best and brightest among them. Here you can go for a ride, chat to

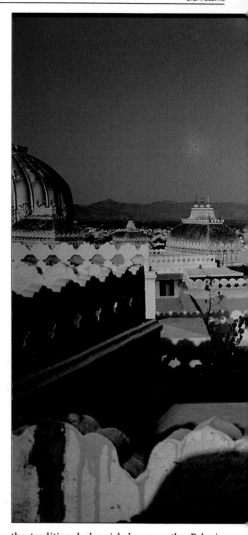

the traditional clannish keepers, the *Rebaris*, about camel lore, and sample still-warm camel milk. The farm welcomes visitors only between 3 and 5 pm. At **Deshnok**, 33 km (20 miles) south of Bikaner, stands the **Karni Mata Temple**, dedicated to the fifteenth-century mystic who prophesied Rao Bika's successes, but more famous as the "rat temple", where swarms of "sacred" rodents are protected in the belief that they are shortly to be reincarnated as gifted humans. Lured in with grain and sweetmeats, hundreds of rats squeak and scurry across the marble shrine — and over the bare feet of devotees. It's not for the squeamish, and visitors are given stern warnings not to stand on one accidentally. Curiously, even the temple priest and his assistant have rather rodent-like features. The beautiful royal *chhatris*, or cenotaphs, at Devi Kund, eight kilometers

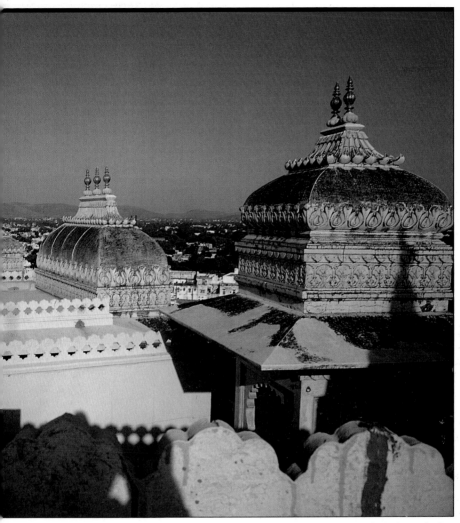

(five miles) from Bikaner, are interesting memorials to the dead of the princely Rathores of Bikaner.

UDAIPUR

Udaipur — a languid lake city strewn with marble palaces, hibiscus-massed gardens, fountain pavilions, and cobbled medieval bazaars — is one of India's most romantic destinations. It offers a dramatic contrast to the desert-bound fortress towns more commonly associated with Rajasthan.

Udaipur, the "city of sunrise", was founded in 1567 by Maharana Udai Singh, on the advice of a sage who told him that if he built his new Mewar capital here it would never be captured. It was timely advice, for his ancestral fortress kingdom at Chittaugarh had just been dealt a fatal blow by Akbar's army.

As Rajasthan's most ancient ruling family, the Mewars bore the title "maharana", or "light of the Hindus", and felt themselves more distinguished than mere maharajas, claiming descent from the sun god Rama. (The royal escutcheon is a defiant-looking sun face.) The proud Mewars suffered the yoke of no foreign power for long, and nursed a bitter grudge against those Rajput clans — most particularly Jaipur's Mansingh — whose kingdoms fell into the hands of the Mughals.

Udaipur had no sooner been founded than Akbar's armies laid siege to it, but despite

ABOVE: The cupolas of the Shiv Niwas Palace provide quiet outlooks over the ancient town of Udaipur.

formidable odds, Udai Singh's heir, the legendary Pratap Singh, kept them at bay for 25 years before finally being overpowered. Successive maharanas were involved in an almost constant round of feudalistic battles and intrigues, and Udaipur achieved a lasting peace — albeit maintained with a superior aloofness — only in 1818 when it came under British control and was rescued, along with the rest of Rajasthan, from the clutches of the Marathas.

Udaipur's most prolific builder was Maharana Jagat Singh, who during the seventeenth century built much of the majestic City Palace. It straddles a sheer natural rock palisade

Shah Jehan; it was from here that he proclaimed himself emperor when his father died. It was on Jagmandir, too, that several British families were given shelter following the Indian Mutiny of 1857.

With its tranquil atmosphere, glittering array of palaces, garden pavilions, and cool lake-fanned breezes, Udaipur is one of Rajasthan's most beguiling cities. You should plan to spend at least four days visiting its many sights and attractions, including several historic temple complexes nearby. Udaipur is at its most beautiful between September and March, and just after the July monsoons.

almost 1.5 km (a mile) in length overlooking Lake Pichola, and is a vision of Rajput grandeur with its riot of kiosks, projecting balconies and turrets, and topped by a gold *kalash* (spire), the symbol of gods or independent kingdoms. Successive rulers kept adding wings until it became the largest and most imposing palace complex in Rajasthan. At the same time, Jagat Singh created an exotic lake citadel — now the famed Lake Palace Hotel — on the island of Jagniwas. He also built the forlornly beautiful palace on the opposite island of Jagmandir, which was later used as an abode-in-exile by Jehangir's rebellious son

ABOVE: At the Karni Mata Temple at Deshnok, near Bikaner, a Rajput girl LEFT observes a "sacred" rat nibbling her proprietary offering of *prasad* or sweetmeats. RIGHT the keeper of the so-called Rat Temple seems unaware of a new addition to his turban.

ACCESS

Indian Airlines links Udaipur with Delhi via Jaipur and Jodhpur, and with Bombay via Aurangabad. The Indian Airlines office, ((0294) 23952, is at LTC Building, Delhi Gate, and the airport is 24 km (15 miles) from town. By rail, the daily *Chetak Express* takes 21 hours to reach Udaipur from Delhi, via Jaipur and Ajmer. The *Ahmedabad Mail* makes the eight-hour journey to and from Gujarat's capital, and also halts at Abu Road Station, about five hours from Udaipur, for those traveling on to Rajasthan's hill station. Daily luxury or RTDC express buses ply to Ahmedabad and all major Rajasthan centers from the main bus stand near the railway line opposite Udai Pole. There are also frequent bus services to surrounding historic attractions such as Eklingi, Ranakpur and, slightly further afield, Chittaurgarh.

HOTELS

The glorious **Lake Palace**, ((0294) 23241-5, fax (0294) 25804, rises from Pichola Lake like a marble confection. Built by Maharana Jagat Singh in 1746, it is now run by the Taj Group as a luxury hotel, complete with shopping arcades, coffee shops, and standard modern rooms, so that only the husk of its original medieval structure remains. Five royal suites, complete with stained-glass windows, glittering mirrored and painted surfaces, and antique furniture, have been painstakingly restored and cost upward of US$150. Pretty interior courtyards and terraces, and a spectacular little marble swimming pool are illuminated at night. A restaurant serving standard five-star fare draws those who aren't guests for sunset drinks and good buffet dinners. Gondoliers dressed in fraying navy-blue tunics ferry guests and visitors back and forth from the marble steps of the Lake Palace to the shore. The locals have never quite gotten over the excitement of having the James Bond movie *Octopussy* filmed here. The Lake Palace operates one-hour boat tours across to Jag Mandir Palace at 5 pm to coincide with dusk's charmed light. These are well worth the cost.

The **Shiv Niwas Palace**, ((0294) 28239, fax (0294) 23823, is an extravagantly elegant five-star hotel — part of a grand eighteenth-century addition to the vast, rambling City Palace. It has served as a royal guesthouse, accommodating the likes of Queen Elizabeth, Jacqueline Onassis, and the Shah of Iran. Massive entrance doors open on to a dazzling courtyard with a clear blue marble Grecian pool. The royal suites, furnished with Belgian chandeliers, four-poster beds, and surplus treasures from the City Palace, range from US$125 to US$300, while the "ordinary" rooms are around US$50. Bookings can be made through the Taj Group of Hotels.

For less-expensive period elegance, try the IDTC-run **Laxmi Vilas Palace Hotel**, ((0294) 29711, on Fateh Sagar Road. Another former palace guesthouse, it has a swimming pool overlooking Fateh Sagar Lake. The neighboring **Anand Bhawan Circuit House,** ((0294) 23256, set on the periphery of a delightful park containing a statue of Maharana Pratap astride his favorite charger, Chetak, has pleasant inexpensive rooms.

Perhaps the best choice for those who don't feel the need for luxury surroundings, but require clean, comfortable, and cheap accommodation, is the **Rang Niwas Hotel,** ((0294) 523891, Lake Palace Road. Located in the shadow of the City Palace, it is another former mansion guest-house, run with boundless enthusiasm by the extremely affable Mr Singh and his two sons. You can arrive at any time of the day or night and be assured of (at least) a stretcher bed in the ping-pong room; or choose from modest but clean US$4 rooms (supplied with buckets of hot water) or charming US$8 to US$12"suites" with nice old furniture, hot water, and mosquito nets. Other attractions are a useful information board in the lobby, a sweet little courtyard, and Udaipur's best rooftop café. Mr Singh is a great organizer — he'll warn against "fiendish" commission-seeking auto-rickshaw wallahs, hire out bicycles, and help coordinate out-of-town tours with other guests to save on taxi fares.

Udaipur also offers two excellent mansion "retreats", both set amid leafy forest at a slight distance from town. **Hotel Shikarbadi**, ((0294) 83200, five kilometers (three miles) away, is a delightful nineteenth-century trophy-stuffed royal hunting lodge, with a swimming pool, old retainers, and leafy gardens. It's good for an overnight stay, and for horse riding at dawn. Rooms are moderately priced and can be booked through the Lake Palace Hotel. Cheaper, and rather more eccentric, is **Pratap County Inn**, ((0294) 23638-9, at Titadhra Village, six kilometers (3.7 miles) from town. Set amid lovely surroundings and there are free horse- and camel-rides.

RESTAURANTS

Udaipur's two fantasy palaces both have pleasant bars and coffee shops and stage excellent candlelit dinners with a choice of Rajasthani, Indian, and Continental dishes, often preceded by puppet shows or musical performances. The Lake Palace offers excellent US$5 *thali* lunches. The sunny rooftop café at the Rang Niwas Hotel is open all day, with modest but well-prepared food and prompt service. Newspapers can be rustled up along with excellent Western-style breakfasts (with perfect two-minute eggs, warm toast, and creamy fruit *lassis*). Main meal dishes offer a choice of Indian, Chinese, or Western food, and are reliably generous and cheap. Another traveler's favorite is the **Mayur Cafe**, opposite the Jagdish Temple down from the City Palace. The excellent cheap food is served promptly by an expert 10-year-old waiter. Highlights here include "Rajasthani Pizza" made with delicious local cheese, "France Frice", "Think-Shakes", and home-baked chocolate cakes. Also try the modern A-framed, aptly-named **Feast Restaurant**, opposite the Saheliyon-ki-Bari Gardens, for pleasant decor, well-dressed waiters, and classic Mughali fare cooked up by the former chief chef at the Lake Palace Hotel. Downstairs is

Udaipur's highly popular fast-food parlor, **Eat-Me-Up**, which serves non-stop *dosas*, hamburgers, french fries, and milkshakes.

SIGHTSEEING

Udaipur's palaces and gardens clustered around the long lakeside boulevards make for a perfect day's cycling or walking. Bike-hire places are found along Lake Palace Road, and usually charge about US$1 to 2 per day. Otherwise you're at the mercy of taxi and auto-rickshaw drivers, who don't use meters and are prone to causing scenes, or tongas drawn by rather feeble-looking nags.

The **City Palace** houses a museum open daily from 9:30 am to 4:30 pm. Visitors pass through an enchanting multi-tiered labyrinth of royal apartments, zenana quarters, courtyards, terraces, and pavilions. Every inch of wall and ceiling has been decorated — much of it by Hindu artisans who came to Udaipur after being expelled from Delhi's Red Fort by the sectarian Aurangzeb — with jewel-colored mosaics, inlaid Chinese tiles, mirror-work niches, and fine paintings. In one of these rooms, the beautiful Mewar princess Krishna Kumari drank poison and saved the kingdom from the wrath of her two rival suitors from neighboring states. Clamber up to the roof gardens and overhanging terraces for views of the lake. There is another interesting museum near the main palace entrance, with fine Rajput miniatures, toys, and royal objets d'art. It is worth buying the museum guide for the detailed information it gives on each room.

Nearby is the eighteenth-century **Tripolia Gate**, with its eight carved marble arches under which the ruler was weighed on his birthday and his weight in gold distributed to his people. Directly behind are the steep stone elephant-steps leading to **Jagdish Temple**, a fine Indo-Aryan temple built by Maharana Jagat Singh in 1651 and notable for its black stone image of Vishnu as Jagannath, Lord of the Universe. You'll emerge into the cobbled Bara Bazaar, which winds its way down to the larger Bapu Bazaar, east of the City Palace, both colorful mêlées overflowing with wooden toys, perfumes, silver trinkets, *pichwai* (cloth paintings), decorative earthenware pots, and giant troughs of bubbling sweetmeats.

To round up, visit the glorious **Gulab Bagh**, or Rose Gardens, laid out in 1881; cycle to the north of the city to see the ornamental **Saheli-yonki Bari** gardens created for the royal concubines, then glide along the **Lake Fateh Sagar**

esplanade, stopping to have tea at **Nehru Park**, a garden island with a restaurant, reached by boat; and visit the fascinating folk museum, **Bhartiya Lok Kala Mandal**, near Chetak Circle, which displays tribal art objects, puppets, masks, dolls, folk deities, and musical instruments and stages an excellent "puppet circus" from 6 to 7 pm. You can also make a pleasant excursion by bicycle to the beautiful royal Mewar *chhatris* at **Ahar**, three kilometers (just under two miles) east of town, where an interesting museum houses archaeological finds. For evening entertainment, traditional Rajasthani dances are performed from 7:30 pm every Tuesday, Thursday, and Saturday at the **Meera Kala Mandir**. ((0294) 23976 for more information.

GENERAL INFORMATION

The main Tourist Information Bureau, ((0294) 23605, is located at the Kajri Tourist Bungalow. Their daily city tours leave from here at 8:30 am and 1:30 pm. There is also an afternoon excursion to **Haldighati** (40 km, or 25 miles away), the site of an historic battle between Maharana Pratap Singh and Akbar; the sacred eighteenth-century shrine to Lord Krishna at **Nathdwara** temple (48 km, or 30 miles away), and the large eighteenth-century temple complex of **Eklingi**, 22 km (13.7 miles) from town. This five-hour tour leaves at 2:30 pm and costs US$2.50. There are also tourist offices at the airport and railway station.

CHITTAURGARH

Some 115 km (72 miles) east of Udaipur, the ancient Mewar capital of Chittaurgarh is the most famous and hallowed of all Rajasthan's fortress citadels. Situated on a 180-m (590-ft)-high precipice, this sprawling, battle-scarred, ghost-ridden fortress was sacked thrice, and thrice won back by the courageous Mewars. With its cannon-shattered battlements, carved marble memorials, and myriad sati palm prints, it is the very symbol of stoic Rajput heroism and sacrifice.

According to legend, the fortress was built by Bhim, one of the five Pandava heroes in the Hindu epic the *Maharabharata*. From the seventh century it was the capital of the Mewars, effectively becoming the ruling seat of Rajasthan and thus coveted by prospective invaders. Its long and traumatic history was a litany of brutal assault during which capitulation to the invading enemy was marked by grisly sacrifice. Preferring death to subjugation, its men drank draughts of opium, donned the saffron robes of

The towering Jai Stambha, or "Tower of Victory" in Chittaugurh.

martyrdom, and rode off for a final orgy of killing known as saka, while their women and children committed jauhaur — mass immolation on giant pyres. Yet great care was always taken to preserve the royal lineage so that the ruler's son and heir could return to lead a guerilla war against the usurpers of the Mewar domain.

The Muslim Sultan of Delhi, Alu-ud-din, was the first to sack Chittaurgarh in 1303, in his frenzied desire to abduct the beautiful Chittaur queen Padmini after having seen her unveiled face in a pool reflection. But his was a bitter victory, since the heroic queen threw herself into the flames beside her Rajput sisters. Chittaurgarh was plundered again in 1535 by the Gujarati sultan, Bahudur Shah; 32,000 Rajput soldiers died in battle, and 13,000 women immolated themselves. Just 30 years later, Chittaurgarh was crushed once more, this time irrevocably, by Akbar's armies, compelling Maharana Udai Singh to found his new capital of Udaipur.

Many visitors find Udaipur a convenient base for a visit to Chittaurgarh, rising early to catch the 5:30 am train, and returning either by express bus or train the same day. Since Chittaugarh has good rail and bus links, it is also a convenient stopping-off place on the rail journey to Jaipur (320 km, or 200 miles) via Ajmer (187 km, or 116 miles) and on the bus trip to Bundi (156 km, or 97 miles). If necessary, stay at **Panna Tourist Bungalow**, ((01472) 41238; it's close to the railway station.

You'll need at least three hours to explore the rambling ruins, which need an experienced guide to bring them alive. Either take the local tour, which starts at the Tourist Office in Janta Lodge at 7:30 am and lasts until 2:30 pm, or hire an approved guide from Chittaurgarh's fort-based Archaeological Survey Office to lead you through the main interest points — starting with their "office", the former **Fateh Prakash Palace**, a large wing of which has been converted into a museum with a rich collection of sculptures from Chittaurgarh's temples and buildings.

See the ruined fifteenth-century **Rana Kumbha Palace**, which houses a Shiva temple, elephant and horse stables, and vaulted underground cellars, in one of which it is thought Maharani Padmini committed *jauhaur*. Also see the Jain and Hindu temples, the beautiful seven-meter (23-ft) -high **Jai Stambha**, the "Tower of Victory" to the south, built to mark Kumbha's victory over the Sultan of Malwa in 1440, and the smaller, squat **Kirti Stambha**, "Pillar of Fame". Husks of ruined palaces are found everywhere, including **Padmini's Palace** at the eastern end of the fort.

MOUNT ABU

Mount Abu is an anomaly. It is Rajasthan's answer to Shimla or Ooty, a lush nineteenth-century hill station dotted with date palms and royal summer palaces, nestled 1,200 m (4,000 ft) up in the craggy, almost biblical-looking, landscape of the Aravallis, the home of the colorfully-clad tribal Bhils. It is also an important center for Jain pilgrimage, with an exquisite temple complex dating back to the eleventh and thirteenth centuries. During the mid-nineteenth century, it suddenly came into vogue as a princely retreat, sprouting stately mansions; later, during the First World War, the British transformed it into a military cantonment, primarily for recuperating shell-shocked soldiers and TB patients. All these influences — as well as its burgeoning popularity as a honeymoon destination for Gujarati Indians, with its rash of kitsch "love hotels" — make it an eccentric, beguiling place to visit.

The origins of Mount Abu are steeped in Hindu lore — it gets its name from "Arbuda", the serpent son of the Himalayas who supposedly rescued Shiva's bull which was stranded in a chasm here; it is also where the gods scooped out the oasis-like Nakki Lake with their "nakks" or nails. Mount Abu is as important to Rajput Hindus as Mount Olympus is to the Greeks for, according to myth, this was where the sage Vashisht lit a sacrificial fire from which the original Rajput warrior clans first emerged.

Like any Indian hill station, Mount Abu is at its most pleasant during the high summer months of March to June. During winter, when the rest of Rajasthan is at its best, Mount Abu can be downright freezing, so be sure to bring sweaters and socks.

ACCESS

Mount Abu can be a convenient place to stop before continuing on to Ahmedabad and Gujarat state. From Udaipur, 185 km (115 miles) away, it can be reached by train or by morning express bus — departing from Udaipur at 8 am and arriving at 2 pm. Book at Udaipur's bus stand or through Taldar Travels, ((0294) 28160, Taldar Building, opposite the Town Hall, whose agents wear stetsons and reflective sunglasses — the height of Udaipur fashion! If you arrive at Abu Road by train, you can either hop aboard a local bus or hire a jeep to make the 27-km (17-mile) winding journey up to Mount Abu. On arrival, you'll find yourself surrounded by pram to pushing "porters", all vying for the task of shunting your luggage to your hotel for a few rupees. Get around locally on foot, by the local "jeep" service, taxi, or by pony. RTDC-conducted morning and afternoon sightseeing tours leave from the Youth Hostel.

HOTELS

Like other hill stations, Mount Abu's hotels offer off-season discounts of up to 50 percent before Indian tourists start arriving in mid-April. Mount Abu has several "luxury" hotels, notably the five-star **Hotel Savera Palace**, ((029742) 3354, Sunset Road, and the three-star **Hotel Hilltone**, ((029742) 3112, located right near the bus station, but these are geared to the "flashy" tastes of Indian tourists. Foreign visitors tend to find the faded, slightly Gothic, elegance of former palace retreats more to their taste. However the nicest place to stay is **Hotel Bikaner Palace**, ((029742) 3121, Delwara Road, set amid leafy grounds with tennis courts and a private lake. Quaintly furnished rooms have nine-meter (30-ft) -high ceilings, hot showers, and are inexpensive. Very large Anglo-Indian meals are available in the former dance hall (look for the purdah slats above), and there is a billiards room in the lounge. **Connaught House**, Delwara Road, is the delightful former summer house of the British Resident attached to the ex-princely state of Marwar (Jodhpur). Owned by the Maharaja of Jodhpur, it has bougainvillea-sprayed bedroom cottages, each with complete privacy, good basic amenities, and simple Indian food. Rates: inexpensive. To book, write to the General Manager, Connaught House, care of Umaid Bhawan Palace, Jodhpur. A homely guesthouse option is the **Mount Hotel**, ((029742) 3150, Dilwara Road. Run by friendly Mrs Bharucha and her son, it serves good authentic Parsi and Indian dishes. If you're determined (and brave enough) to experience the interior of an Indian "love hotel", ask for a honeymoon suite at **Hotel Samrat**, ((029742) 3173, near the taxi stand, and revel in nylon leopard-skin sheets on a bed shaped like a chariot, "his" and "hers" heart-shaped pillows, Khajuraho-motif tiles, curtains, and bath-towels, and non-stop Hindi movies on TV!

Outside the hotels, it's worth sampling the best of Mount Abu's goldmine of excellent Gujarati fare. The town center is full of *thali*-cafés, whose generous platters cost US$1. One of the best of these is Kanak Dining Hall; otherwise stick to the string of friendly open-air eating places near the bus-stand, where barefoot boys in oversized jackets wait on tables. These places are good for spicy sweet ginger tea, *thalis*, *dosas*, and the addictive *pau bhaji* — a steaming hot mixture of pulverized potatoes, vegetables, garlic, ginger, and chillis served with a fried bun.

SIGHTSEEING

North of town, the **Dilwara Jain Temples** are the main attraction. Set on a hill in a mango tree grove, and built between the eleventh and thirteenth centuries, the temples are famous for their complex and intricate marble carvings. It's no exaggeration to say that these carvings alone are worth the journey to Mount Abu. They are so perfect, it is almost impossible to believe they were crafted from a sculptor's chisel. The temples, which deserve several visits, are most beautiful just before dusk. The

temple complex is open to non-Jains only between 12 noon and 8 pm; leather items — shoes, belts, bags, watch-straps, etc. — and menstruating females (as a bold sign declaims) are not permitted inside.

Otherwise, Mount Abu is a picturesque place for walking and relaxing. There are wonderful views from **Guri Shikar**, 15 km (nine miles) at 1,725 m (5,660 ft), the highest point in Rajasthan. At **Achalgarh**, 11 km (seven miles), there is an intriguing Shiva temple, with three stone buffaloes; and the rock-chiselled **Adhar Devi Temple** is reached by a flight of 200 steps. Closer to town are Sunset and Honeymoon points for stunning views and Nakki Lake for boating. The town itself is interesting to stroll around. The Tourist Office, ((029742) 3151, is opposite the bus station. Its opening hours are rather strange — from 7 to 10 am, 12 noon to 2 pm, and 5 to 8 pm — perhaps because there is a Retail Beer shop nearby selling every type of Indian beer to thirsty refugees from "dry" Gujarat.

Entrance hall of the exquisitely carved Dilwara Jain Temples at Mount Abu.

The
Mountain
Trail

SHIMLA

The former summer capital of the British Indian empire, Shimla has colonial ghosts, nineteenth-century cottages with potted geraniums, beautiful alpine scenery, crisp pine-scented air, and monkeys. It sprawls along a 12-km (7.5-mile)-long ridge, 2,200 m (7,218 ft) high in the northwest Himalayan foothills.

The setting for Rudyard Kipling's *Plain Tales From the Hills*, Shimla is thought to have derived its name from "Shamla", a title of the goddess Kali who is revered by local hill people. British officers stumbled on its exceptional scenic charms when driving invading Gurkhas from the region in 1819. Then, in 1822, one Major Kennedy started a trend by constructing permanent residence in Shimla.

The British developed an attachment to this remote Himalayan town that amounted almost to an obsession. During the summer months on the northern plains, government officers would develop a condition known as "Punjab head". The heat was so intense that efficient work and accurate decision-making became well-nigh impossible. Shimla soon became a glamorous summer bolt-hole for the Anglo-Indian elite, the heat-weary, and the invalid, complete with a busy social round of dinners, whist parties, picnics, amateur theatricals, and furtive assignations between young officers and so-called "grass widows", whose husbands labored on the burning plains below. Shimla gained respectability in 1864 when the viceroy Lord Lawrence visited and pronounced it the official summer capital, observing rather soberly, "I believe we shall do more work in one day here than five down in Calcutta". Thus began the great annual exodus of the viceroy with his guards, private staff, and public attendants, along with his secretariat, army headquarters, Foreign Office, the representative of the Indian princes, and a vast entourage of cumbersome file-cases hauled up by pony-drawn tongas, memsahibs, children, and traders. By 1904, the construction of the Kalka–Shimla railway finally provided easy access to the hill station.

Shimla's tiered ridge soon resembled a semi-suburban jumble of fanciful Anglo-Indian architectural styles — red-roofed Swiss chalets with names like Fairy Cottage and Windermere, Tudor and Georgian-style mansions, the Gothic tower of Christ Church with a bell made from a mortar captured in the second Sikh War, and palatial government buildings such as Barnes Court, Kennedy House, and Gordon Castle. The Viceregal Lodge was so luxurious — with a staff of 300 domestics and 100 cooks — that it was said Indian income tax had been invented to pay

for it. No carriages (excepting those of the viceroy and his retinue) were allowed in the center of town, known as the Mall, so residents were carried about in *jhampans*, curtained sedan chairs, or four-man rickshaws by hardy coolies. When Sir Edwin Lutyens, the architect of imperial New Delhi, went to Shimla in 1913, he was apparently appalled, and said, "If one was told the monkeys had built it all one could only say: What wonderful monkeys — they must be shot in case they do it again... ."

Shimla, now the state capital of Himachal Pradesh, has changed surprisingly little in appearance since the days when memsahibs gathered to gossip at Scandal Point. The town itself is very busy, lively and nostalgically "English", with quaint Raj-era hotels and buildings, and beautiful walks through Himalayan mountains thick with oak, deodar, and pine trees. It's a perfect place to indulge in fantasies of the Raj.

The best time to visit is from mid-April to October, the fragrant summer season when hyacinths, rhododendrons, violets, and lilies fill the meadows. Winters are bitterly cold and Shimla is carpeted in snow between December and March. Whatever the time of year, the nights are chilly.

ACCESS

Shimla's nearest airport is at 1,372 m (4,500 ft), and above a sheer drop, at Juberhatti, 22 km (14 miles) away. Vayudoot operates regular flights to and from New Delhi. A good alternative is to take the daily Indian Airlines flight, a train, or a bus to Chandigarh, then proceed the 110 km (68 miles) to Shimla by the charming narrow gauge *Kalka Mail* "toy train", which departs from Kalka, 24 km (15 miles) north of the Haryana state capital. The scenic six-hour journey winds up the original steep track that was built in 1903–1904, and is a collector's item for rail buffs. Shimla's station looks straight out of the series of children's book, *Noddy* with its pretty flower-boxes, gleaming brass, and spic and span coolies in bright red jackets. Several state and luxury coaches run from Delhi and Chandigarh daily, and the trip takes 10 and four hours respectively.

WHERE TO STAY

Shimla attracts droves of holidaying Indians and has a good range of hotels, lodges, and facilities. Accommodation rates drop by 30 to 50 percent during the cold off-season months between November and mid-April.

OPPOSITE: Onion-dome of rustic mosque in Srinagar's old district on the banks of the Jhelum River.

Stay at a choice of old Raj-era hotels which offer a delightful blend of colonial grandeur, eccentric service, and fussy décor with stunning views. In the top bracket, stay either at the **Oberoi Clarkes**, ((0177) 212991, or the **Hotel Cecil**, ((0177) 2073/6041-4, both moderately priced and located on the Mall. The Tudor-style **Woodville Palace Hotel**, ((0177) 72763, is very charming — my personal favorite — surrounded by pine trees right on the edge of town. It was used as a set in *The Jewel in the Crown* series adapted from Paul Scott's *Raj Quartet* by Granada Television. It has moderate rates, spacious period suites crammed with curios and mahogany furniture, plenty of

THE MOUNTAIN TRAIL

hot water, and a pretty garden for afternoon teas served by waiters in cummerbunds. Breakfasts are good, but if you value prompt service at other mealtimes, take a stroll down to the Mall to avoid tiresome waits in the dining room for tepid nursery-style Raj food. The inexpensive **Chapslee Hotel**, ((0177) 78242, is another time-warp gem, located in Lakkar Bazaar.

Cheaper accommodation is much less memorable, and tends to be filled with rowdy Indian honeymooners. Both the **Hotel Holiday Home**, ((0177) 72375, on Cart Road and the - **Hotel Mayur**, ((0177) 72392, behind Christ Church, have inexpensive, comfortable rooms.

OUT AND ABOUT

Shimla is a charming place, with plenty of atmosphere and invigorating country walks. Its

main forum is the crescent-shaped **Mall**, lined with stylish English buildings, ice-cream stalls, and souvenir shops, where everyone goes strolling. You can peer at sepia photographs in musty shop-fronts of 1930's Shimla debutantes and bristle-mustached officers, buy ornately carved walking sticks, Kulu shawls, discarded solar topees, or boxes of faded "at home" cards as souvenirs, and stop for refreshments in one of the many cafés and restaurants. The **South Indian Coffee House** serves excellent snacks and aromatic Mysore coffee.

At the top of the Mall, near the Ridge, is the Gothic **Christ Church**. Built in 1857, it is the second oldest church in northern India. Inside are beautiful stained-glass windows, murals, old oak pews, and fascinating plaques commemorating deceased army regiments. Sunday services are worth attending, just to see the resident organist furiously pounding out *We Plough the Fields and Scatter*. See the mock-Tudor **Gaiety Theater**, where Gilbert and Sullivan tunes were de rigueur, and the grand Scottish Baronial-style **Municipal Buildings**. The church is next to **Scandal Point**, the large open square which got its name 50 years ago when a dashing young Indian prince eloped with a young British memsahib from this spot on horseback. Steep terraces lead down to the crooked, zigzagging levels of **Middle** and **Lower Bazaars**, which brim with local handicraft stalls, cafés, and swarthy-featured Pahari hill tribes.

Visit the **State Museum** for good Pahari-school miniature paintings, costumes, textiles, jewelry, wood-carvings, bronzes, and stone-sculptures. It's open 10 am to 5 pm daily except Monday and every second Saturday. Also see the huge six-storied **Viceregal Lodge** on Summer Hill, which once hosted ceremonial balls and festivities and now houses India's Institute of Advanced Studies, with a fine reception hall and library.

For the best view of Shimla, make the exceedingly steep climb up to **Jackoo Hill** at 3,438 m (11,280 ft), which takes anything from 40 minutes for strapping mountaineers to two hours for mere mortals. At the top is a little temple dedicated to the monkey god Hanuman, presided over by its resident ash-smeared sadhu and his tribe of monkeys. In 1874, Shimla's Victorian society was appalled when a young aristocrat, Charles de Russeth, became a disciple of the Jackoo sadhu, spending his time chanting to monkeys. Known as the "leopard fakir" for his fur head-dress and loincloth, he was India's very first hippie.

Other pleasant walks include **Glen Forest**, four kilometers (two and a half miles) away, a pretty picnic spot with a waterfall near the Annandale racecourse and cricket ground;

Chadwick Falls, two kilometers (one and a quarter miles), for a 67-m (220-ft) waterfall; **Summer Hill,** five kilometers (three miles), to see the elegant Georgian house of **Rajkumari Amrit Kaur** that Mahatma Gandhi stayed in during his visit to Shimla; and **Prospect Hill,** five kilometers (three miles) away.

Good excursions by car or bus include **Wild-flower Hall,** 13 km (eight miles), built by Lord Kitchener in 1903 to rival the Viceregal Lodge, and used as a peaceful hotel; **Kufri,** 16 km (10 miles), a modest winter ski resort with equipment for hire; and **Chail,** 90 km (56 miles), with its summer palace of the Maharaja of Patiala, now run as a hotel, bird-sanctuary, and the world's highest cricket pitch.

GENERAL INFORMATION

The Tourist Office, ((0177) 78311, is located on the Mall and runs useful tours out to surrounding vantage points. The National Book Depot, just up from the Tourist Lift, sells the excellent *Tourist Guide to Shimla,* full of useful information.

THE KULU VALLEY AND MANALI

Kulu Valley, 205 km (127 miles) from Shimla, is famous for its beautiful scenery, apple orchards, and lively tribal music and dances. Enclosed by the last snow range of the Himalayas, with the Dhauladhar and Pir Panjal ranges running parallel to the south, the narrow terraced valley runs north from Mandi through Kulu and Manali all the way up to the Rohtang Pass, at 2,000 m (6,562 ft). The Beas River flows through its fertile, flower-strewn meadows. It's an excellent base for walks, trout fishing, and gentle treks up through pine and cedar forests. Gregarious local hill people dress in traditional home-spun shawls, Kulu caps, wool jackets, and moccasins — all of which make wonderful purchases in the bazaar. They like to work hard, pray hard, and play hard. The region boasts more than 6,000 carved wooden temples, and religious festivities involve much merry consumption of *chang* (the local rice beer) as temple deities are dressed up and borne on elaborate palanquins in torchlight processions.

It's worth making a special trip to the Kulu Valley to see the most exuberant of all Kulu's festivals, Dussehra (September/October), 10 days of exuberant revelry, folk dances, and music played on hill instruments such as *karnal, narsinghas, dhoi,* and drum. All over India, Dussehra is celebrated to commemorate Rama's victory over the demon king of Ravanna. But in Kulu, the god Raghunath is the victorious one

who is the focus of the festivities. Some 200 gods from neighboring villages are carried here on palanquins and chariots to pay him tribute, followed by nightly folk-dancing competitions.

You can reach Kulu's Bhuntar airport, 10 km (six miles) away, by regular Vayudoot flights from New Delhi and Chandigarh. Otherwise, fly to Chandigarh, then make the long 270-km (167-mile) — but exceptionally pretty — journey by road. From Shimla, three buses daily make the hair-raising 205-km (127-mile), eight to nine-hour trip past exhilarating views, perilous drops, and alarming road signs: "Arrive Late In This Life, Not Early In The Next", "Over-takers

Will Meet Undertakers", and "Married Couples, Divorce Speed".

Kulu has few lodging places and restaurants. Both the ITDC **Traveler's Lodge,** ((01902) 79, and the **Kulu Valley Resort,** ((01902) 223 offer moderately priced and comfortable rooms with attached bathrooms and good restaurants. Many travelers prefer to base themselves at **Manali,** a small, picturesque hill station, 42 km (26 miles) — two hours — from Kulu, with better accommodation. The top-bracket hotels include the **Ashok Traveler's Lodge** ((01902) 2331, rates: moderate), **Log Huts** ((01902) 2439, rates: moderate), **Hotel Highland** ((01902) 2399, and **John Banon's Guest House** ((01902) 35, rates: moderate), with well-furnished suites, good food, and wonderful mountain views.

In Kulu, there are pleasant walks to the main seventeenth-century Raghunathji Temple, the Vaishno Devi Temple, and the Bijli Mahadev Temple. There is a good Himachal Pradesh State Museum. Also see two former Kulu capitals, one at Naggar with a castle (now a resthouse) and Jagatsukh, the earlier capital, with many temples.

While in Manali, see nearby **Old Manali Village** and the fourteenth-century wooden

ABOVE: These Kashmiri schoolgirls seem to require little distraction to be lured away from their studies.

Hadimba Devi Temple. The Himalayan Mountaineering Institute can offer advice for treks and has equipment for hire and Sherpas to guide. Trout-fishing licenses are issued through the Tourist Office from the Director of Fisheries, Dehra Gopipur. Good two-day trekking excursions include Hanuman Tibba at 5,929 m (19,452 ft) and to the Rohtang Pass at 4,000 m (13,123 ft). Other worthwhile treks are to Malana, Parbati, Solang, and Seraj valleys and up the Deo Tibba, at 6,000 m (19,685 ft). Beyond the Kulu Valley is the Kangra Valley, with its impressive Kangra fort; further on is Dharmsala, where the Dalai Lama lives in exile with a community of Tibetan refugees.

KASHMIR

Ever since the Mughal emperors made the Vale of Kashmir their summer haven, successive conquerors have fallen captive to the legendary beauty of this land. Nestled high in the Himalayas in India's far north, this lake-studded valley was the "Pearl of Hind" to the Mughals and the playground for the British Raj — a land of lofty snowcapped peaks, alpine forests, lily-strewn waterscapes, orchards of spring-time blossoms, and patchwork meadows of riotous wildflowers.

Kashmir's spectacular natural scenery and bracing alpine climate attract travelers all year round to indulge in nostalgic memories of the Raj on Srinagar's houseboats, or for trekking, trout fishing, and skiing in the Himalayan mountains. Jawaharlal Nehru, himself a Kashmiri, wrote of the land's "strange enchantment" and "fairy magic", and certainly Kashmir feels less like a part of India than a strange Oriental fable.

Nothing gives this impression more than the Kashmiris themselves. Men wear wide-cloaked *chogas,* which in the cold season conceal *kangris,* the small wicker-work baskets of burning coals. Sturdy barefoot urchins rattle their horse-drawn *tongas* through the poplar-lined avenues. And young women wearing brightly patterned layers of garments and candelabra earrings can be startlingly beautiful, with almond-shaped eyes and Tartar cheekbones.

Jammu and Kashmir state is made up of three distinct areas, each very different not only in landscape but also in the heritage, language, and religion of the people.

In the very south, at the periphery of Punjab's hot plains before the foothills of the Himalayas, lies Jammu city, once the stronghold

OPPOSITE: Moored *shikaras* on the glassy surface of Dal Lake, Srinagar.

of feudalistic Hindu and Sikh Dogra rajas, and now a winter capital. To the north, across dense, forested ravines and steep mountain passes, lies Kashmir Valley, an oval plateau 1,500 m (5,000 ft) above sea level, framed by three massive Himalayan ranges — the Karakoram, Zanskar, and Pir Panjal. Srinagar, the state's summer capital, is nestled amid the valley's lakes, meadows, and floating gardens. The third main part of the state, the remote and arid region of Ladakh, is at the northeastern border with China where the 7,000-m (23,000-ft) -high peaks of the Zanskar Range are found. Sometimes referred to as "Little Tibet", Ladakh still looks and feels like a medieval, hermetic Buddhist kingdom, with ancient monasteries hewn into the mountain crags, legions of red-robed monks, and prayer flags fluttering everywhere.

Jammu and Kashmir is 94 percent Muslim, and the residents hold that their cultural links to Central Asia, Afghanistan, Persia, and the Middle East are stronger than those to mostly Hindu India. The area's rich history as a major trading center along the ancient Silk Road is reflected in the potpourri of appearances: sharp — almost Semitic — profiles, fair skin, tawny hair, and hazel eyes.

The region's recorded history stretches back to the early second century BC, when it was renowned as an ancient land of scholars and mystics. Emperor Ashoka (269–232 BC) converted its inhabitants to Buddhism, and Kashmiri missionaries were largely responsible for spreading the doctrine across the mountain passes of the Silk Road to Central Asia, China, and Tibet. A Hindu heyday followed in the seventh and eighth centuries with a line of Karkota kings who gave Kashmir its first impressive monuments and cities. But from the tenth to the fourteenth century, Kashmir entered a dark epoch of feudalistic disarray, in which power passed from a line of ruthless commanders to a Muslim Tibetan prince. When the prince died in 1338, Shah Mir usurped the kingdom and founded the Sultan dynasty. The eighth and most celebrated sultan was Zainul-Abidin — known as Badshah, or Great King — who encouraged studies in Hindu and Buddhist philosophy and patronized literature, dance, and music. Every Kashmiri artisan regards Badshah as a kind of patron saint, for he introduced new arts such as shawl embroidery, carpet making, papier mâché, silver work, and carving, and invited entire guilds of craftsmen in Persia and Samarkand to settle in the valley.

The Mughal emperor Akbar conquered the region in 1857. Declaring Kashmir "my private garden", he amused himself by boating, waterfowling, and indulging in eccentricities such as seeing how many of his valets could fit inside a hollow *chenar* plane tree — 34 was the impressive total! Four generations of Mughal emperors made Kashmir their summer idyll, creating elaborate pleasure gardens, delicate marble pavilions, and intricate irrigation systems still in use today, and eulogizing the vale in poems, songs, and paintings. In the meantime, they brought nearly all of the population under the Muslim faith.

As Mughal power waned in the eighteenth century, Afghan warlords occupied the area from 1752 to 1819, when they were ousted by Ranjit Singh, who conquered the valley and annexed it to his Punjab kingdom. After losing the first Anglo-Sikh war in 1846, the Sikhs could not afford the indemnity of 500,000 imposed by the British, and instead offered them Kashmir. The Dogra Maharaja of Jammu offered London twice the amount, and became the ruler of the combined states of Jammu and Kashmir. His descendants ruled under the British until Independence in 1947.

The strategically situated state has been a battleground in 1948, 1965, and 1971 between India and Pakistan, who still contest Kashmir's sovereignty. Troops from both sides frequently exchange gunfire at the restricted frontier areas, and a tense stand-off is in force at Siachen Glacier, the world's highest battleground at 5,800 m (19,000 ft). At the same time, a section of Kashmir near Ladakh is under dispute between India and China, and is another source of regional tension.

SRINAGAR

Visitors who arrive by air from India's hot and dusty plains often find Srinagar's cool alpine air, chenar-shaded meadows, and soaring snow-clad mountains nothing less than a revelation. With its lake-moored houseboats, Mughal gardens, mosques, and the lure of the nearby Himalayan mountains, Srinagar is easily the most popular destination in northern India and the perfect base from which to explore the rest of Kashmir.

Srinagar, or "city of beautiful scenery", is thought to have originated some 2,000 years ago as a hamlet founded by emperor Ashoka when his daughter Charumati took a fancy to Dal Lake during a pilgrimage to the area. The present city was established in the sixth century by the feudal king Raja Pravarasen II, who created many of the serpentine waterways that still wriggle through the city like backdoor entrances to the sprawling Dal Lake and the smaller, more secluded, Nagin Lake.

Srinagar's old quarters on the banks of the Jhelum River, with their labyrinthine alleys and crooked, Tyrolean-looking houses, appear little changed since the reign of the Mughals.

ACCESS

Most travelers prefer to fly directly to Srinagar, as the overland routes can be arduous. The valley is also a convenient starting point for trips to Ladakh in the northeast and to the trekking trails and hill stations of Himachal Pradesh in the southeast.

Srinagar can be reached by direct flights from Delhi, Ahmedabad, Amritsar, Bombay, and Leh. The Srinagar—Leh flight, which operates twice a week, is one of the world's most spectacular short plane rides, as it glides across snowcapped Himalayan summits. A daily flight service connects Srinagar and Jammu, 293 km (180 miles) away. Srinagar's airport is 18 km (11 miles) out of town, and taxis charge about US$5 each way.

Srinagar's nearest railhead is Jammu, which has direct connections with all parts of the country. Four trains run daily to and from Delhi. The 720-km (450-mile) -trip takes from 10 to 13 hours; a comfortable overnight sleeper is recommended.

There are plenty of "luxury video" buses from Delhi, but this 30-hour marathon must rate as one of India's most grueling journeys. The bus journey between Srinagar and Jammu takes between 10 and 14 hours and has a notorious record of bad accidents. Before departure, it's common to see a skimpily-clad fakir with his holy oil-lamp sprinkle protective water and blossoms on the passive-faced passengers, and place a garland of fresh flowers around the gaudy portraits of Hindu gods on the dashboard. Happily reassured, the driver flicks on his static-laden transistor to its full, mind-numbing, volume, slams his foot down on the accelerator, and takes off on a kamikaze joyride past stunning scenery and ominous road signs — "Is Your Honeymoon Worth Death?" and "Don't Drive So Fast, Your Life Is Waiting." The alternative is to take a taxi, although this works out much more expensive than the airfare.

State buses leave Srinagar and Jammu early each morning. These vary from Rs 120 "super deluxe" to Rs 50 ordinary class. During the peak season, these buses are often sold out days in advance, so try to pre-book seats through the Tourist Reception Centre.

WHEN TO GO

Unlike most of India, Kashmir is transformed by each passing season: harsh snowbound winters, abundant springs, idyllic hot summers, and mellow autumns ablaze with burnished copper, scarlet, and golden-brown leaves. Kashmir is at its most beautiful between April and May, when the melting snow cleanses the lakes, the flower-carpeted meadows are drenched with color, and the almond, walnut, apple, pear, cherry, and apricot orchards burst into fragrant blossoms. The best months for trekking, trout fishing, and water-sports are June and July. In August, Srinagar's lakes are covered with water lilies, the blooms of which are known as "Buddhist flowers". It is scarf-and-sweater weather by mid-October and the winter ski season lasts from December to February.

HOUSEBOATS

By the late nineteenth century, the British had come to regard Kashmir as their cool Himalayan retreat during the furnace-like heat of the Indian summer. But the ruling maharaja balked at this seasonal invasion of his earthly paradise and prohibited the British from owning or building houses on his land, hoping that this would stem the flow of officers, crinolined memsahibs, and entourages of swaddled infants, nannies, and servants. With inventive literal-mindedness, the British created a floating colony of luxurious, carved mock-bungalows on Srinagar's Dal and Nagin lakes, thus launching the fashion for houseboating.

From these drifting cedar-scented Victorian parlors, they issued "at home" cards, drilled their Kashmiri cooks in Mrs Beeton's gastronomic legacy, and went for pleasure cruises in shikaras, the hand-paddled, canopied taxi-gondolas with curtains and mattress-sized cushions on which to recline. Few of the earliest British houseboats survive, but there are many dating from the 1930's, with scrupulously preserved walnut-wood furniture, faded brocade draperies, and biscuit-tin landscapes hung on gingerbread paneling. Most of the houseboats cramming Srinagar's bustling waterways are modern and roomier imitations, with more dependable electricity and plumbing and, during winter, better central heating than the old ones. Their owners compete to woo tourists with colorful awnings, bright flower baskets, and outlandish names such as *Texan Dream, Love-in-the-Mist, Little Dubai,* and *HMS Fairyland* tacked to the roof.

At secluded moorings in the mossed backwaters of lovely Nagin Lake just west of Dal Lake or at the north end of Dal, languid houseboating is a holiday in itself, with somewhat idiosyncratic service provided by the Kashmiri owner's family who live a few steps away in another boat or on the shore. Houseboats range from five-bedroom "five-star deluxe" palaces to modest one-bedroom boats suitable for a couple or a lone traveler. A typical houseboat has two or three bedrooms with attached bathrooms, and dining and lounge rooms fronted by a cupola-style veranda; the more elaborate boats have gaily caparisoned sun decks with chairs, tables, and umbrellas.

There are more than 1,300 boats scattered across the lakes (950 of which are officially approved), so finding one to your taste is not difficult. Travel agents can arrange bookings for a room on a houseboat, or set up special package deals at fixed rates, in which case someone will meet you at Srinagar's airport and

stop at any houseboat that catches your eye, preferably with a "To Let" sign slung across its balcony. Decide first which of the two main houseboat areas you prefer: the livelier and more congested flotilla in lower Dal Lake, running parallel to the Boulevard and just a short shikara hop from the city, or the serene isolated setting of Nagin Lake. On Dal, the most pleasant location for houseboating is along the east-facing backwaters some distance offshore behind Nehru Park. The best location on Nagin is the eastern shore, which has spectacular sunsets and views across snowcapped mountains to the west.

whisk you to your destination with minimal fuss. But this method requires you to rent a houseboat unseen, which is much more of a gamble than booking a hotel room because a holiday aboard a houseboat involves being on fairly intimate terms with the owner, the staff, and often other guests as well, as the living rooms are frequently communal. For this reason, you may prefer to make the choice yourself.

Srinagar's houseboat touts are notoriously pushy, and even turn up at Delhi's airport to accost Kashmir-bound tourists. It is best to consult the Tourist Reception Centre's houseboat bureau to view a list of recommended boats, from deluxe to D-class *doongas*. The office also provides rental rates and a local map which is a useful guide to Srinagar's liquid highways and land layout. Then proceed to Boulevard Road and hire a *shikara*; simply ask the boatman to

During your houseboat "inspection tour", you'll meet enough houseboat owners, staff, and other guests to gain a strong sense of which arrangement is likely to suit you best, as well as some idea of the prevailing rates.

Welcomgroup's five-star houseboats on Nagin Lake are expensive with a choice of rooms and suites, all plushly furnished. The Welcomgroup Gurkha Houseboats can be booked though any Welcomgroup hotel or through PO Box 57, Nagin Lake, ((0194) 75229.

Officially, room rent aboard a deluxe boat costs about US$20, but you'll probably pay US$30, which includes three meals plus "bed" and "four o'clock" tea, as well as free use of the houseboat's *shikara* and dugout canoe.

If privacy is the most important consideration, you may wish to rent a more modest, often equally comfortable, B-class boat, some of which have only one bedroom, but are inexpensive and perfect for a couple. For travelers on a tight budget, D-class houseboats offer comfortable rooms for as little as US$2, and every impish *shikara* boy will know where to find one.

Before you agree on a price with the houseboat owner, make sure that you both understand the terms so as to avoid ill-feeling if mysteriously inflated bills are produced at the end of your stay. Make sure the rate includes ship-to-shore *shikara* rides and, if desired, three meals a day, on the understanding that missed lunches or dinners will be deducted from your bill. Finally, don't let the houseboat owner cajole you

sunbathing nude here. The maharaja capitulated only when Pathan tribesmen from newly created Pakistan stormed the valley in 1948 and Srinagar was about to fall. As he awaited deliverance by Indian troops, he passed the time by ordering a particularly extravagant meal. As he wandered off for a siesta, he nonchalantly instructed his aides, "If they are not here by three, please shoot me." Luckily, he was saved just in time!

The stately 1930's mansion seems to sprawl endlessly, tempting more than one guest to contemplate bicycling down its hallways. The renovated rooms have a comfortable colonial

into paying in advance, which can put you at the mercy of lackadaisical service or mediocre cooking — pay only by the day. Spring, summer, and autumn are the months for delightful, scenic houseboating — not Kashmir's bitterly cold winters, when the houseboats become ice-palaces wedged amidst gray slushy snow.

WHERE ELSE TO STAY

If you sleep easier knowing there is solid ground beneath you, the **Oberoi Palace**, ((0194) 79517 or 71251, is the grandest of all Kashmir's hotels. The former maharaja Sir Hari Singh's palace is set in eight hectares (20 acres) of blossoming gardens with panoramic views across Dal Lake. Mountbatten, during a visit to persuade the maharaja to accede to India upon Independence, shocked the palace servants by

atmosphere, but are expensive — doubles, including breakfast, cost US$80. Afternoons on the front lawn are the Oberoi's forte — perfect for sipping tea and nibbling delicious macaroons from tiered trays while watching bright-orange *shikaras* ripple the lake's mirrored surface. The dining room is Srinagar's best, serving Mughali, Chinese, and European cuisine, and Kashmiri dishes on request. The charming Harlequin Bar is perfect for sundowners. Tucked within the green rolling lawns are a six-hole golf course and a swimming pool.

The **Centaur Lake View Hotel**, ((0194) 77601 or 75631, is a massive, haphazardly designed

---

ABOVE: Experiencing domestic bliss aboard a luxury houseboat is one of Kashmir's most profound pleasures. OPPOSITE: Elaborate gingerbread façades characterize Srinagar's houseboats.

five-star complex set among five hectares (13 acres) on Dal's lakeside, about a half-kilometer (one-third of a mile) from the Oberoi. During the peak season, it is filled with affluent Indian families who are attracted by its recreational facilities — water-skiing, windsurfing, tennis, swimming pool, table tennis, and a private jetty for speedboat and shikara rides — and its secluded holiday camp atmosphere. The restaurants serve Indian and Chinese cuisine. Avoid the coffee shop with its team of absent-minded waiters. The lakeview rooms are best. Rates: moderate.

The **Hotel Broadway**, ((0194) 75621, is in the center of modern Srinagar on Maulana Azad

Road, a short walk from the Tourist Centre and the city's shops, banks, and offices. It's more suited to business travelers than tourists, and is efficient and comfortable with two decent restaurants, one opening on to a secluded garden with a pool. Rates: moderate.

Along Boulevard Road is a row of clean, utilitarian hotels, like Korean lodges, with uniform rooms at roughly similar prices. Try **Hotel Shahenshah Palace**, **Hotel Tramboo Continental**, ((0194) 73914, or **Zamrud Hotel**, ((0194) 73123. **Hotel New Shalimar**, ((0194) 74427, with its rose-trellis archway and café-restaurant set on reclaimed land facing Boulevard Road, is reached by *shikara* and is a good cheap budget hotel option.

The **Hotel Dar-Es-Salam**, a delightful lime-white two-story villa set in a restful garden on Nagin Lake's secluded shore, is a restful oasis

much favored by vacationing diplomats. There are 14 spacious and comfortable double rooms with lake views. Rates: inexpensive. To reserve, write to Hotel Dar-Es-Salam, Nagin Lake, Nandpora Rainawari, Srinagar 190003.

Welcomgroup has renovated the Raj-era **Nedous Hotel**, near the Golf Club on Maulana Azas Road. The russet-colored manor held afternoon quartets and ballroom dances during its heyday in the 1930's, and rivals the new five-star Oberoi Palace.

GETTING AROUND

Nothing is more restful than a *shikara* ride for exploring Srinagar's lakes and winding canals. Or you can borrow your houseboat's canoe and paddle about on your own.

On land, Srinagar is too spread out to be explored conveniently on foot; bicycles are an excellent way of getting around. It is a real pleasure to cycle along the wide lakeside avenues lined with tall chenar trees, past lush paddy fields to the Mughal Gardens, or along the narrow causeway from beneath the Hari Parbat Fort which cuts right across Dal Lake to the Nishat gardens. The many bicycle-hire shops in the Dalgate and Boulevard Road area charge about US$1 for daily hire. Avoid the near-suicidal route through the central city, with its traffic snarls and pollution.

The ubiquitous auto-rickshaws are easy to find and the best option for short city hops, as taxis are more than three times the price. Both rickshaws and taxis are un-metered, so it's necessary to haggle over the price before setting off. Official taxi fares are listed at most taxi stands, as well as at the airport and the Tourist Reception Centre. For excursions out of Srinagar — to Pahalgam, Gulmarg, Sonamarg, Jammu, or even Leh — use a taxi, or for a fraction of the cost, take a bus tour organized by the Tourist Reception Centre.

SRINAGAR A LA CARTE

The rogue-faced *khan-samah*, or cook-boy, who shuffles on to your houseboat at mealtimes can produce perfect breakfasts of fresh crusty Kashmiri bread, boiled eggs, and coffee, but most other meals consist of bland Raj-era, Anglo-Indian fare. If this begins to pall, try to persuade the cook to prepare Persian-influenced Kashmiri food — rice *biriyanis* perhaps, or cigar-shaped shish kebabs marinated in spices and grilled over a makeshift charcoal fire. Given advance warning, some cooks will serve a few of the 36 or so meat courses that make up the Kashmiri *wazwan*, the ceremonial Kashmiri feast prepared for births, circumcisions, weddings, and religious occasions. *Wazas* — chief cooks who get their huge copper cooking pots from an area called Wazpura — pound meat into sausage-like pulp for the popular meatball sized *guzhtaba* and *rista,* served respectively in a creamy sauce and a pepper-red curry. Other favorites include *dhaniwal korma* (mutton rubbed with coriander and cooked in yogurt) and *tabaq-mazh* (grilled spare ribs cooked in yogurt, cashew nuts, poppy seeds, and onions). Try *phirni,* a dessert of vermicelli, crushed almonds, and milk, and the honey-sweet Kashmiri tea known as *kahwa,* flavored with saffron, almonds, and cardamom.

You can sample these specialties ashore at the **Oberoi Palace** (where lunch or dinner for two will cost about US$15), at the **Hotel Broadway,** or the popular **Mughal Darbar** restaurant near the GPO on Shervani Road. **Adhoo's,** one kilometer (half a mile) down the road towards the city, was once famed for its authentic Kashmiri cuisine, but it has become distinctly shabby of late.

Srinagar has few proper restaurants outside the hotels, but there are plenty of excellent, and cheap, café-style eateries along Boulevard Road. The Kashmir Darbar, towards Dalgate, is a favorite tourist's haunt with its frothy cappuccinos, cheese-dripping pizzas, and apple pie, as well as Kashmiri *wazwan* dishes.

The place to try Kashmir's unusual hybrid Chinese cuisine, influenced by nearby Ladakh and Tibet, is **Daitchi,** a gem of a restaurant on Boulevard Road, which serves delicious fried *mo-mo* pastries, Chicken Hong Kong, shredded lamb with hot garlic sauce, and dessert pancakes. It's run by a dedicated Tibetan family who whisk steaming platters on to the table with astonishing speed. A full three-course meal, with rice and Chinese tea, costs around US$5 and is incredibly good value. **Lhasa's,** off the main road close by, also serves good Chinese food; its outdoor garden is packed every night.

For good cheap food, try the **Hotel Paradise Restaurant,** also off Boulevard Road, for excellent South-Indian snacks and Gujarati *thalis.* The **Dal Rock** restaurant at Dalgate serves reliably good Mughlai, Kashmiri, and Chinese dishes, although the dark mirrored interior with its modern flashing lights — ultra-chic by Srinagar's standards — is rather gloomy and cave-like.

Tao's alfresco café is a charming oasis just off the city's Bund promenade on Shervani Road. In this leafy cul-de-sac, you can slump in colorful cane chairs in a garden filled with flowering shrubs, and order cold drinks and snacks. Chinese dishes, notably Manchurian soup, sweet and sour chicken with pineapple, and chow mein, are also served.

The **Lake View** cafeteria is in a picturesque location at the foot of the lakeside Shankaracharya Hill, opposite Nehru Park. Refreshments are served all day on its umbrella-shaded veranda and in the large garden, where groups of devout Muslims gather to pray at twilight. Just opposite is **Nehru Park**, a small island restaurant lit up prettily at night.

Fluffy fresh macaroons and biscuits are a special treat in Kashmir, and there's a score of good bakeries near Dalgate; two of the best are **Jan's Bakery**, beneath the Dal Rock restaurant, and **Moonlight Confectionery**, opposite the Dalgate bridge. Buy a bagful of their specialty,

meringue-topped date slice, to eat with your afternoon tea on the houseboat.

SIGHTSEEING

Shikara Rides and Floating Gardens

Srinagar's pleasures are concentrated on its placid, spring-fed Dal and Nagin lakes, where *shikara* rides prove an addictively indolent form of transport. Spend an hour or two combing the city's backwaters, a network with watery tentacles all along the Jhelum River. The meandering canals are crossed by small Mughal bridges which wobble with the overhead traffic and are flanked by medieval-looking, half-timbered houses buried in bulrush thickets.

Off these liquid corridors are the backwater bayous, where the local river families live in clusters of derelict *doongas* (plain wooden housebarges) with toddlers, mongrels, and chickens scrambling beneath the lines of washing hung on the decks. Gypsy-featured locals dart about in narrow skiffs like dragonflies, collecting water weed, fishing for carp, and stopping to gossip awhile at tiny shops raised on stilts.

ABOVE and OPPOSITE: Cruising by *shikara* provides the most romantic form of transport across Dal and Nagin lakes.

You can turn a *shikara* outing into an all-day expedition by crossing Dal Lake to the **Shalimar Bagh Gardens**. Then paddle across to the southern shore past the **Floating Gardens**, where the thick, buoyant mats of bulrushes are covered with earth and anchored by poles in the deep water. Here you can watch the locals leaning out of their dinghies to harvest cucumbers and melons from these floating beds. The trip takes five or six hours. A *shikara* can be hired at the bottom of the Boulevard for about US$7.

If you have another full day to spare, hire a *shikara* to take you across to the secluded bird sanctuary on the northwest side of Nagin Lake, where Himalayan dippers, golden forktails, and golden orioles circle above the endless banks of flesh-colored water lilies amid dramatic views of the mountain-flanked valley. Go well prepared with a packed lunch, binoculars, and plenty to read, as it takes six hours to reach your destination and three hours to loop back to Dal Lake.

Try to wake early, at about 5 am, to catch the dawn before heading by *shikara* for the floating fruit, flower, and vegetable market where most of Srinagar's fresh produce is bartered and sold. It's a churning riot of activity, with echoing shouts and curses as wizened figures strain to maneuver skiffs loaded with vast stacks of green turnips, wispy yellow mustard-seed plants, and scarlet aubergines. Flowers give this market a festive charm — fragrant bundles of fresh dew-sprinkled wildflowers, hyacinths, and tulips destined for houseboat drawing rooms.

Until your *shikara* reaches upper Dal or secluded Nagin, you'll find that wily merchants are constant companions, deftly nosing their well-laden boats alongside. Hesitate for a second too long and you'll be at the mercy of a well-practiced sales patter — in pidgin French, Italian, German, or Japanese — and held hostage by sinewy arms unraveling carpets or dangling necklaces. All sorts of things turn up on these *shikara* shops — ethnic jewelry, cheap trinkets, Tibetan prayer wheels, precious stones wrapped in chamois, embroidered cloth, carpets, papier mâché boxes, flower seeds, saffron — as well as on the floating supermarkets manned by young urchins with sing-song cries of "cash-shoe-nuts, chocy-ice, flute-juice"! Although it's fun to browse, you'll need to bargain hard.

Mughal Gardens

The pleasure gardens left by the Mughal emperors are as evocative of these legendary rulers as the more famous Red Fort in Delhi or the Taj Mahal in Agra. Kashmir was their summer playground, where they could breathe rose-scented air, gaze across the lake to the snowcapped mountains, frolic with an entourage of saffron-skinned maidens, and — like lotus-eaters — banish thoughts of the hot and dusty plains below.

Scattered alongside upper Dal Lake, the two most beautiful gardens are the Shalimar and the Nishat Bagh, both pavilion-pieces with fountains, water-channels, cascades, and formal quadrangles of terraced wildflowers. By far the most rewarding way of exploring these gardens is by bicycle, which enables you to admire the picturesque scenery at your leisure. Set out in the quiet cool of early morning, when the lake's glassy surface shimmers with diving kingfishers. Glide along the Boulevard, and then simply follow the curving avenues which skirt Dal Lake, past fruit orchards, fields of the bluish spinach-like *haq*, and tiny villages with waving urchins. Alternatively, Shalimar-bound buses leave from Dalgate's main bus-stand — an enjoyable and erratic half-hour journey with villagers, baskets of vegetables, and chickens for company.

The **Shalimar Gardens**, 15 km (nine miles) away, were built in 1616 by the emperor Jehangir as a "garden of love" for his beloved wife, Nur Jehan.

There is a pleasant café in the gardens, where you can watch photographers transform day-tripping city honeymooners into giggling Kashmiri rustics by draping them in traditional wedding finery for coveted family album pictures. In the evenings from 9 to 10 pm during May to October, there is a *son et lumière* show which recounts in English the romance of Emperor Jehangir and Queen Nur. Like all gardens in Srinagar, it is open from sunrise to sunset.

If you're on a bicycle, you will already have passed the second garden, **Nishat Bagh**, or "garden of bliss", five kilometers (three miles) back toward the city. This larger and more ambitious version of the Shalimar was laid out in 1633 by Nur Jehan's brother, Asaf Khan, two years after Nur's death. Set on the lakeside slopes of the Zabarwan mountains, it has steep flights of terraces, leafy walkways, waterfalls, and pavilions. In the distance you'll see Hazratbal Mosque's shimmering marble-white dome against the mist-wrapped Pir Panjal mountains.

These gardens have formed the backdrop to countless Hindi blockbuster movies, which usually manage to include a scene where the heroine — a chaste, doe-eyed starlet in a flowing sari — strikes soulful poses in a leafy bower.

Unfortunately, the oldest garden, **Nasim Bagh**, or "garden of the morning breeze", planned by Akbar in 1586, has become run-down, and few people bother to travel the extra 12 km (7.5 miles) to see it.

Toward the Oberoi Palace lies **Cheshma Shahi**, or "royal spring". The smallest of the gardens, it was begun by Jehangir and completed in 1632 by Shah Jehan, who added vineyards, fountains, and tanks. Its spring is believed to produce waters with magically tonic properties. Set in the slopes above are the ruins andgardens of **Pari Mahal**, once a Buddhist monastery and later converted into a school of astrology by Shah Jehan's son, Dara Shikoh. Stroll here at dusk when the ruins are illuminated, the gardens are at their most picturesque, and the resident peacocks begin their mournful chorus.

Mosques and Monuments

Srinagar's chaotically picturesque old city looks barely changed since the Middle Ages — a jumble of cobbled bazaars, almost Tudor-style multistoried houses built of withered timbers held together by sun-dried mud, and antique wooden mosques. Auto-rickshaws are best for negotiating this Muslim quarter, as would-be cyclists in pursuit of mosques in these twisting alleys risk collisions with impassive cows, a bevy of *burqa*-clad matrons, or stacks of Kashmiri turnips.

If you can, visit Srinagar's mosques on a Friday, the Muslim holy day, when they are full of Muslim men reciting the scriptures of the Koran. Stop first at the city's oldest mosque, within the heart of the old city on the banks of the muddy Jhelum River about six kilometers (a little less than four miles) from Dalgate. Situated within a peaceful graveyard, the **Shah Hamdan Mosque** has an extraordinary exterior of ornate carvings and painted papier mâché. Built between 1373 and 1398, it is named after a prominent Sufi from Persia, whose influence led to the peaceful conversion of millions of Hindus to Islamic mysticism during the fourteenth century.

Like a fanciful illustration for an exotic fairy tale, the mosque's interior glitters with still-bright seventeenth-century papier mâché lacquered colonnades, latticed stairs, whimsical stained glass, and European glass chandeliers. The building signifies the five daily prayers offered to Allah, having five walls, five arches, and a repetition of the number five throughout. Burqa-covered Muslim women file into the screened purdah quarter adjacent to the mosque to whisper their prayers, but neither they nor any non-Muslim are allowed inside — so you will have to content yourself with peering through the doorway, although it's worth visiting regardless.

By rickshaw, the **Jamia Masjid** is less than five minutes away, the largest and most popular mosque in Kashmir. Giant speakers strapped to its square-shaped minarets send the muezzin's cry booming to the faithful across Dal Lake.

Originally built by Sultan Sikandar in 1400, and expanded by his son Zain-ul-Abidin, it was razed to the ground by fire three times and rebuilt each time, although it still retains the original immense deodar pillars, 15 m (50 ft) high, carved from whole trees.

Today's Indo-Saracenic structure can accommodate up to 10,000 worshipers in its peaceful inner courtyard during the main Muslim festival, Id-ul-Fitr, which celebrates the end of Ramadan fasting. Clamber to the top of the minarets for a muezzin's-eye-view of the city.

Along the towering ridge of nearby **Sharika Hill** are the crumbling ruins of the eighteenth-

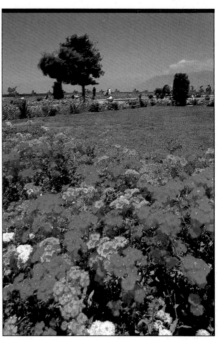

century **Hari Parbat Fort**, built by Atta Mohammad Khan, an Afghan governor. Legend has it that the hill was formed after the goddess Parvati threw a pebble from the heavens, which grew as it fell to crush the wicked water demon, Jalobhava, who dwelt in the depths of a huge lake. Villagers claim that the stones strewn across Hari Parbat are all incarnations of gods from the almost-limitless Hindu pantheon. The emperor Akbar built the surrounding ramparts from local gray limestone in the late sixteenth century, beautifying them with fragrant groves of almond trees. It's worth the invigorating climb for its heady vista across the Kashmir Valley, but there's little to see here. The fort is now an Indian Army watch post, and you'll

ABOVE: Spring blooms at the Shalimar Gardens just outside Srinagar.

need permission from the Director of Tourism to visit.

Continuing along the Sharika hillside and proceeding down the long Gurudwara Naidyat Road, you'll emerge on Dal Lake's western bank. You'll see the elegant white marble **Hazratbal Mosque** in the distance, its Ottoman-style dome flanked by a single minaret like a finger pointed heavenward. Built on the site of the original 600-year-old shrine, it contains the valley's most sacred possession — a strand of the Prophet Mohammed's hair, or the *Moe-e-Muqaddas*, brought to India in 1635 from Medina. The Holy Hair disappeared in December

1963, and black flags flew from houses across the valley. The ensuing riots held the state government to ransom, and calm was only restored five weeks later when the relic was mysteriously restored. On certain Muslim festivals, it is displayed to massed crowds of pilgrims in the outside courtyard.

Back along the Boulevard, just opposite Nehru Park, is the hill path leading to the oldest Hindu shrine in the valley, the **Shankaracharya Temple**, which stands 300 m (1,000 ft) above the city on a hill known as **Takht-I-Sulaiman** (Throne of Solomon). It is thought that the temple was originally built by the emperor Ashoka's son, Jaluka, in around 200 BC, and later enlarged by an unknown Hindu sage in the reign of Emperor Jehangir. A walk (or sprint) up to the shrine, with its superb panoramic views, is a good way to beat houseboat lethargy.

City Walks

Enjoy a sunny morning's walk along the **Bund**, the narrow, poplar-lined, Raj-era promenade near Zero Bridge in the modern city. It's a Kipling's mall of mock-Tudor buildings and musty antediluvian shops with faded advertise-

ments for outdated products, some with gilt porticoes that still bear the insignia of the British crown. On one side of the Bund is the Jhelum River, with steps leading down to parked *doongas*, some of which have been transformed into floating travel agencies, and *shikaras*. Take a *shikara* from the stand opposite Grindley's Bank building and float across to the **Sri Pratap Singh Museum**, housed in an old palace in a quiet backstreet. There's an eccentric collection of stone sculpture from the fourth to the twelfth century, stuffed trophies "bagged" at the turn of the century, old coins, tapestries, and an extensive stamp collection.

If you stroll the Bund's full length, you'll see the old Srinagar Club and the former **British Residency** building, set in well-kept gardens and now used as the Government Arts Emporium.

Heading west, you'll soon find yourself in bustling **Lal Chowk**, Srinagar's business and commercial center, where Kashmiri salesmen shout over the deafening amplified music to try to lure passers-by into their shops. A mélée of shops sell Kashmiri crafts, cheap trinkets, garish mirrored pictures of mosques, and lorry loads of almonds, pomegranate seeds, walnuts, cashews, and dried apricots.

Heading back toward Dal Lake, as you cross the Jhelum River into Srinagar's old city, you'll see the white Regency-style **Baradari Palace**, a former summer palace of the Dogra Maharaja. Deserted and forlorn now, the Baradari once epitomized regal splendor. The maharaja would arrive for his annual visit to the summer capital in a pageant-like river procession, flanked by epauletted oarsmen, gaily caparisoned boats, and a water-borne cabinet.

Shopping

Srinagar is a tempting treasure house of Kashmir's traditional crafts — hand-knotted silk or wool carpets, unique feathery *pashmina* and *shahtush* shawls, exquisite embroideries, ornate papier mâché, and walnut-wood carvings — as well as tailor-made fur coats, leather ware, and saffron.

But be a discerning and hard bargainer. Srinagar breeds money-hungry sales touts like rattlesnakes, and has a surfeit of mass-produced bric—brac aimed at the tourist market. To get an idea of what the legitimate prices are, go first to the **Government Arts Emporium**, Residency Road, or the **Government Central Market**, Exhibition Ground, both open 10 am to 5 pm daily, to see the range of handicrafts sold in Kashmir and the official fixed prices. You'll then be better prepared for browsing in the shops along Boulevard Road and Lal Chowk,

ABOVE: Detail of ornately hand-painted Kashmiri papier mâché box.

and at the better-quality shops along the Bund. Commission sharks who lead you to a particular shop and then loiter inside expect a cut from any purchase you make, which adds to the price considerably.

The most coveted of all Kashmiri handicrafts are the exceptionally fine handmade **carpets**, usually woven in old Persian designs in varying combinations of silk and wool to create a special weave which looks dark from one side and light from the other. They are usually produced on large wooden looms by teams of young boys, and depending on the size and quality can take between six months and four years to complete. Because they are so popular, Srinagar's shops are flooded with inferior mass-produced carpets — particularly those made with cotton-derivative "staple" yarn, which imitates the appearance of silk but is far less durable.

You need to be very careful when choosing a carpet. Check the content and knot of the carpet — regardless of what the salesman tells you. A silk carpet will weigh at least two kilograms (4.5 lb) less than yarn staple or wool. But the true test is to pluck a knot out and burn it — staple yarn ignites instantly, but pure silk smolders. Another test is to check the number of knots per square inch on the reverse of the carpet. A good silk or wool carpet should have around 360 knots per square inch, but the finest carpets have as many as 700 knots. Make sure that you scrutinize the carpet for any design or color faults, and that you are given a certificate of origin to save possible customs duty or VAT payments on your return home. If you want to ship your carpet back, you might feel happier if you make the arrangements yourself. If you don't have time, photograph or mark the carpet under the unfazed salesman's eye. That way he's less likely to send you an inferior or different "replica" of the one you purchased!

Far less expensive are the *namadas*, brightly chain-stitched rugs made from pounded fleece, or the unusual and decorative **crewel-work floor coverings** with an underside of white cotton fabric.

Then there are the legendary **Kashmiri shawls**, prized for centuries by Mughals and maharajas, who employed hundreds of skilled craftsmen to produce the *pashmina, shahtush,* and exquisitely embroidered *jamawar pashmina* shawls, the latter taking as many as 20 years to complete. Akbar launched the practice of giving shawls to foreign dignitaries, and by the late eighteenth century, as trade increased with Europe, they became an item of aristocratic fashion in France. The French empress Josephine possessed between 300 and 400 of these shawls. According to one story, Napoleon — who liked to see her shoulders bared, while she preferred them decoratively draped — would dramatically whisk off her shawl and fling it into the fire, whereupon the empress would calmly send for another one.

By the mid-nineteenth century, the inexpensive mass-produced English imitation Paisley wool and silk shawls almost destroyed the market for exotic, hand-woven Kashmiri shawls. Today, there are efforts to keep the craft alive, and shawls of all qualities are made.

Shahtush shawls are the most legendary of all. Spun from fleece gathered from the throats of ibex goats in Ladakh and Tibet, they are so airy and feathery they can be drawn through a ring, and so warm they can cook a wrapped egg after five hours. Unlike woolen and *pashmina* shawls, *shahtush* is seldom dyed or embroidered. The rare 100 percent pure shawls are mousy brown in color and highly sought after, costing around US$360.

Kashmir's papier mâché goods can be found all over India, but only in Srinagar can you find the most delicate work etched with real gold, not bronze dust or gold poster paint. The making of papier mâché is a laborious process: pulped paper is first soaked in adhesive fluid, dried in a mold for at least a month, then painted with bright designs before being coated with varnish. Traditionally, men and boys do this work, and still use natural extracts for color: coral is ground for red, lapis for blue, charcoal for black, and cardamom for yellow.

Srinagar is also the best place to buy precious pure red **saffron**, which is harvested each autumn from violet-blue crocus flowers just outside the city at Pampore. It is one of only two places in the world where saffron is grown, the other being Spain. Sealed jars of the spice, with the government laboratory's stamp of approval, are available all over Srinagar. When buying loose saffron, one strand only needs to be sampled to judge its quality, for the flavor and fragrance of saffron are unmistakable.

Aside from the state emporiums, the following places located close together on the Bund are good shops and showplaces for contemporary handicrafts. All are run by descendants of the original craftsmen under royal patronage and maintain a deep pride in the quality and tradition of their work. If you would like to see artisans using traditional methods to produce Kashmiri crafts without feeling any pressure to buy, these are the best people to arrange it.

Sadiq's Handicrafts, at Cottage Chinar, next to the GPO, is the place to browse for high-quality shawls, embroideries, *pherans*, crewel work, floor rugs, and tapestries — mostly made with antique designs.

Make sure you visit the establishment of papier mâché artist **Suffering Moses**, nicknamed in the old days by the British, he says, because of his fastidious workmanship. His family established the shop in 1840, and today it contains a small museum of antiques as well as papier mâché of exquisite quality and design, wood carvings, shawls, and embroideries.

Asia Crafts has an excellent collection of fine Persian, Iranian, and Kashmiri carpets, and the upper story is devoted to papier mâché goods.

SRINAGAR AFTER DARK

Kashmir has a unique and particularly vibrant heritage of satirical folk theater, dance, and music. However, these performances are held as part of village fairs and festivals, so tourists generally never get to see them. Only during the Kashmiri marriage season, from October to December, do exuberant wedding processions and hired performers spill out on to Srinagar's streets.

Kashmir's professional entertainers traditionally come from a community known as the Bhands, whose lifestyle is much like that of medieval Europe's strolling players. Their earthy folk plays are potted histories of Kashmir, handed down from generation to generation and filled with slapstick, outrageous costuming, and bawdy puns.

Most hotels and houseboats can arrange for classical musicians and dancers to perform, and for guests to sample a delicious *wazwan* feast aboard the barge-like *doonga* boats which can be hired out for the evening for large parties.

The Sufiana *kalam*, the classic devotional music of the Sufi Muslims, is an unforgettable experience. Often performed by master musicians as an integral feature of important Muslim festivals, this mesmerizing combination of Persian verse and exotic lulling sounds is part worship, part musical frenzy.

Its origins are tied to the cult of Muslim mysticism which took lasting root in Kashmir during the fourteenth century. Sufiana *kalam* is usually performed by three or four musicians who intone verse to the *santoor* (a trapezoid zither), a pair of *tabla*-like drums, and the *saz-i-Kashmir* (a plucked string instrument). Sessions (at which much hookah pipe-puffing is done) last for hours, often until dawn. Devout Sufis believe that these harmonious sounds can send them into a trance-like communion with God. This "music of mystic content" may not whisk casual observers across the great divide, but it is certainly captivating.

A performance of Sufiana *kalam* is rarely advertised in advance; it is usually held for small audiences in private houses. The best way of finding out about a performance is simply to ask around, although the Tourist Reception Centre is unlikely to be of much help. If your houseboat owner can't help, ask at Asia Crafts, Sidiq's Handicrafts, or Suffering Moses.

GENERAL INFORMATION

Srinagar's **Tourist Reception Centre** (TRC) ((0194) 74259, 72644, 734568, and after office hours, 77303, 77305, is just off Maulana Azad Road near Dalgate. It provides virtually all the services you're likely to need during your stay — houseboat and hotel reservations, an Indian Airlines office (((0194) 73270, 73538, 76557), the Railway booking office, the Post Office, a very useful branch of the State Bank of India which stays open from 4 to 7 pm, a bookshop with local maps, and a State Road Transport Corporation bus counter with adjacent depot. It's open 24 hours a day for general information and assistance, but is more efficient during regular office hours (10 am to 5 pm).

There's a camping shop for route information, trekking maps, and equipment — ground sheets, tents, sleeping bags, and trekking boots hired out by the day or week at modest prices. Here also are the departments of Fisheries and Wildlife for information and permits. You can inquire here about accommodation at Dachigam National Park, 22 km (13.6 miles) from Srinagar. This former royal game reserve is notable for its hangul, the Kashmir stag which is related to the Scottish red deer, and Himalayan black and brown bears. Passes to Hari Parbat, and temporary membership of the Kashmir, Srinagar, and Nagin golf clubs is also issued here. There's a restaurant and cheap hostel-style accommodation at the back. The TRC run daily city sightseeing tours, as well as tours to Gulmarg, Pahalgam, Sonamarg, Daksum via Achabal and Kokernag (US$2), and the Mughal Gardens (US$1). Westland 15-seater helicopters can be hired from here to ply between Srinagar, Gulmarg, and Pahalgam, as well as around the city. Round trips to Gulmarg cost US$35, and to Pahalgam, US$50. The TRC also have a bureau at Srinagar's airport which is useful for houseboat information but little else.

For trips further afield, both **Sita World Travel**, ((0194) 78891, Maulana Azad Road, and **Mercury Travels**, ((0194) 78786, in the Oberoi Hotel, are reliable and efficient.

If you're planning to go to Ladakh, or are interested in adventurous trekking, whitewater river rafting, or trout fishing in the Himalayas, it's worth investigating two of

India's top adventure travel agencies, both of which offer flexible package deals that include guides/gillies, trained staff, camp facilities, all meals, and transport. **Tiger Tops Mountain Travel** has a Srinagar office at Houseboat Star of Zanzibar, near Zero Bridge, Jhelum River. Their headquarters in New Delhi, ℂ (011) 521932, 777-1055, fax (011) 777-7483, are at 1/1 Rani Jhansi Road. **Tiger Paw Adventures**, ℂ (011) 616137, is at D-383 Defence Colony, New Delhi.

MOUNTAIN RETREATS

GULMARG

Amid the towering pine-forested Pir Panjal mountains about two hours' drive (52 km, or 32 miles) from Srinagar, Gulmarg is renowned for its spectacular alpine scenery and spring wildflowers which carpet the valley in a solid mass of color.

Gulmarg is both a summer and winter resort. Apart from its exhilarating mountain walks, treks, and pony-rides, it has the world's highest golf course at 2,650 m (8,612 ft) and during winter offers the best skiing on the subcontinent.

Originally called Gaurimarg (after Lord Shiva's wife), Sultan Yusaf Shah renamed it Gul (flower) Marg (meadow) in 1581. But for the muezzin's cry echoing across the valley and its swarthy Muslim hookah-smoking inhabitants, Gulmarg looks like a pastoral Swiss landscape.

Gulmarg's warm season lasts from mid-May to mid-October (May to June for spring flowers) and the peak skiing season is in January to February, when the valley is covered in thick, crunchy snow.

Taxis provide the most comfortable means of enjoying the climb up the mountain slopes along the poplar-lined road with glorious vistas across the Kashmir Valley. The round trip costs about US$20 (few drivers will agree to take you unless you cover their return). For a fraction of the price, take one of the beaten-up buses which leave the Srinagar bus depot next to the TRC.

During the winter months, when the passes are often blocked by snow, buses operate only up to Tanmarg, eight kilometers (five miles) from Gulmarg, and most people cover the final stretch by hired jeep. Even if the pass is open, you might prefer to hire a pony for an hour's ride through the magical hush of the snow-laden forest.

Gulmarg is set for a major onslaught of ski enthusiasts with the recent completion of the

five-kilometer (three-mile) -long Poma gondola ski lift. An ITDC five-star hotel and at least three large lodges now under construction will dramatically change Gulmarg's accommodation facilities. For the moment, the best choice for a relaxed stay is **Hotel Highland Park**, ℂ (01953) 230, 291, which has tiered luxury cottages set amid pretty sloping gardens with reliable hot water and central heating. Rates: expensive. Its fireside bar has an unbeatable view across the valley, but the mock-Bavarian dining room serves bland set meals. Facilities include a sauna, jacuzzi, and car rental. In the spirit of *aprs-ski*, the waiter claimed there was a

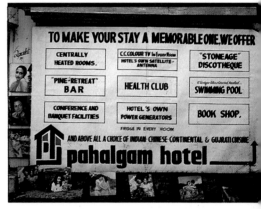

"live disco", but on inspection this appeared to double as a table tennis room!

Hotel Apharwat has very comfortable pinewood-walled double rooms with hot water and heaters plugged in with copper wire by dotty, but well-meaning, staff. Somehow their cook succeeds where all of Gulmarg fails, and serves excellent Kashmiri, Chinese, and Mughal food as well as great mountain-climbing breakfasts. Rates: inexpensive. Other good mid-range options include **Pine Palace**, ℂ (01953) 266, **Nedous**, ℂ (01953) 223, and **Ornate Woodlands**, ℂ (01953) 268. The **Government Tourist Huts** are quaint wooden chalets, each complete with linen, hot-water bottles, and a smoke-stack *bukhara*. These vary in size (a one-bedroom hut will cost US$8) and bookings can be made through the TRC in Srinagar. Alternatively, the state-run Tourist Bungalow atop the hill near the town has simple cheap rooms and an atmosphere of rustic lunacy. I don't think I will ever forget the look of wounded dignity on their aged staffer's face when I suggested he remove an unwelcome mouse: "We don't have that kind of rodent here. That was a rat!"

ABOVE: Enticing sign for trek-weary travelers in the hill-station town of Pahalgam.

It's worth staying for at least a couple of days to explore Gulmarg's mountain trails, either on foot or by pony. Start with the **Outer Circular Walk**, an 11-km (6.8-mile) road which weaves through pine forests and has breathtaking views down to the Kashmir Valley and up to Nanga Parbat (the world's fifth-highest mountain at 8,137 m, or 26,700 ft), Harmukh, Sunset Peak, and Apharwat Ridge. It's an invigorating hour's climb past rippling snow-fed streams and dense cedars to **Khilanmarg** (six kilometers, or just under four miles), a small flower-strewn plateau with stunning views across the mountains and Wular Lake, the largest freshwater reservoir in India. Just across the Apharwat Ridge is **Alpather Lake** (13 km, or eight miles), a deep turquoise lake flecked with floating ice even in high summer. Other good walks include **Ningal Nallah** (eight kilometers, or five miles) and the Muslim shrine of the **Ziarat of Babareshi** (five kilometers, or three miles). For trekking, you can hire a guide/porter from the Tourist Office at about US$5 a day for the three-day hike to the beautiful meadow of **Tosha Maiden** (50 km, or 31 miles), an idyllic camping spot. Start the trek from **Ferozepore Nallah**, five kilometers (three miles) from Gulmarg, which teems with plump rainbow trout and makes a peaceful picnic place. To win a trout for your pine-cone fire, first get the necessary permit from the TRC in Srinagar.

Gulmarg's 18-hole golf course was recently re-laid according to international standards. The small club house issues immediate temporary membership and hires out clubs, shoes, and ball-boys.

During winter, Gulmarg is India's most popular ski resort, and offers a variety of graded slopes of beginner to intermediate standards. Facilities include one chair lift, two rope tows, and two T-bars, as well as heli-skiing up to Khilanmarg which costs US$20. Once the gondola is operating, there will be runs for advanced skiers. High-quality European ski equipment can be hired for modest sums, along with toboggans and ice-skates for Gulmarg's rink.

PAHALGAM

Pahalgam is a charming sleepy valley 96 km (60 miles) from Srinagar, set 2,130 m (7,000 ft) high among snowy peaks and forests of pine, conifer, and sycamore and crisscrossed by the Lidder and Shashnag rivers. Once a lonely shepherd's hamlet, Pahalgam has become a popular hill resort with numerous lodges and rows of shops selling Kashmiri handicrafts. It also serves as a starting point for several major treks across the Himalayas. Here you can angle

for trout in the clear, glacier-fed Lidder River, play golf on a nine-hole course, and take long mountain walks and pony-rides.

If you've hired a taxi from Srinagar, it's worth loitering at several places of interest en route: for the heady sensation of walking through fragrant fields of purple saffron flowers at **Pampore** (13 km, or eight miles), and to see the historic ruins of **Avantipur** (29 km, or 18 miles). This ancient capital of Kashmir, built by King Avantivarman (AD 855–883), has two ninth-century temples dedicated to Vishnu and Shiva. Beyond the Pahalgam turn-off is **Achabal**, a Mughal garden laid out by Shah Jehan's daughter, Jehanara. Nearby is **Kokernag**, famous for its curative springs and, more recently, it's Indo-Danish trout hatchery which provides many of the plump fish that end up on the tables of India's luxury hotels. Back on the Pahalgam route, high on a plateau you'll see the ruins of **Martand**, the huge Sun Temple built by the sixth-century king Lalitaditya.

At Pahalgam you can hire tents, pack-ponies, and trekking and camping equipment, or equipment can be pre-booked at Srinagar's Tourist Office. Rugged individualists will balk at the government-run tent colony with its military rows of tents complete with cots, hot-water bottles, and electricity. For log stoves and cozy rooms with mountain and river vistas, stay at the well-established, moderately priced and fairly luxurious **Hotel Pahalgam** ((26, 52, 78). Good mid-range accommodation is provided by the **Woodstock Hotel** ((27) and the **Hotel Hill Park** ((79). The recently opened alpine-style **Kolahoi Kabin** offers by far the best value for the budget-minded and its restaurant serves good, cheap Kashmiri and Mughal fare. There are several state-run tourist lodges and numerous tourist huts scattered across the valley, some very secluded. Bookings can be made through the Srinagar Tourist Office.

With Pahalgam as your base, there are plenty of walks and treks to explore in every direction, ranging from scenic strolls to tough six-day treks.

Good short excursions include **Mamaleswwara**, a small twelfth-century Shiva temple just one kilometer (a little over half a mile) downstream, and a hike or pony-ride to **Four Points**, a winding route via the scenic Nehru and Shail parks to the "four points" from which there are splendid views across the valley. Even more spectacular is the view from the Hindu temple up on top of the ridge, reached by pony-trail via the Chikarwada Bridge. **Baisaran**, five kilometers (three miles) from Pahalgam, is a picturesque meadow with clusters of yellow mustard-flowers and beautiful views across the valley and the Lidder River. A further 11-km (seven-mile) climb brings you to **Tulian Lake**. At 3,353 m (11,000 ft), the lake is a giant ice-block for most of the year.

Every year, to coincide with the full moon of July/August, thousands of pilgrims from all over India descend on Pahalgam to make the four-day, 47-km (29-mile) journey to the **Amarnath Cave**. At a height of 3,888 m (12,760 ft), the cave is sacred as the house of Shiva. The god of creation is worshiped in his ice-phallic form as *shivling*, a massive stalagmite that waxes and wanes with the moon. The pilgrims are dwarfed by an awesome primeval landscape of vast slate-gray snowcapped peaks and glaciers that shimmer in the moonlight.

Of all Pahalgam's trails, the four-day trek to the base-camp of the 3,600-m (11,800-ft) -high **Kolahoi Glacier** and back (36 km, or 22 miles) is the most popular. Camps are made at **Aru** (11 km, or seven miles), a small sheep-station, and **Lidderwat** (12 km, or 7.5 miles) alongside rushing glacial streams. Instead of returning to Pahalgam, a further three days' trekking will take you to **Sonamarg** in the Sindh Valley, the smallest, and some say the loveliest, of Kashmir's hill stations. Trekkers often pass through Sonamarg en route to the Zoji La Pass on the arduous 10-day trail to Ladakh across the main Himalayan range. Sonamarg is also a good base for several short treks: to **Thajiwas Glacier** (three kilometers, or just under two miles), and the scenic high-altitude, trout-filled lakes of **Vishansar** (4,084 m, or 13,400 ft), **Kishansar** (3,810 m, or 12,500 ft), and **Gangabal** (3,658 m, or 12,000 ft). This region is a paradise for anglers during August and September, when there is plenty of trout and mahseer.

JAMMU

Few of Kashmir's fabled charms are found in Jammu, the state's bustling commercial winter capital, with its ungainly urban sprawl across the banks of the Tawi River against a backdrop of sandstone foothills, small lakes, temples, and a ruined fort.

Little is known of the city's early history. According to legend, it was founded by the ninth-century king Jambulochan, who built his monumental Bahu Fort overlooking the Tawi. In 1730, the region fell under the control of the warlike Dogra Rajputs, whose descendants retained power over the merged Jammu and Kashmir state until Independence. During the eighteenth and nineteenth centuries, Jammu was the center of a minor artistic renaissance, and its artists created the exquisite court miniatures known as the Pahari school.

Most tourists regard Jammu merely as a stopover after a long bus or train journey on their way to Kashmir Valley, Ladakh, or the hill stations of Himachal Pradesh. But Jammu has several interesting places to visit and it's worth staying at least half a day.

HOTELS

Jammu has only two well-established "luxury" hotels, both moderately priced. The four-star **Asia Jammu Tawi**, ((0191) 43932, 48261 is some distance from the city center at Nehru Market, but near the railway station and airport. The staff are friendly and efficient, and facilities include a swimming pool, health club, beauty parlor, J&K Tourist Office, travel counter, and a good restaurant. Double air-conditioned rooms are US$30, or you can opt for "fan-cooled" rooms which are just as comfortable but half the price. **Hotel Jammu Ashok**, ((0191) 43127, 43864, opposite the Amar Mahal Museum, is a slightly cheaper option.

In the mid-range bracket, the **Hotel Mansar**, ((0191) 46161, 43610, at Dennis Gate, is inexpensive and is centrally located with a decent restaurant.

Jammu's lodges have a reputation for being cheap and awful. They're clustered mainly around the Tourist Reception Centre (TRC) in Mir Chowk. The best of this fairly motley crew is **Apsara Hotel**, on Shahidi Chowk, which has clean doubles at US$3, or **Tawi View Hotel**, ((0191) 43752, 43930, at Maheshi Gate, with doubles with bath for US$4.

The main **Jammu TRC**, ((0191) 5421, 42231, on Veer Marg in Mir Chowk, offers basic rooms, very cheap, with attached baths but no air-conditioning in bunker-style blocks, and the smaller tourist office at the railway station has several retiring rooms — useful for an early morning train journey.

RESTAURANTS

Both the Asia Jammu Tawi and Ashok hotels have excellent and reasonably priced Indian restaurants — and both offer good breakfasts of fruit juice, eggs, toast, and coffee for. Elsewhere, head for Veer Marg, Jammu's main restaurant "strip" which is cluttered with small chai and *thali* stalls. Tucked away here are **Dragon**, Jammu's only Chinese restaurant; **Kwality**, with its tri-cuisine menu and reliably good Mughal fare; and **Silver Inn**, for "multi-cuisine".

The **India Coffee House** (open 8:30 am to 5 pm) in the exhibition grounds serves freshly brewed coffee and delicious South Indian snacks.

SIGHTSEEING

Make time for Jammu's two art galleries. The best is the **Dogra Art Gallery**, Gandhi Bhawan, facing the New Secretariat. Set up in 1954, it houses nearly 600 paintings, as well as terracottas, medieval weapons, sculpture, and ancient tar-leaf manuscripts. Many of these exquisite Mughal miniatures were commissioned by Dogra kings, whose patronage led to the development of the local Pahari and Basholi schools. The gallery has only a selection of its full collection on display; to see more, approach the

curator. Open every day except Monday, 11 am to 5 pm during winter and 8:30 am to 1:30 pm in summer.

The **Amar Mahal Museum**, overlooking the Tawi River, was built for Raja Amar Singh in 1907. This extravagantly turreted mock-French chateau now displays the royal collection of rare Pahari miniatures and manuscripts. The imposing ancestral portraits of the Rajput Dogra kings convey much more of the region's history than any book: a heavily-jowled race of flint-eyed monarchs whose plump jewel-bedecked hands never stray far from their swords. Open every day during winter from 10 am to noon, 3 to 5 pm, and from 5 to 7 pm in summer, with half-days on Sundays.

From here it's a 10-minute auto-rickshaw ride to the historic remains of the **Bahu Fort**, located five kilometers (three miles) above the town. Its ramparts swarm with devotees of the evil-eyed, black-faced goddess in the small Kali temple. Beneath the fort are the sloping terraces of the Bagh-I-Bagu Gardens, a pleasant spot in which to stroll and take tea at the small pavilion

restaurant with a view across Jammu and the Tawi River.

Make a last stop at the **Ragunnath Temple**, dedicated to Lord Rama, the interiors of which are coated with gold. Built in 1835 by Maharaja Gulab Singh, it is the most impressive of a cluster of nineteenth-century temples located within the lively and colorful bazaar area in the city center, just five minutes' walk from the tourist office.

GENERAL INFORMATION

Jammu's main Tourist Reception Centre, ((0191) 48172, is in Mir Chowk near the main bus-stand and is open 10 am to 5 pm. There's a second, and rather chaotically-run, office in the railway station, where the Post Office is also located. Neither office runs sightseeing tours or offers city maps, which have been declared a security risk. The Mir Chowk TRC houses the Indian Airlines office, ((0191) 42735, 47577. The main shopping areas of Jammu are Veer Marg, where there's a well-stocked Government Emporium, Raghunath Bazaar, and Hari market.

LADAKH

Ladakh, or "Land of the Passes", is a region of stark beauty north of Kashmir that remains an unspoilt citadel of Buddhist religion and Tibetan culture locked within a snowy fortress of Himalayan gorges. Travelers have titled the area "Little Tibet", "the Moonland", and the "Last Shangri-La" — all with some degree of truth. Leh, the area's ancient capital, sits on a 3,555-m (11,663-ft) -high plateau in the Indus Valley, and is dominated by a royal palace reminiscent of the Potala in Lhasa. The city is dwarfed by the ocher-hued crags of the mighty Karakoram mountains, and is largely populated by Tibetan refugees who fled their homeland after China invaded in 1959.

India, China, and Pakistan all have contesting claims over parts of Ladakh, which for centuries served as a strategic junction on the medieval Silk Road between Sinkiang (Xinjiang) in China and routes to the Indian plains and Persia. Ladakh was virtually closed to the outside world for most of the post-Independence period, until New Delhi in 1974 decided for reasons of tourism to open up the region. But the area still remains virtually untouched, retaining much of its character as a hermetic kingdom where a "divine" monarchy and powerful priests ruled over nomadic tribes who eked out a living from farming yaks, goats, juniper berries, and barley crops.

ABOVE: A remote hamlet is tucked amid dramatic mountain scenery in Ladakh. OPPOSITE: Gorgeously-hued prayer flags fluttering from Leh Gompa. OVERLEAF: Street scene in Leh town.

Sparsely vegetated and as ruggedly inhospitable as the Sahara, Ladakh is home to the legendary snow leopard. Tibetan eagles soar across the sky, while herds of wild Zanskari horses run in herds across the plains. Its tough, Tartar-featured inhabitants have imbued the landscape with the colorful legends and tantric cults of Tibetan Buddhism. The religion is thought to have been first brought to Ladakh in the third century by missionaries sent by Ashoka, and the doctrine became mingled with the indigenous animistic Bon faith and ancient Hindu tantric cults. Prayer flags flutter from every household rafter, *chortens* or shrines of holy relics dot the

seven months a year, Leh airport is Ladakh's only link with the outside world. The unpredictable, high-altitude weather sometimes results in canceled or aborted flights. Make sure your schedule is flexible enough to accommodate an extra day or two to return, just in case you are left stranded waiting for the next available flight.

For variety, fly one way and drive the other. The 430-km (267-mile) -long road from Srinagar to Leh takes two days and allows time to acclimatize to Ladakh's rarefied altitude. The road is open between June and October and crosses the Kashmir–Ladakh

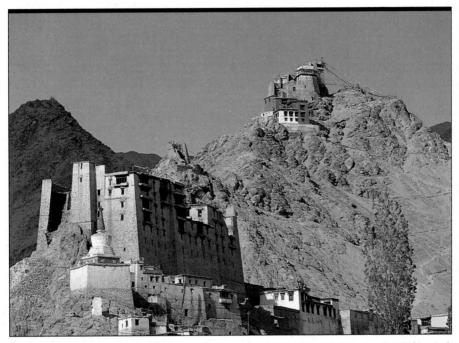

wayside, and villagers carry prayer wheels about with them like fetishes. The region is famous for its perilous cliff-top *gompas*, or Buddhist monasteries, which are brightly painted with murals of tantric gods and laden with gilded gem-studded statues of Buddha, religious icons, carvings, and scroll paintings or thangkas. Many have in recent years been restored and refurbished from donations by tourists, some of whom serve among the red-robed monks.

ACCESS

Reaching Leh is an experience in itself. Ladakh is open to visitors only for six months of the year, as winter freezes the region into isolation. Indian Airlines runs regular flights from Delhi via Chandigarh and Srinagar, with spectacular aerial views across the snowy Himalayas. For

boundary at Zoji La (3,529 m, or 11,578 ft), winding through the Zanskar Range through the Namika La (3,718 m, or 12,198 ft) and Fatu La (4,094 m, or 13,431 ft) passes. Overnight halts are best made at the Muslim hamlet of Kargil, 230 km (143 miles) from Leh, where comfortable accommodation is offered by the Welcomgroup-run Hotel Highlands ((41, rates: moderate) and the Hotel D'Zojila, two and a half kilometers (one and a half miles) from town. This is sensitive border territory disputed by India, Pakistan, and China, with armed guards preventing you from going more than two kilometers (one and a quarter miles) north of the Srinagar–Leh road. It's preferable to make the trip by six-seater jeep or car/taxi, allowing you to stop en route to admire the views and monasteries, particularly Lamayuru, the most hallowed and architecturally impressive of all Ladakh's *gompas*, with 400 monks, 124 km (77 miles) from Leh.

GENERAL TIPS

Ladakh's high altitude and very thin air mean that you'll need to take it very easy for the first few days after arrival. This is when you are most vulnerable to dizziness, headaches, insomnia or nausea, particularly if you fly direct to Leh from Delhi. If the problem persists, consult a doctor immediately. People with heart or lung conditions should take special care. Severe altitude sickness can be fatal, but

as is touching art objects. While you are free to photograph in the *gompas*, Indian soldiers tend to get very excited when tourists take innocent holiday snapshots near bridges, airfields, and military installations, and the ensuing drama and confiscation of film and even cameras is not worth the trouble.

Make sure you have encashed your travelers' checks and foreign currency and have plenty of small denomination rupee notes before arriving in Leh, where both banks and small change are rare.

Finally, you can win big grins from the Ladakhis by peppering your speech with a few

it is more likely to affect overly active trekkers. The only cure is to descend to a lower level as soon as possible.

You should also go prepared for freak temperature changes, bringing light cotton clothes for warm summer days, woolen clothes for nippy nights. Lip salve, sunscreen, sunglasses, hats, and strong walking shoes are essential for all travelers. Binoculars and extra film also come in handy. Local agencies provide tents, mattresses, sleeping bags, and basic utensils for trekkers. The **Tourist Office** ((97) in the Dak Bungalow can give maps and helpful advice for visiting monasteries, trekking, and the current half-day and day rates for hiring jeeps.

A powerful flashlight comes in handy when studying the interiors of dimly lit monasteries. Smoking in the *gompas* is considered very rude,

local words. *Jullay* is an all-purpose greeting that means "hello, goodbye, how are you" all in one. *Katin chey* means "please", while *thukjechey* means "thank-you".

WHEN TO GO

Religious festivals add special gaiety, color, and excitement during visits to the *gompas*. While most festivals occur during the winter months, summer visitors have the opportunity to see the spectacular Hemis festival of masked dances and drama performed by monks held during June and July at **Hemis**

ABOVE: Breathtaking vistas across serrated mountain ranges in Ladakh. OPPOSITE: Cliftop apartments of Leh Palace, now an impressive museum of palace treasures, chapels, shrines, libraries and tombs.

Gompa, 40 km (25 miles) from Leh. All *gompas* have large courtyards where these religious festivities take place, but Hemis stages the most impressive of the genre. Dances are heralded by the discordant crescendo of three-meter (10-ft) -long brass trumpets, drums, and clashing cymbals played by red-robed acolytes in tall hats. Other monks are transformed into demons and gods by ornate padded costumes and garish masks, and they twirl, lunge, and shimmy while holding icons of Bon, Buddhism, and Tantra to enact tales from the scriptures. The victory of good over evil tends to be the basic theme, signifying the destruc-

River rafting in the Indus River can be arranged during the summer (see below).

WHERE TO STAY AND EAT

With more tourists attracted to Ladakh each year, accommodation facilities are improving. Meanwhile, Leh has a range of hotels, lodges, and guesthouses, many of the latter private homes which rent rooms out to foreign visitors. Prices vary a great deal, dropping to half the peak-season rate in the off-season, with many places closed during the winter.

tion of baser characteristics such as greed, lust, and anger, but sometimes monks enter trance-like states and act as oracles, making predictions and answering questions. But the greatest spectacle is seeing thousands of Ladakhi villagers arrive in traditional dress bearing brass samovars containing yak tea. The women wear elaborate robes with long felt head-dresses studded with turquoise and heavy silver jewelry, and the men are swaddled in quilted goncha coats tied with colorful cummerbunds.

Archery contests coincide with every religious festival, and visitors are welcome to try their hand and to join in the music, dancing, and drinking. Check whether your trip coincides with a game of local polo — played at a fast and furious pace on local wild Zanskari ponies on the highest and most spectacular polo ground on the planet.

Upmarket hotels are all moderately priced, and the best and most convenient are the **Kang-Lha-Chhen** ((39) and the **Lha Lha-Ri-Mo** ((101). You could also try the **Hotel Shambala** ((67), located toward the edge of the valley, or the **Hotel Indus** ((166), out of town on the Hemis Road.

Tiger Tops Mountain Travel's **Ladakh Sarai** (11 km, or seven miles) offers comfortable Mongolian-style yurt tents pitched amid willow trees near the old Ladakhi village of Stok, famous for its royal summer palace and archery contests. The circular furnished tents are very cozy, with efficient solar-powered showers and modern toilet facilities. Lighting is provided by lanterns and candles so that the meadow's tranquillity is not spoiled by the sound of generators. Good Western and traditional Ladakhi cuisine is served in a separate dining tent. The Sarai is a good base for trips to the monasteries, short treks, and river rafting on the Indus. Most travel agents can book through the London, Delhi, or Srinagar offices. The same company organizes trekking and rafting in Ladakh.

Ladakhi food does not constitute one of the world's most exciting cuisines. Ladakhis consume lots of roasted barley meal, *tsampa*, as well as quantities of salted yak butter tea and *chang*, a potent barley brew. The better hotels and restaurants serve a choice of Indian, Chinese, and Tibetan dishes. Local chefs excel at delicious *mo mo* steamed dumplings, chow mein, and various other rice and noodle dishes, particularly good at **Dreamland Restaurant**, close to the center of town. Others to try are **Chopstick**, **Potala**, and **Hill Top**.

LEH TOWN

Start your sightseeing with a visit to the abandoned **Leh Khar Palace** (open 6 to 9 am and from 5 pm to 7 pm) which sprawls across Tsemo Hill. It was built by King Singe Namagyl in the sixteenth century, taking its cue from Lhasa's Potala Palace, and still belongs to Leh's royal family who now live in another palace at Stok. Despite its many wall paintings and royal *gompa*, it has a desecrated, pillaged look that dates from the Kashmiri invasion of Ladakh last century. The main attraction is the superb views from its top windows across Leh's fluttering prayer flags. In town, visit the lively marketplace to see elderly Ladakhi women in traditional attire selling vegetables and household goods, spinning, and knitting.

GOING TO THE *GOMPAS*

Sightseeing in and around Leh largely involves scrambling up steep lanes to see cliff-top *gompas*. The drab baked mud exteriors of these monasteries hide colorful tantric frescoes, silk or brocade thangkas, and exquisitely carved statues. *Gompas* are places of worship, isolated meditation, and religious instruction for young monks, as well as the repository of Ladakh's wealth. The approach to a *gompa* is heralded by votive shrines known as *mane* walls and *chortens*. Outer walls and entrances are lined with cylinders of wood or metal mounted vertically on spindles and placed in alcoves which are rotated for prayers.

In Leh, visit the fifteenth-century **Leh Gompa** with its large Buddha (open 7 to 9 am, and 5 to 7 pm) and **Shanka Gompa**, with its gold statues, located two kilometers (one and a quarter miles) away. It takes several

days to see the important *gompas* outside town, using a jeep or taxi. Buses run out to most places, and it is sometimes possible to stay overnight in the monastery. The closest are **Spituk** (eight kilometers, or five miles), with fine Buddha icons, masks, and thangkas, and **Shey** (15 km, or just over nine miles), the ancient seat of the pre-Tibetan kings with a 7.5-m (25-ft) -high copper statue of Buddha. Also see **Phyang** (19 km, or almost 12 miles), a sixteenth-century *gompa* which belongs to the Red Camp sect of Buddhists, and **Thikse** (19 km, or almost 12 miles), a twelfth-century, 12-story clifftop *gompa* with 10 temples full of

statues, images, stupas, and wall-paintings and with views across the green Indus Valley. **Stok Palace** (16 km, or about 10 miles) is the home of Leh's royal family. **Hemis Gompa** (40 km, or about 25 miles), built in 1630, is the wealthiest, best-known, and biggest *gompa* in Ladakh. Its popularity stems from its annual festival which honors Guru Padma Sambhav's birth anniversary. It has Ladakh's most extensive collection of wall-paintings, statues, and thangkas, including the world's largest, which is unfurled every 12 years (the next time in 2004).

ABOVE: Worn, rugged features of an old Ladakhi woman wearing a traditional turquoise necklace. OPPOSITE: The twelfth century Thikse Gompa, one of Ladakh's most important monasteries.

Bombay and the West

BOMBAY

Buddhist Temple

P Budhkar Marg
B Madhukar Marg
To Airport
Maulana Abulkalam Azad Road
Naigum Ro
Jerbai Wadia Road
To Airport
AP Oza Marg
N M Joshi Road
Senapati Behari Marg
G Kadam Marg
Achrya Donde Marg
Babasaheb Ambedkar Road
Hospital Avenue
Ambekar Road
Tokarsi Jivral Rd
Sewri Marg
Currey Road
Com House Gate Road
G D
Jakaria Bunder Road

Dr Annie Besant Road
Dr E Mosses Road
N M Joshi Road
Babasaheb Ambedkar Road
T B Kavam Marg
Reay Road

Race Course

Haji Ali's Tomb

Sane Guruji Road
Com Bapurao Road
JACOB CIRCL
S G MAHARAJ CHOWK
E S Patanwala Marg
Victoria Road
Dr Mascarenhas Road

ARABIAN SEA

Keshavrad Khade Road

Lala Lajpatrai Marg
Arthur Road
Souter St
Motishah Road

Dr Anandrao Nair Road
Maulana Azad Road
Morland Rd
Clare Road
Bat Avant Singh
Magaon Road

J Dadjee Marg
Bombay Central Terminus
J Boman Behram Marg
Dimtimkar Rd
Road
Wadi Bunder

Bhulabhai Desai Road
S K Barodawala Marg
Tardeo Road
P Bapurao Marg
Sukiaji Street
Pupti Rd
JSP Road
Babula Tank Rd

Fly Over N S Patkar
Gopalrao Deshmukh Marg
NANA CHOWK
A Premji
Maulana Shaukatali Road
Jail Road
Patel Road

Kemps Corner

August Kranti
Girgaum Road
Dr Dadasaheb Bhadkamkar Marg
Nanubhai Desai
Padamji Patel Road
Sardar
Sardar
JSP Road
Mohammed Ali Rd
Patel Road

Hanging Gardens
Mani Bhavan (Mahatma Gandhi Memorial)
Marg
Sardar V P Road
Vithalbhai Patel Road
NAL BAZAAR
C P Tank
Bhuleshwar
Nandlal Jani Rd

Kher Marg
Kamla Nehru Park
Netaji Subhash Road
M P Marg
Jagannath
R R M R Marg
Dr B Jaykar Marg
Abdul Rehman
Sheikh Memon
Yusuf Meheralli

Laxmibai Jagmohan Das Marg
Bal Gangadhar
Walkeshwar Road
Chowpatty Beach
Aquarium
Sports Clubs
Marine
Maharshi
Shankar Shet Road
Dr C Hormusji Street
Tilak Marg

Walkeshwan Temple

BACK BAY

Fly Over S Gandhi Marg
Drive
Isl Marine St
Karve Road
Lokmanya
Databai Naoroji Street
D Mello Road

CROSS ISL

Raj Bhavan

MALABAR POINT

Netaji Subhash Road
Sh V Thackersey Marg
Mahatma Gandhi Rd
Cross Maidan
Mahapalika Marg
Azad Maidan
Bombay Victoria Terminus

NARIMAN POINT

Govt of India Tourist Office
Veer Nariman Road
P Mehta Road
Sonarh Marg
G P O
Fort St
W Hirachand Marg
Shoorji V
Mint

D Wacha Road
Madame Cama Road
Jamshedji Tata Road
Maharshi Karve Marg
Gen Bhonsle Marg
Maharshi Karve Marg
Jai Bhai Patel B Y
Shahid Bhagat
Singh Road

N Parekh Marg
C Shivaji
M Marg
Electric House
Gateway of India
P J R Marg

Capt P Pethe Marg
Shahid Bhagat Singh Road

1,000 m

N

BOMBAY

Bombay is a flamboyant and cosmopolitan city, with its fortune barons, chic socialites, movie magnates, street-smart hustlers, and above all, its diverse mixture of races and traditions.

The capital of Maharashtra state, on the west coast, Bombay is India's financial, industrial, and trading center, with a prosperous skyline of gleaming skyscrapers, office towers, and five-star hotels. Bombay strikes a balance between a sort of worldly sangfroid and swaggering vulgarity. There's a fleshy, over-ripe veneer to the place — echoed in the lurid cinema billboards of paunchy villains and voluptuously sequinned heroines that mushroom across town to advertise the latest Hindi *masala* extravaganza. This is where India manufactures her dreams, and cinema-hungry audiences worship stars like demi-gods: Bombay is the single-largest producer of films in the world, with about 800 movies in 12 languages completed in its studios each year.

Every aspect of Bombay is influenced by its mélange of migrant communities. Like New York and Sydney, Bombay's dynamism lies in its mixture of imported cultures — and the adroit pragmatism of its communities of Hindus, Muslims, Parsis, Sikhs, Arabs, Jains, and Jews, many of whom originally settled here several centuries ago. Today the lure of work and wealth is just as strong, drawing thousands of refugees who drift in from the impoverished countryside to construct makeshift *bustee* hovels on any available space in the great beehive. Despite the extreme poverty, Bombay is a beacon of the progressive elements in Indian society and has surpassed Calcutta as the nation's leading city. Its port handles 40 percent of the country's maritime trade, it sports a host of secondary and heavy industries, and its inhabitants provide nearly one third of India's entire income tax revenue.

First-time travelers to India often find Bombay the best choice as a starting point — its relaxed social mores, numerous international-class hotels, thriving nightlife, and its shops and restaurants make it easier to adjust to life on the subcontinent. It is also the gateway to western India, and the ideal starting point for journeys to Goa, Maharashtra, and Gujarat. Virtually all of India can be reached by air or rail connections from Bombay.

A PORT CITY'S PAST

Bombay has been an important trading city with strong links to the West for more than three centuries. Portuguese adventurers in the six-

teenth century coined and adapted a native name for the original seven swampy, malarial islands of "Buan Bahia", or "good bay". The name has stuck, but the islands were long ago reclaimed and transformed into the isthmus upon which now sits one of the world's largest cities. The small archipelago was the base for a succession of Hindu dynasties that ruled until 1348, when Muslim invaders based in Gujarat overran the area. It changed hands again in 1534, ceded by the Islamic conquerors to the Portuguese in exchange for protection from Lisbon's forces against the mighty Mughals of northern India. The Portuguese built several

churches and large fortifications, but little remains of these earliest European occupiers, excepting the walled city at Bassein, still largely intact, some 50 km (31 miles) from Bombay.

Britain entered the scene in 1662, when Catherine of Braganza married Charles II and gave her as her dowry the largest island, Mumbadevi. The six other islands were ceded three years later when the Portuguese retired to the coastal reaches of Goa. Samuel Pepys recorded that the marshy site was "but a poor place, and not really so as it was described to our King." The archipelago was leased out to the East India Company in 1668, which soon capitalized on its worth.

Movie stars achieve the status of demi-gods with Indian audiences. Bombay alone produces some 800 movies a year — a world record.

Scores of Gujarati, Parsi, Arab, Jewish, and Armenian traders and artisans were soon lured to the town, and salt flats around the islands were quickly transformed into a thriving center for trade in spices, silk, precious metals, cotton yarn, and opium. The upsurge in cotton prices during the world shortage caused by the American Civil War, and the opening of the Suez Canal were catalytic events for Bombay. The surplus funds prompted Governor Sir Bartle Frere to undertake a series of ambitious projects. He reclaimed land to link the islands into a single land mass, upon which were built dockyards, railways, spacious boulevards, and grand edifices in the Victorian-Gothic style. Bombay became a true city of Empire.

Early this century, Bombay became the center for the "Quit India" movement led by the leaders of the nationalist movement, Mahatma Gandhi and Jawaharlal Nehru, who became the first Indian Prime Minister after India was made independent in 1948.

EARLY SETTLERS

Most notable of Bombay's many immigrant communities are the Parsis, whose ancestors fled Persia and the religious persecution by the Muslims and migrated to India in the seventeenth century. A formidably successful community that includes many of Bombay's most influential families, the Parsis are Zoroastrians, who venerate fire, water, and earth. Believing the elements too sacred to pollute, the Parsis have a somewhat eerie practice for the disposal of their dead: at the "Towers of Silence" on Malabar Hill (just next to the Hanging Gardens), the dead are left in open wells to be consumed by vultures. Parsis tend to be tolerant in outlook, but generally remain a hermetic community, seldom marrying outsiders. However, Parsi traditions seem to be slowly dying out.

THE CITY

Bombay faces the Arabian Sea, and the original seven islands retain their names as the suburbs of Colaba, Mahim, Mazagoan, Parel, Worli, Girgaum, and Dongri. Metropolitan Bombay comprises five square kilometers (1.9 sq miles) at the tip of the peninsula, into which is squeezed many of the city's 10 million people, its main administrative and commercial offices, docks, and factories. Behind it lies the residential area, covering 22 sq km (8.5 sq miles).

OPPOSITE: A red double-decker bus passes in front of a magnificent Victorian-Gothic municipal building in downtown Bombay — reminders of the city's lasting British legacy.

CLIMATE

Bombay's climate, along with that of most of the western region, is at its best from October to February when the air is fresh, the days balmy, and the nights cool. In March, it becomes appreciably hotter and humid until summer reaches its sizzling zenith in June. Heavy monsoon rains often follow, frequently causing floods. During the cool peak season, and particularly just prior to and during the annual Derby (February to March), Bombay's hotels are thronged with travelers. It can prove extremely difficult to make short-notice connections to other cities, especially Goa, at this time, so it's wise to have all your hotel and travel connections reserved in advance.

TOURING BOMBAY

Getting around metropolitan Bombay is surprisingly straightforward, with most of the essential facilities — ticketing offices, post offices, hotels, restaurants, and shops — located in the thin three-kilometer (two-mile) strip between the Taj Mahal Hotel and Nariman Point. Bombay's meandering inner-city boulevards, narrow alleyways, bazaars, and its invigorating seafront are best explored on foot, but take a taxi to each area of interest and walk about from there. Compared to Delhi, Bombay's taxi-wallahs are models of propriety — they usually take you directly to your destination and use their meters, which are outdated and show a fraction of the real cost. You are wise to look over the driver's shoulder when he is scrutinizing his official "correction rates" card to check the additional amount you need to pay.

Bombay has a rapid electric train system servicing its outer suburbs. Hundreds of thousands of people cram into its open-air cabins each day, burrowing through the human mass when it is time to disembark (a mere 30-second halt at each stop). It is also a pickpocket's paradise, and so crowded during rush hours that commuters scale the sides and cling to the roof — predictably resulting in several fatalities each day. Bearing this in mind, it is quite an adventure to rattle through Bombay's urban landscape, loitering first to admire the clustered gargoyles and Gothic magnificence of the Victoria Terminus, but one recommended for Sundays only when the carriages are virtually empty. Trains leave for the western suburbs from Churchgate and for the eastern suburbs from Victoria Terminus.

Auto-rickshaws cluster around the suburban train stations, but are a rarity in the city center. Along the Apollo Bunder and both ends of Marine Drive are the vintage "Victorias",

horsedrawn carriages perfect for dusk prome-
nades to Chowpatty Beach. Local buses cost
virtually nothing but require much patience as
the destinations and numbers are marked in
Hindi script.

HOTELS

Good accommodation in Bombay can be fiend-
ishly hard to find in the peak January/February
season if you arrive without advance bookings.
The best hotels are often overbooked, so it's
wise to have your reservations confirmed well
in advance.

which provides five-star comfort but lacks the
characterful grace of the old wing. It's wise to
book well in advance for the old wing's spacious
seaview rooms and delightful period suites.

There's a good range of restaurants and bars,
notably the Apollo Bar for "designer" cocktails
and a view across the Arabian Sea, and the
stately Sea Lounge, where the well-heeled dis-
creetly arrange marriages over tiered trays of
cucumber sandwiches. It has a superb bookshop, health club, and swimming pool, a resident astrologer, and its shopping arcades make
interesting browsing. Rates: very expensive; the
modern annex prices are a little cheaper.

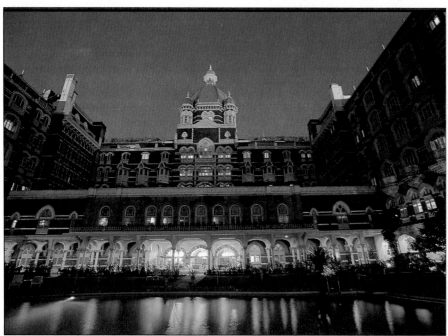

The world-famous **Taj Mahal Hotel**, ((022)
202-3366, fax (022) 287-2711, opposite India Gate,
is the haunt of Bombay's glitterati and probably
the best icon of the city's affluence, blending Rajput, Renaissance, and Gothic architecture. Industrialist Jamshetji Nusserwanji Tata constructed
the hotel in 1903 largely as a reaction against British colonial rulers who barred Indians from their
clubs. The Taj opened its doors to all, provided
they were well-dressed, and epitomized fin de
siecle splendor in its chandeliered salons, protruding bay windows, and marble Turkish baths.
Attached to Tata's edifice is its modern multi-storied annex, the Taj Mahal Intercontinental,

The **Oberoi Bombay Hotel**, ((022) 202-5757,
fax (022) 204-3282, is the Taj's nearest rival, a
monolith of black marble and glass at Nariman Point that outshines the neighboring
Oberoi Towers hotel. The Oberoi offers the most
modern suites and sea views in Bombay, stylish
service, and reputedly the finest dining experiences in town. Rooms are also the city's most
expensive, with singles at US$210, and doubles
US$230 a night. Next door, at the **Oberoi Tow-
ers**, ((022) 202-4343, fax (22) 204-1505, rooms
are from US$175. Both hotels have a varied
range of restaurants, bars, coffee lounges, health
clubs, and shops, but the new Oberoi is undeni-
ably more elegant and more suited to business
travelers.

The **Hotel President**, ((022) 215-0808, fax
(022) 215-1201, 90 Cuffe Parade, is a Taj-group
five-star hotel with an excellent round-the-clock

ABOVE: One of the world's legendary hotels, the Taj
Mahal, boasts spacious suites and rooms overlooking
the ocean and its large pool, as well as first-class
restaurants and modern amenities.

Italian trattoria. Rates: expensive. **The Ambassador Hotel**, ((022) 204-1131, fax (022) 204-0004, on Veer Nariman Road, Churchgate, has distinctive 1930's decor. **The Fariyas**, ((022) 204-2911 fax (022) 234992, off Arthur Bunder Road, Colaba, the **Nataraj Hotel**, ((022) 204-4161 fax (022) 204-3864, 135 Marine Drive, and the art deco-style **Ritz**, ((022) 220141 fax (022) 285-0494, Jamshedji Tata Road, Churchgate, are all pleasant hotels in the moderate to expensive range.

The **Grand Hotel**, ((022) 261-8211 fax (022) 262-6581, 17 Sprott Road, Ballard Estate, is the best of the inexpensive hotels. A pleasant vintage hotel, it has a relaxed atmosphere and a central courtyard. Otherwise try the **Sea Green Hotel**, ((022) 222294, 145 Marine Drive, with views of the Arabian Sea and spacious, comfortable rooms. There's a less expensive annex next door, the **Sea Green South Hotel**, ((022) 221662.

The **Chateau Windsor Guest House**, ((022) 204-3376, next to the Ambassador Hotel, is reliably clean and friendly, and a good economy choice with rooms from US$12. Manager Ashok Aggarwal doubles as a travel agent and is very helpful about any travel plans. The modern **YWCA International Guest House**, ((022) 202-0445, 18 Madame Cama Road, is open to both men and women. Its US$6 rooms are such good value they are frequently booked in advance. Non-YWCA members can pay a "transient membership" fee of US$1.

The best of the other very cheap hotels is **Whalley's Guest House**, ((022) 234206, 41 Mereweather Road, in the Colaba area, a slightly frayed, endearing establishment with huge rooms and balconies.

Both Bombay's airport terminals — the Sahar (international) and Santa Cruz (domestic) — are situated at least an hour's drive from the city. Travelers who prefer a quick getaway can stay directly opposite at the five-star **Leela Kempinski**, ((022) 836-3636, fax (022) 636-0606, or eight kilometers (five miles) from the terminals at Welcomgroup's **Searock Hotel**, ((022) 642-5454, fax (022) 640-8046, at Lands End, Bandra, but ask for a high room facing the sea. There are six restaurants and an elaborate health club. It's worth exploring Bandra itself, which during the days of the Raj was an exclusive British preserve, and to wander through the nearby Linking Road night market.

RESTAURANTS

No other Indian city can rival the quality and diversity of Bombay's restaurants. Here you can find excellent Portuguese-Goan, Iranian, Chinese, Italian, even Polynesian food, as well as every regional cuisine in India. No less exotic are Bombay's own specialties, such as Bombay Duck — feather-light, dried bummelo fish

served crisp from a hot griddle. The famous Parsi *dhanshak* dish, made with fried rice and a chicken or mutton *dhal*, the local pomfret, and the concoctions of *ragada, bhel-puri*, and *pau bhaji* on Chowpatty Beach have also found their way into Bombay's culinary mythology.

There is an almost unlimited variety of restaurants in Bombay — from the most exclusive haunts of the top hotels and glitzy society havens to the proletarian Irani cafés and the city's renowned nocturnal street chef, the Bade-Miyan (meaning "big old Moslem"), who produces delicious brazier-hot kebabs and egg-rotis from his cart behind the Taj Mahal Hotel until one or two in the morning.

For truly exquisite dining, the Oberoi is a sure winner. The sumptuous **Kandahar** restaurant serves faultless North-west Frontier food; the pool-level **La Rotisserie** is excellent for French cuisine, specializing in prime and imported meats; and La Brasserie, open from dawn to midnight, has breakfasts (fresh croissants, perfect freshly squeezed juices) to inspire deep sighs of content from homesick Europeans. Next door at the Oberoi Towers, try the city's only Polynesian restaurant, **The Outrigger**, for seafood specialties.

The Taj Mahal's **Tanjore** restaurant is the best in town for regional Indian cuisine, particularly Hyderabadi, Mughali, and Punjabi specialties, as well as for its evening program of classical Indian dance and music. (Second choice goes to the Oberoi Towers' **Mughal Room**.) Also excellent is the **Golden Dragon**, for authentic Szechuan food.

Outside the hotels, there are literally hundreds of restaurants from which to choose. Currently in vogue with Bombay's glitterati is **China Garden**, ((022) 828-0842, Om Chambers, 123 August Kranti Marg, Om's Corner. This exceptional restaurant serves a variety of regional Chinese cuisine. Locals swear by the **Delhi Durbar**. The upmarket, air-conditioned branch opposite the Regal Cinema in Colaba, ((022) 202035 is popular with affluent Indians for the city's best *biryani* and *dabba gosh* (spicy meat, offal, and onions baked in an earthenware pot). The original **Durbar**, ((022) 359086, in the red-light district of Falkland Road, is easy to find because every taxi-driver knows it.

Good Punjabi fare can be found at the **Sher-e-Punjab** on Bhagat Singh Road, a Sikh enclave where drying turban strips hang from the upper stories, with delicious northern specialties and a distinctive spinach dish made with rye and mustard seeds.

A host of unpretentious vegetarian "clubs" serving the food of South Gujarat, Kutch, and Rajasthan can be found in the central Kalbadevi district. The most famous is the rather basic

Ram Club, opposite the Cotton Exchange and up a dark staircase, for its Rajasthani *thalis*. Close by are **Thakker's Club** and the **Friend's Union Joshi Club**, where the kitchens are part of the dining room, so that you can see your *subze* (vegetarian curries) being assembled. To dine like a true sweet-toothed Gujarati, try **Samrat**, ((022) 220942, J. Tata Road, where dessert precedes the 10-bowl *thali* meal.

The New India Coffee House, Kittridge Road, Sassoon Dock, is the place to try authentic Keralan food, and **Woodlands,** Nariman Point, (202-3499 (there are two other branches in Bombay), has delicious south-Indian mealtime *thalis*.

For Portuguese-Goan lunchtime fare (superlative fish *vindaloo* and, for adventurous palates, chili-hot pork sorpotal), try either **Martin's** at Colaba or the **Cafe Kitchen** in the Fort Market — both are equally good.

You can take your pick of any number of Chinese restaurants, the best among them being **Chopsticks**, ((022) 204-9284, on Veer Nariman Road, with an atmospheric outdoor café extension, and **Nanking Chinese Restaurant,** ((022) 202-0594, Phiroze Building, Shivaji Maharaj Marg, which is especially good for succulent steamed crab, prawns, and lobster at reasonable prices despite its popularity.

For pure idiosyncratic charm, nothing can match Bombay's Irani cafés, the dwindling legacy of the many hundreds founded by staunch Zoroastrian immigrants at the turn of the century, with their marble-topped tables, spindly-legged wooden chairs, salon-style swing doors, illustrated mirrors (often with spidery portraits of the Shah of Iran, George VI, and his Queen Elizabeth), and elderly, white-capped waiters who scuttle around like lizards with a dish in one hand and a tea-towel in the other. Irani cafs are all-day affairs, starting with *brun-maska* hard crusts of buttered Irani bread eaten dipped in *phudhina*, mint tea made with milk and sugar. If Brain Fry In Eggs, or Chicken Dress Gravy seem

best left to the imagination, ask for a *dibbe wala* meal of chicken or mutton instead. The oldest and most famous of the cafés are **Kyani** and **Bastani**, at Dhobi Talao toward the north end of M.G. Road; otherwise try the **Regal Restaurant** and the **Byculla Restaurant**, both of which are near the Byculla railway station, near Victoria Gardens.

Finally, go to **Badshah**, directly opposite Crawford Market, for the best rendition of *falooda*, the multicolored vermicelli and ice-cream drink, fresh grape and pomegranate juice, and the addictive *chikku* (fig) milkshake. And don't miss the **Leopold Cafe**, down the road from the Regal Cinema in Colaba. It's a tropical beatnik haunt with well-thumbed menus, cheap and hearty meals (full English breakfasts for US$1), and chilled beer (try the state-brewed London Diet or Pilsener brands).

NIGHTLIFE

Bombay is the brightest beacon in the largely teetotal subcontinent. Of all Indian cities it has the most thriving array of bars, restaurants, nightclubs, and theaters. It has its fair share of glitterati — land barons, movie producers, starlets, and chic socialites — and is an exciting place to be out on the town.

Of all Bombay's night-time entertainment, to miss seeing a Hindi film would be like going to Stratford-on-Avon without seeing a production of a Shakespeare play. There are literally hundreds of cinemas here, showing a variety of films in Hindi, Marathi, and English. They usually screen at 3, 6, and 9 pm, with a few extra matinees at odd hours. To get acquainted with Bombay's insatiable fascination for celluloid, buy one of the "screen gossip" rags sold at every newsstand (*Star and Style* is especially salacious) and then find out from the local newspaper listings what's showing where. It's most fun to go to one of the old "talkies" cinemas with ornate faades dating to the 1930's: the **Eros** on J.N. Tata Road, Churchgate, the **Metro** on 1st Marine Drive, and the pretty (but run-down) **Opera House**, opposite Chowpatty Beach, are popular and centrally located. If your taxi/auto-driver doesn't know them he's not worth his salt. Otherwise, opt for modern air-conditioned comfort at one of the three cinemas directly opposite Victoria Terminus — the **Excelsior**, the **Empire**, and the **Sterling**.

For the city's best cocktails, jazz, and stunning views, the Oberoi's elegant **Bayview Bar** is a winner. Other haunts for enjoyable sundowners are the neighboring Oberoi Towers' **Supper Club**, with nightly cabaret shows and dancing; the Taj Mahal's **Apollo Bar**, on the 24th floor, with its spectacular views, swaying Goan musicians, 1960's decor, and flared-trousered businessmen clinching deals; and the Ambassador Hotel's revolving **Rooftop Restaurant**.

Bombay's nightclubs start opening their doors at around 10 pm, but don't really get going until past midnight, especially on Friday and Saturday nights. Virtually all are housed within five-star hotels, meaning that unless you are a guest or can sweet-talk your way past the bouncer, you'll need to pay an entry fee. Once inside, drinks — local liquor, unless specified — tend to be expensive.

The best is **1900**, at the Taj Mahal Hotel, a belle époque-style haunt for Bombay's young, fashionable in-crowd, enlivened by the appearance of models and rising film stars. With teased hair and dangling earrings, girls from the wealthy upper class dance like pouting marionettes in the latest Western fashions. At the bar, a few heavy-jowled men wearing gold medallions drink neat whisky in silence, tapping snake-skin shoes in time with the beat until closing time. Open from 9:30 pm, to 3 am, cover charge: US$10.

The **Cellar**, at the Oberoi Towers, is decorated to resemble an Austrian taverna, with waiters clad in alpine breeches. It fails to attract much of a fashionable following. Open from 9:30 pm to 3 am, cover charge: US$3.

A half-hour drive north of Bombay is **Juhu Beach**, a mini-Malibu dotted with the kitch mansions of film stars. Palms fringe an unswimmable beach, but at night it looks suitably romantic — a glittering stretch of cafés, neon lights, and carnival-like stalls along the sands. You'll find **Xanadu**, the most popular of the Juhu clubs, down a narrow staircase next to the Hotel Horizon. Its dark, strobe-lit interior makes the grinning barmen look like they've used Chernobyl toothpaste. Proletarian disco tunes keep this place packed to the rafters on Friday and Saturday nights. Open 9:30 pm to 3 am, cover charge: US$3.

Nearby, the Holiday Inn and the Airport Plaza Hotel have standard discotheques, patronized mostly by airline crews on their stopovers. Not far from Juhu is the Searock Hotel's **Cavern** nightclub in **Bandra**, a 45 minute drive from inner-city Colaba. It has a fake Ali Baba-style interior, dangling camouflage nets, and loud disco medleys. Like 1900, this is a popular place for aspiring starlets in Madonna outfits. Aging talent scouts prop themselves against the bar like corpulent lizards. Open from 9:30 pm to 3 am, cover charge US$5.

Back in the city, it's fascinating to glimpse the seamier underworld of Bombay's so-called "Cages," the lively brothel area located in Colaba's Maulana Shaukatali (Grant) and Falkland Roads, named for the grilled windows through which the painted ladies peer. It's better to drive rather than walk late at night. You could make one last stop at Chowpatty Beach, at the north end of Marine Drive, which is still lively at one or two in the morning. It's a drifting circus of hawkers selling king coconuts, giant balloons, and piping-hot midnight snacks; parents trailing small toddlers; and eccentric sideshows on the moonlit sands.

SIGHTSEEING

City Strolls

You could start your day with a swirled cappuccino and the Bombay edition of the *Times of India* at the Taj Mahal before crossing the road to the **Gateway of India**. This was where King George V

and Queen Mary stepped ashore in 1911, en route to make the startling announcement at the Delhi Durbar that New Delhi was to replace Calcutta as the capital of India. In Bombay, they were welcomed by a hastily constructed white plaster arch on the Bunder pier that was replaced in 1927 by the present Gateway of India, designed by George Wittet, with its cosmopolitan mélange of traditional Hindu, Muslim, and Gujarati styles, notably the minarets and trelliswork *jalis*. India Gate was also the site where on February 28, 1948, the Somerset Light Infantry, to the tune of *Auld Lang Syne*, wrapped up the

OPPOSITE: The Taj Mahal Hotel's "1900" disco is frequented by Bombay's fashionable in-crowd.
ABOVE: Tourist boats moor in front of the Gateway of India, scene of departure ceremonies when Britain left India in 1948, ending more than two centuries of rule.

Union Jack and boarded vessels for England, ending more than two centuries of British rule.

The **Sassoon Docks**, a 1.5-km (0.9-mile) walk south of the Bunder, named after Bombay's famous Sephardic Jew, David Sassoon, are recommended for the dawn spectacle of fishermen unloading their catch. It's a 10-minute walk from here to the tranquil **Afghan Memorial Church of St John the Evangelist**, built in 1847 to commemorate British soldiers killed in the Sind and Afghan campaigns of 1838 and 1843.

Adjacent to the Apollo Bunder is the bustling **Colaba** area — the main tourist center — crowded with antique shops, cheap lodgings (such as the

dehyde by proud Victorian men of science. There's an array of Harappan artifacts, Assyrian tablets, Tibetan-Buddhist sculptures and scrolls (and gruesome carvings from human bone), antique cloisonné-ware, and oil paintings. Open daily except Monday from 10 am to 6:30 pm, with a Rs 5 entry fee (but free on Tuesdays). Next door is the Jehangir Art Gallery (closed on public holidays) and its pleasant Samovar Cafe. Hawkers in this area sell factory seconds — acid-washed denim, cotton dresses, and bright shirts — giant balloons, and garish stuffed animals.

Nariman Point is the place to see small armies of sinewy, white Gandhi-capped *dabba-*

infamous Stiffles Hotel, which bears a quaint resemblance to a New Orleans brothel and lists its room rates in Arabic), cafés, and street-stalls selling a medley of bright shirts, plastic flowers, good leather shoes, and electronic watches. Tucked behind the Taj is the **Royal Bombay Yacht Club**, an oasis of musty, nautical charm.

Nearby is the Wittet-designed **Prince of Wales Museum**, set in a circular garden on Mahatma Gandhi Road, which commemorates that monarch's first visit to India. This leafy marble oasis in the midst of Bombay's bustle contains one of India's best collections of art and artifacts. The natural history section contains numerous strange creatures snared and stored in formal-

wallahs delivering cartloads of tiffin boxes to waiting office workers at lunchtime.

The Fort on Foot

The "Fort area" is a rather elastic term for the area that encompassed the original **Fort St George** cantonment, and is now the heart of civic Bombay. This is a fascinating place to stroll around, with its musty antique shops, architectural monuments, and colorful street-hawkers, notably the sandwich-wallahs who serve multi-layered offerings from boxes strapped around their necks. In this area are some of the most daunting official buildings ever constructed on the outposts of the British Empire. These architectural talismans of the High Victorian age were built when Bombay was flushed with commercial success and governed by an ardent imperialist, Sir Bartle Frere (1862—1867), who imported

ABOVE: Clocktower at Bombay University.
OPPOSITE: Bombay's antique shops attract visitors from all over the world.

British architects to execute a massive palisade of public offices in the fashionable Gothic Revival style.

An excursion into the city's history can begin at the **Bandstand** south of the Oval Maiden, where cricket games are held on Sundays. Fronting the sea is a remarkable collection of buildings, beginning with the Venetian-Gothic **Secretariat**, flanked by Sir Gilbert Scott's 1874 French-Gothic **University Campus**, **University Library**, and the **Rajabai Clock Tower** (excellent for a view over the city). Further along is the **High Court**, completed in 1878. In the noon-day sun, bewigged lawyers flit about in its large courtyard like black crows, and affidavits are painstakingly drafted under flapping palm-mat awnings. The smaller building next to it is the **Public Works Building**, and adjacent to it is James Trubshawe's **Central Telegraph Office**.

An alternative tour starts from **Hautatama Chowk**, formerly Flora Fountain, where a short walk east brings you to Horniman's Circle and **St Thomas' Cathedral**, whose foundation stone was laid in 1675. The ornate faade was a gift from the East India Company, and the cathedral still exhibits the chairs King George and Queen Mary occupied during their visit in 1911, and a profusion of brass plaques and marble figures.

Beyond the cathedral is a stately sweep of buildings, including the Doric-style **Town Hall**, designed by Col. Thomas Cowper. Opened in 1833, it also functions as the Asiatic Society Library, the oldest and largest library in the city. The basement contains many cloth-covered statues of former colonial rulers, removed after Independence. Beyond this you can glimpse the **Mint**, built in 1829 (permission to visit requires an application to the Mint Master).

But the greatest building of all is the magnificently preposterous **Victoria Terminus** at the north end of the Fort, designed by Frederick William Stevens in 1888. Its faade teems with contorted gargoyles, turreted spires, and a petrified menagerie of rats, peacocks, and snakes. A life-size statue of Queen Victoria once stood in front of the faade, but it has been relocated (with regal hauteur intact) to a corner of the Bombay Zoo. At dusk, the throngs of suburb-bound workers beneath the giant arches give Victoria Terminus the appearance of a metropolitan Hades, watched over sternly by busts of the founding company chairman and his managing director. Lady Dufferin, vicerine when the terminus was completed, thought it "much too magnificent for a bustling crowd of railway passengers."

The Markets

Crawford Market, built by Arthur Crawford in 1867, is the most grandiose market building

in India. Tattered sunlight turns the dust into incense-scented screens as you wander through the chaotic maze of cool passages, each a division of wares. The best time to visit is around seven in the morning, when armies of slender coolies balance silvery basins of fresh fish on their heads, chickens run riot, and immense troughs of fruits and vegetables are unloaded amidst a cacophony of squeals, shouts, and thuds. It has immense character: here you find sly Marwari traders hawking false mustaches and crocheted caps, the frail leaf-like dried bummelo fish, giant sacks of grain, brightly colored spices, caged Assam parrots, labrador puppies,

and fighting cocks. If you crane your neck, it's possible to make out Rudyard's father, Lockwood Kipling's bas reliefs on the market's faade.

Within a two-kilometer (just over a mile) radius of Crawford Market and concentrated between Victoria Terminus and Maulana Shaukatali (Grant) Road are literally dozens of specialist bazaars set amidst a labyrinth of temples, mosques, and narrow, spindly seventeenth-century Gujarati houses. It's easy to spend hours strolling from one bazaar to another. Even Bombayites throw up their hands in mock despair when asked to name them all, but listed here are some of the most interesting. North of Crawford Market, off Abdul Rahman Street, are the **Zaveri** and adjacent silver bazaars, where plump merchants recline on white cushions while prospective wives barter for gold and diamond jewelry — the more ostentatious the better. Around the corner is the sneeze-inducing dry fruits and spices bazaar, called **Mirchi Gully**, where every conceivable kind of chili is sold, along with piles of Afghani almonds and pistachio nuts.

For rows of glittering brass and copper, go to the **Bhuleshwar** area at the top of Kalbadevi Road, where you can also visit the Mumbadevi temple and tank, reconstructed from the original built in 1737 and a shrine of the Koli or fisherfolk, whose sacred goddess gave Bombay its name.

To the north, on Mutton Street, is the best of them all: **Chor** or **Thieves Bazaar**. Stroll past retired car engines to the antique section of the market where grandfather clocks, intricately carved rosewood furniture, chinaware, nautical instruments, and His Master's Voice gramophones are sold by shrewd dealers. The rest of Chor bazaar gets more peculiar — secondhand army surplus, rows of shoelaces, and even a section for stolen airline headphones. The **leather market** in Dhaboo Street is just parallel and worth exploring for wallets, bags, and shoes.

The Marine Promenade

Locals never call Marine Drive by its new name, Netaji Subhash Road; they prefer to call it "Queen's Necklace" for its sparkle of lamps at night. Reclaimed as recently as 1920, it stretches along the seafront from Nariman Point to Malabar Hill and is well-patronized by early morning joggers, king-coconut sellers, and courting couples. Towards the Chowpatty end is the **Taraporewala Aquarium**, which is worth a visit. Opened in 1951, it houses a wide variety of marine and freshwater fish, and even sells fish and chips at its small café! Open 11 am to 8 pm weekdays (except Monday) and 10 am to 8 pm on Sundays, with a Rs 5 entrance fee.

At the north end of Marine Drive is **Chowpatty Beach,** a stretch of sand offering donkey-rides, candy-floss, and piping-hot midnight snacks. This is also the focus for political rallies and where the **Ganesh Chaturthi** festival is staged every year during September's full moon. Bombayites are devoted to this plump, elephant-headed fellow, the deity of material advancement, and honor him with a massive parade along Marine Drive with as many as 6,000 Ganesh images, some towering to nine meters (30 ft) and strung with flashing lights and blaring loudspeakers. The grand finale is the immersion of these effigies in the sea at Chowpatty Beach and the cheers from the crowd as they either buckle and sink or float gaily toward the horizon. In the late nineteenth century, when political meetings were banned by the British, the early Independence move-

ment used the Ganesh festival as a way of communicating political messages through dance and drama.

From dawn to dusk, Chowpatty Beach is a drifting circus of scrawny beggars, hawkers, aimless sadhus with long tousled hair, and scrums of young men in flared trousers. Families flock here on Sundays, wandering from the donkey stand to impromptu wrestling competitions and the triple row of Bombay's best fast food vendors. Here is the place to sample *channa bhatura, bhel-puri, ragada*, and the queen of Bombay's snacks, *pau bhaji,* a spicy vegetable gravy served with a fried bun.

It's about a 15-minute stroll to August Kranti Gardens, and **Mani Bhavan** — a little brown house at 19 Laburnam Road — is just parallel. This was Mahatma Gandhi's residence during his visits to Bombay between 1917 and 1934.

From here, Gandhi launched many of his famous *satyagraha* (non-violence) campaigns. Today, Mani Bhavan is a museum housing replicas of Gandhi's daily utensils, ascetic bed, spinning wheel, and well-worn sandals. There's a section depicting the Mahatma's life through a collection of dolls, a picture gallery, and an excellent library. Also on exhibit are copies of historic documents signed by Gandhi. Open from 9:30 am to 6 pm, except Sunday. Entrance fee Rs 5.

Malabar Hill

At the top of nearby Malabar Hill are the **Hanging Gardens**, which were landscaped in 1881 and immediately became popular with memsahib watercolorists as a locale for botanical sketches. Despite the Gothic-sounding name, the gardens are very sedate but do have one intriguing attraction — a gardener who trans-

forms his hedges into astonishing abstract art compositions.

Adjacent to the gardens in a private enclave and hidden by dense foliage is the **Tower of Silence**, the round stone construction in which the Parsis place their dead to be devoured by vultures. These structures are designed in much the same way as a lobster-net — to prevent vultures from flying out with body parts in their talons. A series of towers have been built since Aungier leased the Parsi community the one-square kilometer (0.4-sq mile) site in 1673, and today the area is potentially some of the most valuable real estate in Bombay, but is ardently protected by the Parsis. Visitors are strictly forbidden.

Bombay's swish Marine Drive, is known as the "Queen's Necklace" for its sparkle of lights at night.

Just across the road is the **Kamala Nehru Children's Park,** with its colorful playground, floral clock, and spectacular views across Back Bay, Chowpatty Beach, and Marine Drive. Just near the park's entrance is the **Naaz Cafe,** where the top terrace is the best place for a chilled beer at sunset.

At the **Adishwarji Jain Temple,** on B.G. Kher Marg, just down the road from the gardens, you can admire the intricate marble carvings, many of great antiquity, which were placed here after the temple's construction in 1903. Its upper story contains exquisite silver doors, and the ground floor has rows of recesses with statues of Jain

can be found here alongside the skyscrapers. On the southern tip, Malabar Point, is **Raj Bhavan,** the Chief Minister's residence, which is closed to the public but can be seen from Marine Drive. Nearby is the **Walkeshwar Temple,** dating back to the eleventh century, where legend has it Rama stopped to make a devotional lingam on his way to rescue his kidnapped wife, Sita, from the clutches of the evil Ceylonese god-king.

Opposite is the **Banganga Tank,** where Rama is supposed to have shot an arrow into the scorched earth when he was thirsty. Today the ancient stone stairs are used to dry clothes and

tirthankaras. One of the most colorful Jain ceremonies to witness here is the Siddh-Chakra, a purification ritual before marriage. (The best time to see it is just before the marriage season begins in December to January). The young men undergoing the ritual wear dhotis and cover their faces with the distinctive Jain gauze mask (to discourage the swallowing of insects), and sit amidst elaborate patterns of blossoms and symbolic *thali*-dishes, humming scriptures with the temple priests as musicians play stirring tunes — all recorded by proud parents on their video cameras.

Malabar Hill and the neighboring suburb of **Breach Candy** are Bombay's most exclusive addresses, where much of the city's famed socializing takes place. Majestic eighteenth-century mansions with ornately carved faades and marble fountains writhing with naked nymphs

the tank's mythically pure water has turned to a chocolate-colored swill.

Haji Ali's Tomb and Dhobi Ghats

Little is known about Haji Ali, the turreted mausoleum built in the late eighteenth century at the end of a rocky causeway reached only at low tide near Mahalaxmi. According to popular belief, the tomb was built in memory of a merchant who renounced his wealth and lived on the barren rocks after a pilgrimage (hajj) to Mecca. His sister, Ma Hajiani, became his companion in ascetic suffering and a mausoleum was built for her a little distance away on Worli Bay. This is not the place to leave your shoes unguarded — the tomb is full of quick-eyed beggar urchins eager to whisk away your sneakers. Muslim pilgrims have developed a ritual to deal with the row of pitiful, wailing beggars who perform *khel* (beggar's tricks) along the narrow walkway — they exchange rupees for a handful of paise and distribute the equivalent of a few grains of rice to each one. At the entrance are dozens of stalls selling sticky white (and sickly sweet) *prasad*, reflective-glass scripture pictures, *burqa* (the encompassing garment worn by Muslim women), and plug-in Taj Mahal baubles, which shine in the dark. There's also the **Hajiali Juice Center,** which makes the best fresh juice in town. Also try their specialty, *sitafel* (custard-apple), and pomegranate juice.

Two of Bombay's elite social institutions, the ultra-proper Willingdon Club and the **Mahalaxmi Race Course,** are close by. The racecourse is named for the goddess of the nearby Hindu temple, who is the deity of wealth. The annual Derby here in February and March creates a frenzy of social activity. Stroll to the **Mahalaxmi Junction** station over-bridge to see Bombay's dhobi ghats, where hundreds of dhobi-wallahs (washermen) live and work. It's a giant maze of troughs, bubbling with suds and echoing with the noise of stains being tirelessly whacked out of the city's laundry. Like the *dabba*-wallahs, the dhobi-ghats operate almost infallibly on a system of hieroglyphic squiggles on each piece of fabric to identify the owner.

The Museum Round-up Tour

The **Victoria and Albert Museum** is situated in spacious gardens close to the entrance of the Jijamata Udyan in Byculla, which was once the premier European suburb in Bombay. The museum has many Indian paintings, antique coins, and weaponry, but its highlight is "Bombay: a Photorama", which portrays the story of Bombay from 1661 to 1931 through a series of old prints, maps, and 250 old and rare photographs. It is open every day except Wednesday.

The **Victoria Gardens** are Bombay's best and largest, laid out in 1861 with broad paths, ornamental ferneries, and many rare species of tropical plants. A blackboard near the entrance lists "flowering" attractions of the day. The **Bombay Zoo** is here, and children can take elephant, camel, and pony rides. Open Thursday—Tuesday from 8 am to 6 pm.

The **National Maritime Museum** is the only one of its kind in India, with a rich collection of naval and maritime memorabilia dating back to the time of Alexander the Great. It's located on Middle Island, a coastal battery owned by the Western Naval Command, and reached by tourist boats which leave from the nearby Gateway of India. Open between 2 pm and 5:30 pm on Saturdays and 10 am and 5 pm on Sundays and public holidays.

The **F.D. Alpaiwalla Museum,** located at Khareghat Memorial Hall in Khareghat Colony, houses an extensive collection of antique memorabilia, Gandhara sculptures, 80 albums of picture postcards, fragments of Sir John Marshall's Taxila excavations, Chinese porcelain, and a mummified hand from Egypt.

The **Nehru Planetarium** in Worli has daily star-gazing shows in English at 3 pm and 6 pm (except Mondays), admission US$0.50.

OUT OF BOMBAY

On a small green island just 10 km (six miles) northeast of the Apollo Bunder are four magnificent rock-cut cave temples of Elephanta,

dating from AD 450 to 750 and dedicated to Lord Shiva. It's an hour's journey to **Elephanta Island** and ferries leave every hour between 9 am and 2 pm from the Gateway of India. The deluxe boats are preferable because they have archaeology graduates as guides.

Long before Bombay came into existence, Elephanta Island was the capital city of the Silahara dynasty (first century AD) and was called Gharapuri, "place of idols". Much later, the Portuguese claimed part of the island and renamed it after discovering a massive elephant sculpture, which now stands in the Victoria Gardens. Portuguese soldiers used the carved temple deities for target practice, and natural decay has added to the damage. From the primitive wooden jetty, the caves are reached by an easy climb (or palanquins for those who don't mind being hoisted up the hill by four semi-naked men). The cave temples contain a combination of Hindu, Jain, and Buddhist iconography, and the sinuous, enraptured figures were considered shockingly Dionysian by the straitlaced Christian visitors. On Sundays and public holidays, Elephanta Island is unbearable, with

OPPOSITE: Haji Ali's Muslim tomb of mysterious origin. ABOVE: Boats used for tours of the Elephanta Caves.

Bombay and the West

199

creaking ferry-loads of fellow tourists and a motley crowd of persistent hawkers. Avoid the rabble by taking the earliest boat during the week.

The **Kanheri Caves**, 42 km (26 miles) from Bombay, are far more impressive. This is one of the largest of a series of Buddhist rock-cut monasteries in western India, cut into the hills and valleys of the mountain chain known as the Western Ghats, of which the most famous are at Ajanta and Ellora. The pillars are hewn from the rock in such a way that they appear to support the weight of the mountain above. There are 109 caves in all, dating from about the first to the ninth century AD, and all are excavated from a gigantic circular rock.

The earlier caves belong to the Hinayana phase of Buddhist architecture. Many served as simple monks' quarters and are of little interest, but caves 1, 2, and 3 are notable for their massive pillars, sculptures, and stupas. Most impressive is cave 3, a Buddhist *chaitya* (or chapel), with its monumental pillars and elaborate images of Buddha.

The ruins at **Bassein**, 77 km (48 miles) from Bombay on the mainland, make a perfect picnic spot. This is where the Portuguese built a walled city overlooking the sea after taking possession of the territory from its Muslim rulers in 1534. It grew into a grand settlement, with cathedrals and elegant homes where the fiercely Jesuit Portuguese aristocrats, the Hildalgos, lived in dissolute splendor, using Bassein as a naval base for converting the natives, often under threat of death, and amassing considerable wealth. They were forced to flee suddenly in 1739 during an invasion by the local Mahratta army, and the ruins now serve as a poignant reminder of Portuguese rule. Trains run to Bassein Road station from Victoria Terminus, and the settlement ruins are only four kilometers (2.5 miles) away. It's best to make this a full day's excursion.

GENERAL INFORMATION

The Maharashtra Tourism Development Corporation (MTDC) runs well-organized conducted city bus tours that bulldoze through the main places of interest. Daily, except Mondays, at 9 am to 1 pm, and 2 pm to 7 pm. Other guided tours include daily boat trips to the Elephanta Caves at 10 am to 2 pm and 2:30 pm to 6:30 pm, and a full day's excursion that includes the Kanheri Caves, the Lion Safari Park, and Juhu Beach, at 10 am to 7 pm.

MTDC Office, CDO Hutments, Madame Cama Road. ((022) 202-6713, 202-7762.

India Tourism Development Corporation (ITDC), ((022) 242-3343.

Government of India Tourist Office, 123 Maharshi Karve Road, opposite Churchgate station. ((022) 293144. Open 9 am to 5 pm, alternate Saturdays 9 am to 12:30 pm, closed Sundays.

Useful Reading

The monthly *Bombay Calling* has an extensive directory for all hotels, restaurants, information centers, travel reservation offices, museums, etc and is available from hotels and news-stands. The Government of India Tourist Office also publishes a fortnightly diary of cultural events in Bombay.

THE WESTERN TRAIL

From Bombay, travelers usually explore western India by one or a combination of three routes through **Goa**, **Maharashtra**, and **Gujarat**. Many make Goa's sandy, palm-lined beaches and colonial Portuguese sights their first priority. But both Maharashtra and Gujarat are equally rewarding destinations, though they are often neglected by tourists.

In Maharashtra, carved from the bare rocks of the Deccan Plateau, are India's finest ancient cave sculptures and frescoes at Ellora and Ajanta.

Gujarat's capital, Ahmedabad, contains many relics of its grand Mughal past and fine art and textile museums. Nearby, the former princely capital, Vadodara (Baroda), is a stately city of Gothic palaces, parks, and museums. But the real pleasures lie in rural Gujarat, from its northern tip at the Rann of Kutch, the home of brightly attired tribal nomads, through the Sasan-Gir wildlife sanctuary and elaborate Jain temples in the south.

GOA

BALMY DAYS AND PORTUGUESE RELICS

Goa is justifiably famous for its dazzling 100-km (62-mile) sweep of palm-lined coastline fringed by the turquoise Arabian Sea. Unspoilt and rustic, Goa's fertile green plains are covered with cashew, mango, and jackfruit groves, and criss-crossed by the Mandovi and Zuari rivers, from which rise forested hills up to the Western Ghats mountain range.

Goa has a seductive Latin atmosphere that feels peculiarly unIndian, and is perfect for relaxing, swimming, sunbathing, and eating seafood.

The Mauryan Empire established settlements along this coastal sweep in the third century BC and the area passed through a succession of rulers in seesaw wars and conflicts between the Muslims from the north and the Hindu-dominated dynasties of the south.

But Goa owes its exotic personality to the Portuguese, who seized it from the Bijapur kings of the Deccan in 1510 under the command of Afonso Albuquerque after failing to secure a base on the Malabar coast further south. Traders from Lisbon used Goa as well as the smaller possessions of Diman and Diu to the north in Gujarat as staging posts for plying the eastern spice routes to Indonesia and Sri Lanka to amass fortunes from ginger, pepper, nutmegs, and saffron.

Zealous missionaries followed, and their terrifying threats of a fiery hell prompted mass conversions of local Hindus, aided by the arrival of an Inquisition party in 1560. At the height of its prosperity, Goa was a magnificent city, full of majestic cathedrals and mansions, some of which can still be seen in old Goa today. But Portuguese power declined rapidly after the seventeenth century, falling prey to occupation by the Dutch in 1603, and later by the British during the Napoleonic wars in Europe. During the full-blown days of the Raj, Goa was regarded as a quaint and harmless vestige, appreciated for its cheap wine. A British guide book of 1898, *Picturesque India*, referred to Goa as "a pathetic wilderness of ruined churches and palaces". The Portuguese held control until 1961, when the remaining colonials were thrown out in a largely bloodless invasion by India.

The colonial heritage is apparent everywhere, in the street tavernas, dilapidated Iberian-style villas, women's preference for frocks over saris, and numerous smatterings of Portuguese in the local Konkan vernacular.

Although India has some 6,000 km (3,700 miles) of coastline, most of it is completely undeveloped and Goa is India's most superior beach resort. This is as much due to its variety of beautiful beaches and hotels as it is to the gregarious Goanese who have a Mediterranean enthusiasm for their hybrid cuisine and locally brewed *feni*, a coconut, palm, or cashew whiskey.

WHEN TO GO

India has few destinations where it is possible to feel comfortable all year round, but Goa is one of them. It's best to visit between October and February, but the monsoon period of June to September is often dramatically beautiful. Sadly, Goa's famous pre-Advent Carnival (held late February to early March), once an exuberant, bacchanalian ritual of floats and costumes, has become drab of late owing to political disputes between its organizers. If you are in Goa for any major Christian festival or for the *Novidades* harvest celebration on August 24, it's likely that bull-fights will be staged, advertised by word of mouth only. During Easter and Christmas, Goa dons full sixteenth century-style regalia for remarkable processions in Old Goa's ghost city of cathedrals and basilicas.

HOW TO GET THERE

By far the most enjoyable way of arriving in Goa is by steamer from Bombay, which operates daily except Tuesday between October and May, but closes down during the June—September monsoon months. The boat leaves from Bombay's Ferry Wharf at around 10 am and drifts into Goa early next morning. Berths can be reserved, but even so, it is best to arrive early to claim your place as operators often double-book. A deluxe cabin on the upper deck costs between Rs 235 and Rs 300 but is recommended over the rigors of traveling in the congested cargo class. However, the lower deck is a mere Rs 48 and for many travelers proves a more interesting experience. Meals and beer are served on board. The return journey from Goa leaves daily except Wednesday; again, berths can be booked in advance.

Goa's Dabolim airport is connected by Indian Airlines flights from Bombay, Delhi,

Bangalore, Cochin, and Trivandrum. Panaji, the capital, is 27 km (16.8 miles) away and the resort beaches are even further, so it's worth utilizing the free reception coaches provided by the major hotels for prospective guests. Otherwise, there's a US$1.50 airport bus into town.

Train journeys to Goa's Vasco da Gama station, some 30 km (18.6 miles) from Panaji, take 22 hours from Bombay and 46 hours from New Delhi. The route from Bombay slices through some spectacular scenery, but the New Delhi journey can be arduous. Luxury buses take 16 hours from Bombay, but most are notorious video-coaches. The best choice is MTDC's air-conditioned "luxury" bus, with no video, departing at 3 pm daily (US$8).

GETTING AROUND

Goa looks deceptively tiny on the map, but in reality it is very spread out, and transport is needed to appreciate its varied landscape. Taxis are freely available for day hire. Hiring a motorbike is far more exhilarating, and rates are best negotiated on a weekly basis. Your hotel should be able to arrange a newish vehicle, but make sure you wear a crash helmet as the local constabulary often extract "simple police fines" from bareheaded tourists.

Goa's four main towns are connected by a regular bus service. **Panaji**, the center, is close to Dona Paula and Miramar beaches; **Mapusa** (13 km, or eight miles) has bus connections along the northern coast; **Margao** (34 km, or 21 miles) is very Portuguese, with fine parks and old mansions, and connects to the southern beaches of Majorda, Colva, Benaulim, Betelbatim, and Betel; and **Vasco da Gama** (30 km, or 18.6 miles) is close to the Oberoi Resort at Bogmalo Beach. The nicest way to explore Old Goa from Panaji is by taking a mid-morning ferry for a languid chug down the Mandovi River. The tourist office runs enjoyable evening river cruises from Panaji's jetty at 6 pm. Full moon nights are spectacular, with dinner and lively Portuguese music and dancing on deck.

SIGHTSEEING

Panaji

Panaji still looks and feels like a sleepy Portuguese town. It is set along the southern bank of the salty Mandovi River, with broad avenues spilling into cobbled squares, grand public buildings, red-tiled houses, narrow lanes, and tavernas.

OPPOSITE: Goan scenes: TOP: Aguada Beach. BELOW: Restaurant on Baga Beach.

Start with the **Secretariat** building, originally built by the Sultan of Bijipur who quartered his Arabian horses and elephants in the Moorish courtyard. The Portuguese rebuilt it in 1615 as the official residence for viceroys and generals. Beyond Largo Da Palacio (Palace Square) is Panaji's lively quay where the steamer from Bombay arrives each morning. Nearby is the baroque **Church of the Immaculate Conception**, with its distinctive twin towers. Just beyond the church is the residential Fontainhas area, a languid maze of shuttered, balustraded villas, painted ochre, blue, or mint green, behind which plump matrons slice spinach for the lunchtime Goan favorite, *caldo verde*. This area is full of musty, antiquated shops selling sacks of raw cashews and lumps of Goa's mango-flavored cheese. Shadowed lanes reveal cafés where old men in straw hats gather to sip feni in the siesta hours. For a spectacular view across the town, take a 15-minute walk up to **Altino Hill** and the **Patriarch Palace**, where Pope John Paul II stayed during his 1986 visit.

Old Goa: Conquistadors and Cathedrals

The Portuguese called their prized Indian possession "Goa Dourada", or Golden Goa, but it was not the beautiful beaches they were referring to. Portuguese wealth and power was concentrated in Old Goa, its "Rome of the Orient", where the vast hybrid oriental-baroque cathedrals are layered with African gold.

In the sixteenth century, Goa was famed for its eight square kilometers (three square miles) of majestic churches, monasteries, convents, and stately mansions, boasting a larger population than Lisbon, Paris, or London. Old Goa was abandoned after a series of virulent plagues in 1534, 1635, and 1735 that wiped out nearly 80 percent of the population. The survivors created Panaji, nine kilometers (5.5 miles) away, as the new capital in 1835. Today, Old Goa is still fairly deserted, and its lime-white churches hover above the jungle like a Christian Angkor Wat.

The **Basilica of Bom Jesus**, completed in 1604, contains a remarkable Baroque gilded altar. In an airtight silver and glass casket lie the sacred remains of St Francis Xavier, Goa's patron saint, who spent his life spreading Christianity through the Portuguese colonies. His mottled skull is eerily lit by a naked bulb. Beneath the basilica is a beautifully sculpted mausoleum donated by the Grand Duke of Tuscany. Xavier died in China in 1552, and his mummified corpse criss-crossed the globe before it was brought to Goa in 1613. For a "small donation" you can view his silver-encased feet. Every 10 years, the basilica becomes a mad throng of pilgrims for the "public veneration" of the skeleton. A small gallery displays portraits and

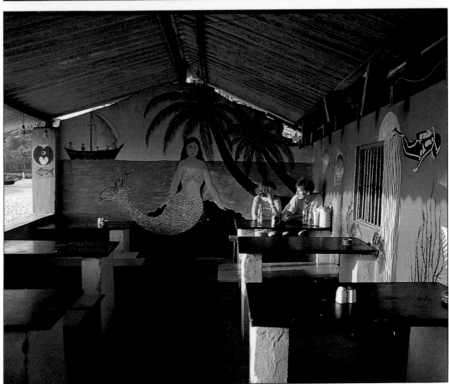

various relics attributed to the famous saint. The basilica is open 9 am to 6 pm daily (open 10 am Sundays for service).

Across the road is the majestic **Chapel of St Catherine**, completed in 1619 and dedicated to St Catherine of Alexandria, a pagan girl who became an ardent Christian and was later beheaded on the very same day, November 25, that Afonso Albuquerque gunned his way down the Mandovi to wrest Goa from the Muslims. Many regard the cathedral as Asia's largest and most magnificent Christian church, a grand renaissance structure with an ornate gilded interior. Beautifully detailed panels around the center

The **Church of St Cajetan**, near old Goa's ferry wharf, was built by Italian friars to resemble St Peters' basilica in Rome. Look for the **Viceroy's Arch**, the ceremonial entranceway for disembarking Portuguese governors. On Monte Santo (holy hill) is the **St Augustine Tower**, all that remains of what was once Goa's biggest church. Opposite is the buttressed, fortress-style **Convent of St Monica**, India's largest nunnery. A gate leads to the secluded **Church of Our Lady of the Rosary**, one of the earliest built in Goa, which contains the tomb of Dona Caterina, wife of the tenth governor and the first Portuguese woman to venture to Goa.

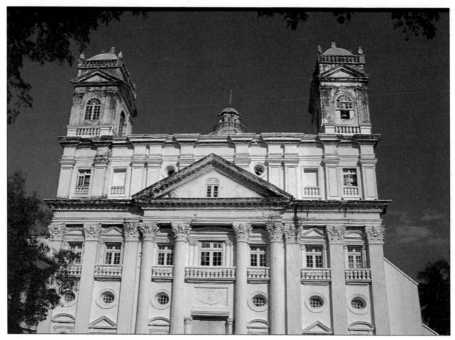

altarpiece depict St Catherine's life. The font is believed to have been used by St Francis Xavier. The cathedral has five bells, one of which is the "Golden Bell", one of the biggest in the world, which was used to announce the burning of pagans and heretics during the Inquisition.

The nearby **Convent and Church of Francis of Assisi**, built in the rare Manueline style, was originally a small Franciscan chapel. It was completely remodeled in 1661 with gilded, beautifully carved woodwork, exquisite panel frescoes, and fascinating gravestones bearing coats of arms. It houses the Archaeological Museum, which has a gallery of portraits of Portuguese governors and viceroys and a notable collection of ancient Indian sculpture recovered from Goan Hindu shrines sacked by both Muslims and Christians in fits of religious monomania.

Stately Mansions

The tourist department in Panaji can provide a list of 20 private villas and mansions which can be visited by appointment. Some are more than 400 years old and still lived in by the original families, with very beautiful collections of Portuguese colonial and Indian furniture and fittings. The Alvarez mansion in Margao and that of cartoonist Mario Miranda at Lotulim are well worth a visit. Don't turn up on their doorsteps without ringing first, as these are private residences.

Sea and Sand

If you're not heading straight for the main luxury resorts at Aguada and Bogmala beaches, then you face a daunting array of beaches and hotels from which to choose. Generally, the northern coastline is popular for a good range of hotels, beaches, and restaurants, while the southern coast is more primitive and secluded, though it contains two of Goa's resort hotels.

The Northern Beaches

North of Fort Aguada are the twin beaches of **Calangute** and **Candolim**, a seven-kilometer (4.3-mile) sandy stretch scattered with dozens of hotels and lodging houses and, on the beach-front, makeshift bars and restaurants made from wood and palm leaves. Children cross the sands to tempt reclining tourists with their fruit baskets, and at dawn each morning fishermen unload their catch. During the mid-1960's, when hippies began colonizing Goa's beaches—to the

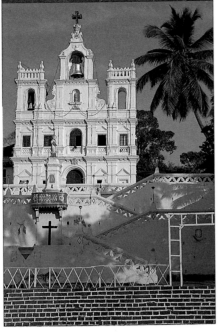

slightly outraged astonishment of local villagers —Calangute became the center of Flower Power adherents. Stalls in Calangute still do a roaring trade in leather G-strings, hessian trousers, and ethnic sandals.

Two kilometers (just over a mile) further north is **Baga Beach**, backed by a steep hill and probably one of the best of the northern beaches. Its uncluttered sands have an authentic feel, with traditional fishing boats hauled past the high-tide mark, and chaperoning nuns and schoolchildren spending the siesta under the coconut palms. Baga also has a good windsurfing school.

From Baga's northern headland, it's a 10-minute walk to **Anjuna Beach**, a faded paradise for the "love generation" who live in crude matting shacks along the cliff face. The nude sunbathing attracts squads of Indian men, who are sometimes known to conceal cameras in their

pockets. Daily life here centers on exhibitionist yoga, Frisbee games, and the smoking of vast amounts of hashish from elaborate pipes. Worthwhile Anjuna institutions are the Wednesday flea market and the Friday evening Haystack, the brainchild of Goa's most noted musician, August Braganza, whose backyard turns into a canopied showcase for local talent, with folk dances, singing, and music performed and good Goan food served.

The small rocky inlets of **Chapora** and **Vagator** are three kilometers (just under two miles) further north. Chapora is overlooked by the ruins of a Portuguese fort, built in 1717, with fine views from the ramparts. Vagator is more idyllic and secluded, with only one good hotel. A number of local residents here rent out rooms in the village, and it's possible to rent an entire house for US$150 per month.

The Southern Beaches

Bogmalo is small by Goan standards and largely patronized by guests of the Oberoi's luxury resort which dominates the crescent-shaped bay. For secluded beauty, **Colva**'s 40-km (25-mile) stretch of powdery sand and pristine, warm water is Goa's most paradisical. Away from the main cluster of tourist lodgings and beach cafés, you can virtually have the sands to yourself.

WHERE TO STAY

Panaji

Hotel Mandovi, Goa's oldest, D.B. Bandodkar Road, ((0832) 6270-9, still has a certain charm despite suffering from a 1960's décor overhaul. Nothing has changed much since Evelyn Waugh stayed here and observed that the hotel bookshop contained only cheap detective novels, sex psychology, and rationalist education books. Rates: inexpensive.

Hotel Fidalgo, 18th June Road, ((0832) 6291-9, is more modern but fairly characterless. Inexpensive.

The Northern Beaches

The **Fort Aguada Beach Resort**, ((0832) 276201 fax (0832) 217733, is Goa's premier resort at Sinquerim, Bardez. Built by the Taj Group within extensive gardens and the ruins of a seventeenth-century fort, the hotel building has tasteful sea-facing rooms, some with terraces.

On the hillside are tiers of self-contained cottages, perfect for a couple. On an even higher level is **Aguada Hermitage Villas**, ((0832) 276201 fax (0832) 276044, a series of elite dwellings used for the 1983 Commonwealth heads of government conference, with one cottage named after

ABOVE: Church of Immaculate Conception, Panaji, Goa. OPPOSITE: Church of St Cajetan in old Goa.

Britain's former Prime Minister Margaret Thatcher. These cost about US$200. Overlooking the seemingly endless white sands of Calangute Beach, the **Fort Aguada**, is perfect for a lazy, luxurious holiday and has an impressive sports complex with good instructors for waterskiing, windsurfing, fishing, scuba diving, and parasailing.

Next door, right on the beach, is the affiliated **Taj Holiday Village**, ℂ (0832) 276201, fax (0832) 276045, rates expensive to very expensive with less expensive functional cottages, and access to all Fort Aguada's facilities.

On Baga Beach, **Hotel Baia Do Sol**, ℂ (0832) 276084-5, fax (0832) 21415, offers the best accommodation. Literally set on the sands, it has casual, well-kept rooms, a great outdoor seafood restaurant, and excellent value riverside cottages. The helpful staff can arrange motorbikes, river cruises, waterskiing, fishing, and traditional folk dances.

The **Ronil Beach Resort**, a modern Spanish-style resort around a freshwater swimming pool with an outdoor restaurant is highly reccommended and moderately priced. A last Baga Beach option is **Cavala**, which offers simple, rooms without air-condition-

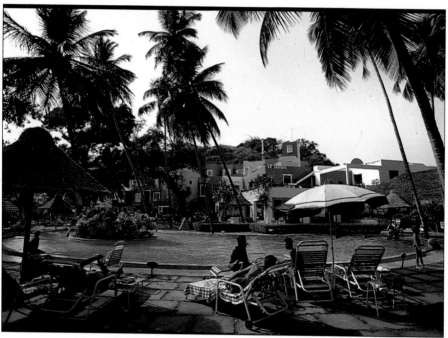

On Calangute Beach, the best choice is the **Varma Beach Resort**, ℂ (0832) 276077 with large, moderately priced, well-kept, air-conditioned rooms and three small cottages, situated just across the road from the Taj Village. Excellent breakfasts of piping-hot Goanese bread, eggs, fruit, and delicious coffee. Nearby is **Villa Ludovici** (which is exactly the way V.S. Naipaul's "House for Mr Biswas" ought to look) with quaint inexpensive rooms and **O'Sombreiro**, a veranda restaurant serving home-cooked Goan dishes, lobster, and prawns. The secluded **Essa Beach Resort**, ℂ (0832) 92, has a choice of pleasant seafacing rooms. Cheap.

ing and has a quaint bar and good Goanese restaurant.

Vagator Beach Resort, ℂ (0832) 262918, has the only worthwhile accommodation on the other northern beaches, with charming beachfront cottages and cheaper rooms in the main building. There is an excellent open-air restaurant.

The Southern Beaches

The **Oberoi Bogmalo Beach Resort**, ℂ (0832) 2191, fax (0832) 2510, is only 10 minutes from the airport, with pleasant rooms; small balconies face either the sea or a beautiful rear garden. The resort boasts excellent water-sports, a freshwater swimming pool, health club, and a variety of restaurants serving good traditional Goan and seafood dishes. And Colva, Goa's most spectacular beach, is close by. Rooms are expensive

ABOVE: One of Goa's upmarket beach resorts. OPPOSITE: Maharashtra girl hawking handicrafts on the beach.

but drop to almost half during the low season from May to September.

Colva's **Hotel Silver Sands**, ℂ (0832) 21645, has good, air-conditioned rooms, but it's preferable to stay at **Golden House Cottages**, much cheaper and a pleasant five-minute walk from the beach. Run by a gentle fishing family, you can dine like a king on fresh crab and lobster every night.

Cicade de Goa, Vainguinim Beach, Dona Paula, ℂ (0832) 3301, was designed by Indian architect Charles Correa to create the feeling of a Moorish village. The Goan-style rooms and courtyards have views across the Zuari estuary and Mormugao harbor. Excellent facilities, including good poolside and indoor restaurants. Rates: expensive.

Prainha Cottages, Dona Paula, ℂ (0832) 44162. These 13 tasteful, white stucco cottages with bougainvillea-fringed balconies are set among palm trees in a secluded, black-sanded bay. Very clean and restful, with the family-run O'Pescador seafood restaurant a two-minute walk away. Rates: expensive.

Accommodation Footnote: The state-run tourism department offers a reasonable range of unembellished but well-kept tourist hotels and cottages in Goa's main towns and on Bardez, Calangute, Colva, and Bicholim beaches.

GOA A LA CARTE

All over Goa, from city restaurants to the simplest village taverna, it's possible to eat magnificently. Here the unique hybrid cuisine finds a perfect companion in the famous *feni* — a potent local brew made from cashew, coconut palm, or apple. Goans are particularly proud of their robust cuisine, and never turn down an invitation to dine at a family home, where the most authentic food is found.

Indianized Portuguese dishes are usually spicy, but delicious, such as *xacuti*, a high-powered dish of either mutton or chicken with a coconut masala sauce, or *caldinhe*, a delicately seasoned fish dish. These are usually accompanied by *pau*, a small soft bread roll leavened with palm toddy. Pork is a staple meat and is used in *chourisso*, a sausage, and *sorpotal*, pig's liver pickled in a savory sauce.

But the real splendor of Goan cuisine is in the numerous preparations of fresh seafood — king prawns, lobster, kingfish, oysters, mussels, shrimps, and crabs — roasted, grilled, or curried in mouthwatering ways. Goan wines are unexceptional, though much cheaper than other Indian varieties, and all come in screw-top bottles. It is easy to develop a taste for feni, which is best taken diluted with soda. The smoother, double-distilled variant flavored with cumin, ginger, or sarsaparilla makes an unusual drink.

Eating Out

Every Goan has a list of favorite eating places, and the only bias tends to be proximity, as Goa is very spread out. Most of the main hotels have good indoor and outdoor restaurants, but the following places are highly recommended.

The outdoor **Beach House** restaurant at the Taj Village has simple wooden benches on the sand under a thatch roof, where

you can enjoy exceptional Goan and seafood specialties.

But the best place to head for after sunset is **Casa Portuguesa**, Baga Beach, an exquisitely restored Portuguese villa owned by Francisco Sousa, a wealthy Goan lawyer. This may well be India's most elegant restaurant, with candlelit tables spread through the Iberian-style vaulted rooms, small veranda, and tropical garden. It serves classic Portuguese dishes and standard Goan fare, including such delicacies as Whole Shark *Rachieada*, Mussels in Wine, and Grilled Oysters. Goa's cognoscente flock here as much for the wonderful food as to hear Francisco perform *fado*, the lugubrious Portuguese love songs. Try either to book or to come early — the Casa Portuguesa serves only dinner and fills up at about 9 pm.

On the Baga beachfront is **St Anthony's Bar**, which has been part of Goan mythology since it opened in 1968. This weathered beach shack, with its peeling formica-top tables, slumbering dogs, and rock-bottom prices, serves everything with a Midas touch, from fruit whips and waffles to grilled mackerel and clams cooked in coconut sauce. **Lilly's** authentic Goan restaurant on Vagator Beach is run by an enterprising Indian woman who was expelled from Mozambique by the Portuguese in the sixties in retaliation for the Indian occupation of Goa.

For good Goan and seafood dishes, also try **O'Coqueriro**, at Porvoim (four kilometers, or 2.5 miles, from the Panaji bridge), the popular **O'Pescador** restaurant at Dona Paula, and **La Paz** and **Zuari Hotel**, both at Vasco. In Panaji, the old Mandovi Hotel's **Rio Rico** has excellent Goan dishes in a period atmosphere, with its antiquated waiters insisting on silver service, its faded chintz, and the view across casuarina trees to the Mandovi River, although it is plagued with the sound of an electric organ playing *Swannee River*.

GENERAL INFORMATION

Government of India Tourist Office, Communidade Building, Church Square, Panaji. ((0832) 43412.
Tourist Information and Tour Counter, Tourist Home, Patto Bridge, Panaji. ((0832) 45583, 45715, 44757.

HOW TO GET THERE

Overnight Ferry Service: Bombay: New Ferry Wharf, Mallet Bunder. ((0832) 864071. Panaji: V.S. Dempo (Travel Division) opposite the Port Jetty, D.B. Bandodkar Marg, Panaji. ((0832) 3842.

MUSEUMS AND ART GALLERIES

Archaeological Museum and Portrait Gallery, Old Goa. ((0832) 46006. 10 am to 12 pm and 1 pm to 5 pm. Closed Fridays.
Archives Museum of Goa, Arhirwad Building, 1st floor, Santa Inez, Panaji. ((0832) 46006. 9:30 am to 1 pm and 2 pm to 5:30 pm. Closed Saturdays, Sundays, and public holidays.

ABOVE: Dusk at Bogmalo Beach, Goa.

MAHARASHTRA

LEGACY OF STONE

Set high on the dry, weathered Deccan Plateau, Maharashtra's craggy heartland stands in stark contrast to the tropical bustle of Bombay, the state capital. A rural patchwork of thatch-huts, fields of giant sunflowers, cotton, and mustard plants, and deep, dried-out ravines, Maharashtra has an eerie, primitive beauty. The state was once the center of the mighty Maratha empire, which ruled much of central India during the seventeenth century, waging fierce battles with Muslim invaders. Much earlier, however, between the second century BC and thirteenth century AD, the area witnessed the creation of the finest of all cave temples and monasteries in India, a technical *tour de force* carved from solid rock with brilliant technical and artistic skill. These are the famous caves at **Ajanta** and **Ellora**, some 60 in total, near the city of Aurangabad. The work of itinerant communities of Buddhist (and later Hindu and Jain) monks who had among their ranks exceptionally skilled sculptors and artists, the caves at Ajanta and Ellora are so exquisite in their execution that they rank with the Taj Mahal, the temples of Khajaraho and Kanchipuram, and the ruined city of Fatehpur Sikri as the country's greatest wonders.

Today's tourists pass through the musty cave recesses to marvel at the skill and beauty of these caves, but for earlier generations of largely illiterate devotees they were an overwhelming visual sermon, enshrining the history of myth, religion, and architecture of ancient India.

After Buddhism declined in India, these cave masterpieces were neglected and fell into obscurity under layers of earth and vegetation until 1819, when a group of British soldiers stumbled upon a cave while tiger hunting on the Deccan Plateau.

AURANGABAD

Although primarily used as a base for the cave temples of Ajanta and Ellora, Aurangabad has several historical attractions and some very interesting Buddhist caves of its own. Originally called Khadke, it was later renamed during the Mughal emperor Aurangzeb's reign from 1650 to 1670. Aurangabad is surrounded by crumbling fortifications and contains several fine Mughal monuments, including Aurangzeb's duplicate Taj Mahal, the Bibi-ka-Maqbara, built as a mausoleum for his wife.

GETTING THERE

From Bombay there is a daily direct flight, leaving at 6:15 am and arriving at 6:55. It's worth bearing in mind that the MTDC tours to both Ellora and Ajanta leave at around 8 am, which makes it difficult if you have to search for a hotel first. You can also fly to Aurangabad direct from Udaipur, Jaipur, and Delhi.

Trains run to Aurangabad from Bombay, but this is a long, awkward journey (eight to nine hours) involving a change at Manmad junction. It's still a popular route, however, and you are required to book four days in advance from Bombay. Jalgaon is the nearest railhead for the Ajanta Caves (56 km, or 35 miles, from Aurangabad), and both Manmad and Jalgaon are linked to Bombay, Delhi, and Calcutta.

Of the overnight buses which ply the winding, mountainous route to Aurangabad, the best choice is the MTDC air-conditioned coach, which leaves Bombay at 8:30 pm. There are frequent buses to both Ellora (29 km, or 18 miles) and Ajanta (106 km, or 66 miles), but you may prefer to take either or both of MTDC's daily, well-conducted full-day Ellora and City Tour and the Ajanta Excursion. The former covers Daulatabad Fort, Grishneshwar Temple, Ellora Caves, the Aurangabad Caves, tomb at Khuldabad, Bibi-ka-Maqbara, and Panchakki, while the latter covers the Ajanta viewpoint and the Ajanta Caves.

These tours are a very economical way of covering all the main areas of interest in and around the city, and their accompanying guides are all knowledgeable archaeology graduates.

For those who prefer to study India's finest cave temples at leisure, an organized tour can be frustrating. If you are pressed for time, it is possible (but tiring) to see everything in one day. A hired Ambassador taxi (seats four) will cost around US$35 for the day, and there are many pleasant picnic spots along the way if you bring a packed lunch.

The best season to visit is October to November, after the monsoon, when the fields brim with sunflower plantations, or December to March, when it is comfortably warm and sunny. As early as April to May, Maharashtra becomes unpleasantly hot, and a supply of mineral water is an absolute necessity.

HOTELS

Aurangabad's best tourist class hotels are the **Welcomgroup Rama International**, ((02432) 84441-4, fax (02432) 83468, and the **Ajanta Ambassador Hotel**, ((02432) 82211, fax (02432) 82367, both centrally located on Airport Road and moderately priced with pleasant décor and facilities at around US$35 a night. Just down the road is the cheaper, recently opened **Hotel Raj-doot**, ((02432) 29991, with unremarkable but clean accommodation. In the heart of Aurangabad town is the moderately priced Hotel **Aurangabad Ashok**, ((02432) 20520-9, fax (02432) 31328, in Dr Rajendra Prasad Marg. If you are traveling on a budget, eschew the cluster of rather nasty hotels around the railway station and try the MTDC Government Holiday Camp in Station Road, with reliably basic rooms (plus mosquito nets) for US$4.

EATING OUT

Both the **Rama International** and the **Ajanta Ambassador** have good Indian/continental restaurants, with almost doting service and evening sitar recitals. The **Mingling Restaurant**, attached to the Hotel Rajdoot, is currently in vogue with Aurangabad's safari suit and pearl set for its excellent Mughlai fare, spotless kitch pastel decor, and crooning *ghazal* singers who perform at both lunch and dinner. By comparison, the adjacent **Shaolin Chinese Restaurant** looks murky and decrepit, but locals swear by its extensive menu of Indianized Chinese food, all laced with chili to please local palates and not a chopstick in sight.

The **Tandoor**, near the railway station on Begumpura Road, is very popular for its Punjabi specialties and definitive version of chicken *tikka*. Otherwise try the **Food Walla's Bhoj Restaurant**, on Station Road, for good vegetarian fare.

GETTING AROUND

Aurangabad is a small, rather sleepy, town, with all the useful tourist facilities — railway station, central bus stand, hotels, restaurants, and tourist office — fairly close together. Auto-rickshaws seem to outnumber taxis, and are the best way to negotiate Aurangabad's narrow back-alleys, where the Muslim influence is strongly evident in street-side mosques and *burqa*-clad women. With its better facilities, Aurangabad is perfect as a base for daily excursions to Ajanta and Ellora, and you should plan to spend at least two days here to see everything properly.

SIGHTSEEING

Aurangabad Caves

Few visitors to Aurangabad venture up the stony hillside rock-cleft three kilometers (just under two miles) out of town to see these unfinished, but still magnificent, cave temples. There are 10 of them in all, excavated by Buddhist monks between the third and the seventh century AD. It's convenient to start with the western group of caves by walking "backwards" from cave 10 to cave 6. Amongst this group, cave 7 is by far the most spectacular, with its central frieze depicting an enormous Siddhartha on the verge of his transformation into Buddha, praying for protection from eight fears — sword, fire, chains, shipwreck, lions, snakes, crazed elephants, and the writhing demons of death. Cave 6 has a curious mixture of Hindu and Buddhist iconography that indicates the gradual absorption of Buddhist thought into Hinduism.

From these caves, it's a rambling 20-minute stroll across to the eastern side of the hill where caves 1 to 5 are located. Cave 4 is the only *chaitya*, or temple, in the series, all the others being *viharas*, or monastery prayer halls.

It is best to travel to the caves by solid Ambassador taxi — the alternative, an autorickshaw, is much bumpier. The caves are open from sunrise to 6 pm. A stroll back to Aurangabad is a pleasant finale, and it's easy to find your bearings: just stride across the empty plains towards the white minarets of the Taj-clone, Bibi-ka-Maqbara, and from here you can hire a rickshaw for a ride back into town.

The orthodox Mughal emperor Aurangzeb built the Bibi-ka-Maqbara in 1679 for his wife, known as Rabia Durrani, ordering his architects to construct a masterpiece that would outshine his father Shah Jehan's then recently completed Taj Mahal in Agra. Thrifty even in his grief, Aurangzeb's mausoleum is far less ornamental, costing 300 times less than its immortal rival. Open from sunrise to 10 pm.

Overlooking Aurangabad's Kaum River in the heart of the city is the **Panchakki,** an impressive pre-Mughal water mill harnessed to operate large grain-grinding stones. It was built in 1624 to commemorate the memory of the Sufi saint Baba Shah Musafir, whose tomb lies nearby. Open from sunrise to 10 pm.

Aurangabad is famous for its *himroo* shawls, cotton brocade, *bidri* ware, and Aurangabad silk, but the antiquated traditional handloom methods are rapidly disappearing. It's worth paying a visit to one of the few family businesses existing in the city. The most characteristic is the Aurangabad Himroo Factory in Shahganj, opposite Gandhi Square, where the owner and arch-weaver, A.H. Qureshi, will explain the technique and mourn the death of the trade, while his spindly fingers blur in the motion of knotting and threading.

RIGHT: Carved out of solid rock over a period of some 400 years, the Ellora caves are the most elaborate cave temples in India.

Daulatabad Fort

A remarkable medieval fortress towering high on a pyramidal hill above the dusty plains some 13 km (eight miles) from Aurangabad, Daulatabad's eerie beauty is full of references to its former despotic rulers and bloody history. Originally it was the capital of the Yadava dynasty in the thirteenth century, who called it Devagiri, or "hill of the gods". It caught the quixotic imagination of the mad Delhi sultan, Muhammed Tughlaq, who captured the fortress, renaming it Daulatabad, or "fortunate city", for his new capital. His unfortunate subjects were forced to walk 1,100 km (680 miles) here from

Delhi in 1327; then, only 17 years later, he realized the impracticality of the location and marched the remaining survivors back again.

The medieval equivalent of Fort Knox, Daulatabad is surrounded by six kilometers (3.7 miles) of thick walls, rows of terrifying spikes at its entrance to deter charging elephants, a huge moat that once seethed with hungry crocodiles, and dead-end passages where trapped intruders ended their lives under vat-loads of boiling oil.

With its labyrinth of musty passages, Daulatabad is fascinating to wander through, but bring a torch to avoid stumbling in its dark stairwells. Just inside the entrance gate is the 60-m (197-ft) -high Chand Minar pillar, built in 1435 as a monument of victory. From the dried-out moat, it's a half-hour climb to the top, passing the blue-tiled Chini Mahal Palace where prestigious nobles were kept prisoner. On the hill's crest stands a formidable cannon engraved with Aurangzeb's name, and there's a black, spiralling pit once used to hurl burning coals down on to invaders. Open from sunrise to sunset.

Aurangzeb's Grave

When Aurangzeb died in 1707, he was buried according to his instructions in a bare earth grave open to the sky at Khuldabad ("heavenly abode"), 26 km (16 miles) from Aurangabad on the route to Ellora. Once a fortified village (Aurangzeb built the battlements around it), its most interesting monument is the Karbala, or holy shrine of Deccan Muslims, which contains the remains of many historical figures. In his will, Aurangzeb stated that his funeral costs were to be covered only by the four and a half rupees earned from the sale of caps sewn by the emperor himself. As a final request, the money earned from the sale of his hand-copied Korans was to be divided amongst holy men on the day of his death. It would have displeased Aurangzeb to see the decorative marble screen that surrounds his grave — a donation from the wealthy Nizam of Hyderabad. As contrived as this austerity must have seemed, it came to symbolize Aurangzeb's troubled legacy, for although his descendants were to rule fitfully for another century and a half, Aurangzeb was the last of the Great Mughals. Standing in this tranquil sunlit spot, you may find your musings on this theme interrupted by a meaningful cough by the elderly mosque keeper with a carrot-colored beard, a well-thumbed Koran, and a monetary gleam in his eyes.

Ellora

Some 29 km (18 miles) from Aurangabad are the most elaborate cave temples in India. Although Buddhist monks began excavating in the seventh century, the site grew to include Hindu and Jain temples as the Buddhist faith waned in popularity toward the end of the seventh century. There are 34 caves — 12 Buddhist (AD 600–800), 17 Hindu (around AD 900), and five Jain (AD 800–1000) — and they are numbered in that order as you progress from south to north.

It's convenient to start with the Buddhist caves first, though these are the least interesting. Ten of these can be traced to the Mahayana schism of Buddhism by their contemplative images of Buddha vilified by the more orthodox relic-worshiping Hinayana sect which was responsible for building caves 1 and 7. The wealthy merchants who financed the construction of these caves did so in the belief that their pious contributions helped them to accumulate religious merit. Cave 10 is the only *chaitya* of the group, with its immense Buddha on a lion throne, surrounded by attendants and fronted by a nine-meter (29.5-ft) -high stupa.

If you're on the MTDC tour you'll be whisked speedily past most of the Hindu temples, stopping to admire in detail only the most spectacular. This is cave 16, the Kailasha Temple, named after Shiva's mountain home in the Himalayas. It was built by 7,000 stonecutters, working in squadrons constantly over a period of 150 years during the Rashtrakuta dynasty in the eighth century, an expenditure in manpower and rupees equal to that of conducting a major protracted war.

Carved from a single rock as large as the Parthenon in Athens, the Kailasha Temple is an awesome feat of engineering: begun from the top (much of which is now open to the sky) and chiseled down to the floor, creating arches, passageways, towers, and ornate friezes along the way. A bridge at the entrance leads to an enclosed courtyard, where immense flagstaffs and stone elephants surround the main two-storied shrine and Nandi pavilion. The cool, sandal-

Ajanta

It's a long, winding drive from Aurangabad to the Ajanta caves (104 km, or 65 miles), but at journey's end is one of the world's most fascinating collections of wall paintings and frescoes. Unfortunately, the wall paintings are becoming progressively bleached by exposure to the atmosphere and, despite efforts by experts to preserve them with sealing fluids, are slowly fading away. The light wreaks havoc with the delicate colors, so the caves are kept in murky darkness. Come prepared with a strong flashlight, or pay the "lighting charge" at the entrance. For a small sum, a wizened attendant in a Nehru cap will

wood-scented interior chambers are filled with ornate Dravidian sculptures depicting stories from the *Ramayana*.

The Jain temples are a short stroll to the north. Although noteworthy for their delicacy and detail, the Jain temples appear rather anemic after the energetic brilliance of the Kailasha Temple. The "Assembly Hall of Indra", cave 32, is the most interesting of this group, with its simple ground floor enlivened by curving lotus reliefs on the ceiling, and the upper story is notable for its decorative friezes and lotus-design columns. The shrine is dedicated to Mahavira, the last of the 24 Tirthankas and founder of the Jain religion.

There are several hotels near Ellora if you want to spend more time looking at the caves, but none are particularly good. The best (and nearest to the caves) is the **Kailash Hotel, (** 43.

try to reflect rays of sunlight into the cave using a sheet of corrugated iron. If you're not with a tour, it's advisable to hire a "deluxe" guide from the entrance (the bone fide ones wear accredited badges).

The 30 caves chiseled into Ajanta's crescent-shaped granite gorge represent the highest artistic achievement of the Buddhist monks who arrived here in the second century BC to establish a monastic retreat. Most of the caves were completed by the second century AD; the others date from the fifth to the seventh century, before the site was mysteriously abandoned for nearby Ellora. For hundreds of years, the caves were obscured under thick foliage, and this accounts

ABOVE: Entrance to the Ellora caves. OPPOSITE: Daulatabad Fort has an eerie beauty and a bloody history.

for the near-perfect state of preservation in which they were found.

The caves are a perfect showcase for understanding the progression of Buddhist art and thought. The early Hinayana school disapproved of earthly pleasures, believing that the best way to attain salvation was through pain. Caves 8, 9, 10, 12, and 13 date from the older Hinayana period, and images of Buddha are notably absent. In the second century BC, the more worldly Mahayana school's liberal ideas shocked Hinayana Buddhists to the core, but created a renaissance in Indian art. Here the frescoes are full of Brueghel-like scenes, far more

4 is the largest *vihara* (residence) cave, supported by 28 pillars. Along with caves 17, 19, and 26, it has the best sculptures in the group. The oldest cave is cave 10. The caves are open from 9:30 am to 5:30 pm.

The best local accommodation is five kilometers (three miles) away in Fardapur, with a choice between the **Guest House**, ((02432) 4874, and the **Holiday Resort**, ((02432) 4713, both of which offer cheap, clean rooms and meals. The tourist hostel directly opposite the caves has extremely surly staff, and it's restaurant should not be trusted with anything more complex than fresh-lime sodas.

diverting than the central theme of the Ajanta caves, the life and times of Buddha. This more realistic and sensual art reached its zenith under the Gupta dynasty, AD 320—647.

All the caves at Ajanta are monolithic: scooped out to create a complex granite husk complete with pillars, faades, dormitories, and galleries of sculpted Buddhas, all carved from the same piece of rock. Beneath the frescoes are layers of clay, cow dung, powdered rice husk, and lime plaster. Crushed pebbles, ochre, and ground lapis lazuli were used as colors, and applied with squirrel-hair brushes. Cave 1 is the largest and most impressive of the Ajanta caves, with the best frescoes and relief carvings. Caves 2, 16, 17, and 19 also contain beautiful frescoes. Cave

The Ajanta caves boast one of the world's most fascinating collections of wall paintings and frescoes.

GENERAL INFORMATION

Government of India Tourist Office, Krishna Vilas, Station Road, ((02432) 20417. **Government of Maharashtra Tourist Office**, Holiday Camp, Aurangabad ((02432) 24713.

GUJARAT

WOVEN COLORS AND CREEDS

Few travelers venture to Gujarat, yet the state is saturated with historical attractions and, as a relatively untrodden tourist trail, has retained much of its traditional lifestyle. Gujarat is a colorful mixture of modern and old-age cultures.

In Gujarat's capital, Ahmedabad — one of India's most highly developed commercial cities — the whole city grinds to a halt during the siesta hours from noon to 4 pm, and camels continue to traipse its main streets as they have done for centuries. Rural Gujarat appears barely touched by the twentieth century — villagers still wear traditional dress and practice skilled crafts, particularly weaving and wood carving.

Gujarat contains many of the ancient sites of Hindu mythology. The story goes that the Somnath shore temple in the south was built by Soma, the Moon God, to mark the creation of the universe. Legend also places Lord

known as Saurashtra, had 282 princely states in an area roughly the size of Ireland.

Mahatma Gandhi, who was born in Gujarat's Porbander state, believed that his penchant for pacifism and social reform was an inherent Gujarati trait and took the motto "non-violence is the supreme religion" from the Jains. More noticeably, Gujaratis are renowned for their shrewd business acumen, and many have emigrated and now thrive in communities around the world.

A good mini-tour of Gujarat begins with **Ahmedabad** and covers the main destinations of the Jain pilgrimage centers of **Palitana** and

Krishna's kingdom at Dwarka, on Gujarat's west coast. Its first communities appeared with the Indus Valley civilization in about 2500 BC, and the world's earliest Asian and Western literature refers to the value of Gujarat's trade goods. Anti-caste Buddhists and Jains ruled until the end of the eighth century, and the latter are still a dominant force in Gujarat today, being responsible for the state's almost total vegetarianism. During India's Middle Ages, these peaceful cultures were invaded by the feudal Hindu Rajputs, and for several centuries much of the present state fell under first Muslim, then Mughal, rule. Opportunistic Portuguese traders established key ports in Damen and Diu on the southern coast, retaining possession until 1961. With the expansion of the British Empire, mainland Gujarat was governed by the British, while the southern Kathiawar peninsula, now

Junagadh, the **Sasan-Gir Wildlife Sanctuary** and **Somnath Temple** in the south, and palace-filled **Vadodara** in the southeast. Adventurous travelers can explore the northern **Rann of Kutch**, a salt desert inhabited by the colorful nomadic Malderi tribe. Most of Gujarat's hotels are inexpensive and simple, but are subject to a sliding state-imposed luxury tax that can add 30 percent to the bill.

WHEN TO GO

Gujarat has an abundance of fairs and festivals throughout the year, but it's well worth coinciding with the **Makara Sankranti Kite Festival** on January 14, or the **Navrati Festival** which celebrates the goddess Amba, held on the cusp of September to October, with nine days of impromptu street dances and *bhavai* folk theater.

The mild winter months from November to March are the best times for Gujarat, although the monsoon season has its own charm. Bring light clothes for the day and a sweater for winter evenings.

AHMEDABAD: GATEWAY TO GUJARAT

Ahmedabad's congested urban sprawl contains the husk of an original city built by the Muslim ruler Ahmed Shah during the fifteenth century, and much grand Islamic architecture

still stands. Toward the end of the sixteenth century, Ahmedabad had a thousand mosques, cenotaphs, and tombs, all surrounded by carefully kept gardens. In 1615, Sir Thomas Roe, the British emissary to Emperor Jehangir in Delhi, described Ahmedabad as being "as large as London, the handsomest city in Hindustan and perhaps the world". It was here that Mahatma Gandhi founded his *ashram* and later launched his famous Salt March to protest British hegemony. Now an industrial center plagued by pollution and noise, Ahmedabad is no longer a beautiful city, but visitors will find it has many pockets of unexpected charm. It has fine museums and boasts a cultivated patronage of the arts that is quite unique in India. Beyond the remains of the medieval wall and its stone gateways, in the Byzantine confusion of Ahmedabad's old city, are many sixteenth-century

havelis, so delicately carved they resemble wooden cobwebs, and the *pols*, or living quarters, of the artisan and merchant communities. At almost any hour, weavers, hand-block printers, and wood-workers can be seen in these musty lanes toiling over their work.

Despite Gandhi's legacy, communal enmities run deep in Ahmedabad, which has seen grisly clashes between its Muslim and Hindu communities in the old city.

HOW TO GET THERE

There are daily flights to Ahmedabad's airport (eight kilometers, or five miles, away) from Bombay, Delhi, Calcutta, Jaipur, and Jodhpur, and you can also fly there from Vadodara, Bangalore, Madras, Hyderabad, Aurangabad, and Srinagar. From Ahmedabad there are air connections to Gujarat's main cities, notably Vadodara, Keshod, Jamnagar, Rajkot, Porbandar, Bhuj, and Bhavnagar. Daily trains run there from Bombay (the 492-km, or 306-mile, trip takes nine hours by fast mail train and 15 hours by normal service). If you have the stamina, it's fun to experience a lengthy train ride at least once, and the Delhi to Ahmedabad (626 km, or 390 miles, 24 hours) has a drawn-out charm. It stops at Ajmer, Jaipur, and Mount Abu, and passes through dry desert tundra, enlivened by clusters of nomadic camels, brilliant splashes of dandified tribal dress, vendors who wander through the swaying train, and itinerant musicians who jump aboard and sing evocative Rajasthani *ragas*.

There are bus services from Bombay, Mount Abu, and Udaipur, and from Ahmedabad to destinations throughout the state.

WHERE TO STAY

There are only two good hotels, both in the heart of the city overlooking the river and frequently booked out. The **Ritz Hotel**, Lal Darwaja, ((0272) 393637, is a quaint establishment, originally an eighteenth-century family home, set in a secluded garden with prompt service and characterful, air-conditioned rooms. Inexpensive. **Hotel Cama**, Khanpur Road, (305281-9, fax (0272) 305285 is pleasant and modern, with efficient staff, car rental, a liquor shop, good chemist, and a restaurant that serves delicious lunchtime *thalis*. Rates: moderate. Otherwise, try either the **Rivera Hotel**, ((0272) 304201-7, fax (0272) 302327 or the **Ambassador**

OPPOSITE and ABOVE: Pockets of unexpected charm are found in the bustling city of Ahmedabad, such as the Manek Chowk market area where sacred cows wander at will.

Hotel, ℭ (0272) 353244, in the cheap to moderate range, both on Khanpur Road. If you're on a low budget, try the **Circuit House**, Shahibagh, ℭ (0272) 65033. The **Gandhi Ashram Guest House,** ℭ (0272) 407742, six kilometers (3.7 miles) away opposite Gandhi's Ashram, is a pleasant option, with peaceful, balconied rooms set in a small garden at a very reasonable price, with a good restaurant attached.

EATING OUT

Ahmedabad's best evening entertainment and authentic Gujarati cuisine is a 15-minute drive south of the city center, at the mock-Gujarati **Vishalla** village, on Sarkhej Road. It's best to arrive no later than 8:30 pm, and then to wander about the decorated mud huts where artisans pot, weave, and make *paan*. The excellent Vechaar Utensils Museum situated here houses a remarkable collection of 2,500 metalware utensils collected from all over Gujarat — including betel nut cutters, hookahs, guns, unique vessels for milking camels, and dowry items — and stays open until 10 pm.

To the accompaniment of folk music or a traditional puppet show, dinner is taken in true cross-legged Gujarati style, served on a brass *thali*. A superb feast of subtly spiced vegetable dishes, fragrant rice, lightly fried *puris*, and chutneys, followed by mugs of sweet buttermilk, and outrageously sweet *jalebis* for dessert. Lunch is equally pleasant, served from 11 am to 1 pm.

Both the **Ritz** and the **Cama** have good restaurants, but Ahmedabad's modest, proletarian-style eating houses are more authentic. The best of these are the popular **Hotel Chetna**, next to the Krishna Talkies on Relief Road, with all-you-can-eat *thalis* for US$1.50, **Hotel Sabar** (opposite the Cama), and **Gopi**, near the Town Hall.

Gujaratis are usually strict vegetarians. Popular dishes include *undhyoo*, a winter dish of aubergines, potato, broad beans, and sweet potato buried under a hot fire, *srikand*, hot *puris* eaten with rich candied yogurt, and *khaman dhokla*, a chick-pea flour cake.

Gujarat makes India's best ice-cream, crammed with fruit and nuts, and with unusual seasonal favorites such as custard apple and cashew. Gujaratis have a fetish for it, and there's a parlor on every block. For the best range, try **Havmor** on Relief Road, or the **Vadilal Soda Fountain**, Bhadra.

SIGHTSEEING

The domes and minarets of the Muslim mosques, pavilions, and monuments built

during the fifteenth century are dotted throughout central Ahmedabad. Built of local honey-colored stone, these structures are a fusion of austere Islamic design and ornately decorative Hindu art, and mark the birth of the Indo-Saracenic style. The most beautiful are within the heart of the city. **Rani Sipri's Mosque and Tomb** (1514) is believed to have been built by a wife of Sultan Mehmood Begada after he executed her son in a fit of anger. Nearby is the **Rani Rupmati's Mosque** (1440), with its exquisite traceries and *jali* screens.

The gracious Friday mosque, **Jumma Masjid** (1424), was built by Ahmed Shah, the

city's founder. According to local myth, the large black stone slab near the main door once formed the base of a Jain idol, which was buried upside down and trampled on to express distaste for other religions. Just outside the mosque's east gate is **Ahmed Shah's Tomb**. Women are refused entry to the central chamber. The tombs of his queens are across the street, but almost impossible to find in the dense bazaars.

Sidi Saiyad's Mosque (1430), close to the river end of Relief Road, was built by one of Ahmed Shah's slaves. Its pierced marble lattice-work arches are alone worth coming to Ahmedabad to see. Their design and workmanship outshine even the windows of the Taj Mahal in Agra. Unfortunately, the mosque now forms part of a traffic island.

Also a Muslim creation, and unique to Gujarat, are the ornately carved *baolis* (step wells), resembling watery amphitheaters. The most beautiful is the **Adalaj Vav**, built in 1499 by Queen Rudabai of the Waghela dynasty, with its richly carved ornamental friezes and five-story structure, 19 km (12 miles) from the city. Closer at hand is the **Dada Hari** *baoli* in town (closed for siesta 1 to 4 pm), with spiral staircases and decorative friezes.

Just outside the Delhi Gate, to the north of the old city, lies the white marble **Hatheesingh Temple**, a well-patronized Jain citadel erected in 1848 by a wealthy merchant.

For restful strolls, the **Kankaria** artificial lake, almost 1.6 km (a mile) long, is four kilometers (2.5 miles) southeast of the city. Built by the Sultan Qutb-ud-Din in 1451, it has an island palace where Emperor Jehangir and his beautiful empress Nur Jehan came to escape from the dust of Ahmedabad. Today, it's refreshingly peaceful, with lakeside cafés, boating, and a well-stocked zoo. The **Sarkej** monuments, 10 km (six miles) southwest of the city, make a pleasant excursion. This was once an isolated oasis around a stone-stepped *baoli*. The remnants of the palace, pavilions, mosque, and tombs, built by Sultan Mehmud Shah Beghara and his queen Raj Bai in around 1460, are of an elegant, unembellished design.

Gandhi's Ashram

The Sabarmati Ashram (six kilometers, or 3.7 miles, from Ahmedabad) was founded by India's most famous Gujarati, Mahatma Gandhi (1869—1948) in 1915. He moved here two years later with his wife, Kasturba, and remained until 1930. This was where he launched his great civil disobedience movement which led to the freeing of India after two and a half centuries of British rule. It was from here that Gandhi began his famous Dandi march in 1930 to protest the British Salt Law, which effectively barred Indians from the salt business. Of all the memorials throughout India associated with Gandhi, this small collection of whitewashed thatched cottages and personal possessions is the most moving. Open from dawn until the close of the nightly sound and light show (conducted in Hindi, Gujarati, and English on different nights), the Ashram contains a pictorial history of Gandhi's life, a handicrafts center, and a spinning wheel factory. The English sound and light show is held on Wednesdays, Fridays, and Sundays at 8:30 pm.

Pols and Pigeons

Old Ahmedabad is thick with bazaars and tiny shops selling a wonderful array of treasures. **Manek Chowk** is the old city's main marketplace, a bustling mélée where merchants sell an array of embroidered beadwork, silver

jewelry, antique carved wooden doorways, trays of spices, quaint stuffed toys, regimental silver, and brass teapots. For serious shoppers, this is where the best variety of Gujarat's distinctive fabrics is to be found. Look especially for handpainted or wood-blocked prints in the traditional black, maroon, red, and ochre patterns, *bandhana* (tie-dyed) silks and cottons, *zari* (gold) work; and the unusual patola silk sari, a traditional design woven with tie-dyed threads much coveted by Gujarati girls and costing anything from US$120 to US$1,800 depending on the quality. If you're uncertain as to whether you are getting a bargain or being

thoroughly hoodwinked, try either **Gurjari Handicrafts Emporium** or **Bangshree**, opposite Vidhyapith, both back in the commercial part of the city on Ashram Road, which offer a good range of traditional products at government prices.

This is Ahmedabad's oldest residential area, divided into confusingly dense pols or culs de sac, which house extended families or clans. Ask directions for the **Doshiwada-ni-pol**, where the most beautiful of the old *havelis* are found. Often only one room wide, they can be as high as five stories and are covered with beautiful carvings. Sadly, these are rapidly being dismantled and sold as antiques or placed in museums. In this

Ahmedabad is a city of mosques, temples and monuments. OPPOSITE: Jami Masjid, known as the Friday mosque. ABOVE: Hutheesingh Temple.

area you'll see bird-feeding squares, called *parabdis*, where the nature-respecting Jains throw grain to the pigeons. In this most dense part of the old city, it's common to see men wearing the distinctive Gujarati dress — the white, pin-tucked and embroidered tunic worn to almost girlish effect — and *burqa*-clad women.

Museums

Ahmedabad's museums are wonderful, though they tend to be closed during the siesta hours and on state holidays. The best is the **Sarabhais' Calico Museum**, a rare collection of textiles

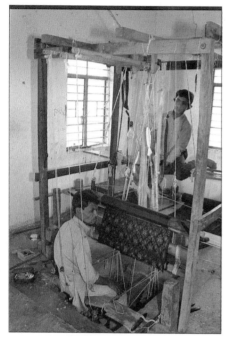

costumes, decorations, and crafts (open 9 to 11 am, 4 to 7 pm, closed Wednesdays), and the **Tribal Museum** in Gujarat Vidyapith, Ashram Road (open weekdays 4:30 to 5:30 pm), provide a good introduction to Gujarati culture and mythology.

The **N.C. Mehta Museum**, housed in Le Corbusier's Sanskar Kendra Municipal Museum, Paldi, has a fine collection of Indian miniature paintings. Open Tuesday to Sunday, 11 am to noon, 3 to 5 pm. The **Vechaar Utensils Museum** in the Vishalla village (see EATING OUT, page 218) is open Monday to Saturday, 5 to 11 pm, Sunday 5 to 10 pm.

dating to the seventeenth century housed in the gardens of the family mansion in Shahibag, the old elite Civil Lines. There's also an extensive reference library on textiles which can be seen on request. Open April—June, 8:30 to 10:30 am, July to March, 11 am to noon and 3 to 5 pm, open daily, except Wednesdays and public holidays. The Sarabhais are the barons of India's textile industry, a talented Jain family who made their fortune during the cotton boom last century, and live in great style in the leafy compound surrounding the museum. The stately old Sarabhai mansion can be visited, and is now a center for Hindu studies.

The **Shreyas Folk Art Museum**, off Circular Road, which displays a unique array of tribal

OUT OF AHMEDABAD: LOTHAL

The famous archaeological ruins at Lothal, 87 km (54 miles) from Ahmedabad, are well worth a day's excursion. It was once an important Harappan port which traded with Eygpt and Mesopotamia in around 2400 to 1500 BC, and is thus the earliest known civilization in the subcontinent. Other major Harappan sites are in Pakistan at Mohenjo-Daro and Harappa. Discovered in 1954, excavations reveal a systematically planned port city, with a scientific knowledge of the tides applied to its underground drains, planned streets and houses with baths and fireplaces, burial grounds, and dockyards. Terracotta figurines, ivory and shell objects, beads, bangles and semi-precious stones, painted bowls, bronze and copper

ABOVE LEFT: Textile factory at Aurangabad.
ABOVE RIGHT: Darwaza Market, Ahmedabad.

implements, and seals with Indus Valley script are on display at an excellent on-site museum.

GENERAL INFORMATION

Government conducted tours covering the city's sights leave each day from the Lal Darwaja bus-stand at 8 am and 2:30 pm, costing Rs 12. These are useful if you have very little time and for getting your bearings. Contact the Tourist Office for details on their longer (four or five days) tours around north and south Gujarat and Saurashtra, costing about US$30 to US$40. **Tourist Corporation of Gujarat**, H.K. House, Ashram Road, ((0272) 449683, Open 10:30 am to 1:30 pm, 2 to 5:30 pm.

There are also tourist counters at the airport and railway station.

JAIN FOOTSTEPS

PALITANA

The most revered of the Jains' five temple-covered sacred hills, Palitana's nearby **Shatrunjaya Hill** is a marble jungle of some 863 magnificent Jain temples, some of which date back to the eleventh century. The other sacred hills are at Girnar, near Junagadh, Mount Abu in Rajasthan, Parasnath in Bihar, and Gwalior in Madhya Pradesh.

Jainism became a powerful force in the sixth century BC, largely in reaction to strict, caste-bound Hinduism. It was founded by Prince Mahavira (559–527 BC), the 24th and last Jain Tirthankara, or saint, who became a *jina*, or conqueror of spiritual knowledge, and his disciples, Jains.

The temple complex, known as the "abode of the gods", is a marvel of complex architecture, each temple within a *tuk*, or enclosure, and richly ornamented with carved spires and towers.

The temple chambers are frequently thronged with Jain pilgrims who prostrate themselves before the rows of impassive-looking idols, whose eyes gleam out fiercely in the gloom. Wiry, shaven-headed priests administer to the temple duties and keep a watchful eye out for tourists who neglect to leave their shoes at the door. A stern sign at the entrance to the complex forbids menstruating women to enter, lest they defile the temple's purity. Largest and most ornate temple is the Chaumukh temple, built by a wealthy banker in 1618 in the hope of saving his soul. But most pilgrims make a bee-line for the most sacred temple, dedicated to Sri Adishwara, the first Tirthankara, whose image is studded with gold and enormous diamonds.

An unusual addition is the Angar Pir, a Moslem shrine, where childless women make offerings of miniature cradles and pray for children.

The magnificence of these temples is due largely to the Jain belief that reincarnation and salvation can be influenced by, amongst other things, temple building and *ahimsa*, reverence for all life. The truly devout are not only complete vegetarians, excluding even eggs and milk from their diet, but also wear white gauze masks to prevent the accidental swallowing of small insects.

It's best to make Palitana an early morning expedition, before the heat makes climbing the four kilometers (2.5 miles) of steps unbearable. At dawn, the route throngs with white-clad pilgrims, the aged and disabled carried in *dolis*, string sedan chairs, which are also utilized by exhausted tourists. Priests hand a ticket to each leaving visitor who, after an hour's tiring descent, can exchange it for a restorative breakfast of sweetmeats and sugary tea. Open from 7 am to 7 pm, when even the priests withdraw to leave the gods to themselves.

Where to Stay

Palitana, 215 km (134 miles) from Ahmedabad, has many resthouses but these are exclusively for Jain pilgrims. There's a choice of either the state-run **Hotel Sumeru Toran**, (227, on Station Road, or the **Hotel Shravak**, (328, opposite the bus station, offering rooms or dormitories and cheap *thalis* at mealtimes. If hunger strikes at odd hours, try the popular snack alley next to the Shravak.

It's far preferable to stay in the larger port city of **Bhavnagar**, 56 km (35 miles) away, at the **Nilambag Palace Hotel**, ((0278) 24222. This local maharaja's former palace has charming, inexpensive, period suites.

General Information

Bhavnagar, 244 km (152 miles) from Ahmedabad, has the nearest airport, with regular train and bus services for visiting Palitana. From Ahmedabad, there's a train which takes between nine and 11 hours and stops just before Palitana, at Sihor. Express buses take four hours.

JUNAGADH

A picturesque city of much archaeological importance, Junagadh is rather off the beaten track, but of great significance to Jains for the sacred, temple-covered **Girnar Hill** nearby, which is no less impressive than Palitana, and a much gentler climb at only 2,000 steps! Betrothed couples come to worship at the topmost Amba Mata temple to ensure a harmonious marriage. It's a good place to spend a day before continuing on to Sasan-Gir wildlife sanctuary, 58 km (36 miles) away.

Junagadh is thought to date back to around 250 BC, when the Mauryan emperor Ashoka ordered his edicts inscribed on a boulder, which can still be seen on the way to Girnar Hill. On Junagadh's outskirts lies **Uparkot**, a walled city with its own palace, Jami Masjid, and Buddhist caves with spiral staircases, built by the militaristic Chudasamal Rajputs during the ninth century. It was the scene of an epic 12-year siege over the heart of a beautiful potter's daughter who rejected the advances of a neighboring king and married the Rajput ruler of Junagadh instead. In 1094, the Junagadh raja was slain — in a Pyrrhic victory, since the coveted woman committed sati shortly afterwards.

In town, see the **Rang Mahal**, the nineteenth-century palace now used as government offices, in which the dog-loving Nawab of Junagadh staged canine weddings and gave each of his 800 dogs its own room with a telephone and servant. At the time of Partition, the Nawab wished to have his tiny state merged with Pakistan, and having failed to do so, lived in disgraced exile. Within the palace is the **Durbar Hall** museum, with palace relics, weaponry, and a portrait gallery. Open 9:30 to 11:45 am, 3 to 5:30 pm. The tourist office is right next door.

Also see the ornate **Maqbara**, the royal mausoleum, with minarets and spiral staircases; the **Sakkar Bagh** museum and zoo; and the **Rupayatan Institute for Handicrafts** where craftsmen work on traditional embroidery and patchwork.

GENERAL INFORMATION

There are a number of small, cheap hotels in Junagadh, but none is very good. Try **Hotel Vaibhav**, close to the bus station, which has a mirrored dining room with good *thalis* and excellent mango milkshakes. The nearest airport is Keshod, 47 km (29 miles) away, with flights from Bombay and Ahmedabad. The *Somnath Mail* runs between Ahmedabad and Veraval/Somnath via Junagadh, a 13-hour journey. Buses connect Junagadh with Ahmedabad, Vereval/Somnath, Palitana, and the Sasan-Gir.

SOMNATH

According to Hindu myth, Somnath Temple, which overlooks the Arabian Sea, was built by Soma, the Moon God, at the dawn of creation. Archaeologists date the shore temple to around the first century AD.

Although destroyed and rebuilt more than seven times, the present temple retains much of its legendary beauty. By the sixth century, Somnath was renowned as the richest temple in India, and consequently was sacked by the Mahmud of Ghazni, who required a vast caravanserai of elephants, camels, and mules to carry all the gold and precious ornaments. Over the next 700 years, the temple was repeatedly smashed, then rebuilt by devout priests. The Mughal Aurangzeb, vowing to crush the "heretical" temple, powdered it to dust in 1706. Only in 1950 was it restored to its present state.

Somnath contains one of the 12 *jyotirlingas*, or Shiva shrines, in India and has two major festivals: the vibrant **Kartika Poornima**, a village fair with traditional dance, theater, and chanting of vedic hymns, held in November/December, and the **Mahashivratri**, held in February/March, which attracts hundreds of thousands of Indian pilgrims.

It's best to visit at sunrise or sunset, when the priests perform an elaborate ritual to worship Shiva.

The nearby government-run **Prabhas Patan Museum** is very disorganized, but contains ancient relics of the various versions of Somnath Temple. Open 9 am to noon, 3 to 6 pm daily, except Wednesday.

Somnath has only one decent hotel — the **Hotel Mayuram**, Triveni Road ((Prabhas Patan 362, 268). Somnath's only source of tourist information is the Manager of the Somnath Temple Trust whose office is next to the temple.

SASAN-GIR

One of India's finest wildlife sanctuaries, set in 1,295 sq km (500 sq miles) of lush deciduous forest, the Sasan-Gir is the final refuge of the rare Asiatic lion, once found throughout the Middle East and both north and east India, but hunted as a coveted trophy item during the British Raj era. The famine of 1899 so decimated the Asiatic lion population that Lord Curzon cancelled his shoot at Gir, where he was the guest of the Nawab of Junagadh. Curzon persuaded the Nawab to protect the remaining lions, who now number around 200. The sanctuary is open from mid-October to mid-June, but the cool season between November and February is the best time for sighting the lions, who generally retire to the forest's interior during the summer. The forest also has wild boar, bears, panthers, antelopes, hyenas, leopards, and the unusual Indian *chowsingha* (antelope) whose buck has four horns. The monsoon months of July to September are good for seeing almost 200 varieties of birds.

The Gir Forestry Department organizes "lion shows" by guide-conducted jeeps, and ensures that lions can be viewed at close range by sending trackers on early morning missions to stake out large groups of lions. Shows take place each Sunday between 3 and 6 pm, and can be booked from the Forest Lodge between 4 and 6 pm. If you wish to explore the sanctuary on your own, it's possible to hire a jeep and guide. Within the Gir Forest are the scenic **Tulishyam Hot Springs**, 90 km (56 miles) from the sanctuary's entrance, where you can bathe in the natural sulfur springs and, if desired, find cheap accommodation at the Holiday Camp Lodge.

GENERAL INFORMATION

There are two lodges, both of which are state-run and inexpensive, with good facilities. The three-star **Lion Safari Lodge**, (21 has upper-story rooms overlooking the reserve. Otherwise try the **Forest Guest House.**

The Gujarat State Tourism Corporation offers a special two-day package tour to Sasan-Gir, which includes reception at Keshod, 90 km (56 miles) away, the nearest airport (an 80-minute flight from Bombay), accommodation at the Forest Lodge, sanctuary tour, and visit to Somnath. The Government Gujarat Tourist Office, Dhanraj Mahal, C. Shivaji Road, Bombay, ((022) 2024925, will supply further details.

VADODARA (BARODA)

Located 120 km (75 miles) southeast of Ahmedabad, the former capital of the vastly wealthy Gaekwads (whose name means "protector of cows") of Baroda is a city of sprawling parks and lakes, palaces and museums, with a campus atmosphere. Predictably, perhaps, its charms are muted by ugly industrial expansion. It's a good base for excursions to the beautiful ruined fort of **Champaner,** 47 km (29 miles) away.

SIGHTSEEING

On the city's periphery is the **Lakshmi Vilas Palace**, a Gothic-domed, Indo-Saracenic extravaganza with a 150-m (500-ft) faade. It was completed in 1890 for the Maharaja of Sayajirao, who campaigned against purdah and tried to introduce a form of separation for unhappily married women. His legendary wealth included the Baroda collection of jewels, a pearl carpet studded with diamonds, rubies, emeralds, and woven with gold, and

thick gold anklets worn by the palace elephants. Unfortunately, the palace and its fabulous collection of armor and sculpture is rarely open to the public.

Back in the city, the **Baroda Museum and Art Gallery** in the **Sayaji Park** (complete with a zoo, miniature train, and large lake) has an excellent collection of Mughal miniatures and European paintings. Open Fridays and Sundays from 9:30 am to 4:45 pm, and Saturdays, 10 am to 5:45 pm. Nearby is the **Maharaja Fateh Singh Museum**, the Gaekwad's lavish art collection, which includes works by Titian, Raphael, Murillo, and displays of Graeco-Roman, Chinese, Japanese, and Indian paintings. Situated within the palace grounds, the museum is open Tuesdays to Sundays from 9 am to noon, 3 to 6 pm from July to March, 4 to 7 pm from April to June.

Old Baroda's faded splendor is best appreciated by visiting several of the Gaekwad's smaller palaces scattered around the city, the most impressive being the **Pratap Vilas Palace**, now used as the Railway Staff College. The **Maharaja Sayajirao University of Vadodara** is a grand palisade of Gothic-inspired architecture leading to Sayaji Park, with a renowned Arts faculty that organizes regular evening performances by India's top artistes. Its Art College is considered one of India's best. Other places to see are the **Kirti Mandir**, the Gaekwad's family vault, and the exquisite **Tambekarwada**, a four-story *haveli* covered with murals. Managed by the Archaeological Survey of India, it is open daily and hard to find, so obtain directions from the Tourist Office opposite the railway station. The **Naulakhi** well, just near the Lakshmi Vilas Palace, is a good example of Gujarati *baoli*, or step-well. The Islamic **Maqbara** has beautiful filigree carvings, and the **Sarsagar Lake** is good for boating.

Some 47 km (29 miles) northeast of Vadodara, the ruins of **Champaner**, Sultan Mahmud Shah Begda's fortified fifteenth-century palace-town, and its grand Jami Masjid mosque lie on the flame-red Pavagadh Hill. It's a sight worth seeing, and it's possible to stay at Champaner's Holiday Home.

General Information
Vadodara connects by air with Delhi and Bombay, and by rail with Ahmedabad, Bombay, and Delhi. The only five-star accommodation is the **Welcomgroup Vadodara**, R.C. Dutt Road, ((0265) 330033, fax (0265) 330050, with a swimming pool, excellent Mughali restaurant, and a good travel counter. **Hotel Surya Palace**, ((0265) 330011, fax (0265) 333888, is moderately priced, and comfortable with an excellent restaurant for great value Gujarati *thalis*.

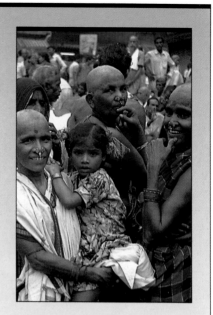

Calcutta
and
the East

CALCUTTA

Calcutta offers unexpected charms, perhaps all the more striking when contrasted with the image of impoverishment it is more widely associated with. It is easily the country's most fascinating city, a unique and compelling mixture of Raj-era relics, Bengali culture and communist politics. The state capital of West Bengal, it is one of the world's largest cities with a population of more than 11 million people.

Once Calcutta was the second city of the British empire after London, and it remains above all a monument to imperial decline, for it is the most British of all Indian cities. It has a legacy of patrician English Classical buildings, fine museums, the university, the prestigious Royal Asiatic society, the Botanical Gardens and its Pall Mall stretch of exclusive social clubs, not to mention the Edwardian spoonerisms so beloved by the local English press.

Calcutta is the action-packed center of the exuberant Bengali culture, and here literature, politics and the visual and performing arts thrive as the city's ruling passions. The Bengalis are a civilized, gregarious people, given to volatile outbursts but quick to smile and offer their help and hospitality. Calcutta is India's "Left Bank" with its "café society, Bohemian airs, political argument and love of gossip," noted Trevor Fishlock, the author of India File.

The city both mocks and fulfills a prophecy, apparently attributed to Lenin, that the "road to world revolution lies through Peking, Shanghai and Calcutta." For over a decade, flags emblazoned with the hammer and sickle have fluttered from the state Secretariat, the former British Writers Building. Its central Maiden has statues of Lenin and the local hero Subhas Chandra Bose who courted both Hitler and the Japanese during World War II in the hope that they would rid India of the British, dying before his plans came to fruition in a wartime plane crash. With deliberate tongue in cheek, Calcuttan authorities renamed the historic Clive Street after Bose, just as they renamed the street in which the American consulate is located after Ho Chi Minh during the Vietnam war.

By Indian standards, Calcutta is comparatively young. It was founded for trade and profit in 1690 by Job Charncock, the local agent of the British East India Company. Desiring a permanent trading post in wealthy Bengal, Charncock selected the site of three villages amid swamp and jungle. One of these was called Kalikata, named by locals after the most fearsome goddess in the Hindu pantheon, Kali, the destroyer. These early settlers lost no time in Anglicizing it to Calcutta and erecting the first Fort William

near the present Dalhousie Square six years later. They faced heavy losses, not only from random bloodshed when defending their patch from regional Muslim officials, but because their immune systems balked at a whole host of hitherto unknown diseases. Calcutta became known as Golgotha or "Place of Skulls" long before it was to earn the sobriquet "City of Palaces" for the Palladian mansions and grand English classical buildings that rose with the city's fortunes. Mortality rates of the European population during the eighteenth century climbed to above 50 percent, and the British penchant for excessive quantities of port, wild boar and puddings may not have helped matters.

Calcutta grew steadily as trade prospered. Opportunistic merchants soon began reaping vast profits in jute, tea, indigo, cotton, silk and minerals, luring scores of young men to make the 18-week journey from England to work as Company hacks or "writers," banking on making their fortunes by dabbling in free trade. The British Residency of Calcutta received a temporary set-back when Fort William was attacked by the Nabob of Murshidabad in 1757, recaptured by Robert Clive, who arrived too late to rescue 123 Europeans who perished in an underground cellar, that later came to be called the "Black Hole of Calcutta."

Soon Calcutta boasted a second, well-fortified fortress town, and in 1772, it was proclaimed the capital of British India by its first Governor, Warren Hastings. The grand imperial architecture is the relic of Calcutta at its zenith, when the British lived and worked behind the iron gates of their splendid homes, offices and social clubs, attended by ever-increasing tiers of servants. James Morris set the scene for the ghosts of the past in Pax Britanica: "In the evenings, the richer British box-wallahs emerged in top hats and frock coats to promenade the Maiden, driving steadily here and there in broughams, hansoms and victorias, exchanging bows and transient assessments." During the nineteenth century, Calcutta was the focus for the early independence movement, motivating the British to shift the vice-regal seat to Delhi in 1911. After Independence it lost its commercial clout with the waning of colonial-based trade, when new industries sprang up in Bombay — and its grand imperial infrastructure fell into neglect and decay.

Calcutta's modern reality is one of impossible overcrowding, pavement slums, congested traffic, inoperable phones, daily electricity blackouts, with water shortages alternating with floods — living conditions that by any standards are intolerable. It was Kipling's "city of dreadful night... the packed and pestilential town." It is true that Calcutta is a virtual synonym for dreadful squalor. It remains off the beaten track for many travelers, and tales of the city's suffering and filth do not add to its attractions. Yet Calcuttans defend their city with a kind of fierce pride, and few would choose to live anywhere else, including its two most famous personalities — Mother Teresa, a Calcuttan by adoption and the famous film-maker Satyajit Ray. Tourists who come to sample its peculiar, yet stimulating attractions will discover that above all, this city radiates the unforgettable triumph of life, laughter and the human spirit against tremendous odds, and few fail to be moved by its unique energy.

WHEN TO GO

"Enough to make a doorknob mushy." So said Mark Twain of Calcutta's intensely humid climate, created that way by its proximity to the sea and low altitude. For comfort, avoid its torrential monsoon from June to September, and visit instead during November to February. Calcutta explodes with revelry during its spectacular three-week **Durga Puja** festival in September/October, when tinseled glitter, colorful pageantry, music, dance and infectious gaiety spill out on the streets. This is the Bengal version of Dussehra, celebrating the goddess Durga, destroyer of evil, portrayed as riding a tiger. On the final day, floats of ornate idols are paraded through the main boulevards, later dunked in the Hooghly at sunset, accompanied by cheering crowds, flashing strobes and Hindi "disco" music.

Calcuttans adore festivals, and are as enthusiastic about the Diwali and the Muslim Id as they are about Christmas, the latter culminating in a grand candlelight mass at St Paul's Cathedral. Since there are about 20 official holidays in the Bengali year, it's rare to arrive without something going on. Bengali New Year in April/May is riotous but hot.

A BIRD'S EYE VIEW

Calcutta is immense. Its greater area sprawls for some 102 sq km (39 sq miles), and just crossing the relatively compact, but very congested city center can easily take an hour by taxi. For the visitor the most relevant part of Calcutta is its central core, which sprawls along the west bank of the Hooghly River from the Zoological Gardens in the south to the Howrah Bridge some five kilometers (three miles) north. Over the bridge is the industrial ship-building and jute industry heartland, and the beautiful Botanical Gardens. The inner city core is the huge green expanse of the Maiden, hugged by the bustling strip popularly known as Chowring-

hee, now renamed Jawaharlal Nehru Road, where most of the hotels, restaurants, travel and airline offices are found. At the southern end of Chowringhee you'll find the Government of India Tourist Office on and nearby the Birla Planetarium, St Paul's Cathedral and the Victoria Memorial. Slightly north lies BBD Bagh (Dalhousie Square), where the GPO, the international telephone office, the West Bengal Tourist Office, various railway reservation offices, the Writers Building and the American Express office are located.

TRANSPORT

Calcutta can be a dastardly city for getting around in. Visitors are often perplexed by its duplication of street names, since nobody seems to know whether to use the old Raj-era or new post-Independence version. Even maps aren't consistent. The best way to deal with Calcutta's anarchic traffic is treat it as one of the city's most amazing "sights" — an endless heaving tide of garishly painted lorries, double-decker buses, clanging trams, bullock carts, with man-powered rickshaws pulling decorously perched passengers, weaving to and fro. Astonishing things happen on the streets — during one short ten-minute ride for example, I witnessed a naked sadhu casually wander past, a flock of goats milling past the university gates, rows of cycle-rickshaws pulling school-children kept "safe" for their parents in cages and a Calcutta "ambulance," actually an Ambassador taxi with a man waving a red flag leaning out the window making siren noises!

Rush hour literally lasts all day, easing up only in the early hours of the morning and after seven at night. The new subway — India's first — has helped to solve some of Calcutta's transport problems. After years of tunneling, delayed by waterlogging with the annual monsoon, it has opened a four kilometer (two and a half mile) stretch of an astonishingly clean and efficient alternative to the bedlam above. It's still only half completed, running from Tollygunge in the south to Esplanade, but eventually will run all the way out to Dum Dum Airport. Many tourists make use of it to get out to Kalighat, which takes 10 minutes by the underground contrasted with up to an hour's drive.

Taxis and auto-rickshaws provide the most comfortable transport, found at any hour around the Sudder Street area. Both refuse to use their meters, but are prepared to bargain on a fixed fare beforehand. Buses are a test of Darwinian fitness — watch Calcutta's office-workers hurl themselves like human javelins or cling desperately to dangling hands while attempting to board — then decide whether this mode of transport is for you.

Calcutta is the world's last stronghold of the human-powered cart rickshaw — originally introduced by the Chinese immigrants during the eighteenth century, and now an enduring symbol of the city. Over 30,000 ply the inner city trade, and they have their own union for protection against Calcutta's authorities who have often tried to eradicate them as an embarrassing reminder of human degradation. Tourists often feel guiltily imperialistic perched above a struggling rickshaw wallah — but it's worth remembering that they depend on miserly wages (and generous tips) to fill their stomachs. At night they hook themselves into their contraptions to slumber. For short hops, they can be invaluable for weaving in and out of clogged traffic.

ACCESS

Indian Airlines run direct flights to Calcutta from Delhi, Bombay, Bangalore, Bagdogra (for Darjeeling), Bhubaneswar, Hyderabad, Madras, Varanasi, Patna and Port Blair in the Andaman Islands. Various international carriers connect it with Rome, London, Bangkok, Tokyo, Dubai, New York, Osaka, Moscow, Kathmandu and Dhaka. and domestic flights.

Calcutta's Dum Dum Airport complex combines both international and domestic services and is the most efficient clean and well-organised complex in the country. It's named after a small-arms factory nearby, which in 1898 produced the notoriously effective Dum Dum bullet, which punched fist-sized holes into tribal Afridis and was banned after the Boer War. It's best to get a pre-paid taxi for the 40-minute ride into the city center, costing about US$5 either way. There's also a US$1 airport bus which stops at Chowringhee, near the Oberoi Grand and Sudder Street, but this service becomes irregular in the evenings.

There are two rail stations, but travelers are most likely to enter the city through the teeming bedlam of Howrah station, just over the Howrah bridge, which has overnight and day rail services out to most major destinations, including Madras (33 hours), Delhi (16 hours), Bombay (36 hours), and Varanasi (12 hours). Give yourself at least an hour to reach Howrah by taxi from the city center. The less congested Sealdah station, 20 minutes north-east of the city, services Darjeeling (24 hours).

HOTELS

Calcutta's **Oberoi Grand**, ((033) 292323 fax (033) 291217, 15 Jawaharlal Nehru Road, is one of India's most stylish and efficient hotels, rated

by frequent business travelers as their personal favorite, even compared favorably by some with London's Savoy Hotel. Tucked behind Chowringhee's bustling arcades, it is a haven of luxury, with its sweeping Georgian faade, brass-buttoned bell-hops, immaculate 1930's style marble interior, and staff in period uniforms. Its fortunes are a mini-chronicle of Calcutta: originally built as a fantasy home by one Colonel Grand in the late nineteenth century, then sold to an entrepreneurial Armenian, and during World War II became a glorified doss-house for British troops, known locally as Mrs Monks Guest House. It's now the Oberoi

chain's flagstaff hotel, miraculously managing to function in Calcutta, a city notorious for its frequent power cuts, tainted water and non-operative telephones. It has a beautiful swimming pool and terrace garden, excellent health club facilities including saunas, Turkish baths, gymnasiums and massage-cum-beauty parlors. It offers Calcutta's best restaurants, cultural Dances of India performances, a stylish cocktail lounge, an airy 24-hour coffee shop and the city's only discotheque, the Pink Elephant, full of brass palm trees, flashing strobes, and the latest tunes, but open only to guests and club members. Other facilities include a well-equipped business center, shopping arcade, travel desk and in-house astrologer. Stylish comfort extends to all rooms, with their pastel pink, marble and mahogany decor. Rates: very expensive.

The Taj Group opened their **Taj Bengal**, ((033) 248-3939, fax (033) 248-1776, in late 1989, at 34B Belvedere Road in Alipore in residential south Calcutta. Other than that, the only real luxury alternative to the Oberoi is the **Tollygunge Club**, ((033) 410616, 120 Deshapran Sasmal Road, also in south Calcutta. Set amid a

---

ABOVE: A nag-drawn *tonga*, or traditional horse-drawn taxi, outside Howrah Station.

beautiful 81-hectare (200-acre) estate, this historic club-house was built in 1788, and for a time became the residence of the desposed sons of Tipu "Tiger" Sultan. During the heyday of the British Raj, it became the most exclusive of all European clubs. It's run by an English couple, Bob and Anne Wright, and facilities include polo and horse-riding fields, squash and tennis courts and a swimming pool. Rates: inexpensive and non-members must advance book.

The **Fairlawn Hotel** ((033) 244460, 245-1510, 13A Sudder Street, is delightfully eccentric, trussed up like a Brighton boarding house. It is dominated by its formidable Armenian pro-

prietress, Mrs Smith, whose entourage includes a fleet of lap dogs and a corps of beaming retainers in faded khaki and Nehru caps. Once the entrance gate is closed, Calcutta's tumultuous street-life recedes (although rickshaw boys bed down on the pavement outside) and the guest can unwind in the small leafy courtyard strewn with cane chairs, statues and fairy-lights. Rooms are very pukka — with floral drapes, lace dollies, and old fashioned baths — and you'll have a "bearer" assigned to your room to bring "bed-tea" and Britannica biscuits, collect washing for the *dhobi wallah* and refill water. Mealtimes are sounded with a resounding gong, with as many as four courses ritually served in a dining room crammed with extraordinary monarchist memorabilia. The daily Anglo-Indian menus read like samples from a Victorian handbook for memsahibs in the tropics, frequently delicious, particularly the fish course. With its homely, time-warp atmosphere, the Fairlawn often steals nostalgic British guests away from the more luxurious Oberoi, and attracts an interesting array of travelers, who are more or less thrown into each other's company. Videotaped

The Oberoi Grand Hotel, considered by many Calcuttans to be the epitome of elegance and the good life.

episodes of *The Good Life, Yes Minister* not to mention the nuptials of Prince Charles and bride Diana, can be viewed in the lounge. Rates are moderate and include three huge meals a day.

After the Fairlawn everything else pales into insignifiance. But of other pleasant centrally located Raj-era options, try the moderately priced three-star **Park Hotel**, ((033) 297336, fax (033) 297343, 17 Park Road, which offers comfortable rooms or the inexpensive **Hotel New Kenilworth**, ((033) 242-8394, fax (033) 242-5136, 1-2 Little Russell Street, conveniently located close to the tourist office and government emporiums. Just around the corner, the **Astor Hotel**, ((033) 242-9957, 15 Shakespeare Sarani, is a quaint inexpensive Tudor-style establishment in a peaceful courtyard with evening barbecues. Then there's the **Great Eastern Hotel**, ((033) 248-2331, 1-2 Old Court Road, whose once-considerable charms are barely perceptible through a haze of grime and tat, although it still charges inflated room rates because Rudyard Kipling stayed there for a few months typing out dispatches for the *Civil and Military Gazette*.

Sudder Street has the greatest concentration of cheap tourist lodges. At 2 Sudder Street is the **Salvation Army Red Shield Guest House**, ((033) 242895, with spartan, but spotless fan-cooled singles rooms with attached bath. Dorm beds cost US$1, and guests can use communal bathrooms. Budget travelers rate it highly, although its water supply is not always up to scratch. It's possible to put valuables into "safe-keeping" at the front desk. Another popular and cheap tourist lodge is the **Shilton Hotel**, ((033) 245-1512, a few doors away, at 5A.

Calcutta's YMCA's are quite grand. The most creakily Gothic of all, the **YMCA**, ((033) 292192, on Jawaharial Nehru Road, was originally built in 1902, and has a spooky "Turn of the Screw" feel. It still retains its mystifying plaque "No pets or private servants allowed!" it's unisex, and the room rate — US$10 for singles, US$15 for doubles — is expensive by YMCA standards, but includes three hearty meals a day, plus tanin-saturated "bed-tea".

RESTAURANTS

It's possible to dine at the Oberoi Grand on Russian caviar, blinis and champagne at Rs 1,000 a shot, if it suits your whim and pocket — it's also possible to join the hungry queue outside the "begger's restaurant" — run by beggers for beggers — just outside Sealdah station, where for Rs 1 you are given a plate, made from melded leaves, heaped with rice, dal and chapatis. Given the wide array of excellent restaurants in between, it can be surprisingly difficult to sample Calcutta's exotic Bengali cuisine. That's because most Calcuttan families tend in eat in — believing, quite rightly, that home cooking is best. This may stem partly from tradition and partly because Bengali dishes rely heavily on subtle herbs, fresh fish and mustard oil—a combination of which does not keep well together for long. Traditionally, meals are served course by course on plantain leaves. When Calcuttans go out, they like to do so in style — opting for swish European, Chinese or north-Indian food, and "cabarets" with Goan bands — both of which are affected by the state's partial prohibition on Thursdays and Saturdays.

The **Suruchi** at 89 Elliot Road, near Sudder Street, gets the highest praise from locals for its typical Bengali dishes. It's best to concentrate on their fresh fish dishes, particularly doi mach, an unforgettable curry of river fish, yogurt, ginger, raisins and spices; dabey chingri shell-fish baked with coconut; maccher paturi steamed mustard fish; delicious but bony smoked hilsa fish, and prawns sauteed in mustard oil and spiced with coriander and garlic. All are eaten with a variety of rice dishes or with loochi a deep-fried bread, and hot, syrupy mango chutney. Bengali sweets are positively devilish for sugar-addicts — usually milk and curd based, like barfi, rosgulla, rasmalai, and sandhesh — all made to tantalize the taste buds. Another favorite Bengali dessert is misthi dohi, a sweet curd with raw jaggery.

The Oberoi Grand offers the best Mughali, Szechuan and French food in Calcutta with such sophisticated food and stylish décor that it barely seems possible that the "City of Dreadful Night" hovers outside. The city's elite adore **La Rotisserie** for its classic French cuisine, with such decadent delights as Strasbourg goose liver and truffles, Scottish pheasant, fresh rainbow trout, and New Zealand prime steak — all flown in fresh. Desserts are no less appetizing, and there's an extensive wine list (at extensive prices). A full-blown dinner for two, without imported wine, costs around US$100, or you can sample their good-value set lunch buffets, and the dinner-time "Dances of India" performance, every night at 6:30 pm (except Tuesdays).

Calcutta's main drag, Park Street, is festooned with faded neon, garish "cabaret" club porticoes and shop faades left over from the thirties and forties, crammed with the city's best-loved restaurants.

The **Sky Room**, ((033) 294362 at N° 57 is the most quirkily elegant with its Art Deco decor, fake "sky" ceiling, and old-fashioned waiters clad in spotless white. Order their excellent Bengali and Mughali dishes, all beautifully served on silverware. Here it's possible to buy 1930's style brocade ties (displayed at the front counter)

now back in fashion. It's best to pre-book as city-smart locals flock here in their chiffon-clad and Bengali-dhotied droves, but be forewarned, no alcohol is sold here. Other well-patronized haunts for standard tri-cuisine include **Kwality**, at N' 17, one of the biggest and best of the chain, the **Moulin Rouge** at N' 31, fronted by a fake windmill faade, and the **Blue Fox** at N' 55. Just behind Sudder Street, **Amber**, 11 Waterloo Road is the place to sample north-Indian Punjabi food.

Calcutta's Chinese immigrants have endowed the city with numerous authentic regional Chinese restaurants, still mainly catering to the small colony who patronize them for their Peking duck, other homely dishes and continuous green tea. One of the best is **How Hwa**, Mirza Ghalib Road, which offers a staggering 32 different kinds of soups, including the house specialty, Chimney Soup, a mélange of prawn wantons, fish, crab meat and home-made bean curd cooked with a garlic-ginger stock in a Mongolian hot-pot. Special dishes can be ordered in 24 hours in advance, notably luscious roasted Peking duck served with plum sauce, scallions and pancakes. Other popular "Chinese" include the **Nanking**, 22 Blackburn Lane, and the Peiping, 1/1 Park Street, (with its partitioned sections a concession to Muslim patrons), renowned for its steamed garlic and ginger fish and giant king prawns.

Flury's, on Park Street, is a classic Raj-era tearoom with an adjoining pastry shop. it's open early for British breakfasts of baked beans on toast, and is a popular rendezvous place for all-day pastries, club sandwiches and Vienna coffees. **Kathleen's**, 12 Free School Street, at the end of Sudder Street, also has a great restaurant-cum-bakery, always well patronized since Calcuttans adore their cream cakes! Backpackers gravitate to the **Blue Sky Café**, in Sudder Street, which bills itself "The Only Café for You Kind of People!" and serves good fruit lassis, Western-style breakfasts, and burgers.

If you're strolling down College Street's "book strip" don't miss one of Calcutta's most lively hang-outs, the **Indian Coffee Worker's Co-operative**, at 15 Bankim Chatterjee Street nearby. It occupies the cavernous Albert Hall, noted as the venue for the First National Congress Conference in 1885. Climb up the "balcony seat" for a delicious iced coffee and observe this hub of political and cultural discussion, echoing to the sounds of urgent Bengali, wafts of highbrow English and emphatic fists on tables. Calcutta's Bengali students may look threadbare, and exist only on coffee and cigarettes, but they sure know their Marxist dialectics. Giant fans dangle like low propellers, waiters flit about dressed in bizarre plumed caps, soiled white uniforms and cummerbunds. It's a great place to strike up conversations, and dine well for next to nothing.

"Cabaret-restaurants", provide the glitz for Calcutta's nightlife, and the most famous is **"Trinca's"** at 17B, just outside the Park Hotel. It might be "Exotic Mina and the Twisters", a plump mulatto from Trinaded in a lame dress crooning to the accompaniment of bandsmen in sequinned large lapelled suits one night, or "Shaheed and the Goanese All-Stars" the next.

SIGHTSEEING

Going "sightseeing" in Calcutta is almost an anachronism. Many travelers stay for weeks, becoming so fascinated by its unbelievably tumultuous street-life that they spend all their time in a half-intoxicated dread-state, combing through the cobbled streets of the decaying imperial center, fossicking in bazaars and simply being a witness to the city's incredible pace of life. At the end of their stay, they've probably worn out their shoe leather, but may not have seen many of Calcutta's historic "sights" at all.

A successful itinerary is planned on the basis of geographical proximity rather than attempting to see things in a particular order. Walking the long distances between general localities can not only become confusingly complicated if following a less-than accurate Calcutta street map, but gets exhausting too. So hail some form of transport — be it mechanical, animal, or in the case of Calcutta, even human — and move on to wherever else seems the most interesting. The tours devised below are tailor-made for this approach, best spread over several days of sightseeing.

CITY TOUR

If you're staying in the central Chowringhee/Sudder Street area, the most decadent start to any sightseeing is breakfast in the Oberoi Maidens, followed by a short stroll down Chowringhee, now called Jawaharlal Nehru Road. It's lined with decaying Palladian palaces and mansions, formerly inhabited by the wealthy and powerful British and Bengali bhandralok, the enterprising Westernized Indian middle class. Today they are used as commercial offices, amid Chowringhee's frenetic melee of garish movie billboards, bazaars, cafés, and hotels.

The Maiden

Across the road is the **Maiden**, Calcutta's three-kilometer (two-mile) -long Hyde Park where everything from massive political rallies to early

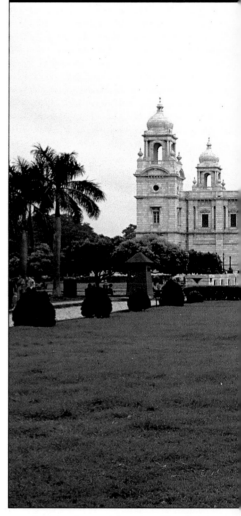

morning yoga lessons takes place. Itinerant performers, ash-smeared sadhus and tired tourists alike enjoy the shade of its leafy trees, and it's also famous as the venue for the "Mukta Mela," a sort of informal cultural fair held from time to time, in which poets recite their verses to one another, artists discuss their canvases and free-thinkers bring along their soap-boxes. The Maiden was created in the wake of the massacres of the Indian Mutiny of 1857, when the British decided to replace their original Fort William near Dalhousie Square with a new more massive and impregnable version, whose white-washed fortifications and trenches overlook the Hooghly River further west. The Maiden was originally designed to give the fort's cannons a clear line of fire — today it echoes to the sound of cricket shots. Indian cricket was actually born on the Maiden with a two-day white flannel match in 1802 between the "Old Etonians" versus a "Calcutta" brigade of East India Company nabobs.

To the south lies the Royal Calcutta Turf Club, which has an active season from November to mid-March, but draws India's horse-mad elite for its climactic annual Queen Elizabeth II Derby in January.

At the southern end of the Maiden rises the dazzling white marble **Victoria Memorial**, one of the most pompous, grandiloquent edifices ever built by the British in India. When the Poet W.H. Auden visited during the fifties, he recorded being vastly amused when a freelance guide told him that it had been designed by the same man who created the Taj Mahal! It has been called an imperial "blamanche" of Classical and Mughal architecture, and it was in fact inspired by the Taj Mahal, with its four rudimentary

minarets, gleaming white dome and exterior of solid Macarana marble.

It was commisioned by Lord Curzon, Viceroy of India, and raised entirely with money from voluntary contributions, as the ultimate compliment to Queen Victoria after her death in 1901. Built between 1906 and 1921 at a cost of Rs 7.5 million, it's set amid 26 hectares (64 acres) of lawns, fountains, herbaceous borders and dotted with statues of former British rulers which used to adorn street corners all along Chowringhee and the Maiden. Looking dourly imperious, the Empress of India sits enthroned in bronze at the entrance marble staircase, wearing the regal Order of the Star of India. Above her, a 4.9-m (16-ft) -high bronze winged Angel

Families picnicking in the lush statuary-dotted gardens of the pompously grand Victoria Memorial.

of Victory is poised to fly from atop the central dome.

Inside houses the most remarkable collection of memorabilia of British India ever amassed under one roof — 3,500 exhibits on 25 galleries. The entrance dome is etched with the text of Queen Victoria's proclamation speech of herself as Empress, while the surrounding galleries are crammed with pageant-like paintings relating to the major episodes in the monarch's life (coronation, marriage to Albert, baptism of her son and heir Edward VII, going riding with her faithful retainer, John Brown, pompish celebrations of the golden and silver jubilees, and

his grand tour of Jaipur in 1876, the works of the Victorian artists, Thomas and William Daniells, and Johann Zoffany's portrait of William Hastings and his family. Rare extant documents, treaties, an armory and a Historic Calcutta exhibition complete the fascinating collection. The Publications Office sells excellent catalogues, books and posters. It's open Tuesdays to Sundays, from 10 am to 4:30 pm from March to October, and until 3:30 pm during November to February, closed on public holidays.

St Paul's Cathedral, barely five minutes walk across the gardens is the first Church of England cathedral of British India, built in 1847

many others) as well as several of her personal possessions: the baby-grand piano on which she played as a child, her personal writing desk and embroidered armchair. There are even scrapbooks of her letters in Hindustani, for she was tutored in the language by her favorite India attendant Abdul Karim. Entire wings are lined with portraits and busts of famous British figures, who each in their own way added their contribution to British India, including Robert Clive, General Stringer Lawrence (father of the Indian army), Lord Bentinck who outlawed suttee, William Makepeace Thackeray who was born here, and Florence Nightingale, who only ever took a distant interest in India. Among the many excellent paintings, look especially for Burne-Jones's portrait of Rudyard Kipling, Verestchagin's monumental depiction of the Prince of Wales, (the future King Edward VII) making

with East India Company funds as their Gothic imitation Canterbury Cathedral. Inside see the ornate communion plate presented by Queen Victoria, Burne-Jones's stained glass west window, Francis Chantrey's statue of Bishop Heber and Sir Arthur Blomfield's mosaics around the altar.

Further south-east lies the **Zoological Gardens,** off Belvedere Road, open sunrise to sunset, its main attraction being a captive rare white tiger from Rewa.

Opposite is **Raj Bhawan**, the Government House from which Viceroys ruled India until 1911. It was built in 1803 upon the orders of the Governor General of Bengal, Lord Wellesley who was determined to have a palace equal to his station. He tactfully omitted to mention how palatial his palace was, only sending the bill to his superiors in London when it was safely completed, and the East India Company was forced to foot the cost — then two million rupees. However future viceroys found this replica of Kedleston Hall in Derbyshire very much to their tastes. Inside is a grand marble hall dominated by 12 busts of Caesar, staircase sphinxes — and the various contributions left behind by previous occupants: Warren Hasting's gravel from Bayswater, Lord Ellenborough's Chinese cannon on a brass dragon, Lord Curzon's fretted-iron lift. It's now the part-residence of the Chief Minister and part-Secretariat of West Bengal, not open to the public.

Close by, along Council House Street, you'll find the Greco-colonial **St John's Church**, Calcutta's oldest British cemetery. It was built in 1787, modelled on London's St Martin-in-the-Fields and used as a temporary cathedral by the East India Company's burgeoning populace until St Paul's Cathedral was completed. Its quaint interior is dominated by Zoffany's Raj-version of the "Last Supper", whose saintly disciples actually resemble their less-than angelic sitters, a corps of young clerks, who Zoffany later wryly noted, passed the time taking swigs at brandy bottles. Within the overgrown churchyard, crammed with moss-encrusted masonry, one of the oldest tombstones belongs to Job Charnock, who died in 1692, two years after founding Calcutta. Admiral Watson, who supported Clive in retaking Calcutta from Suraj-ud-daula, is also buried here. Other tombstones illustrate the perils faced by the early British settlers — premature deaths caused by heat, exotic malaises, too much port or ill-fated adventures.

From here, it's a 20 minute stroll down to **Dalhousie Square**, now renamed **BBD Bagh**, in memory of Benoy, Badal and Dinesh, three freedom-fighting Bengali martyrs. For more than 150 years, Dalhousie Square was British India's headquarters, and it is still Calcutta's commercial hub. Bengali bureaucrats, lawyers, stockbrokers and businessmen deftly pick their way past beggers, coolies, shattered pavements and rattling trams. To Western eyes, this imperial muddle of dilapidated Victorian buildings, swept-up Doric colonnades, grand mahogany doors and Romanesque-lettered brass nameplates looks eerily familiar, yet with its overlapping chaotic squalor, almost like a sort of post-Holocaust London. Half-naked men and boys briskly lather themselves in muddy gushes sloshed from burst pipes and clean their teeth with neem twigs; thin pavement clerks hunch over battered Remingtons typing out applications for queues of illiterates; tiny urchins chatter over shared chapatis. Once this was Job Charnock's Tank Square, where bheesties or water carriers serviced the houses of the early European settlers. The tank still brims today,

and its high fence does nothing to discourage early morning swimmers and tribes of dhobi-wallahs, who tirelessly thwack spirals of cloth against the concrete slopes. The square is dominated by the huge 14-storied **Writer's Building**, built in 1880, with its Early English porticos and burnt–sienna faade crowned by rooftop statues who strike allegorical poses representing imperial ethos: Justice, Virtue, Faith, Charity, and so on. Originally it was just a squat barrack-house where the runtish clerks or "writers", who came out with the East India Company, lived and worked. As Benaglis are apt to explain, India's notoriously complex bureaucracy dates back to

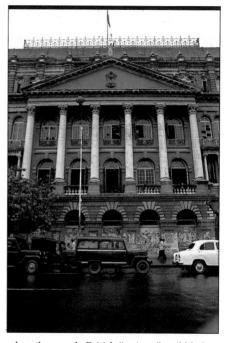

when these early British "writers" scribbled records of business transactions in this very building, now used as the Secretariat of Communist West Bengal. Their modern counterparts, the Bengali bapus carry on the tradition of painstakingly-typed letters, receipts and memoranda in triplicate. Tourists who venture inside, usually seeking permission to go the Sunderbans or Darjeeling, find labyrinthine passages, branching off into dusty cavernous rooms where peons shuffle papers, sip tea and wile away time in a trance against pyramids of yellowing files. To the west of Dalhousie Square is the imposing Corinthian-pillared **GPO**, which occupies the

---

ABOVE: Imposing façade of the Writer's Building in BBD Bagh. OPPOSITE: The Marble Palace is the "Miss Haversham" of grand Calcutta mansions, full of cobwebbed charm.

site of the original Fort William that was demolished by the Nabob Siraj-ud-Daulah in 1756. Calcutta's infamous "black hole", was actually a guard room that stood at the north-east corner of the GPO, but since independence all indications of its presence have been removed, save a tiny brass plaque. It's fascinating to walk along Netaji Subhas Road, Calcutta's main business strip adjoining the square, lined with the old British commercial houses that continue to flourish in Indian hands. Whiffs of tea grow stronger nearer **R.N. Mukherjee Street**, where the city's tea auctions are held, brawny coolies lug stacks of paper for printing industries, and frenzied dealing goes on at the Lyon's Range Stock Exchange, just beyond Clive Street.

A PATCHWORK OF LEGACIES

Howrah Bridge
The colossal cantilevered bridge is the city's most famous landmark. The 27,000-ton plank joining Calcutta with the jute-mill and ship-building settlement of Howrah across the khaki waters of the Hooghly opened in 1943 and is now one of the busiest bridges in the world with some two million people crossing it daily. No other sight captures Calcutta's hectic energy quite so dramatically — from dawn until late into the night it's a permanently choked tide of sardine-can buses, taxis, hideously polluting trucks, buffalo-drawn carts, clanging hordes of bicycles and rickshaws. Sprightly laborers balancing mountainous loads weaving in and out among the larger vehicles. Astonishingly, during high summer, this steel mesh bridge expands some four feet each day in the heat, shrinking back to normal during the night. Beneath it along the river banks, is a constant jamboree of itinerant masseuses, barbers, and flower sellers.

The Marble Palace
Some three kilometers (nearly two miles) north of the city center off Chittaranjan Avenue, lies one of Calcutta's most extraordinary sights. This Palladian mansion and its ornamental garden was built in 1835 by a wealthy Bengali merchant, Raja Rajendra Mullick, who had been orphaned at three and given an English guardian, Sir James Hogg, by the Supreme Court. He started building at the age of 16, amassing an eclectic mix of 126 varieties of marble to line the floors, wall panels and tables. Pelicans and peacocks strut through the colonnaded inner courtyard, and tiny stairwells lead to rooms and apartments crammed with ornate objets d'art and paintings studiously collected from auctions and dispossessed households across the globe — all slowly consumed by Dickensian decay,

mildew and dust. Lurking somewhere in this charmed gloom hang oils by Titian, Sir Joshua Reynolds, Murillo and Rubens — amid a jumble of Venetian glass, statues of Greek gods, enormous chandeliers, Parisian furniture, gilt goblets from Bohemia and Teutonic stag heads. An unusually nubile-looking Queen Victoria dominates a red marble room, facing many po-faced plaster busts. Guests are free to wander through between the hours of 10 am and 4 pm, although it's not a museum, but the Mullick family's private home. Respecting the wishes of Mullick senior, their allow beggar children to play in their fairy-tale garden, and provide free meals for queues of destitutes every day at noon. It's closed on Monday and Thursdays.

Nearby, off Rabindra Sarani, is the **Rabindra-Bharati Museum**, the stately ancestral home of the gifted and influential Tagore family. This is where India's famous poet, philosopher and fervent nationalist, Rabindranath Tagore was born and later died. His talents as poet won him the Nobel Prize in 1913, and he also composed the song Jana Gana Mana Adhinayaka which was adopted as the National Anthem after Independence. It's a fascinating treasure trove filled with family heirlooms, manuscripts and paintings. It's open from Monday to Friday from 10 am to 7 pm, Saturdays 10 am to 1 pm, and Sundays, 11 am to 2 pm.

It's a 15-minute drive north-east to the **Jain Temple**, built by the fabulously rich Birla family in 1867. It's actually a collection of four pagoda-like shrines set in geometrical gardens and ponds. They have exquisite interiors encrusted with mirror-glass mosaics, Venetian glass, gilt dome ceilings and precious stones, inlaid by a jeweler — all dedicated to Sitalnathji, tenth of the 24 Jain tirthankars (prophets).

Returning to the city center, make a short detour to the junction of Rabindra Sarani and Zakaria Street, to see the magnificent **Nakhoda Mosque**, whose giant two 46-m (150-ft) -high minarets and copper-green domes are visible from afar. It's the center of Calcutta's Muslim community, modeled on Akbar's tomb at Sikandra near Agra and able to accommodate up to 10,000 people during major festivals. The most spectacular of these is Muharram, when the surrounding streets come alive with bands, and men dancing like whirling dervishes with long curving swords.

Back in central Calcutta, round off sightseeing with a visit to the historic **South Park Cemetery**, in Park Street, a leafy enclosure congested with classical mausoleums of Calcutta's distinguished Europeans, replacing St John's cemetery in 1767. Among those buried here is William Hickey's wife Charlotte Barry; Colonel Charles Russell Deare, who perished in the fight against

Tipu Sultan; Colonel Kyd, the founder of the Botanical Gardens; the early Indologist William Jones, founder of the Royal Asiatic Society, the novelist William Makepeace Thackeray's father, and sons of Charles Dickens and Captain Cook. Among the crumbling tombstones is that of Rose Aylmer, a young beauty who captured Thackeray's heart but died in her late teens after eating infected pineapple. The custodian is full of stories, and it's open all day.

Goddess Kali and the Sisters of Mercy

Take the underground metro to Kalighat to see the temple of Calcutta's patron goddess, Kali, the malevolent destroyer, located about 10 minutes walk from the station. The present temple was built in 1809, but this site of **Kali Khetra** — from which Calcutta derived its name — has long been associated with legend. It is said to be the home of Kali, "the black one," who rose as an incarnation of Devi, Shiva's wife. The story goes that Shiva was so distraught about when Devi died, that the other gods feared he would pound the earth to dust in his grief. So Vishnu surreptitiously removed Devi's offending corpse from Shiva's sight, slicing it into 52 pieces. One of her severed toes fell here, becoming Kali. Devi represented Shiva's feminine energy in its manifold forms. Thus she took on many incarnations, of which Kali and the more saintly Durga, (the focus of Calcutta's annual Durga Puja festival), are the most important. Rather unappetisingly, the temple is notorious for its daily animal sacrifice — usually goats or sheep — when pilgrims are whipped into a frenzy, scrabbling up the marble stairs to make puja of sweetmeats, flowers or coconuts. Kali is usually depicted as a gorgon-like creature with beady red eyes, dripping with blood, and triumphantly holding up weapons, snakes, and severed heads in her ten arms. Of all the Hindu deities, her wrath is most feared, and hence revered most slavishly. The temple is open until 10 pm.

Nirmal Hriday, the Place of the Pure Heart, the most famous of Mother Theresa's homes for the dying, stands beside the Kali temple in a former pilgrim's hostel, at 54A Lower Circular Road, ((033) 247115. Visitors are allowed during the early morning and between 4 and 6 pm. It's here that dying men and women with nothing and no one come to be cared for by the Sisters of Mercy in their distinctive white blue-bordered saris, before "going home to God". Mother Theresa started alone in 1948 in a Calcutta slum, and since then the Missionary Sisters have grown to more than a 1,000-strong and a separate Brotherhood has also been formed. Under her auspices, the Sisters and Brothers now operate over 81 schools, 325 mobile dispensaries serving 1,600,000 people annually, 28 family planning centers, 67 leprosy clinics and 32 homes for dying destitute men and women. It's easy to see why this iron-willed crusader has earned world-wide admiration for her courageous efforts to redress Calcutta's overwhelming human suffering.

Bengali Biblomania

Calcuttans pride themselves on being a literary people. The British began the trend, founding the prestigious Royal Asiatic Society and the National Library here, but the Bengalis were behind Calcutta's nineteenth century literary renaissance that gave zeal to the early independence movement. There are more than 800 newspapers in the state, more than 1,600 poetry magazines, and the bulk of India's creative theater emerges from here. Even the subway system reflects Calcutta's mania for poetical message, one station almost entirely covered in Tagore's poems and artistic doodles. Provocative graffiti crams the city's walls, usually a compelling mixture of the poetic and the political.

Nowhere is the Bengali obsession with words so amply illustrated than the city's Portabello Road of books, **College Street**, near the university, where the air is trapped with dust particles from thousands upon thousands of books — stacked high on the pavement, in tiny stalls, spilling out from large awnings. You'll find almost anything here in almost every language — Victorian lithographs to Russian textbooks — along this kilometer-long strip. Nearby is the **National Library,** the grand former residence of the British Lieutenant Governor, with its eight million books, including rare manuscripts. For brand-new books go to the **Oxford Book Company** on Park Street.

Arrive well primed for Calcutta by reading Geoffrey Moorehouse's classic 1971 Calcutta, published by Penguin — easily the most fascinating in-depth study around. Dominique Lapierre's City of Joy is less critically acclaimed, but makes compulsive reading.

Terracotta Pompeii

The unsung heroes of Calcutta's spectacular Durga Puja parade are the idol-makers who fashion clay gods by the thousands. Squatting in cotton lunghis, deftly molding wet mud over straw cones, these pavement artisans work in the community known as **Kumar Tulli,** or **"Potter's Lane"**, located near the river in north Calcutta, just off Chitpur Road. Unpainted, yet extraordinarily life-like terracotta images of Durga, Kali, Ganesh and Laxmi and many other gods clutter the streets to bake in the sun, looking eerily like a kind of terra-cotta Pompeii. Later they will be painted up in gaudy colors, threaded with tinsel and dressed in glittering costumes as part of the Durga Puja's mammoth float parade.

CULTURE AND CRAFTS ROUND-UP

Of all Indian cities, Calcutta has the most fascinating array of museums, art galleries and cultural "happenings."

Keep an eye out for what's on by consulting the daily Amrita Bazaar Patrika and Sunday Telegraph newspapers, or consult the tourist office's Calcutta This Fortnight leaflet. Opposite the Calcutta Club on Acharaya Bose Road is an excellent information center and box office for the arts. The most active hall is **Rabindra Sadan,** ((033) 449936 on Cathedral Road, Calcutta's cultural hub, where Indian dancers, writers and musicians perform. You're bound to find something happening most nights. Other main halls include the **Academy of Fine Arts, Birla Academy** and the **Sisir Mancha.** It's worth catching a performance of Indian classical dance, particularly the eastern dance styles of Manipuri, Odissa and Chahau, usually recounting stories from the Mahabharata or the Ramayana.

Of Calcutta's 30 or so museums, make time for the country's largest, and most extensive, the **Indian Museum,** located at the junction of Chowringhee and Sudder Street. Founded in 1814 to house the burgeoning collection of the prestigious Asiatic Society, it's a huge Classical-style building with a Corinthian portico and a cavernous proscenium-style arch auditorium. Its vast collection is spread across six departments: archaeology, anthropology, zoology, geology, botany and art. Look especially for its fine coin collection, textiles, *bidri* ware, Indian miniature paintings, and the Sunga and Gandhara sculpture. Intriguing oddities abound, including giant prehistoric coconuts, an eight-legged, four-eared preserved goat, bangles from the belly of a captured crocodile. At the entrance, get a map to help you find your way around its giant corridors, some barely disturbed, with priceless treasures sharing dust-filled rooms with nesting pigeons. It's open daily except Mondays from 10 am to 4:30 pm. Equally impressive is the **Austosh Museum of Modern Art,** housed in Calcutta University on College Street, a fabulous showcase of the rich artistic legacy of eastern India, with sculpture, folk-art, textiles and fine collection of Kalighat paintings and terracottas. It's open from Monday to Friday from 10:30 am to 5 pm with half-days on Saturdays.

Of others to explore, the following are closed on Mondays unless otherwise specified. The **Academy of Fine Arts,** Cathedral Road, open 3 to 8 pm. The **Birla Academy of Art and Culture,** 108-9 Southern Avenue, open 4 to 8 pm. The **Birla Planetarium** at 96 J. Nehru Road, the largest and best organized in India, well patronized by city workers for its air-conditioned environment during the hot summers — most seem to doze off during the soothing drone of its lectures! There are at least two English sessions daily between 2:30 and 6:30 pm.

You can visit the preserved home of **Netaji Subhas Chandra Bose,** the errant Indian nationalist leader who joined forces with the Japanese during World War II, at 38/2 Lala Lajpat Rai Sarani, open Monday to Friday from 6 to 8 pm and on Sundays 9 am to 12 pm. The **Nehru Children's Museum,** 94 J. Nehru Road, open noon to 8 pm. The **Royal Asiatic Society,** 1 Park Street, open for studying only from Monday to Friday noon to 7 pm. The **State Archaeological Museum,** 33 Chittaranjan Avenue, open Monday to Friday 11 am to 5:30 pm, Saturdays from 11 am to 2 pm.

SHOPPING

Calcutta is an oasis of traditional Bengali handicrafts and textiles. Try browsing first at the **Bengal Home Industries Association,** at 57 Jawaharlal Nehru Road and the **West Bengal Government Sales Emporium** on Lindsay Street. Stars to search for include the village terra-cotta figurines, made throughout rural Bengal as icons of occupation; rice-measuring bowls made from wood inlaid with brass, often in a shell design; brass oil lamps crafted to resemble figures or animals; conch-shell bangles, carved ivory, delicate silver jewelry and dolls made from papier mâché or cotton. The queen of Bengali textiles is the Baluchari brocade sari, noted for its highly complicated floral and story-telling motifs, developed by eighteenth century Gujurati migrants. Delicate cotton and lace embroidery is another speciality, best bought at the **All Bengal Women's Home** at 89 Elliot Street. Round off any shopping with a visit to the historic **Hogg's Market,** now known as **New Market,** tucked behind the Oberoi Grand. Its Victorian red-brickwork and awnings were built almost a century ago, and it remains Calcutta's chief bartering place, particularly for its brimming animal and bird mart. Squads of eager porters rush up to prospective buyers, offering to lug your purchases around in panier-like baskets before you've even bought them.

Bystanders wait for some temple action outside the Kali Temple at Kalighat.

AROUND CALCUTTA

THE BANYAN BOULEVARD

Across the Hooghly's banks, south of Howrah, are India's most beautiful **Botanical Gardens** — a perfect bolt-hole from Calcutta proper. It's a 40 minute drive (20 km or 11.4 miles) from the city center. Laid out by one Colonel Kyd in 1786 as a pleasure retreat for the East India Company, it stretches for about a kilometer along the riverfront, with palm, orchid and cacti houses, a her-

barium, lakes and altogether some 30,000 varieties of tropical plants and trees. It was at these gardens that the tea now grown in Assam and Darjeeling was first developed. Its world-famous attraction is its 225 year-old banyan tree, the largest on earth. It has a circumference of 417 m (1,367 ft) and some 1,600 aerial roots, resembling a small forest, not a single tree. It's most pleasant to make this a morning exursion, taking a ferry cruise across the Hooghly from Chandpal or Takta Ghats, checking first that the Botanical Gardens Ghat is open.

THE BELUR MATH

Some 10 km (6.2 miles) north, still on the east bank of the Hooghly, is the **Belur Math**, the headquarters of the Ramakrishna Mission. This was established in 1898 by Swami Vivekananda, resuscitating the ideals of the sage Rama Krishna who preached the essential unity of all religions. Illustrating this belief, it looks like a church, Hindu temple or mosque — depending on the way you look at it.

On safari in the Sunderbans. ABOVE: A tawny Royal Bengal tiger. OPPOSITE TOP: Pastoral peace as the sun sets over the marshlands. OPPOSITE BOTTOM: Waiting for a boat to ferry passengers through the mangrove swamps.

General Information

The best Government of India Tourist Office, ℂ (033) 242-1402, 443521, is at 4 Shakespeare Sarani. It's both friendly and well-stocked with information, particularly helpful for advice about permit requirements for Darjeeling. The West Bengal Tourist Bureau, ℂ (033) 248-8271 is at 3/2 BBD Bagh. Both the state and national tourist offices have counters at the airport. Both run daily morning and afternoon conducted city tours, good for orientation if you don't have time to sightsee at leisure, and getting out to far-flung sights.

In the Dalhousie Square (BBD Bagh) area, you can make overseas calls at to the Central Telegraph Office at 8 Red Cross Place and collect Poste Restante letters at the large GPO. The Foreigner's Registration Office, ℂ (033) 44301 is at 237 Acharya J C Bose Road. Lastly, you'll save yourself much time and energy by entrusting your travel plans/predicaments to a reliable travel agent. Good ones to try include the Travel Corporation of India, ℂ (033) 445469, or Mercury Travels (ℂ (033) 443555 both at 46C Jawaharlal Nehru Road, or Sita World Travels, ℂ (033) 240935, 293003, at 3B Camac Street.

Indian Airlines can be reached at ℂ (033) 260730, 263390, 39 Chittaranhan Avenue. For rail bookings, there are two main offices situated quite close together, both within BBD Square (Dalhousie Square): Eastern Railways, ℂ (033) 222291, at 6 Fairlee Place, BBD Square, and South Eastern Railways, ℂ (033) 235074, Esplanade Mansions, 14A Strand Road. You can waste hours negotiating endless reservations queues, so if possible, let a travel agent handle your bookings. The main bus terminus for city and state transport is off Jawaharlal Nehru Road.

MANGROVES AND TIGERS

The **Sunderbans,** which lies 131 km (81 miles) east of Calcutta where the Ganges spills into the Bay of Bengal sea, is the world's largest mangrove swamp and the home of the magnificent Royal Bengal tiger. Few tourists ever venture to this vast 2,500 sq km (965 sq miles) esturine land of mud flats, mangroves and dense forest, which sprawls across to Bangladesh and is accessible only by riverine waterways. Among those who returned impressed was Alfred Hitchcock, who begged former prime minister Indira Gandhi to let him make a horror film here, writing that it was the most "devilish, foreboding landscape" he had ever seen. She turned Hitchcock down, having already refused him permission to film in the Taj Mahal. However lonely or perilous its landscape, it is certainly crammed with spectacular wildlife. Tribal villagers who eke out a living by honey collecting and fishing here wear brightly painted masks on the backs of their

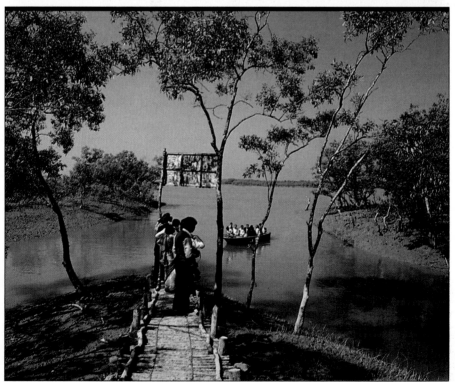

heads to lessen their chances of becoming tiger fodder. This is the largest natural habitat of tigers in the world, with some 300 roaming free in the central Project Tiger reserve. Among other wildlife, you have a good chance of seeing wild boar, jungle cat, spotted deer, giant crocodiles, king cobras, lizards and monitors including the rare Salvator lizard. Part of the Sunderbans is the **Sajnakhali Bird Sanctuary.**

The main embarkation point for river cruises through the sanctuary is **Canning,** 54 km (33.5 miles) from Calcutta, reached by car, train or bus. It's possible to hire private launches, but safest and easiest to go on the conducted trips

run by the West Bengal Tourist Bureau, who operate a luxury launch, which has sleeping quarters and armed guard for Project Tiger areas, and can anchor in mid-channel to stay overnight. Accomodation can also be had at the **Sundar Cheetal Lodge** at Sajnakhali. It is best visited from mid-September to mid-March. Foreign visitors have to contact the Secretary, Department of Forest and Tourism, Government of West Bengal, Writer's Building, Calcutta.

THE EASTERN TRAIL

From Calcutta you have a diverse array of destinations no more than an hour's flight away. To the west is rural **Bihar,** which has many pilgrimage places sacred to Buddhists. To the north lie the cool, exotic Himalayan destinations of **Darjeeling, Sikkim** and the north-east-

ern frontier states. To the south is lush, temple-dotted **Orissa**, while off the south-eastern coast lie scattered the beautiful virgin **Andaman** and **Nicobar** archipelago.

If you plan a visit to Darjeeling or the Andaman and Nicobar islands, but particularly to any of the north-eastern states, you'll be required to obtain special visas and permits in advance. In the case of Darjeeling and the Andaman capital, Port Blair however, permits may be issued upon arrival, provided you make the journey by air. It's advisable to check with the Tourist Office or the travel agencies listed above for any up-to-date stipulations or changes and general information on these more politically delicate areas.

BIHAR: THE BUDDHIST TRAIL

Buddha lived and preached most of his life in the north-eastern state of rural Bihar. Of especial interest to Buddhists, Bihar is off the beaten track for most tourists.

In the sixth century BC Pataliputra, the site of Bihar's modern capital **Patna**, became the capital of the Magadhans, and later the Mauryans and of other successive empires that promoted Buddhist culture and philosophy.

Within the state, **Bodhgaya** is a hallowed place for Buddhists and where Buddha achieved his enlightenment beneath the Bodhi Tree. Close by are **Nalanda,** with the ruins of the world's oldest university and **Rajgir,** capital of the Magadha empire, and the place where Buddha and Mahavira (founder of the Jain faith) lived in retreat and delivered sermons.

DARJEELING

Darjeeling was the unsurpassed "Queen of the Hill Stations" during the British Raj, the goal of jaded Europeans seeking to revive their tempers amid its refreshing cool charm and lovely scenery, far away from muggy Calcutta. It is an exotic patch of Anglo–Himalaya, perched on the Ghoom–Senchal Ridge at an altitude of 2,134 m (7,000 ft), with magnificent views across Mt. Kanchenjunga and Mt. Everest. Its surrounding landscape has range upon range of snowy cloud and mountain peaks, with steeply sloping conifer forests and terraced tea plantations. The lively town is a labyrinth puzzle of interlacing steps, chalet-style huts and colorful bazaars selling handicrafts, the famous Darjeeling tea, and an object of much practical value in Darjeeling — the umbrella. Its cobbled streets bustle with all the races of the Himalayas, often in colorful tribal costume: the martially formidable Gurkhas, the famous mountaineering Sherpas, Nepali women swaddled in red flannel, their chests hung with huge silver and turquoise necklaces, Mongol-featured urchins, elfin Lepchas and fair-skinned Sikkimese, Tibetan Lamas in saffron robes, Gurung farmers from western Nepal, and serene-faced Bhutanese. Stunted ponies lumber up and down the steps, taking market goods on the way down to town, and giggling apple-cheeked school-children on the way up, bundled in large baskets.

Until the beginning of the eighteenth century, Darjeeling was ruled by the Rajahs of Sikkim, who lost their domain to invading tribes

the Himalayan Mountaineering Institute. It's also a botanist's paradise, with over 4,000 species of flowers. Nearby destinations include Tiger Hill, which offers incomparable views of the Himalayas, and the **Ghoom Monastery,** dedicated to Maitreya, said by the Tibetans to be the "Buddha Yet to Come."

Darjeeling is of course renowned throughout the world for its tea. However, what is so good for the tea plantations is not always so good for the visitor. The torrential monsoon, which erupts from mid-June to mid-September, can blot out the views, wash out the roads and seriously dampen the pleasure of a visit to

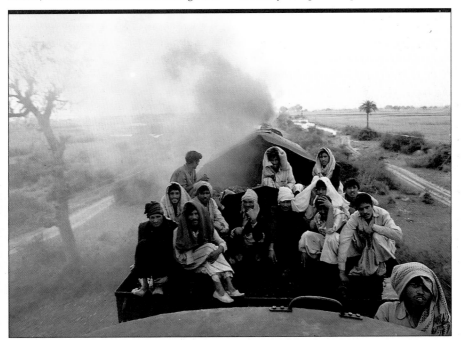

of Gurkhas from Nepal in 1780. Two British officers stumbled on this remote Shangri-La in 1828, realizing its potential as a strategic link in the Nepal/Tibet mountain passes, as well as a hill-station sanatorium. At that time, locals called their home "Dorje Ling" or "Place of the Thunderbolt". According to legend, Darjeeling was struck by a mystic thunderbolt of the Lamaist religion, said to be the scepter of Indra, Lord of the Gods, which supposedly fell on the site known as Observatory Hill.

Darjeeling is steeped in British legacies, nattily preserved in Anglican, Scottish and Roman Catholic churches, Tudor-style cottages, village squares, the polo ground — but above all in the tea plantations — begun by the British using seeds smuggled from China.

Darjeeling is a major base for trekking expeditions in the eastern Himalayas, the center of

Darjeeling. The hill station is most sunnily idyllic during March to mid-June when rhododendron, magnolia and hollyhocks bloom. Views across to the divine mass of the Himalayas are at their most crisply spectacular during the wintry months of mid-September to December, when Darjeeling is carpeted with snow. Visitors should come prepared with an umbrella, a light raincoat and some warm clothing for the nippy evenings.

PERMITS

Darjeeling is classified as a so-called "sensitive area" by the Indian Government, due in part to the activities of the GNLF (Gurkha National

Impoverished villagers swaddled against steam fumes as they are sped on a ticketless journey through the arid hinterland of Bihar.

Liberation Front). There's a real possibility at the present time of meeting strikes and violence, both of a random and directed kind.

You won't require a permit if flying up to Darjeeling, as your passport will be automatically stamped when you arrive at Bagdogra airport, allowing you to stay for 15 days. It's wise to check with tourist authorities before leaving, as the situation is sometimes prone to changes.

A special permit to visit for seven days must be obtained in advance by those who travel there by train. Arrive early (10:30 am opening time) with your passport and rail tickets, and you may have your case "expedited." Alternatively, you may approach the Political Department, 3rd Floor at the Writer's Building.

Once you're actually in Darjeeling, it's not very easy to extend your stay, but if you want to chance your luck, approach the Darjeeling Foreigner's Registration Department, ((0354) 2261, in Laden-La Road.

HOW TO GET THERE

Indian Airlines operates daily direct flights to Bagdogra airport from Delhi, Calcutta, Patna, Imphal and Guwahati. Bagdogra airport is 90 km (56 miles) away from Darjeeling and reached either by a 3-hour drive by airport bus, taxi or jeep; or by taking the famous miniature two-foot narrow gauge "Toy Train", completed in 1881, from nearby Siliguri/New Jalpaiguri.

The "express" *Darjeeling Mail* (12 hours) leaves Calcutta's Sealdah Station daily at 7:15 pm, bound for New Jalpaiguri. Reservations can be made at the Eastern Railways Booking Office, Fairlee Place, Calcutta. The last leg of the journey takes place on a miniature railway, (about three departures daily) which chugs, puffs and winds through deep jungles, tea gardens and pine forests, culminating in the famous "Agony Loop" just outside Darjeeling. Train addicts have called it India's greatest train journey, but mere mortals often find that the spectacular scenery begins to pall at the crawling pace of 10 kph (6 mph). It frequently takes much longer than its advertised time of seven to eight hours, and some travelers reported arriving in Darjeeling in the small hours after an epic 12 hour run, finding all hotels closed. Check with the tourist office in Calcutta whether the Toy Train is running, as there have occasionally been times when the service has been disrupted. You'll reach Darjeeling much faster (and get the same views) by express bus, although you'll also anticipate a hundred deaths! Quirky roadside warnings, like "Lovers, Don't Leap!" or "Beware of Fall-

ing Trucks" quickly convince you that it's not just you being neurotic.

ROOM WITH A VIEW

Darjeeling offers a wide-range of hotels, many with breathtaking mountain and valley views. Prices vary a good deal according to season and most hotels include meals in their tariffs. Whatever your accommodation, you'll require heating facilities (Darjeeling gets bone-pinchingly chilly) and a window across the surrounding landscape.

Luxury chateau-style accommodation is best at **Hotel Everest**, ((0354) 2616-8, rates: expensive), 29 Gandhi Road. Rooms have superb views, and facilities include a reliably good restaurant, shopping arcade, health club and beauty salon. The **Windamere**, ((0354) 54041-2 fax (0354) 54043, rates: moderate), Bhanu Sarani, The Mall, has a delightfully eccentric Raj-era ambience — rather like Calcutta's Fairlawn — with homely log fires in the bedrooms and a "hottie" magically slipped beneath the floral bedspread at night. There's a fusty library, bar, sweet garden, miniature golf course and badminton court. Good quality Indian, Chinese and Continental dishes are guaranteed to restore the body and soul after a long day's traipsing.

Spectacular views from all rooms are just as good at the **Luxury Tourist Lodge**, Bhanu Sarani (((0354) 2611; rates: economy), where rooms have good heaters. Breakfast and dinner are included in the room tariff.

The most sought budget accommodation is the **Youth Hostel**, (((0354) 2290; rates: very cheap), Dr Zakir Hussain Road. It's absurdly good value at US$3 for a double room with attached bathroom, with skid row US$0.75 dormitory beds. It's often full, being very popular, since not only is it dirt cheap, clean and equipped with hot showers, but being situated high up on the ridge, it has fantastic views. Its drawback is that its location requires a mandatory 15 minute puffing ascent from the bus or rail stations. The best alternative budget option is the **Shamrock Hotel**, Upper Beachwood Road, family-run and spotlessly clean, with buckets of hot water supplied on request. Room 13 has the best mountain views.

Darjeeling is not renowned for its appetizing cuisine. Addicts of traditional Tibetan momos, steamed mincemeat balls flavored with onion

Bathed in bright Himalayan sunshine, the ornate Yiga Chhoiling monastery is worthy of a detour in Ghoom.

and ginger, will have a field day — otherwise expect your taste-buds to remain untantalized. The best food is found at the **Windamere,** otherwise go to **Glenary's,** in Laden-La Road, for quaintly cummerbunded waiters but unexceptional mainstream Indian dishes, or to **Chowrasta,** Chowrasta Square, an open-air café serving good-value vegetarian south Indian fare. Another popular rendezvous place is the Himalaya, near the Post Office, with freshly baked Tibetan bread, non-greasy chips, omelets and apple-pancakes. If all else fails — Darjeeling tea and the dry, locally produced Kalimpong cheese help quell hunger pangs.

ORIENTATION

Only the most dedicated sightseer could rise bright and early for energetic expeditions on the first day in Darjeeling. Its high altitude leaves most people feeling slightly enervated for at least a day or so. Bearing this is mind, allow yourself at least three days to see Dajeeling's main attractions — which can be covered on foot if you've a penchant for healthy, rugged walking. Alternatively, you can inquire at the Tourist Bureau, ((0354) 54050, 1 Laden-La Road about hiring private taxis, jeeps, Land-rovers for getting about, as well as picking up their useful local map. Ponies might look spindly, but their sturdy knobbled legs are bred for lugging heavy loads around — including visiting tourists.

On the first day, develop your Himalayan sea legs by winding your way around Darjeeling town's two main thoroughfares — Laden-La, officially known as Nehru Road leading up to Chowrasta Square, a bustling strip where you'll find most of the hotels, restaurants, shops, banks, cinemas and the Tourist Bureau — and Cart Road at the bottom of the steep ridge, which is crammed with winding bazaars overflowing with odd-shaped vegetables, putrid-smelling Tibetan potions, and colorful Himalayan handicrafts — a mixture of Nepali, Tibetan, Sikkimese and Bhutanese folk art, wooden carvings, woven fabric, knits, carpets, local jewelry, and bric—brac. Look especially for the interesting, well-organized **Tibetan Self Help Centre**, established in 1959 to assist Darjeeling's large Tibetan refugee community (who fled China-occupied Tibet to India along with the 13th Dalai Lama) create their own cottage industry workshops, and crammed with curios, carpets, leather work, jewelry and wood carvings. Also visit **Hayden Hall,** where Tibetan women in striped tunics sell their brilliantly-hued knitted creations. Darjeeling's main markets pack away their baskets and stalls all day Thursday, while shops are shuttered on Sundays and half-day Saturdays. **Cart Road** is where the rail and bus stations, as well as the taxi stand, are located.

HIGH ON THE HIMALAYAS

Witnessing dawn is Darjeeling's ultimate experience. The curtain is raised and there it is: Mt. Kanchenjunga — and, on a clear morning — Mt. Everest, standing tremendously in the background, surrounded by Markala, Lhotose and several other Eastern Himalayan peaks, their snows flushed rosy-pink with first light, fringed by glittering pyramids of ice, snow and rock.

The best vantage point is **Tiger Hill**, at an altitude of 2,590 m (8,482 ft), situated 11 km (6.9 miles) away. On a clear day, you'll become part of a noisy, exhaust-spluttering convoy along the mountain roads all sharing the same objective. Sightseeing buses and jeeps make the hour-long trip there each morning, arriving at 4 am to await dawn. To avoid the melee, stay overnight for an early rising at the simple, but adequate **Tiger Hill Tourist Lodge**, ((0354) 2813 rates: very cheap, which has a strategic location on a scenic plateau directly facing Mt. Kanchenjunga.

It's worth making the sturdy 40-minute trek from the Tiger Hill viewing platform to **Ghoom Buddhist Monastry**, the largest and most famous religious center of its kind in Darjeeling, with an entrance of fluttering prayer flags. It was established in 1850 by a Mongolian astrologer-monk, and contains a giant seated image of Maitreya, the "Buddha to Come", surrounded by bowed-headed Yellow Sect Buddhists, sticks of incense, bells, drums and ornate thangka scrolls. You can ask to view a collection of precious Buddhist manuscripts, and will be asked for a small donation in return. The fun part of this excursion is returning to Darjeeling by another miniature "toy train", which leaves from Ghoom's small station, a half-hour scenic trip.

FLORA AND FAUNA

In town there are plenty of attractions worth a look. Start with the institutions founded by zealously scholarly "mad-dog" British butter-

ting its inmates — mostly Siberian tiger, Himalayan black bear, deer, panda and black jaguar — up in squalid little cages.

Also worth visiting is the **Himalayan Mountaineering Institute**, famous for its training courses, it also has a museum with fascinating photos, equipment and exhibits relating to famous mountaineering expeditions. It's open daily 9 am to 5 pm (summer), 9 am to 4 am (winter). Close by, there's an interesting, well-manicured cemetery of former Raj residents, also containing the tomb of nineteenth century Alexander Krs, a Hungarian orientologist who traveled to Darjeeling set on establishing that

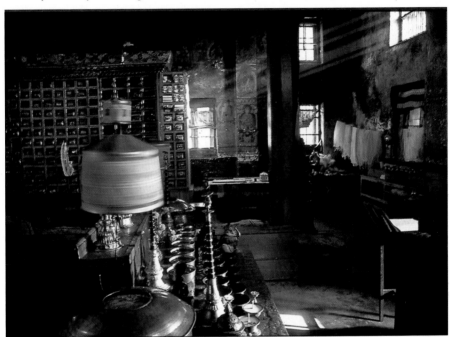

fly-catching botanists: **The Bengal Natural History Museum**, set up in 1903, is quite simply a taxidermist's heaven. Expertly presented, it's eccentric enough to warrant a visit purely for the sensation of being "watched" by 4,300 beady stuffed animals and insects, all captured, or stuffed into chloroform bottles, along the Eastern Himalayan belt. It's open from 10 am to 4 pm, closed Thursdays. **Lloyd's Botanical Gardens**, laid out in 1865 with beautiful orchid hot-houses containing over 2,000 species and a representative collection of the flora of the Sikkim Himayalas. It's open from 6 am to 5 pm and admission is free. Take directions from the gardens to Victoria Road, then proceed along the pretty half-hour walk to the **Victoria Falls** — one of the most beautiful, secluded strolls in the area, although the waterfall itself is hardly impressive. Darjeeling's **Zoo** is notorious for shut-

Tibetan and Hungarian peoples shared a common ancestry. He became a national hero to the Tibetan people after publishing his dictionary and grammar of the Tibetan language.

Kalimpong, 51 km (32 miles) from Darjeeling, makes a pleasant day's excursion. This scenic mountain bazaar town, perched at an altitude of 1,250 m (4,100 ft) has spectacular views, picturesque hill-folk and flower nurseries.

TEA PLANTATIONS

Darjeeling is one of the world's most famous tea-growing centers, producing India's most

ABOVE: The brass-studded interior of the Ghoom Monastery famous for its enshrined image of the Maitreya Buddha. OPPOSITE: The magical spectacle of dawn unfolding over the lofty peaks of Mount Kanchenjunga above Darjeeling.

celebrated tea, its refined taste apparently due to its uniquely favorable climate. Altogether, the hill station is dotted with some 78 tea plantations which employ some 48,000 people, many of them Nepalis, and produces some 10.5 million kilos (23 million pounds) of tea annually, all of which is packed in giant tea crates and sent off to Calcutta's tea auctions. Pure Darjeeling tea is so expensive — from US$5 to US$120 for a single kilo — that it's usually blended with leaves from other areas. India is still the largest consumer of its own tea, but the Soviet Union is a major importer of the thoroughbred Darjeeling tea, which they mix with

their own leaves and then sell off as "pure" Russian Tea! The traditional way of judging tea is to take a pinch in the curl of your hand, then breathe on it to moisten the leaves, and judge the quality from the aroma. Darjeeling's leaves end up at the world's longest tea tasting table at Calcutta's Nilhat House, where highly trained tannin testers fastidiously sip, sniff and swill in the practiced manner of wine-tasters.

You're welcome to visit the **Happy Valley Tea Gardens,** three kilometers (1.9 miles) from the center of town, to see how tea is produced in the so called "orthodox" method, in which the fresh leaves are placed in "withering" troughs, dried

out by high-speed fan, then successively rolled, pressed and painstakingly fermented on a conveyer belt. Finally the tea is sorted out into grades of Golden Flowery Orange Pekoe (unbroken leaves), then Golden Broken Orange Pekoe, Orange Fanning and Dust (broken leaves). It's open daily, except Mondays, from 8 am to noon, and 1 to 4:30 pm, open only from 1 to 4:30 pm on Sundays.

RECREATION

Just combing this hillside town's vertiginous slopes should be enough to ensure that most visitors sink into their beds at night with their muscles aching all over. If all this pony-riding and strolling don't satisfy athletic urges for the great outdoors, try golfing at the Senchal Golf Club, one of the world's highest; fishing on the Rangeet River at Singla, (8 km or 5 miles) or at the Teesta River at Riyand, (41 km or 25 miles), first obtaining permits from the District Officer. Darjeeling's treks are another popular option, since they are short — two to three days to a week — easily managed and covering spectacular scenery. If you decide to embark on an organized trek, with Sherpa guides, ponies and tents, contact either **Summit** or **Himal Ventures,** both located at Indreni Lodge, ((0354) 2710, or **Tenzing Kanchenjunga Tours,** ((0354) 3508, 1/D B. Giri Road. These agencies will arrange everything for the equivalent of US$12 a day. If you decide to go it alone, trails are well marked with plenty of good lodges for overnight stays along the routes.

The most popular trails go to **Sandakphu, Tonglu** and **Phalut,** all offering marvelous views of the whole Kachenjunga range and Mt. Everest. For detailed information on various trekking possibilities, contact the Tourist Bureau in Darjeeling. You'll also need to notify the Foreigner's Registration Office, and permission is usually granted on production of your permit.

SIKKIM

Button-holed between Bhutan and Nepal, Sikkim was a remote independent Himalayan kingdom until it was annexed by India in 1975. It still has a hermitic flavor, with its Buddhist monasteries, prayer flags fluttering from pagoda-style houses and red-robed lamas chanting mantras to the sound of drums and man-size horns, all against the breathtaking backdrop of the mighty Kanchanjunga range. The Sikkimese are a friendly mix of Lepcha, Bhutanese and Nepalese communities, and their land offers beautiful mountain scenery, good trekking, exotic varieties of fauna and flora. It boasts 600 species of orchid. The best season to visit is during February to May and October to December. Get there by flying to

---

ABOVE: Layered tea gardens at the Happy Valley Plantation are typical of the landscape of Darjeeling. OPPOSITE: Tibetan-style façade of Rumtek Monastery, 24 km from Gangtok in Sikkim.

Calcutta and the East

Bagdogra, then make the 125 km (77 miles) journey to the capital, **Gangtok,** either by helicopter, taxi or bus. In the capital, comfortable moderately priced accommodation is best at the Nor-Khill Hotel, ((03592) 23186, the **Hotel Tashi Delek** ((03592) 22991, and the **Ashok Mayur** ((03592) 2825.

In Gangtok visit the **Tsuklakhang Palace,** the **Institute of Tibetology,** the **Orchid Sanctuary,** the **Cottage Industries Institute,** the **Enchey Monastery** and **Deer Park.** Make trekking excursions to **Bakkim** and **Dzongri.** Sikkim has remarkable monasteries at **Pemayangtse, Tashiding, Rumtek** and **Phodang,** which have vivid

wall frescoes, exquisite silk brocade thangkas or hangings, rare hand-painted scrolls, magnificent carvings and precious icons of silver and gold. Devotees seek blessings by walking in circles around small Buddhist monuments called chortens. Sikkim's religious festivals are celebrated in the monastery courtyards with lively mask dances by ornately costumed lamas.

The Tourist Information Centre, ((03592) 2064, in Gangtok bazaar can assist with tours, car and guide hire. Good trekking firms in Gangtok are Sikkim Himalayan Adventure, Yak and Yeti Travels and Snow Lion Travels.

THE NORTH-EAST

The north-east is India's last frontier, and regrettably is mostly forbidden to travelers

hoping to explore this vast fertile region of rice paddies, mountains and jungle, wedged between Nepal and China to the north, Bangladesh to the west and Burma to the east. Connected to the rest of Hindu-dominated India by a sliver of territory above Bangladesh, its inhabitants have cultural affinities more toward South East Asia than the subcontinent.

Arunachal Pradesh, Nagaland and Tripura states and the territory of Mizoram are sensitive border zones and off limits. But visitors who do not mind the lack of comforts and can tolerate some restrictions on their movements can, with prior planning, visit the states of Assam, Meghalaya and Manipur. Traveling here yields magnificent scenery and exotic wildlife and the experience of one of the least known areas of the globe. The north-east is the home to many tribal peoples, with many different cultures, languages and an infectious love of festivals, music and dance. Part of the Indian government's policy of banning outsiders stems from the government's fear that wholesale exposure to newcomers could spell doom for these unique cultures.

ASSAM

Assam may be synonymous with fine tea, but exotic wildlife reserves are its principal attraction, and home to India's rare one-horned rhinoceros that Marco Polo called the "hideous unicorn". The state capital **Guwahati** lies on the banks of the great Brahmaputra, classified in Hindu cosmology as India's only male river. The city has some grand Hindu temples, but is primarily an airport gateway to the north-east and a jump-off spot for visiting the wild-life reserves. You can either fly there directly from Calcutta, or make the 24-hour journey by train. New Delhi is 40 hours away, even on the express Assam Mail. In Guwahati, the best bet is **Hotel Bramaputra Ashok**, ((0361) 542653, MG Road. Rates: moderate. In town, visit the **Kamakshya Temple**, which honors the Hindu goddess Shakti, the essence of female energy, and the **Assam State Zoo and Museum.** Chug 20 km (12miles) up the Brahmaputra by steamer to visit the silk-weaving community at **Sualkashi,** where the rich Endi, Muga and Pat silks are made. The Tourist Information Centre, ((03561) 24475, is on Station Road. The best season to visit is January to March and Novem-ber to December, and the Assamese mark the harvesting season with *bihus*, festivals cele-brated by bathing in the Brahmaputra.

WILDLIFE PARKS

Kaziranga Wildlife Sanctuary is located north-east of Guwahati on the banks of the Brahmaputra. Assam's premier nature park has some 430 sq km (158 sq miles) of steamy primeval forest which can be explored by elephant, car and boat. It is home to some 1,000 rhinos, 800 wild elephants and 700 wild buffalo, along with swamp deer, hog deer, ti-gers and Himalayan bears. The rhinos are watched closely by park guards, but about 30 are believed to be killed illegally each year by poachers, as Chinese value rhino blood, skin and bones for medicinal brews, and pay up to US$200 for an ounce of powdered horn, prized as a reputedly potent aphrodisiac.

Kaziranga can be reached by air from Calcutta to **Jorhat,** 84 km (52 miles) from the park, or the 235 km (146 mile) trip from Guwa-hati can be made by bus or taxi through ver-dant rice paddies and thatched hut villages. Stay in the ITDC **Kaziranga Forest Lodge,** making reservations in advance through the Divisional Forest Officer, Sibasagar Division, PO Box Kaziranga.

Manas Wildlife Sanctuary is nestled in the Himalayan foothills bordering Bhutan, 175 km (108 miles) north-west of Guwahati. It has 270 sq km (104 sq miles) of riverine forest that attracts many varieties of bird and animal life, and was the site where Project Tiger was launched. Stay at the **Forestry Department Bun-galow or the Manas Tourist Lodge,** bookable through the Division Forest Officer, Wildlife Division, Sarania, Guwahati.

MEGHLAYA

Only 100 km (62 miles) from Guwahati, Megh-laya's capital of **Shillong** is 1,495 m (4,900 ft) high, a pretty Raj-era hill station with land-scape and climate that British colonialist called the "Scotland of the East." It is pleasant most of the year for its quaint cottages, waterfalls, pine groves and flowers, as well as to see dancing by the local Khasi, Jantia and Garo tribes. Avoid the monsoon. **Cherrapunji,** just 60 km (37 miles) away, is reported to be the wettest place on the planet, with an annual average rainfall of

nearly 11.5 m or 40 ft! **Shillong** is a regional melting pot, and **Bara** bazaar bustles with col-orful costumed Nagas, Mizos and Manipurs from the neighboring states. There are Naga-style woven rugs, silver jewelry, bamboo handicrafts and rare butterflies compressed in glass to buy.

Arrive via Guwahati and stay at the modest **Hotel Pinewood Ashok,** ((0364) 223116 rates: inexpensive). In town, play golf at an 18-hole course, and go fishing on Umiam Lake, 16 km (10 miles) away.

MANIPUR

Bordering Nagaland, Mizoram and Burma, **Ma-nipur** is rich in tribal culture, wooded hills and lakes. Visit the capital, **Imphal** for its spectacular Rash Lila festival of Manipuri dance in Octo-ber/November. Stay at the **Hotel Ranjit,** ((0385) 220382, rates: cheap on Thangal Bazaar. See the golden **Shri Govindaji** temple museum. Visit the tribal village of **Moriang** (folk culture), 37 km (23 miles) away. Buy woven goods and local handicrafts in the large **Khwairamband** bazaar.

ABOVE: Gangtok's bustling marketplace.
OPPOSITE: Youthful Buddhist monks in Sikkim.

ENTRY FORMALITIES

Given that some parts of these areas are open to visitors, foreign tourists will need a separate permit for each state. The permit may specify that only part of the state can be visited and many are valid for only seven days. If planning to visit this area, try to obtain all the necessary papers from your Indian mission before leaving home, as some states can require up to four months notice. If booking the trip in India, apply for permits at any Foreigners Registration Office. For the most up-to-date information, contact the Deputy Secretary, Ministry of Home Affairs, Government of New Delhi, (F-10), North Block, New Delhi 110001.

ORISSA

Tucked alongside the north-eastern coastline off the Bay of Bengal, this green, semitropical state is one of India's undiscovered gems — it is said that if one knows Orissa, one knows India. To a visitor's eyes, this quiet, rural state seems barely industrialized at all. Its capital, Bhubaneswar is surrounded by intricate beehive-sculpted temples and tiny villages of ocher-red mud huts whose exteriors are traced with pretty rice-flour patterns. Its unspoiled pastoral landscape is a patchwork of palm and cashew plantations, pools covered with mauve water-hyacinths, conspicuously empty of tourists, yet busy with ebony-skinned villagers dressed in loincloths, bullock-carts and plumaged parakeets flickering through the trees.

Orissa has a rich culture, colorful festivals and distinctive folk art. What's more, it even has white-sanded beaches, a tantalizing local cuisine, and a growing network of luxury hotels — in other words, a perfect place just to switch off and relax. For generations, Bengalis have come here to escape the squalor, poverty and rampant social divisions of Calcutta. It's only a matter of time before foreign tourists start flocking to Orissa too.

Above all else, Orissa is famous for its astonishing number of magnificent Hindu and Jain temples. The state is best visited with a view to exploring its compact "temple triangle," beginning with the state capital, **Bhubaneswar**, a cathedral city of more than 500 temples, built during the heyday of Oriyan Hindu culture between the seventh and fifteenth centuries, some of the most superb religious architecture the world has ever produced. It also has Jain and Buddhist caves, fine museums, and beautiful botanical and zoological gardens. The seaside resort of **Puri** lies 61 km (38 miles) away, a vital

pilgrimage center where life revolves around the famous temple of Lord Jagannath, culminating in one of India's most extraordinary and spectacular festivals, the Ratha Yatra, held every summer.

Just 31 km (19 miles) along the coastal road from Puri, past paddy fields and villages, is **Konarak,** with its magnificent, densely-carved Sun Temple built in the shape of a huge chariot.

Recorded history documents Orissa's earliest ruler as Kalinga, a powerful warlord who lost his domain to Ashoka, the powerful Mauryan emperor, in 260 BC at a battlefield near modern-day Bhubaneswar. According to lore, Ashoka was so repulsed by the bloody carnage he witnessed here that he pledged to renounce warfare, taking up the Buddhist faith of non-violence and compassion. To commemorate his epoch-making conversion, he left a famous set of rock edicts at Dhauli, 8 km, (5 miles) south of Bhubaneswar.

Buddhism rapidly declined however, and Jainism took root, reaching its zenith during the second century BC under the Chedi king, Khavravela, who encouraged monks to create the excavated cave temples of Udayagiri and Khandagiri, 8 km, (5 miles) west of Bhubaneswar. By the seventh century, Orissa had adopted Hinduism, like much of south India, and entered its golden age of temple architecture.

Under successive Hindu Kesari and Ganga kings, the temple for Lord Jagannath was built at Puri; the cult of Shiva, or Shaivism, inspired the creation of many temples in Bhubaneswar, and the worship of Surya, the Sun God,

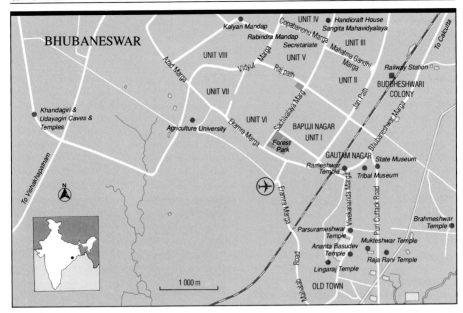

flourished, culminating in Konarak's famous Sun Temple, built during the thirteenth century.

Yet Muslim invasions from both the north and the southern kingdom of Golconda resulted in the overthrow of the Hindu rulers, not to mention the decimation of countless temples. Thereafter, Orissa was claimed successively by the Afghans, the Marathas, and the British in 1803.

Orissa is at its most steamy, lush and beautiful just after the monsoon in October, and comfortable to visit until February when the mercury starts to climb. Puri is pleasant and popular as a bolt-hole from Calcutta all the year round. Otherwise, it's well worth braving heat and human waves to witness the Rath Yatra festival held every June to July. Pre-monsoon breakers (May to June) produce the best coasters if you like body-surfing. Puri and Bhubaneswar make the best bases for day-long excursions — there are few hotels of any repute at Konarak.

GETTING THERE

You can fly to Bhubaneswar daily from Calcutta, and there are direct flights from Hyderabad and Varanasi.

It can be more fun to make the journey by overnight train — at least one way. Bhubaneswar is on the main Calcutta to Madras railway line so there are plenty of trains to Bhubaneswar, as well as trains terminating at Puri. From Calcutta, take the "super-fast" overnight Coromandel Express to Bhubaneswar (7 hours) or the slower pilgrim-packed Howrah-Puri Express

(12 hours). Bhubaneswar also has direct rail links with Hyderabad, Delhi and Bombay.

BHUBANESWAR

In ancient times, Bhubaneswar was known as Ekamrakshetra, one of five religious cities in the ancient Kalingan state which now comprises modern-day Orissa. Locals will tell you that Lord Shiva makes his "holidays" here, ranking it second only to Varanasi as his favorite "resort." Here in Bhubaneswar, Shiva is known as Tribuhuvaneswara or "Lord of the Three Worlds," from which the city derives its name. In its heyday, between the seventh to the fifteenth centuries, it was a magnetic and powerful pilgrimage center. More than 7000 sandstone temples once fringed its sacred Bindusagar "Ocean Drop," tank, said to contain water from every holy stream, river and pool in India, and hence a great place for washing away sins. All but 500 or so were destroyed during the Mughal conquest of the sixteenth century. Among these are many perfectly preserved examples of the profusely carved Oriyan style of temple architecture.

Modern Bhubaneswar is delightfully rural for a state capital that administers the affairs of 25 million Oriyans — largely free of pollution, traffic and high-rise buildings. Its hallowed temples are concentrated in the old town, very exotic with its cobbled alleys, palm groves and frangipani trees dotted around the khaki-colored Bindusagar Tank, where local lads go spear-fishing for sacred fish.

GETTING AROUND

In town, use taxis, auto-rickshaws or buses. Go temple-hopping by cycle-rickshaw; these are often wired up with black sun-umbrellas. Bicycles can be hired easily through any hotel, perfect for a day's excursion.

The OTDC Tourist Information Center, ((0674) 50099, Jayadev Marg, near Pantha Niwas Tourist Bungalow runs useful sightseeing tours. The city tour (8:45 am to 6 pm daily, except Monday) costs US$2, and covers Bhubaneswar's major temples, the Udayagiri and Khandagiri caves, Nandankanan Park and Dhauli. There's also a regular Puri/Konarak tour (9 am to 6 pm). Both have good guides and leave from the Pantha Niwas Tourist Bungalow. You can also hire trained guides and private cars for sightseeing here. Expect to pay about US$25 for a round trip from Bhubaneswar to Puri and Konarak, or US$15 one way.

Otherwise, frequent local buses make the 1½ hour journey to Puri, leaving from the main bus station. Buses to Konarak can be irregular, and it's wise to check departures with the tourist office before planning your day. From Puri to Konarak, regular minibuses take passengers on a "fill-her-up" basis for the 35 minute, 30 km (18.8 miles) ride. If you take an early-morning bus from Puri and an afternoon bus back (or on to Bhubaneswar), you'll have ample time to see the Sun Temple.

WHERE TO STAY

The **Hotel Oberoi Bhubaneswar**, ((0674) 56116, 56320 fax (0674) 440898, Nayapalli, offers luxury accommodation at remarkably reasonable rates. One of India's most beautiful hotels, its distinctive, temple-inspired design features polished sandstone, Oriyan décor and brass lamps throughout, with a lovely swimming pool and tennis courts set in palm-dotted landscaped gardens. A choice of restaurants offer excellent food, ranging from local specialities to Mughali, Western and Chinese. Facilities include a health club, shopping arcade, travel desk and beauty salon with car-hire for temple-hopping. It's located seven kilometers from the capital. There's a courtesy shuttle service between the airport and the hotel.

Within the city center, choose from three moderately priced hotels, all close to the temples. Best is the **New Kenilworth Hotel**, ((0674) 54330-1 fax (0674) 56147, at Gautam Nagar, which has comfortably furnished rooms, efficient staff and good restaurants and travel desk. Breakfast at their coffee shop — delicious yogurt, fresh fruit, toast, eggs and coffee — is astoundingly good at only US$1.50. Around the corner, the ITDC-run **Kalinga Ashok**, ((0674)

53318, is quite stylish, and its useful facilities include a bank, several restaurants, travel agency, swimming pool and doctor. **Hotel Swosti**, ((0674) 54178-9 fax (0674) 407524, on Janpath is slightly cheaper, with immaculately clean rooms, friendly staff, excellent restaurant, and good facilities including bank, shopping arcade, travel counter and bar.

Hotel Prachi, ((0674) 52689 fax (0674) 403287, rates: inexpensive), further along Janpath, is functional and clean, with good food, swimming pool and tennis courts. The state-run **Pantha Niwas Tourist Bungalow**, (((0674) 54515, rates: inexpensive to cheap) is located

close to the temples on Lewis Road, offers practical comfort: each room comes with fans, mosquito net and shower. It also has dorm rooms. It's right next door to the tourist office and is the departure point for sightseeing tours. Similar quality can be found at the big, well-kept **Bhubaneswar Hotel**, (((0674) 51977, rates: cheap) directly behind the railway station.

EATING OUT

Orissa's cuisine is similar to that of Bengal — liberal quantities of fresh seafood (lobster, prawns, crab and fish), traditionally cooked with coconut milk or curd, and given zing with pinches of *fenugreek* and mustard seeds. Order an Oriyan *thali* for starters — fluffy white rice, *bekti* or *rui* fish, vegetable dishes, including the staple green, *kara saag* (spinach), delicate *puris*, rounded off with the local caramel custard, *chena purd patha* (cheese-burnt-sweet) or *khiri*, rice cooked with milk, sugar, cardamoms and cashew nuts.

Other delicious specialties to look out for are *dahi maccha* fish cooked with curd and coriander; *saag bhaja*, fried spinach; and *khajun khata*, an unusual combination of tomato cooked with dates. Local curd is devastatingly rich and creamy — perfect with fresh fruit for breakfast.

A pleasant ride north of town, the **Hotel Oberoi** offers the most stylish dining experience — its **Pushpaneri** restaurant has exceptional Oriyan and Indian fare (both vegetarian and non-vegetarian) for around US$6 per head.

style and form developing, expanding and refining before your eyes.

Oriyan temple design was governed by mathematical formulae, even down to the most seemingly innocuous detail. All follow an essential structure consisting of an entrance porch (*jagamohan*) and an inner sanctum for the image of the deity (*deul*), above which a ribbed conical tower (*shikara*) rises. Endless additions could be incorporated — sub-shrines, halls where offerings could be made, and dancing halls for the ritualized dance that later blossomed into the lithe, exotic Orissi style. The exterior was always lavishly carved with geometrical designs, flow-

You'll also dine well at slightly cheaper prices at the **Hotel Swosti** and the **Hotel Kalinga Ashok,** both of which offer incredibly good value lunchtime Oriyan *thalis*, as well as offering a diverse range of Indian, Continental and Chinese food. Few restaurants are worth visiting outside the hotels — most are glorified grubby tea stalls — although the **Angar South Indian Restaurant**, near Station Square, is very popular for its excellent Indian-style breakfasts.

THE TEMPLE TRAIL

Bhubaneswar's famous temples are best covered leisurely on your own, preferably in the quiet cool of early morning. By concentrating on a cluster of impeccably preserved temples, you will be taken on a curator's walk though five centuries of temple architecture, able to see

ers, animals, mythological figures, humans and gods. In the earlier, squat shrines, these carvings are simple story-telling devices, but in the later extravagant, tapering temples, the stone comes alive with sharp precision, and provocative female figures appear, at their most poutingly playful at the Rajarani and Brahmesvara temples and at the Sun Temple at Konarak, where scrutiny of close-up detail reveals some highly athletic dalliances.

What to See

Bhubaneswar's eleventh century **Lingaraj Temple**, dedicated to Shiva as Lord Lingaraj, or

ABOVE: Post-monsoon ablutions at the Mukteshwar Temple in Bhubaneswar. OPPOSITE: Detail of an exquisitely ornate frieze adorning the Rajarani Temple in Bhubaneswar.

"Lord of the Universe," is considered the pinnacle of Oriyan architecture, but it's so sacred to Hindus that "heathens" aren't allowed inside, and instead are restricted to peering at it from a platform (erected for Lord Curzon) outside the compound wall. Binoculars are useful; otherwise you'll see the temple's ornately carved 46-m (150-ft) -high spire, covered with sculpted lions crushing elephants, said to symbolize the re-emergence of Hinduism over Buddhism. There's little else for foreigners to look at except elderly temple priests napping under a giant Banyan tree. The temple is dedicated to Lord Shiva, and the granite lingam which represents him is dutifully lathered each day with water, milk and bhang (hashish). Amazingly, the entire walled compound contains some 50 small shrines, each of importance to the gift-bearing devotees. Thousands of pilgrims gather here for the major Shivrati festival in February/March, holding candles on the night of the full moon as the Lingaraj deity is ritually bathed in the nearby Bindusagar tank to mark his birth anniversary.

Skirting the eastern side of Bindusagar is a cluster of about 20 smaller temples. Look especially for the small, decorative **Sisneswar Temple** and the double-storied **Vaital Deul Temple**, both dating to the eighth century, the latter thought to be be a tantric shrine where humans were once sacrificed for the presiding eight-armed deity, Kapalini, depicted wearing here with garlands of skulls and reclining on a corpse. It's one of the few non-Shiva temples in Bhubaneswar, being dedicated to the Goddess Durga.

At the top of Tankpani Road, you'll find the **Parumeshwar Temple** (seventh century) said to be the home of Ganesh's brother Parumeshwar (Muruga). It's the best preserved of all Bhubaneswar's most ancient temples, and has detailed bas-reliefs of elephant and horse processions. Close by is the **Mukteshwar Temple** (ninth century), with its exquisite carved lotus entrance canopy, each petal bearing an image of a deity. Within its enclosure are many mango and jackfruit trees, plus a pint-sized sacred tank, where childless women bathe on the full moon of March/April to become fertile.

Continuing along Tankpani Road, look out for the **Rajarani Temple**, (twelfth century) set in pretty gardens. It is a "love temple," covered with coyly erotic carvings of women and couples, built by a Rajah for his wife, the Rani — hence the name. Once the Rajah was interred within, the temple became a mausoleum and was no longer used for worship.

Finally, the **Brahmeshwar Temple** (eleventh century) lies on the outskirts of the old city. It's actually a complex of shrines, notable for its elaborate exterior carvings, particularly its

dancing girls, and higher up, the Orissan lion, which was hunted to extinction during the British Raj.

If you care to take a look, just across the field from the Brahmeshwar Temple are the part-excavated ruins of **Sisupalgarh**, thought to be the remains of the city founded by Ashoka, occupied from the third century BC to the fourth century AD.

In town, also visit the **Orissa State Museum,** opposite the Kalinga Ashok for its rich collection relating to Orissa's history, culture, architecture and many tribal people, open 10 am to 5 pm every day except Monday.

The Tribal Research Bureau is located here, filled with sheaves of yellowing theses on Orissa's 62 distinct tribal groups of aboriginal people whose ancestors existed before the Aryan invasion of India. These "hunter-gatherers" live according to their own customs in the mountain ridges of the central Orissa. Among the better known are the Kondhs, the bugbear of British missionaries for their reluctance to give up their habit of human sacrifice — today slaughter is mostly confined to roosters, goats and bullocks. Then there are the Bondas, famous in India for their licentious attitude to premarital sex, and the fact that their young women choose their husbands on the basis of their sexual skills. Other major tribes are the Juangs, the Santals, the Parajas, the Koyas and the Godabas.

OUT OF TOWN

Either take the OTDC tour or hire a taxi for the afternoon to round-off Bhubaneswar's sights. Some 8 km (5 miles) into the surrounding countryside lie the twin hills of **Udaigiri** and **Khandagiri**, honeycombed with ancient Jain and Buddhist caves. Scattered at various levels, they were hollowed out by monks during the reign of Kharavela, the Kalinga emperor during the second century BC. Udayagiri has 44 caves, many extensively carved. The most historically interesting is the Hathi Gumpha or Elephant Cave, which contains one of India's most important extant Pali scripts — a detailed record of Kharavela's religious, military and civil accomplishments. Khandagiri has 19 caves, and is crowned by a series of Jain temples.

Ashoka's famous **Dhauli Edicts** are about 8 km south of Bhubaneswar, carved on a giant rock overlooking the plain below where the climactic Kalinga battle took place. The 13 inscriptions are still remarkably legible after 2000 years. Above them, the elephant carved out of the rock above symbolizes Buddha, and is the earliest known sculpture in Orissa. The hill is topped by the modern white Shanti Stupa, or Peace Pagoda, built by Japanese Buddhists and visible for miles and notable for its marked resemblance to a UFO, with its five antennae-like "umbrella" representing the Buddhist virtues of faith, hope, compassion, forgiveness and nonviolence.

The extensive **Nandankanan Park**, 20 km (12.5 miles) away, is a scenic wildlife and botanical garden, unique as the only place where the rare white tiger has ever been bred in captivity. It's also India's largest Lion Safari Park in India, measuring over 20 hectares (50 acres). It's also home to rhinos, monkeys, gharials, pelicans, pythons, brown bear and India's rare white crocodile. Buses run visitors out on regular "wildlife patrols." There are pleasant facilities at the Tourist Cottages or Forest Rest House. It's open 7 am to 6 pm during April to September, and 7:30 am to 5 pm, September to March. Local buses ply there every hour from Bhubaneswar.

SHOPPING FOR CRAFTS

Orissa was traditionally known as "Utkal," or "Land of Art" for its talented communities of sculptors, painters, potters, weavers and embroiderers whose skills created her exquisite temple complexes and kept her rulers beautifully garbed — today these arts are kept alive in Orissa's timeless villages. By far the most popular tourist purchase is Orissa's famous colorful patchwork appliqué, fashioned into sun umbrellas, hanging lanterns, canopies and cushions, and her silk and cotton hand loom ikat design textiles. Other good buys include the animal motif papier mach masks originally used for epic play; patachitra paintings on muslin cloth; etched palm-leaf manuscripts, silver filigree jewelry, soapstone and wood carvings, brass and bell metal work and shellcraft. At Puri you can buy little carved replicas of Lord Jagannath and his brother and sister.

In Bhubaneswar the best places to shop are the **Utkalika Handicrafts Emporium** and the **Handloom Cooperative Society**, both in the Market Building halfway up Rajpath. These give an overview of contemporary Orissan crafts, with everything sold at fixed prices. They can also arrange visits to see skilled craftsmen at work.

Throughout the state, you'll find lanes, neighborhoods and sometimes, entire villages devoted to one particular craft. Wander into any of these areas, and you'll be welcome to watch the work in progress, meet the family and, if you like, make a purchase. All of this commercial activity comes to a head in **Pipli**, 20 km (12.5 miles) en route from Bhubaneswar to Puri, where the main street consists entirely of stalls aimed at passing tourists. The speciality here is colorful

appliqué work, often utilizing decorative motifs of animals, birds and flowers. Much of has become rather mass-produced, although there are still elderly artists who still remember how to make the delicate elaborate work of the last century. Others to visit include the bell-metal village of **Belakati**, 9 km (5½ miles) from Bhubaneswar; the palm-etcher's village of **Ragurajpur**, just outside Puri; and the beautiful fresco-covered houses of **Pathuria Sahi** or "Stone Carver's Lane" in Puri itself.

In the major bazaar areas, such as that around the Jagannath Temple in Puri, bargaining is expected, and whittling down prices is

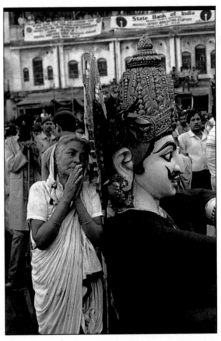

part of the fun, carried out with bantering good humor. By contrast, the individual artists working from their homes tend to quote fair prices for their work — exceedingly low in relation to the painstaking time, skill and talent which has gone into its making.

PURI

Fringed by sand dunes and casuarina trees, Puri is one of India's four holiest places, a goal for countless pilgrims, from ash-smeared fakirs to Bombay film-stars. It's also India's Brighton,

ABOVE: An white-clad widow clasps her hands and gazes with fretful adoration at a garish painted idol before the commencement of the Rath Yatra or Car festival in Puri.

a popular seaside resort with a rambling country-club style hotel, dilapidated Bengali villas and conical-capped lifeguards.

Puri is home to the "Formless One," Lord Jagannath, said to represent the primordial essence of the cosmos. His palatial apartment is the twelfth century **Jagannath Temple**, the focus of this atmospheric, worship-obsessed town. He is an incarnation of Lord Krishna, and one of the reasons for his popularity is that all castes are equal before him.

Millions have dropped to their knees before his image — a white-faced, legless, brightly-painted wooden idol with glaring eyes. Stumpy arms emerge from his forehead, which glitters with a large diamond. He shares the temple with his black-faced brother Balaram, and his yellow-faced sister, Subshadra. He commands more than six thousand "servants" who dedicate their lives to him, either as priests, temple wardens or pilgrim guides, altogether forming a complex hierarchy of 37 orders and 97 classes. Like an infant emperor, Lord Jagannath has his teeth brushed, his face anointed, his fine clothes changed, his body given a fragrant sandalwood-

scented bath and laid out for siesta. Meals are placed before him and later removed — untouched but sanctified. None of these age-old ceremonies may be witnessed by a non-Hindu, for the temple is a forbidden citadel to outsiders.

Puri's religious fervor reaches a spectacular pitch during the **Rath Yatra**, the "Car Festival," held during June and July. To celebrate Krishna's journey from Gokul to Mathura, the images of Lord Jagannath and his siblings are hauled through Puri on vast raths (chariots) to the nearby Gundicha Mandir (garden house) for

their annual week's holiday, before being dragged back home.

Puri becomes massed with hundreds of thousands of delirious, swaying humans, riveted by the spectacle of three huge wooden chariots, as large as houses, and surmounted by decorated pavilions where the three gods sit on brocade cushions for their mile-long journey. The largest is Jagannath's, some 14 m (45 ft) high, 11 m (35 ft) square and supported by 16 wheels, each 2.1 m (7 ft) tall — adding the word Juggernaut to the English language. Ritual decrees that each wagon is pulled by 4,200 men, girdled with thick rope, and accompanied by musicians bashing cymbals, drums and horns in wild abandon. People press forward, throwing rice, marigolds, and coconut shards for blessings, and cases of frenzied self-sacrifice beneath the wheels are not unknown. After delivering the gods back home, the chariots are broken up and the discarded timbers are sold as sacred relics.

Four faces of devotion at Puri's Rath Yatra. Clockwise from ABOVE LEFT: Fierce gaze from a shaven-headed woman, one of thousands, has dedicated her locks to Lord Jagganath; A "servant" of Lord Jagganath bears a totemic staff in the image of his master; Ash-smeared *sadhu* or holy man; A Shaivite or follower of Lord Shiva, his forehead smeared with the phallic symbol of the lingam.

ON THE BEACH

Puri's endless white sand beach is good for long strolls, fresh air, sun-bathing, swims; watching sunrises, sunsets and local fishermen dressed in loincloths and conical hats repairing nets and putting out to sea in their catamarans. Local urchins tag along, selling shells, cloth and semi-precious gems. Pilgrims take a holy dip, staggering and giggling in the surf getting their clothes drenched, believing that its extremely salty waters will, in the words of a local guide, "bring broadness of mind and do away with all meanness."

Tourists preparing to don skimpy swimsuits will soon discover that sun-bathing is considered highly eccentric in Orissa — what goes in Goa does not "go" here. The sight of partially exposed flesh causes local fishermen to stampede across the sands, rapt at having cornered a rare Westerner on their shores. You'll be pep-

pered with friendly invitations to explore their village, become a star guest at a seafood sizzle-up on the sands or spend a day going fishing with them. It's certainly fascinating to watch their catamarans being constructed on the sands, made from solid tree trunks, split longitudinally and bound together. When they're not being used, they're untied and the planks laid out on the beach to dry out, like giant matchsticks.

Strong currents fringe the shoreline, resulting in Puri's eccentric corps of elderly "life-

guards", actually retired fishermen, easily recognized by their wicker-work hats. They'll lead you down to surf with heroic displays of chivalry, then "guard" your clothes for a few rupees. One Dutch traveler related that he was snatched by a current out to sea, and started shouting for help, only to see the "lifeguard" wave encouragingly from the shore, while his traveling companions had to swim out to rescue him!

Unfortunately, locals seem to use much of their otherwise glorious beach as a public latrine — a good reason for escaping to the more pristine, (hygienic) sands at Gopalpur-on-sea, further south.

WHERE TO STAY

Stay at the **South Eastern Railway Hotel**, ((06752) 2063 rates:moderate, a delightful pre-World War I establishment set in a manicured garden on sand's edge, originally built as the grand residence of one Lady Ashworth. It was taken over the Bengal Nagpur Railway and opened as a hotel in 1925. It's now run by the South Eastern Railway, but still referred to as the "BNR." Rooms are kept spotless, with sand whisked out twice a day, and have quaint four-posters, mosquito nets, porcelain baths, sea-facing shuttered windows, and adjoining verandahs. Some are grander than others and priced accordingly. Convalescent bath-chairs are set for taking "bed tea" and "after tea," delivered by hotel "boys" wearing cummerbunds and

BNR hats with big brass buttons. Huge quantities of Raj-era food are served downstairs in the dining room, included within the room rates, but open to non-residents. Signs in the hallway request silence during the siesta hours. Facilities include billiards, table tennis, bar and library. The manager is friendly and helpful, particularly for travel arrangements. As you open your shutters in the morning, life-guards wave hopefully from the gate, cooing, "Sahib, Madam, beach is ready and waiting!"

Other accommodation will seem characterless by comparison. Best of Puri's many resorts is **Hotel Prachi Puri**, (((06752) 2114, rates: moderate), located at the west end of Puri beach. It offers Puri's best Indian, Continental and Chinese food, and has a pretty outdoor bar. The **Pantha Niwas Tourist Bungalow** (((06752) 2740; rates: cheap) has clean comfortable rooms, with an attached restaurant for good mealtime *thalis*.

Small guesthouses provide cheap accommodation for those who like to travel rough, most clustered towards the eastern end of the beach. In current vogue with back-packers are the **Sea Foam Hotel** and the **Z Hotel**, both clean, with fans, mosquito nets and the option of shared or attached bathrooms. Puri's skid row is the big, modern **Youth Hostel**, ((06752) 424, where dormitory beds segregate the sexes.

THE MAIN DRAG

All sandy tracks in Puri lead to its broad central **Baradand** or **Grand Road** which runs from the Jagannath Temple to the Gundicha Mandir. It's nicest to visit at sunset, when gas lamps and candles form a flickering action-packed strip of jostling pilgrims, prospecting beggars, bullock carts, cycle-rickshaws, and street stalls selling trinkets, vegetarian snacks, and religious paraphernalia.

The magnificent **Jagannath Temple** stands at the center, built during the twelfth century by the Kalingan king Chodaganga. It is Orissa's tallest temple, and its 65 m high (212 ft) spire is a landmark for miles around. Each of its four gates has an animal theme: horse (south), elephant (north), tiger (west) and lion (east). Pilgrims enter by the Lion Gate to pay respects to Lord Jagannath, laden with gifts of coconuts and flowers. Devout women emerge bald-headed, having offered their shining tresses as a symbol of sacrifice. In front of the main entrance is a beautiful pillar, uprooted from the Sun Temple at Konarak.

Non-Hindus aren't allowed inside, but can peer over the walls on a nearby viewing platform on the roof of the Raghunandan Library. A sign inside warns "Be Aware of Monkeys," and

you are given a big stick, just in case. From here you'll get a clear view all the way down to the Gundicha Mandir, Lord Jagannath's summer temple. On the way down, ask to see the library's good collection of antique Pali manuscripts can be available on request — you'll be asked for a donation in any case.

UP THE COAST

If you're looking for a place to get away from it all with clean private beaches, head for Gopalpur-on-Sea, three hours drive south of Puri.

Comfortable accommodation is found at the **Oberoi Palm Beach Hotel** ((0821) 8123 rates: moderate, a charming British country house-style resort just 100 meters from the empty golden sands. Excellent facilities include good restaurants, car rental, badminton and tennis, and arrangements can be made for riding, sailing and fishing. It's 172 km (107 miles) from Bhubaneswar and 16 km (10 miles) from the Berhampur railway station which links with Bhubaneswar and Calcutta. It's a good base for an excursion to Chilka Lake, on the coast between Puri and Gopalpur-on-sea, a beautiful island-dotted bird sanctuary best seen at sunrise by taking a boat out from Balligan or Rambha.

KONARAK

The thirteenth century **Sun Temple** stands on a desolate stretch of blowing sand, an awesome relic of Konarak's ancient legacy as a busy center of Orissan culture and commerce. This unique ruin was conceived as an immense

ABOVE: Frenzied devotees hurl themselves on a fragment of a painted wooden *rath* or chariot.
OPPOSITE: Seething crowds and enough medieval pageantry to rival a Cecil B. de Mille epic at the Rath Yatra.

stone chariot which pulls the Sun God, Surya, across the heavens. Steps ascend to the main entrance, flanked by seven gigantic straining horses, representing the seven colors of the prism. Around its base are 24 huge wheels, each signifying the changing cycle of the sun. The entire structure is covered with carvings, sculptures, figures and bas-reliefs. It was designed so that the sun's first rays would strike first the dancing hall, then the hall of audience, and finally the head of the Sun God in the main temple, harnessing its energy and life-force. According to popular lore, it was here that the cult of sun-worship began some 5,000 years

1243–1255. The main temple has fallen into ruins, yet a remaining audience hall is proof of the colossal scale on which the temple was executed. Every aspect of contemporary life was recorded in its painstaking carvings, from courtly procedures like law, administration, civic life and war to erotic imagery of human love as marvelous and detailed as those seen at Khajuraho. Originally the temple had a huge spire, soaring to 70 m (277 ft), and was nicknamed the "Black Pagoda" by early mariners navigating their passage to Calcutta, apparently due to the superstition that the temple's iron filings lured unwary ships to the shore.

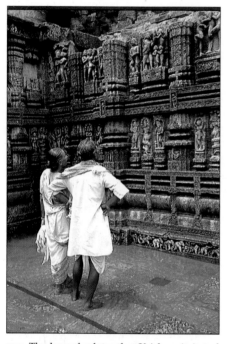

ago. The legend relates that Krishna, irritated by a disrespectful son-in-law, Samba, cursed him with leprosy, and advised him to do penance for the sun-god Surya for 12 years. Once cured of his disease, Samba erected a small temple to Surya — said to be buried beneath the present temple.

The Sun Temple was commissioned by King Narasimha of the Ganga dynasty to commemorate his victorious expansion into Bengal, and as a symbol of Hindu might against the encroaching Muslims. It took 1200 masons and sculptors, and 12,000 laborers 12 years to complete between

Outside the temple grounds, there's a small but interesting **museum** which houses excavated sculptures and fragments, and stocks Debala Mitra's inexpensive guide to Konarak here. It's open 10 am to 5 pm, closed on Fridays.

Konarak's deserted, beautiful beach may tempt some travelers to stay on. The **Tourist Bungalow** (¢ 21 rates: cheap) is next to the temple, has clean rooms with fans and attached baths.

ANDAMAN AND NICOBAR ISLANDS

This chain of 321 virgin tropical islands stretches across the eastern Bay of Bengal, midway between India and the tip of Sumatra. Only 38 of the islands are inhabited. The

ABOVE: Elderly *dhoti*-clad couple admire friezes worn to a spidery frailty after seven centuries of exposure to the elements at the Sun Temple in Konarak. RIGHT: One of 24 gigantic wheels adorning the base of the Sun Temple.

archipelago possesses a smoldering primitive beauty, with dense forests woven with canopies of vines and deserted white-sand beaches lapped by clear turquoise waters. This exotic, unspoilt landscape hardly feels part of India at all.

Port Blair, the Andamans' capital, is tranquil and rustic, with wooden houses smothered in bougainvillea, scenic views across to nearby islands, and an unpolluted wharf with old ships and cackling seagulls.

There is still something unconquered and mysterious about much of the archipelago, which is home to six aboriginal tribal groups, each with different physiognomies, languages, and beliefs that have changed little since the Paleolithic age. Many of these indigenous tribes are hostile toward intruders, be they government officials carrying presents of plastic buckets, watches, or chocolates, or gaping tourists fumbling for their cameras. Islands inhabited by these tribes are now off limits to casual visitors. Only the xenophobic and handsome Sentinelese, who live on North Sentinel Island, have remained completely isolated from the world, repulsing all intruders with their expertly hurled two-meter (6.5-ft) poisoned arrows. The Greater Andamese from the north, the Jarawas from the Middle Andamans, and the Nicobarese and Shompens from the Nicobar Islands simply prefer to be left alone. Others, like the naked, body-painted Onges from South Andaman, a tribe of hunters and gatherers, have become quite blasé about visits from anthropologists and curious onlookers, and eagerly swap their tasseled G-strings for polyester nighties or T-shirts, and their fresh fish for tins of baked beans.

The powerful Marathas from central India first annexed the Andaman and Nicobar islands in the late seventeenth century as a convenient base for plundering British, Dutch, and Portuguese merchant ships. After several attempts, the British finally ousted the Marathas in the nineteenth century and established a penal colony at Port Blair in the aftermath of the 1857 Indian Mutiny, earning the archipelago the notorious sobriquet "kala pani", or "water of death". During World War II, the Andamans were the only part of India to be occupied by the Japanese, who between 1942 and 1945 massacred large numbers of prisoners and local tribespeople.

Port Blair's main industry is the export of timber, and vast areas of its teak, mahogany, and rosewood forests have been razed. The capital has a mixed community of mainland Indians and Burmese, and makes a perfect base for exploring the nearby coral reefs.

ENTRY FORMALITIES

Foreigners require a permit to visit the Andaman and Nicobar islands, but this is easily obtained from the authorities on arrival at Port Blair, regardless of whether you arrive by air or ship. The permit is valid for 15 days, but it can be extended. It applies only to Port Blair's municipal area and the nearby coral reef islands of Jolly Buoy, Red Skin, Cinque, Neil, and Havelock. Permits are issued from the **Tourist Office** (((03192) 20694) in the Secretariat building on VIP Road, Port Blair. You'll have to make another visit to get a "departure" stamp in your passport before leaving. Those wishing to visit other islands need to approach the Ministry of Home Affairs, Government of India, North Block, New Delhi, but the southern Nicobar Islands are completely off limits to foreign tourists, as are any islands inhabited by tribal groups.

ACCESS

Indian Airlines operates four flights weekly to Port Blair and back from Calcutta and Madras. The flight takes about two hours.

The other alternative is to make the three-day sea crossing to Port Blair from either Calcutta or Madras. Schedules can be irregular, particularly during the monsoon months, and the lurching journey can induce seasickness, but those with a yen for sea travel will find glamour in being adrift in the Bay of Bengal, sighting dolphins and sharks, and being privy to the slightly farcical shipboard atmosphere with its salty seadog captain, aged bearers in soiled caps, and sinewy Dravidian ship-boys. It's certainly much cheaper than flying — one-way fares range from deluxe air-conditioned private cabins with attached bathrooms at around US$35, Class B at US$22, and Class C at US$20, all the way down the scale to US$4 bunk class, with fold-down planks. Shipboard meals cost extra and tend to be monotonous thali affairs, although the Western-style breakfasts are good. To book berths or inquire about the next sailing, contact the Shipping Corporation of India, ((033) 239456, 13 Strand Road in Calcutta, or their Madras agents, KPV Sheikh Muhammed Rowther and Co., ((044) 510346, 41 Linghi Chetty Street. The SCI also have an office in Bombay at 229–232 Madame Cama Road.

WHEN TO GO

The Andamans are at their most idyllic between mid-November and mid-May, when the weather is generally warm with cooling sea breezes. Port Blair's "off" season coincides with the monsoon period (late May to early October), when it has a steamy, primeval beauty but snorkeling and scuba diving become impossible.

HOTELS

Welcomgroup Bay Island, ((03192) 20881 fax (03192) 83367, is a spacious, well-designed resort hotel atop Marine Hill, fitted out with local and natural wood furniture. The rooms all have balconies, which provide breathtaking views across Phoenix Bay. Both the bar and restaurant overlook the sea, and hotel fare includes Indian, Burmese, and local seafood dishes. Rates: moderate. Facilities include a seawater pool (there is no attached beach), health club, indoor games, and video screenings of several interesting films on the tribal people of the islands. Mrs Vasan operates the hotel's travel desk, and her efficiency and prodigious knowledge of the islands make this service far superior to that provided by the sleepy tourist office. She'll take rapid care of any ticketing, and can arrange transport facilities (taxi, boat hire, helicopter rides) as well as snorkeling and scuba equipment.

Andaman Beach Resort, ((03192) 21462, is modern and functional with a beachfront location at Corbyn's Cove, Port Blair's most swimmable beach. The hotel supplies equipment for windsurfing, water-skiing, sailing, scuba diving, snorkeling, and fishing. Other facilities include a restaurant, bar, travel desk, and tennis courts. Rates: moderate.

Good inexpensive options include the **Shompen Hotel,** ((03192) 20360, at Middle Point, which has friendly service, a restaurant, and rooms with attached bathrooms and the popular **Megapode Nest,** ((03192) 2207, Haddo, overlooking Phoenix Bay, both bookable through Port Blair's Deputy Director of Tourism ((03192) 20694. There are also two quite pleasant government guesthouses, one atop Marine Hill and one in Corbyn's Cove: both offer clean, basic accommodation.

The two resort hotels have the town's only established restaurants — otherwise go to Aberdeen Bazaar to stock up on provisions and delicious local fruits, or sample fish patties and samosas from cheap *chai* cafés. The **Annapurna Café,** near the Shompen Hotel, serves good fish and chips and mealtime *thalis*.

SIGHTSEEING

What most people have in mind when they visit the Andamans archipelago is a week or two of idyllic leisure, hopping from one secluded oyster-shell bay to another, basking in clearwaters, and exploring the underwater enchantment of colorful coral reefs. But Port Blair has its own charm, and it's worth spending a day or two making a relaxed bicycle tour of its sights.

Start with the **Cellular Jail,** the eerie edifice constructed by the British in 1906 and used to incarcerate many hundreds of "dangerous" Indian political prisoners until 1938. Set on the sea coast of Atlanta Point, it resembles a vast wheel, with the central watchtower joined by seven triple-storied wings, all pocketed with hundreds of tiny crypt-like cells where prisoners were kept in solitary confinement. For the British, it was a highly effective way of paralyzing the Independence movement: elite and literate freedom fighters shared their plight of isolation, hard labor, and brutal torture with common criminals, and many were driven to insanity and suicide.

But by far the worst atrocities took place during the Japanese occupation of Port Blair from 1942 to 1945, when there were mass executions of prisoners as well as villagers suspected of being spies for the Allied forces.

The prison grounds are open from 9 am to noon and 2 to 5 pm every day, and a son et lumire show is scheduled to begin in early 1989. There are several informative booklets for sale at the entrance booth.

Winding down the road to Aberdeen Jetty you'll find the **Marine Museum,** a dusty chamber which has over 350 pickled exhibits of different species, charts of tropical fish, shells, coral, and an exotic collection of turtle eggs. Come here before you start scuba diving so you'll recognize what lurks beneath the Andamans' ocean waves. It's open 8:30 am to 12:30 pm and 1:30 to 4 pm, but is closed on Sundays and public holidays.

From here it's a hilly climb through Aberdeen Bazaar up to the **Anthropological Museum,** which has a fascinating collection of photographs and descriptions of the Andaman and Nicobar tribal groups, and displays of ceremonial costumes and objects, such as crab claw pipes, flax tassel G-strings, leaf-palm umbrellas, human mandible necklaces, and nautilus shell cups. But there is frustratingly little solid information, and if you wish to know more about the region's tribal people, try to strike up a conversation with the head researcher in residence, Mr Baha. The museum is open from 9 am to noon and 1 to 4 pm, closed Saturdays and public holidays. From here, ask for directions to the nearby **Cottage Industries Emporium,** which sells delicate shell jewelry, shell-lamps, and a wide range of local handicrafts. It's open 8:15 am to 12:30 pm and 1 to 4:45 pm except during the weekend.

Halfway down the road leading to Chatham Wharf is Port Blair's well-kept **Mini Zoo**, which houses an array of indigenous plumed birds, monitor lizards, wild boars, macaque monkeys, bears, and deer. There's also a crocodile breeding farm, and a captivating Painted Stork, as poised and eccentric as an old count in a multicolored tuxedo. It's open from 7 am to noon, 1 to 5 pm, and is closed on Mondays. The two last stops are eccentric Port Blair tourist attractions: the gigantic Victorian-era Chatham Saw Mill, and the Wimco Match Factory, where most of India's matchsticks are made.

HARBOR CRUISES

The tourist office employs old khaki-clad sailors to run afternoon cruises on quaint, brass-studded Bristol boats, which meander around the harbor stopping at places of interest and return just as sunset casts a molten light over the landscape. First stop is at the Bamboo Jetty Market, where excited islanders in folded-up dhotis and large lapels haggle passionately for fish, jackfruit, and Tupperware. The most interesting stop on this trip is at **Viper Island**. The first prison for chain-gang convicts in British India was built here in 1867; later it was used for female prisoners. Ironically, the view from the gallows — all that remains of the prison — is one of incomparable loveliness. The boat leaves from the end of the Phoenix Bay dockyard at 3 pm.

There's also an early morning cruise from the same jetty across to **Ross Island**, which was once a well-fortified cantonment from which the British could survey their penal settlement in style, well protected from convicts and naked "heathen" tribespeople. Established in 1858, Ross Island had a splendid Georgian-style Residency, a combined officers' mess and club, colonial bungalows, a church and graveyard, numerous administrative offices, and even a printing press and swimming pool. Its residents dressed formally for dinner, as though they were dining in a Pall Mall club. Lady Duff Cooper once spent a night here while fleeing Singapore for England, and thought it very "select". Banyan trees now have the crumbling settlement in a macabre embrace that resembles flesh grafted on to stone. Spotted deer and peacocks run wild and take shelter in the deserted buildings. The island is occupied by the Indian Navy, and is open to visitors only until 12:30 pm. The Tourist Information Centre, (20380, at the Tourist Home in Haddo, can confirm boat timings.

BEACH PARADISE AND CORAL REEFS

The easiest way to arrange a visit to the outer islands is to contact either Island Travels, Aberdeen Bazaar, ((03192) 21358, their branch at the Bay Island Hotel, or the TCI travel desk at the Andaman Beach Resort. They'll give you an update on which islands are open to visitors, and save you the hassle of hiring a boat or organizing helicopter transport to **Havelock** and **Neil** islands (where it's possible to stay overnight at PWD bungalows). They'll also arrange snorkeling and scuba diving equipment. To organize your own trip, contact the Marine Department or the Oceanic Company, on M.G. Road, Middle Point. Boat trips include visits to the paradisical uninhabited islands of **Red Skin**, **Jolly Buoy**, and **Cinque** (actually a handful of small islands connected by sandbars), all fringed by beaches and sheer blue waters with visibility up to six meters (20 ft). The calm lagoons enclosed by coral reefs around these islands are particularly good for snorkeling and diving — just like floating through a huge aquarium with shifting kaleidoscopic hues and technicolor tropical fish. As you cruise between the islands, you'll quite often see gamboling dolphins, flying fish, and large sea crocodiles.

If you plan a diving trip to the Andamans, be sure to avoid the monsoon period between June and September when the sea is turbulent, khaki-colored, and massed with venomous jellyfish. During this period of sudden squalls, boat-owners usually refuse to take tourists to the outer islands.

Two enjoyable excursions from Port Blair are just an hour's drive away. **Chiriya Tapu** is a magnificent beach at the southern tip of the South Andamans, surrounded by lush mangrove swamps. Rare exotic birds can be seen by early risers, and there's plenty of good fishing to be had in the mangrove creeks. You can stay overnight at a guesthouse set atop a hill overlooking the sea. On the west coast lies **Wandoor Beach**, with secluded clear waters and rich coral reefs. It's a convenient base for exploring nearby **Jolly Buoy** and **Red Skin** islands.

Across the Deccan

HYDERABAD

Capital of Andhra Pradesh, Hyderabad is India's sixth largest city. The beautiful architectural relics of its legendary Muslim grandeur are rapidly being swallowed up by an ugly industrial hinterland that sprawls across to Secunderabad, the modern twin capital. Yet locked within Hyderabad's heart are countless layers of its medieval Islamic heritage. Magnificent mosques and peeling nineteenth-century courtly mansions stand cheek by jowl with a shanty town of modern buildings and factory shacks.

With a skyline distinguished by slender minarets, Hyderabad represents a curious Muslim foothold in the south's Hindu heartland. It was founded in 1591 by the Qutub Shahi dynasty, a line of Muslim rulers who had ruled the mainly Hindu subjects of the surrounding southern Deccan since the fourteenth century. Mohammed Quli, the fourth of the Qutub Shahis, built his new capital near the Musi River as an alternative to his cramped, disease-ridden fortress city at Golconda, 11 km (seven miles) away, which today lends its name to locally produced wine.

Hyderabad's first major monument remains its most magnificent emblem: the Charminar arch, which straddles the city's original grid of broad intersecting boulevards. As a thriving trading center, Hyderabad — and the lure of its local diamond industry — proved irresistible to the Mughal emperor Aurangzeb who captured the region in 1650. In the wake of Aurangzeb's death in 1707, Hyderabad was snatched up in 1713 by one of the dead emperor's most trusted generals, Mir Kamruddin Khan, of the Asaf Jahn dynasty. He retained his Mughal title, Nizam-ul-Mulk, and became the independent ruler of Hyderabad.

Successive Nizams amassed legendary fortunes, despite having part of their Deccan domain chipped down to the size of Italy by the French, the Marathas, and the British. When the tenth and last Nizam, Mir Osman Ali Khan, came to power in 1911, he was arguably the richest man in the world. His giant palace teemed with some 11,000 servants (38 were required to dust the chandeliers, while others did nothing except grind spices) entire wings were used to house mammoth quantities of precious jewels and gold bullion, and he used egg-sized diamonds as paperweights. Yet the Nizam's parsimony was equally fabled: he wore the same oil-streaked fez and soiled jacket for 30 years, was said to knit his own socks, and haggled over the price of local Charminar cigarettes. When India gained its independence in 1947, the Nizam flatly refused to relinquish his control of the state, grimly hanging on for two years before

Across the Deccan

Indian troops massed at his borders forced him to capitulate.

Hyderabad's landscape is fringed by its boulder-strewn Banjara Hills, once the rugged home of a gypsy tribe from distant Rajasthan and now an elite enclave. The Banjara tribespeople still add their colorful presence to the city's bazaars, their women costumed in rustic Rajput finery, with heavy, jingling jewelry and embroidered camel slippers. It's most pleasant to visit the city between October and February, when it is fanned by cool breezes from its numerous reservoirs. But from March onwards, Hyderabad becomes unbearably stifling, with the waves of dry, sauna-hot air reducing even determined sightseers to a dehydrated frazzle.

ACCESS

Indian Airlines operates daily direct flights to Hyderabad from Delhi, Bangalore, Bombay, Madras, and Calcutta, and regular flights from Bhubaneswar.

Alternatively, Vayudoot provide direct links from Goa, Bangalore, and Mysore. Hyderabad is connected by train to all major Indian cities, and popular rail journeys to south Indian destinations include the 19-hour trip to Bangalore and the 15-hour overnight express to Madras. Both these trains can be taken from the central Kachiguda station, saving the drive to the main station in Secunderabad, eight kilometers (five miles) away. As elsewhere in India, the express overnight trains are freqently booked out, so try to reserve your sleeper as soon as possible. Regular buses ply between Hyderabad and Bangalore, Madras, and Bombay.

HOTELS

The **Krishna Oberoi**, ((0842) 222121, fax (0842) 223079, Road No. 1, Banjara Hills, is Hyderabad's most elegant luxury hotel with plush pastel decor, indoor fountains, and impeccably efficient staff. It's situated 10 minutes from the airport amid landscaped gardens which overlook the city. (From the top floors you can see Golconda Fort, 13 km, or eight miles, away). Comfortable, tastefully furnished double rooms come with all the latest Indian mod-cons — push-button telephones, vast televisions linked to cable TV, and mini-bars. Rates: expensive. Its two stylish restaurants, which offer excellent Hyderabadi and Chinese cuisine, are heavily patronized by the city's elite, and there's also a good bar and 24-hour coffee shop. Facilities include a very modern health club with grounds

OPPOSITE: Care-worn and ash-smeared old man of Hyderabad.

for squash, tennis, and golf, a beauty parlor, swimming pool, travel desk, and the adjacent Krishna Plaza, a slick shopping arcade.

Situated close by is **Hotel Banjara,** ((0842) 222222, fax (0842) 222218, which lacks the Oberoi's polish but has good facilities, including several restaurants, a small swimming pool, shopping arcade, beauty salon, and lakeside boating. The **Ritz Hotel,** ((0842) 233571, Hillfort Palace, is more central and has far more character. Built in a Scottish baronial style, this former palace is now a charming — if slightly dilapidated — hotel smothered with whitewash, dusty chandeliers, and bright bougainvillea creepers. The dining room serves Indian, continental, and Chinese food, but has dreary 1950's décor and a befuddled evening band called the "The Minarettes". There are tennis courts and a small pool which is used by locals for swimming lessons. Spacious, air-conditioned ground floor rooms with quaint furniture are best. Rates: inexpensive.

For inexpensive accommodation, try the **Rock Castle Hotel,** ((0842) 222541, Road No. 6, Banjara Hills, a colonial-era lodging house now slightly run-down but still quaint, with friendly staff and good food. Within the city center, **Hotel Sarovar,** ((0842) 237638, on Secretariat Road has clean, comfortable rooms and an excellent all-day South Indian restaurant with generous *thalis*. The towering annexe under construction next door will offer four-star accommodation at much higher rates. For cheap accommodation try **Hotel Taj Mahal,** ((0842) 237988, 237993, on King Kothi Road, in Abids, the city's bustling shopping area, which is very popular with budget travelers. There's a pleasant rooftop café, and a colorful array of freelance gurus hovering at the entrance, sometimes catnapping under black umbrellas. One sign reads: "Mr Bakshi, the world's greatest scientific palmist who can solve all life's problems!"

RESTAURANTS

For sophisticated dining and good service: the Oberoi hotel has two plush restaurants, both overlooking cascading fountains: **Firdaus** for faultless Persian-influenced Hyderabadi Mughali dishes — with delicious baronial *raan*, tandoor leg of lamb — and the **Szechuan Garden** for regional Chinese food.

Hotel Banjara's evening **Kebab-e-Bahar** outdoor terrace restaurant is deservedly popular for its Mughali dishes, aromatic kebabs, and handkerchief-thin *roomali rotis*. But no visit to Hyderabad is complete without an authentic experience of the city's Islamic culture in one of the Irani cafés: always cheap, filthy, full of capped Muslims, *burqa*-clad matrons, marble-topped tables, and glittering mosaic walls. The

best (cleanest) to try are the **Hotel Madina,** near the Charminar, and **Rainbow Restaurant** on Abid Road (also known as Mahatma Gandhi Road). Specialties to order include *haleem,* a spiced mutton curry cooked with delicately pounded wheat; *paya,* chicken soup served with flat bread, and *pauna,* sweet spiced tea. Local sweetmeats include *ashrafi,* an edible "coin" stamped with a Mughal seal, and *badam ki jali,* almond-studded halva. Good south Indian food is found at **Hotel Sampurna International** and **Kamath Hotel** near the Indian Airlines office in Saifabad. Well-heeled locals favor a handful of "classy" restaurants, all heavily air-conditioned with fake rococo, mirror-lined décor and a pulsating disco beat, serving good Mughali, Chinese, and continental dishes: **Golden Deer** restaurant and bar, just opposite the Santhosh cinema in Abids; the rooftop **Palace Heights** nearby (just look up, you can't miss its towering neon sign); **Fifth Avenue** and **Blue Fox,** both next to each other on Lakdiakapol. The **Indian Coffee House,** in the Secretariat grounds, has delicious hot or cold coffee and south Indian snacks — good for a break after visiting the nearby Government Archaeological Museum in the Public Gardens. It's open 9:30 am to 5 pm.

SIGHTSEEING

Hyderabad is very spread out, so it's worth having a definite strategy before setting off for a day's sightseeing. Golconda Fort (see page 273) is best enjoyed in the cool early morning, leaving you free to explore the city's museums, mosques, and markets in the afternoon. Conducted city tours are convenient time-savers, but offer only a fleeting glimpse of Hyderabad's real charm, which is concentrated in its vibrantly colorful bazaars. Personal guides and transport can be hired at the Tourist Information Bureau and if you're set on cycling the 11 km (seven miles) out to Golconda Fort — a pleasant, relatively straightfoward route if you've got a map on hand — hotels should be able to advise on bicycle hire.

Mosques, Markets, and Museums

At the heart of the old walled city stands Hyderabad's emblematic **Charminar**, a magnificent archway framed by four tapering minarets, each 56 m (184 ft) high. It was built in 1591 by Muhammed Quli Qutub Shahi as a sort of architectural talisman against a plague that was devastating the newly-founded city. You can make the spiraling ascent up to a tiny second-floor mosque for views across the city. The image of the Charminar follows you all across India on the country's No. 1 brand of glorified *beedi* cigarettes. It's open from 9 am to 4:30 pm, and expect to find its cavernous interior teeming with swaddled alms-seekers.

Just beyond the Charminar, you'll see the colossal **Mecca Masjid**, the largest mosque in South India. Construction began under Muhammed Quli Qutub Shahi in 1614, but it was finished as an act of Islamic faith by the next conqueror of the Deccan, the Mughal emperor Aurangzeb, in 1687. Modeled on the famous mosque at Mecca, it's built on an awe-inspiring scale with lofty monolithic pillars, vast calligraphy-emblazoned archways, and towering gold-tipped 30-m (100-ft)-high minarets. Pigeons and hornets swoop around it like dark clouds and build nests in its inaccessible upper regions. Against its severe granite walls, the interior glitters in contrast with dangling Belgian chandeliers, and decorative marbled inscriptions from the Koran. This is Hyderabad's principal place of Muslim worship, and during Fridays and Muslim festivals it can accommodate more than 10,000 kneeling devotees. During the Muslim holy month of Ramadan, many thousands more spill across the streets outside. To the left of the courtyard is a marbled row of the Nizam's decorative tombstones — their womenfolk lie beneath flat tablets. Old men with hennaed beards commiserate with each other in the shadows, and ragged urchins sprawl across the tombstones. The mosque's workers scatter grain across the courtyard for bedraggled flocks of goats, pigeons, chickens, and in the courtyard's far right-hand corner is a solid black marble seat, brought from Iran 200 years ago. Locals say that those who sit on it are destined to return to Hyderabad — you'll have to find that out for yourself!

From here, any number of cobbled lanes will plunge you into the bustling, medieval pantomime of Hyderabad's **Old Bazaar.** Wind your way through crowded alleys strewn with sandalwood screw-curls and dung, side-step loitering buffaloes and knots of conversing merchants, and charge bravely through the riotous traffic.

Crocheted-capped merchants gossip on upturned flower-pots; *burqa*-clad women with heavily kohl-rimmed downcast eyes flit by; and craftsmen stoop over spun silver or run plump fingers through rows of pearls. The lanes glitter with glass bangles and open sacks dot the pavement with the color and scent of every imaginable spice. Hyderabad is a major pearl processing center for pearls from the Middle East, Japan, and China, and loose pearls can be purchased at about 20 percent of London prices — and although in many shops you might bargain over the price, you can also pay by credit card. Himroo brocades, delicate silver jewelry, rare Urdu books or decadently gilded Korans, lacquered sandalwood toys, and traditional *bidri* work with its distinctive silver designs against black metal are the best products to buy.

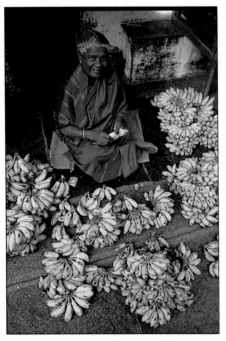

Several old and decaying city palaces lie within walking distance of the bazaar area. They include the **Panch Mahal**, **Chow Mahala**, **King Kothi**, and **Baradari** palaces, the latter notable for the battalions of Amazonian female sepoys, used to patrol the palace's zenana, or women's quarters, during the reign of Nizam Ali in the eighteenth century. Court documents as well as local lore record that this Nizam made his Italian mistress the colonel in charge of these female soldiers. But having gained military clout, she lost her original appeal for the Nizam, and he resolved to remove her. Acting on a tip-off, she escaped to Poona (now Pune, in Maharashtra state) accompanied by her loyal female sepoys, where she lived until her death. The next resident of the Baradari was a prime minister renowned for his elegant eccentricities, who trained his soldiers to ride ostriches in the

gardens. By far the most extravagant of these palaces is the **Faluknuma Palace**, five kilometers (three miles) south, a palatial neoclassical mansion fronted by a vast marble stairway and vestibule fountains. It was built in 1897, and was used as the Nizam's guesthouse, accommodating touring viceroys and graced by British royalty. Its grand gilt-edged reception room is left just as it was, cluttered with period furniture, chandeliers, and figurines. To visit, contact the tourist office or apply to Mr Asadullah, the Secretary of the Nizam's Trust Fund, near Lal Bahadur Stadium.

Located on the south bank of the Musi River, the **Salar Jung Museum** is one of Hyderabad's highlights. It houses the extraordinary private collection of the eclectic Nabob Salar Jung III, who served as prime minister to the Nizam of Hyderabad early this century until he resigned in 1914 to devote himself to the serious pursuit of collecting. The Nabob traveled incessantly, immense reserves of gold, and the sight of his sallow, serious face caused ripples of excitement taking with him Europe's leading auction houses. He died in 1949, aged 60 and a bachelor, and his priceless collection of over 35,000 exhibits from all over the world spans 35 galleries, each devoted to a certain theme. There's a vast range of Indian antiques — family heirlooms, sculptures, paintings, manuscripts, textiles, ivory and jade carvings, arms and armour — as well as galleries devoted to Middle Eastern, Far Eastern, and European art, with novelty collections of toys and antique clocks. The top floor contains an India researcher's gold-mine — the Nabob's library of over 60,000 books, many original historical documents and rare state annals. In one corner, an army of plaster busts, a veritable Who's Who of British Empire builders, gathers dust, with their faces turned to the wall like errant children. There's a ground floor cafeteria for tea and snacks. The museum is open daily except Fridays from 10 am to 5 pm, and bags and cameras must be deposited at the entrance.

On the other side of the River Musi lies the former **British Residency,** a fine Greco-colonial building fronted by two crouching sphinxes, built in 1803, and now used as a college. Other nearby architectural relics include the remarkable ocher-red **High Court** and the **Osmania Hospital,** both built in the Indo–Saracenic style in the late nineteenth century.

The **Government Archaeological Museum**, adjacent to the imposing colonial-era Indo–Saracenic Secretariat near the Public Gardens has a fine collection of antique Indian sculpture, prehistoric utensils, coins, manuscripts, old arms, eighteenth-century *bidri*-ware, textiles, and china. Close by is the **Ajanta Pavilion,** which displays full-size copies of the Ajanta frescoes. The gardens are good for a peaceful stroll away from the city's choatic muddle. Rather incongruously, just outside the Secretariat, a row of medicine men seem to have claimed their turf, selling a lurid array of peacock feathers, musty pills, tiger teeth, flayed buffalo skin, and cats' and rats' tails.

If you're going to visit any zoo in India, then make it the **Nehru Zoological Park**, located just outside the old city walls on Bangalore Road, quite near the Charminar. Wandering around its lush, well-landscaped, miniature lake-studded 121-hectare (300-acre) enclosure

the Public Gardens. During the reign of the Qutab Shahis, royal proclamations were announced from here, with drum rolls for effect. Built by the mega-wealthy Birla family and decorated with ornate bas-reliefs depicting scenes from the Hindu epics, the temple is open to all castes and creeds. It's liveliest at sunset, when crowds clamor to offer scented garlands and coconuts — a symbol of a fulfilling life — to the temple deity, Lord Venkateshwara. So many coconuts are offered, in fact, that a sign says: "Please Leave Your Coconuts Here" at a locker used to babysit coconuts at the rate of 10 paise an hour! Hawkers sell medicinal bottles of

makes an enjoyable afternoon's excursion. Some 1,600 animals and 240 species of birds live in the near-natural surroundings. The highlight is undoubtedly the **Lion Safari Park**, with its free-roaming herds of lions. It's about a 20-minute walk from the zoo's main entrance, and every 15 minutes between 9:30 am and 12:15 pm and 2 to 4:30 pm, crowded mini-buses leave for a "safari" circuit. There are several cafeterias, and leafy grounds for picnics. During the hot season, avoid visiting in the afternoon, when the animals are slumped in deep siesta. The **National History Museum**, **Aquarium**, and **Ancient Life Museum** are worth visiting, located just near the entrance. The complex is open between 9 am and 6 pm daily, except Monday.

If you're still in need of stimulation, visit the **Birla Mandir** (Naubat Prahad), the modern white marble temple atop a rocky hill opposite

"Guaranteed Pure Ganga Water", plastic trinkets, and candyfloss at the temple's entrance. On the adjacent hill stands the **Birla Planetarium** (Adarsh Nagar), which offers "Japanese Technology Sky Theater" and English sessions at 11:30 am, 4 and 6 pm daily (Sundays at 11:30 am, 3:45 and 6 pm).

Golconda Fort

The majestic ruins of this rambling fortress capital have an almost biblical quality, looming high above dusty, sepia scrubland, 11 km (seven miles) west of Hyderabad. Golconda was the virtually impregnable medieval citadel of the Qutub Shahi kings, a city fabled for its exotic bazaars

OPPOSITE ans ABOVE: Everything from silver and pearls to daily fruit and vegetables are on sale at Hyderabad's bustling and colorful bazaars.

selling diamonds, silver jewelry, and precious gems. Its mines produced the legendary Orloff, Regent, and Kohinoor diamonds.

Eyewitness accounts by Marco Polo and the seventeenth-century French traveler Jean-Baptiste Tavernier spread the legend of Golconda's decadence and wealth. Founded in the thirteenth century by the Hindu Kakatiya kings of Warangal, it was originally just a simple hilltop mud settlement called "Golla" (shepherd) "Konda" (hill). Golconda was ceded to the powerful fourteenth-century Muslim Bahmani rulers, and later passed into the hands of the Persian Qutub Shahi dynasty, who ruled the surrounding region between 1518 and 1687. Under the Qutub Shahis, Golconda emerged as a formidable stronghold; built entirely of solid granite boulders, it seemed almost part of the mountain itself. The city within its walls, had a complex civil and military administration, gem-studded royal palaces, mosques, harem quarters with interior fountains, Turkish baths, assembly halls, pavilioned gardens, and even a mortuary. Water was raised by an ingenious system through laminated clay pipes and Persian water wheels gushed water through the fountains and irrigated the flower-strewn roof gardens at the citadel's heights. One of Golconda's most intriguing features is its acoustical system, which enables a handclap sounded at the gates to be heard clearly right up in the citadel. Golconda was virtually impregnable: it was encircled by some seven kilometers (four and a half miles) of triple-tiered ramparts dotted with eight formidable iron-spiked gates, 87 semicircular watchposts, and a wide moat. It withstood eight months under seige by Aurangzeb's armies, falling only when a turncoat general betrayed the Qutub Shahis and allowed the enemy's forces to stream through the grand entrance gate. Aurangzeb annexed Golconda as part of his empire in 1687, and the fortress citadel soon crumbled into decline.

Golconda's fragmented ruins and winding medieval passages come to life with the help of a knowledgeable guide — but it's also the sort of place that is nice to ramble about in at will, making discoveries of your own. Experienced guides can be hired from the tourist bureau, or you can buy the very informative *Guide of Golconda Fort* which has a its clearly marked map.

Northwest of Golconda lie the **Qutub Shahi Tombs**, a necropolis of more than a dozen magnificent domed tombs built for the Qutub Shahi rulers and their families set amid peaceful gar-

dens. The tombs are reminiscent of the famous Lodhi tombs of Delhi, and the finest is that of Muhammed Quli Qutub Shahi, the founder of Hyderabad, which rises to a height of 55 m (180 ft).

GENERAL INFORMATION

The Andhra Pradesh Tourist Information Bureau, ((0842) 556493, 556523, first and fifth floors, Gargan Vihar, Mukkaram Jahi Road, provide local information, city maps, and tickets for their conducted city tours (8 am to 6 pm every day except Friday). For booking and travel arrangements, both Indian Airlines, ((0842) 36902, 72051, and Vayudoot, ((0842) 36902, are located at Safiabad, and good travel agents include Trade Wings, ((0842) 30545, 3 Public Gardens Road, and Sita World Travel, ((0842) 223628, Sita House, Hyderguda.

THE DECCAN TRAIL TO BANGALORE

From Hyderabad, many travelers head straight for Karnataka's capital, Bangalore, picking up the popular route through Mysore to Ooty. Few venture southwest across the Deccan Plateau's arid, boulder-strewn terrain to explore its deserted medieval cities, forts, and temples — the legacy of the powerful Mughal, Chalukya, Telegu, and Hoysala kingdoms who made this region their battleground. Those who make the effort — involving long, hot hours of bus and train travel — will be richly rewarded. The region is full of decaying architectural treasures and rustic towns where life seems barely to have changed for centuries. A good network of state-run hotels offer overnight facilities at all main destinations.

Ideally, you could spend a week or so on the Deccan trail, starting in north Karnataka with **Bidar**, 130 km (81 miles) from Hyderabad, the former capital of the Muslim Bahmanis, with its well-preserved fifteenth-century city fort, palaces, pavilions, and fine tombs; and the fabulous medieval walled city of **Bijapur**, described by historian James Grant Duff as "exceeding anything of its kind in Europe". Bijapur was the sixteenth-century stronghold of the Adil Shahi dynasty, whose legacy of majestic monuments includes the Gol Gumbaz, with a massive dome said to be second in size only to that of St Peter's in Rome, and a "whispering gallery" where the slightest whisper echoes inside the dome 12 times over. To the south lie a clustered trio of sculptured caves and stone temple sites — **Badami, Pattadakal,** and **Aihole** — dating back to the sixth century when the early Chalukya

OPPOSITE: The palatial Neo-Dravidian style Vidhana Soudha, which houses Bangalore's Secretariat and Legislature.

kings ruled the region. But the culmination of the Deccan trail is found in the splendid isolation of **Hampi**, the fourteenth-century kingdom of the mighty Vijaynagars, whose Hindu empire was the largest in India's history. Its impressive medieval ruins — full of fortified battlements, palaces, temples, pavilions, shrines, baths, and bazaars — spread across 26 sq km (10 sq miles). From Hampi you can link up to Bangalore, 358 km (222 miles) away, either by rail or express bus. For more detailed information on these destinations, and how to reach them, consult with the Government of India Tourist Office in Hyderabad, at its new location in the A.P. Tourist Information Bureau, Gargan Vihar, Mukkaram Jahi Road.

BANGALORE

Karnataka's state capital is an attractive, efficient city with a well-planned grid of treelined boulevards, stately old public buildings, and beautiful gardens. Dubbed India's "Silicon Valley" for its burgeoning computer industry, Bangalore is the country's main center for scientific and technological research, eclipsing the city's traditional industries of coffee-trading, stud farm horse-breeding, and indefatigable movie-making. There's a cosmopolitan, almost campus-like, air to Bangalore, which has a constant stream of foreign business travelers and draws people from all over India for higher education, business opportunities, and research. It's an ideal base for planning trips through South India, with several interesting sights of its own, plenty of good hotels, and a thriving nightlife with an array of restaurants, bars, and thirties-era art deco cinemas.

Legend has it that Kempe Gowda, a feudal chief from the Vjayanagar kingdom, founded Bangalore, which means "city of boiled beans", in 1537 in memory of the spot where he was offered a meal of beans by a kindly hermit when lost in the forest. His medieval mud fort was later enlarged and rebuilt in stone by the Muslim leader Hyder Ali and his son, Tipu Sultan, in the late eighteenth century. After defeating Tipu "Tiger" Sultan at Srirangapatna, the British arrived in 1809 to build a cantonment, and present-day Bangalore is dotted with Raj-era bougainvillea-shrouded bungalows, churches, clubs, pavilioned gardens, quaint shopping malls, as well as racing grounds and breweries. Ironically, it was the Maharaja of Mysore who produced the most extravagant parody of Victorian England in his Bangalore Palace, a vast, ivy-swathed turreted model of Windsor Palace, now eerily silent amidst its large gardens on the outskirts of the old cantonment town.

Set high above the stifling plains, Bangalore is a popular summer bolt-hole, though its climate is pleasant all year round. The city's extensive parks — notably Cubbon Park and Lal Bagh — are at their best during January and August, and it can be fun to participate in the horse-racing mania that grips Bangaloreans between November and March and from mid-April to July.

ACCESS

Bangalore has excellent air connections to the rest of India, with daily direct flights to Bombay, Delhi, Hyderabad, and Madras, as well as regular services to Ahmedabad, Calcutta, Cochin, Coimbature, Goa, Trivandrum, and other centers. India's second-flag airline, Vayudoot, operates between Bangalore and Mysore, Hyderabad, and Tirupati. Daily express trains run to Bangalore from all major Indian cities, and popular journeys include the seven-hour *Brindhavan Express* or *Bangalore Mail* from Madras, the twice-weekly 38-hour *Karnataka Express* from Delhi, and the 27-hour trip from Bombay. Bangalore is also well-serviced by state coaches from all the main Indian cities, with an efficient daily network of buses plying throughout southern and central India. When planning a long bus journey, try to avoid the notorious "video coaches", which feature Hindi movies in "glorious technicolor" as a ploy to lure customers. Insomniacal Indians seem to adore these spoof extravaganzas full of wet saris, paunchy villains, and dance sequences on wildly elaborate sets. Most video coaches carry the sign "If the Video Fails We Are Not Responsible", but alas, it never does.

HOTELS

Welcomgroup's **Windsor Manor Sheraton**, ((080) 226-9898, fax (080) 226-4941, 25 Sankey Road, is very stylish, with meticulous Regency-style décor throughout — from the lobby's balustraded marble staircase to the staff uniforms — prompt service, excellent restaurants, and a poolside barbecue. Rooms are plush, pastel-colored, and fitted with cable TV. Rates: moderate. Facilities include a swimming pool, health club, beauty salon, bookshop, travel counter, and business desk. A classic English bar serves pints of chilled draught beer. **West End Hotel**, ((080) 226-9281, fax (080) 220-0010, Race Course Road, run by the Taj Group, is Bangalore's oldest hotel. Set in eight hectares (20 acres) of landscaped gardens, and despite a characterless modern annex, it still radiates Raj-era charm. Ask for a Victorian room in the original whitewashed hotel, where rooms come with balconies, wicker furniture, and huge British bathtubs. Rates: expensive. There's a good pool, several restaurants, and the lawns are perfect for candlelit cocktails. **Taj Residency**, ((080) 558-4444 fax (080) 558-4748, 14 Mahatma Gandhi Road, is a modern, five-star hotel with extensive facilities aimed at business travelers. Its restaurants and bar are considered top-notch by locals. Rates: moderate.

In cheap bracket, try the **Hotel Hoysala**, ((080) 365311, 212 S.C. Road, Seshadri Puram for reliably clean rooms; the **New Victoria Hotel**, ((080) 584076-7, 47–48 Residency Road, for vintage charm; or **Luciya International**, ((080) 224145-8, 6 O.T.C. Road, which offers comfortable rooms, a restaurant, and a tourist bus service. Accommodation in the very cheap range are crammed around the central market area. One of the best is **Sudha Lodge**, ((080)

605420, 6 Cottonpet Main Road, with simple, clean lodgings, hot and cold water, and friendly owners. If this is full, try the **Tourist Hotel** on Race Course Road, a rabbit warren of clean cubicle-style rooms.

BARS AND RESTAURANTS

Bangalore is the only south Indian city with a thriving nightlife, and most travelers find it a welcome oasis of good restaurants, bars, English-style pubs, and even a discotheque. It's also the only place in India which makes decent draught beer, best sampled at **The Pub**, Church Street. Modeled on an English pub, it comes complete with stained-glass windows, bar stools, and the daily draught on tap is only US$0.50 per glass. It's open from 11:30 am to

10:30 pm. Just next door you'll find **Mac's Fast Food,** a casual eatery with (buffalo meat) hamburgers, french fries, pizzas, and shakes. Other pubs to try include **Ramda Pub,** off M.G. Road, Indiana, St Patrick's Complex, Residency Road, and **Waikikee,** 11 Brigade Road.

Of the leading hotels, the **Windsor Manor** has several elegant restaurants serving particularly good Indian, North-west Frontier, Chinese, and continental food. Discriminating locals flock to the lobby-level Royal Derby, a classic London tavern which serves excellent pub lunches with a pint of draught beer. In town, try **Princes,** Curzon Complex, Brigade Road, the

Excellent Andhra-style food, served on a banana leaf platter, can be found at both **Amaravathi,** off M.G. Road, and **RR Plantation Leaf,** opposite The Pub in Church Street. **Woodlands Hotel,** 5 Sampangi Tank Road, offers delicious south-Indian vegetarian food, with as-much-as-you-can-eat bargain mealtime *thalis* and delicious freshly squeezed grape juice. At Bangalore's clean, proletarian Udipi cafés — located mainly around the Gandhi Nagar–Chickpet area near the rail and bus stations — it's possible to dine well on delicious south Indian fare for less than US$0.50! One of the best to try, the **Dai Vihar,** is a few doors down from the Badami

last word in Bangalore chic, with its plush Regency decor, potted palms, and tailored waiters. A blow-out three-course meal of Waldorf Salad, Prawns Crème Gratin, and Chateaubriand Steak, plus coffee comes to around US$10. Right next door is the **Knock-Out Disco,** the city's only discotheque, where overweight sari-clad ladies wobble with their husbands under flashing strobe lights. Entry is free to Princes' restaurant customers — otherwise there's a US$3 entrance fee. It's open from Tuesday to Thursday. Other local favorites, with good and reasonably priced Mughali, Chinese, and continental dishes, are the **Blue Fox,** at 80 M.G. Road, with its old-time band and two-step dance-floor; and the **Jewel Box** and **Koshy's Parade Cafe,** both with vintage waiters and excellent food, located within the quaint Raj-era Koshy's Corner, opposite St Mark's Cathedral on Church Road.

House Tourist Office on N.R. Square. It has cheap *thalis,* fresh fruit juices, and great *lassis* mixed in a machine that looks just like a 1920's dentist's drill. There's a quaint **Indian Coffee House** at 78 M.G. Road for early breakfasts with good strong coffee. It's full of amusement value — with its aged waiters in Nehru caps, worn convict-like cotton uniforms, and walls plastered with faded posters of Mahatma Gandhi.

SIGHTSEEING

Bangalore's few places of interest are concentrated around its large sprawling gardens. In the city center, it's worth making a promenade down Vidhana Vidhi (Bangalore's Champs-Elysées) to see an extraordinary Raj-era palisade of Greco-colonial public buildings bordering Cubbon Park. Here you'll see India's most impressive **Post Office,** the sienna-colored **High Court** (given a medieval look by straw "tatties" nailed up to keep out the sun), and the ash-red public library. The most magnificent building of all stands on the north side of the park — the palatial **Vidhana Soudha,** which houses the Secretariat and Legislature. Built in 1954, this four-story Neo-Dravidian-style citadel is worth a closer look. Permission to visit after 5:30 pm can be obtained from the Under Secretary (Protocol), Dept. Social and Administrative Reforms, Vidhana Soudha (**℡** (080) 79401).

The **Government Museum** is located on Kasturba Road. Established in 1886, it has 18 wings displaying an extensive collection of sculptures, coins, artifacts, inscriptions, and paintings excavated from both the neolithic-period Chandraval site and the great Harappan site at Mohenjodhao in Sind Province, as well as a portrait gallery with rare miniatures and paintings of the bejewelled, sybaritic Tanjore and Mysore rulers. The **Venkatappa Art Gallery** is a spacious modern extension, and houses many paintings by Venkatappa, who was court painter to the Mysore maharaja early this century. Works by India's top contemporary artists are also on display. It's open every day except Wednesday from 9 am to 5 pm. Neither the **Technological Museum** nor the **Aquarium** close by are really worth visiting. This could be a useful time to visit the Tourist Office, almost directly across the road, for information on sightseeing tours. At the entrance to **Cubbon Park,** opposite, it's impossible to miss one of the few imposing statues of Queen Victoria allowed to remain standing in India. Laid out in 1864, the park's wide sweeping green has original wrought-iron benches and is relaxing for sunset strolls.

About four kilometers (2.5 miles) south of the city's bustling market area stands Bangalore's historic **Kempegowda Fort,** Hyder Ali's eighteenth-century stone reconstruction of the orginal mud fort. Inside the fort walls is Tipu Sultan's wooden palace, with just enough elaborate paintwork surviving on the walls, niches, and twirling columns to give an idea of its former glory. Don't miss the tiny museum here; the antique etchings, documents, and family portraits provide a pocket history of the legendary Muslim leader Tipu Sultan (British India's arch rival) and his life and times. It's open from 6 am to 6 pm daily, and is particularly worth seeing if you plan to visit Tipu Sultan's fortress capital, Sriringapatna, 125 km (77.5 miles) away. The finely wrought marble temple almost directly adjacent to Tipu's palace will undoubtedly catch your eye — it's the Venkataramanaswamy Temple, built by the Wodeyars in the seventeenth century.

Bangalore's beautiful **Lalbagh Botanical Gardens,** situated a two kilometer (just over a mile) taxi ride southeast of the city center, were laid out over 100 hectares (240 acres) by Hyder Ali in 1760 with exotic plants supplied by ambassadors from Persia, Kabul, Mauritius, and France. With much zeal, the British added nineteenth-century pavilions, pebble paths lined with elegant lamps, fountains, flower-beds, and a beautiful cast-iron glasshouse modeled on Crystal Palace. Every afternoon, a band comprised of aged pensioners in epauletted costumes sends warbling, reedy notes from a bygone era wafting across the park. Magnifi-

cent flower shows are held twice a year — on August 15 to mark Independence Day and on January 26, Republic Day. From the gardens, you can make a detour up the nearby Bugle Hill to see the **Bull Temple** with its 6.2-m (20-ft)-high stone monolith Nandi bull, which locals claim grows larger every year. Close by is the **Ganesh Temple,** with a devotional idol of the elephant-headed god carved in 110 kilos (243 lb) of solid butter! Amazingly, it never seems to melt, and when it is ritually cut up every four years and meted out to pilgrims, another replica is created from the proceeds donated by wealthy patrons.

Cultural entertainment in Bangalore is best from March to April, being the peak season for performances of traditional Karnataka dance and music. Performances are always listed alongside the cinema guide in the city's daily *Deccan Herald.* Otherwise inquire at the Chowdiah Memorial Hall, Sankey Road, or Bharatiya Bhavan, on Race Course Road, where the shows are usually held.

ABOVE: Exuberantly-colored powders coaxed into finger-swirled pyramids, terra-cotta pots and dangling necklaces make up some of the *puja* items sold at this stall in Mysore's Devaraja Market. OPPOSITE: The Lalbagh Botanical Gardens in Bangalore.

GENERAL INFORMATION

The Karnataka Tourist Office, ((080) 578901, at 10/4 Kasturba Road, Queen's Circle, is the most efficient of a handful of offices dotted around the city. It's worth investigating a number of the well-planned and reasonably priced sightseeing tours on offer. Aside from useful city tours, there's an excellent 16-hour tour out to Mysore, Srirangapatna, and Brindhaven Gardens, with various overnight tours to the Hoysala temple towns of Belur and Halebid, the Vijayanagar ruins of Hampi, Ootacamund, and the wildlife sanctuaries of Bandipur and Nagarhole.

For air bookings, Indian Airlines, ((080) 79413, is located in the Cauvery Bhavan complex in District Office Road.

MYSORE

Mysore once held sway as Karnataka's princely capital, and an aura of faded grandeur still lingers in this leisurely city of angel-cake palaces, manicured gardens, and treelined avenues. Eclipsed by bustling, industrial Bangalore as the modern capital, Mysore is a quaintly rustic town with thirties-era architecture. This is India's "Sandalwood City", where much of the country's incense is produced, filling the air with dusky whiffs of jasmine, sandalwood, musk, and rose.

Mysore's name stems from Mahishasura, a ruthless demon king who, according to Hindu lore, tyrranized the people of this region until he was slaughtered by the goddess Chamundi. The city has been the seat of a succession of powerful ruling dynasties of the south since ancient times. The first to leave a significant legacy were the Hoysalas, who governed the area from the twelfth to the fourteenth century and were renowned for their patronage of art and architecture. Their magnificent temples and buildings can be seen at nearby Somnathpur, Belur, and Halebid. The Wadiyar maharajas then made Mysore their capital, ruling until 1759 when their kingdom was snatched away by the monarch's own commander-in-chief, the renegade Hyder Ali. In 1799, the British defeated Tipu Sultan, Hyder Ali's powerful son, annexed half his state, and restored an infant Wadiyar heir to the Mysore throne. The British set about expanding their empire in the south, and the Wadiyar maharajas ruled more or less under the protective thumb of the Raj until Independence in 1947. The British referred to prosperous, semi-democratic Mysore as a "model princely state", and adored attending the domain's lavish royal extravanganzas. The most famous of these was the annual *khedda,* a ritual round-up of wild elephants, with specially con-

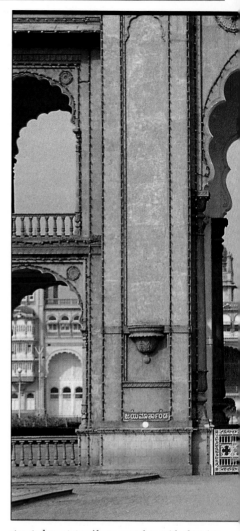

structed spectators' huts complete with electricty and running water, as well as evening entertainment in the form of banquets and a full-piece orchestra — all in the middle of dense jungle.

Today, Mysore boasts India's most spectacular Dassera festival (called Dussehra in northern India). Held during September/October, it celebrates the goddess Chamundi's victory over Mahishasura. This 10-day carnival of dance and musical festivities climaxes with a stunning procession of richly caparisoned elephants, liveried cavalry, and regal silver and gold carriages, accompanied by parading bands, flower-strewn floats, and fireworks.

ACCESS

Vayudoot flies to Mysore from Bangalore and Hyderabad, although Bangalore (140 km, or

87 miles) is the nearest destination for making Indian Airlines connections with most parts of the country. From Bangalore, buses depart throughout the day for the three-hour journey, or there's a regular train service which takes slightly longer.

HOTELS

There are two luxury palace-hotels, both moderately priced quirkily grand and built by the Maharaja of Mysore during the thirties. The most conveniently located is **Lalitha Mahal Palace Hotel**, ((0821) 27721, fax (0821) 33398, on T. Narasipur Road overlooking the city, an immense former guest palace painted with a confectioner's palette of white marble, lemon yellow, pale blue, and peppermint green. Its dome was designed after St Paul's Cathedral in London. Suites are crammed with rickety period furniture, and open on to balustraded terraces. Moderately priced. **Rajendra Vilas Palace**, ((0821) 22050, is a charming European-style villa set high on Chamundi Hill. Both the rooms and the former royal staff are delightfully archaic. There are stunning views across Mysore from the garden pavilions, especially at night. Transport is essential for getting up and down the hill. Rooms are inexpensive. In the city center, **Quality Inn Southern Star**, ((0821) 27217 fax (0821) 32175, 13 Vinoba Road, is modern and efficient. Rates: inexpensive. In the same league but slighty out of town is **Hotel**

ABOVE: A scalloped archway frames Amber Villas, the fantasy palace built for the Maharaja of Mysore, a passionate Anglophile who also created a replica of Windsor Palace on the outskirts of Bangalore.

Dasaprakash Paradise, ((0821) 26666, 105 Vivekananda Road, Yadavagiri, Mysore's top Indian-style hotel. It has a superb south Indian vegetarian restaurant. Heartily recommended for its comfortable colonial charm is **Hotel Metropole, (** (0821) 520681, 5 Jhansi Laxshimibai Road, in the city's heart. It has affable khaki-clad staff, rattan-lined verandas, and leafy gardens for sipping cold beers at twilight. Spacious Raj-era rooms have mosquito net-clad bedsteads and old tiled bathrooms. Rates: inexpensive. Excellent Indian, Chinese, and Western dishes are served at the restaurant. Across the road is the KSTDC-run **Hotel Mayura**

Hoysala, ((0821) 25349, 31766, the best of the mid-range hotels. This quaint old building has clean, very cheap single rooms comfortable air-conditioned suites in the cheap range. A courtyard restaurant serves good travelers' fare, and the Tourist Office is just next door. Another good cheap option is **Hotel Dasaprakash, (** (0821) 24444, in Gandhi Square, with a vegetarian restaurant and an ice-cream parlor. Cheaper budget lodges are crammed around the central Gandhi Square area, but you'll find the best value for money at **Hotel Anugraha, (** (0821) 520581, in the Thejus Complex, Sayaji Rao Road; **Hotel Durbar, (** (0821) 20029, has balcony doubles with attached bathrooms, and a popular rooftop caf; and the **Hotel Indra Bhavan, (** (0821) 23933, on Dhanvantri Road.

RESTAURANTS

Adventurous eaters will favor Mysore's unexpectedly good streetside south Indian cafés in and around Dhanvantri Road over the predict-

able fare provided by the main hotels. Try **RRR Restaurant** on Gandhi Square, or **RR Plantation Leaf** on Chandraguptha Road, for delicious Andhra Pradesh-style *thalis* served on a banana leaf. **Hotel Dasaprakash**'s cafeteria serves freshly prepared South Indian snacks throughout the day and great mealtime "tiffins" with 15 or so assorted dishes. Freshly squeezed grape juice is their specialty, though it's much nicer if you ask them to leave out the sugar. Opposite the Amber Vilas is the **Gun House**, formerly the royal armory and now a pleasantly restored restaurant with an outside terrace. It's open from mid-morning for drinks and snacks, with excellent Mughali dishes and a Goan band at night. **Hotel Shilpashi**, in CPC Building, Gandhi Square, is a travelers' favorite for relaxed evening dining. There's a good bar and the pretty rooftop restaurant serves excellent Mughali food, as well as Chinese and Western-style dishes. Another popular establishment is the **Punjabi Restaurant and Bombay Juice Centre**, 397 Dhanvantri Road, for good North Indian dishes and fluffy cappuccinos. It's run by an eccentric proprietor who bears an uncanny resemblence to *Coronation Street's* Ena Sharples in drag. **New Bombay Tiffinys**, near the Thesus Complex on Sayyaji Rao Road, is renowned for its overwhelming array of Indian confectionery, with an upstairs café for sampling them with a glass of chilled *lassi*. The vintage **Cold Drinks House** (founded in 1934 as the Brahman Soda Factory), Sardar Patel Road near Gandhi Square, has excellent chilled sweetened milk and fresh fruit juices served in clean glasses with straws. It's run by the spritely Mr Rao, who swears that his good health is due to his grandfather's recipe for delicious Sarsparilla Soda.

SIGHTSEEING

Mysore is pleasantly small, so most of its sights can easily be covered on foot or in short hops by taxi or auto-rickshaw. The Tourist Office runs excellent all-day city sightseeing tours that include visits to Brindhavan Gardens and excursions to Somnathpur and Sriringpatna. The city tour starts with **St Philomena's Church**, three kilometers (two miles) north of town. Built in 1931, this neo-Gothic cathedral with its two tapering spires and dazzling medieval-style stained-glass interior appears to have been uprooted from rural France and set down again on the other side of the world. In town is the **Sri Chamarajendra Art Gallery**, housed in the eighteenth-century Jaganmohan Palace near Gandhi Square, with many fine oil portraits of Mysore's royal family, miniature paintings, and all sorts of antique treasures including fine pieces of sculpture, Hoysala carvings, and rare musical instruments. It's open daily from 8 am to 5 pm. There's a brief stop at the **Zoological Gardens**, on Lalitha Palace Road, open daily 8 am to 5 pm, where over 1,500 species of animals and birds reside in leafy captivity.

The city's main attraction is **Amber Vilas,** the late maharaja's palace, a lavish Arabian Nights fantasy of domes, turrets, archways, and fluted colonnades which stands amid garden pavilions in the town center. Designed by the English architect Henry Irwin in the Indo–Saracenic style, it was built over a period of 15 years (1897–1912) to replace the former pal-

shoes must be left at the entrance. Avoid the nightmarish crowds during weekends and public holidays, and return on Sunday evenings when Amber Villas, lit up by thousands of flame-colored bulbs, looks like an illuminated mirage. The tour goes to **Chamundi Hill** (13 km, eight miles, by road, or four kilometers, 2.5 miles, by climbing the seventeenth-century pilgrims' steps), a picnic spot 1,065 m (3,500 ft) above the city. It was named for the goddess Chamundi, the family deity of the Mysore rulers. Atop the hill is the 2,000-year-old **Chamundeshwari Temple**, with its sculpted multi-tiered pyramidal tower added only three centuries

ace which had been partially destroyed by fire. Only the public quarters of this rambling fairytale palace are open to view, as this is still a royal residence. It's filled with eccentric enchantments: a vast Durbar Hall dotted with candy-striped gilt pillars, lined with giant murals depicting the life of the maharaja, and topped by a beautiful stained-glass roof. One extravagant room is followed by another, each a confused marvel of styles, with Italianate furniture, Byzantine mosaics, the local Hoysala-style carvings, solid silver doors, art deco statues, sweeping marble staircases, and plumed ostrich-feather chairs with *punkah-wallah* attachments. A fascinating portrait gallery is incorporated within the palace, with another museum of paintings and royal relics in the courtyard near several ornate temples. The palace is open daily from 10:30 am to 5:30 pm. Cameras and

ago. Nearby is the lurid statue of the ferocious demon Mahishasura — complete with a caddish, cheesy leer — who, according to legend, met his death at the hands of the vengeful goddess Chamundi, thus bringing peace to the local people. Halfway down the hill you'll see the 4.9-m (16-ft) -high **Nandi**, Shiva's holy bull, hewn in 1859 from a single black boulder with wreaths of carved bells and garlands.

The tour ends with a visit to the beautifully terraced **Brindhavan Gardens**, 19 km (12 miles) from Mysore, laid out against the Krishnarasagar Dam on the Cauvery River. Evenings have a gala atmosphere, with the whole park illuminated like a fluorescent fishbowl with sparkling

ABOVE: Victorian-era steam-train and an old Austin colorfully adapted into a bogie are two of the exhibits at Mysore's Rail Museum.

lights and cascading computer controlled fountains synchronized with music! It's possible to stay overnight at the ex-palace **Hotel Krishnajasagar** ((0821) 57222 rates: inexpensive, and views across the gardens, or at the **KSTDC Tourist Home**, rates: very cheap.

Back in Mysore, one of the city's highlights is the **Devaraja Fruit and Spice Market**, located behind Gandhi Square. It's an intoxicating maze-like strip of heaped flowers, incense stalls, and exotic fruit. Even if you're not shopping for Mysore's famous incense, sandalwood handicrafts, or silks, it's fun to stroll through the city's excellent emporiums. Among the best are **Cauvery Arts and Crafts Emporium** on Sayaji Rao Road, **Karnataka Silk Industries Corporation** on Mananthody Road, and the **Government Sandalwood Oil Factory**, located in the city's southern outskirts, where you can watch the distilling process and see how incense is made and then browse in the shop (open Monday to Saturday 9 to 11 am, 2 to 4 pm).

Train buffs should visit the **Rail Museum**, in KRS Road near the railway station, with its rows of vintage engines, decadent royal coaches, signals, and Raj-era memorabilia. Open daily from 10 am to 1 pm, and from 3 to 5 pm.

It's well worth making an excursion to the island fortress at **Sriringapatna**, 16 km (10 miles) from Mysore, standing between two tributaries of the Cauvery River and was once the stronghold of the powerful eighteenth-century Muslim ruler Hyder Ali and his legendary son, Tipu Sultan. Tipu Sultan was British India's most mercilessly powerful foe. He led two successful battles against East India Company forces before finally dying while defending his fortress capital against Lord Wellesley's army in 1799.

Tipu's larger-than-life persona, virulent hatred of Englishmen, and obsession with surrounding himself with tigers (both live and symbolic) make him one of India's most flamboyant historical figures. One of his most famous artifacts now lies in the Victoria and Albert Museum — the so-called Tiger Man Organ, an ingenious mechanical toy which represents a gleeful tiger swallowing a petrified English sahib.

Only sprawling battle-scarred ruins remain of Tipu Sultan's splendid fortress, although the dungeon where many British soldiers were imprisoned has been preserved. To the right of the entrance, look for a small plaque commemorating the exact spot where the fatally wounded leader died. Also see Tipu's mosque with its twin minarets and the ancient multi-columned **Sri Ranganathawamy Temple**, built in AD 894, with its large reclining image of Vishnu in his *avatar* as sea-serpent and central brass pillar.

Tipu Sultan's magnificent summer palace, **Daria Daulat Bagh**, and the family mausoleum,

the white-domed **Gumbaz** — with its interior lacquered with Tipu's tiger stripe emblem — stand unscathed amid ornamental gardens outside the fort. The Indo–Islamic palace, built in 1784 almost entirely of wood, has an extravagant multicolored interior of gilded walls and ornate arches. Stylized eighteenth-century frescoes depict the lifestyles of the Muslim nabobs and famous battle scenes, each full of symbolic intrigue. Upstairs is a fascinating museum displaying an array of Tipu's tiger-studded possessions, documents, and lithographs, as well as fine ink drawings of him and his family. The palace is open from 9 am to 5 pm daily.

THE HOYSALA TEMPLES

No visit to Karnataka is quite complete without appreciating the artistic grandeur of the Hoysala dynasty in the magnificent temple architecture found at **Somnathpur**, **Belur**, and **Halebid**. The Hoysala dynasty ruled the surrounding region between about AD 950 to 1310 when they were crushed by the iconoclastic Muslim rulers of Delhi. The finesse and artistry of these Hoysala temples is remarkable, with the fine-grained black stone so finely chiseled that it attains the lace-like delicacy of carved sandalwood or ivory. Hoysala temples typically have origami-pleated walls, ascending friezes, rise from a star-shaped platform, and unlike other south Indian temples have no towering *goporams*.

HASSAN

Hassan, 187 km (116 miles) northwest of Bangalore or 120 km (74 miles) northwest of Mysore, is a convenient base for visiting **Belur** and **Halebid**, and can be reached easily by rail or bus. The **Hassan Ashok Hotel**, (68731, provides the most comfortable accommodation, or there's a choice of several budget hostels. En route, make a detour to **Sravanabelagola**, 93 km (58 miles) from Mysore, to see its astonishing 1,000 year-old 17-m (56 ft) -high monolithic statue of the naked Jain saint Lord Gomateswara. Every 12 years, there's a near riot here as Jain pilgrims clamber up scaffolding to pour thousands of pots of water, milk, curds, ghee, flowers, vermilion, and saffron across the saint's implacable face in a sacred anointing ritual.

BELUR

Belur, 39 km (14 miles) from Hassan, which flourished as the Hoysala capital 800 years ago, contains the ornately carved **Chennakeshava Temple**, built in 1116. According to local lore, the Muslim conquerors came to Belur intent on razing this temple, but left awed by its magnificence. Every deity in the Hindu pantheon is said to be represented here, and some many times over.

HALEBID

Halebid, 16 km (10 miles) away, offers the equally splendid double-shrined **Hoysalesvara Temple**, built in 1126 and considered one of the most skilled architectural feats in the world. As you walk around the temple, the carved walls begin to seem like a voluminous scroll unfurled before your eyes, laden with an infinite variety of ornamental decoration. Nearby, an open-air museum displays an excellent collection of Hoysala-period sculpture salvaged from other temples. The Tourist Office runs day tours to Belur and Halebid every Wednesday, Friday, and Sunday.

SOMNATHPUR

Somnathpur, built in the thirteenth century, was the last of the Hoysala temples and is the culmination of their artistic achievement.

The triple-shrined temple, dedicated to Keshava, stands on a star-shaped base within a cloistered enclosure and is covered with panels of exquisite sculpted friezes depicting narratives from the great Hindu epics, the *Ramayana, Mahabharata,* and *Bhagavad Gita.* It ranks alongside the temples of Khajuraho and Bhubaneswar for the skilled execution and delicacy of its exterior carvings, and is especially noted for the six horizontal bands of decorative friezes ascending with lathe-turn precision from the temple base. The temple is open from 9 am to 5 pm daily. For a more informed account of the temple's history, ask the curator for a copy of P.K. Mishra's *The Hoysalas.*

KARNATAKA'S WILDLIFE SANCTUARIES

From Mysore, two of Karnataka's loveliest wildlife sanctuaries are only a couple of hours' driving distance away. **Bandipur Wildlife Sanctuary** in the Nilgiri foothills, lies 80 km (50 miles) south on the Mysore–Ooty Road. Amidst Bandipur's lush 400 sq km (154 sq miles) of bamboo, teak, and rosewood jungle live many elephants, leopards, Indian bison, spotted deer, macaques, and a great variety of bird-life. It's possible to observe the animals at close range, particularly elephant herds, from the road, from atop an elephant, or from a boat on the Moyer River. The best season is from September to April. Accommodation (which must be pre-booked) as well as all transport within the

forest is arranged through Bandipur's Forest Lodge and Guest House. Write to the Field Director, Project Tiger, Government House Complex, Mysore, or ((0821) 20901, 24980.

Nagarhole National Park, 94 km (58 miles) southwest of Mysore, in the beautiful Kodagu district, is famous for its coffee. The park spans 294 sq km (114 sq miles) of tropical forest, undulating streams, and swampland. It's inhabited by tigers, elephants, leopards, sloth bears, wild boar, several species of crocodile, and a rich variety of bird-life. Nagarhole, which translates as "snaking water", is crisscrossed with meandering streams thick with plump mahseer for fishing. Arrangements for hiring jeeps, elephants, and boats, for visiting Heballa elephant training camp, are made either through the hotel or Nagarhole's Forest Department. Delightful accommodation is offered by Tiger Top's riverside Kabini River Lodge, located just outside the park, which includes a converted royal hunting lodge. Excellent food is served, and there's a well-stocked bar. They also run the safari-style Karapur Tented Camp, six kilometers (four miles) into the forest, and both are open to coincide with the park's season from mid-September to mid-June, and bookable through Jungle Lodges and Resorts, 348/9 Brooklands, 13th Main, Rajmahal Villas Extension, Bangalore, or ((080) 362820.

OOTACAMUND (OOTY)

Set 2,285 m (7,500 ft) high in the lush Nilgiri Hills at the apex of Tamil Nadu, Kerala, and Karnataka, "Ooty" was the former summer headquarters of the British Government of Madras. Ooty was their mock-Sussex retreat: a bracing, eucalyptus-scented region of softly undulating hills grazed by plump Jersey cows, rhododendron-lined country roads, Victorian gingerbread cottages, milky streams thrashing with trout, and a cobbled town bazaar called Charing Cross. Today, India's elite spend their summers in a "Snooty Ooty" slightly gone to seed, playing snooker in the Ooty Club (a young subaltern called Neville Chamberlain first invented snooker here in 1875) and attending the annual fox-hunting, garden, and dog galas.

Ooty derives its name from the local Toda word *udhagamandalam,* or "village of huts". The area's original settlers were the Todas, a cattle-worshipping tribe whose women often have as many as four husbands apiece, and still live in small beehive huts on Ooty's outskirts. John Sullivan, the Collector of Coimbature and avid botanist who founded the first European settlement here, stumbled across Ooty's idyllic scenery in 1819 during one of his nomadic searches for rare flowers. By 1869, Ooty was the southern summer capital and an icon of Victorian India with its full social season and pastoral round of "at home" calls, horse-riding, and punting on the lake. Indian royalty soon followed, each vying to build a more extravagant palace than the last.

Raj relics survive everywhere in the pavilioned Botanical Gardens, the Anglican church spires, the nineteenth-century shops, and the dwindling community of British pensioners who preferred to stay on after Independence.

Ooty's main industry is oil extraction, particularly from the eucalyptus trees introduced during the nineteenth century, but also from

major rail junction, with an efficient network of trains to all the main cities.

From Mysore, the 159-km (100-mile) bus journey takes about four hours. The route corkscrews up thickly forested slopes dotted with precarious alpine villages, past the sun-drenched glades of Karnataka's Bandipur and Tamil Nadu's Mudumalai wildlife sanctuaries where elephants and monkeys loiter by the roadside. Mysore–Ooty buses leave the depot throughout the day, but the 6:15 am bus is best for quieter roads.

If you're heading for Coimbature from Ooty, the quickest option is the three-hour bus

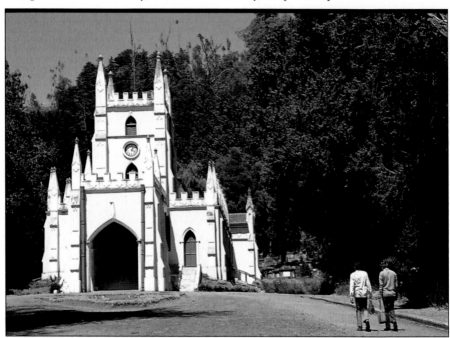

lemongrass, geranium, clove, and camphor. Tea plantations in the neighboring hills produce distinctive blends of masala, chocolate, and cardamom tea. Ooty's popular "season" lasts from September to October and from April to May, but the place is far more peaceful and less expensive during February and March. In winter and during the nippy (sometimes downright freezing) monsoon months, bring warm woolens and waterproof shoes to guard against sudden flash floods.

ACCESS

Ooty's nearest airport is at **Coimbature,** 88 km (55 miles) away, with direct flights to Madras, Bombay, and Bangalore. Coimbature is also a

trip. But be warned: this is a white-knuckle affair, as the bus tends to hurtle down the switchback roads. Between 20 and 30 buses leave Ooty station each day. The best option, though, is India's most enchanting rail journey. Ooty's vintage Swiss miniature train steams slowly down the steep slopes via the Coonoor Hills with their soaring rainforests and waterfalls to the lowland railhead of Mettapalayam. There's a 2:55 pm departure from Ooty which arrives in Mettapalayam in time to connect with the 7:30 pm *Nilgiri Express* (which also stops in Coimbature an hour later en route to Madras).

HOTELS

Savoy Hotel, ((0423) 2572, 4142-7, fax (0423) 3318, Club Road, which first opened in 1841,

The Raj-era parish church of St Stephen's in Ooty.

Across the Deccan

offers deluxe rooms in the original old hotel or in whitewashed cottages, both with comfortable thirties-era furniture and wooden floors, at US$30-35. On nippy winter nights, aged retainers shuffle in with hot-water bottles and light the wood fires. Good Anglo–Indian cuisine is served in the rosewood-paneled dining room, with afternoon cream teas served on the lawn. Mr Gordon at the front desk can arrange pony-riding, trout-fishing, golf, and visits to nearby tea plantations.

Hotel Fernhill Imperial, ((0423) 3910-7, a vast Swiss Alpine-style former summer palace of the Maharaja of Mysore, offers views across the blue Nilgiri mountains, romantically overgrown gardens, pavilions, and tennis courts. Each room is different. The multi-chambered suites at US$30 a night are filled with Edwardian furniture, old sepia photographs, and dusty objets d'art. The service is theatrically bad. Meals are served in the opulent Gothic-style ballroom. Hotel Palace, ((0423) 3931, has a similar vintage charm. It is the Nizam of Hyderabad's former retreat, complete with an annex for his summer "wives". Double rooms are US$15.

For mid-range accommodation, try Hotel Mayura Sudarshan, ((0423) 3828, Hotel Tamil Nadu, ((0423) 2543, or Hotel Nilgiri Dasaprakash, ((0423) 2434, famed for its south Indian vegetarian restaurant; all offer clean, simple double rooms from US$6-12. The YWCA, ((0423) 3008, Anandagri, which takes both men and women, is particularly good value. It has carpeted single rooms with log-fires and a good restaurant. The Youth Hostel, ((0423) 3665, has cheap dormitory beds for US$1. For lakeside vistas — most pleasant during the peaceful off-season — stay at Hotel Lakeview, ((0423) 3580 located outside town overlooking Ooty Lake.

During the off-season, hotels and lodges reduce their rates substantially.

RESTAURANTS

Ooty's main bazaar area is crammed with eating places catering for the seasonal droves of Indian tourists, but the Hotel Hills Palace, at 66 Commercial Road, has particularly good Gujaratimealtime *thalis* and a never-ending menu with something to please everyone from fussy Brahmans to brain-eating Zoroastrians. Your status as a "meat-eater or not, sahib?" is demanded at the door, as a kind of food apartheid is in force: partition walls separate the carnivorous types from the herds of herbivores. Up the road is Tandoor Mahal, good for Mughali and tandoor dishes, and the ice-cream parlour next door serves creamy concoctions made with real strawberries, figs, and mango. Both Chungwah, on Commercial Road, and

Shinkows, on Commissioner's Road, are run by Chinese families whose curry-laced Sino–Indian dishes are quite appetizing. Tehrani's, opposite the Youth Hostel, caters for Western tastebuds with delicious pizzas (made with Ooty's Cheddar cheese), baked beans on toast, and apple pie. King Star, "The English Confectionery" opposite the Tourist Office, sells moreish filled chocolates and divine fudge by the kilo. Prohibition is in force, but both the Savoy and Fernhill Palace hotel bars serve liquor without demanding permits.

SIGHTSEEING

Ooty's charming landscape provides a soothing break from the scorched lowlands, with plenty of opportunities for long strolls in the Nilgiri Hills, horse-riding, boating on the lake, or simply relaxing in rickety Raj-era splendor. Ooty town is very small, and its sights are easily covered on foot in a day; longer distances can be covered by bus, taxi, or auto-rickshaw.

Start with the terraced Botanical Gardens, a sprawling 21-hectare (50-acre) manicured paradise created by the Marquis of Tweedale in 1847 and brimming with some 650 varieties of plants. Visitors can buy seedlings and fresh-cut flowers from the curator's office. Ooty's "season" reaches its peak during May, with the annual Flower Show and Dog Show. A half-hour climb up the main winding path past ornamental floral beds and exotic thickets is the grand Raj-era Government House, still used by the Tamil Nadu Governor as a summer retreat. At the top of the ridge is a Toda community, whose lifestyle has been "modernized" with concrete shacks and Western-style clothing. (To see a Toda settlement where the tribespeople live traditionally in tiny domed huts and wear decorative tattoos, vivid handwoven shawls, and corkscrew curls, go to Kandal Mund, a village nine kilometers, or 5.5 miles, from Ooty.) From the Gardens' high cast-iron entrance gates, it's a 20-minute stroll back along Garden Road (turning left at Higgins Road) to St Stephen's, a parish church set in an English cemetery. It was built during the early nineteenth century with immense teak beams pillaged from Tipu Sultan's palace at Srirangapatna. Nearby is Spencer's Store, an old British emporium with 1940's merchandise and excellent local Cheddar and Wensleydale cheeses, and the red-brick Scottish Nilgiri Library, opened in 1868, where old men wearing pince-nez and mufflers study dated copies of Punch magazine and glance disapprovingly at intruders.

Just down the road, near the Savoy Hotel, is the Ooty Club (more properly called the

Ootacamund Planter's Club). From here, either jump aboard a bus or take a two-kilometer (one-and-a-quarter-mile) stroll to Ooty's scenic **lake,** the main focus of activity for coy honeymooners and large, raucous family groups. The **Boat House** (open from 8 am to 6 pm) hires out row-, paddle-, and motorboats, and also has facilities for fishing. A handpainted sign proclaims: "Rowers are available for rowing capacity including the rower's rowing cooly charges extra!" Nearby is a children's toy railway which circles the lake, and a small snack bar. At the open-air market by the lakeside, you can hire ponies for about US$3 an hour, with or without a hired escort, to trot along Ooty's mountain trails. You can also arrange to have ponies delivered to your hotel for a day excursion.

Ooty's **bazaar,** which stretches from Hospital Road and Commercial Road down to Charing Cross, is good for a leisurely stroll. There are all sorts of musty oddities: Chinese tailors who still use 1930's pattern books, shops specializing only in rosewood pipes and walking sticks, and photographers' shops displaying "Box Brownies" and yellowing photographs of pale-skinned debutantes. For the best collection of antique silver Toda jewelry go to **Suraaj,** about midway down the main bazaar (with a twin shop at the Savoy Hotel), and buy embroidered Toda shawls from a cluster of shops near Charing Cross. The bazaar is crammed with tiny shops selling oils, tea, and delicious Nilgiri honey. The Tourist Office at Charing Cross seems consistently to lack useful Ooty maps and pamphlets; you'll have better luck at Higginbothams bookshop nearby.

OOTY EXCURSIONS

Aside from walking, pony-riding, boating, and a scenic golf course open to paying non-members, anglers will find excellent trout and carp fishing in streams at Avalanche Emerald, and Parson's valleys, as well as in Ooty Lake. A license and tackle are available from the Assistant Director of Fisheries, ((0423) 2232, Fishdale, near the bus-stand.

There are plenty of invigorating walks across the hills, particularly to **Wenlock Downs,** eight kilometers (five miles) away, with impressive views across the Nilgiri Hills to **Dodabatta Heights,** 10 km (6.2 miles), which looms behind the Botanical Gardens and is the highest peak in Tamil Nadu at nearly 3,000 m (9,845 ft). Take a bus there from the main bus-stand, and enjoy spectacular views all the way down to the Coimbature lowlands from the topmost observation point. From there, it's a glorious 45-minute walk back to town, descending past tea gardens, forest thickets, and rolling meadows. (If you start

to wilt, there are plenty of buses plying the route back to town.) Nearby picnic spots include **Catherine Falls** and **Elk Hill** (both eight kilometers, or five miles), and **Kodanad View Point** (16 km, or 10 miles) for superb views across the hazel-colored mountains, and the hill station of **Coonoor** (13 km, or eight miles), where you can stay overnight at the delightful Raj-era **Hampton Manor,** ((04264) 6244 or 2244, on Church Road, offering period suites. Visits to **Glen Morgan** (24 km, or 15 miles), one of the most beautiful tea estates in the region, can be arranged through Mr Gordon of the Savoy Hotel. Given advance notice, the estate owners will guide visitors around and explain the tea production process; they can also arrange an afternoon tea.

To visit **Mudumalai Wildlife Sanctuary**, 64 km (40 miles) away, take the two-hour express bus to **Theppukady,** where the sanctuary's reception center is located. Mudumalai covers some 320 sq km (about 125 sq miles), a dense, deciduous hill forest wedged between Bandipur and Wynad sanctuaries. Its remoter regions are exceptionally rich in wildlife, and can be explored by jeep or atop elephants on a four-seater howdah. You're likely to see tigers, panthers, wild bears, spotted deer, gaur (Indian bison), sambar, reptiles (including the scaly ant-eater), and a great variety of bird life. The park also contains an Elephant Camp, where the harnessed heavyweights are tutored in the logging trade. The best season to visit is February to May, and you can conveniently arrange accommodation and in-park transport whilst in Ooty through the District Forest Officer (North), ((0423) 2235. There are lots of options ranging from basic dormitory beds in forest lodges to the most comfortable deluxe rooms for US$5 to US$10 at **Bamboo Banks Farm House** in Musingudi Village.

GENERAL INFORMATION

The Tourist Office, ((0423) 2416, situated in the Super Market building, Charing Cross, runs daily sightseeing tours around Ooty, as well as to Coonoor and Mudumalai Wildlife Sanctuary. Talk to S.D. Vincent, Venus Travels, at Hotel Weston, ((0423) 3700, about ticketing or transport arrangements.

OPPOSITE: A village woman carries firewood across a rustic meadow in Ooty.

Madras
and the
Temple
Towns

TAMIL NADU

Tamil Nadu, India's most southerly state — dubbed India's Bible Belt — brims with magnificent architecture, exotic pageantry, and age-old traditions — the legacy of the South's ancient Dravidian culture. Following the route from Madras through Kanchipuram, Mahabalipuram, and Madurai — the main trio of temple towns — you'll see some of India's most impressive temple architecture and experience the warmth and color of rustic Tamil Nadu.

TEMPLE ARCHITECTURE OF THE SOUTH

Dravidian architecture and sculpture achieved its zenith with the construction of vast, imposing temple complexes. These were not the single buildings of further north, but sprawling edifices in which the main shrine was lost amidst a warren of passages, sweeping pillared halls, courtyards, bazaars, and sacred bathing pools. Encased by concentric outer walls and dominated by gigantic, multi-tiered *goporum* gateway towers, they are stunning in their rich decorative detail. These places of worship were also public forums, where villagers would come to gossip, listen to devotional readings from ancient palm leaf manuscripts, and debate administrative and court matters.

Dravidian temple architecture follows a basic pattern, regardless of a temple's size, with a rectangular ground plan dominated by the distinctive *goporum*, believed to exert talismanic protection over the temple complex. Often rising to a height of more than 50 m (164 ft), these archways swarm with cavorting deities and mythological creatures — some human and some fantastic hybrids — which act out scenes from the great Hindu epics. Up until Independence, caste Hindus barred harijans, or so-called "untouchables", from entering the temples, so these poor pariahs could only worship the deities on the *goporums*, getting cricked necks in the bargain. Nowadays, temple authorities bow to modern public taste and have them painted up in an outrageous technicolor gloss, disfiguring their great antiquity.

Inside the temple complex stands the pyramid-shaped *vimana*, the wall and tower over the main shrine. This is entered through *mandapas*, cool cloistered passages. In the later Dravidian temple complexes, the designs of these passages became more elaborate, culminating in the so-called "thousand-pillared halls", although rarely do these halls contain this exact number. For instance, Madurai's

famous Meenakshi Temple's Hall of Thousand Pillars actually has only 997. Each temple also has its own sacred tank, several smaller shrines, often a score of ceremonial elephants, and its own ornate *ratha,* or wooden temple chariot. On the annual chariot festival day, the *ratha* is mounted with ornate bronze idols and paraded through the town in a ritual climax of religious fanfare. Most temples you'll encounter in Tamil Nadu's temple towns bar non-Hindus from entering the inner shrine, the sacred *sanctum sanctorum,* but there's still much to admire, with each detail crafted as though that particular panel, door, or fresco was in itself an individual work of art.

SOUTH INDIAN CUISINE

While south Indian dishes are often very hot, they are tempered with plenty of cooling fresh yogurt, grated coconut, and rice, and are generally much lighter on the palate than the rich, ghee-laden cuisine of the north. Fish is always plentiful along the coastal stretches of the south, and you can usually take your pick of pomfret, lobster, mussels, prawns, and crabs, traditionally cooked with spice-laced coconut milk.

The easiest way to order is to request a "tiffin" *thali,* which will either be served the traditional way on a banana leaf or on a large round metal tray. Even in modest cafés — known variously as *udipi vihars,* tiffin houses, and military hotels (the latter denoting non-vegetarian) — you'll be given six or so assorted vegetarian dishes that are constantly refurbished, a dollop of steaming rice, *papads,* puffed wheat *puri,* fresh *dahi* (yogurt), chutneys, and mango pickle. You'll soon catch on to the south Indian way of using fingers as expert all-purpose eating utensils — and marvel how Madras girls manage to make this look almost graceful — but remember to observe the Indian etiquette of using only your right hand, as using the left will earn you horrified glances from neighboring tables. You'll notice how the locals scrub their hands scrupulously clean before settling down to their finger-scrum meal. Don't touch the water which is slapped down as soon as you sit down; stick to bottled drinks, or well-boiled tea and coffee.

Typical south Indian staples include a dozen varieties of *dosa,* a crispy-thin rice pancake filled with spiced vegetables; *idli,* steamed fermented rice cakes; *vadai,* doughnut-shaped, black peppercorn-studded balls of deep-fried lentils and rice; and *utthapam,* a

OPPOSITE: Weathered stone bulls guard the seventh century Shore Temple at Mahabalipuram.

thick rice pancake which always comes with a topping — akin to a pizza — of tomatoes, onions, and green chilies. All are accompanied by fresh coconut chutney and *sambhar*, a spicy lentil dish, and make a nourishing protein-packed meal in themselves. Soothe away the chilies with a *lassi*, freshly squeezed fruit juice, or refreshing fresh coconut milk sipped straight from the husk with a straw. The finale to any meal is always a cup or two of the local filtered coffee, which is hard to beat anywhere in the world. Don't be alarmed at the waiter's antics if he starts sloshing the boiling brew from one beaker to another at rapid speed — he's performing "coffee by the yard", a south Indian courtesy which froths and cools it down to drinking temperature!

MADRAS: THE SOUTHERN GATEWAY

As a gateway to Tamil Nadu, Madras offers relative comfort, good cuisine, and a refined charm to travelers embarking on a tour through the state's temple heartland. Tamil Nadu's tropical seaside capital is full of commercial bustle, yet despite its sprawling skyline, it lacks the brash poverty of India's three larger cities — Bombay, New Delhi, and Calcutta — and has a languid, almost rustic, atmosphere that reflects the essence of south India. This is partly due to its breezy, surf-sprayed locale on the eastern Coromandel Coast, but also to the city's irrepressibly affable, Dravidian-featured, dark-skinned Tamils, whose easy-going ways, lilting language, vivacious culture, and devastatingly hot cuisine give even the seasoned India traveler the odd sensation of encountering another nation altogether.

Four centuries ago, Madras was still Madraspatnam, a small fishing village within a region that was ruled over by the greatest dynasties of the south, the Cholas and the Pallavas. Yet Madras has a long, colorful history of association with seafaring traders and missionaries: St Thomas the Apostle was thought to have been martyred here in AD 72, and Arab, Chinese, and Phoenician merchants first began trading along the Coromandel Coast some 1,500 years ago. A Portuguese cathedral bears witness to a transient occupation by traders from Lisbon during the fourteenth century.

In the early seventeenth century, Madras played a strategic role in the history of the British in India, long before India Britannica was a gleam in Queen Victoria's eye. The city's founder, Sir Francis Day, arrived with the East India Company in 1639, and leased 10 km (six miles)

of coastal territory from a descendant of the Raja of Vijayanagar to build Fort St George. The garrison camp within the fort's walls became known as "White Town;" outside sprang up Madraspatam or "Black Town" where the Indian community lived, many of whom were employed as weavers for the cloth trade. This was the husk of modern Madras, which rapidly eclipsed the East India Company's original settlement at Surat on India's northwest coast. In 1688, James II granted Fort St George the first municipal charter in India, and by 1740, Company trade represented over 10 percent of the entire British public revenue. At this time, however, the Company faced a formidable rival in the French who were just as intent as the British on reaping profits from India. They finally came to blows after war broke out in Europe — first the War of the Austrian Succession (1740–1748) then, with reversed alliances, the Seven Years War (1756–1763). The French attacked and took Fort St George in 1746, although in the pause between the two European wars, Madras was restored to the British in exchange for Cape Breton Island in North America. Madras was barely back in British hands before another battle for supremacy in the south followed — but this time the British defeated the French in a dramatic, unexpected assault on nearby Arcot in 1751, taking it against a force twice its size and saved only by timely reinforcements. From this battle emerged one of British India's lasting heroes — the young Robert Clive, who had persuaded his commander to let him seize Arcot and who later became the governor of Madras.

By 1772, Calcutta had become the most important British city, and Madras, despite its busy commerce, grand Victorian buildings, spacious mansions, and glorious coastline, was destined to be the most provincial of British India's quartet of major capitals. Nowadays, Madras combines its old legacy with a sprawling manufacturing belt for its main industries — textiles, tannery, cycles, and automobiles. It's also a major producer of films, and gaudy cinema billboards are the city's trademark.

Madras offers the perfect introduction for a first-time India traveler, as it lacks the intensity, crowds and strain of Bombay, New Delhi, and Calcutta, and is both unusually spacious and easy to negotiate. Madrassis are often ingenuously friendly, forever flashing mirthful grins at passing tourists. Somehow, long after you've left Madras, you'll be charmed by its simplicity — the men perfectly at ease in a knotted, sarong-style *lunghi,* and the women with fragrant blossoms wound into their hair with the same artless grace.

ACCESS

International travelers can fly direct to Madras from Colombo, Kuala Lumpur, Singapore, Shahjah, and Abu Dhabi, and British Airways operate direct flights from London three times a week. Madras is the most convenient base from which to explore south India, with direct Indian Airlines flights to Ahmedabad, Bangalore, Bombay, Calcutta, Cochin, Delhi, Hyderabad, Madurai, Port Blair, Trivandrum, and several other centers. Both the smart domestic terminal and the international airport are situated quite close together about 15 km (nine miles) from the city. If arriving by air, there's a PTC bus service (from 5 am to 10 pm) running between both airports and the city, which drops passengers at Egmore railway station and most major hotels on request. Madras port has passenger shipping links with Penang, Singapore, and Port Blair.

Madras has two railway stations: Egmore, which serves most of south India, and Central for the rest of India. Both are located quite close together in the city center near Poomallee High Road. Popular train journeys include the overnight *Madras–Cochin Express* (departs 7:20 am, arrives 9:40 am), the *Madras–Madurai–Quilon Mail* (departs 7 pm, arrives Madurai 6:40 am, Quilon, 2:45 pm), the *Bangalore Mail* (seven hours), and the *Hyderabad Express* (16 hours). From either station, you can make the short city hop north to Fort St George or eight kilometers (five miles) south to the Guindy National Park. Avoid bottleneck queues for rail tickets and head for the Indrail office on the second floor of the Central station, open from 10 am to 6 pm. Trains are generally slower, but safer, than the battered sardine-tin state buses which make traveling long distances a grueling endurance test. Both the Tamil Nadu State Transport and the privately-run Tiruvalluvar Transport Corporation have their terminals off Esplanade Road. If you intend to do much traveling by bus, buy the monthly *Jaico Time table* from any newsstand, which lists all destinations, revised schedules, and fares in south India.

THE CITY

Despite its ever-expanding boundaries, Madras is refreshingly flat, spacious, and uncrowded. Most of the city's sights are concentrated around three main areas. The historic seafront, **Fort St George**, site of the original East India Company settlement, is bordered by bustling **Georgetown** to the north — you'll find the main bazaars, budget hotels, and Raj-era architecture dotted around its main boulevard, Netaji Subhash Bose Road (known by old Madras-hands

as Parry's Corner). Close by are the two main railway stations, **Central** and **Egmore**, and the two main long-distance bus terminals. To the south, **Anna Salai Road**, also known as Mount Road, is the city's main 16-km (10-mile) -long boulevard and its commercial nerve center — here you'll find many state tourist offices, emporia, shops, restaurants, consulates, airline offices, and many of the top-range hotels and restaurants. Further south lies the **Guindy/Adyar** area, bordered by Elliot's Beach, with the nearby attractions of the Guindy reserves and temples. Along the Adyar River, one of the city's major waterways, stands a leafy pocket of grand old mansions, including the Madras Club, the Raja's Chettinad Palace, and the Theosophical Society.

Like most of the southern region, Madras has a balmy, hot climate throughout the year, although it reaches sunstroke levels between March and May when temperatures average 37°C (99°F) — compared by one eighteenth-century English diarist to standing within the "oppressive influence of a steam furnace" — and in the July to September months the area is prey to heavy monsoon rains and coastal squalls, sending huge breakers crashing on to the beachfront sands. The most comfortable time to visit is during its short-sleeved winter from mid-December to February, when the city comes alive with music and dance festivals, with performances of *Bharatanatayam* and classical music every evening. The English daily *The Hindu* offers a useful daily entertainment guide. It's certainly worth timing your visit to coincide with south India's most exuberant festival, **Pongal**, which celebrates the early harvest during four riotous, rice-throwing days during mid-January. You'll watch in amazement as Madras goes cattle-crazy, with people adorning their sacred cows with turmeric, garlands of flowers, sugarcane, coconut, and mango leaves, parading them through the crowded bazaars, and even staging bull rodeos on Marina Beach.

GETTING AROUND

Madras's streets can seem quite intimidating to the first-time visitor, with streets and lanes arranged in haphazard fashion and many of the old British place-names still in currency, despite an official emphasis on new, tongue-twisting, post-Independence names. To save problems, it's often worth asking someone to write in Tamil the names of places you want to visit before setting out. It's most enjoyable to explore Madras by taxi, stopping off at the city's three main sightseeing areas and then simply strolling at whim. You'll find cabs at any of the major hotels and at the main railway station, and can also hail them in the street. Fares are very reasonable and you can always bargain for a day rate, giving a list of the places you wish to see. Auto-rickshaws can do the same job for much less, taking you as far as the airport if desired, and cycle-rickshaws are perfect for negotiating the frenetic back-alleys of the city center, but remember to agree on the fare before climbing aboard. Madras has an easy-to-use city bus system — almost orderly compared to India's other main cities — and if you plan to cover much distance this way, buy the useful *Hallo Madras* booklet for a list of all the city bus routes.

Otherwise, the tourist office runs excellent conducted tours, staffed by knowledgeable guides, which whisk you to all the main places of interest in an afternoon. You'll get a good overview of Madras this way, and can always return to Fort St George and the Government Museum — where the tour stops are tantalizingly brief — for a less-harried inspection. The tours leave daily at 2 pm from outside the ITDC office at 154 Anna Salai Road.

Bicycles are perfect for gliding along Madras's flat Italianate Marina Parade for panoramic views across the steel-gray Bay of Bengal and lungfuls of salty, incense-scented air, dodging balloon-sellers, donkeys, fakirs, and family scrums. If you follow your nose southward, you'll eventually arrive at Elliots Beach, 11 km (seven miles) away, where the sea starts to look inviting enough for a swim.

HOTELS

The stately **Hotel Connemara**, ((044) 852-0123 fax (044) 852-3361, Binny's Road, has served as both a nabob's palace and a British residency and is an elegant oasis within the city's business district. Its ornately carved wooden lobby is filled with centerpieces from a dismantled antique Dravidian temple, and service is splendidly efficient. Ask to be put in the delightful old wing overlooking the pool, with spacious, luxurious Raj-era rooms. Facilities include possibly the best bookshop in Madras, a choice of bars, a good shopping arcade, travel desk, beauty salon, several excellent restaurants, a coffee shop, and a pastry shop. Rates: moderate.

Two other five-star hotels with similar room rates are located near the city center. There's the **Welcomgroup Chola Sheraton**, ((044) 828-0101 fax (044) 827-8779, 10 Cathedral Road, which has executive business facilities, a good swimming pool, a variety of restaurants including the city's best North-west Frontier cuisine at its replica of the Maurya Sheraton's famous Bukhara restaurant in New Delhi. The best rooms for panoramic city views are those on the top floor. The **Taj Coromandel**, ((044) 827-2827 fax (044)

825-7104, 17 Nungambakkam High Road, provides luxury accommodation despite its drab concrete exterior. As with the Sheraton, the top-floor rooms are the best. Of several restaurants, the Taj's Mysore restaurant is particularly worthwhile for Mughali and regional Indian specialties, with evening Bharatanatayam dance performances and musicians. **Welcomgroup Park Sheraton**, ((044) 499-4104, fax (044) 499-7101, 132 Mowbray's Road, lies about 15 minutes' drive from the city center and is popular with business travelers for its comfort and efficiency. Facilities include excellent Indian and Chinese restaurants, a health club, and a large swimming pool which at night sets the scene for an evening barbecue. Rates: expensive.

Good centrally located and inexpensive hotels include the **Hotel New Victoria**, ((044) 825-3638, 3 Kenneth Lane, Egmore; and the **Hotel Imperial**, ((044) 825-0376, fax (044) 825-2030, 14 Whannels Road, Egmore, set in gracious gardens and courtyards. Both have good Chinese, Indian and continental restaurants. A little less expensive and good value is **Hotel Maris**, ((044) 827-0541, right next door to the Chola Sheraton and despite its unexciting, utilitarian decor. In more secluded, downtown Mylapore are two reliably good and clean inexpensive hotels, both on Dr Radhakrishnan Road. At No. 69 is **Hotel Savera**, ((044) 827-4700, and at No. 72, **New Woodland's Hotel**, ((044) 827-3111, which has the added attraction of an excellent, cheap south Indian vegetarian restaurant.

But by far the best hotel in the very cheap range is **Broadlands Lodge**, ((044) 845573, 848131, 16 Vallabha Agraham Street, opposite Star Talkies in Triplicane. It's an immaculate old Moorish merchant's house with pastel-blue shutters — a traveler's oasis with simple rooms, a sunroof, a peaceful garden courtyard strewn with deck chairs and swing-seats, room-service meals, and boiled and filtered water. Proprietor Mr Kumar anticipates most essential needs: here you can make international calls, leave valuables and luggage in a safehold, hire bikes, and use the well-stocked, multilingual library. The accommodation choice is single rooms, doubles with attached bathrooms, and the coveted rooftop cottage. The rooftop terrace, popular for sunbathing, overlooks a large modern mosque. Broadlands' staff are a cast of characters, particularly Laxmiah, the rotund comic barber/masseur with his 1920's leather doctor's bag filled with archaic scissors and lotions — but he works wonders with a five-day bristle or an aching back.

If Broadlands' full, other good economy options worth trying are the **Tourist Home**, ((044) 825-0079, 21 Gandhi Irwin Road; the **YMCA** in Westcott Road, opposite the Royapetah Hospital, which offers both men and women basic, clean single rooms; or the **YWCA Guest House and Camping Ground**, ((044) 39920, at 1086 Poonamallee High Road.

RESTAURANTS

For stylish dining, try Hotel Connemara's outdoor mock-rustic **Raintree** restaurant, which serves the delicious Tamil Nadu Chettinad cuisine. Specialties include *chettinadu meen kozambu,* an aromatic fish curry, *kozhi varutha,* a subtly spiced chicken curry, and *paayasam,* a moist rice pudding with almonds, raisins, and

cardamoms. Each of the four main hotels has a potpourri of good restaurants and bars, but some are outstanding: the Chola Sheraton's **Peshawri** for superb North-west Frontier food; the Taj Coromandel's **Mysore** for a variety of Indian regional dishes and evening dance performances; and the **Golden Dragon** for Chinese food. Both the Hotel Connemara and the Welcomgroup Adyar Park offer outstanding buffet lunches — with a pick-and-choose mixture of Indian, Chinese, and Western dishes — complete with dessert and coffee for around US$5 per head.

For those with a newly-acquired enthusiasm for the almost exclusively vegetarian south Indian cuisine, Madras is a gold mine for good, extraordinarily cheap restaurants and it's fun to experience south Indian cuisine in more authentic surroundings.

Amaravathi, ((044) 476416, 1 Cathedral Road, is nothing less than an eating experience, and won the city's 1987 Best Restaurant Award for its superb Andhra-style food. Try their crab *masala* and *sora puttu,* grilled fish with spices, or opt for their spectacular set meal, served on a banana leaf. This includes a variety of vegetarian dishes, fish, prawns, or chicken, and, if desired, curd and fluffy rice, which the waiter liberally sprinkles with a fine lentil powder and hot ghee, leaving the traditional tamarind paste up to your discretion. Your fingers are supposed to do the rest (you're given finger bowls and hot towels before and after the meal), but if you find the idea off-putting just ask for a fork and spoon.

Other excellent south Indian restaurants to try are **Woodlands Drive-In** restaurant near the top of Cathedral Road, open daily for early morning breakfasts of fresh *idlis, dosas,* and *vadas,* with generous *thali* platters served for lunch and dinner; **Hotel Dasaprakash**'s pleasant rooftop restaurant on Poonamallee Road; and **Mathura** restaurant, on the second floor, Tarapore Towers, Anna Salai Road, which specializes in regional vegetarian fare, with a bewildering array of *thali* choices. Here you can dine on the pretty fairy-lit terrace or in air-conditioned comfort.

Along Anna Salai Road, you'll find an overwhelming variety of small eating houses, most open all day serving simple *dipi,* south Indian *thalis,* snacks, and frothed-up *lassis.* One of the best is **Mansara**, at 819 Anna Salai, and highlights here include their immense mealtime *thalis,* fresh grape juice, their "Family Rost", a one-meter (three-foot)-long *dosa* (only served if at least five people solemnly swear they will eat it!), and the urchins in pixie caps who wheel trolleys to and fro like dim-sum ladies in a Hong Kong restaurant. Nearby is one of the city's historic cafés, the **Coronation Durbar Restaurant**, just off Anna Salai at 123 Waljara Road. Head straight for its pleasant rooftop garden restaurant for cheap, reliably good Indian, continental and Chinese dishes. Just opposite the Tourist Office in Spencer's Building — the Harrods of the Raj — is **Fiesta**, extremely popular with tourists and students for its all-day fruity ice-cream, milk shakes, and good Indian and continental food. Outside the hotels, the best Chinese restaurant is **Chinatown**, opposite the Chola Sheraton on Cathedral Road, where the Madras chic converge for excellent Szechuan and Chinese regional dishes amidst an attractive bold red and green decor, dangling Chinese lanterns, and monkey-box screens. The **Chungking**, 67 Anna Salai, is another local old-time favorite for Sino–Indian fare. Set in a quiet leafy cul-de-sac above a musty music shop, it serves good garlic prawns, sweet and sour pomfret, and spring rolls. When you feel you can't look at another *thali*, try the **Taco Tavern**'s good vegetarian Mexican tacos and pizzas, located in the Willingdon Estate Building on Commander-in-Chief Road.

SIGHTSEEING

There are two main aspects to sightseeing in Madras — the historic Raj-era architecture within the city's environs and a host of surrounding attractions in the southern Guindy/Adyar area. If you're taking the con-

Survey Office), **Wellesley House**, and the original Officers' Mess (1780–1790), now converted into the **Fort St George Museum**. There's an extraordinarily rich collection of East India Company memorabilia, including original historical documents, a superb portrait gallery, armory, coins, medals, uniforms, antique clocks, and furniture. The museum's highlights include many fine original eighteenth-century lithographs and paintings by the Daniell brothers; a painting attributed to George Chinnery depicting the East India Company's plump adventurer Major Stringer Lawrence companionably walking with the Nabob of Carnatic; and a tiny

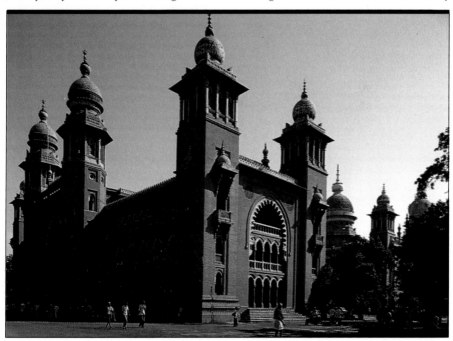

ducted tour, you'll first stop at **Fort St George**, established by the East India Company in 1641. The husk of the fort's original "White Town" still stands, much of it rebuilt after the French surrendered the fort in 1749. The ghosts of the Company's East Indiamen still seem to linger in these Georgian gesso-surfaced buildings.

The imposing eleventh-century **Governor's House**, with its grand black Charnockite Corinthian columns, now serves as the city's Legislative Assembly and Council, as well as the offices of the State Secretariat. Its marble-like surface is actually *chunam*, a hard plaster made from ground shells which gleams with high polish. Party men come to chat in the cool of the nearby **Cornwallis Cupola**, above which soars India's tallest flagpole. Other fine historic buildings include **Clive House** (next to the Archaeological

wooden cage into which one Captain Phillip Anstruther of the Madras Artillery, a huge, bearded officer, was squashed from September 1839 to February 1840 after he was captured in China while on some forgotten imperial mission. He spent his time sketching on old scraps of bark, the result of which so impressed his captors that they built him a slightly larger cage for more arm movement! Admission is free and the museum is open daily except Fridays from 9 am to 5 pm.

The oldest Anglican church in the East, **St Mary's Church** stands in a leafy, shaded corner of the garrison and still attracts a large

ABOVE: The bulbously-domed Indo-Saracenic High Court is the second largest judicial building in the world. OPPOSITE: Army *jawan* bicycles past a historic building within Fort St George.

congregation of Madras Christians. Designed by William Dixon and built from solid stone between 1678 and 1680 this exquisite chapel is suffused with the spirit of early Empire. Its courtyard is paved with some of the oldest British tombstones in Asia. The church's interior is cluttered with ornate marble sarcophagi decorated with mourning angels. Job Charncock, the founder of Calcutta, who rescued his Indian mistress from her suttee pyre, baptized their three daughters at the church font; Lord Robert Clive married at an altarpiece captured from the French at Pondicherry; and eight former governors lie buried within its environs. Permission can be granted to look at the register of baptisms, marriages, and burials dating from 1680. St Mary's Church is open daily from 8:30 am to 5:30 pm.

Just north of the fort, near Parry's Corner, stands the bulbously domed, ash-red **High Court**, reputed to be India's most remarkable Indo–Saracenic structure and the second-largest judicial building in the world, after London. Designed by Henry Irwin (who designed the Mysore Palace) and J.H. Stephens in 1892, it towers surrealistically over the bustling chaos of modern Madras. If you're on a tour bus, you will probably make a mental note to return for a more lingering inspection. You're free to wander through to its grand central cupola, where impromptu affidavits can be typed out by spectacled, cross-legged peons, and through its vaulted arcades where black-cloaked lawyers, wigs askew, converse in the shade of giant sparrow-infested matted *tatties*. Other spectacularly pompous Victorian buildings clustered nearby to include in your own tour of Madras are the Southern Headquarters of the State Bank of India and the General Post Office further north. Westward from here stands the Indo–Saracenic Central Railway Station with its classic clock-tower, Moore Market, and the Government Museum and National Art Gallery, all of which were designed by Irwin, one of the most prolific architects of the Raj period.

The tour stops next at the **Government Museum** in Pantheon Road, Egmore. First opened in 1857, it is one of the country's best museums, with entire wings devoted to natural history and archaeological relics. Its highlight is India's most extensive collection of Dravidian bronze sculpture, mainly from the Pallava (AD 700–900) Chola (AD 850–1350) and Vijaynagar (1350–1600) periods. Pallava bronzes are easily identified by their elongated grace and distinctive oval faces. The Cholas achieved an artistic peak with their robustly sensuous and ornately-clad bronzes, their archetypal females dressed in bejeweled harem pants, exposing boyish waists, perfect navels, and protruding breasts. Perhaps

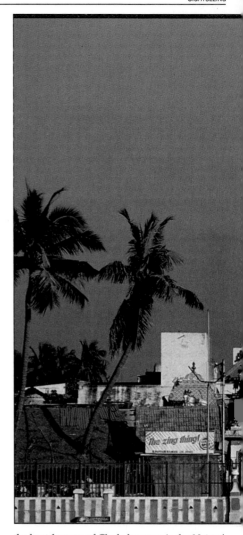

the best-known of Chola bronzes is the *Nataraj*, or Shiva, in a cosmic dance pose framed by a decorative ring. Also on display are many rare second-century Buddhist sculptures and the immense Amaravati stupa, said to have been erected over Gautama Buddha's relics. A pebble path leads to the turreted and domed **National Art Gallery**, which has a fine collection of old and modern paintings, including rare Rajput-, Mughal-, and south Indian-style paintings. Both complexes are open from 10 am to 5 pm daily except Friday, and there's a small cafeteria for cool drinks and snacks.

Heading southward, the next stop is **Valluvar Kottam**, in Nungambakkum, a giant concrete memorial to the ancient poet-saint Thiruvalluvar, impressive only for its ornate "temple chariot" shrine, a replica of the famed temple chariot at Tiruvarur. Opened in 1976, its vast

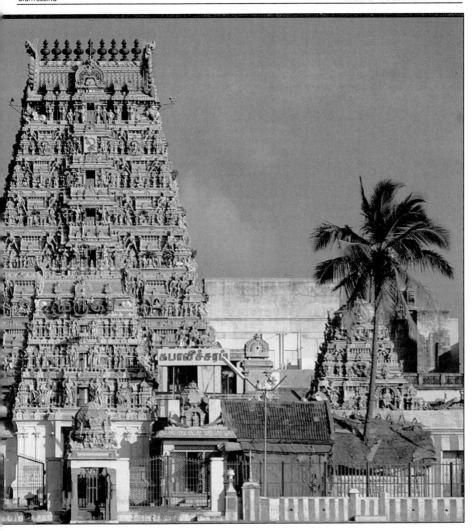

auditorium looks like an aircraft hanger, and contains 1,330 of the poet's verses inscribed on granite tablets.

A further six kilometers (3.7 miles) south lies the **Guindy Snake Park**, the brainchild of American conservationist Romunlus Whitiker. It houses a fascinating, well-documented reptilium, with over 200 species of snakes, lizards, crocodiles, tortoises, and spiders, all living in pits. Look especially for the massive 11-m (33-ft) -long Regal Python and the very poisonous Russells Viper, whose fangs inspired the invention of the hypodermic needle, and the swarming "Snake-Worship Termite-Hill", decked with flowers and lamps every Friday. There's an impressive hourly bout of unfanged snake handling, and you can witness venom extraction on Saturdays and Sundays between 4 and 5 pm. The fully-fledged research

center here manufactures anti-venom for snakebite cures. It's open every day from 8:30 am to 5:30 pm.

You can return later to visit the nearby **Raj Bhavan**, a former governor's Banqueting Hall built in the style of a Greek temple, with grand Corinthian and Ionic columns and marble terraces. It was commissioned by Edward Clive, son of Lord Robert Clive, in 1802. Renamed Rajaji Hall, and used for important public functions, it is open to visitors from 10 am to 6 pm daily. It lies on the periphery of the **Guindy National Park**, a 121-hectare (300-acre) reserve only eight kilometers (five miles) from central Madras. It

ABOVE: Kapaleeswarar Temple in Madras, dominated by a giant multi-tiered pyramid goporum (gateway) that is believed to exert a protective influence over the temple complex.

was once part of the governor's gigantic domain, and rare black buck, spotted deer, cheetah, civet cats, jackals, mongoose, and monkeys roam wild. You can return for an enjoyable day's excursion, either taking the urban train or the No. 45 bus from Anna Square.

Crossing the Cooum River into the historic Mylapore district, the tour continues to the **Kapaleeswarar Temple**, off R.K. Mutt Road down an alley lined with hawkers selling flowers, sacred ash, and tulsi-wood beads. It's a magnificent example of Dravidian temple architecture, dominated by a towering *goporum* gateway writhing with colorful, ornately-carved mythological figures.

The present Shiva temple was built by the Vijaynagar kings in the sixteenth century on the site of an earlier temple destroyed during the Portuguese occupation of Mylapore in 1566. Its spacious flagstone-paved courtyard has a bustling, forum-like atmosphere. It is best visited at sunset, when the temple priest conducts the evening *puja*, or worshiping ceremony, to a backdrop of cymbals, flutes, gongs, smoldering incense, and muttered prayers. Pilgrims stream in, clutching blossoms, shredded coconuts, and rice-strands and stopping to have their temples smeared with a blood-red *tikka* mark. The colorful 11-day *Arupathumoovar* festival staged here every March to April is most spectacular on the eighth day, when bronze images of the 63 *nayanmars*, or devotees of Lord Shiva, are paraded around the courtyard. You can also unearth treasures — silks, jewelry, and traditional brass vessels — from the tiny shops surrounding the temples.

Another ancient temple is the **Krishna Parthasarathy Temple** on Triplicane High Road. The tour makes a paddle-stop at **Elliots Beach**, the Long Beach of Madras, which is more peaceful than Marina Beach but not recommended for swimming. You'll notice a small memorial facing the sea, erected in the memory of a sixteenth-century Danish sailor called Schimdt who fell in love with a beautiful Tamil girl. So disconsolate was Schimdt when his mistress drowned at sea that he set sail, vowing to comb the waves in search of her body, and was never seen again. The tour finishes at the **San Thome Cathedral Basilica** on the Main Beach Road, said to contain the mortal remains of St Thomas the Apostle, who was martyred by stone-throwing assailants in AD 72 at the nearby hillock (you'll see it on your way in from the airport) now called **St Thomas Mount**. The present Gothic cathedral, with sepia-colored towers and lovely stained-glass windows, was built in 1896 on a site occupied by several churches since the original fourteenth-century Portuguese church. If you venture to St Thomas

Mount, you'll find a little chapel and a cell, said to have been his dwelling, with holes in the ground worn away by his knees in constant prayer.

The Theosophical Society

It's worth making a special visit to the stately nineteenth-century mansion housing the **Theosophical Society**, located amid an oasis of 100 hectares (247 acres) of forested parkland on the southern banks of the Adyar River. The Society, whose advocates essentially explored the spiritual nature of man, was co-founded in 1875 by the Russian Madame Blavatsky and her American financial mentor, Colonel Henry Olcott, who established their world headquarters in Madras two years later. A tireless traveler, Madame Blavatsky survived a disastrous marriage at the age of 14, and despite being described as "fat, unprepossessing and irascible", went on to build an impressive international organization, astounding skeptics by such feats as materializing a shower of roses. In her later years, she taught that evolution would soon dispense with the human sexual organs and that there would be two spinal cords in the body. Among those profoundly influenced by her doctrines were the poet W.B. Yeats, the artists Kandinsky and Mondrian, India-reformer Annie Besant, and Oscar Wilde's wife, Constance. There's an enormous library — open from 9 to 10 am and from 2 to 4 pm — stacked with some 17,000 books and many ancient manuscripts encompassing all religions and philosophies. You can picnic undisturbed in the leafy gardens which are massed with ancient banyan trees, and house a spiritual supermarket of a church, Buddhist and Hindu temples, a Zoroastrian shrine, and a mosque. The Society is open daily from 8 to 11 am and from 2 to 5 pm except Sundays, and the gardens from sunrise to sunset.

Nearby is the **Kalashetra Centre**, where students come from all over India (and overseas) to study Bharatanatayam, possibly India's most ancient classical dance form, traditionally performed by *devadassis*, young girls dedicated to south Indian temples.

Beaches and Bazaars

Marina Beach stands between Madras and the deep-blue Bay of Bengal. This 13-km (eight-mile) -long mustard-yellow sandy strip fringed by palms and casuarina trees is not exactly the French Riviera, but its balmy seafront throbs with activity. By twilight it throngs with milling families, resembling a sort of shantytown Hades of lamp-lit stalls, pavement entertainers, and wandering hawkers. Along its Italianate Raj-era esplanade lie several imposing public buildings facing the ocean — the Nabob's Palace, the

University, Presidency College, and the new lighthouse. Along Marina Beach are parks dotted with statues of famous Tamil writers and sages, flanked at either end by memorials to two former Chief Ministers, the late C.N. Annadurai and M.G. Ramachandran, who was a former matinee idol known for his Superman roles before he turned to politics. Fishing fleets bob into shore on their catamarans (from the Tamil, meaning "tied-logs") just before dusk, providing an interesting spectacle as they pile their seething catch on the sands and haggle with waiting marketers. Walking southward, at the junction of Pycroft Road and South Beach

heyday, Blacktown had an added oriental swagger in its shifting population of merchants from Portugal, China, Europe, and Arabia, who all added their personality to this historic grid of interlocking streets filled with crumbling facades and decaying godowns. A good walking tour starts at **Armenian Street**, just off Parry's Corner or Netaji Subhash Chandra Bose Road. You can't miss the **Armenian Church**, built in 1724, with its whitewashed interior hung with icons and paintings, and a leafy inner courtyard and cemetery containing the gravestone of a Christian who died in 1630, the earliest in Madras. The church is beautifully maintained, with

Corner, you'll reach the **Aquarium** and the historic eighteenth-century **Ice House**, which used to store immense chunks of ice brought by ships from American lakes before the days of refrigerators and air-conditioners. If you're serious about swimming, head out for **Golden Beach**, about 21 km (13 miles) south of Madras, where the sea is clean and calm, or simply head for the beach resorts of Mahabalipuram, 61 km (38 miles) away.

Back in the city, much of Madras's maritime history is crammed into the spice-laden cobbled bazaars of central **Georgetown**, west of the dock area and north of Fort St George. When King George V visited Madras in 1911, he raised his eyebrows at Blacktown, the original East India Company's indelicate sobriquet for the native quarter, and suggested it be renamed. During Madras's late seventeenth-century trading

a fascinating array of documents relating to the history of Armenians in India, yet has no priest or congregation. Clustered nearby, you'll find the **China Bazaar** and **Portuguese Church Street**. For livelier street-life go to the modern **Burma Bazaar**, located directly opposite the Customs House on First Line Beach Road near Parry's Corner. It's full of cheap electronics smuggled from the Gulf, fake Rolex watches, murky bottles of Johnny Walker, reflective sunglasses by the case-load, and shifty salesmen. Moving southwest toward Anna Salai Road, **Evening Bazaar** is riddled with tiny alleys each specializing in different household items. Its musty antique shops are open until about 9:30 pm.

ABOVE: Windbreaking palm trees along lonely coastal stretch in Tamil Nadu.

ENTERTAINMENT

Enthusiasts of Indian classical dance and music should time their visit to Madras to coincide with the annual cultural bonanza held during December and January, when performances are staged each evening. A dozen cultural halls stage performances throughout the year, notably the **Kalashetra Centre,** the **Music Academy Raja Annamalai Hall,** and the **Fairlands Tourist Exhibition Centre** on Marina Beach. The week's upcoming events are listed in Friday's *The Hindu.* Otherwise, this is your once-in-a-life-

sistible brightly painted terra-cotta horses known as *ayyanars,* traditionally made through-out Tamil Nadu as symbolic protection of home and hearth. Purchases can be shipped home, usually with minimum fuss, through either Beanie and Company Shipping Division, ℂ (044) 26894, Armenian Street, and KPV Sheikh Muhammed Rawther and Company, ℂ (044) 10346, 202 Linghi Chetti Street.

The best, and most convenient, items to buy are inexpensive, good quality silks, cottons, and handloom fabrics. **Co-Optrex,** Kuralagam, on N.S.C. Bose Road, has the most extensive range, with a ground floor devoted just to silks and

time chance to experience the outrageous for-tunes and lachrymose antics of south Indian cin-ema. The best centrally located air-conditioned cinemas are Sathyam, Devi, and Safire, and if that only whets your appetite, approach the Tourist Office about arranging a visit to one of Madras's film studios.

SHOPPING

Madras is one of India's largest cottage indus-try centers for textiles, glazed Thanjuver pot-tery, leather ware, and numerous types of handicrafts. Treasure-hunters will also find Madras full of musty curio shops and excellent well-stocked state emporia, and may find themselves making improbable "impulse" buys of giant brass-studded temple doors, elaborate south Indian temple lamps, or irre-

handloom fabrics, sold at fixed prices. **India Silk House,** on 846 Anna Salai Road, also has an excellent range. If you're beginning to feel rather travel-worn, Madras is the perfect place to stock up on fresh cheap cotton garments, many of them "export seconds" in the latest designs. Try **Hanif Bros,** 15-A, Nungambakkam High Road, for quality "Madras plaid" shirts, or simply comb an almost endless line of hawk-ers' wares along Anna Salai Road. Here you'll also find the state emporia, of which Tamil Nadu's **Poompahur** (at 818), Kerala's **Kairali** (at 138), Karnataka's **Kaveri** in the LIC Building, and the **Victoria Technical Institute** (at 765), are the best.

Poompahur has an especially good range of bronze figures, all reproductions of original tenth- to twelfth-century Chola sculptures. Interesting curio shops to poke through for sculpture, Raj-era relics, brass, and paintings include **N. Balakrishnan and Company**, 62 Montieth Lane, the **Heritage**, 135 Anna Salai Road, **Kalimuthi**, Krishnamuthi Mudali Street, next to Triplicane High Road, and **Aparna Art Gallery**, 781 Anna Salai Road. However, bear in mind that faking antiques is a well-developed business throughout India, and that it's illegal to take anything more than a hundred years old out of the country. Reproductions are often excellent, provided they are presented and priced as such and not as the genuine article. Excellent quality leatherware — stylish luggage, wallets, jackets, belts, and shoes — is best at **Sarala Art**

Centre, at the Hotel Connemara. The **Reptile House**, 161 Anna Salai Road, is also worth a try. And its neighbor, **Higginbothams Bookshop**, established in 1844, is the city's largest.

GENERAL INFORMATION

The **Tamil Nadu Government Tourist Office**, ((044) 869685, 143 Anna Salai Road, is friendly, efficient, and well-stocked with city maps and leaflets, as well as information on upcoming dance performances. Here you can book the Madras city tour, as well as the highly rewarding day tour to Kanchipuram, Thirukalikundram, and Mahabalipuram, which leaves at 7:30 am and returns at 6 pm daily. There's even a week-long package tour which covers all important destinations in south India, which leaves every Saturday at 6:30 am and costs

US$70. Boarding points are at the express bus-stand and outside the Government of India Tourist Office, 154 Anna Salai Road. Otherwise, consult the encyclopedic monthly booklet, *Hallo Madras*, found at every newsagent and most hotels, which has an exhaustive list of all airline offices, information centers, and travel agents likely to be of use.

THE TEMPLE TOWNS

Tamil Nadu's main trio of temple towns — **Kanchipuram, Mahabalipuram**, and **Madurai** — offer the perfect introduction to the cultural fabric of south India, with its Hindu faith, rustic simplicity, and deep respect for tradition.

At least two days are recommended for relaxed enjoyment of both Kanchipuram and Mahabalipuram, with excellent accommodation at the latter. Buses ply from these temple towns to Madurai, but it's more interesting and comfortable to return to Madras first along the scenic coastal road, and then take either the daily flight, eight-hour train trip, or deluxe bus to Madurai.

KANCHIPURAM

Kanchipuram, or "Golden City", 76 km (47 miles) southwest of Madras, is one of the most spectacular of Tamil Nadu's pilgrimage centers. The skyline of this rustic town is massed with towering *goporums*, for within its environs stand no less than a thousand ancient temples, many of them well-preserved masterpieces of Dravidian architecture. Kanchipuram is one of India's Seven Sacred Cities, but differs from the others — Varanasi, Mathura, Ujjian, Hardwar, Dwarka, and Ajodhya — in that it offers worship to both Shiva and Vishnu, rather than one or the other. Few of Tamil Nadu's temple towns are as interesting and beguiling to explore as Kanchipuram, with its almost constant festival pageantry, exquisite temples, swarms of kohl-eyed children, and tiny hut porticoes decorated with rice-powder *kolam*. Outside the entrance to the main temples, wizened hawkers sell assorted piles of blossoms, coconuts, powdered ash, camphor, sugar lumps (a symbol of wealth), incense sticks, conch shells, and sacred threads for Brahmans, the latter with a point-of-sale mantra hummed over it!

Kanchipuram is also renowned for its brightly colored, fine-quality silk, and silver

OPPOSITE and ABOVE: South India is well known for its traditional dance and drama. Special performances are held in Madras in December and January.

and gold brocaded fabrics. In the surrounding countryside, skeins of brilliant silk and cotton hang to dry beneath the trees, and the town itself is a hive of weaving activity: back alleys are matted with silk threads and hum with the click-clacking of looms.

Kanchipuram first flourished as the capital of the Pallava dynasty, great patrons of art who ruled much of the far south between the sixth and eighth centuries. The Pallavas were prolific builders who also turned their talents to establishing the traditions of silk-weaving and the choreography of Bharatanatayam dance, performed within pillared halls by barefoot *devadassis,* half-hidden by silken veils, who lived within the temple enclosures.

Of all the Pallava kings, Mahendravarman I (600–630), a dramatist and poet, encouraged the most inspired developments in Dravidian — the Pallava term for Tamil Nadu — temple architecture. His reign witnessed not only some of the monolithic *rathas,* or "chariot temples", carved out at Mahabalipuram, but also the beginnings of the towering *goporum* gate-towers clustered with writhing deities that became a Dravidian temple trademark. In its heyday, Kanchipuram was not just a major religious pilgrimage center, but also a seat of learning, attracting scholars, sculptors, artists, and musicians. The sixth-century sage Shankaracharya, who has been called the "Brahman Aquinas", set up an episcopal seat here which exists to this day. But by the ninth century, the Pallavas were on the wane, and Kanchipuram fell to a succession of rulers — the Cholas, the Badami Chalukyas, and the Vijaynagar rajas — all of whom stamped their own artistic style on the elaborate temples that can be seen today.

To see Kanchipuram at its exuberant best, try to time your visit to coincide with one of the major temple festivals. The most spectacular is the "car festival" held at the Kamakshiamman Temple on the lunar cusp of February and March, when temple deities are paraded in elaborately decorated wooden chariots against an extravagant backdrop of firecrackers, fairs, street acrobats, and folk theater. Similar festivals are held on a smaller scale by every temple to celebrate the south Indian new year during April, when the equally carnival-like *Brahmothsavam* festival also takes place.

Access and Accommodation

Kanchipuram is easily reached from Madras, either by regular bus services or daily trains from Madras, connecting at Chengalpattu. If you're taking the TTDC tour, which leaves Madras at 6:45 am and returns at 6 pm, you'll make only a brief morning stop at the main temples. It's best to explore at your own leisurely pace,

staying overnight at the TTDC-run **Hotel Tamil Nadu,** ((04112) 22562, Kamatshi Sannathi Street, near the railway station, which is cheaply priced and serves good south Indian fare. Bicycles are perfect for cruising Kanchipuram's flat, spacious streets, and there are plenty of bike-hire places. There is no tourist office, but the Archaeological Survey Office opposite the Kailasanatha Temple can usually supply maps.

Sightseeing

Scattered in and around Kanchipuram are some 1,000 temples, about 200 of which are within

the city itself. Only a handful are especially outstanding, and these are mainly clustered toward the northern end of the town, near the bus station.

There are a few basic guidelines to bear in mind before setting off on your temple tour. First, all "living" temples (where pilgrims still come to make *puja* worship) take a siesta break between 1 and 4 pm, so that early mornings and late afternoon are best for sightseeing. Secondly, be prepared for a barrage of dirty beggars and frantic, credential-waving "guides", and remember that one stern-faced "No!" is more effective than a dozen apologetic smiles. But have

ABOVE: Temple wall buttressed by stone guardians in the pilgrimage town of Kanchipuram. OPPOSITE: Courtyard view of the Ekambareshwara Temple in Kanchipuram.

plenty of spare change at hand anyway in case you get talking with temple priests or custodians, whose knowledge is genuine and their tales often fascinating. They will sometimes let you clamber to the top of temple *gopora* for stunning views, but they'll expect a token of thanks, something in the realm of Rs 10 to Rs 20.

The **Kailasanthar Temple**, located east of the town center down Nellukkara and Putteri Streets, is one of Kanchipuram's earliest and most exquisite temples. It's a masterpiece of early Dravidian architecture, with a small prototypical *gopora* and *mandapam*, and its sculptures, carved reliefs, and overall design poses a

Temple, with its soaring 57-m (187-ft) -high *rajagoporum* and massive fortress-like outer walls built by the Vijaynagar king Krishna Devaraja in 1500. Dedicated to Shiva, this is Kanchipuram's largest, most magnificent "living" temple, spread across nine hectares (22 acres). It was originally built by the Pallavas, and became a fusion of successive Chola and Vijaynagar craftsmanship. Within the dim coolness of its airy sandalwood-scented enclosures, the barefoot pilgrims seem dwarfed. Long pillared hallways lead to a monkey puzzle of ornately-carved enclosures, small shrines, and the inner *sanctum sanctorum*. Within a tiny courtyard

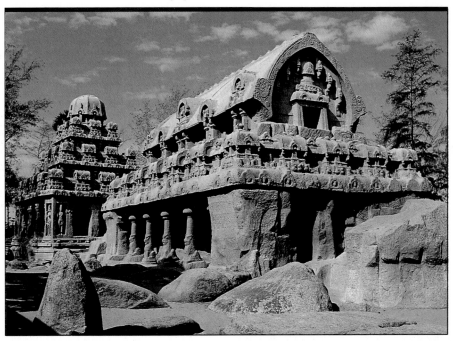

vitality and austere elegance closer in style to the monolithic rock-cut temples at Mahabalipuram. It was built entirely in sandstone by the Pallava king Rayasimha in the late seventh century, with the more elaborate frontispiece added later by his son, Mahendravarman III. Within the temple pavilion stand the three telltale signs of a "living" temple where pilgrims gather to worship Lord Shiva: the Nandi bull (Shiva's trusty steed), the tall *durajasthamba* flagstaff, and the *balipitha*, shaped like an inverted lotus leaf, where offerings are made. The temple's inner courtyard wall contains many miniature shrines, and if you peer closely, some of these have the fragments of beautifully painted stucco-work frescoes, just enough to give an impression of the temple's original splendor.

To the left of the nearby Nellukkara and Putteri Streets junction lies the **Ekambareshwara**

stands a gnarled mango tree, said to be some 2,500 years old. The temple was built around this tree, and owes its name to a corruption of *Eka Amra Nathar*, Lord of the Mango tree. Novice priests seem to materialize like ghosts from the shadows — some are barely eight years old, already self-assured, with sacred threads twined across their chests, heads shaved but for a tuft of hair.

A five-minute stroll further left, you'll find the **Kamakshiamman Temple**, with its large watchtower *goporums*. Built by the Cholas during the fourteenth century, it is one of India's three holy places dedicated to Sakthi (the goddess Parvati when she married Lord Shiva), considered particularly auspicious for marriage-blessings. Close by is the large Vishnu temple, the **Vaikuntha Perumal**, built by the Pallavan emperor, Nadivarman II, in the seventh century.

It has beautiful lion-pillared cloisters and sculpted bas-reliefs around the main shrine, portraying the history of the Pallavas and the wars fought by them. Another impressive Vishnu temple is the Vijaynagar **Varasdaraja Temple**, with its 30-m (98-ft) -high *gorporum*, thousand-pillared hall, and many ornate sculptures, among which is a huge chain carved out of a single piece of stone. But these are only the most famous of the town's temples, and you're bound to stumble across countless discoveries of your own, including fascinating weaving workshops. If you're serious about shopping, drop in at the **Weaver's Service Centre**, at 20 Railway Station Road, or **Srinavas Silk House**, at 17A T.K. Nambi Street, for reasonably priced selections of fine silks and brocades. Kanchipuram's delightful **India Coffee House** just down Gandhi Road, serves excellent cold coffee.

TIRUKKALIKUNDRAM

The TTDC tour makes a brief stop at this small pilgrimage town, 50 km (31 miles) from Kanchipuram and 15 km (nine miles) from Mahabalipuram. It's notable for its medieval Shiva temple atop the 160-m (525-ft) -high Vedagiri hill, where two eagles are said to come to be fed by temple priests every day at noon. Legend has it that these two eagles are actually saints who stop to rest at this temple on their daily flight between the holy cities of Varanasi and Rameswaram. But somehow, the birds have either "just been" or are "delayed", when visitors clamber up to witness this daily ritual! The vertiginous climb up the hill's 500 granite-hewn steps is the equivalent of a Jane Fonda work-out and earns you spectacular views. The less-fit get themselves slung into baskets for an alarming swaying ascent at the hands of the dandi-wallahs, whose one false step could send their human baggage plummeting all the way down! Another much larger Shiva temple stands within the village center and houses Tamil Nadu's "Lourdes" — a tank believed to have healing powers. Locals swear that every 12 years, a conch mysteriously rises from its waters, a phenomenon which attracts streams of pilgrims. These conchs are displayed in the Shiva temple.

MAHABALIPURAM (MAMMALLAPURAM)

This popular seaside resort lies on the gloriously empty white-sanded Coromandel Coast, 65 km (40 miles) east of Kanchipuram, or 58 km (36 miles) south of Madras, and is easily reached by bus. It began as a seaport almost 2,000 years ago, and was known to Phoenician,

Arab, and Greek traders. Between the seventh and tenth centuries, it thrived as a busy trade center established by Narasimhavarman I, nicknamed *"mamalla"* or "great wrestler", hence the village's original name of Mamallapuram. The Pallavas left an astonishing legacy of unique monolithic rock-cut temples, caves, massive bas-reliefs, and one remaining shore temple — and these are the oriental marvels that visitors flock to see today.

Collectively, these open-air structures are the earliest known examples of Dravidian architecture in existence, built by the Pallava kings during a creative frenzy of temple-build-

ing in the seventh century. Mysteriously, the Pallavas deserted the site, and these ancient architectural treasures lay undiscovered until the late eighteenth century.

You could start your tour close to the village center, with the most famous of the bas-reliefs: the immense **"Arjuna's Penance"**, a huge 27-m (88-ft) -long and nine-meter (30-ft) -high frieze crammed with a Noah's Ark of beasts, birds, and mythological figures — including life-sized elephants — sculpted across a whaleback-shaped rock. Built during the reign of Narasimhavarman Pallava (circa 630–670), archaeologists have long debated whether it portrays the Mahabharata fable in which the mortal Arjuna undergoes penance to Lord Shiva for his guilt in killing his fellow humans alongside Krishna; or the mythical tale of the descent of the holy river Ganges to the earth — depicted by a natural fissure in the rock face. To the right, you'll see Lord Shiva letting the floodwaters flow through his hair, preventing the world from being destroyed by the impact of its descent. Either way, the panel is nothing less than a brilliant piece of

ABOVE: Gypsy waifs are eerily dwarfed beside Krishna's gravity-defying "Butterball" on the mountain slopes of Mahabalipuram. OPPOSITE: Ancient stone-hewn temples within the group of the Five Rathas at Mabalipuram.

artistry, filled with realistic, humorous touches: cavorting mice at the elephants' feet, a deer scratching its face with its hoof, and an emaciated hermit doing penance by standing on one foot, whose ascetic posturing is mocked by a cat striking the same pose.

The nearby hillside is dotted with eight *mandapams,* shallow rock-cut cave temples, each sculpted with fine bas-reliefs depicting scenes from Hindu mythology, although two were left unfinished. The finest and largest of these is the **Krishna Mandapam**, which shows Krishna using Mount Govardhann as a sort of protective umbrella to save his flocks of shepherds and animals from Indra, a vengeful rain-god. Take the path just left of the "Penance" for an easy climb up the hill — site of several scattered temple *mandapams,* and **Krishna's Butterball**, a massive boulder precariously balanced on the hill's slope. For stunning views across Mahabalipuram, climb the tall lighthouse at the rear of the hill, open to visitors until noon. Just below the lighthouse, the **Mahishasuramardhini Cave**, fronted by a lion-pillared portico, has especially exquisite reliefs, with bas-reliefs of Lord Vishnu sleeping on the coils of the serpent Adisesha and of the Goddess Durga, better known as Kali, seated on a lion about to kill the buffalo-headed demon, Mahishasura.

Back on Beach Road, take the road to your left for a 15-minute walk down to the casuarina tree-sheltered sandy clearing containing the monolithic seventh-century **Five Rathas**. Each of these miniature "temple chariots" is a stupendous work of art, sculpted into architecture from gigantic boulders, and covered with ornate porches, pillars, and statuary. Although these temples have stylistic links to early Buddhist chapels and monasteries, they contain the embryonic forms of later Dravidian architecture — the *goporums, vimanas,* and multi-pillared halls. They are named after the Pancha Pandava, the five hero brothers of the epic *Maharabharata,* and guarded by three stone guardians: a lion, an elephant, and a nandi-bull.

Of Mahabalipuram's ancient "Seven Pagodas", only a single desolate **Shore Temple** stands on the coastline, at the end of the main Beach Road. Built by the Pallava king Rajasimha during the late seventh century, this simple, pagoda-roofed structure is one of south India's oldest temples. Assaulted by the elements, many of the temple's exquisite reliefs have been worn to obscurity, but its original splendor is still visible. This two-spired temple is unique in that it houses shrines to both Shiva and Vishnu, the latter containing a splendid 2.5-m (eight-feet) -long bas-relief of Vishnu reclining on his serpent couch. A rear chamber contains rem-

nants of a 16-sided granite phallic lingam, which originally touched the ceiling, and a bas-relief depicting a sacred cow forever in the throes of sacrificial slaughter. Rows of stone bulls guard the temple courtyard. The temple's modern neighbor is a bulbously ugly nuclear power plant, visible 10 km (six miles) further up the coastline.

Back in town, there's a good open-air museum, dozens of tiny souvenir shops, and a government-funded **School of Sculpture**, where sculptors create excellent replicas of ancient Indian carvings in marble, soapstone, and granite, all sold at reasonable prices. It's diagonally opposite the bus-stop and is open from 9 am to 1 pm, and 2 to 6 pm, closed Tuesdays. Local information is provided by the tourist office, ((04113) 232, in East Raja Street, and the useful *Guide to Mahsbalipuram* booklet.

Hotels

For a winning combination of comfortable lodgings, excellent food, and a perfect, quiet stretch of surf for swimming, go to **Silversands Beach Resort** ((04113) 2228, about two kilometers (1.2 miles) along the coast. It has sea-facing air-conditioned deluxe rooms or deluxe beach villas, all with tasteful south Indian decor. Good Indian, continental, and Chinese food is served, but fresh seafood dishes here are simply outstanding. Rates: inexpensive. The ITDC-run **Ashok Temple Bay Resort**, ((04113) 2251, is slightly more expensive yet is less stylish, despite secluded cottages, a swimming pool, restaurant, and bar. The TTDC-run **Shore Temple Beach Resort**, ((04113) 235, 268, is cheap-range resort option, with a complex of double-tiered cottages right on the sands. There's a simple cafeteria-style restaurant, swimming pool, and

tennis court. Shoe-string budget lodges in town include the **Mamalla Bhavan**, ((04113) 250, and the ITDC-run **Youth Camp**, near the Shore Temple, which has dormitory beds for US$1, and spartan mosquito-infested rooms for US$2. Some visitors swear by the "authentic" experience of lodging with village families, paying about US$4 per week for the local version of "bed and breakfast" — *charpoy* and *chai*. Of a host of friendly, ramshackle budget beach-cafés, try the **Village Restaurant**, the **Sunset**, and the **Rose Garden** for excellent fresh seafood and travelers' fare.

ABOVE: A wandering showman orchestrates a beachfront battle between a mongoose and a cobra near the Shore Temple.

The **Mahabalipuram–Madras Road** is worth several stops. This 58-km (36-mile) -long coastal ribbon of road takes you first to the **Crocodile Farm**, which lies 16 km (10 miles) from Mahabalipuram. Like Madras' Snake Farm, it was established by Romulus Whitaker to breed rare species of crocodiles in captivity. Visitors peer down into large swampy enclosures housing some 516 reptiles. "Jaws 3", the largest captive crocodile in India, is the star attraction, and crowds form to watch him chew his way through a lunch of bandicoots and beef steaks.

At the sleepy historic fishing village of **Covelong**, 20 km (12 miles) from Mahabalipuram, the remains of an old fort have been converted into the Coromandel Coast's finest luxury resort: the five-star, **Fishermen's Cove**, ((04114) 268, run by the Taj Group and comparable to their Fort Aguada resort in Goa. There's a choice of well-furnished, sea-facing rooms outfitted with all modern conveniences, or private beach cottages right on the sands. Facilities include wind-surfing, car rental, a lovely swimming pool, terrace restaurant and bar, shopping arcade, and business services. Rates: inexpensive to moderate.

Just 18 km (11 miles) short of Madras is the **Cholamandalam Artists Village**, a seaside commune started during the sixties where a community of artists, sculptors, and potters live and work. There's a continual exhibition of works for sale, and visitors are often invited in to meet the artists. Those with a creative bent can stay at a clean, simple guesthouse and attend workshops in batik-dyeing, sculpture, painting, or fabric-printing.

MADURAI

Lying 472 km (293 miles) south of Madras, Madurai is one of India's oldest and most illustrious cities, an oasis of traditional Tamil culture dominated by magnificent towering temple complexes. Founded over 2,500 years ago on the lushly fertile banks of the Vaigai River, it retains much of its distinctive heritage, along with a leisurely old-world charm. The most famous of all Tamil Nadu's pilgrimage centers, Madurai's overwhelming attraction for visitors is the giant fortress-like medieval **Meenakshi Temple,** with its nine soaring stucco-work *goporums*. Acknowledged as the finest, and one of the largest, examples of Dravidian architecture, it embraces much of the city with ever-rippling rings of stone battlements, tanks, and corridors. The elaborate ebb and flow of its temple life has changed little for centuries, and its exotic bazaars hum with a carnival atmosphere and are full of temple-of-

ferings, barefoot devotees, sacred ash-smeared mystics, and wailing music. Tiny shops are full of unexpected treasures — traditional brass temple lamps, jewelry, handwoven silks, tie-dye fabrics, and stone carvings.

Legend tells how Madurai, "the city of nectar", was formed by a single drop of water shaken from Lord Shiva's locks, in answer to a prayer of the Pandyan king Kulasekera for a new capital during the sixth century BC. The Pandyas ruled much of south India from Madurai until the thirteenth century, initiating a renaissance of Tamil literature, art, and architecture as the seat of the *Sangam*, or Tamil Academy. The city fell to the Cholas during the eleventh and twelfth centuries, and was to change hands several times — first to the Delhi Sultans, then the Vijaynagars, followed by the cultivated Nayak rulers who built Madurai as we see it today, laid out in the pattern of a lotus flower with the immense Meenakshi Temple at its core. The Nayaks ruled from 1599 to 1781, when they were ousted by British troops who destroyed the temple's defenses, filled in its moat fort, and built four broad streets known as the *veli*, or "outer streets", which now mark the limits of the old city. You'll find most of Madurai's sights concentrated here, as well as the budget lodges, restaurants, the main Tourist Office (((0452) 22957, West Veli Street), GPO, bus stations, and railway station. Madurai's modern cantonment area lies on the northern banks of the Vaigai River — there's little to see here, but this is where the better hotels are located. Allow yourself at least two days for leisurely sightseeing, either on foot or by handy cycle-rickshaw, nicest in the cool of early evening.

The best time to visit is the cool season from October to March, but it's worth coming a little later for the most spectacular month-long **Chithirai Festival** in April and May, when Madurai explodes with bizarre and wonderful pageantry for the "marriage" of Goddess Meenakshi and Lord Sundareswarar. As many as 10,000 pilgrims stream into the city each day. The **Teppam**, or **"Float" Festival** which is just as interesting, is held during January and February at the Mariamman tank's island temple.

Access

Madurai is easily accessible from Madras, with a choice of a daily flight, an eight-hour train journey, and frequent buses. From either Kanchipuram or Mahabalipuram, buses take about 10 wearisome hours. Madurai is also connected by air to Cochin and Bangalore, and well-connected by rail directly with Bangalore, Quilon, and — for temple-addicts — the other major Tamil temple cities of Rameswaram,

Tiruchirapalli (Trichy), Thanjavur (Tanjore), and Tirupati. Buses ply to all major south Indian centers, and from here, Kanya Kumari, the "Land's End" of India, is only 150 km (94 miles), a six-hour bus journey. From Kanya Kumari you can conveniently continue travelling through Kerala state by taking the early morning express bus to Kovalam beach, a pleasant three-and-a-half-hour trip.

Hotels

Of Madurai's two top-class hotels, the best is the Taj Group's three-star **Pandyan Hotel, (** (0452) 42471, Race Course Road, set in a pretty garden with pleasant, well-furnished rooms. Rates: inexpensive. It has Madurai's best restaurant, and useful facilities include a car rental, travel agency, bank, beauty parlor, and shopping arcade. Otherwise, try the similarly priced **Hotel Madurai Ashok, (** (0452) 42531, Algarkoil Road, which has clean rooms, or the more central, cheaply priced TTDC-run **Hotel Tamil Nadu, (** (0452) 424-6568, West Veli Street, with good air-conditioned doubles, even cheaper "fancooled" rooms and classic south Indian meals. You'll see dozens of very cheap hotels and cafés clustered along Town Hall Road within the old town, but **Hotel Apsara, (** (0452) 31444, West Masi Street, rates high with travelers. Outside the hotels, good, simple south Indian breakfasts and *thali* meals can be had at **Amutham** and the **Indo–Ceylon Restaurant**, both on Town Hall Road.

Sightseeing

Located in the center of the old town, the magnificent **Meenakshi Temple** is the classic monument to Madurai's Dravidian heritage, and seethes with an astonishing profusion of sculpted figures, ornamental pillars, and cloistered courtyards. Much of this massive complex — which covers six hectares (15 acres) — was built during the seventeenth century by the Nayak kings, although the Vijaynagar rulers renovated it extensively. It comprises two main sanctums, one dedicated to the goddess Meenakshi — a "fish-eyed" Pandyan princess born with three breasts, one of which miraculously disappeared when she met her true love, Shiva, in the form of Lord Sundareswara, up on Mount Kailasha; the other is dedicated to her famous consort, Shiva himself. Of four leviathan tapering *goporums* surrounding the temple complex, the southern gateway eclipses them all with a height of nearly 50 m (164 ft). Within are five smaller *goporums*, enclosing two slender, gilt-smothered *vimanas*, or central shrines. Highlights include its famous **Musical Pillars** — 22 tapering rods, each carved out of a single block of granite, which sound an arpeggio of

musical notes when tapped; and the ornate **Hall of a Thousand Pillars**, actually 985, with two small shrines standing in the space reserved for the remaining 15 pillars. Part of the hall has been turned into a museum with a fascinating, though poorly-lit, display of antique art treasures, sculpture, religious icons, and photographs charting the development of Dravidian architecture. There's plenty to see — one enthusiastic visitor said he spent two entire days wandering through its imposing enclosure — and only the inner sanctum is barred to non-Hindus. Evenings can be spent very pleasantly listening to temple music performed outside the Meenakshi Amman shrine between 6 to 7:30 pm and 9 to 10 pm. The main temple complex is open daily from 5 am to 12:30 pm and 4 to 10 pm, and there's a peculiar rule that photos can only be taken between 1 and 4 pm on payment of Rs 5.

A short 10-minute cycle-rickshaw ride brings you to the seventeenth-century **Tirumalai Nayak Palace**, a vast Indo–Saracenic abode notable for its elegant domes, colonnades, and pavilions. As a sort of south Indian Versailles, it so captivated Lord Napier, the Governor of Madras during the 1860's, that he restored it, although today it is only a quarter of its original size. Its imposing Main Hall, as big as a football field, was originally Tirumalai Nayak's boudoir, where he was royally entertained by dancers, musicians, and court fakirs. The courtyard outside was used for religious pageants and gladiatorial fights. Open from 8 am to 4 pm daily, there's a museum and a good sound and light show here daily at 6:45 pm, relating the history of the Nayak dynasty.

There are several other places of interest. The **Mariamman Teppakkulam Tank**, built in 1646, with its picturesque island temple reached by boat, lies five kilometers (three miles) east of the city center. There's a good **Gandhi Museum**, five kilometers (three miles) north of the city center, which houses many of the Mahatma's personal relics, including the bloodstained dhoti he was assassinated in and his glasses. Within the same complex is the **Government Museum** and various south Indian crafts and textile displays, all open daily between 10 am to 1 pm and 2 to 6 pm except Wednesdays.

From the central bus-stand, you can take a N° 5 bus out to the impressive rock-cut temple of **Tirupparankundrum**, eight kilometers (five miles) away. Carved into the side of a mountain, it is one of the six holy shrines of Subrahmanya, the second son of Shiva, and throbs with colorful activity as pilgrims, holy-men, and holidaying Indians come armed with lamp-lit bowls, coconuts, garlands, and incense for Shiva's blessings.

The Deep South Trail

KERALA: COCONUTS AND CATHEDRALS

Kerala instantly disarms travel-weary visitors with its beautiful, shimmering beaches, sun-filtered glades of palm trees, and green lowlands.

Villagers claim their land was created by the war-mongering god Parashurama, who was persuaded to change his bloodthirsty ways and throw away his axe. So noble was his gesture, the legend goes, that when the axe fell from heaven it landed in Southern India and formed the fertile Malabar Coast on the Arabian Sea.

This narrow, verdant strip of land is one of India's wealthiest states, criss-crossed with mossed backwaters and bursting with paddy fields and coconut, rubber, and cashew plantations. Cut off from the rest of India by the towering Sahyadri mountain range to the east, Kerala evolved a distinctive culture of dance, drama, and temple arts under the royal Chera dynasty, and defied even the Mughal's efforts to incorporate it into their empire.

Although isolated by land, Kerala claims an unusually cosmopolitan history. Missionaries were among its earliest visitors: St Thomas the Apostle is believed to have established the earliest Christian colony in Kerala in AD 52, followed by Syrian Christian settlers from Alexandria, whose cathedrals and churches still attract large congregations throughout the state. Kerala's lush Malabar coast lured legions of ancient Phoenician, Chinese, Arab, and Jewish traders in search of ivory, pepper, spices, incense, and myrrh. In the period spanning the fifteenth to the seventeenth century, Kerala became the battleground for numerous colonizing struggles between the Portuguese, the French, the Dutch, and, finally, the British, who gained control in 1795.

Modern Kerala — "land of the Cheras", or "land of *kera*" (coconuts) — was created in 1956 by the joining together of lands that comprised the ancient kingdoms of Tranvancore, Cochin, and Malabar. A year later, the people of Kerala were the first in the world to voluntarily elect a Communist regime. Today, religious piety and Marxist–Leninism are the reigning passions. Novelist Arthur Koestler described the state as "a kind of tropical Marxist Ruritania, where Cabinet Ministers were known to consult their horoscopes to deduce the Party-line from the stars and Catholic missions, deriving from St Francis Xavier, were still the most important cultural influence."

Kerala does not suffer from the extreme poverty found in the larger northern cities of Bombay, Delhi, and Calcutta. The state boasts a literacy rate of 70 percent and one of the lowest birthrates in India. The balmy climate is softened by strong sea breezes and is most pleasant from December to January, although it's still comfortable to travel between October and March.

TRIVANDRUM

Trivandrum, Kerala's languid seaside capital, sprawls over seven hills covered with colonial-era government buildings and traditional wooden houses hidden among lush parks and gardens.

Trivandrum was originally called Thiru Ananthapuram, or "abode of the snake", after an ancient myth that it was the home of Anantha, the sacred serpent often depicted curling around Lord Vishnu's body. Raja Marthanda Varma of Travancore made this his capital in 1750 and dedicated his entire kingdom to Lord Vishnu, the god of creation. He decreed that he and his successors would be the *dasis*, or servants of Vishnu. The present ex-raja still makes a daily morning pilgrimage from his palace to the Padmanabhaswamy Temple to prostrate himself before the reclining image of the family deity.

Most travelers prefer the sunny indolence of Kovalam's beaches, which are only 13 km (eight miles) away, and visit Trivandrum for a full-day tour of its museums, art galleries, temples, and zoo.

ACCESS

Trivandrum's airport is a useful jumping-off point for Air India, Air Lanka, or Indian Airlines flights to Sri Lanka and the Maldives. Indian Airlines flies direct from Madras, Cochin, Bombay, Goa, Bangalore, and Delhi. Kerala offers some of India's most enjoyable train journeys — gentle swaying rides past spectacular palm-fringed coastal backwaters and vast fields busy with *lunghi*-clad rice-planters. Many travelers make the 18-hour, 920-km (570-mile) journey from Madras by the *Trivandrum Mail*, and then continue up Kerala's coastline to Cochin, 219 km (136 miles) away, by a combination of train, backwater trails, and buses.

From Trivandrum, KSRTC runs frequent buses to all the main cities in Kerala as well as long-distance services to Madras, Madurai, Mysore, and Bangalore; all leave from the bus depot opposite the railway station. If you're planning to take the backwater trip from Quilon (71 km, or 44 miles), buses start at 7:30 am for Ernakulam/Cochin and pass through Quilon about two hours later. There's also a daily bus

OPPOSITE: Bustling street scene in the Connemara Market, Trivandrum.

to the Thekkady Wildlife Sanctuary (272 km, or 170 miles) which takes eight hours.

Locating the right bus at Trivandrum's bus depot can be quite infuriating, as destinations are written in Malayam script and there are no bus bays, so that you have to join the melée each time a bus arrives to find out if it is the one you want. It's usually possible to find a seat on these buses but near impossible to book.

HOTELS

The three-star **Luciya Continental**, ((0471) 73443, near the old East Fort, is Trivandrum's

has a cafeteria-style coffee shop that serves reliably good south Indian *thalis* and refreshing fruit *lassis*. Others include **Hotel Arulakam**, ((0471) 330488, on Station Road, which attracts many Indian tourists, is spartan, but clean. There's a good all-day vegetarian restaurant with plentiful *thalis* at the lobby level. **Hotel Aristo**, ((0471) 63622, located at Aristo Junction, near the railway station, has a pretty cottage-style exterior and very cheap, pleasant rooms. Find rock-bottom accommodation at the **YMCA Guest House**, ((0471) 330059, in Palatam, and the **Youth Hostel**, ((0471) 71364, in the Veli area of Trivandrum.

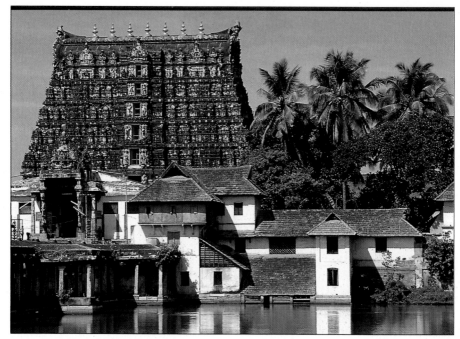

most luxurious hotel. It is comfortable and inexpensive, and has novelty suites in Arabic, Chinese, and Keralan styles, and the city's best restaurant for Indian and continental fare. The KTDC-run **Hotel Mascot**, ((0471) 438990, is a quaint colonial bungalow set in a leafy part of town expanded to accommodate Soviet trade delegations and legions of Russian tourists. The nicest rooms are on the top floor. It's very conveniently located, with the Indian Airlines office just opposite, and the museum, zoo, and tourist office within a 10-minute walk away. Rates: inexpensive. A good cheap-range option is **Hotel Chaithram**, ((0471) 331421, near the railway station on Thampanoor Road which

RESTAURANTS

Trivandrum has plenty of small eating houses which serve very good south Indian vegetarian food for next to nothing. One of the best is **Arul Jyothi**, just across the road from the Secretariat, where plentiful *thalis* with fresh red grape juice cost only US$0.50. They serve "rocket roasts", immense paper-thin *dosas* curved up like stetsons and served with *sambhar* and coconut chutney, and have a large selection of delicious *lassis* and sweets. Other good places to try include the excellent vegetarian restaurant at **Hotel Woodlands**, the **Indian Coffee House** (north of Statue Road and between the museum and the Secretariat), and the **Khyber Restaurant**, near Station Road, which also has Chinese and Western food. The railway station's cafete-

ABOVE: The multi-storied Padmanabhaswamy Temple in Trivandrum makes an easy landmark in the low-lying capital.

ria must be India's cleanest, with delicious and very cheap *thalis* and south Indian snacks served with a mug of steaming cardamom tea.

SIGHTSEEING

Trivandrum's most famous sight is the **Padmanabhaswamy Temple**, which has a seven-storyed *goporum,* or pyramid-shaped archway, writhing with carved mythological figures. Raja Marthanda Varma poured much of his personal wealth into glorifying this temple in 1733 as his tribute to Lord Vishnu. Non-Hindus are not allowed inside, and can only admire its ornate exterior — the interior has fine murals and reliefs — and observe male devotees self-consciously disrobing on the temple stairs, partly concealed behind their wives. Clad in their rented Rs 1 dhotis, they disappear into the cool, sandalwood scented interior, from which is heard occasional humming and the clang of a temple bell. Two major temple festivals take place here in March to April and October to November, each lasting 10 days and climaxing in processions of caparisoned elephants, devotees carrying golden deities on palanquins, and marching musicians, all led by the dhoti-clad maharaja down to the sea.

It's worth timing your visit around noon to catch the daily procession of temple priests. Then stroll through the back streets branching off Mahatma Gandhi Road for a poke through the government emporium, and the book and antique shops dotted throughout the area. Look out for Kairali, the excellent government handicrafts emporium, opposite the Secretariat.

From here it's a short rickshaw ride north to Trivandrum's magnificent hilltop **Zoo and Botanical Gardens** (64 acre or 26 hectare), which are open daily and have several museums within the grounds. The **Napier Museum** is a brightly turreted pagoda designed in 1880 by an English architect to honor the Governor of Madras, Lord Napier. It houses a superb collection of rare eighth-century, Chola-period sculpture, stone carvings, delicate antique jewelry, intriguing musical instruments, and memorabilia from the royal Travancore household. An excellent guidebook with anecdotes about the various items on display is sold at the front desk. The museum is open from 10 am to 5 pm except Mondays and Wednesdays. Other museums include the **Sri Chitra Art Gallery**, with its fine collection of contemporary Indian paintings, and the **Aquarium**, which has natural history displays of ghoulish stuffed specimens.

The **Connemara Market**, which is easily found by its entrance archway near the Secretariat along M.G. Road, is an interesting place to wander through: a joss-scented strip lined with merchants squatting under black umbrellas like wizened monkeys, wiry boys splashing water on heaped blossoms, and chickens running among piles of mangoes, jackfruit and coconuts. This is the city's colorful market forum, where everything from wedding finery to pet parrots can be found.

EXCURSIONS FROM TRIVANDRUM

Trivandrum makes a good base for visiting **Kanya Kumari**, also known as Cape Comorin, 87 km (54 miles) to the southeast in neighboring Tamil Nadu state. This is India's "Land's End", where the waters of the Arabian Sea, Indian Ocean, and the Bay of Bengal merge. Hindu pilgrims throng to its beachfront ghats, or steps, in the belief that bathing in these waters washes away their sins. It's a spectacular, wind-blown location, with nothing but endless sky and sea on the horizon, and its sunsets and sunrises are unique. On full moon nights, sunset and moonrise occur simultaneously, hovering together like a tangerine and a golf ball. It's worth staying overnight to see at least one sunset and one sunrise.

The TTDC-run **Hotel Tamil Nadu,** ((04653) 71209 has a beachfront locations, rooms overlooking the sea, and mealtime *thalis*. Rates: cheap. To get there, you can either take a local bus from Trivandrum (or Kovalam Beach), or go on the US$3 day-tour organized by the Kerala Tourist Development Corporation (KTDC), which leaves at 7:30 am and returns at 9 pm and also covers Kovalam Beach and **Padmanbhapuram Palace**, which is 32 km (20 miles) from Kanya Kumari and 55 km (34 miles) from Trivandrum. This is one of Kerala's most impressive buildings, built in 1550 for the Travancore rulers of this former capital city. It's a marvel of design and delicate craftsmanship, built of teak wood with Chinese-influenced low gabled roofs with elaborate carved interiors opening out on to private courtyards and some 40 panels of murals throughout. As you wander through, look for the carved open hall where the king held court, and the ornate council chambers, dance hall, temple, women's quarters, and the palace tower, where the topmost room was reserved for the god Vishnu, complete with murals and a bed — the maharaja occupied the room just beneath it. The complex is open daily, except Mondays, from 7 am to 9 pm.

GENERAL INFORMATION

The Tourist Information Centre, ((0471) 61132, on Park View Road, Trivandrum, is very friendly, informative, and conveniently located just opposite the gateway entrance to the zoo, gardens, and museum. You can ask here about Kathakali dance performances run by the Trivandrum Kathakali Club.

The KTDC office, ((0471) 330031, Station Road, Thampanoor, runs good sightseeing tours around the city, Padmanabhapuram palace, Kanya Kumari, and to Thekkady Wildlife Sanctuary.

KOVALAM

Kerala's dramatic Malabar coast is a continuous stretch of unspoilt, white-sanded bays, but

main beach, just to the south, resembles a seaside commune crammed with budget hotels, well-tanned tourists, and cheap restaurants serving delicious fresh seafood and Western-style dishes.

It's not a place for peaceful solitude. Garrulous fisherwomen try to barter their haul of wriggling crabs or sackfuls of pawpaw for your wristwatch, and semi-nude body-surfers attract regular busloads of daytripping Indians. Swimmers should keep close to the shore as Kovalam's waters are renowned for dangerous undertows that frequently carry the unwitting out to sea. After a record 11 deaths in 1986, a

the only beach resort is at Kovalam, just 13 km (eight miles) from Trivandrum. Here you'll find a series of small, sheltered coves with powder-soft sand, fringed by palm groves and paddy fields. Kovalam is perfect for unwinding after a bout of travel, with its good range of hotels, beach cafés, and plenty of sun and surf.

Compared to Goa's sprawling sands, Kovalam's two main beaches are quite contained and both within easy strolling distance of each other. At one end is Kovalam's five-star Beach Resort, landscaped across a palm-lined hillside with its own secluded bay. The other

Kovalam's lush scenery and palm-fringed beaches are a perfect location for tropical indolence. ABOVE: Poolside vista from the Kovalam Ashok Beach Hotel. OPPOSITE: A seemingly endless stretch of unspoilt coastline.

long-term Kovalam resident, clothes-designer Tim Heineman, an American citizen born in Tamil Nadu who has adopted Indian nationality, formed India's first professional team of lifeguards, who rescue an average of two swimmers a day.

ACCESS

Kovalam is only 13 km (8 miles) from Trivandrum and can be reached either by taxi, which costs about US$6 one way, or a bus service every half-hour from platform 19 at Trivandrum's city bus depot opposite the Padmanabhaswamy Temple.

Kovalam's optimum season is from September to April, after which the summer's heat and the monsoon send most tourists fleeing to Kashmir and the Himalayas.

HOTELS

Kerala's luxury five-star resort, the **Kovalam Ashok Beach Resort**, ((0471) 65323, is stunningly located atop a palm-scattered cliff face. Of a Mediterranean-style design which has won awards from the Royal Institute of British Architects, it sprawls across several tiers that drop down to the beach. but has become quite run-down. Facilities include an extensive yoga and massage center, water-sports (including waterskiing, motorboats, and paddleboats), a large pool, and a tennis court. Kovalam's only bank is located within the main lobby. Either stay in the main hotel building, or at the Kovalam Grove, a cluster of self-contained cottages, each with a terrace, along the seafront sands. For quaint vintage splendor, stay at a suite in the 100-year-old Halcyon Castle, the Maharaja of Travancore's former summer palace with beautiful views across the Lakshadweep Sea. Rates moderate to expensive.

The KTDC-run **Hotel Samudra**, ((0471) 54242, overlooking the adjacent secluded bay, is pleasant and inexpensively priced.

Along the main tourist beach, **Rockholm**, ((0471) 306, just above the lighthouse, has a winning combination of spacious, clean rooms (complete with vases of fresh flowers), a friendly management, the beach's most attractive balcony restaurant, and a well-thumbed library. Try to snare one of the coveted rooftop rooms for privacy and a spectacular view. Rates: cheap. Just opposite is **Sharma Cottages** which rents rooms cheaply to long-staying tourists. Nearby, both **Hotel Seaweed**, ((0471) 60806, and **Hotel Samudra Tara**, ((0471) 54242, offer comfortable rooms. There are also many very cheap lodging houses along the main beach. You might try the **Hotel Moonlight**, ((0471) 584311, near the Kovalam Post Office, with incredibly spotless, spacious rooms run by the solicitous Mr Anand, or **Hotel Neelakanta**, basic but clean. Just outside is Tim Heineman's "Rags Express" shop, which sells clothes especially devised for travelers in India. The hottest-selling item is his "travel pants", with ingenious interior pockets for passports, airline tickets, and travelers' checks.

RESTAURANTS

The ex-fishermen chefs who staff Kovalam's many beach cafés are culinary dynamos, serving up delectable seafood as well as popular Italian, Chinese, English, and French dishes.

Rockholm Hotel's **Balcony Restaurant** has an enchanting view, and serves chilled beer, excellent seafood dishes, and strong, fragrant coffee. Portions are gargantuan by Kovalam standards.

The **Lucky Coral** rooftop restaurant above Hotel Seaweed is almost as pleasant, and plays Talking Heads and David Bowie for its music-conscious patrons. Try Fish Welewska, served with a veloute sauce with shrimps or Lobster Thermidor.

On the beach, **Hotel Searock's Café** has a talented Goan chef, whose classic Goan dishes are as good as his grilled or baked seafood served with the house lemon-butter garlic sauce. This is also the place for an excellent "executive breakfast", with your toes in the sand and a crumpled copy of yesterday's *Indian Express*.

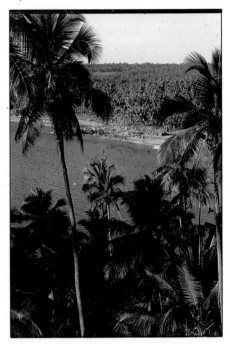

But for almost unbelievably good value and haphazard charm, both **My Dream**, which serves the best fish and chips in the subcontinent, and the **Black Cat** (for delicious garlic prawns and hot banana pancakes) are heartily recommended.

BEACHES

Apart from these two beaches, there's an almost endless unspoilt coastline to explore. Further south, strung between Kovalam's candy-striped lighthouse and a mini Taj Mahal-style mosque perched on the headland's tip, is a sheltered, slightly more private, beach. In the opposite direction, the almost deserted bay just beyond the Hotel Samudra (past Kovalam's Beach Resort) makes a pleasant afternoon's excursion and is safe for swimming. From here, the beaches get more bewitching the further you stroll.

It's worth rising early one morning to witness Kovalam's fishing community hauling ashore their catamarans and proudly inspecting the morning's catch of tuna, squid, crabs, lobster, sharks and, occasionally, an illicit turtle. From the lighthouse, it's a 10-minute walk across the headland to the fishing village, with a small path leading down to the beach. En route, stop by at the Marine Research Laboratory, which has displays of local marine life and the methods used to catch them. There is also an extensive library, though you must first request permission from the custodian to browse.

THE BACKWATERS

The palm-fringed, balmy backwaters, or *kayals*, stretch along the coastal strip from Quilon to Cochin. Local ferries chug gently through this unexpected version of rural India, providing one of south India's most profound pleasures: a cruise in the heart of a tropical Venice. Go armed with a large floppy hat, a pair of binoculars, a zoom-lens camera, and a bagful of oranges and delicious fresh cashew nuts for optimum enjoyment. Local ferries from **Quilon, Alleppey,** or **Kottayam** — the main backwater towns — cost less than the cashew nuts and offer an *African Queen* fantasy plowing through winding waterways that are peopled by slender riverbank dwellers, and heady with the scent of frangipani and ripe jackfruit trees.

It's also possible to hire a small boat for a watery jaunt for US$7 an hour, or if you can muster a large group, there are government barges which seat 15 and cost US$20 for four hours. Be sure to agree on the payment details with the boatman before embarking on your journey.

It's worth traveling to Alleppey and Kottayam for the late August/early September 10-day Onam harvest festival, when the backwaters churn with colorful water carnivals and snake boat races. The most spectacular is the Nehru Trophy Boat Race, held in Alleppey on the second Saturday of August, when boats carrying up to 100 paddlers each compete in a colorful regatta.

The backwaters are best visited from December to February, because by early March the heat becomes oppressive and the swarms of mosquitoes can be deflected only by applying continual lathers of repellent.

The picturesque town of Allepey is a favorite setting out point for barge cruises through Kerala's winding coils of backwaters.

QUILON

On the edge of Ashtamudi Lake, 73 km (45 miles) from Trivandrum, Quilon is the most picturesque of the *kayal* towns. It's full of pastel-painted wooden villas and labyrinthine alleys, and policemen wearing quaint Raj-style topees. It's also one of Kerala's most historic ports: the Phoenicians, Persians, Greeks, Romans, and Arabs all used Quilon as a stopover for plying the backwaters. From the seventh to the tenth century, the Chinese established a busy trading base here, leaving a visible legacy of low-slung, pagoda-style architecture and Chinese fishing nets. This strategic, fertile district later became a source of rivalry between the Portuguese, Dutch, and British. It's still possible to see the dilapidated ruins of an old Portuguese fort near Thangasseri Beach, three kilometers (almost two miles) away.

Travelers come to Quilon to embark on the longest and most varied of the backwater routes. It takes eight and a half hours to meander along the 85-km (53-mile) stretch to Alleppey. There are two ferries daily, but you'll see more if you take the earlier one which departs at 10 am and glides into Allepey just after dusk. (This trip can also be made in the opposite direction.)

It's worth staying overnight in Quilon for one of Kerala's best accommodation surprises, the charming lakeside **Tourist Bungalow**, a former British Residency set in leafy gardens on the outskirts of town. Pristine rooms are furnished in local wooden furniture, all with shower, tub, and hot water and very cheap. The stately balcony-level drawing room is full of old Raj-era memorabilia. It's always popular, so book in advance in writing or through a KTDC office.

The more central **Hotel Sudarshan**, ((0474) 75322, on Parameswar Nagar, is only 10 minutes' walk from the ferry jetty, and has very cheap, fan-cooled rooms or more expensive air-conditioned ones. You can dine well at either of its two restaurants on a choice of Indian, Chinese, and European specialties, or opt for cheap, delicious vegetarian *thalis* at Hotel Guru Prasad on Main Street.

ALLEPPEY

Alleppey, 83 km (52 miles) from Quilon, is a small, picturesque, oriental Amsterdam, with interlocking canals and bridges, and a center for backwater cruises.

From here you can take the two-and-a-half-hour scenic cruise to Kottayam, which for many is quite long enough to enjoy the *kayals*. Gliding along the canals, which cross the extensive

Vembanad Lake stretching north to Cochin, you'll see flotillas of dug-outs laden with coconuts, and lovely inland lagoons snaking into narrow, waterlily-covered stretches.

Ferries leave for Kottayam throughout the day, starting at 5 am, but the early morning or mid-afternoon departures ensure optimum comfort. There's an alternative, and equally beautiful, four-hour round-trip from Alleppey inland to Changanacherry, with frequent ferries from 6 am to 4:45 pm.

The bus-stand and boat jetty are fairly close together; Alleppey has no rail connection with other destinations in Kerala.

THE DEEP SOUTH

The two-star **Alleppey Prince Hotel**, ((0411) 3752, on A.S. Road, on the National Highway, provides very comfortable US$10 to US$15 rooms in a pleasant setting a short distance out of town, and has a good restaurant and swimming pool. Just opposite the boat jetty is **Hotel Komala**, ((0411) 3631, with a choice of air-conditioned doubles for US$10 or non air-conditioned for US$4.

St George Lodge, ((0411) 61620, is popular for its friendly staff and very cheap spotless rooms with attached bath, or try the modern **Sheeba Lodge**, near Hotel Komala, for similar prices.

At the **Indian Coffee House**, a five-minute rickshaw ride from the center, waiters clad in ornate turbans and striped cummerbunds serve excellent filter coffee and cheap meals in a simple but relaxing café — perfect for frittering

away an hour or so before setting out for the backwaters. For good vegetarian *thalis,* try **Shree Durga Bhavan** restaurant in the Udipi Hotel on Cullen Road.

KOTTAYAM

Less than 30 km (18 miles) from Alleppey, and situated slightly inland from the Malabar coast, Kottayam is a busy commercial city, famous for its rubber, tea, coffee, pepper, and cardamom plantations, and primarily visited by tourists as a stopping-off point on the way to the Periyar Wildlife Sanctuary, 117 km (73 miles) away. A stronghold of the Syrian Christian sect, which has existed in Kerala since AD 190, Kottayam has many beautiful churches, including the Valiapalli Church, five kilometers (three miles) northwest of the railway station, which contains a cross believed to have come from the original church founded by St Thomas the Apostle in Cranganore.

Kottayam is part of the rail network and has two bus stations: a local depot and an interstate stand that is roughly a kilometer (just over half a mile) from the boat jetty.

Stay at **Vembanad Lake Resort**, ((0481) 564866, Kodimatha, five kilometers (three miles) out of town, with peaceful, pleasant cheap rooms. Regardless of where you choose to stay, take the mid-morning Alleppey–Kottayam ferry and arrive at the Vembanad at lunchtime to order Keralan specialties such as *karimeen,* a local freshwater fish prepared in a fiery sauce of onions, green chilies, and spices, and a variety of vegetarian dishes eaten al fresco by the lakeside at Kottayam's best restaurant.

The brand-new **Hotel Sears**, ((0481) 563013, on Shastri Road, a five-minute rickshaw ride from the railway station, has good-value. In town, stay either at **Anjali Hotel**, ((0481) 563661, on KK Road with a good coffee shop and clean, comfortable, air-conditioned inexpensive rooms, or at the unusual **Tourist Bungalow**, a former British officers' barracks, with spacious antiquated rooms. Very cheap. It's a 15-minute trek from the boat jetty, and you'll need to ask for directions, as it's a little difficult to find.

PERIYAR (THEKKADY)

The **Periyar Wildlife Sanctuary** is one of the most beautiful forest stretches of the south. Set in the Cardamom Hills near the border with Tamil Nadu, it is a 777 sq km (300 sq mile) jungle refuge for tigers, elephants, bison, antelope, sloth bear, otter, monkeys, and the occasional panther or leopard. Among the sanctuary's creepers, spice vines, and blossoming trees, bird-watchers may spot darters, flycatchers, hornbills, blue-winged parakeets, bulbuls, herons, and egrets.

This is the finest Indian sanctuary for watching and photographing wild elephants, and as a member of Project Tiger, it has 40 of India's 3,000 or so remaining tigers. The enormous Periyar Lake, 24 sq km (9.3 sq miles) in area, was created in 1895 by the British government in Madras for use in irrigation, but it became part of the newly formed sanctuary in 1934. While cruising along the shore in a motorboat, you can watch herds of elephants, bison, deer, and the occasional tiger, grazing at the water's edge.

sive. On the lake's edge, **Aranya Niwas Hotel**, ((04869) 22023, has comfortable rooms ranging from cheap to inexpensive. In the rather tatty dining room, gravy-stained waiters rush around with such creations as "Lassie", "Mutton Fuyong", "Raw Eggs", and "Two Numbers, Only". Far more enjoyable is the quaint, three-roomed **Government Rest House**, although this is frequently full, or the KTDC-run **Periyar House**, ((04869) 22026, about a kilometer (just over half a mile) away in the forest, with pleasant airy rooms, hot water, and food that is worth the hike.

At Kumily town, five kilometers (three miles) away, the **Lake Queen Tourist Home**, opposite the post office is another pleasant option. It's best to book in advance for hotels in Periyar, which can be done through any KTDC office; otherwise, ask the staff at the tourist office in Kumily to check which hotels have rooms available. They'll also give you useful boat-trip tickets, maps, and walking/trekking permits.

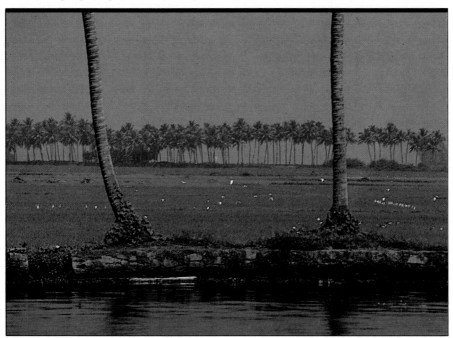

ACCESS

There are bus connections to Periyar from all main cities in Kerala, but the most popular scenic route is from Kottayam, 117 km (73 miles) away. The four- to five-hour journey winds up to a 305 m (1000 ft) plateau of leafy cardamom, pepper, and coffee plantations.

HOTELS

The **Lake Palace Hotel**, (via operator) 2384, has the most romantic location for overnight stays. This large old bungalow sits on a small island on Thekkady Lake, has a good bar and restaurant, and guests have been known to spot tigers from the windows of their rooms. Rooms have an antiquated Raj-era charm. Rates: inexpen-

SIGHTSEEING

Tickets for the motorboat cruises on Lake Periyar, which last for 1½ hours, are available from the Wildlife Office, near the boat jetty. You're likely to see more if you take the earliest boat

ABOVE: Rice-beds create lush headlands all the way along the backwater trail.

at 7 am, when the misty waters resemble England's Lake District, and the herds come down for their morning drink.

The Wildlife Office also organizes three-hour group treks through the forest, which are most informative about the sanctuary's flora and fauna, but frustrating as the noise of so many people frightens most animals away. A far more satisfying alternative is to hire a private Wildlife Office guide to take you to the best vantage points and *machans,* or tree houses, so that you see far more wildlife at close range. The Wildlife Office can also arrange elephant rides and private boat rides.

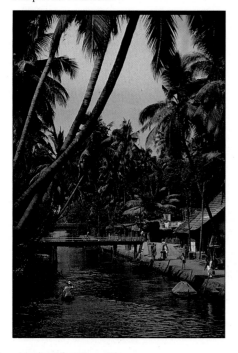

COCHIN

Cochin is Kerala's largest and most beautiful city, with its lush islands, backwaters, faded colonial architecture, and an unusual history. It comprises the Fort Cochin/Mattancherry southern peninsula, the modern business district on Ernakulum mainland, and Willindon, Bolgatty, Gundu, and Vypeen islands. It is one of India's biggest naval bases and busiest ports, exporting vast amounts of coir, rubber, seafood, and spices to foreign countries. Despite its bustling harbour, Cochin is full of languid charm and is perfect for exploring on foot or by boat.

ABOVE: Swaying palms dwarf a canal-side village along the backwaters.

Phoenician, Israelite, Greek, Roman, Arab, and Chinese traders all visited or settled in this tropical port, leaving behind Muslim, Christian, and Jewish communities that still exist today. It was Cochin's Jews who founded the first large community, over 1,000 years ago. These were the "black Jews", who arrived as early as AD 52 from Yemen and Babylon to trade olive oil and dates for peacocks and spices, and intermarried with the local population. Another wave of Jewish refugees came from Spain in the fifteenth century and were given protection by the Raja of Cochin. These "white Jews" were more insular and frowned on mixed marriages; they still exist, though in ever-dwindling numbers, today.

Vasco da Gama took Cochin for Lisbon in 1502, but the Dutch, who coveted its spices, incense, myrrh, and ivory, usurped the Portuguese in 1663. Then in 1795 the city passed to the British. Fort Cochin and Mattancherry Island are littered with the architectural relics — Dutch Palaces, Portuguese churches, and British bungalows — of these conquerors.

ACCESS

Cochin can be reached by daily direct flights from Madras, Trivandrum, Bangalore, Goa, Bombay, and Delhi. There are also direct train routes linking the city with all major cities. Daily trains service nearby destinations from Cochin: an Ernakulam–Kottayam train at 7 am and 5:30 pm, and the Ernakulam–Quilon service at 11:30 am.

Buses depart from the Central Bus Station on Stadium Road in Ernakulam, with regular shuttles several times daily to Trichur, Alleppey, Quilon, Thekkady, and Trivandrum, and links to major cities in neighboring Karnataka and Tamil Nadu states.

WHERE TO STAY

The **Malabar Hotel, (** (0484) 346811, 340010, fax (0484) 340297, Willingdon Island, is by far the best hotel in Cochin, with air-conditioned rooms tastefully decorated with woven rugs and wicker furniture. Set on the edge of the island with its own lawns and jetty, it has a glorious view across the busy harbor to Mattancherry Island. The hotel has a swimming pool, restaurant, unexceptional coffee shop, and bar and, as part of the Taj-Group, it is being expanded to a total of 100 sea-facing rooms. Located right next to the tourist office, the hotel is convenient to the airport and a short ferry or taxi ride from either Fort Cochin or Ernakulam. Rates: moderate.

Also on Willingdon Island is the inexpensively priced **Casino Hotel, (** (0484) 666821, fax (0484) 340001 just up the road. Built in the 1950's, it lacks a harbour view, but is very efficient, with a pleasant old wing. There's a swimming pool and an excellent seafood restaurant that has one drawback — an intrusive live band crooning Western numbers each night. Both hotels have boat services to neighboring islands. Cheaper options on this pleasant island include the **Maruthi Tourist Home,** ((0484) 6365, and just next door, **Island Inn,** ((0484) 666816.

For travelers in search of faded elegance, the 250-year-old **Bolgatty Palace Hotel,** ((0484) 355003, has antique furniture, ceiling fans, mosquito nets draped on four-poster beds and a languid terrace for sipping afternoon beers. Located on the narrow, palm-fringed Bolgatty Island, this was once a Dutch Palace and later the British Residency. Run by the state government, it is deluged with Indian holidaymakers during peak season, and becomes a haven of peace only during off-season. Rates: cheap.

In Ernakulam, stay at the three-star, **Sea Lord Hotel,** ((0484) 352682, Shanmugham Road, with good air-conditioned rooms. Rates: cheap. Another choice in the cheap bracket with optional air-conditioning is **Hotel International,** ((0484) 353911, and cheaper still is **Woodlands Hotel,** ((0484) 351372, 351719, both on Mahatma Gandhi Road. The latter has an excellent vegetarian restaurant. **Biju's Tourist Home,** ((0484) 369881, is the best of the budget hotels with rooms, including baths, very friendly staff, and a convenient location opposite the ferry jetty.

On Fort Cochin, **Hotel Seagull,** ((0484) 28128, Calvety Road, overlooks the harbor and the Chinese fishing nets in a sleepy, cul-de-sac of pastel-hued villas, just five minutes' walk from the jetty. It has pleasant very cheap rooms with bath and a popular balcony restaurant. Otherwise, the spartan **PWD Tourist Rest Home,** ((0484) 25797, near the beach, offers basic accommodation with a big advantage — mosquito nets.

RESTAURANTS

Kerala cuisine is distinctive for its variety of spicy, coconut-flavored dishes and fresh seafood specialties. The **Riceboat Restaurant** at the Malabar Hotel is decorated to resemble Kerala's cargo boats. The walls are adorned with paddles and coolie hats, and their seafood specialties are very good, especially the prawn shashlik Oriental.

In Ernakulam, the **Sealord Restaurant,** at the Sealord Hotel, serves a special fish Veronique (stuffed with grapes), and offers a range of delicious seafood dishes. **Swagath,** the bustling upstairs eatery at Dwarka Hotel on M.G. Road, is a favorite of Cochin's locals for its air-condi-

tioned annex and generous *thalis*. It offers a staggering array of dishes including the massive mini-*thali*, or the "executive power lunch" *thalis*, as well as good *lassis* and south Indian specialties. **Woodlands,** just down the road, is also recommended for excellent cheap vegetarian *thalis*. Just behind the Dwarka Hotel is Cochin's best Chinese restaurant, the **Chinese Garden,** which serves excellent seafood dishes. The **Indian Coffee House,** opposite the ferry jetty, serves strong, freshly ground coffee, Western-style omelets, and "butter jam" toast as early as 6 am. **Jancy Cafe,** on Shanmugam Road, serves delicious south Indian snacks, with particularly good fluffy *iddlies* and crisp, doughnut-shaped *vadas*.

SIGHTSEEING

If you take a ferry to the historic Fort Cochin/Mattancherry district, you'll alight at the old docks, now a sprawling neighborhood of shuttered merchants' houses and warehouses. Almost directly opposite is the elegant **Mattancherry Palace,** set in a cluster of mango trees. Built by the Portuguese in 1557, it was presented to the Cochin raja, Veera Kerala Varma (1537–1567), in exchange for trading privileges. It was later repaired by the occupying Dutch, gaining the misnomer "Dutch Palace". An annex of the Mattancherry is now a museum. One room contains portraits of former Cochin rajas, a line of imperious mandarin-like faces with fixed, inscrutable gazes; another displays a collection of their elaborate costumes, including ornate robes, brilliant turbans, silk parasols, and an ivory palanquin. The upstairs bedchambers are adorned with seventeenth-century frescoes depicting lively scenes from the Indian epics, the *Ramayana* and the *Mahabharata,* painted with colors created from charcoal, lime, leaves, and flowers. Open from 10 am to 5 pm every day except Friday and public holidays.

Near Mattancherry Palace, up a winding street filled with interesting antique shops and heady with the scent of pepper, cardamom, and cloves, is **Jewtown.** The Jews of Cochin once numbered as many as 4,000, but today only eight families remain, with many families having emigrated to Israel, Australia, and Canada. Almost hidden at the end of a cul-de-sac is the **Jewish Synagogue.** Built in 1568, it is the oldest synagogue in the Commonwealth. It was destroyed by the Portuguese in 1662, and rebuilt by the Dutch in 1664. Its interior glitters with nineteenth-century Belgian chandeliers, hand-painted eighteenth-century Chinese willow-pattern tiles, and in one corner, a brass pulpit and gold raja's crown. Jackie Cohen, the synogogue's custodian, has an expert knowledge of Jewish settlements in Asia, and displays the synagogue's prized possessions on request: a papyrus whorl that is an ancient copy of the Great Scrolls of the Old Testament and the copperplate grants of privilege made by the Cochin rajas to the Jewish merchant Joseph Rabin. The synagogue is open from 10 am to noon, and from 3 to 5 pm every day except Saturday and Jewish holidays.

By cycle or rickshaw, it's two kilometers (one and a quarter miles) to the northern isthmus of **Fort Cochin**, a neighborhood of pastel-washed villas, sixteenth century bastions, and cobbled streets. Along the way, stop to watch Cochin's

fishermen working their Chinese fishing nets, first introduced by visitors from the court of Kublai Khan, whose influence also remains throughout Kerala in pagoda-style temples, conical fishermen's hats, and Chinese methods of making porcelain and paper. The filmy blue nets, suspended from poles lashed together and cantilevered out over the water, are counterbalanced with a primitive system of rock-weights. To see them in action, return an hour before dusk, when the nets look like giant birds dipping in and out of the water with their silvery cargo.

It's a 10-minute stroll through the winding streets to **St Francis Church**, established by Portuguese Franciscan friars in 1504. This unadorned structure, originally made from wood and later rebuilt in stone, is the oldest European church in India. As invaders conquered Cochin, it passed from the Catholic Portuguese to the Protestant Dutch and the British Anglican, and today functions as a Church of Southern India. The Portuguese explorer Vasco da Gama, who landed in Cochin in 1498 and was known to have terrorized the natives by slicing off the noses, ears, and hands of his captives, was buried here in 1524, although his remains were shipped back to Lisbon 14 years later. The tombstones of da Gama and other settlers, written in Portuguese on one side, and Dutch on the other, can be seen in St Francis Church.

A short stroll south, down Prince Street, is the Roman Catholic **Santa Cruz Church**, built in 1557, with a mock-marble interior painted in lurid colors.

Across the water, on **Gundu Island**, is an old Raj-era coir factory where weavers use the area's abundant supply of coconut husks to fashion practical doormats, ropes, and matting.

The easiest way to become acquainted with Cochin is to take the KTDC's boat tour. It leaves twice a day (9:30 am and 1:30 pm) from Ernakulam's boat jetty opposite the Sealord Hotel, and includes a stop at Bolgatty Palace. The tickets must be purchased at the tourist office, not on board the boat.

If you have a free afternoon, Cochin's scenic backwaters between Ernakulam and Varpaoja make a pleasant trip. The ferry leaves from Ernakulam's main jetty every hour, and takes two hours each way.

In Ernakulam, see the **Cochin Archaeological Museum** in Durbar Hall Road, with its assortment of exhibits plucked from the Cochin royal family's collection. Otherwise buy teas, spices, and fresh cashewnuts in Ernakulam market, and meander along Mahatma Gandhi Road where various emporiums sell *lunghis* the colorful cloth worn tied at the waist, rosewood carvings, jewelry, and Kathakali masks. At the government emporium, look out for a curious collection of Hindu deities with bobbing heads in contemporary garb, with Hanuman, the Monkey god, dressed up like a Japanese *yakuza!*

KATHAKALI

A performance of the traditional Kathakali dance is one of Cochin's highlights. This form of dance theater, dating back 500 years, can be seen nightly, with explanation and narration, all over the city. By tradition, all dancers are male and wear elaborate costumes and mask-like make-up to mime stories from the great Hindu epics, the *Ramayana* and the *Mahabharata*. Arrive early for the performance and peer backstage to see the lean, athletic performers transform themselves into oversized deities attired in bulky tutu-like burlap underskirts, layers of bright garments, heavy jewelry, and head-dress. The make-up is highly symbolic: green denotes the hero king or god, and black and red denote demons. The actor slips a seed from the *cunlappuvu,* or eggplant vine, under his eyelids to make his eyes red.

As much an act of worship as a highly dramatic folk theater, Kathakali is traditionally performed by the flickering light of temple-lamps, accompanied by musicians and a chanting Brahman priest. Artistes use a vast repertoire of acrobatic eye movements, dramatic facial expressions, and perfect muscle control that require years of training. In Ernakulam, there are three equally good daily performances: at the **Cochin Cultural Centre**, ((0484) 353732, at the Durbar Hall Ground next to the Cochin Museum, from 6:30 to 8 pm; **Art Kerala**, Menon and Krishna Annexe, from 7 to 8:30 pm and **See India Foundation**, ((0484) 369471, Kathathi–Parambil Lane, from 7 to 8:30 pm.

GENERAL INFORMATION

Government of India Tourist Office, ((0484) 6045, Willingdon Island (next to the Malabar

"tusker" elephants, each carrying a Brahman priest seated under silk parasols and giant feathers. After dusk, there's a massive fireworks display which lasts until dawn.

Trichur's most remarkable feature is its magnificent Vadakkunath Temple complex in the low-slung, wooden pagoda style unique to Kerala's traditional temple architecture. The main temple shrine contains a curious three-meter (10-ft) mound of hardened cows' ghee, or clarified butter, under which a devotional lingam dedicated to Lord Shiva is completely embedded. The shrine also contains a panel of exquisite murals narrating the epic *Mahabharata.*

Hotel). Open 9 am to 2 pm daily except Sunday. Contact the KTDC Tourist Reception Centre, ((0484) 353234, Shanmugham Road, Ernakulam, to make reservations for the conducted boat tours around Cochin.

OUT OF COCHIN: TRICHUR

Trichur, a picturesque pilgrimage town just south of the Nilgiri Hills, set amongst paddy fields and coconut and pineapple plantations, makes an enjoyable overnight excursion from Cochin, 80 km (50 miles) away. If you're visiting Kerala during late April to early May, it's worth planning your itinerary around Trichur's exuberant Pooram procession, the most spectacular of Kerala's temple festivals. Trichur's streets explode into rich pageantry, with a day-long parade of 30 gaily caparisoned

A museum and a zoo with a renowned collection of snakes are the other attractions. In Trichur, stay either at the **Ambassador Hotel** or the **Government Guest House**. If you've discovered a fascination for Kathakali dance, it's well worth making the 27-km (17-mile) trip to Cheruthuruthy where the **Kerala Kala Mandalam**, the state's renowned Kathakali dance school, is located. The instructors are usually delighted to let you watch their rigorous early morning training sessions, and there are evening dance performances.

ABOVE LEFT and RIGHT: Two faces of Kathakali dance artistes, displaying the traditional elaborate make-up and stylized dress. OPPOSITE: A vestige of the Portuguese legacy in the old European enclave of the Fort Cochin.

Travelers'
Tips

GETTING THERE

Getting to India is easy. The nation's main gateways of Calcutta, New Delhi, Bombay, and Madras are serviced by most major international airlines. Each airport is linked to the rest of India by its internal air network. It is best to book tickets well in advance, so that you have a firm reservation with the airline of your choice and a date around which to begin planning travel arrangements within India. When booking your international flight, seats on internal Indian Airlines flights can also be booked through your travel agent.

AIR INDIA

Flagship Air India offers flights from Asian capitals, Australia, Europe, the Middle East, Africa, the Soviet Union, and North America.

FROM EUROPE

The London *Independent*'s travel section is good for checking out tours and package deals. Many cut-price flights are offered by Arab or Asian airlines, which often make long stopovers and can be delayed in obscure or bizarre locations. It is much better to pay the extra amount and take a direct flight on an established international carrier which at least gives a certain guarantee of arriving on time. Air India, Alitalia, Air France, British Airways, Air Canada, Japan Airlines, Lufthansa, Delta, SAS, Swissair, Singapore Airlines, Thai Airways, and Qantas all have good, regular and reliable services to India. Reliable London travel agencies for low-cost tickets are **Trail Finders Travel Centre** at 194 Kensington High Street, W8 7RG, ((0171 938-3939 fax (0171) 938-3305 and at 42-50 Earls Court Road, London W8 6FT, (0171) 938-3366; and **STA Travel**, UK telephone sales enquiries and bookings ((0171) 937-9962. Typical fares being quoted at press time (London to Delhi) were £231 one way or £385 return, but prices depend very much on the carrier and tour operator.

From the UK and Europe, bargain-hunting can be rewarded by some remarkably cheap deals. ("Bucket shops" advertise in the newspapers and in magazines like *Time Out, LAM*, and the *Australasian Express*.)

FROM AUSTRALASIA

Travelers from Australasia often stop off in India for very little extra cost on the grand overland route to Europe. It's possible to get cheap or Apex fares to Singapore, Bangkok or Hong Kong, and then fly on to India from there.

Advance-purchase return fares from Australia to London or other European cities with India as a stopover cost around A$1,500. The price varies according to the season and destination in India, and Sydney and Perth offer the cheapest deals. Travel Specialists, 7 Piccadilly Arcade, 222 Pitt Street, Sydney 2000, has a good reputation.

FROM THE UNITED STATES

American visitors, for whom India is virtually the opposite side of the world, are provided with limited direct air connections and are advised to explore discount fares offered in New York, Los Angeles, and San Francisco, mostly by Asian carriers. Only a few airlines, notably Air India, Delta, and United, service India directly. New York has the greatest frequency of direct flights to New Delhi, Bombay and Madras, and has at least one weekly flight to Calcutta. The cheapest return fares to India are around US$1,000. Check the Sunday travel sections of papers like the *New York Times,* the *Los Angeles Times* or the *San Francisco Examiner/Chronicle.* Cheaper fares can be found through discounts offered by several Asian airlines. American travelers may wish to forsake the direct-flight option and and travel to India via London or from an Asian gateway city. From Hong Kong, Bangkok and Singapore you can find one-way flights for around US$230 to US$300.

VISAS

A tourist visa is required for all visitors to India, and it is absolutely imperative to receive clearance from India's local embassy before departing. Visas take two days to issue if application is made in person and four weeks for mailed applications. Immigration officials steadfastly refuse to allow entry to anyone without proper documentation, and most airlines check the passports of all India-bound passengers as in the past they have borne the cost of deporting numerous travelers.

Indian officials usually grant a four-month (120-day) stay, and charge the reciprocal equivalent of what your country charges for Indians to enter. If you plan to stay longer than the 120 days' tourist visa limit, you can apply to any Superintendant of Police in all district headquarters, and the **Foreigner's Regional Registration Offices** in Bombay, Calcutta and Madras. In Delhi the **Foreigner's Registration Office**, ((011) 331-8179, is at 1st Floor, Hans Bhawan, Tilak Bridge, New Delhi 110-002. Special permits for entry into "restricted areas" are requested from the Under Secretary, Foreigner's Division, at the

Ministry of Home Affairs, Lok Nayak Bhawan, Khan Market. After the six-month period, officials prefer you to leave, and Indian missions will be reluctant to grant you another entry visa for at least a year.

CUSTOMS

Visitors are allowed to carry in one duty-free bottle of spirits and 200 cigarettes. But customs officials are ever-vigilant about items that may be sold at great profit, and require all foreigners to declare gold, jewelry, and electronic goods, particularly video cameras, which are subject to a 280 percent duty. They will write the serial number of the item on the back page of your passport, and the item must be produced when you leave the country.

India has heavy penalties for smuggling, and unless you really desire a jail term, don't even think about bringing in any illicit goods or smuggling in expensive items. Recent political extremism in India has led to greatly enhanced security, so do not be surprised if after you have been cleared through Customs, your bags are run through an X-ray machine. The four main international airports have red and green channels, and customs officials will be available at the red channel for any foreigners wishing to register dutiable goods. Visitors with more than US$1,000 in cash or travelers' checks are also required to obtain currency declaration forms. There is no restriction on how much money you may bring in, but when you leave you may be asked to show exchange receipts from a state-owned bank to prove that the hard currency was not swapped on the black-market.

CURRENCY

Currency is based on the decimal system, with 100 paise to the rupee, which is available in denominations of 1, 2, 5, 10, 20, 50, 100 and 500.

The exchange rate at press time was Rs 100 to US$3.20. Exchanging cash and travelers' checks can be a hassle, involving the filling in of endless forms and being referred to at least four different officers before you get the money in your pocket. For this reason, it is often best to change a sizable sum of money at a time so as to minimize the time spent on such procedures. Your passport is essential identification for changing money, and travelers' checks generally have a better rate of exchange than cash.

It can be difficult to change a Rs 500 note on the street, so it is wise to get some small change

at the bank for rickshaws, tips, and fending off persistent street urchins.

There is also a reluctance to accept any bills that are ripped or worn, so be careful that your change does not include notes that will prove difficult to get rid of. Banks and five-star hotels will graciously accept this exhausted currency.

Credit cards have found widespread acceptance at shops and restaurants across India, and you will find the American Express and Visa logos in some of the most distant and obscure locations. While plastic is a convenient way of reserving travel funds, most private shopkeepers will try to charge you the percentage that they are meant to pay the card company. It is rare that wily traders can be persuaded out of this uncharitable state of mind, so be prepared to pay three percent for American Express, and six percent for credit cards such as Visa and Diners Club.

However, plastic is an advantage when paying in five-star hotels, which will add a seven percent "luxury tax" for food and accommodation if you are paying with foreign currency.

Foreigners are generally required to use hard currency to settle accounts at hotels, but can use rupees if they present an encashment certificate proving the source of their local currency was an official bank. This system is chaotic, and you can repeatedly use the same certificate, which may not have any correlation to the rupees you are spending.

WHEN TO GO

It is possible to go to India at any time of the year and avoid extreme heat and monsoons, provided you select the right area. When it is blisteringly hot in the south, it can be crisply pleasant in Delhi and the Himalayas.

In general, the optimum season to travel to northern India — to Delhi, Agra, and Rajasthan — is between September and March, although it can get very cold during the winter months of December and January. It is best to avoid the plains during the hot months between April and June. Southern India is hot all the time, but is best between November and February. To the east, a combination of heat, humidity, and monsoon again makes November to February the most comfortable time to visit. The Himalayas are best appreciated between May and July, so unless you have been bitten by the ski-bug, avoid the winter snows. The extreme pre-monsoon heat, the torrential rain, and the post-monsoon humidity apply everywhere, at varying times, between May and September.

WHAT TO TAKE

Naturally, it is best to travel as lightly as possible if you want to avoid your trip becoming an endurance test, and unless you have a safe base to leave luggage, confine yourself to one main bag. You'll find it near impossible not to accumulate purchases as you travel, so that you'll leave with considerably more than what you did when you arrived. A sound lock, preferably a combination lock is constantly useful to guard against having your luggage pilfered. Always keep all your important documents in your hand luggage: passports, air tickets, credit cards, insurance policies, and immunization certificates etc.

The type of clothing you take is naturally based on your destination. Many travelers, believing that India is a land of perpetual heat and dust, have landed in New Delhi in mid-winter with a bag full of breezy Hawaiian shirts. Read the international temperature guide in your local newspaper before deciding your wardrobe. For most of the year, the most practical clothing for India will be loose cotton clothes and sensible walking shoes. Sunglasses provide essential protection against the relentless sun.

There are other items worth taking to India so that you can more easily cope with the unforeseen. Bring spare passport photographs as these are often required for permits to restricted areas. A basic first aid kit should include Lomotil tablets (non-antibiotic pills for diarrhea), sunscreen, water purification pills, multi-vitamins, aspirin, insect repellent and antiseptic cream. As far as toiletries go, bring whatever you feel you couldn't live without for more than a week. Indian chemists usually have a baffling array of pharmaceuticals, but are short on good quality shampoo, cosmetics, sun-tan lotion, razors, dental floss, contraceptives and tampons.

Photographic film should be purchased outside India, as items sold in India have often been spoiled from being unrefrigerated. A small torch will provide illumination during power cuts and while exploring caves and gloomy ruins. Electrical appliances such as hair dryers, travel irons, and shavers must run on 220 volts. A small pair of binoculars can be useful for spotting wildlife.

India has a great range of bookshops which stock most leading titles, so it is not necessary to bring with you all the reading material you think you might need.

It can be a good idea to carry a supply of music cassettes, film, cigarettes, alcohol, toiletries, lighters, and pens to be given away as gifts in return for favors or hospitality.

HEALTH

IMMUNIZATIONS

Prevention is always the best cure. A course of immunization vaccinations and a supply of malaria tablets are essential to safeguard you against most of the dreaded maladies India has to offer. These are not essential requirements for entering the country unless you have arrived from Africa, South America, or any area infested with smallpox, yellow-fever, or cholera.

Vaccinations are recommended against cholera, typhoid, tetanus, and hepatitis A. These diseases can easily be contracted and will not only put you in hospital, but may well impair your health permanently. Have your injections at least a fortnight before departing, so that the immunizations have time to take full effect and you can recover from any lingering reaction. Cholera vaccines remain active for six months. The vaccine against hepatitis A, gamma globulin, is effective for two months, so those intending a longer stay should ask for a double dose.

Also make sure that your teeth are in good order, as Indian dentistry can look fearsomely antiquated to Western eyes! If you have capped teeth, you may want to take spare caps and a glue kit. India's swirling dust spells pure hell for travelers who wear contact lenses, so it's more comfortable to wear glasses.

Malaria is a widespread problem, particularly during the monsoon and in tropical areas where mosquitoes are rampant, and there are numerous theories as to the pros and cons of anti-malaria preparations. There is evidence that long-term use can be damaging to the retina and the liver, and many travelers prefer to smother themselves with mosquito repellents and string up nets around their beds at night. Also, pills do not offer complete protection. However, many people who have contracted a severe case of malaria have survived only because they were on a course of pills.

Doctors usually prescribe Chloroquine tablets, which can be taken either daily or weekly. Pregnant women should avoid Chloroquine, and instead take Proguanil, while an anti-malarial syrup is available for children. Other alternatives, known by the brand names Fansidar, Faladar, Antemal, and Methidox, can trigger adverse reactions. It's best to start taking the tablets 10 days before departure, which will give you a chance to change them if they don't agree with you. For full protection, you are supposed to continue taking them for six weeks after you leave the country, as malaria germs are incredibly resilient.

Anti-malarial tablets are overpriced in the United States, where a single course can cost up to US$100 on prescription, compared with US$10 in Europe, Britain, or Australia. In most parts of Asia, anti-malarials are sold without a prescription and cost only US$1.

Rabies vaccinations are now available, but as a general rule, avoid stray dogs and monkeys. Macaque monkeys may look cuddlesome as they gambol across ancient forts and temples, but they can become vicious if they decide to take food from you. If bitten by any animal, clean the wound thoroughly and then admit yourself into the nearest hospital for the 14-day-long series of injections to thwart the potentially fatal disease.

ON THE ROAD

The budget travelers' slogan "Eat Well, Sleep Hard" was probably coined in India, where your health is more important than the bumpy beds you may have to endure. It's quite normal to experience a few minor bodily hiccups in adjusting to the Indian diet and climate, especially during the first few days after arrival when your system is particularly sensitive. There are plenty of tales about India's holiday-ruining ailments, but if you observe some basic rules you should return home in good shape.

Food and drink tend to be the biggest worries for most visitors. Since most diseases in the subcontinent are waterborne, you will need to be particularly careful about your liquid consumption, especially as several liters of fluid a day is necessary to stave off dehydration from India's notoriously hot and dusty summer months.

No matter what old India-hands tell you, avoid any water that has not been boiled for at least 10 minutes and filtered or sterilized with water purification tablets. Always inquire whether water served in hotels and restaurants has been processed, as water that has only been filtered may still harbor a few resilient bugs. Indian Airlines serves unfiltered, un-boiled water on its flights, and it is best to carry on planes, buses, and trains a few bottles of mineral water. When ordering bottled water, make sure that the seal is removed before your eyes, since crafty vendors and waiters have been known to top bottles up with tap water so that they can make a little money on the sly. Also avoid ice cubes, which are, after all, just frozen water. You'll need to take twice as much water on train or bus journeys as you think you will consume, and if your supply runs out, stick to hot tea, soft drinks, or juicy oranges. It's a good idea to bring an all-purpose plastic cup with you, so that you

avoid using dirty *chai* glasses which can carry hepatitis. Get into the habit of brushing your teeth with boiled, bottled, or even soda water, and try to remember not to swallow water while you practice arias in the shower!

Adjust to the highly-spiced Indian diet slowly, sticking for the first couple of days to fairly bland dishes like rice, yogurt, breads, and boiled eggs. In general, it is risky to eat street food prepared by pavement vendors, raw vegetables, un-peeled or unsterilized fruits, and food with a high water content, such as lettuce, tomatoes, and watermelon. India has a fantastic array of vegetarian dishes and many travelers avoid

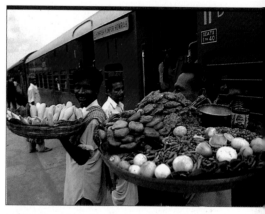

red meats and pork as these can contain nasty parasites. Poultry is usually safe but can contain salmonella, particularly if it is under-cooked, and it is advisable to choose chicken *tikka* over chicken tandoori as the former dish is equally as tasty but cooked more thoroughly, being served off the bone. Seafood is best eaten in the coastal regions and avoided inland, as refrigerated trucks have been known to break down.

However, you must not be overly fastidious or you will miss sampling the remarkable fare that India offers. Food freshly cooked and sold straight from the brazier at roadside *dhabas*, or cafés, is delicious and usually safe. Ice-cream can be a breeding ground for typhoid when thawed and re-frozen, but is also a most delicious treat, particularly in the dairy state of Gujarat. The best rule is to eat at places with a high turnover so that the food served is usually fresh. Ironically, five-star hotels often produce tummy troubles as they serve food with sauces and dressings such as mayonnaise that are best left alone. Be sensible, and if something looks or smells borderline, do not eat it. Smaller restaurants often do not provide utensils, in keeping with the Indian custom of eating with one's right

ABOVE: Platform hawkers sell their spicy wares as a train stands to a halt at a rural station.

hand, and so it is best to wash your hands before chowing down.

If you are smitten by diarrhea or an upset tummy, treat all spiced and oily foods as taboo. Eat sparing amounts of bland boiled rice, yogurt, and bananas, and drink plenty of black tea and water. It is best to try and work the bugs out of your system, but if your travel itinerary demands an immediate calmed stomach, take some Lomotil tablets to halt diarrhea. Avoid taking antibiotics immediately, as these will kill the bugs but also any other bacterial resistance you have accumulated, making you susceptible for a second bout. If problems persist for more than two days, particularly if accompanied by fever, consult a doctor as you may be suffering from dysentery, an illness that will require treatment.

ACCOMMODATION

India has a vast array of accommodation, from opulent palaces to seedy dives, and as tourism becomes a major industry, service standards have generally improved.

In this guide, accommodation has been divided into categories which fall into set price ranges, as follows: Very Expensive: US$130 plus; Expensive: US$80 to $130; Moderate: US$40 to $80; Inexpensive: US$20 to $40; Cheap: US$10 to $20; and Very Cheap: US$10 and below.

Five-star hotels are the scene of much socializing in the major cities and are usually up to international standards, having an array of restaurants, health clubs, business centers, and all essential services.

Information on Goverment run hotels and accommodation can be obtained from the Tourist Reception Centre (RDTC Ltd), Bikaner House, Pandera Road, New Delhi, ((011) 383837 fax (011) 382823).

Rajasthan has many former palaces converted into hotels, and it is worth staying in one of these for an unforgettable experience of comfort, cuisine and service amid architectural magnificence — a pleasant change from the modern hotels of the West.

Former lodges of British colonial rulers provide solid and often sumptuous accommodation in the hill stations, and wildlife parks often have comfortable bungalows run by state authorities.

Quite frequently, you will arrive at your hotel and the staff will deny all knowledge of your booking, usually because your room has been given to a guest willing to pay a higher price. In such a situation, have ready all the paperwork necessary to prove your booking, and usually a room will suddenly become vacant.

Cheap accommodation is typically clustered around bus or rail stations, and despite being spartan, is usually available for under US$5 a night. If you are traveling through malaria-infested areas and see slogans declaring "get blood test for all fever cases", this is a cue to use a mosquito net. Cotton nets are better than nylon because the natural fabric breathes and allows your sweat to evaporate from the net, cooling you underneath. If you have no net, turn on a ceiling fan — mosquitoes hate direct air currents so this will hopefully ward them off.

Always lock up your luggage when you leave your room if your accommodation is in any way disreputable. The real thieves, sad to say, are usually other foreign tourists who have fallen on hard times or are into hard drugs. French and Italian junkies have the worst reputation for ripping off everything you own, so if you see any one acting suspiciously, change hotels or take protective measures by either carrying your cash and passport with you or leaving it with the hotel manager for safekeeping.

TOURIST INFORMATION

The main **Government of India Tourist Office** is in Delhi, ((011) 332-0005 and 333-0008, at 88 Janpath and is open from 9 am to 6 pm daily except Sundays offers answers to queries about all Indian destinations. **State Tourist Offices** in Delhi are useful for gathering specialized material and are either at Kanishka Shopping Plaza, 19 Ashok Road (Jammu and Kashmir, Kerala, Madhya Pradesh); C-4 Chanderlok Building, 36 Janpath (Rajasthan, Uttar Pradesh, Himachel Pradesh, and Haryana); B-1 Baba Kharak Singh Marg, (Andhra Pradesh, Assam, Gujarat, Karnataka, Maharashtra, Orissa, Tamil Nadu and West Bengal) or at Hotel Janpath (Sikkim).

Tourist information can also be obtained from the following overseas offices of the Government of India Tourist Office:
Australia
Sydney: 65 Elizabeth Street, Sydney, NSW 2000, ((02) 232-1600.
Canada
Toronto: 60 Bloor Street, West Suite No. 1003, Ontario M4W 3B8, ((416) 962-3787/88.
Thailand
Bangkok: Singapore Airlines Building, 3rd Floor, 62/5 Thaniya Road, (235-2585.
United Kingdom
London: 7 Cork Street, London W1X 2AB, ((0171) 437-3677/8.
United States of America
Los Angeles: 3550 Wilshire Blvd, Suite 204, California 90010, ((213) 380-8855.

Chicago: 230 North Michigan Avenue, Illinois 60601, ((312) 236-6899/7869.
New York: 30 Rockefeller Plaza, Room 15, North Mezzanine, NY 10020, ((212) 586-4901/2/3.

GETTING AROUND

India is different for everyone. Some people swear that a rough-and-tumble style of traveling is the only way to get close to its soul. Others enjoy adventurous sightseeing, but not at the expense of comfort.

Perhaps the best strategy is the middle ground of traveling independently with an emphasis on comfort. Try to strike a balance between insulation from India's grand panorama that comes from the cloistered atmosphere of organized tours and five-star hotels, and being snared in by the day-to-day hassles of tight budget traveling.

Most people underestimate India's size, and many travelers' itineraries have been thrown out of kilter by failing to appreciate the considerable time it takes to cover distances. The country has a remarkable transport infrastructure that somehow always gets you where you want to go, and mostly it is a trade-off between time by train and money by plane.

DOMESTIC AIRLINES

Until quite recently there was little alternative to flying Indian Airlines, India's main domestic carrier. It is still the main carrier, however both Jet Airways and Demania Airways cover major tourist routes with daily flights. There are several other private airlines with less extensive routes including Modiluft, Jagson, Archana and East West.

The general enquiry/reservation numbers in India for the above airlines are:

Indian Airlines: (main offices) Bombay, (202-3031; Calcutta, ((033) 262548; Delhi, ((011) 331-3732; Madras, ((044) 478333.

Jet Airways: Bangalore, ((080) 588354; Bombay: ((022) (022) 838-6311; Delhi, ((011) 372-4727; Goa, ((0832) 221472; Hydrabad; ((0842) 239076; Madras, ((044) 825-7914. In London, England, ((0181) 970-1500

Demania Airlines: Bombay, ((022) 810-2525; Calcutta, (033) 475-9652; Delhi, ((011) 687-9279; Goa, ((0832) 433942; Madras, ((044) 828-0610. In London, England, ((0171) 724-3038.

Flights on these airlines generally cost about double that of a first-class rail ticket, but the investment is usually worthwhile for covering vast distances that take days by train.

Try to buy tickets well in advance and ensure that seats are confirmed, as flights are typically overbooked. If you purchase your ticket with rupees, you will be asked to produce a bank receipt to prove your foreign currency was changed at a bank. Foreigners pay 50 percent more than residents, but are given a higher priority on flights and greater flexibility in changing tickets.

Political extremism has made tight security a facet of Indian air travel, so ensure that any pocket-knives are stashed inside your checked luggage, and expect batteries to be confiscated as these are designated as capable of powering a bomb.

Indian civil aviation is very overstressed

and it is best to give yourself plenty of time between connections as planes are frequently delayed.

Indian Airlines offer several discount travel schemes. The "Youth Fare", restricted to 12- to 30-year-olds, gives a 25 percent discount on the US dollar fare for any internal flight for up to 90 days. The "Discover India" scheme offers 21 days' unlimited travel for a flat US$400. The "Tour India" ticket is similar (US$300 for 14 days spread over six sectors of the country), as is the "Wonderfare" ticket (US$200 for seven days). With all these schemes, you are allowed to visit no airport more than once, except for the purpose of a connecting flight or when in transit.

ABOVE: Luckily for these hardy travelers, India is a land of endless horizons and few life-endangering tunnels.

RIDING THE RAILS

The Indian rail system was established by the British largely as a means of transporting troops and extracting raw materials, and it remains one of the more beneficial colonial legacies, carrying more than three billion passengers each year on its services that ply across the country. In contrast to the brisk, buckled-up anxiety of a plane journey, Indian train trips are made vivid by one's fellow passengers, and a ticket buys a front-row seat for the greatest drama on earth — the human condition.

The network services the most far-flung areas of the country, and no visit to India would be complete without experiencing a train journey, which remains the most practical and reliable form of travel. There are several scenic routes worth taking during the day, but it is generally best to cover longer distances by overnight sleeper, which will save you money and time.

From first-class air-conditioned sleeper to third-class bench, there will be a mode of rail travel to suit your budget. A quota of berths are reserved for tourists, but these are rapidly allocated so it is best to book well in advance. The system works surprisingly well, and many an astonished traveler has arrived at a remote station to see a clerk open an immense ledger in which their name is listed for a reserved seat.

ABOVE: A second-class carriage scene.

Ticketing is computerized along the main trunk routes, where there are also international travel bureaus that save you the inconvenience of queuing for hours in the main ticket hall.

Not all trains have first-class compartments, and the second-class compartments are usually overcrowded. Even if you have reserved a berth, and it can be difficult to avoid unlikely bed partners. An old man may respectfully request that he be allowed to perch on the edge of your seat, and when you consent, he may be joined by many relatives. In a totally crammed train, it would look very selfish for you to want to take so much room when such people have so little. For this reason, request the top bench that unfolds from the wall. These cannot be shared and usually provide a cozy location for a good night's sleep.

Thieves do prey upon snoozing travelers, so be sure to use your luggage as a pillow. Dining cars are rare on Indian trains, as snacks and refreshments are sold by hawkers at each station. For a more comfortable journey it is best to take along some food and bottles of mineral water.

Indrail Passes are particularly good value for those planning an extended tour of India by train. Passes are issued for periods of 1,2,4,7, 8,21, 30, 60 and 90 days. They must be purchased in foreign currency by foreign nationals or by Indians living abroad and can be obtained from all main railway stations in India or through your travel agent. Their are three prices, Fully airconditioned; first class/AC sleeper; and second class. The prices for travel for seven days in these categories is US$270/$135/$71 and for 90 days, US$960/$480/$210. Railway timetables are available from most large stations; the most useful ones are the *All India Railway Timetable* and the concise but comprehensive *Trains at a Glance.*

Travelers who enjoy luxury may want to experience the "Palace on Wheels," a remarkable eight-day rail tour through Rajasthan aboard sumptuous carriages belonging to erstwhile maharajas. Scarlet-turbaned waiters serve Indian and continental cuisine as you chug through the desert state aboard the vintage train, which has private cabins with showers. The tour rolls out from Delhi and stops at Jaipur, Chittaurgarh, Udaipur, Jaisalmer, Jodhpur, and Bharatpur/Fatehpur Sikri/Agra. The tour runs between October and May. To request space or for information call or fax Amtour Vacations, 15760 Ventura Blvd #803, Encino, Ca 91436, USA. ((1) 818 386 fax (1) 818 386-9079.

BUSES

Buses are less comfortable than trains, but are cheaper and go to more obscure locations not reached by rail. Buses are another quintessential Indian experience, and no one quite forgets the near-collisions above mountain ravines or the constant blaring of horns. The latest addition to the fleets are "video buses", coaches that have mounted behind the driver a television set showing the latest Hindi-language films. While these productions yield remarkable insights into the dynamics of India, the soundtracks ensure insomnia and, unless you have come equipped with earplugs, it is advisable to slip the conductor Rs 30 with the instruction that the video is broken. At the height of summer, it is worth paying extra to travel aboard an air-conditioned vehicle.

URBAN TRANSPORT

Indian towns and cities usually have bus and sometimes rail systems, but most travelers find it best to get around by taxi and auto-rickshaw, for which there are certain ground rules.

Drivers will often insist their meter is not working so that they can charge more; and if you accept this principle, always agree on a price before setting off. It can be helpful to ask a local what a fair price should be. If there is a queue of auto-rickshaws, the lead driver may turn you down if he feels the fare is too low to justify losing his place at the front of the line. If this is the case, just go to the last driver, who will have little to lose by taking you to your destination, even if it is nearby.

Auto-rickshaws are the cheapest and most convenient way of negotiating short distances, but are best avoided for longer trips as it is invariably a rough ride, and the vehicle are prone to break down and have accidents.

Taxis are about double the price, but it is worthwhile paying for the added comfort and speed. The vehicle will either be the ubiquitous Ambassador, a clanking 1957 Morris Oxford still produced in India, or the Padmini, a zippier 1950's-model Fiat.

Drivers usually treat their vehicle reverently, rather like sacred cows, and know weird and wonderful ways to keep them functioning. I once saw a taxi-wallah beat his engine back to life with a rock. Drivers will also wait quite happily if you want to retain them while you go off for an hour or so of sightseeing or shopping, but you must agree to pay a waiting charge of about Rs 40 per hour. Drivers are also entitled to charge on top of the meter a 25 percent "night charge" between 10 pm and 6 am. Different rules apply in different cities, and it is best to check with hotel personnel as to the correct local rate.

COMMUNICATIONS

TIME

Indian Standard Time is 5½ hours ahead of Greenwich Mean Time and 9½ hours ahead of US EST. However time is a very elastic concept in India. Indeed in Hindi, the same word is used to describe both "yesterday" and "tomorrow."

POSTAL SERVICES

Mail services in India are generally good, although it's best to make sure that staff frank letters to ensure that the stamp is not immediately peeled off and resold — a common practice. Sending a parcel abroad can be a complicated, time-consuming business. Either bear with excess luggage or get government emporiums to ship your shopping home.

TELEPHONES

Until quite recently India had one of the world's oldest telephone systems, an archaic network established by the British during Queen Victoria's reign. Blessedly, the government has updated its mechanical exchanges with digital systems and most numbers are obtainable by direct dialing. Use the area code (indicated in parentheses in this book) if dialing from outside the area and the local number only if in the area. To reach a subscriber in India from overseas, dial your overseas access number, then "91" for India, the area code (dropping the initial "0") and the number.

If you are staying in a good city hotel, it is quite easy to make calls internationally or long-distance within India by direct dialing. Otherwise, calls must be made from crowded booths at the local post office.

Hotels usually whack a stiff service charge on telephone calls, so it is worth checking their terms before you begin a calling binge.

TELEX, TELEGRAMS, AND FACSIMILE

Domestic and international telex and telegram services in India are fairly reliable and reasonably priced. Again, you have a choice of either queuing up at the GPO or using the facilities of a large hotel. The advantage of the telex is that it gives you a record of having reconfirmed hotel or flight bookings, and can be a highly useful piece of paper if knowledge of your booking is denied.

Facsimile facilities have yet to make an impact in India. Most five-star hotels have business centers with fax services, but rates tend to be pricey, with an additional 10 percent service charge for an international destination.

Filing information by a computer modem through a telephone line can be erratic, as one line hit will disrupt the data flow, but after two or three attempts the message is usually received at the other end.

MEDIA

India has a large number of English-language dailies and hundreds of vernacular newspapers, for one of its beauties is an unshackled press. The dailies, written in a dense Edwardian prose packed with remarkable colloquialisms, become an addictive beginning to the day if you wish to understand the complexities of Indian politics. The *Times of India* is the largest in circulation and, along with the *Statesman of Calcutta*, plots a centrist path. The *Indian Express* is anti-government and prone to printing glaring exposés on its front page. The *Hindu of Madras* has a strong science section and solid coverage of southern India, while the *Hindustan Times* is pro-government and good for getting the views of the status quo. The *Telegraph* and the newly-created *India Post* are more upbeat, with solid features and good photographs. Newspapers also advertise ongoing cultural events, but the coverage is haphazard, with events often being advertised after they have occurred. Major cities usually have a weekly journal dedicated to local events, such as the capital's *Delhi Diary*, *Bombay Calling* and *Hallo Madras*, brimming with practical information and directory listings.

Sunday newspapers contain matrimonial columns that amply illustrate how Indian marriages are frequently transactions based on pragmatic assessment. For women, a "wheatish complexion" is an asset, and both sexes are rated by their caste, profession, income, and prospects.

More in-depth coverage is found in news magazines, such as The *Illustrated Weekly* or *Sunday*. But the best read is *India Today*, a fortnightly publication crammed with well-written and well-researched articles covering all aspects of Indian life.

The government controls the electronic media, and All India Radio and the two-channel Doordarshan television network are notoriously dull, essentially reporting on news of process (politicians planting trees) or cricket matches. Television does have its high points, notably the screening of soap operas based on the Hindu epics. The programs enjoy a massive following, with entire villages turning out to watch a television set that has been garlanded and blessed for the weekly showing.

India has the world's largest film industry, annually churning out more than 1,000 films compared with Hollywood's paltry 400. The industry is centered in Bombay, and the finished products usually resemble to the Western eye 1940's-style pantomimes of heroes, villains, and damsels in distress bursting into song between gun battles.

Cinema has been seriously undermined throughout the country by the rise of the video. Cassettes of new Western films are pirated and appear in India within weeks of their release in the United States or Europe.

INDIA'S NIGHTLIFE

Nightlife is virtually non-existent in small towns and villages, but New Delhi, Bombay, and Calcutta have discos and an array of cultural events that will keep you out until the wee hours.

Wealthy, well-educated, and socially elite Indians tend to lead incredibly hectic social lives, and simply adore formal dress functions, which is what the winter wedding season is all about. Visitors drawn into well-connected party circles will encounter a high-powered series of social engagements in private homes, five-star hotels, and exclusive clubs. Here, dress, manners, and informed conversation count for everything. Time-honored tradition ensures that while guests are plied with drinks, food often doesn't arrive until past midnight. By the time it does, your surroundings may have become an amiable blur of perfume, silk brocade saris, handlebar mustaches, and tinkling laughs. Most guests tend to eat very quickly, then melt away into the night. Whiskey on an empty stomach followed by rich, spicy food taxes the body, and the best counter-measure is to have a snack before going out and then to drink and eat lightly.

Discos are found in most five-star hotels in the big cities, but cover charges and bar prices tend to be outrageously high. Hotel guests are charged only a nominal amount, but high membership fees deter all but the wealthy sons and daughters of the shakers and movers.

BENEATH THE WHIRLING FAN

Every visitor to India encounters its bureaucracy, the leviathan that runs the affairs of the nation's multitudes.

Many formalities in India require bouts of form-filling, but anything slightly more complex — like getting a refund on a railway ticket or permission to go to a restricted area — can escalate into a Kafkaesque adventure. India's bureaucratic warrens usually house rows of bespectacled shrunken clerks, cowering peons in faded khaki shuffling about delivering sahib's tea, whirring fans, and great sheaves of yellowing files held down by paperweights or quite literally bound by "red tape". The expression was born in India during the early days of the British Civil Service, when red ribbons were first used to hold together official documents.

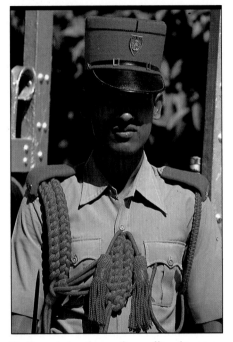

To the untutored eye, these office dens may appear totally haphazard — bustling with people and transactions, while replies to your queries may appear confusing, or even cryptic. You may find yourself wondering what originally launched you on your bureaucratic odyssey in the first place.

But take heart. Be assured that behind every formality lies a reason. By following some general ground rules, keeping reasonably patient, and always maintaining a sense of humor, you'll find things can get done. As a foreigner, it is sometimes difficult to understand all the labyrinthine ins-and-outs of the system. Since transactions can often be frustrating and time-consuming, use an age-old management technique: delegate responsibility. Most hotels can produce a number of willing young men who for a small tip will wait in long queues to purchase tickets at airline offices, rail or bus stations. In local parlance, they will "do the needful" while you follow your own schedule. Always check that the person you are about to trust with your money has been vetted by hotel staff. Travel agencies in India tend to charge only nominal rates for their services, and often secure bookings magically through their own quotas, even on services you've been assured are completely "full up".

More important procedures, such as extending one's visa or seeking a permit to visit a restricted area, require making a personal appearance. Often all that is required is a stamp and an indecipherable scrawl in the right place on the right piece of paper by the right official, but without this your holiday may be ruined. Officials tend to take a very dim view of foreigners who arrive in India without a visa, over-stay, or wind up in areas deemed strategically "sensitive".

The trials and eventual triumphs of dealing with officialdom in India are just part of adjusting to the pace of life on the subcontinent. Never underestimate the power of the person wielding the needed rubber stamp, and always conduct your business in a very polite, but reasonably firm manner.

Officials usually sit in a cramped room and deal with hundreds of people daily, all of whom think their case is more important than yours, so it is easy to see why any display of rudeness or arrogance can go against the grain. Heat and inexplicable delays can drive even paragons of patience to tantrums, but try to remember that India is run according to different rules.

Jovial small talk and a zestful handshake with the appropriate official will go a long way toward getting your case cleared. Some travelers swear that a tip oils the cogs, and this may work in distant regions. But most Indian officials staunchly oppose the suggestion of a bribe, and unless a demand is clearly made, do not risk being arrested for trying to corrupt an officer of the government of India.

BAKSHEESH, BEGGING AND BARGAINING

One of the first words a traveler learns in India is **"baksheesh"**. Loosely translated, it is something you pay to get things done — a little gift or a bribe, a payment for services rendered or even to get rid of a pest. It is usually a small amount, generally less than Rs 10.

ABOVE: An Indian policeman wearing a *kepi* in Pondicherry, Tamil Nadu, once a French enclave.

Beggars moan "baksheesh, sahib", on street corners. Taxi drivers keep their palms out and demand "baksheesh" after you've just given them the correct fare. The judicious use of baksheesh can save you many tedious hours of queue-waiting, while a boy waits for you for a few rupees. Begging is a part of Indian life, despite being officially illegal. India in many ways forces a traveler to make choices, and the baksheesh decision is one for which there can be no guidance. Coping with beggars is all part of traveling in India.

The most deserving of your sympathy are the lepers, multiple amputees, and other

misfortunes whose permanent, life-crippling diseases prohibit them from doing much else. Elderly women begging on the streets are invariably widows, who have a lowly place in society once their husband has died. Half-naked children with large eyes can be very endearing, but are often employed by local rackets who make begging a profession. Mothers with screaming babies whom they deliberately pinch should come much lower on the compassion scale.

Bargaining is one of India's great institutions. Once you have experienced the satisfaction of whittling down the price of a carpet, silver necklace or carved statue, no shopping expedition in India will ever be the same again. Traders expect their customers to haggle, and are inwardly astonished if items are purchased without even a hint of dissent.

Bargaining requires a little acting ability — traders do their showmanship routine, offering syrupy tea, and pulling out stock so that their shop takes on the appearance of a sty-pen — and you should do your part by appearing disinterested in the items you most covet, by picking out

little defects, and disdainfully scorning the prices being quoted. The last stage of bargaining involves getting up, shaking your head and commenting on how the price is just too high. Usually you won't get far before having your shirt sleeves tugged back inside, with prices dropping with each shrug of your shoulders. Bear in mind that no merchant worth his salt is going to sell at anything less than his cost price — and they'll often try to sell goods at up to 70 percent higher than that.

The main thing to remember is that bargaining is only the means to an end. When you see something that you really want, or that you know will make a perfect gift for someone, don't feel that if you can't whittle the price down then it's not worth having. In India as anywhere, quality and fine workmanship will always come with a price-tag attached.

TRAVELERS' HINDI

Hullo/Goodbye   *Namaste*
Goodbye/See you again   *Phir milenge*
How are you   *Aap kaise hain*
Very Good   *Bahut Acha*
Bad   *Kharab*
Please   *Kripaya*
Thank you   *Dhanyavad, Shukriya*
Yes   *Han, Anchi*
No   *Nahi*
Excuse me   *Maaf Karna*
What is your name   *Aap ka naam kya hai*
My name is John   *Meera naam John hai*
What is the time   *Kya bara hai*
Where is the ...   *Kahan hai ...*
How much is this   *Kitne ka hai*
Too much   *Bahut zyada hai*
Lower your price   *Kum karo*
Left   *Bai*
Right   *Dai*
Stop   *Roko/Bas*
Go Straight   *Seedha jaaiye*
Hurry up   *Jaldi kare*
Slow Down   *Aahista*
Go away   *Chale jao or Chelo*
Big   *Bada*
Small   *Chhota*
Beautiful   *Sundar*
Toilet   *Bakhana*
Train   *Gadi*
Prayer   *Puja, pratha*
Sleep   *Sana*
Friend   *Dosta*
Smile   *Muskarana*
Bill please   *Bill lao*
Water   *Panni*
Rice   *Chawal*
Fruit   *Phal*

ABOVE: Ritual beggars at Dasaswanadh Ghat in Varanasi.

Vegetables   *Sabzi*
Bread   *Chapati*
Tea   *Chai*
Coffee   *Kafi*
Milk   *Dudh*
Sugar   *Chini*
Laundry   *Dhobi*
O.K.   *Achha*

Numbers

1	*ek*
2	*do*
3	*teen*
4	*char*
5	*panch*
6	*chhe*
7	*saat*
8	*aarth*
9	*nau*
10	*das*
20	*bis*
30	*tish*
40	*chalish*
50	*pachash*
60	*sahath*
70	*setur*
80	*aashi*
90	*numba*
100	*sau*
1000	*hazar*

GLOSSARY OF COMMON FOODS, CUISINES AND DISHES

Mughali food. Strongly meat-based cuisine, very rich, redolent of thick yoghurt, onions and exotic spices.

Common dishes

roomali   snack or meal of (handkerchief) *rotis* or parathas, layered and stuffed with minced meat or *paneer* cheese.

dal makhni   dish of rich spiced lentils with coriander.

shahi paneer   cheese in cream and tomatoes.

khatte alloo   spiced potato.

baingan mumtaz   stuffed eggplant.

Firni   a kind of exotic rice pudding served in earthenware bowl.

kheer   a rich thickened milk with raisins and nuts.

khulfi   Indian ice-cream accompanied by transparent sweet vermicelli called *falooda*.

subze   spiced vegetable dishes.

dosa   south Indian crisp rice pancake often with a mashed potato filling served with *sambhar*.

Rogon josh   curried lamb.

gushtaba   spicy meat pounded to paté-consistency, formed into balls and simmered in spiced yogurt.

idlis   steamed rice-cake eaten with fresh coconut chutney.

sambhar   a chilli-laced lentil soup.

biryani   chicken or lamb in orange-flavored rice, sprinkled with rose water, almonds and dried fruits.

tandoori   clay oven-baking, of chicken, meat or fish marinated in herbs.

thali   a large round metal tray filled with little bowls that are constantly refilled.

Unleavened breads (baked clinging to the side of a tandoor clay oven):

chapati   crispy bread.

romali roti   hankerchief-thin bread.

Naan   fluffy, yoghurt-leavened bread.

paratha   millet based, sprinkled with cumin, sesame, caraway, or stuffed with peas, onions or potato.

khulcha bhatura   a soft doughy bread eaten with spicy chick-peas.

dosa   a form of crepe made from lightly fermented rice flour and stuffed with spiced potato eaten with fresh coconut chutney and *sambhar*.

Sweet milk/curd-based puddings and confections:

kulfi   ice-cream, flavored with cardamom, pistachio nuts and saffron.

rasgullas   cream cheese balls in rose syrup.

burfi   halva sweets, covered in wafer-thin silver paper.

gulab jamun   spongy ground almond balls, served dripping with honeyed syrup.

jalebi   cartwheel-shaped sweets, served dripping with honeyed syrup.

paan   a mixture of betel nut and spices wrapped in a betel leaf.

Drinks:

nimbu   lime soda, served sweet, salt or plain.

lassis   yogurt-based drink.

Reading List

History and Religion

BASHAM, A.L., *The Wonder That Was India*, London, 1967, reprint 1985.

GANDHI, M.K., *An Autobiography or The Story of My Experiments With Truth*, first published 1927–1929, London, 1982.

HIBBERT, C., *The History of the Indian Mutiny*, London, 1980.

KEAYS, JOHN, *Into India*, 1973.

KEAYS, JOHN, *India Rediscovered*, London, Collins, 1988.

MEHTA, VED, *Mahatma Gandhi and His Apostles*, London, 1982.

MOOREHOUSE, G., *India Britannica*, London, 1983

SPEAR, P. AND THAPAR, R., *A History of India*, vols. 1 and 2, 1978.

THAPAR, ROMILA, *A History of India*, vol. 2, Pelican, 1980.

WATFORD, F., *A Concise History of India*, London 1974.

Novels, Travel Writing, and Commentaries

ACKERLEY, J.R., *Hindoo Holiday*, London, 1931.

ALLEN, CHARLES (ed.), *Plain Tales From The Hills*, London, 1973.

BANNERJEE, B., *Panther Panchali*, London, 1968.

CAMERON, JAMES, *Indian Summer*, London, 1974.

COLLINS, L. AND LAPIERRE, D., *Freedom At Midnight*, India, 1976.

FISHLOCK, TREVOR, *India File*, London, 1983.

FORSTER, E.M., *A Passage To India*, London, 1924.

JHABVALA, R, *To Whom She Will*. The first of many novels set in India.

LAPIERRE, DOMINIQUE, *The City of Joy*, Century, 1986.

NAIPAUL, V.S., *An Area Of Darkness*, London, 1964.

NAIPAUL, V.S., *A Wounded Civilization*, London, 1977.

RUSHDIE, S., *Midnight's Children*, London, 1981.

THEROUX, PAUL, *The Great Railway Bazaar*, London, 1980.

WOOD, M., *Third Class Ticket*, London, 1984.

FOOTNOTE:

Backpackers, and anyone planning an extensive tour of India should invest in *India: A Travel Survival Kit*, Melbourne, Lonely Planet Publications, 3rd Edition 1987, while anyone with a serious interest in the country's wildlife sanctuaries will find invaluable *Indian Wildlife*, written by Samuel Israel, Toby Sinclair and Bikram Grewal, Insight Guides, APA Productions, Singapore 1987.

Photo Credits

Quick Reference A–Z Guide
to Places and Topics of Interest with Listed Accommodation, Restaurants and Useful Telephone Numbers

A accommodation, general advice 336
Agra 92–101
  access 94–95
  accommodation
    Agra Ashok ((0562) 361223 96
    budget lodges 96
    Clarks Shiraz ((0562) 361421 96
    Grand Hotel ((0562) 364014 96
    Hotel Amar ((0562) 360696 96
    Hotel Lauries ((0562) 364536 96
    Hotel Mumtaz ((0562) 361771 96
    Mughgal Sheraton ((0562) 361701 96
    Taj-View Hotel ((0562) 361171-8 96
  attractions
    Agra Fort 97–98
    China-ka-Rauza 99
    Emperor Babur's Ram Bagh Garden 99
    Itmad-ud-Daulah 98–99
    Sikandra 99
    Taj Mahal 93, 96–97
  environs
    Bharatpur Bird Sanctuary
      (Keoladeo National Park) 99, 102–103
    Fatehpur Sikri 99, 100–102
  history 92–99
  restaurants 96
  shopping 99
Ahmedabad 216–221
  access 217
  accommodation
    Ambassador Hotel,
      ((0272) 353244 217–218
    Circuit House, ((0272) 65033 218
    Gandhi Ashram Guest House,
      ((0272) 407742 218
    Hotel Cama, ((0272) 305285 217
    Ritz Hotel, ((0272) 393637 217
    Rivera Hotel, ((0272) 304201-7 217
  attractions
    Ahmed Shah's Tomb 218
    Dada Hari *baoli* (step well) 219
    Doshiwada-ni-pol 219
    Hatheesingh Temple 219
    Jumma Masjid 218
    Manek Chowk 219
    N.C. Mehta Museum 220
    Rani Rupmati's Mosque 218
    Rani Sipri's Mosque and Tomb 218
    Sarabhais' Calico Museum 220
    Shreyas Folk Art Museum 220
    Sidi Saiyad's Mosque 218
    Tribal Museum 220
    Vechaar Utensils Museum 220
  environs
    Adalaj Vav *baoli* (step well) 219
    Lothal archaeological ruins 220
    Sabarmati Ashram 219
    Sarkej monuments 219
  history 217

  retaurants 218
  shopping 219
    hand printed fabrics 219
  tourist information 221
    Tourist Corporation of Gujarat,
      ((0272) 449683 221
Aihole 274
airlines, domestic 337
Ajanta 208, 213, 215
  – *see also* Aurangabad
  accommodation
    Guest House, ((02432) 4874 215
    Holiday Resort, ((02432) 4713 215
  attractions
    caves and frescoes 215
Ajmer 130
  accommodation
    Hotel Khadim, ((0145) 2490 130
  attractions
    Adai-din-ka-Jhonpra mosque 130
    Dargah shrine 130
    festival of Urs 130
Alleppey 322, 324
  accommodation
    Alleppey Prince Hotel, ((0411) 3752 324
    Hotel Komala, ((0411) 3631 324
    St George Lodge, ((0411) 61620 324
  attractions
    backwater cruises 322
    Onam harvest festival 322
  environs
  when to visit 322
Alwar 128
  – *see also* Sariska
  accommodation
    Lake Palace, ((1442) 3764 128
  attractions
    Sariska Tiger Reserve 128–129
    Vinay Vilas Palace 129
Amber 127
  – *see also* Jaipur
Amritsar 89
  attractions
    Akal Takht 89
    Golden Temple 89
    Jalliawalla Bagh 89
Andaman and Nicobar Islands 242, 262–265
  – *see also* Port Blair
  entry permits 263
    Tourist Office, ((03192) 20694 263
  when to go 263–264
Andhra Pradesh 269
Aranchal Pradesh 250
  architecture
    Dravidian 293, 309, 312
    goporums 31
    Islamic 32
    medieval fortresses 32
    Mughal 33

rock-hewn temples 29
southern 31
arriving in India 332
  customs and formalities 333
  from Australasia 332
  from Europe 332
  from the United States 332
  visas 332
  what to bring 334
Assam 250
Aurangabad 208–214
  access 209
  accommodation
    Ajanta Ambassador, ℂ (02432) 82211 209
    Aurangabad Ashok, ℂ (02432) 20520-9 209
    Hotel Rajdoot, ℂ (02432) 299991 209
    Welcomgroup Rama International,
      ℂ (02432) 84441-4 209
  attractions
    Ajanta Caves 215
    Aurangabad Caves 209–210
    Panchakki water mill 210
    shopping and handicrafts 210
  environs
    Ajanta Caves 213, 215
    Aurangzeb's Grave 212
    Daulatabad Fort 212
    Ellora Caves 208, 212–213
  restaurants 209
  tourist information 215
    Government of India Tourist Office,
      ℂ (02432) 20417 215
    Government of Maharashtra Tourist
      Office, ℂ (02432) 24713 215
  when to visit 209

B | **Badami** 274
Bagdogra 249–250
Baksheesh, begging and bargaining 341–342
Bandipur Wildlife Sanctuary 285
Bangalore 276–280
  access 276
  accommodation
    Hotel Hoysala, ℂ (080) 365311 277
    Luciya International, ℂ (080) 224145-8 277
    New Victoria Hotel, ℂ (080) 584076-7 277
    Sudha Lodge, ℂ (080) 605420 277
    Taj Residency, ℂ (080) 558-4444 277
    West End Hotel, ℂ (080) 226-9281 276
    Windsor Manor Sheraton, ℂ (080) 226-9898 276
  attractions
    Bull Temple 279
    Ganesh Temple 279
    Government Museum 279
    High Court 279
    Karnataka dance performances 279
    Kempegowda Fort 279
    Lalbagh Botanical Gardens 279
    Post Office 278
    Venkatappa Art Gallery 279
    Vidhana Soudha 279
    Vidhana Vidhi 278
  environs
    Sriringapatna 279
    Venkataramanaswamy Temple 279
  history 276
  nightlife 277
  restaurants 277–278

tourist information 280
  Karnataka Tourist Office, ℂ (080) 578901 280
Baroda *See* Vadodara
Belakati 257
  – *see also* Bhubaneswar
Belur 280, 284
  attractions
    Chennakeshava Temple 284
Benares *See* Varanasi
Bharatpur 99, 102–103
  accommodation
    Forest Lodge, ℂ (05644) 22722 103
    Golbagh Palace Hotel, ℂ (05644) 3783 103
    Saras Tourist Bungalow, ℂ (05644) 3700 103
  attractions
    Jat Palace and Museum 103
    Keoladeo National Park 102–103
    Lohagarh (Iron) Fort 103
Bhavnagar 221
  accommodation
    Nilambag Palace Hotel, ℂ (0278) 24222 221
Bhubaneswar 253–257
  accommodation
    Bhubaneswar Hotel, ℂ (0674) 51977 254
    Hotel Oberoi Bhubaneswar, ℂ (0674) 56116 254
    Hotel Prachi, ℂ (0674) 52689 254
    Hotel Swosti, ℂ (0674) 54178-9 254
    Kalinga Ashok, ℂ (0674) 53318 254
    New Kenilworth Hotel, ℂ (0674) 54330-1 254
    Pantha Niwas Tourist Bungalow,
      ℂ (0674) 54515 254
  attractions
    Brahmeshwar Temple 256
    Dhauli rock edicts 252
    Khandagiri and Udayagiri cave temples 252
    Lingaraj Temple 255
    Mukteshwar Temple 256
    Orissa State Museum 256
    Parumeshwar Temple 256
    Rajarani Temple 256
    Sisneswar Temple 256
    Sisupalgarh excavated ruins 256
    Vaital Deul Temple 256
  environs
    Dhauli Edicts carved rocks 256
    Nandankanan Park 257
    Udaigiri and Khandagiri Jain and
      Buddhist caves 256
  getting around 254
  history 253
  restaurants 254–255
  shopping 257
    Belakati 257
    Handloom Cooperative Society 257
    Orissan handicrafts 257
    Pipli 257
    Utkalika Handicrafts Emporium 257
  tourist information 254
    OTDC Tourist Information Center,
      ℂ (0674) 50099 254
Bidar 274
Bihar 242
Bijapur 274
Bikaner 144–147
  access 144
  accommodation
    Dhola Maru Tourist Bungalow, ℂ (0151) 5002 145

Gajner Palace, ((0151) 3239 *145*
Lallgarh Palace, ((0151) 61963 *144*
attractions
  bazaars *146*
  Bikaner Jail *146*
  Ganga Singh Golden Jubilee Museum *146*
  Junagarh Fort *145–146*
  Lullargh Palace Museum *145*
environs
  Camel Breeding Farm *146*
  Karni Mata Temple "rat temple" *146*
restaurants 145
Bodhgaya *242*
Bombay *187–200*
accommodation
  Chateau Windsor Guest House,
      ((022) 204-3376 *191*
  Grand Hotel, ((022) 261-8211 *191*
  Hotel President, ((022) 495-0808 *190*
  Leela Penta Hotel, ((022) 836-3636 *191*
  Natraj Hotel, ((022) 204-4161 *191*
  Oberoi Bombay Hotel, ((022) 202-5757 *190*
  Oberoi Towers, ((022) 202-4343 *190*
  Ritz Hotel, ((022) 220141 *191*
  Sea Green Hotel, ((022) 222294 *191*
  Sea Green South Hotel, ((022) 221662 *191*
  Searock Hotel, ((022) 642-5454 *191*
  Taj Mahal Hotel, ((022) 202-3366 *190*
  The Ambassador Hotel, ((022) 204-1131 *191*
  The Fariyas, ((022) 204-2911 *191*
  Whalley's Guest House, ((022) 234206 *191*
  YWCA International Guest House,
      ((022) 202-0445 *191*
attractions
  Adishwarji Jain Temple *198*
  Afghan Memorial Church *194*
  Bhuleshwar Bazaar (brass and copper) *196*
  Bombay Zoo *199*
  Chor or Theives Bazaar (bric-a-brac) *196*
  Chowpatty Beach *196*
  city strolls *193, 195*
  Colaba district *194*
  Crawford Market *195*
  Dhobi ghats *198–199*
  F.D. Alpaiwalla Museum *199*
  Fort area *194*
  Ganesh Chaturthi festival *196*
  Gateway of India *193*
  Haji Ali's Tomb *198*
  Hanging Gardens *197*
  High Court *195*
  Jehangir Art Gallery *194*
  Kamala Nehru Children's Park *198*
  Mahalaxmi Race Course *199*
  Mani Bhavan Gandhi Museum *196*
  Marine Drive *196*
  Mirchi Gully *196*
  Nariman Point *194*
  National Maritime Museum *199*
  Nehru Planetarium *199*
  Prince of Wales Museum *194*
  Royal Bombay Yacht Club *194*
  Sassoon Docks *194*
  Secretariat *195*
  specialist bazaars *195*
  St Thomas' Cathedral *195*
  University Library *195*

  Victoria and Albert Museum *199*
  Victoria Gardens *199*
  Victoria Terminus *195*
  Walkeswar Temple *198*
  Zaveri Bazaar (silver) *195*
climate 188
environs
  Bassein ruins *200*
  Elephanta Island *199*
  Kanheri Caves *200*
getting around 188, 190
history 187
nightlife 192–193
restaurants 191–192
  (Chinese) China Garden, ((022) 828-0842 *191*
  (Chinese) Chopsticks, ((022) 204-9284 *192*
  (Chinese) Nanking, ((022) 202-0594 *192*
  (French) La Rotisserie, ((022) 202-5757 *191*
  (Gujarati) Samrat, ((022) 220492 *192*
  (Indian) Delhi Durbar, ((022) 202035 *191*
  (Indian) Durbar, ((022) 359086 *191*
  (Indian) Tanjore, ((022) 202-3366 *191*
  (Keralan) Woodlands, ((022) 202-3499 *192*
  (Northwest)Kandahar, ((022) 202-5757 *191*
  (Polynesian) The Outrigger,
      ((022) 202-4343 *191*
  (Szechuan) Golden Dragon,
      ((022) 202-3366 *191*
tourist information 200
  Government of India Tourist Office,
      ((022) 293144 *200*
  India Tourism Development Corporation
      (ITDC), ((022) 242-3343 *200*
  Maharashtra TDC, ((022) 202-6713,
      ((022) 202-7762 *200*
Buddhism *26, 51–52*
Buddhist art *28–29*
  famous sites *29*
bus travel, long distance *338*
C Calcutta *227–242*
access 229
accommodation
  Astor Hotel, ((033) 242-9957 *230*
  Fairlawn Hotel, ((033) 244460, 245-1510 *230*
  Great Eastern, ((033) 248-2331 *230*
  Hotel New Kenilworth, ((033) 242-5136 *230*
  Oberoi Grand, ((033) 292323 *229*
  Park Hotel, ((033) 297336 *230*
  Shilton Hotel, ((033) 245-1512 *230*
  Taj Bengal, ((033) 248-3939 *229*
  Tollygunge Club, ((033) 410616 *229*
  Salvation Army Red Shield Guest House,
      ((033) 245-1512 *230*
  YMCA, ((033) 292192 *230*
attractions
  Academy of Fine Arts *238*
  Ausotosh Museum *238*
  BBD Bagh (Dalhousie Square) *235*
  Birla Academy of Art and Culture *238*
  Birla Planetarium *238*
  College Street *237*
  Durga Puja festival *228*
  GPO Building *236*
  Howrah Bridge *236*
  Indian Museum *238*
  Jain Temple *236*
  Kali Khetra Temple *237*

Kumar Tulli "Potter's Lane" 237
Nakhoda Mosque 236
National Library 237
Nehru Children's Museum 238
nightlife 232
Nirmal Hriday 237
R.N. Mukherjee Street 236
Rabindra Sadan concert hall 238
Rabindra-Bharati Museum 236
Raj Bhawan 234
Royal Asiatic Society 238
Sisar Mancha concert hall 238
South Park Cemetery 236
St John's Church 235
St Paul's Cathedral 234
State Archaeological Museum 238
The Maiden 232
The Marble Palace 236
Victoria Memorial 233–234
Writer's Building 235
Zoological Gardens 234
environs
Belur Math 240
Botanical Gardens 240
getting around 228–229
history 227
restaurants 230–231
(Bengali) Surachi 231
(Bengali/Mughali) Sky Room,
((033) 294362 231
(French) La Rotisserie (Oberoi Grand),
((033) 292323 231
shopping 238
All Bengal Women's Home 238
Bengal Home Industries Association 238
New Market (Hogg's Market) 238
West Bengal Government Sales
Emporium 238
tourist information 240, 251
Foreigner's Registration Office,
((033) 44301 240
India Tourist Office, ((033) 242-1402 240
Tourist Information Centre,
((0361) 24475 251
West Bengal Tourist Bureau,
((033) 248-8271 240
travel bookings 240
Eastern Railways, ((033) 222291 240
Indian Airlines, ((033) 260730, 263390 240
Mercury Travels, ((033) 443555 240
Sita World Travels, ((033) 240935,
(293003 240
South Eastern Railways, ((033) 235074 240
Travel Corporation of India,
((033) 445469 240
when to visit 228
Canning 242
caste system 23, 30, 50
Cherrapunji 251
Chittaurgarh 150–151
accommodation
Panna Tourist Bungalow, ((01472) 41238 152
access 152
attractions
Chittaurgarh fortress citadel 150–152
history 150
Christianity 53

Cochin 326–329
access 326
accommodation
Biju's Tourist Home, ((0484) 369881 327
Bolgatty Palace Hotel, ((0484) 355003 327
Casino Hotel, ((0484) 666821 326327
Hotel International, ((0484) 353911 327
Hotel Seagull, ((0484) 28128 327
Island Inn, ((0484) 666816 327
Malabar Hotel, ((0484) 346811, 340010 326
Maruthi Tourist Home, ((0484) 6365 327
PWD Tourist Rest Home, ((0484) 25797 327
Sea Lord Hotel, ((0484) 352682 327
Woodlands Hotel, ((0484) 351372 327
attractions
backwater cruises 328
Cochin Archaeological Museum 328
Cochin Cultural Centre, ((0484) 353732 329
Ernakulam Market 328
Fort Cochin 328
Gundu Island 328
Jewish Synagogue 327
Jewtown 327
Kathakali dance performances 328
Mattancherry Palace 327
Santa Cruz Church 328
See India Foundation, ((0484) 369471 329
St Francis Church 328
environs
Trichur 329
history 326
restaurants 327
tourist information
Government of India Tourist Office,
((0484) 6045 329
KTDC Tourist Reception Centre,
((0484) 353234 329
Coimbature 286
– see also Ootacamund (Ooty)
communications 339
Coonoor 288
– see also Ootacamund (Ooty)
accommodation
Hampton Manor, ((0264) 6244 288
attractions
Glen Morgan Tea Estate 288
Corbett National Park 89
Covelong 312
– see also Mahabalipuram
accommodation
Fishermen's Cove, ((04114) 268 312
credit card acceptance 333
currency and exchange 333
customs and formalities 333
D Dachigam National Park 172
Darjeeling 242–247
access 244
accommodation
Hotel Everest, ((0354) 2616-8 244
Luxury Tourist Lodge, ((0354) 2611 245
Windamere, ((0354) 54041-2 244
Youth Hostel, ((0354) 2290 245
attractions
Cart road 246
Chowrastra Square 246
fishing 248
Happy Valley Tea Gardens 248

Hayden Hall 246
Himalayan handicrafts 246
Himalayan Mountaineering Institute 247
Laden-La (Nehru Road) 246
Lloyd's Botanical Gardens 247
Mt. Everest views 246
The Bengal Natural History Museum 247
Tibetan Self Help Centre 246
trekking 243, 248
Victoria Falls 247
Zoo 247
environs
Kalimpong 247
Senchal Golf Club 248
Tiger Hill 246
restaurants 246
tourist information 244
Darjeeling Foreigner's Registration
Department, ((0354) 2261 244
Tourist Bureau, ((0354) 54050 246
travel permits 244
trekking tours 248
Himal Ventures, ((0354) 2710 248
Summit, ((0354) 2710 248
Tenzing Kanchenjunga Tours,
((0354) 3508 248
Datia 109
attractions
Gobinda Palace 109
Daulatabad Fort 212
– see also Aurangabad
Delhi 69–89
accommodation
Ashok Hotel, ((011) 600412 75
Ashok Yatri Niwas, ((011) 332-4511 75
Blue Triangle Family Hostel,
((011) 310133 75
Centaur Hotel, ((011) 545-2223 75
Claridges, ((011) 301-0211 75
Hotel Ambassador, ((011) 463-2600 75
Hotel Imperial, ((011) 332-5332 75
Hotel Marina, ((011) 332-4658 75
Hyatt Regency Delhi, ((011) 688-1234 75
Le Meridien Hotel, ((011) 371-0101 75
Lodhi Hotel, ((011) 436-2422 75
Maurya Sheraton (Welcomgroup),
((011) 301-0101 75
Nirula's, ((011) 332-2419 75
Oberoi Maidens, ((011) 252-5464 75
Roshan Villa Guest House,
((011) 331-1770 75–76
Taj Mahal Hotel, ((011) 301-6162 75
The Holiday Inn Crowne Plaza,
((011) 332-0101 75
The Oberoi, ((011) 436-3030 75
The Taj Palace Hotel, ((011) 301-0404 75
Vivek Hotel, ((011) 523015 76
YMCA Tourist Hostel, ((011) 311915 75
YWCA International Guest House,
((011) 311561 75
attractions
Ashokan Pillar 83
Bird Hospital 82
Chandni Chowk bazaars 82
Civil Lines 82
Connaught Place 69, 72, 83
Crafts Museum 87

Digambar Jain Mandir 82
Doll's Museum 87
Feroz Shah Kotla 87
festivals 74, 86
Flagstaff Tower 83
Humayan's Tomb 72, 84
India Gate 69, 84
Indira Gandhi Memorial 87
Jama Masjid mosque 82
Janpath 72
Jantar Mantar Observatory 83
Kotawali (police station) 82
Laxmi Narayan Temple (Birla Temple) 83
Lodhi Gardens 72, 84
Lothian Road 83
Maidan 84
Metcalfe House 83
Mughal Gardens 84
Mutiny Memorial 83
National Museum 87
National Museum of Modern Art 88
Nehru Museum 87
Nicholson Cemeteries 83
nightlife 78
Nizamuddin (14th century Sufi village) 86
Old Delhi 79
Old secretariat 83
Purana Qila 86
Qatb Minar 84
Rail Museum 87
Raj Ghat 87
Rashtrapati Bhawan (PresidentialPalace) 69, 72
Rashtrapati Bhawan complex 72, 83
Red Fort (Lal Qila) 69, 72, 79–82
Safdarjang Tomb 72, 84
Sansad Bhawan (Parliament) 83
Shah Jehan's Medieval Walled City 79
shopping 82, 88–89
shopping areas 72
Sikh Gurudwara Sisgani 82
Spice Market 82
St James Church 82
Tibet House Museum 88
Tughlaqabad 84
Zoo 86
history 72—72
restaurants 76–78
(Afghani) Khyber ((011) 252-0867 77
(Chinese) Taipan ((011) 363030 78
(Chinese) Tea House of the August Moon
((011) 301 0404 78
(French) La Rochelle ((011) 363030 78
(Italian) Valentino's ((011) 609911 78
(Mediterranian) Taverna Cyprus
((011) 600412 78
(Mughali) ((011) 301-3201 76
(Mughali) Dum Pukht ((011) 301-0101 76
(Mughali) Haveli ((011) 301-0404 76
(Mughali) Kandahar ((011) 363030 76
(Mughali) Karims ((011) 698300 77
(north-west Indian) Bukhara
((011) 301-0101 76
(Polynesian/southeast Asian) Bali Hi
((011) 391-0101 78
(seafood) Fisherman's Wharf
((011) 698123 78
(south Indian) Dasaprakash ((011) 690391 77

(south Indian) Woodlands ((011) 619422 77
Frontier ((011) 600412 76
tourist information
Foreigners' Registration Office,
((011) 331-8179 332
Government of India Tourist Office,
((011) 332-0005 and 333-0008 89
transportation
Auto-rickshaws 74
taxis 74
Deshnok 146
– *see also* Bikaner
attractions
Karni Mata Temple "rat temple" 146
Dhauli 252
– *see also* Bhubaneswar
Dundlod 129
– *see also* Shekhavati

E **Eklingi** 150
– *see also* Udaipur
Ellora 212
– *see also* Aurangabad
accommodation
Kailash Hotel, (43 213
attractions
Ellora Caves 212–213

F **Fardapur** 215
– *see also* Ajanta and Aurangabad
Fatehpur Sikri 100–102
accommodation 102
history 93
festival calendar 54–55, 58–60
fresco centers *See* Shekhavati

G **Ganges River** *See* Varanasi
Gangtok 249–250
accommodation
Ashok Mayur, ((03592) 2825 250
Hotel Tashi Delek, ((03592) 22991 250
Nor-Khill Hotel, ((03592) 23186 250
attractions
Cottage Industries Institute 250
Enchey Monastery and Deer Park 250
Institute of Tibetology 250
Orchid Sanctuary 250
Tsuklakhang Palace 250
environs
Bakkim 250
Dzongri 250
Pemayangtse 250
Phodang 250
Rumtek 250
Tashiding 250
tourist information 250
Tourist Information Centre, ((03592) 2064 250
getting around India
buses 338
domestic airlines 337
raiways 337
urban transport 339
Ghoom 243
– *see also* Tiger Hill
Gir 223
– *see also* Sasan-Gir Wildlife Sanctuary
Goa 200–208
access 201–202, 208
Bombay: Overnight Ferry Service,
((022) 864071 208

Panaji: V.S. Dempo (Travel Division),
((0832) 3842 208
accommodation
Aguada Hermitage Villas,
((0832) 276201 205
Cicade de Goa, ((0832) 3301 207
Essa Beach Resort, ((0832) 92 206
Fort Aguada Beach Resort, ((0832) 276201 205
Hotel Baia Do Sol, ((0832) 276084-5 206
Hotel Fidalgo, ((0832) 6291-9 205
Hotel Mandovi, ((0832) 6270-9 205
Hotel Silver Sands, ((0832) 21645 206
Oberoi Bogmalo Beach Resort,
((0832) 2191 206
Prainha Cottages, ((0832) 44162 207
Taj Holiday Village, ((0832) 276201 206
Vagator Beach Resort, ((0832) 262918 206
Varma Beach Resort, ((0832) 276077 206
attractions
Archaeological Museum and Portrait
Gallery, ((0832) 5941 208
Archives Museum of Goa, ((0832) 6006 208
Baga and Anjuna Beaches 205
Basilica of Bom Jesus 202
Bogmalo beach 205
Calangute and Candolim beaches 205
Chapel of St Catherine 204
Chapora and Vagator beaches 205
Church of Our Lady of the Rosary 204
Colva beach 205
Convent and Church of Francis of Assisi 204
Convent of St Monica 204
Old Goa 202
Panaji 202
St Augustine Tower 204
stately mansions 204
The Church of St Cajetan 204
getting around 202
history 201
restaurants 207–208
tourist information 208
Government of India Tourist Office,
((0832) 43412 208
Tourist Information and Tour Counter,
((0832) 45583, 45715, 44757 208
when to visit 201
Gopalpur-on-sea 261
– *see also* Puri
accommodation
Oberoi Palm Beach Hotel, ((0821) 8123 261
attractions
golden sands 261
environs
Chilka Lake bird sanctuary 261
Gujarat 200, 215–217
attractions
Makara Sakranti Kite Festival 216
Navrati Festival 216
tourist information
Government Gujarat Tourist Office,
((022) 202-6886 223
Gulmarg 173–174
accommodation
Hotel Highland Park, ((01953) 230, 291 173
Nedous, ((01953) 223 173
Ornate Woodlands, ((01953) 268 173
Pine Palace, ((01953) 266 173

attractions
    Alpather Lake 174
    golf course 174
    mountain walks and climbs 174
    skiing 173
    trekking 174
Guwahati 250
accommodation
    Hotel Bramaputra Ashok,
        ((0361) 542653 251
attractions
    Assam State Zoo and Museum 251
    Kamakshya Temple 251
    Kaziranga Wildlife Sanctuary 251
    Manas Wildlife Sanctuary 251
    Sualkashi silk weaving center 251
Gwalior 108–109
access 108
accommodation
    Tansen Hotel ((0751) 340371 109
    Usha Kiran Palace ((0751) 323213 109
attractions
    Gwalior Fort 108
    Jai Vilas Palace 108–109
environs
    Datia 109
    Orchha 109
H Haldighati 150
    – see also Udaipur
Halebid 280, 285
attractions
    Hoysalesvara Temple 285
Hampi 275–276, 280
Hassan 284
accommodation
    Hassan Ashok Hotel, ((8172) 8330 284
environs
    Belur 284
    Halebid 284
    Sravanabelagola 284
health and precautions 334–335
Hemis Gompa 181
    – see also Ladakh
Hinduism 26, 46, 48–50
history
    Alexander the Great 23
    ancient India 22
    arrival of Europeans 35
    art and artifacts 45
    Aryans 23
    Ashoka 26, 28
    Bactrian Greeks 28–29
    British Raj 36–38
    Dravidian kingdoms 27–28
    Dravidians 22
    early Western invaders 23
    Gandhi and independance 38–39
    Guptas 29–30
    India under Nehru 40
    Indira Gandhi 40
    Indus Valley Civilization 22
    Kushans 28
    Mauryas 26
    medieval fortresses 32
    Mughals 32–34
    Muslim invasions 31
    Sungas 28

    Tamil kingdoms 31
    Tughlaqs 32
Hyderabad 268–274
access 269
accommodation
    Hotel Banjara, ((0842)222222 270
    Hotel Sarovar, ((0842) 237638 270
    Hotel Taj Mahal, ((0842) 237988, or
        (237993 270
    Krishna Oberoi, ((0842) 222121 269
    Ritz Hotel, ((0842) 233571 270
    Rock Castle Hotel, ((0842) 222541 270
attractions
    Ajanta Pavilion 272
    Ancient Life Museum 273
    Aquarium 273
    Baradari Palace 272
    Birla Mandir (Naubat Prahad) temple 273
    Birla Planetarium 273
    British Residency 272
    Charminar 270
    Faluknuma Palace 272
    Government Archaeological Museum 272
    High Court 272
    King Kothi Palace 272
    Lion Safari Park 273
    Mecca Masjid 271
    National History Museum 273
    Nehru Zoological Park 273
    Old Bazaar 271
    Osmania Hospital 272
    Panch Mahal 272
    Salar Jung Museum 272
environs
    Golconda Fort 273
    Qutub Shahi Tombs 274
getting about 270
history 269
restaurants 270
shopping 271
    pearls and jewelry 272
tourist information 274
    Andhra Pradesh Tourist Information Bureau,
        ((0842) 556493, 556523 274
travel bookings 274
    Sita World Travel, ((0842) 223628 274
    Trade Wings, ((0842) 30545 274
    Vayudoot Airlines, ((0842) 36902 274
when to visit 269
I Imphal 251
accommodation
    Hotel Ranjit ((0385) 220382 (Imphal) 251
attractions
    Moriang folk village 251
    Rash Lila festival of Manipuri dance
        (Oct/Nov) 251
environs
India, general information
    border regions 21
    river systems 21
    getting around the country 337
    when to visit 333
Indian Airlines 134, 148
    – discount travel scheme 337
    – general information 337
    Bangalore, ((080) 79413 280
    Bombay, ((022) 202-3031 337

Calcutta, ℂ (033) 264433 enquiries; ℂ (033) 263135 reservations; 260730, 263390 *240*
Delhi, ℂ (011) 462-4332 enquiries; ℂ (011) 462-0566 reservations; ℂ 331-3732 *337*
Hyderabad, ℂ (0842) 36902, 72051 *274*
Jammu, ℂ (0191) 42735, 47577 *176*
Jodhpur, ℂ (0291) 28600 or 20909 *134*
Madras, ℂ (044) 825-1677 enquiries; ℂ 827-7888 reservations; ℂ 478333 *337*
Srinagar, ℂ (194) 73270, 73538, 76557 *172*
Udaipur, ℂ (0294) 23952 *148*
Varanasi, ℂ (0542) 44537 *117*
Indian bureaucracy and officialdom *341*
Indian classical literature *93*
  Mahabharata *93*
Indian dances *60*
Indian festivals and fairs *54–55, 58–60*
Indian food and drink *62–63, 293–295, 327*
  precautions *335–336*
Indian languages
  Sanskrit *23, 29*
Indian mail services *339*
Indian music *60*
Indian railways and services *338*
  "Palace on Wheels" *338*
  Indrail passes *338*
Islam *52*
Jainism *50–51*
Jaipur *121–127*
  access *121–122*
  accommodation
    Achrol Lodge, ℂ (0141) 72254 *123*
    Bissau Palace, ℂ (0141) 74191 *123*
    Gangaur Tourist Bungalow, ℂ (0141) 371641 *123*
    Havali Hotel, ℂ (0141) 75024 *123*
    Jai Mahal Palace, ℂ (0141) 371616 *123*
    Khasa Khoti, ℂ (0141) 375151 *123*
    Khetri House, ℂ (0141) 69183 *123*
    Mansingh Hotel, ℂ (0141) 378771 *123*
    Narain Niwas Guesthouse, ℂ (0141) 563448 *123*
    Raj Mahal Hotel, ℂ (0141) 381757 *123*
    Rambagh Palace, ℂ (0141) 381919 *122*
    Samode Haveli, ℂ (0141) 540770 *123*
    Teej Tourist Bungalow, ℂ (0141) 374373 *123*
  attractions
    Central Museum (Albert Hall) *125*
    City Palace *124*
    Hawa Mahal *124*
    Jantar Mantar astronomical observatory *125*
    Old Royal City *124*
    shopping *127–128*
  environs
    Amber Palace *127*
    Gaitor *127*
    Nahargarh (Tiger) Fort *127*
    Samode *128*
    Sanganer palace ruins *128*
  restaurants *123–124*
  tourist information *128*
    Tourist Office, ℂ (0141) 69714 *124*
  when to visit *121*
Jaisalmer *137–144*
  access *138*
  accommodation
    Fort View Hotel, ℂ (02992) 2214 *140*
    Hotel Narayan Niwas, ℂ (02992) 2408 *139*
    Hotel Neeraj, ℂ (02992) 2442 *139*
    Jaisal Castle, ℂ (02992) 2362 *139*
    Moomal Tourist Bungalow, ℂ (02992) 2392 *139*
  attractions –143
    camel safaris *142–143*
    Desert Festival *138*
    Fort *140–141*
    Gadisar Tank *140*
    Holi Festival *139*
    Mandir Palace *141*
    Manik Chowk market *142*
    Nathamal-ki-Haveli *141*
    Patwon-ki-Haveli *141*
    Salim Singh Haveli *141*
    shopping *141–142*
  environs
    Amar Sagar Jain temple *143*
    Bada Bagh (Big Garden) *143*
    Khuri *144*
    Lodurva *143*
    Sam sand dunes *143*
  history *137–138*
  restaurants *140*
  when to visit *138*
Jammu *175–176*
  accommodation
    Asia Jammu Tawi, ℂ (0191) 43932, 48261 *175*
    Hotel Jammu Ashok, ℂ (0191) 43127, ℂ 43864 *175*
    Hotel Mansar, ℂ (0191) 46161, 43610 *175*
    Jammu TRC, ℂ (0191) 5421, 42231 *175*
    Tawi View Hotel, ℂ (0191) 43752, 43930 *175*
  attractions
    Amar Mahal Museum *176*
    Bahu Fort *176*
    Dogra Art Gallery *176*
    Ragunnath Temple *176*
  restaurants *175*
  tourist information
    Tourist Reception Centre, ℂ (0191) 48172 *176*
Jhansi *109*
Jhunjhunu *129–130*
  – see also Shekhavati
Jodhpur *130–137*
  access *133*
  accommodation
    Adarsh Niwas Hotel, ℂ (0291) 26936 *134*
    Ajit Bhawan, ℂ (0291) 20409 *133*
    Ghoomar Tourist Bungalow, ℂ (0291) 44010 *133*
    Hotel Kalrni Bhawan, ℂ (0291) 30157 *133*
    Umaid Bhawan Palace, ℂ (0291) 33316 *133*
  attractions
    Government Museum *135*
    Jaswant Thada cenotaph *135*
    Mehrangarh Fort *134–135*
    Sardar Bazaar *135*
    Umaid Bhawan Palace *133*
    Umaid Public Gardens and Zoo *135*
    village visits *135–137*
  environs
    Rathmore Marwars (necropolis) *135*
    Rohet Castle *136*
  history *132–133*
  restaurants *134*
  tourist information *134*

Jorhat *251*
attractions
Kaziranga Wildlife Sanctuary *251*
Judaism *53*
Junagadh *221–222*
access 222
accommodation 222
attractions
Girnar Hill Jain Temple complex *221*
Maqbara royal mausoleum *222*
Rang Mahal palace *222*
Rupayatan Institute for Handicrafts *222*
Sakkar Bagh Museum and Zoo *222*
Uparkot walled city *222*
K **Kalibangan** *22*
history 22
Kanchipuram *305–309*
access 307
accommodation
Hotel Tamil Nadu, ((04112) 22562 *307*
attractions
"car festival" *307*
Brahmothsavam festival *307*
Ekambareshwara Temple *308*
Kailasanthar Temple *308*
Kamakshiamman Temple *308*
towering goporum gate-towers *307*
Vaikuntha Perumal *308*
Varasdaraja Temple *309*
shopping 309
silk and handicrafts *305*
when to visit 307
Kanya Kumari *319*
– *see also* Trivandrum
accommodation
Hotel Tamil Nadu, ((04653) 71209 *319*
Karnataka *274, 276, 278–285*
Kashmir *161–162*
history 162
Kaziranga *251*
– *see also* Jorhat
accommodation 251
attractions
Kaziranga Wildlife Sanctuary *251*
rhinos, elephants, wild buffalo, swamp deer,
hog deer, tigers Himalayan bears *251*
Keoladeo National Park, Bharatpur *102–103*
accommodation see listing under Bharatpur
Kerala *316–317, 319, 322, 324–325, 327, 329*
backwater cruises 322
Khajuraho *103–108*
access 105
accommodation
Chandella Hotel ((076861) 2054 *105*
Jass Oberoi ((076861) 2085 *105*
Khajuraho Ashok ((076861) 2024 *105*
Rahil Hotel ((076861) 2062 *105*
Tourist Bungalow ((076861) 2064 *105*
attractions
Archaeological Museum *106*
medieval temples *106–108*
environs
Raja Café *108*
restaurants 105
Khimsar *137*
attractions
Royal Castle *137*

Konarak *252, 261–262*
accommodation
Tourist Bungalow, (21 (Konarak) *262*
attractions
Sun Temple *253, 261*
Kottayam *324*
accommodation
Anjali Hotel, ((0481) 563661 *324*
Hotel Sears, ((0481) 563013 *324*
Vembanad Lake Resort, ((0481) 564866 *324*
attractions
Onam harvest festival *322*
environs
backwater cruises *322*
Kovalam *320–321*
access 320
accommodation
Hotel Moonlight, ((0471) 584311 *321*
Hotel Samudra Tara, ((0471) 54242 *321*
Hotel Samudra, ((0471) 54242 *321*
Hotel Seaweed, ((0471) 60806 *321*
Kovalam Ashok Beach Resort,
((0471) 65323 *321*
Rockholm, ((0471) 306 *321*
attractions
lush scenery and palm-fringed beaches
Marine Research Laboratory
unspoilt coastline to explore
restaurants 321
when to visit 320
Kulu *159*
attractions
Himachal Pradesh State Museum *159*
Raghunathji Temple *159*
Kulu Valley *159*
access 159
accommodation
Kulu Valley Resort, ((01902) 223 *159*
Traveler's Lodge, ((01902) 79 *159*
attractions
Dussehra festival *159*
handicrafts *159*
L **Ladakh** *176–183*
access 180–181
attractions
Hemis festival *181*
Hemis Gompa *183*
tourist information
Tourist Office, (97 (Leh) *181*
when to visit 181–182
languages *See* Indian languages
Leh *180, 182*
– *see also* Ladakh
accommodation
Hotel Indus, (166 (Leh) *182*
Hotel Shambala, (67 (Leh) *182*
Kang-Lha-Chhen, (39 (Leh) *182*
Lha Lha-Ri-Mo, (101 *182*
attractions
Leh Gompa *183*
Leh Khar Palace *183*
Shanka Gompa *183*
environs
Spituk, Shey, Phyang Thikse and Hemis
Gompas *183*
Stok Palace *183*
restaurants 182

Lothal *22, 220*
– *see also* Ahmedabad
history 22

M **Madhya Pradesh** *62*
Madras *295–305*
access 296
accommodation
    Broadlands Lodge, ((044) 845573, or
       (848131 *297*
    Hotel Imperial, ((044) 825-0376 *297*
    Hotel Maris, ((044) 827-0541 *297*
    Hotel New Victoria, ((044) 825-3638 *297*
    Hotel Savera, ((044) 827-4700 *297*
    New Woodland's Hotel, ((044) 827-3111 *297*
    Taj Coromandel, ((044) 827-2827 *297*
    Tourist Home, ((044) 825-0079 *297*
    Welcomgroup Chola Sheraton,
       ((044) 828-0101 *297*
    Welcomgroup Park Sheraton,
       ((044) 499-4104 *297*
    YWCA Guest House and Camping
       Ground, ((044) 39920 *298*
attractions
    Anna Salai Road *296*
    Armenian Church *303*
    Armenian Street *303*
    Burma Bazaar *303*
    China Bazaar *303*
    Clive House *299*
    Cornwallis Cupola *299*
    Elliots Beach *302*
    Evening Bazaar *303*
    Fort St George *296, 299*
    Fort St George Museum *299*
    Georgetown *303*
    Government Museum *300*
    Governor's House *299*
    Guindy Snake Park *301*
    High Court *300*
    Hotel Connemara, ((044) 810051, 82166 *297*
    Ice House *303*
    Indian classical dance *304*
    Kalashetra Centre *302*
    Krishna Parthasarathy Temple *302*
    Marina Beach *302*
    National Art Gallery *300*
    Portuguese Church Street *303*
    Raj Bhavan *301*
    San Thome Cathedral Basilica *302*
    St Mary's Church *299*
    St Thomas Mount *302*
    Theosophical Society *302*
    Valluvar Kottam *300*
    Wellesley House *299*
environs
    Cholamandalam Artists Village *312*
    Golden Beach *303*
    Guindy National Park *301*
    Kapaleeswarar Temple *302*
     Arupathumoovar festival *302*
festivals
    Dance and Arts Festivals *59–60*
getting around 296–297
history 295
restaurants 298
    Amaravathi, ((044) 476416 *298*
shopping 304–305

tourist information
    Tamil Nadu Government Tourist Office,
       ((044) 869685 *305*
when to visit 296
Madurai *305, 312–313*
access 312–313
accommodation
    Hotel Apsara, ((0452) 31444 *313*
    Hotel Madurai Ashok, ((0452) 42531 *313*
    Hotel Tamil Nadu, ((0452) 424-6568 *313*
    Pandyan Hotel, ((0452) 42471 *313*
attractions
    Chithirai Festival *312*
    Gandhi Museum *313*
    Mariamman Teppakkulam Tank *313*
    Meenakshi Temple *312–313*
    Teppam, or "Float" Festival *312*
    Tirumalai Nayak Palace *313*
environs
    Tirupparankundrum *313*
restaurants 313
tourist information
    Tourist Office, ((0452) 22957 *312*
when to visit 312
Mahabalipuram (Mammallapuram) *305, 309–312*
accommodation
    Ashok Temple Bay Resort, ((04113) 2251 *311*
    Mamalla Bhavan, ((04113) 250 *311*
    Shore Temple Beach Resort,
       ((04113) 235, 268 *311*
    Silversands Beach Resort, ((04113) 2228 *311*
attractions
    "Arjuna's Penance" *309*
    Crocodile Farm *311*
    Five Rathas sculpted chariots *310*
    Krishna Mandapam *310*
    Krishna's Butterball *310*
    Mahishasuramardhini Cave *310*
    open air museum *310*
    School of Sculpture *310*
    Shore Temple *310*
environs
    Covelong *312*
tourist information
    tourist office, ((04113) 232 *310*
Maharashtra *200, 208*
Mahayana Buddhism *26*
Manali *159–161*
accommodation
    Ashok Traveler's Lodge, ((01902) 2331 *159*
    Hotel Highland, ((01902) 2399 *159*
    John Banon's Guest House,
       ((01902) 35 *159*
    Log Huts, ((01902) 2439 *159*
attractions
    fishing (trout) *161*
    Hadimba Devi Temple *161*
    mountaineering *161*
    Old Manali village *159*
    trekking *161*
Manas *251*
– *see also* Guwahati
accommodation
    Forestry Department Bungalow *251*
    Manas Tourist Lodge *251*
attractions
    Manas Wildlife Sanctuary *251*

Mandawa *129*
– *see also* Shekhavati
Manipur *251*
Mapusa *202*
– *see also* Goa
Margao *202*
– *see also* Goa
media *340*
Meghlaya *259—251*
Mettapalayam *286*
– *see also* Ootacamund (Ooty)
Mohenjo-daro (Pakistan) *22*
Moriang *251*
– *see also* Imphal
attractions
woven goods and handicrafts *251*
Mount Abu *152–153*
access 152
accommodation
Hotel Bikaner Palace, ((029742) 3121 *153*
Hotel Hilltone, ((029742) 3112 *153*
Hotel Samrat, ((029742) 3173 *153*
Hotel Savera Palace, ((029742) 3354 *153*
Mount Hotel, ((029742) 3150 *153*
attractions
Dilwara Jain temples *153*
environs
Achalgarh *153*
Guri Shikar *153*
mountain trekking and travel bookings 172
restaurants 153
Mukundagh *129*
– *see also* Shekhavati
Mysore *280–284*
access 280–281
accommodation
Hotel Anugraha, ((0821) 520581 *282*
Hotel Dasaprakash Paradise, ((0821) 26666 *282*
Hotel Dasaprakash, ((0821) 24444 *282*
Hotel Durbar, ((0821) 20029 *282*
Hotel Indra Bhavan, ((0821) 23933 *282*
Hotel Krishnajasagar, ((0821) 57222 *284*
Hotel Mayura Hoysala,
((0821) 25349, 31766 *282*
Hotel Metropole, ((0821) 520681 *282*
Lalitha Mahal Palace Hotel,
((0821) 27721 *281*
Quality Inn Southern Star, ((0821) 27217 ·*281*
Rajendra Vilas Palace, ((0821) 22050 *281*
attractions
Amber Vilas *283*
Dassera festival *280*
Devaraja Fruit and Spice Market *284*
Rail Museum *284*
Sri Chamarajendra Art Gallery *282*
St Philomena's Church *282*
Zoological Gardens *283*
environs
Bandipur Wildlife Sanctuary *285*
Brindhavan Gardens *283*
Chamundeshwari·Temple *283*
Chamundi Hill *283*
Nagarhole National Park *285*
Sriringapatna Fort *284*
restaurants 282
shopping 284

N **Nagaland** *250*

Nagaur *137*
attractions
Camel Fair *137*
Mughal fort *137*
Nalanda *242*
Nandankanan Park *257*
– *see also* Bhubaneswar
attractions
Lion Safari Park *257*
rhinos, monkeys, gharials, pelicans, pythons,
brown bear and India's rare white
crocodile *257*
Nathdwara *150*
– *see also* Udaipur
New Delhi
See Delhi
Newalgarh *129*
– *see also* Shekhavati
nightlife, general *340*

O **Ootacamund (Ooty)** *285–288*
access 286
accommodation
Hotel Fernhill Imperial, ((0423) 3910 *287*
Hotel Lakeview, ((0423) 3580 *287*
Hotel Mayura Sudarshan, ((0423) 3828 *287*
Hotel Nilgiri Dasaprakah, ((0423) 2434 *287*
Hotel Palace, ((0423) 3931 *287*
Hotel Tamil Nadu, ((0423) 2543 *287*
Savoy Hotel, ((0423) 2572 *286*
Youth Hostel, ((0423) 3665 *287*
YWCA, ((0423) 3008 *287*
attractions
bazaar *288*
Botanical Gardens *287*
fishing on Ooty Lake, ((0423) 2232 *288*
Nilgiri Library *287*
Ooty Club *287*
Ooty Lake *288*
St Stephen's Parish Church *287*
walks in the hills *288*
environs
Kandal Mund traditional Toda village *287*
Mudumalai Wildlife Sanctuary *288*
restaurants 287
tour bookings and travel arrangements
Venus Travels, ((0423) 3700 *288*
tourist information
Tourist Office, ((0423) 2416 *288*
Orchha *109*
attractions
Chatturbhu Temple *109*
Jehangir Mahal *109*
Laxmi Narain Temple *109*
Raj Mahal *109*
Orissa *242, 252–257, 259, 261–262*
when to visit 253
Osian *137*
attractions
Jain and Hindu temples *137*

P **Pahalgam** *174–175*
accommodation
Hotel Hill Park, (79 (Pahalgam) *174*
Hotel Pahalgam, (26, 52, 78 (Pahalgam) *174*
Woodstock Hotel, (27 (Pahalgam) *174*
attractions
Achabal gardens *174*
fishing (trout) *174*

Kashmiri handicrafts *174*
Mamaleswwara Shiva temple *174*
trekking and pony trekking *174*
environs
Amarnath Cave *175*
Avantipur ancient Kashmir capital *174*
Kokernag springs *174*
Kolahoi Glacier *175*
Martand Sun Temple *174*
Sonamarg hill station *175*
Palitana *221*
access *221*
accommodation
Hotel Shavrak, (*328* *221*
Hotel Sumeru Toren, (*227* *221*
attractions
Shatrunjaya Hill Jain temple complex *221*
Panaji *202, 205*
– *see also* Goa
Patna *26, 242*
history *26*
Pattadakal *274*
Periyar (Thekkady) *324–325*
access *325*
accommodation
Aranya Niwas Hotel, ((04869) *325*
Lake Palace Hotel, (2384 (via operator) *325*
Periyar House, ((04869) 22026 *325*
attractions
cruises on Lake Periyar *325*
Periyar Lake *325*
Periyar Wildlife Sanctuary *324–325*
Phalut *248*
– *see also* Darjeeling
Pipli *257*
– *see also* Bhubaneswar
Port Blair *263*
access
Shipping Corporation of India, ((033) 239456
(in Calcutta) *263*
accommodation
Andaman Beach Resort, ((03192) 21462 *264*
Megapode Nest, ((03192) 2207 *264*
Shompen Hotel, ((03192) 20360 *264*
Welcomgroup Bay Island, ((03192) 20881 *264*
attractions
Anthropological Museum *264*
Cellular Jail *264*
harbor and island cruises *265*
Marine Museum *264*
Mini Zoo *265*
environs
Chiriya Tapu beach *265*
outer islands bookings *265*
Island Travels, ((03192) 21358 *265*
restaurants *264*
shopping
Cottage Industries Emporium *264*
tourist information *263–264*
Port Blair's Deputy Director of Tourism,
((03192) 20694 *264*
Tourist Office, ((03192) 20694 *263*
travel bookings *263*
(Calcutta): Shipping Corporation of India,
((033) 239456 *263*
(Madras): KPV Sheikh Muhammed Rowther
and Co, ((044) 510346 *263*

postal services *339*
Punjab *89*
Puri *252, 257–261*
accommodation
Hotel Prachi Puri, ((06752) 2114 *261*
Pantha Niwas Tourist Bungalow,
((06752) 2740 *261*
South Eastern Railway Hotel,
((06752) 2063 *259*
Youth Hostel, ((06752) 424 *261*
attractions
Baradand *261*
Jagannath Temple *258, 261*
Pathuria Sahi or "Stone Carver's Lane" *257*
Rath Yatra festival *252, 258*
environs
Gopalpur-on-sea *259, 261*
shopping
Ragurajpur *257*
Pushkar *130*
accommodation
Hotel Sarovar, ((0145) 2040 *130*
attractions
Camel and Cattle Fair *130*

Q Quilon *322*
accommodation
Hotel Sudarshan, ((0474) 75322 *322*
attractions
backwater cruises *322*
Tourist Bungalow *322*
environs
backwater cruises *322–325*

R railway network and services *338*
Rajasthan *62, 119–153*
Rajgir *242*
Ranakpur *136–137*
Ranthambhore *128*
access *128*
accommodation
Castle Jhoomer Baori Forest Lodge,
(620 *128*
attractions
wildlife sanctuary *128*
religion *46–53*
Buddhism *26, 51–52*
Christianity *31*
Hinduism *24, 26, 30, 49–50*
Islam *31, 52*
Jainism *26, 50–51*
Judaism *31*
Mahayana *26*
Sikhism *52*
the Buddha image *29*
Zoroastrianism *52*
Ropar *22*
history *22*
Ross Island *265*
tourist information
Tourist Information Centre, (20380 *265*

S Sajnakhali *242*
accommodation
Sundar Cheetal Lodge *242*
attractions
Sajnakhali Bird Sanctuary *241–242*
Samode *128*
– *see also* Jaipur
access *128*

Sandakphu *248*
– *see also* Darjeeling
Sariska *128*
accommodation
  Sariska Palace, (22 (Sariska) *128*
  Tiger Den Tourist Bungalow, (42 (Sariska) *129*
attractions
  Sariska Tiger Reserve *129*
Sarnath *116–117*
– *see also* Varanasi
attractions
  Archaeological Museum *116*
  festival *117*
Sasan-Gir Wildlife Sanctuary *222–223*
access *223*
accommodation
  Lion Safari Lodge, (21 (Gir) *223*
attractions
  lions, wild boars, bears, panthers, antelopes,
    hyenas, leopards *222*
  Tulishyam Hot Springs *223*
tourist information
  Government Gujarat Tourist Office,
    ((022) 202-6886 *223*
Secunderabad *269*
– *see also* Hyderabad
Shekhavati *129*
access *130*
accommodation
  Castle Dundlod, ((0141) 61611 *129*
  Castle Mandawa (24 (Mandawa) *129*
  Desert Camp, ((0141) 75358 *129*
  Roop Niwal Haveli, ((0141) 75358 *129*
attractions
  frescoes and *havelis* *129*
Shillong *251*
accommodation
  Hotel Pinewood Ashok, ((0364) 23116 *251*
attractions
  fishing on Umiam Lake *251*
  golf *251*
Shimla *157–159*
access *157*
accommodation
  Chapslee Hotel, ((0177) 78242 *158*
  Hotel Cecil, ((0177) 2073/6041-4 *158*
  Hotel Holiday Home, ((0177) 72375 *158*
  Hotel Mayur, ((0177) 72392 *158*
  Oberoi Clarkes, ((0177) 212991 *158*
  Woodville Palace Hotel, ((0177) 72763 *158*
attractions
  Chadwick Falls *159*
  Gaity Theater *158*
  Glen Forest *158*
  Gothic Christ Church *158*
  Jackoo Hill *158*
  Municipal Buildings *158*
  Prospect Hill *159*
  Rajkumari Amrit Kaur Georgian house *159*
  shopping and handicrafts *158*
  State Museum *158*
  Viceregal Lodge *158*
  walking trails *158*
  winter sport *159*
environs
  Kufri ski resort *159*
  Wildflower Hall *159*

  history *157*
  tourist information *159*
  Tourist Office, ((0177) 78311 *159*
  when to visit *157*
Sikar *129*
– *see also* Shekhavati
Sikhism *52*
Sikkim *242, 248–249*
Somnath *222*
accommodation
  Hotel Mayuram, (362, 268 (Prabhas Patan) *222*
attractions
  Kartika Poornima festival *222*
  Mahashivratri festival *222*
  Prabhas Patan Museum *222*
  Somnath Temple *222*
Somnathpur *285*
attractions
  Somnathpur Temple *285*
Sonamarg *175*
– *see also* Pahalgam
Sravanabelagola *284*
Srinagar *162–173*
access *163*
accommodation
  Centaur Lake View Hotel, ((0194) 77601 or
    75631 *165*
  Hotel Broadway, ((0194) 75621 *166*
  Hotel New Shalimar, ((0194) 74427 *166*
  Hotel Tramboo Continental,
    ((0194) 73914 *166*
  houseboats *163–165*
    Welcomgroup Gurkha Houseboats,
      ((0194) 75229 *164*
  Oberoi Palace, ((0194) 79517 or
    71251 *165*
  Zamrud Hotel, ((0194) 75263 *166*
attractions
  Baradari Palace *170*
  Cheshma Shahi Gardens *168*
  city walks *170*
  Dal and Nagin lakes *167*
  Floating Gardens *168*
  floating market *168*
  Hari Parbat Fort ruins *169*
  Hazratbal Mosque *170*
  houseboats *163–164*
  Jamia Masjid Mosque *169*
  Mughal Gardens *168*
  Nagin Lake Bird Sanctuary *168*
  Nishat Bagh Gardens *168*
  Shah Hamdan Mosque *169*
  Shalimar Bagh Gardens *168*
  Shalimar Gardens *168*
  Shankaracharya Temple *170*
  shikara rides *168*
  shopping *170–171*
  theater and dance *172*
environs
  Dachigam National Park *172*
getting around *166*
restaurants *167*
mountaineering *161*
  Tiger Paw Adventures (in New Delhi),
    ((011) 616137 *173*
  Tiger Tops Mountain Travel (in New Delhi),
    ((011) 521932 or 777-1055 *173*

tourist information
  Srinagar's Tourist Reception Centre (TRC)
    ((0194) 74259 or after office hours
    ((0194) 77303 172
travel further afield 172
  Mercury Travels, ((0194) 78786 172
  Sita World Travel, ((0194) 78891 172
Sriringapatna 284
  – see also Mysore
Stok 182
  – see also Ladakh
  accommodation
    Ladakh Sarai (Mongolian-style yurt tents),
      reservation (Delhi), ((011) 521832,
      771095 182
  attractions
    Royal Summer Palace 182
Sunderbans 240
  – see also Sajnakhali, Bird Sanctuary
Tamil Nadu 292–293, 295, 305, 307–313
telephones 339
Theppukady 288
  accommodation
    Bamboo Banks Farm House,
      ((0423) 2235 288
  attractions
    Mudumalai Wildlife Sanctuary 288
Tiger Hill 243
  – see also Darjeeling
  accommodation
    Tiger Hill Tourist Lodge, ((0354) 2813 246
  attractions
    Ghoom Buddhist Monastry 246
    Himalayan viewing platform 246
Tirukkalikundram 309
  attractions
    Shiva temple 309
Tonglu 248
  – see also Darjeeling
tourist information 336
  – see also under city names
  Australia (Sydney), ((02) 232-1600 336
  Canada (Toronto), ((416) 962-3787/8 336
  England (London), ((0171) 437-3677/8 337
  India (Delhi), Government of India Tourist
    Office, ((011) 332-0005 and 333-0008 336
  Thailand (Bangkok), ((2) 235-2585 336
  U.S.A.
    (Chicago), ((312) 236-6899/7869 337
    (Los Angeles), ((213) 380-8855 336
    (New York), ((212) 586-4901/3 337
travel advice on the road 335
Trichur 329
  attractions
    Pooram festival 329
Tripura 250
Trivandrum 317–320
  access 317–318
  accommodation
    Hotel Aristo, ((0471) 63622 318
    Hotel Arulakam, ((0471) 330488 318
    Hotel Chaithram, ((0471) 331421 318
    Hotel Mascot, ((0471) 438990 318
    Luciya Continental, ((0471) 73443 318
    YMCA Guest House, ((0471) 330059 318
  attractions
    Aquarium 319

    Padmanabhaswamy Temple 319
    Sri Chitra Art Gallery 319
    The Connemara Market 319
    Zoo and Botanical Gardens 319
  environs
    Kanya Kumari 319
    Kathakali dance performances 320
    Kovalam Beach 319
    Padmanbhapuram Palace 319
  restaurants 318
  tourist information
    KTDC office, ((0471) 330031 320
    The Tourist Information Centre,
      ((0471) 61132 319
Udaipur 147–150
  access 148
  accommodation
    Anand Bhawan Circuit House,
      ((0294) 23256 149
    Hotel Shikarbadi, ((0294) 83200 149
    Lake Palace, ((0294) 23241-5 148
    Laxmi Vilas Palace Hotel,
      ((0294) 29711 149
    Pratap County Inn, ((0294) 23638-9 149
    Rang Niwas Hotel, ((0294) 523891 149
    Shiv Niwas Palace, ((0294) 28239 149
  attractions
    Bhartiya Lok Kala Mandal folk
      museum 150
    City Palace 150
    Gulab Bagh, or Rose Gardens 150
    Jagdish Temple 150
    Nehru Park 150
    Saheliyonki Bari Gardens 150
    Tripolia Gate 150
  environs
    Ahar archaeological museum) 150
    Eklingi temple complex 150
    Haldighati 150
    Nathdwara temple 150
  history 147
  restaurants 149–150
  tourist information 150
    Tourist Information Bureau,
      ((0294) 23605 150
Uttar Pradesh 62
Vadodara 223
  access 223
  accommodation
    Hotel Surya Palace, ((0265) 330011 223
    Welcomgroup Vadodara,
      ((0265) 330033 223
  attractions
    Baroda Museum and Art Gallery 223
    Kirti Mandir 223
    Lakshmi Vilas Palace 223
    Maharaja Fateh Singh Museum 223
    Maharaja Sayajirao University of
      Vadodara 223
    Maqbara 223
    Naulakhi baoli (step-well) 223
    Pratap Vilas Palace 223
    Sarsagar Lake 223
    Sayaji Park 223
    Tambekarwada haveli 223
  environs
    Champaner ruined fort 223

Varanasi *110–117*
  access *112*
  accommodation
    Clarks Varanasi, ((0542) 46771 *112*
    Hotel de Paris, ((0542) 46601 *112*
    Hotel Taj Ganges, ((0542) 42480 *112*
    India Hotel, ((0542) 45127 *112*
    Tourist Dak Bungalow, ((0542) 43413 *112*
    Varanasi Ashok, ((0542) 46020 *112*
  attractions
    Benares Hindu University *115*
    Durga Temple *115*
    festivals *112*
    Golden Temple *115*
    shopping *117*
    the City *115*
    the Ghats *113–115*
    Tulsi Manas Temple *115*
  environs
    Ramnagar Fort *115*
    Sarnath *116–117*
  history *110*
  restaurants *112–113*
  tourist information *117*
Vasco de Gama *202*
  – see also Goa
visas *332–333*
vocabulary *342*
W when to visit India *333*
wildlife *62*
wildlife sanctuaries *61–62, 128, 172, 222, 251, 285, 288, 324*
  directory *62*
winter sports *159, 173*
  Shimla *159*
Z Zoroastrianism *52*

Illustrated Blueprints to Travel Enjoyment

INSIDER'S GUIDES

The Guides That Lead